BIG IDEAS MATH®
Modeling Real Life

Grade 7
Advanced

Ron Larson
Laurie Boswell

Big
Ideas
Learning™

Erie, Pennsylvania
BigIdeasLearning.com

Big Ideas Learning, LLC
1762 Norcross Road
Erie, PA 16510-3838
USA

For product information and customer support, contact Big Ideas Learning
at **1-877-552-7766** or visit us at ***BigIdeasLearning.com***.

Cover Image:
Valdis Torms, cobalt88/Shutterstock.com

Front Matter:
xix Heyourelax/iStock/Getty Images Plus; **xx** Valengilda/iStock/Getty Images Plus; **xxi** Juanmonino/E+/Getty Images; **xxii** stockcam/iStock/Getty Images Plus; **xxiii** supergenijalac/iStock/Getty Images Plus; **xxv** tawan/Shutterstock.com; **xxvi** uatp2/ iStock/Getty Images Plus; **xxvii** carlosgaw/E+/Getty Images; **xxviii** Georgethefourth/iStock/Getty Images Plus; **xxix** ©iStockphoto.com/ryasick; **xxx** ©iStockphoto.com/Eric Isselée; **xxxi** peepo/E+/Getty Images; **xxxii** tropper2000/iStock/Getty Images Plus

Printed in the U.S.A.

IBSN 13: 978-1-63708-401-4

3 4 5 6 7 8 9 10—25 24 23 22

One Voice from Kindergarten Through Algebra 2

Written by renowned authors, Dr. Ron Larson and Dr. Laurie Boswell, *Big Ideas Math* offers a seamless math pedagogy from elementary through high school. Together, Ron and Laurie provide a consistent voice that encourages students to make connections through cohesive progressions and clear instruction. Since 1992, Ron and Laurie have authored over 50 mathematics programs.

Each time Laurie and I start working on a new program, we spend time putting ourselves in the position of the reader. How old is the reader? What is the reader's experience with mathematics? The answers to these questions become our writing guides. Our goal is to make the learning targets understandable and to develop these targets in a clear path that leads to student success.

Ron Larson

Ron Larson, Ph.D., is well known as lead author of a comprehensive and widely used mathematics program that ranges from elementary school through college. He holds the distinction of Professor Emeritus from Penn State Erie, The Behrend College, where he taught for nearly 40 years. He received his Ph.D. in mathematics from the University of Colorado. Dr. Larson engages in the latest research and advancements in mathematics education and consistently incorporates key pedagogical elements to ensure focus, coherence, rigor, and student self-reflection.

My passion and goal in writing is to provide an essential resource for exploring and making sense of mathematics. Our program is guided by research around the learning and teaching of mathematics in the hopes of improving the achievement of all students. May this be a successful year for you!

Laurie Boswell

Laurie Boswell, Ed.D., is the former Head of School at Riverside School in Lyndonville, Vermont. In addition to authoring textbooks, she provides mathematics consulting and embedded coaching sessions. Dr. Boswell received her Ed.D. from the University of Vermont in 2010. She is a recipient of the Presidential Award for Excellence in Mathematics Teaching and later served as president of CPAM. Laurie has taught math to students at all levels, elementary through college. In addition, Laurie has served on the NCTM Board of Directors and as a Regional Director for NCSM. Along with Ron, Laurie has co-authored numerous math programs and has become a popular national speaker.

Big Ideas Learning would like to express our gratitude to the mathematics education and instruction experts who served as our advisory panel, contributing specialists, and reviewers during the writing of *Big Ideas Math: Modeling Real Life*. Their input was an invaluable asset during the development of this program.

Contributing Specialists and Reviewers

- **Sophie Murphy**, Ph.D. Candidate, Melbourne School of Education, Melbourne, Australia
  Learning Targets and Success Criteria Specialist and Visible Learning Reviewer

- **Linda Hall**, Mathematics Educational Consultant, Edmond, OK
  Advisory Panel and Teaching Edition Contributor

- **Michael McDowell**, Ed.D., Superintendent, Ross, CA
  Project-Based Learning Specialist

- **Kelly Byrne**, Math Supervisor and Coordinator of Data Analysis, Downingtown, PA
  Advisory Panel and Content Reviewer

- **Jean Carwin**, Math Specialist/TOSA, Snohomish, WA
  Advisory Panel and Content Reviewer

- **Nancy Siddens**, Independent Language Teaching Consultant, Las Cruces, NM
  English Language Learner Specialist

- **Nancy Thiele**, Mathematics Consultant, Mesa, AZ
  Teaching Edition Contributor

- **Kristen Karbon**, Curriculum and Assessment Coordinator, Troy, MI
  Advisory Panel and Content Reviewer

- **Kery Obradovich**, K–8 Math/Science Coordinator, Northbrook, IL
  Advisory Panel and Content Reviewer

- **Jennifer Rollins**, Math Curriculum Content Specialist, Golden, CO
  Advisory Panel

- **Becky Walker**, Ph.D., School Improvement Services Director, Green Bay, WI
  Advisory Panel

- **Anthony Smith**, Ph.D., Associate Professor, Associate Dean, University of Washington Bothell, Seattle, WA
  Reading/Writing Reviewer

- **Nicole Dimich Vagle**, Educator, Author, and Consultant, Hopkins, MN
  Assessment Reviewer

- **Jill Kalb**, Secondary Math Content Specialist, Arvada, CO
  Content Reviewer

- **Janet Graham**, District Math Specialist, Manassas, VA
  Response to Intervention and Differentiated Instruction Reviewer

- **Sharon Huber**, Director of Elementary Mathematics, Chesapeake, VA
  Universal Design for Learning Reviewer

Student Reviewers

- Jackson Currier
- Mason Currier
- Taylor DeLuca
- Ajalae Evans
- Malik Goodwine
- Majesty Hamilton
- Reilly Koch

- Kyla Kramer
- Matthew Lindemuth
- Greer Lippert
- Zane Lippert
- Jeffrey Lobaugh
- Riley Moran
- Zoe Morin

- Deke Patton
- Brooke Smith
- Dylan Throop
- Jenna Urso
- Madison Whitford
- Jenna Wigham

Research

Ron Larson and Laurie Boswell used the latest in educational research, along with the body of knowledge collected from expert mathematics instructors, to develop the *Modeling Real Life* series. The pedagogical approach used in this program follows the best practices outlined in the most prominent and widely accepted educational research, including:

- *Visible Learning*
  John Hattie © 2009

- *Visible Learning for Teachers*
  John Hattie © 2012

- *Visible Learning for Mathematics*
  John Hattie © 2017

- *Principles to Actions: Ensuring Mathematical Success for All*
  NCTM © 2014

- *Adding It Up: Helping Children Learn Mathematics*
  National Research Council © 2001

- *Mathematical Mindsets: Unleashing Students' Potential through Creative Math, Inspiring Messages and Innovative Teaching*
  Jo Boaler © 2015

- *What Works in Schools: Translating Research into Action*
  Robert Marzano © 2003

- *Classroom Instruction That Works: Research-Based Strategies for Increasing Student Achievement*
  Marzano, Pickering, and Pollock © 2001

- *Principles and Standards for School Mathematics*
  NCTM © 2000

- *Rigorous PBL by Design: Three Shifts for Developing Confident and Competent Learners*
  Michael McDowell © 2017

- *Universal Design for Learning Guidelines*
  CAST © 2011

- *Rigor/Relevance Framework®*
  International Center for Leadership in Education

- *Understanding by Design*
  Grant Wiggins and Jay McTighe © 2005

- Achieve, ACT, and The College Board

- *Elementary and Middle School Mathematics: Teaching Developmentally*
  John A. Van de Walle and Karen S. Karp © 2015

- *Evaluating the Quality of Learning: The SOLO Taxonomy*
  John B. Biggs & Kevin F. Collis © 1982

- *Unlocking Formative Assessment: Practical Strategies for Enhancing Students' Learning in the Primary and Intermediate Classroom*
  Shirley Clarke, Helen Timperley, and John Hattie © 2004

- *Formative Assessment in the Secondary Classroom*
  Shirley Clarke © 2005

- *Improving Student Achievement: A Practical Guide to Assessment for Learning*
  Toni Glasson © 2009

Instructional Design

A single authorship team from Kindergarten through Algebra 2 results in a logical progression of focused topics with meaningful coherence from course to course.

FOCUS

A focused program reflects the balance in grade-level standards while simultaneously supporting and engaging you to develop conceptual understanding of the major work of the grade.

The **Learning Target** and **Success Criteria** for each section focus the learning into manageable chunks, using clear teaching text and Key Ideas.

2.1 Multiplying Integers

Learning Target: Find products of integers.

Success Criteria:
- I can explain the rules for multiplying integers.
- I can find products of integers with the same sign.
- I can find products of integers with different signs.

 Key Idea

Ratios

Words A **ratio** is a comparison of two quantities. The **value of the ratio** a to b is the number $\frac{a}{b}$, which describes the multiplicative relationship between the quantities in the ratio.

Examples 2 snails *to* 6 fish

$\frac{1}{2}$ cup of milk *for every* $\frac{1}{4}$ cup of cream

Algebra The ratio of a to b can be written as $a : b$.

Laurie's Notes, located in the Teaching Edition, prepare your teacher for the math concepts in each chapter and section and make connections to the threads of major topics for the course.

Laurie's Notes

Chapter 5 Overview

The study of ratios and proportions in this chapter builds upon and connects to prior work with rates and ratios in the previous course. Students should have an understanding of how ratios are represented and how ratio tables are used to find equivalent ratios. Tape diagrams and double number lines were also used to represent and solve problems involving equivalent ratios.

a Single Authorship Team

COHERENCE

A single authorship team built a coherent program that has intentional progression of content within each grade and between grade levels. You will build new understanding on foundations from prior grades and connect concepts throughout the course.

The authors developed content that progresses from prior chapters and grades to future ones. In addition to charts like this one, Laurie's Notes give your teacher insights about where you have come from and where you are going in your learning progression.

One author team thoughtfully wrote each course, creating a seamless progression of content from Kindergarten to Algebra 2.

Through the Grades		
Grade 7	**Grade 8**	**High School**
• Use samples to draw inferences about populations. • Compare two populations from random samples using measures of center and variability. • Approximate the probability of a chance event and predict the approximate relative frequency given the probability.	• Construct and interpret scatter plots. • Find and assess lines of fit for scatter plots. • Use equations of lines to solve problems and interpret the slope and the y-intercept. • Construct and interpret a two-way table summarizing data. Use relative frequencies to describe possible association between the two variables.	• Classify data as quantitative or qualitative, choose and create appropriate data displays, and analyze misleading graphs. • Make and use two-way tables to recognize associations in data by finding marginal, relative, and conditional relative frequencies. • Interpret scatter plots, determine how well lines of fit model data, and distinguish between correlation and causation.

Grade 1	Grade 2	Grade 3	Grade 4	Grade 5	Grade 6	Grade 7	Grade 8
			Operations and Algebraic Thinking		**Expressions and Equations**		
oblems involving and subtraction 0. roperties of ns. th addition and ion equations. s 1–5, 10, 11	Solve problems involving addition and subtraction within 20. Work with equal groups of objects. Chapters 1–6, 15	Solve problems involving multiplication and division within 100. Apply properties of multiplication. Solve problems involving the four operations, and identify and explain patterns in arithmetic. Chapters 1–5, 8, 9, and 14	Use the four operations with whole numbers to solve problems. Understand factors and multiples. Generate and analyze patterns. Chapters 2–6, 12	Write and interpret numerical expressions. Analyze patterns and relationships. Chapters 2, 12	Perform arithmetic with algebraic expressions. Chapter 5 Solve one-variable equations and inequalities. Chapters 6, 8 Analyze relationships between dependent and independent variables. Chapter 6	Write equivalent expressions. Chapter 3 Use numerical and algebraic expressions, equations, and inequalities to solve problems. Chapters 3, 4, 6	Understand the connections between proportional relationships, lines, and linear equations. Chapter 4 Solve linear equations and systems of linear equations. Chapters 1, 5 Work with radicals and integer exponents. Chapters 8, 9
							Functions
							Define, evaluate, and compare functions, and use functions to model relationships between quantities.

You have used number lines to find sums of positive numbers, which involve movement to the right. Now you will find sums with negative numbers, which involve movement to the left.

Using Number Lines to Find Sums

a. Find $4 + (-4)$.

Draw an arrow from 0 to 4 to represent 4. Then draw an arrow 4 units to the left to represent adding -4.

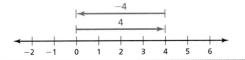

Throughout each course, lessons build on prior learning as new concepts are introduced. Here you are reminded that you have used number lines with positive numbers.

Rigor in Math: A Balanced Approach

Instructional Design

The authors wrote every chapter and every section to give you a meaningful balance of rigorous instruction.

RIGOR

A rigorous program provides a balance of three important building blocks.

- **Conceptual Understanding**
  Discovering why
- **Procedural Fluency**
  Learning how
- **Application**
  Knowing when to apply

Conceptual Understanding

You have the opportunity to develop foundational concepts central to the *Learning Target* in each *Exploration* by experimenting with new concepts, talking with peers, and asking questions.

EXPLORATION 1 **Understanding Quotients Involving N**

Work with a partner.

a. Discuss the relationship between multiplication your partner.

b. **INDUCTIVE REASONING** Complete the table. The for dividing (i) two integers with the same sign a different signs.

Expression	Type of Quotient	Quotie
$-15 \div 3$	Integers	
$12 \div (-6)$		
$10 \div (-2)$		

Conceptual Thinking

Conceptual questions ask you to think deeply.

29. **MP** **NUMBER SENSE** Without solving, determine whether $\dfrac{x}{4} = \dfrac{15}{3}$ and $\dfrac{x}{15} = \dfrac{4}{3}$ have the same solution. Explain your reasoning.

EXAMPLE 1 **Graphing a Linear Equation in Standard Form**

Graph $-2x + 3y = -6$.

Step 1: Write the equation in slope-intercept form.

$$-2x + 3y = -6 \qquad \text{Write the equation.}$$
$$3y = 2x - 6 \qquad \text{Add } 2x \text{ to each side.}$$
$$y = \frac{2}{3}x - 2 \qquad \text{Divide each side by 3.}$$

Step 2: Use the slope and the y-intercept to graph the equation.

$$y = \frac{2}{3}x + (-2)$$

slope ⟶   ⟵ y-intercept

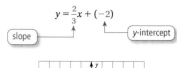
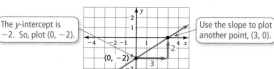

The y-intercept is -2. So, plot $(0, -2)$.

Use the slope to plot another point, $(3, 0)$.

$(0, -2)$

Procedural Fluency

Solidify learning with clear, stepped-out teaching and examples.

Then shift conceptual understanding into procedural fluency with *Try Its, Self-Assessments, Practice,* and *Review & Refresh.*

STEAM Video: "Trophic Status"

STEAM Applications

Begin every chapter with a fun, engaging STEAM video to see how math applies to everyday life. Apply what you learn in the chapter with a related *Performance Task*.

Name_____ Date_____

Chapter 3 **Performance Task**

Chlorophyll in Plants

What is needed for photosynthesis? How can you use the amount of chlorophyll in a lake to determine the level of biological productivity?

Photosynthesis is the process by which plants acquire energy from the sun. Sunlight, carbon dioxide, and water are used by a plant to produce glucose and dioxygen.

Before:
6 Carbon Dioxide + 6 Water ⟶ Glucose + 6 Dioxygen
After:

1. You want to make models of the molecules involved in photosynthesis for a science fair project. The table shows the number of each element used for each molecule. Let x, y, and z represent the costs of a model carbon atom, model hydrogen atom, and

Molecule	Number of Atoms		
	Carbon	Hydrogen	Oxygen
Carbon Dioxide	1	0	2
Water	0	2	1

Daily Application Practice

Modeling Real Life, *Dig Deeper*, *Problem Solving*, and other non-routine problems help you apply surface-level skills to gain a deeper understanding. These problems lead to independent problem-solving.

36. **DIG DEEPER!** The *girth* of a package is the distance around the perimeter of a face that does not include the length as a side. A postal service says that a rectangular package can have a maximum combined length and girth of 108 inches.

a. Write an inequality that represents the allowable dimensions for the package.

b. Find three different sets of allowable dimensions that are reasonable for the package. Find the volume of each package.

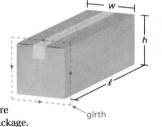

girth

THE PROBLEM-SOLVING PLAN

Problem-Solving Plan

Walk through the Problem-Solving Plan, featured in many examples, to help you make sense of problems with confidence.

1. **Understand the Problem**
   Think about what the problem is asking, what information you know, and how you might begin to solve.

2. **Make a Plan**
   Plan your solution pathway before jumping in to solve. Identify any relationships and decide on a problem-solving strategy.

3. **Solve and Check**
   As you solve the problem, be sure to evaluate your progress and check your answers. Throughout the problem-solving process, you must continually ask, "Does this make sense?" and be willing to change course if necessary.

Embedded Mathematical Practices

Encouraging Mathematical Mindsets

Developing proficiency in the **Mathematical Practices** is about becoming a mathematical thinker. Learn to ask why, and to reason and communicate with others as you learn. Use this guide to develop proficiency with the mathematical practices.

1 One way to **Make Sense of Problems and Persevere in Solving Them** is to use the Problem-Solving Plan. Take time to analyze the given information and what the problem is asking to help you plan a solution pathway.

Look for labels such as:
- Explain the Meaning
- Find Entry Points
- Analyze Givens
- Make a Plan
- Interpret a Solution
- Consider Similar Problems
- Consider Simpler Forms
- Check Progress
- Problem Solving

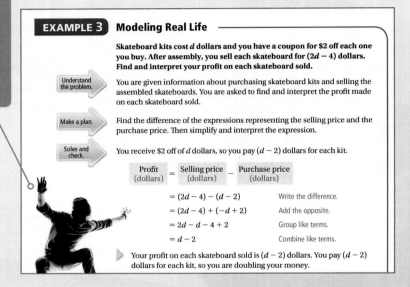

EXAMPLE 3 **Modeling Real Life**

Skateboard kits cost d dollars and you have a coupon for $2 off each one you buy. After assembly, you sell each skateboard for $(2d - 4)$ dollars. Find and interpret your profit on each skateboard sold.

Understand the problem. You are given information about purchasing skateboard kits and selling the assembled skateboards. You are asked to find and interpret the profit made on each skateboard sold.

Make a plan. Find the difference of the expressions representing the selling price and the purchase price. Then simplify and interpret the expression.

Solve and check. You receive $2 off of d dollars, so you pay $(d - 2)$ dollars for each kit.

$$\underset{\text{(dollars)}}{\text{Profit}} = \underset{\text{(dollars)}}{\text{Selling price}} - \underset{\text{(dollars)}}{\text{Purchase price}}$$

$$= (2d - 4) - (d - 2) \qquad \text{Write the difference.}$$
$$= (2d - 4) + (-d + 2) \qquad \text{Add the opposite.}$$
$$= 2d - d - 4 + 2 \qquad \text{Group like terms.}$$
$$= d - 2 \qquad \text{Combine like terms.}$$

Your profit on each skateboard sold is $(d - 2)$ dollars. You pay $(d - 2)$ dollars for each kit, so you are doubling your money.

2 **Reason Abstractly** when you explore a concrete example and represent it symbolically. Other times, **Reason Quantitatively** when you see relationships in numbers or symbols and draw conclusions about a concrete example.

Look for labels such as:
- Make Sense of Quantities
- Use Equations
- Use Expressions
- Understand Quantities
- Use Operations
- Number Sense
- Reasoning

a. Represent each table in the same coordinate plane. Which graph represents a proportional relationship? How do you know?

Drops of red

Drops of blue

Math Practice

Reasoning
How is the graph of the proportional relationship different from the other graph?

b. Which property can you use to solve each of the equations modeled by the algebra tiles? Solve each equation and explain your method.

46. (MP) LOGIC When you multiply or divide each side of an inequality by the same negative number, you must reverse the direction of the inequality symbol. Explain why.

Math Practice

Make Conjectures
Can you use algebra tiles to solve any equation? Explain your reasoning.

3 When you **Construct Viable Arguments and Critique the Reasoning of Others,** you make and justify conclusions and decide whether others' arguments are correct or flawed.

Look for labels such as:

- Use Assumptions
- Use Definitions
- Use Prior Results
- Make Conjectures
- Build Arguments
- Analyze Conjectures
- Use Counterexamples

- Justify Conclusions
- Compare Arguments
- Construct Arguments
- Listen and Ask Questions
- You Be the Teacher
- Logic

36. (MP) APPLY MATHEMATICS You decide to make and sell bracelets. The cost of your materials is $84.00. You charge $3.50 for each bracelet.

a. Write a function that represents the profit P for selling b bracelets.

b. Which variable is independent? dependent? Explain.

c. You will *break even* when the cost of your materials equals your income. How many bracelets must you sell to break even?

Look for labels such as:

- Apply Mathematics
- Simplify a Solution
- Use a Diagram
- Use a Table
- Use a Graph

- Use a Formula
- Analyze Relationships
- Interpret Results
- Modeling Real Life

4 To **Model with Mathematics,** apply the math you have learned to a real-life problem, and interpret mathematical results in the context of the situation.

BUILDING TO FULL UNDERSTANDING

Throughout each course, you have opportunities to demonstrate specific aspects of the mathematical practices. Labels throughout the book indicate gateways to those aspects. Collectively, these opportunities will lead to a full understanding of each mathematical practice. Developing these mindsets and habits will give meaning to the mathematics you learn.

5

To **Use Appropriate Tools Strategically**, you need to know what tools are available and think about how each tool might help you solve a mathematical problem. When you choose a tool to use, remember that it may have limitations.

Look for labels such as:
- Choose Tools
- Recognize Usefulness of Tools
- Use Other Resources
- Use Technology to Explore
- Using Tools

d. Enter the function $y = \left(\frac{1}{10}\right)^x$ into your graphing calculator. Use the *table* feature to evaluate the function for positive integer values of x until the calculator displays a y-value that is not in standard form. Do the results support your answer in part (c)? Explain.

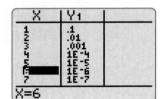

Math Practice

Use Technology to Explore
How can writing $\frac{1}{10}$ as a power of 10 help you understand the calculator display?

6

When you **Attend to Precision**, you are developing a habit of being careful in how you talk about concepts, label work, and write answers.

Look for labels such as:
- Communicate Precisely
- Use Clear Definitions
- State the Meaning of Symbols
- Specify Units
- Label Axes
- Calculate Accurately
- Precision

Add 1.459 + 23.7.

$$
\begin{array}{r}
1 \\
1.459 \\
+\ 23.700 \\
\hline
25.159
\end{array}
$$

← Insert zeros so that both numbers have the same number of decimal places.

Math Practice

Calculate Accurately
Why is it important to line up the decimal points when adding or subtracting decimals?

49. **MP** **PRECISION** Consider the equation $c = ax - bx$, where a, b, and c are whole numbers. Which of the following result in values of a, b, and c so that the original equation has exactly one solution? Justify your answer.

| $a - b = 1, c = 0$ | $a = b, c \neq 0$ | $a = b, c = 0$ | $a \neq b, c = 0$ |

MP STRUCTURE Tell whether the triangles are similar. Explain.

14.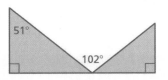

15.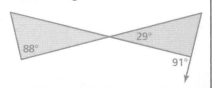

7

Look For and Make Use of Structure by looking closely to see structure within a mathematical statement, or stepping back for an overview to see how individual parts make one single object.

Find the sum of the areas of the faces.

Surface Area	=	Area of bottom	+	Area of a side	+	Area of a side	+	Area of a side	+	Area of a side	
S	=	49	+	35	+	35	+	35	+	35	= 189

Look for labels such as:
- Look for Structure
- Look for Patterns
- View as Components
- Structure
- Patterns

Math Practice

Look for Patterns
How can you find the surface area of a square pyramid by calculating the area of only two of the faces?

35. MP REPEATED REASONING You have been assigned a nine-digit identification number.

a. Should you use the Fundamental Counting Principle or a tree diagram to find the total number of possible identification numbers? Explain.

b. How many identification numbers are possible?

8

When you **Look For and Express Regularity in Repeated Reasoning**, you can notice patterns and make generalizations. Remember to keep in mind the goal of a problem, which will help you evaluate reasonableness of answers along the way.

Look for labels such as:
- Repeat Calculations
- Find General Methods
- Maintain Oversight
- Evaluate Results
- Repeated Reasoning

Making Learning Visible

Knowing the learning intention of a chapter or section helps you focus on the purpose of an activity, rather than simply completing it in isolation. This program supports visible learning through the consistent use of learning targets and success criteria to ensure positive outcomes for all students.

> Every chapter and section shows a **Learning Target** and related **Success Criteria**. These are purposefully integrated into each carefully written lesson.

4.4 Writing and Graphing Inequalities

Learning Target: Write inequalities and represent solutions of inequalities on number lines.

Success Criteria:
- I can write word sentences as inequalities.
- I can determine whether a value is a solution of an inequality.
- I can graph the solutions of inequalities.

Chapter Learning Target:
Understand equations and inequalities.

Chapter Success Criteria:
- ☐ I can identify key words and phrases to write equations and inequalities.
- ☐ I can write word sentences as equations and inequalities.
- ☐ I can solve equations and inequalities using properties.
- ☐ I can use equations and inequalities to model and solve real-life problems.

> The **Chapter Review** reminds you to rate your understanding of the learning targets.

▶ Chapter Self-Assessment

As you complete the exercises, use the scale below to rate your understanding of the success criteria in your journal.

1	2	3	4
I do not understand.	I can do it with help.	I can do it on my own.	I can teach someone else.

6.1 Writing Equations in One Variable (pp. 245–250)

Learning Target: Write equations in one variable and write equations that represent real-life problems.

> Review each section with a reminder of that section's learning target.

Write the word sentence as an equation.

1. The product of a number *m* and 2 is 8.

QUESTIONS FOR LEARNING

As you progress through a section, you should be able to answer the following questions.
- What am I learning?
- Why am I learning this?
- Where am I in my learning?
- How will I know when I have learned it?
- Where am I going next?

Success Criteria, and Self-Assessment

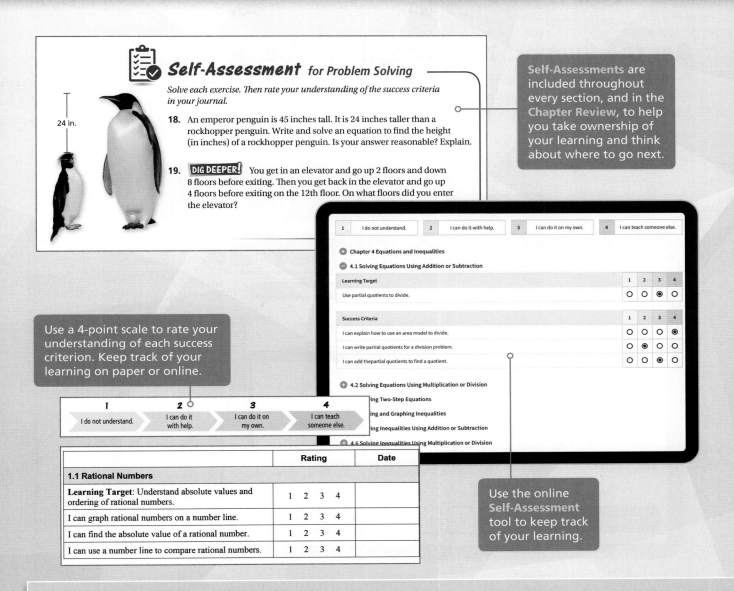

Self-Assessment for Problem Solving

Solve each exercise. Then rate your understanding of the success criteria in your journal.

24 in.

18. An emperor penguin is 45 inches tall. It is 24 inches taller than a rockhopper penguin. Write and solve an equation to find the height (in inches) of a rockhopper penguin. Is your answer reasonable? Explain.

19. **DIG DEEPER!** You get in an elevator and go up 2 floors and down 8 floors before exiting. Then you get back in the elevator and go up 4 floors before exiting on the 12th floor. On what floors did you enter the elevator?

Self-Assessments are included throughout every section, and in the **Chapter Review**, to help you take ownership of your learning and think about where to go next.

| 1 | I do not understand. | 2 | I can do it with help. | 3 | I can do it on my own. | 4 | I can teach someone else. |

⊕ Chapter 4 Equations and Inequalities

⊖ 4.1 Solving Equations Using Addition or Subtraction

Learning Target	1	2	3	4
Use partial quotients to divide.	○	○	◉	○

Success Criteria	1	2	3	4
I can explain how to use an area model to divide.	○	○	○	◉
I can write partial quotients for a division problem.	○	◉	○	○
I can add the partial quotients to find a quotient.	○	○	◉	○

⊕ 4.2 Solving Equations Using Multiplication or Division

...ing Two-Step Equations

...ing and Graphing Inequalities

...ing Inequalities Using Addition or Subtraction

⊕ 4.6 Solving Inequalities Using Multiplication or Division

Use a 4-point scale to rate your understanding of each success criterion. Keep track of your learning on paper or online.

1	2	3	4
I do not understand.	I can do it with help.	I can do it on my own.	I can teach someone else.

Use the online **Self-Assessment** tool to keep track of your learning.

	Rating	Date
1.1 Rational Numbers		
Learning Target: Understand absolute values and ordering of rational numbers.	1 2 3 4	
I can graph rational numbers on a number line.	1 2 3 4	
I can find the absolute value of a rational number.	1 2 3 4	
I can use a number line to compare rational numbers.	1 2 3 4	

Ensuring Positive Outcomes

John Hattie's *Visible Learning* research consistently shows that using learning targets and success criteria can result in two years' growth in one year, ensuring positive outcomes for your learning and achievement.

Sophie Murphy, M.Ed., wrote the chapter-level learning targets and success criteria for this program. Sophie is currently completing her Ph.D. at the University of Melbourne in Australia with Professor John Hattie as her leading supervisor. Sophie completed her Master's thesis with Professor John Hattie in 2015. Sophie has over 20 years of experience as a teacher and school leader in private and public school settings in Australia.

Strategic Support for Online Learning

Get the Support You Need, When You Need It

There will be times throughout this course when you may need help. Whether you missed a section, did not understand the content, or just want to review, take advantage of the resources provided in the *Dynamic Student Edition*.

Use the **Self-Assessment** tool to keep track of your understanding of the section's success criteria.

Take notes throughout the lesson using the **My Notes** function. These notes will be organized by chapter and section.

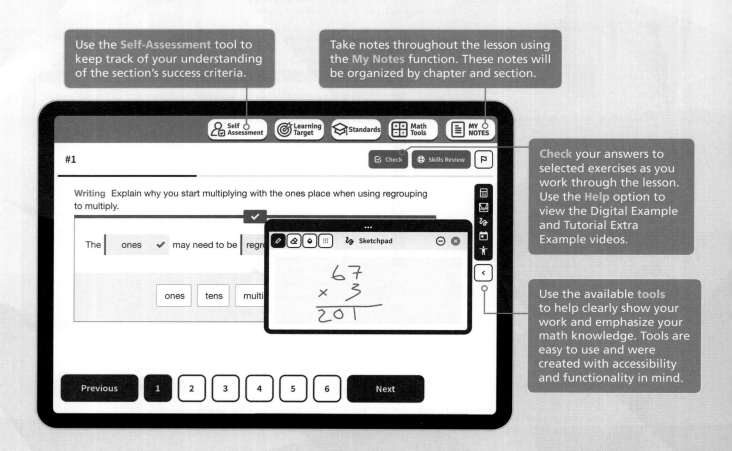

Check your answers to selected exercises as you work through the lesson. Use the **Help** option to view the Digital Example and Tutorial Extra Example videos.

Use the available **tools** to help clearly show your work and emphasize your math knowledge. Tools are easy to use and were created with accessibility and functionality in mind.

USE THESE QR CODES TO EXPLORE ADDITIONAL RESOURCES

Multi-Language Glossary

View definitions and examples of vocabulary words

Skills Trainer

Practice previously learned skills

Interactive Tools

Visualize mathematical concepts

Skills Review Handbook

A collection of review topics

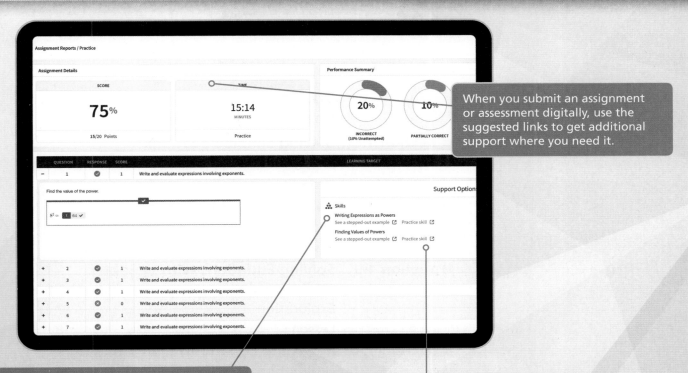

When you submit an assignment or assessment digitally, use the suggested links to get additional support where you need it.

Choose a skill to review and watch a video to see a stepped-out example of that skill. Whether you get a question incorrect, or want a second explanation, these videos can provide additional help with homework.

Choose a skill and launch the **Skills Trainer** for additional practice on that skill. Practicing repeated problems with instant feedback can help build confidence when solving problems.

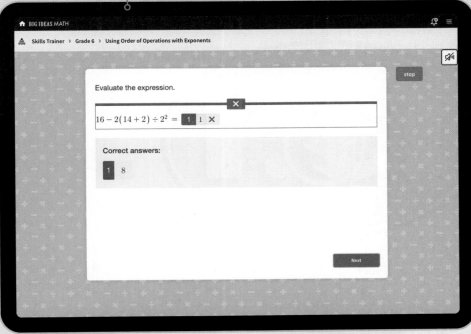

Equations

■ Major Topic
■ Supporting Topic
■ Additional Topic

Transformations

Angles and Triangles

■ Major Topic
■ Supporting Topic
■ Additional Topic

Graphing and Writing Linear Equations

5 Systems of Linear Equations

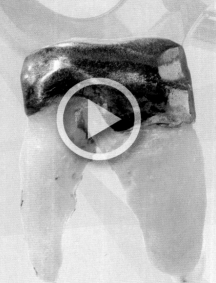

■ Major Topic
■ Supporting Topic
■ Additional Topic

Data Analysis and Displays

6

Functions

■ Major Topic
■ Supporting Topic
■ Additional Topic

Exponents and Scientific Notation

9 Real Numbers and the Pythagorean Theorem

■ Major Topic
■ Supporting Topic
■ Additional Topic

Volume and Similar Solids

A Equations and Inequalities

■ Major Topic
■ Supporting Topic
■ Additional Topic

Probability

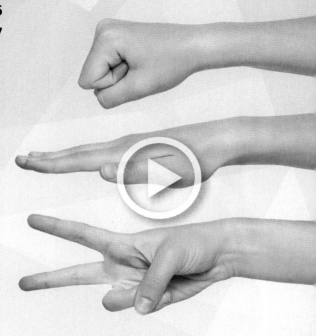

Statistics

■ Major Topic
■ Supporting Topic
■ Additional Topic

Geometric Shapes and Angles

Surface Area and Volume

■ Major Topic
■ Supporting Topic
■ Additional Topic

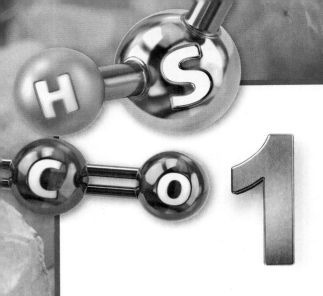

1 Equations

Chapter Learning Target:
Understand equations.

Chapter Success Criteria:
- ☐ I can identify key words and phrases to solve equations.
- ☐ I can write word sentences as equations.
- ■ I can explain how to solve equations.
- ■ I can model different types of equations to solve real-life problems.

STEAM Video: "Training for a Half Marathon"

Training for a Half Marathon

A half marathon is a race that is 13.1 miles long. How can a runner develop a routine to help train for a half marathon?

Watch the STEAM Video "Training for a Half Marathon." Then answer the following questions.

1. Alex and Enid are training for a half marathon. They run four days each week, as shown in the table. How far do they have to run on Saturday to average 4.75 miles per running day in Week Nine?

	Distance Ran (miles)			
	Monday	**Wednesday**	**Friday**	**Saturday**
Week Six	2.5	2.6	2.4	7.0
Week Seven	3.3	2.8	2.9	7.0
Week Eight	3.3	3.1	2.6	8.5
Week Nine	3.7	3.0	4.1	x

2. Assuming they meet their goal on Saturday in Week Nine, what is the average number of miles per running day over the 4 weeks in the table?

Target Heart Rates

After completing this chapter, you will be able to use the concepts you learned to answer the questions in the *STEAM Video Performance Task*. You will be given information about a person's heart rate.

Resting heart rate

$$\left.\begin{array}{l} \textbf{Day 1} = x \\ \textbf{Day 2} = x \\ \textbf{Day 3} = x \\ \textbf{Day 4} = x \\ \textbf{Day 5} = 58 \end{array}\right\} \quad \text{5-day average} = 62$$

You will be asked to find the range of a person's target heart rate. What factors might affect the range of a person's target heart rate?

Getting Ready for Chapter

Chapter Exploration

1. **Work with a partner. Use algebra tiles to model and solve each equation.**

   a. $x + 3 = -3$

   $\boxed{+} = +1$ $\boxed{-} = -1$ $\boxed{+} = x$

   $\boxed{+}\;\boxed{+}\,\boxed{+}\,\boxed{+} = \boxed{-}\,\boxed{-}\,\boxed{-}$ Model the equation $x + 3 = -3$.

   $\boxed{+}\begin{smallmatrix}\boxed{+}\,\boxed{+}\,\boxed{+}\\\boxed{-}\,\boxed{-}\,\boxed{-}\end{smallmatrix} = \begin{smallmatrix}\boxed{-}\,\boxed{-}\,\boxed{-}\\\boxed{-}\,\boxed{-}\,\boxed{-}\end{smallmatrix}$ Add three -1 tiles to each side.

   $\boxed{+} = \begin{smallmatrix}\boxed{-}\,\boxed{-}\,\boxed{-}\\\boxed{-}\,\boxed{-}\,\boxed{-}\end{smallmatrix}$ Remove the zero pairs from the left side.

   $\boxed{+} = \boxed{}$ Write the solution of the equation.

   b. $-3 = x - 2$

   $\boxed{-}\,\boxed{-}\,\boxed{-} = \boxed{+}\,\boxed{-}\,\boxed{-}$ Model the equation $-3 = x - 2$.

   $\begin{smallmatrix}\boxed{-}\,\boxed{-}\,\boxed{-}\\\boxed{+}\,\boxed{+}\end{smallmatrix} = \boxed{+}\begin{smallmatrix}\boxed{-}\,\boxed{-}\\\boxed{+}\,\boxed{+}\end{smallmatrix}$ Add two $+1$ tiles to each side.

   $\boxed{-} = \boxed{+}$ Remove the zero pairs from the each side.

   $\boxed{} = \boxed{+}$ Write the solution of the equation.

   c. $x - 4 = 1$ **d.** $x + 5 = -2$ **e.** $-7 = x + 4$

   f. $x + 6 = 7$ **g.** $-5 + x = -3$ **h.** $-4 = x - 4$

2. **WRITE GUIDELINES** Work with a partner. Use your models in Exercise 1 to summarize the *algebraic steps* that you can use to solve an equation.

Vocabulary

The following vocabulary term is defined in this chapter. Think about what the term might mean and record your thoughts.

literal equation

1.1 Solving Simple Equations

Learning Target: Write and solve one-step equations.

Success Criteria:
- I can apply properties of equality to produce equivalent equations.
- I can solve equations using addition, subtraction, multiplication, or division.
- I can use equations to model and solve real-life problems.

EXPLORATION 1

Using Properties of Equality

Work with a partner.

   a. You have used the following properties in a previous course. Explain the meaning of each property.

- Addition Property of Equality
- Subtraction Property of Equality
- Multiplication Property of Equality
- Division Property of Equality

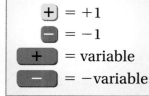

   b. Which property can you use to solve each of the equations modeled by the algebra tiles? Solve each equation and explain your method.

Math Practice

Recognize Usefulness of Tools

Can you use algebra tiles to solve any equation? Explain your reasoning.

   c. Write an equation that can be solved using one property of equality. Exchange equations with another pair and find the solution.

Key Ideas

Remember

Addition and subtraction are inverse operations.

Addition Property of Equality

Words Adding the same number to each side of an equation produces an equivalent equation.

Algebra If $a = b$, then $a + c = b + c$.

Subtraction Property of Equality

Words Subtracting the same number from each side of an equation produces an equivalent equation.

Algebra If $a = b$, then $a - c = b - c$.

EXAMPLE 1 **Solving Equations Using Addition or Subtraction**

a. **Solve $x - 7 = -6$.**

$$x - 7 = -6$$ Write the equation.

Undo the subtraction. $\longrightarrow$ $\underline{+7 \quad +7}$ Addition Property of Equality

$$x = 1$$ Simplify.

▷ The solution is $x = 1$.

Check

$$x - 7 = -6$$

$$1 - 7 \overset{?}{=} -6$$

$$-6 = -6 \checkmark$$

b. **Solve $1 = w + 6$.**

$$1 = w + 6$$ Write the equation.

Undo the addition. $\longrightarrow$ $\underline{-6 \qquad -6}$ Subtraction Property of Equality

$$-5 = w$$ Simplify.

▷ The solution is $w = -5$.

Check

$$1 = w + 6$$

$$1 \overset{?}{=} -5 + 6$$

$$1 = 1 \checkmark$$

c. **Solve $y + 3.4 = 0.5$.**

$$y + 3.4 = 0.5$$ Write the equation.

Undo the addition. $\longrightarrow$ $\underline{-3.4 \quad -3.4}$ Subtraction Property of Equality

$$y = -2.9$$ Simplify.

▷ The solution is $y = -2.9$.

Try It Solve the equation. Check your solution.

1. $b + 2 = -5$ **2.** $-3 = k + 3$ **3.** $t - \dfrac{1}{4} = -\dfrac{3}{4}$

 **Key Ideas**

Multiplication Property of Equality

Words   Multiplying each side of an equation by the same number produces an equivalent equation.

Algebra   If $a = b$, then $a \cdot c = b \cdot c$.

Division Property of Equality

Words   Dividing each side of an equation by the same number produces an equivalent equation.

Algebra   If $a = b$, then $a \div c = b \div c, c \neq 0$.

> **Remember**
>
> Multiplication and division are inverse operations.

EXAMPLE 2 **Solving Equations Using Multiplication or Division**

a.   **Solve $-\dfrac{3}{4}n = -2$.**

$$-\frac{3}{4}n = -2 \qquad \text{Write the equation.}$$

$$-\frac{4}{3} \cdot \left(-\frac{3}{4}n\right) = -\frac{4}{3} \cdot (-2) \qquad \text{Multiplication Property of Equality}$$

$$n = \frac{8}{3} \qquad \text{Simplify.}$$

▶ The solution is $n = \dfrac{8}{3}$.

> **Math Practice**
>
> **Maintain Oversight**
> Describe the relationship between $-\dfrac{4}{3}$ and $-\dfrac{3}{4}$. Then explain why it makes sense to multiply each side of the equation by $-\dfrac{4}{3}$.

b.   **Solve $\pi x = 3\pi$.**

$$\pi x = 3\pi \qquad \text{Write the equation.}$$

Undo the multiplication. →
$$\frac{\pi x}{\pi} = \frac{3\pi}{\pi} \qquad \text{Division Property of Equality}$$

$$x = 3 \qquad \text{Simplify.}$$

▶ The solution is $x = 3$.

> **Check**
>
> $\pi x = 3\pi$
>
> $\pi(3) \stackrel{?}{=} 3\pi$
>
> $3\pi = 3\pi$ ✓

Try It   **Solve the equation. Check your solution.**

4. $\dfrac{y}{4} = -7$

5. $-\dfrac{2z}{3} = 6$

6. $0.09w = 1.8$

7. $6\pi = \pi x$

EXAMPLE 3 **Identifying the Solution of an Equation**

What value of k makes the equation $k + 4 \div 0.2 = 5$ true?

A. -15 **B.** -5 **C.** -3 **D.** 1.5

$k + 4 \div 0.2 =$	5	Write the equation.
$k + 20 =$	5	Divide 4 by 0.2.
$\underline{-20}$	$\underline{-20}$	Subtraction Property of Equality
$k =$	-15	Simplify.

The correct answer is **A**.

> **Check**
> $k + 4 \div 0.2 = 5$
> $-15 + 4 \div 0.2 \overset{?}{=} 5$
> $-15 + 20 \overset{?}{=} 5$
> $5 = 5$ ✓

Try It **Solve the equation. Check your solution.**

8. $p - 8 \div \dfrac{1}{2} = -3$ **9.** $q + \left| -10 \right| = 2$

Self-Assessment for Concepts & Skills

Solve each exercise. Then rate your understanding of the success criteria in your journal.

WRITING **Are the equations equivalent? Explain.**

10. $x + 3 = 4$ and $x = 1$ **11.** $-\dfrac{y}{5} = 2$ and $y = 10$

12. **OPEN-ENDED** Write an equation that you can use the Division Property of Equality to solve.

SOLVING EQUATIONS **Solve the equation. Check your solution.**

13. $-5 = w - 3$ **14.** $-\dfrac{2}{3}n = 8$

15. $p - 9 \div \dfrac{1}{3} = 6$ **16.** $q + \left| 3 \right| = -5$

17. **WHICH ONE DOESN'T BELONG?** Which equation does *not* belong with the other three? Explain your reasoning.

| $x - 2 = 4$ | $x - 3 = 9$ | $x - 5 = 1$ | $x - 6 = 0$ |

EXAMPLE 4 **Modeling Real Life**

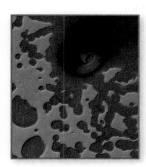

The temperature in a crater on Mars is 0°C at 1 P.M. The temperature decreases 8°C every hour. When will the temperature be −50°C?

To determine when the temperature will be −50°C, find how long it will take the temperature to decrease by 50°C. Write and solve an equation to find the time.

| **Verbal Model** | Change in temperature (°C) | = | Hourly change in temperature (°C per hour) | • | Time (hours) |

Variable Let t be the time for the temperature to decrease 50°C.

Equation -50 $=$ -8 • t

> The changes in temperature are negative because the temperatures are decreasing.

$-50 = -8t$ Write the equation.

$\dfrac{-50}{-8} = \dfrac{-8t}{-8}$ Division Property of Equality

$6.25 = t$ Simplify.

The temperature will be −50°C at 6.25 hours after 1 P.M., or 6 hours and 15 minutes after 1 P.M.

▷ So, the temperature will be −50°C at 7:15 P.M.

Self-Assessment for *Problem Solving*

Solve each exercise. Then rate your understanding of the success criteria in your journal.

18. A shipwreck is 300 meters away from a diving station. An undersea explorer travels away from the station at a speed of 2 meters per second. The explorer is x meters away from the station and will reach the shipwreck in 100 seconds. What is the value of x?

19. You conduct an inventory for a hardware store and count 40 rolls of duct tape. Your manager wants to keep 7 boxes of duct tape in stock. If each box holds 8 rolls of duct tape, how many boxes should you order? Justify your answer.

20. **DIG DEEPER!** Your fitness tracker overestimates the number of steps you take by 5%. The tracker indicates that you took 7350 steps today. Write and solve an equation to find the actual number of steps you took today.

1.1 Practice

 Go to *BigIdeasMath.com* to get HELP with solving the exercises.

▶ Review & Refresh

Evaluate the expression.

1. $(3^2 - 8) + 4$
2. $1 + 5 \times 3^2$
3. $4 \times 3 + 10^2$

Identify the terms, coefficients, and constants in the expression.

4. $11q + 2$
5. $h + 9 + g$
6. $6m^2 + 7n$

Write the phrase as an expression.

7. the quotient of 22 and a number a

8. the difference of a number t and 9

▶ Concepts, Skills, & Problem Solving

USING PROPERTIES OF EQUALITY Which property of equality can you use to solve the equation modeled by the algebra tiles? Solve the equation and explain your method. (See Exploration 1, p. 3.)

9.

10.

SOLVING EQUATIONS USING ADDITION OR SUBTRACTION Solve the equation. Check your solution.

11. $x + 12 = 7$
12. $g - 16 = 8$
13. $-9 + p = 12$

14. $2.5 + y = -3.5$
15. $x - 8\pi = \pi$
16. $4\pi = w - 6\pi$

17. $\dfrac{5}{6} = \dfrac{1}{6} + d$
18. $\dfrac{3}{8} = r + \dfrac{2}{3}$
19. $n - 1.4 = -6.3$

20. **MP MODELING REAL LIFE** A discounted concert ticket costs $14.50 less than the original price p. You pay $53 for a discounted ticket. Write and solve an equation to find the original price.

21. **MP PROBLEM SOLVING** A game of bowling has ten frames. After five frames, your friend's bowling score is 65 and your bowling score is 8 less than your friend's score.

   a. Write and solve an equation to find your score.

   b. By the end of the game, your friend's score doubles and your score increases by 80. Who wins the game? Explain.

SOLVING EQUATIONS USING MULTIPLICATION OR DIVISION **Solve the equation. Check your solution.**

22. $7x = 35$

23. $4 = -0.8n$

24. $6 = -\dfrac{w}{8}$

25. $\dfrac{m}{\pi} = 7.3$

26. $-4.3g = 25.8$

27. $\dfrac{3}{2} = \dfrac{9}{10}k$

28. $-7.8x = -1.56$

29. $-2 = \dfrac{6}{7}p$

30. $3\pi d = 12\pi$

31. **(MP) YOU BE THE TEACHER** Your friend solves the equation. Is your friend correct? Explain your reasoning.

$-1.5 + k = 8.2$
$k = 8.2 + (-1.5)$
$k = 6.7$

32. **(MP) STRUCTURE** A gym teacher orders 42 tennis balls. The tennis balls come in packs of 3. Which of the following equations represents the number x of packs?

$x + 3 = 42$ $\qquad$ $3x = 42$ $\qquad$ $\dfrac{x}{3} = 42$ $\qquad$ $x = \dfrac{3}{42}$

33. **(MP) MODELING REAL LIFE** You clean a community park for 6.5 hours. You earn $42.25. How much do you earn per hour?

34. **(MP) MODELING REAL LIFE** A rocket is scheduled to launch from a command center in 3.75 hours. What time is it now?

35. **(MP) MODELING REAL LIFE** After earning interest, the balance of an account is $420. The new balance is $\dfrac{7}{6}$ of the original balance. How much interest did it earn?

36. **(MP) MODELING REAL LIFE** After a cleanup, algae covers 2 miles of a coastline. The length of the coastline covered after the cleanup is $\dfrac{1}{3}$ of the previous length. How many miles of the coast did the algae previously cover?

Launch Time
11:20 A.M.

Roller Coasters at Cedar Point	
Coaster	Height (feet)
Top Thrill Dragster	420
Millennium Force	310
Valravn	225
Rougarou	?

37. **(MP) PROBLEM SOLVING** Cedar Point, an amusement park in Ohio, has some of the tallest roller coasters in the United States. The Rougarou is 165 feet shorter than the Millennium Force. What is the height of the Rougarou?

SOLVING AN EQUATION Solve the equation. Check your solution.

38. $-3 = h + 8 \div 2$

39. $12 = w - |-7|$

40. $q + |6.4| = 9.6$

41. $d - 2.8 \div 0.2 = -14$

42. $\dfrac{8}{9} = x + \dfrac{1}{3}(7)$

43. $p - \dfrac{1}{4} \cdot 3 = -\dfrac{5}{6}$

44. **GEOMETRY** The volume V of the prism is 1122 cubic inches. Use the formula $V = Bh$ to find the height h of the prism.

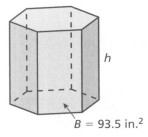

$B = 93.5$ in.^{2}

SOLVING AN EQUATION Write and solve an equation to find the value of x.

45. The angles are complementary.

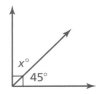

$x°$

$45°$

46. The angles are supplementary.

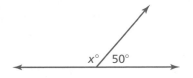

$x°$ $50°$

47. **CRITICAL THINKING** Which of the operations $+$, $-$, $\times$, and $\div$ are inverses of each other? Explain.

48. **MP LOGIC** Without solving, determine whether the solution of $-2x = -15$ is *greater than* or *less than* -15. Explain.

49. **OPEN-ENDED** Write a subtraction equation and a division equation so that each has a solution of -2. Justify your answer.

50. **MP MODELING REAL LIFE** Ants of a particular species can carry 50 times their body weight. It takes 32 ants of that species to carry the cherry shown. About how much does each ant weigh?

4800 mg

51. **MP REASONING** One-fourth of the girls and one-eighth of the boys in a grade retake their school pictures. The photographer retakes pictures for 16 girls and 7 boys. How many students are in the grade?

52. **DIG DEEPER!** You use a crowdfunding website to raise money. The website keeps 5% of each donation. Five of your friends each donate the same amount. The total funding you receive is $47.50. How much does each friend donate?

53. **CRITICAL THINKING** A neighbor pays you and two friends $90 to paint her garage. You divide the money three ways in the ratio $2 : 3 : 5$.

    a. How much does each person receive?

    b. What is one possible reason the money is not divided evenly?

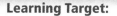

1.2 Solving Multi-Step Equations

Learning Target: Write and solve multi-step equations.

Success Criteria:
- I can apply properties to produce equivalent equations.
- I can solve multi-step equations.
- I can use multi-step equations to model and solve real-life problems.

EXPLORATION 1

Finding Angle Measures

Work with a partner. Find each angle measure in each figure.
Use equations to justify your answers.

a.
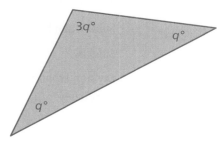

b.
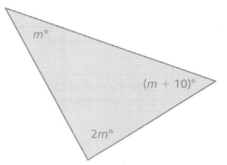

c.
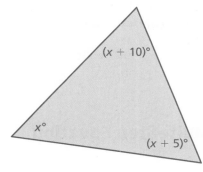

d.
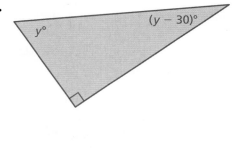

Math Practice

Find Entry Points
How do you decide which triangle to solve first? Explain.

e.
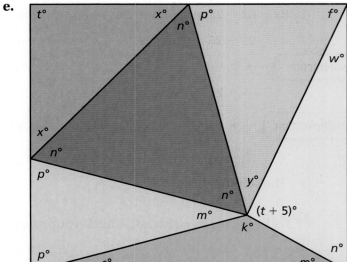

1.2 Lesson

 **Key Idea**

Solving Multi-Step Equations
To solve multi-step equations, use inverse operations to isolate the variable.

EXAMPLE 1 **Solving a Two-Step Equation**

Solve $3x + 15 = 24$.

$3x + 15 = 24$		Write the equation.
Undo the addition. → $-15 \quad -15$		Subtraction Property of Equality
$3x = 9$		Simplify.
Undo the multiplication. → $\dfrac{3x}{3} = \dfrac{9}{3}$		Division Property of Equality
$x = 3$		Simplify.

Check

$3x + 15 = 24$

$3(3) + 15 \overset{?}{=} 24$

$24 = 24$ ✓

▷ The solution is $x = 3$.

Try It Solve the equation. Check your solution.

1. $2z - 1 = -5$ **2.** $-3z + 1 = 7$ **3.** $\dfrac{1}{2}x - 9 = -25$

EXAMPLE 2 **Solving a Multi-Step Equation**

Solve $8x - 6x - 25 = -35$.

$8x - 6x - 25 = -35$		Write the equation.
$2x - 25 = -35$		Combine like terms.
Undo the subtraction. → $+25 \quad +25$		Addition Property of Equality
$2x = -10$		Simplify.
Undo the multiplication. → $\dfrac{2x}{2} = \dfrac{-10}{2}$		Division Property of Equality
$x = -5$		Simplify.

▷ The solution is $x = -5$.

Try It Solve the equation. Check your solution.

4. $-4n - 8n + 17 = 23$ **5.** $10 = 3n + 20 - n$

EXAMPLE 3 **Using the Distributive Property to Solve an Equation**

Solve $2(1 - 5x) + 4 = -8$.

$2(1 - 5x) + 4 = -8$	Write the equation.
$2(1) - 2(5x) + 4 = -8$	Distributive Property
$2 - 10x + 4 = -8$	Multiply.
$-10x + 6 = -8$	Combine like terms.
$\underline{\quad -6 \quad -6\quad}$	Subtraction Property of Equality
$-10x = -14$	Simplify.
$\dfrac{-10x}{-10} = \dfrac{-14}{-10}$	Division Property of Equality
$x = 1.4$	Simplify.

Math Practice

Look for Structure
Show how to solve the equation without using the Distributive Property.

 The solution is $x = 1.4$.

Try It Solve the equation. Check your solution.

6. $-3(x + 2) + 5x = -9$ **7.** $5 + 1.5(2d - 1) = 0.5$

 Self-Assessment *for Concepts & Skills*

Solve each exercise. Then rate your understanding of the success criteria in your journal.

SOLVING AN EQUATION Solve the equation. Check your solution.

8. $-5x + 1 = 31$ **9.** $\dfrac{1}{3}x - 9 = -12$

10. $-n - 6n + 4 = 53$ **11.** $14 = 6n + 6 - 2n$

12. $-8(x + 1) + 2x = -32$ **13.** $3 + 4.5(2d - 3) = 7.5$

14. WRITING Write the sentence as an equation, then solve.

> 2 more than 3 times a number x is 17.

15. OPEN-ENDED Explain how to solve the equation $2(4x - 11) + 9 = 19$.

16. CRITICAL THINKING How can you solve $3(x + 2) = 9$ without distributing the 3?

EXAMPLE 4 **Modeling Real Life**

Find the number x of miles you need to run on Friday so that the mean number of miles run per day is 1.5.

Day	Miles
Monday	2
Tuesday	0
Wednesday	1.5
Thursday	0
Friday	x

 Understand the problem.

You are given the number of miles you run each day from Monday through Thursday. You are asked how many miles you need to run on Friday so that your daily average for the five days is 1.5 miles.

Make a plan.

Write and solve an equation using the definition of *mean*.

Solve and check.

$$\frac{2 + 0 + 1.5 + 0 + x}{5} = 1.5 \qquad \frac{\text{sum of the data}}{\text{number of values}} = \text{mean}$$

$$\frac{3.5 + x}{5} = 1.5 \qquad \text{Combine like terms.}$$

$$5 \cdot \frac{3.5 + x}{5} = 5 \cdot 1.5 \qquad \text{Multiplication Property of Equality}$$

$$3.5 + x = \quad 7.5 \qquad \text{Simplify.}$$

$$\underline{-\ 3.5} \qquad \underline{-\ 3.5} \qquad \text{Subtraction Property of Equality}$$

$$x = 4 \qquad \text{Simplify.}$$

Check You run $2 + 1.5 + 4 = 7.5$ miles in 5 days. So, the mean number of miles run per day is $\frac{7.5}{5} = 1.5$. ✓

▷ So, you need to run 4 miles on Friday.

 Self-Assessment for Problem Solving

Solve each exercise. Then rate your understanding of the success criteria in your journal.

Day	Action Figures
Monday	55
Tuesday	45
Wednesday	53
Thursday	44
Friday	x

17. Find the number x of action figures that a small business needs to produce on Friday so that the mean number of action figures produced per day is 50.

18. **DIG DEEPER!** A hard drive is 80% full and has 12,000 MB of free space. One minute of video uses 60 MB of storage. How many minutes of video should be deleted so that the hard drive is 75% full?

19. A teacher spends $354 on costumes and microphones for six cast members in a play. Each cast member receives a costume that costs $38 and a microphone that costs c. What did the teacher spend on each microphone? Justify your answer.

1.2 Practice

 Go to *BigIdeasMath.com* to get HELP with solving the exercises.

▶ Review & Refresh

Solve the equation.

1. $y + 8 = 3$

2. $h - 1 = 7.2$

3. $5 = -2n$

4. $-3.3m = -1.1$

Write the decimal as a fraction or mixed number in simplest form.

5. -0.2

6. 3.82

7. -0.454

8. -0.125

▶▶ Concepts, Skills, & Problem Solving

FINDING ANGLE MEASURES Find each angle measure in the figure. Use equations to justify your answers. (See Exploration 1, p. 11.)

9.
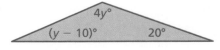

10.
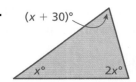

SOLVING AN EQUATION Solve the equation. Check your solution.

11. $10x + 2 = 32$

12. $19 - 4c = 17$

13. $5x + 2x + 4 = 18$

14. $2 = -9n + 22 - n$

15. $1.1x + 1.2x - 5.4 = -10$

16. $\frac{2}{3}h - \frac{1}{3}h + 11 = 8$

17. $6(5 - 8v) + 12 = -54$

18. $21(2 - x) + 12x = 44$

19. $8.5 = 6.5(2d - 3) + d$

20. $-\frac{1}{4}(x + 2) + 5 = -x$

MP YOU BE THE TEACHER Your friend solves the equation. Is your friend correct? Explain your reasoning.

21.
$$-2(7 - y) + 4 = -4$$
$$-14 - 2y + 4 = -4$$
$$-10 - 2y = -4$$
$$-2y = 6$$
$$y = -3$$

22.
$$3(y - 1) + 8 = 11$$
$$3y - 3 + 8 = 11$$
$$3y + 5 = 11$$
$$3y = 6$$
$$y = 2$$

23. **MP STRUCTURE** The cost C (in dollars) of making n watches is represented by $C = 15n + 85$. How many watches are made when the cost is $385?

6 ft

x

x

24. **MP** **MODELING REAL LIFE** The height of the house is 26 feet. What is the height *x* of each story?

25. **MP** **MODELING REAL LIFE** After the addition of an acid, a solution has a volume of 90 milliliters. The volume of the solution is 3 milliliters greater than 3 times the volume of the solution before the acid was added. What was the original volume of the solution?

26. **MP** **PROBLEM SOLVING** A grocer prepares free samples of a salad to give out during the day. By lunchtime, the grocer has given out 5 fewer than half the total number of samples. How many samples did the grocer prepare if she gives out 50 samples before lunch?

27. **GEOMETRY** What is the length of the missing base of the trapezoid?

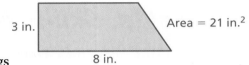

3 in.

8 in.

Area = 21 in.²

28. **MP** **MODELING REAL LIFE** You order two servings of pancakes and a fruit cup. The cost of the fruit cup is $1.50. You leave a 15% tip. Your total bill is $11.50. How much does one serving of pancakes cost?

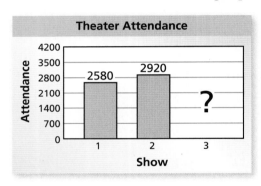

Theater Attendance

2580   2920   ?

29. **MP** **PROBLEM SOLVING** How many people must attend the third show so that the average attendance per show is 3000?

30. **DIG DEEPER!** Divers in a competition are scored by an international panel of judges. The highest and the lowest scores are dropped. The total of the remaining scores is multiplied by the degree of difficulty of the dive. This product is multiplied by 0.6 to determine the final score.

   a. A diver's final score is 77.7. What is the degree of difficulty of the dive?

Judge	Russia	China	Mexico	Germany	Italy	Japan	Brazil
Score	7.5	8.0	6.5	8.5	7.0	7.5	7.0

   b. **CRITICAL THINKING** The degree of difficulty of a dive is 4.0. The diver's final score is 97.2. Judges award half or whole points from 0 to 10. What scores could the judges have given the diver?

1.3 Solving Equations with Variables on Both Sides

Learning Target: Write and solve equations with variables on both sides.

Success Criteria:
- I can explain how to solve an equation with variables on both sides.
- I can determine whether an equation has one solution, no solution, or infinitely many solutions.
- I can use equations with variables on both sides to model and solve real-life problems.

EXPLORATION 1

Finding Missing Measures in Figures

Work with a partner.

a. If possible, find the value of x so that the value of the perimeter (in feet) is equal to the value of the area (in square feet) for each figure. Use an equation to justify your answer.

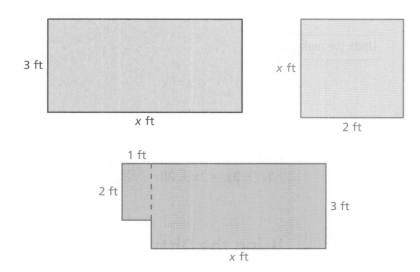

Math Practice

Use Operations
What properties do you need to use to solve for x in each figure?

b. If possible, find the value of y so that the value of the surface area (in square inches) is equal to the value of the volume (in cubic inches) for each figure. Use an equation to justify your answer.

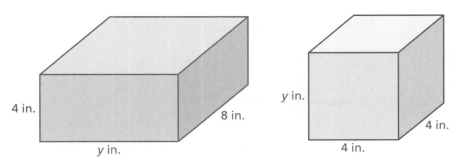

c. How are the equations you used in parts (a) and (b) different from equations used in previous sections? Explain how to solve this type of equation.

1.3 Lesson

 **Key Idea**

Solving Equations with Variables on Both Sides

To solve equations with variables on both sides, collect the variable terms on one side and the constant terms on the other side.

EXAMPLE 1 **Solving an Equation with Variables on Both Sides**

Solve $15 - 2x = -7x$. Check your solution.

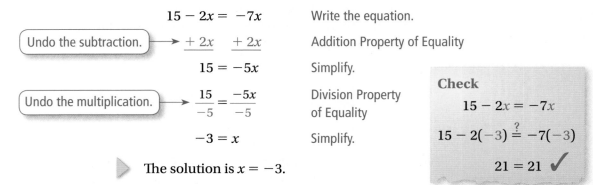

$$15 - 2x = -7x \qquad \text{Write the equation.}$$

Undo the subtraction. → $\quad \underline{+\ 2x \qquad +\ 2x} \qquad$ Addition Property of Equality

$$15 = -5x \qquad \text{Simplify.}$$

Undo the multiplication. → $\dfrac{15}{-5} = \dfrac{-5x}{-5} \qquad$ Division Property of Equality

$$-3 = x \qquad \text{Simplify.}$$

Check
$$15 - 2x = -7x$$
$$15 - 2(-3) \stackrel{?}{=} -7(-3)$$
$$21 = 21 \ \checkmark$$

▷ The solution is $x = -3$.

Try It Solve the equation. Check your solution.

1. $-3x = 2x + 20$

2. $2.5y + 6 = 4.5y - 1$

EXAMPLE 2 **Using the Distributive Property to Solve an Equation**

Solve $-2(x - 5) = 6(2 - 0.5x)$.

$$-2(x - 5) = 6(2 - 0.5x) \qquad \text{Write the equation.}$$

$$-2x + 10 = 12 - 3x \qquad \text{Distributive Property}$$

Undo the subtraction. → $\quad \underline{+\ 3x \qquad\qquad +\ 3x} \qquad$ Addition Property of Equality

$$x + 10 = \quad 12 \qquad \text{Simplify.}$$

Undo the addition. → $\quad \underline{-\ 10 \qquad -\ 10} \qquad$ Subtraction Property of Equality

$$x = 2 \qquad \text{Simplify.}$$

▷ The solution is $x = 2$.

Try It Solve the equation. Check your solution.

3. $6(4 - z) = 2z$

4. $5(w - 2) = -2(1.5w + 5)$

Some equations do not have one solution. Equations can also have no solution or infinitely many solutions.

When solving an equation that has no solution, you will obtain an equivalent equation that is not true for any value of the variable, such as $0 = 2$.

EXAMPLE 3 **Solving an Equation with No Solution**

Math Practice

Look for Structure
How can you use the structure of the original equation to recognize that there is no solution?

Solve $3 - 4x = -7 - 4x$.

$$3 - 4x = -7 - 4x$$ Write the equation.

$$\underline{+\ 4x \qquad\quad +\ 4x}$$ Addition Property of Equality

$$3 = -7 \quad \boldsymbol{\times}$$ Simplify.

▷ The equation $3 = -7$ is never true. So, the equation has no solution.

Try It Solve the equation.

5. $2x + 1 = 2x - 1$ **6.** $6(5 - 2v) = -4(3v + 1)$

When solving an equation that has infinitely many solutions, you will obtain an equivalent equation that is true for all values of the variable, such as $-5 = -5$.

EXAMPLE 4 **Solving an Equation with Infinitely Many Solutions**

Solve $6x + 4 = 4\left(\dfrac{3}{2}x + 1\right)$.

Check Choose any value of x, such as $x = 2$.

$$6x + 4 = 4\left(\dfrac{3}{2}x + 1\right)$$

$$6(2) + 4 \overset{?}{=} 4\left[\dfrac{3}{2}(2) + 1\right]$$

$$12 + 4 \overset{?}{=} 4(3 + 1)$$

$$16 = 16 \ \checkmark$$

$$6x + 4 = 4\left(\dfrac{3}{2}x + 1\right)$$ Write the equation.

$$6x + 4 = \quad 6x + 4$$ Distributive Property

$$\underline{-\ 6x \qquad\quad -\ 6x}$$ Subtraction Property of Equality

$$4 = 4$$ Simplify.

▷ The equation $4 = 4$ is always true. So, the equation has infinitely many solutions.

Try It Solve the equation.

7. $\dfrac{1}{2}(6t - 4) = 3t - 2$ **8.** $\dfrac{1}{3}(2b + 9) = \dfrac{2}{3}\left(b + \dfrac{9}{2}\right)$

EXAMPLE 5 **Writing and Solving an Equation**

The circles are identical. What is the area of each circle?

A. 2   **B.** 4

C. 16π **D.** 64π

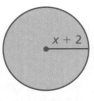

The radius of the green circle is $x + 2$ and the radius of the purple circle is $\frac{4x}{2} = 2x$. The circles are identical, so the radius of each circle is the same. Write and solve an equation to find the value of x.

$$x + 2 = 2x \qquad \text{Write an equation. The radii are equal.}$$
$$\underline{-\,x \qquad\quad -\,x} \qquad \text{Subtraction Property of Equality}$$
$$2 = x \qquad\quad \text{Simplify.}$$

When $x = 2$, the radius of each circle is 4 and the area of each circle is $\pi r^2 = \pi(4)^2 = 16\pi$.

 So, the correct answer is **C.**

Try It

9. **WHAT IF?** The diameter of the purple circle is $3x$. What is the area of each circle?

Self-Assessment *for Concepts & Skills*

Solve each exercise. Then rate your understanding of the success criteria in your journal.

10. **OPEN-ENDED** Write an equation with variables on both sides that has a single solution of -1. Explain how to solve your equation.

MP **STRUCTURE** Without solving, determine whether the equation has one solution, no solution, or infinitely many solutions. Justify your answer.

11. $3(x - 1) = -3$ 12. $6x + 6 = 6(x + 1)$ 13. $z + 1 = z + 6$

SOLVING AN EQUATION Solve the equation. Check your solution, if possible.

14. $-7x = x + 24$ 15. $8(3 - z) = 4z$ 16. $2(t - 3) = 2t - 6$

17. **WRITING AND SOLVING AN EQUATION** The squares are identical. What is the area of each square?

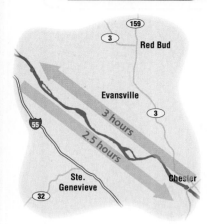

EXAMPLE 6 **Modeling Real Life**

A boat travels x miles per hour upstream on the Mississippi River. On the return trip, the boat travels 2 miles per hour faster. How far does the boat travel upstream?

The boat travels the same distance upstream as on the return trip. The speed of the boat on the return trip is $(x + 2)$ miles per hour. Write and solve an equation to find the distance upstream.

Distance upstream   *Distance of return trip*

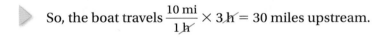

Rate upstream (miles per hour)	•	Time (hours)	=	Rate on return trip (miles per hour)	•	Time (hours)

$$x(3) = (x + 2)(2.5)$$ Write an equation.

$$3x = 2.5x + 5$$ Distributive Property

$$\underline{-2.5x \quad\quad -2.5x}$$ Subtraction Property of Equality

$$0.5x = 5$$ Simplify.

$$\frac{0.5x}{0.5} = \frac{5}{0.5}$$ Division Property of Equality

$$x = 10$$ Simplify.

The boat travels 10 miles per hour for 3 hours upstream.

 So, the boat travels $\dfrac{10 \text{ mi}}{1 \text{ h}} \times 3 \text{ h} = 30$ miles upstream.

Self-Assessment for Problem Solving

Solve each exercise. Then rate your understanding of the success criteria in your journal.

18. Your cousin renews his apartment lease and pays a new monthly rent. His new rent is calculated by applying a discount of $50 to his original rent and then applying a 10% increase to the discounted amount. What was your cousin's original monthly rent when his new rent is 5% greater?

19. **DIG DEEPER!** You and your friend race on a trail that is 10 miles long. In each situation, does your friend pass you before the end of the trail? Justify your answer.

     a. You have a four-mile head start and jog at 6 miles per hour. Your friend bikes at 8 miles per hour.

     b. You have a five-mile head start and run at 7 miles per hour. Your friend bikes at 17 miles per hour.

? Go to *BigIdeasMath.com* to get HELP with solving the exercises.

▶ Review & Refresh

Solve the equation. Check your solution.

1. $-9z + 2 = 11$

2. $-3n - 4n - 17 = 25$

3. $-2(x + 3) + 5x = -39$

4. $-15 + 7.5(2d - 1) = 7.5$

Find the volume of the solid.

5.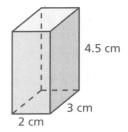
4.5 cm
3 cm
2 cm

6.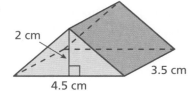
2 cm
3.5 cm
4.5 cm

7.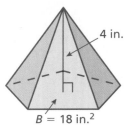
4 in.
$B = 18$ in.^{2}

▶▶ Concepts, Skills, & Problem Solving

FINDING MISSING MEASURES IN FIGURES If possible, find the value of x so that the value of the surface area (in square inches) is equal to the value of the volume (in cubic inches). Use an equation to justify your answer. (See Exploration 1, p. 17.)

8.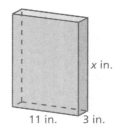
x in.
11 in. 3 in.

9.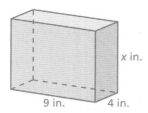
x in.
9 in. 4 in.

10.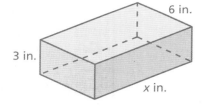
6 in.
3 in.
x in.

SOLVING AN EQUATION Solve the equation. Check your solution.

11. $m - 4 = 2m$

12. $3k - 1 = 7k + 2$

13. $6x = 5x + 22$

14. $-24 - 8p = 4p$

15. $12(2w - 3) = 6w$

16. $2(n - 3) = 4n + 1$

17. $2(4z - 1) = 3(z + 2)$

18. $0.1x = 0.2(x + 2)$

19. $\frac{1}{6}d + \frac{2}{3} = \frac{1}{4}(d - 2)$

20. **MP YOU BE THE TEACHER** Your friend solves the equation shown. Is your friend correct? Explain your reasoning.

$$3x - 4 = 2x + 1$$
$$3x - 4 - 2x = 2x + 1 - 2x$$
$$x - 4 = 1$$
$$x - 4 + 4 = 1 - 4$$
$$x = -3$$

21. **MP MODELING REAL LIFE** Write and solve an equation to find the number of miles you must drive to have the same cost for each of the car rentals.

$20 plus $0.50 per mile $30 plus $0.25 per mile

SOLVING AN EQUATION Solve the equation. Check your solution, if possible.

22. $x + 6 = x$

23. $3x - 1 = 1 - 3x$

24. $3x + 15 = 3(x + 5)$

25. $4x - 9 = 3.5x - 9$

26. $\frac{1}{3}(9x + 3) = 3x + 1$

27. $5x - 7 = 4x - 1$

28. $\frac{1}{2}x + \frac{1}{2}x = x + 1$

29. $2x + 4 = -(-7x + 6)$

30. $5.5 - x = -4.5 - x$

31. $-3(2x - 3) = -6x + 9$

32. $10x - \frac{8}{3} - 4x = 6x$

33. $6(7x + 7) = 7(6x + 6)$

34. **MP YOU BE THE TEACHER** Your friend solves the equation shown. Is your friend correct? Explain your reasoning.

$-4(2n - 3) = 12 - 8n$
$-8n + 12 = 12 - 8n$
$-8n = -8n$
$0 = 0$
The solution is $n = 0$.

35. **OPEN-ENDED** Write an equation with variables on both sides that has no solution. Explain why it has no solution.

36. **MP MODELING REAL LIFE** A cable television provider charges $75 for installation and $39.96 per month for a basic entertainment package. A satellite television provider offers free installation and charges $13.32 per month for service for each television. Your neighbor subscribes to the cable provider the same month you subscribe to the satellite provider. After how many months is your neighbor's total cost the same as your total cost when you own three televisions?

37. **MP MODELING REAL LIFE** A pizza parlor makes 52 pizza crusts the first week of summer and 180 pizza crusts each subsequent week. A diner makes 26 pizza crusts the first week of summer and 90 pizza crusts each subsequent week. In how many weeks will the total number of pizza crusts made by the pizza parlor be twice the total number of pizza crusts made by the diner?

38. **MP PRECISION** Is the triangle an equilateral triangle? Justify your answer.

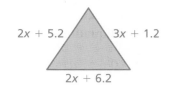

$2x + 5.2$ $3x + 1.2$

$2x + 6.2$

GEOMETRY Find the perimeter of the regular polygon.

39.
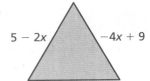
$5 - 2x$ $-4x + 9$

40.

$3(x - 1)$
$5x - 6$

41.
$x + 7$
$\frac{4}{3}x - \frac{1}{3}$

42. **MP** **PRECISION** The cost of mailing a DVD in an envelope using Company B is equal to the cost of mailing a DVD in a box using Company A. What is the weight of the DVD with its packing material? Round your answer to the nearest hundredth.

Packing Material	Company A	Company B
Box	$2.25	$2.50 per lb	$8.50 per lb
Envelope	$1.10	$2.50 per lb	$8.50 per lb

43. **WRITING** Would you solve the equation $0.25x + 7 = \frac{1}{3}x - 8$ using fractions or decimals? Explain.

44. **MP** **NUMBER SENSE** The weight of an object is equal to $\frac{3}{4}$ of its own weight plus $\frac{3}{4}$ of a pound. How much does the object weigh? Explain.

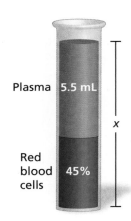

Plasma 5.5 mL

Red blood cells 45%

x

45. **MP** **STRUCTURE** Fill in the blanks in three different ways to create an equation that has one solution, no solution, and infinitely many solutions.

$$7x + 3x + 10 = -2\left(\boxed{} x + \boxed{}\right)$$

46. **MP** **MODELING REAL LIFE** The volume of red blood cells in a blood sample is equal to the total volume of the sample minus the volume of plasma. What is the total volume x of blood drawn?

47. **MP** **PROBLEM SOLVING** One serving of oatmeal provides 16% of the fiber you need daily. You must get the remaining 21 grams of fiber from other sources. How many grams of fiber should you consume daily? Justify your answer.

48. **DIG DEEPER!** The floor of a six-foot-wide hallway is painted as shown, using equal amounts of white and black paint.

a. How long is the hallway?

b. Can this same hallway be painted with the same pattern, but using twice as much black paint as white paint? Explain.

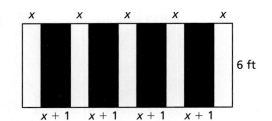
x x x x x
6 ft
$x + 1$ $x + 1$ $x + 1$ $x + 1$

49. **MP** **PRECISION** Consider the equation $c = ax - bx$, where a, b, and c are whole numbers. Which of the following result in values of a, b, and c so that the original equation has exactly one solution? Justify your answer.

| $a - b = 1, c = 0$ | $a = b, c \neq 0$ | $a = b, c = 0$ | $a \neq b, c = 0$ |

1.4 Rewriting Equations and Formulas

Learning Target: Solve literal equations for given variables and convert temperatures.

Success Criteria:
• I can use properties of equality to rewrite literal equations.
• I can use a formula to convert temperatures.

EXPLORATION 1

Rewriting Formulas

Work with a partner.

Math Practice

Find General Methods

When does it make more sense to use the formulas you wrote in part (a) than the original area and volume formulas?

a. Write a formula for the height h of each figure. Explain your method.
   • A parallelogram with area A and base b
   • A rectangular prism with volume V, length ℓ, and width w
   • A triangle with area A and base b

b. Write a formula for the length ℓ of each figure. Explain your method.
   • A rectangle with perimeter P and width w
   • A rectangular prism with surface area S, width w, and height h

c. Use your formulas in parts (a) and (b) to find the missing dimension of each figure.

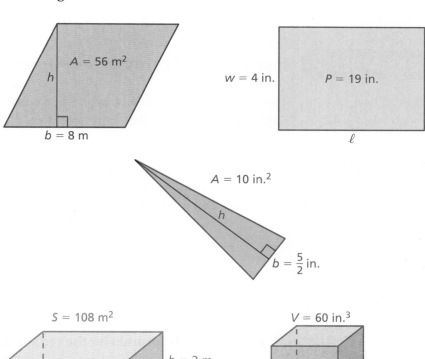

$A = 56$ m^2
h
$b = 8$ m

$w = 4$ in.
$P = 19$ in.
ℓ

$A = 10$ in.^{2}
h
$b = \frac{5}{2}$ in.

$S = 108$ m^2
$h = 3$ m
$w = 4$ m
ℓ

$V = 60$ in.^{3}
h
$B = 12$ in.^{2}

An equation that has two or more variables is called a **literal equation**. To rewrite a literal equation, solve for one variable in terms of the other variable(s).

EXAMPLE 1 Rewriting an Equation

Solve the equation $2y + 5x = 6$ for y.

$2y + 5x = 6$	Write the equation.
$2y + 5x - 5x = 6 - 5x$	Subtraction Property of Equality
$2y = 6 - 5x$	Simplify.
$\dfrac{2y}{2} = \dfrac{6 - 5x}{2}$	Division Property of Equality
$y = 3 - \dfrac{5}{2}x$	Simplify.

Undo the addition. →

Undo the multiplication. →

Try It Solve the equation for y.

1. $5y - x = 10$ **2.** $4x - 4y = 1$ **3.** $12 = 6x + 3y$

EXAMPLE 2 Rewriting a Formula

The formula for the surface area S of a cone is $S = \pi r^2 + \pi r \ell$. Solve the formula for the slant height ℓ.

$S = \pi r^2 + \pi r \ell$	Write the formula.
$S - \pi r^2 = \pi r^2 - \pi r^2 + \pi r \ell$	Subtraction Property of Equality
$S - \pi r^2 = \pi r \ell$	Simplify.
$\dfrac{S - \pi r^2}{\pi r} = \dfrac{\pi r \ell}{\pi r}$	Division Property of Equality
$\dfrac{S - \pi r^2}{\pi r} = \ell$	Simplify.

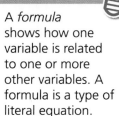

Remember

A *formula* shows how one variable is related to one or more other variables. A formula is a type of literal equation.

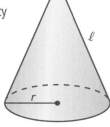

Try It Solve the formula for the red variable.

4. Area of rectangle: $A = bh$ **5.** Simple interest: $I = Prt$

6. Surface area of cylinder: $S = 2\pi r^2 + 2\pi rh$

◀)) Multi-Language Glossary at *BigIdeasMath.com*

 **Key Idea**

Temperature Conversion

A formula for converting from degrees Fahrenheit F to degrees Celsius C is

$$C = \frac{5}{9}(F - 32).$$

EXAMPLE 3 **Rewriting the Temperature Formula**

Solve the temperature formula for F.

$C = \frac{5}{9}(F - 32)$	Write the temperature formula.
Use the reciprocal. → $\frac{9}{5} \cdot C = \frac{9}{5} \cdot \frac{5}{9}(F - 32)$	Multiplication Property of Equality
$\frac{9}{5}C = F - 32$	Simplify.
Undo the subtraction. → $\frac{9}{5}C + 32 = F - 32 + 32$	Addition Property of Equality
$\frac{9}{5}C + 32 = F$	Simplify.

▷ The rewritten formula is $F = \frac{9}{5}C + 32$.

Try It

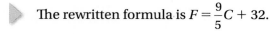

7. Solve the formula $F = \frac{9}{5}C + 32$ for C. Justify your answer.

 Self-Assessment *for Concepts & Skills*

Solve each exercise. Then rate your understanding of the success criteria in your journal.

8. **REWRITING A FORMULA** The formula for the circumference of a circle is $C = 2\pi r$. Solve the formula for r.

9. **DIFFERENT WORDS, SAME QUESTION** Which is different? Find "both" answers.

Solve $4x = 6 + 2y$ for y.	Solve $6 = 4x - 2y$ for y.
Solve $2y - 4x = -6$ for y.	Solve $2y - 4x = 6$ for y.

EXAMPLE 4 **Modeling Real Life**

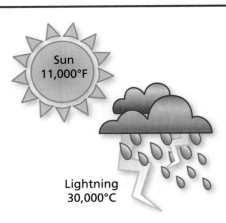

Which has the greater temperature?

Understand the problem.
You are given the temperature of the Sun in degrees Fahrenheit and the temperature of lightning in degrees Celsius. You are asked which temperature is greater.

Make a plan.
Convert the Celsius temperature to Fahrenheit. Then compare the temperatures.

Solve and check.

$$F = \frac{9}{5}C + 32$$ Write the rewritten formula from Example 3.

$$= \frac{9}{5}(30,000) + 32$$ Substitute 30,000 for C.

$$= 54,032$$ Simplify.

▷ Because $54,032°F > 11,000°F$, lightning has the greater temperature.

Another Method Compare the temperatures in degrees Celsius.

When $F = 11,000$, $C = \frac{5}{9}(F - 32) = \frac{5}{9}(11,000 - 32) \approx 6093$.

Because $30,000°C > 6093°C$, lightning has the greater temperature. ✓

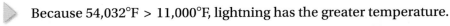

 Self-Assessment for Problem Solving

Solve each exercise. Then rate your understanding of the success criteria in your journal.

10. Room temperature is considered to be 70°F. The temperature outside is currently 23°C. Is this greater than or less than room temperature?

11. A bird flies at a top speed of 20,000 meters per hour. The bird flies 30,000 meters without stopping.

    a. For how many hours did the bird fly if it flew at top speed?

    b. In part (a), did you rewrite a formula to find the number of hours the bird flew, or did you use another approach? Explain.

12. A ball pit is in the shape of a cylinder with a lateral surface area of 245 square feet. The diameter of the ball pit is 312 inches. What is the height of the ball pit? Justify your answer.

1.4 Practice

? Go to *BigIdeasMath.com* to get HELP with solving the exercises.

▶ Review & Refresh

Solve the equation. Check your solution, if possible.

1. $-2x = x + 15$

2. $4(z - 3) = 2z$

3. $x - 8 = x - 1$

4. $5(4 + t) = 5t + 20$

Find the unit rate.

5. 60 miles in 5 hours

6. $8.50 : 5 ounces

7. 9 pounds per 6 crates

▶ Concepts, Skills, & Problem Solving

REWRITING FORMULAS Solve the formula for the height of the figure. Then use the new formula to find the height. (See Exploration 1, p. 25.)

8. $A = \dfrac{1}{2}bh$

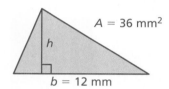

$A = 36 \text{ mm}^2$

h

$b = 12 \text{ mm}$

9. $V = Bh$

$V = 36 \text{ in.}^3$

h

$B = 6 \text{ in.}^2$

IDENTIFYING LITERAL EQUATIONS Is the equation a literal equation? Explain.

10. $y = 4$

11. $t + 8y = 7$

12. $z = 4x + 9y$

REWRITING AN EQUATION Solve the equation for y.

13. $\dfrac{1}{3}x + y = 4$

14. $3x + \dfrac{1}{5}y = 7$

15. $6 = 4x + 9y$

16. $\pi = 7x - 2y$

17. $4.2x - 1.4y = 2.1$

18. $6y - 1.5x = 8$

19. **MP YOU BE THE TEACHER** Your friend rewrites the equation $2x - y = 5$. Is your friend correct? Explain your reasoning.

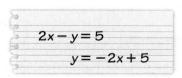

$2x - y = 5$

$y = -2x + 5$

REWRITING A FORMULA Solve the formula for the red variable.

20. $d = rt$

21. $e = mc^2$

22. $R - C = P$

23. $P = a + b + c$

24. $B = 3\dfrac{V}{h}$

25. $D = \dfrac{m}{V}$

26. **(MP) MODELING REAL LIFE** The formula $K = C + 273.15$ converts temperatures from degrees Celsius C to Kelvin K.

    a. Convert 200 degrees Celsius to Kelvin.

    b. Solve the formula for C.

    c. Convert 300 Kelvin to degrees Celsius.

27. **(MP) PROBLEM SOLVING** The formula for simple interest is $I = Prt$.

    a. Solve the formula for t.

    b. Use the new formula to find the value of t in the table.

I	$75
P	$500
r	5%
t	

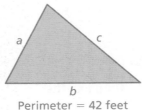

28. **GEOMETRY** Use the triangle shown.

    a. Write a formula for the perimeter P of the triangle.

    b. Solve the formula for b.

    c. Use the new formula to find b when a is 10 feet and c is 17 feet.

Perimeter = 42 feet

29. **(MP) REASONING** The formula $K = \dfrac{5}{9}(F - 32) + 273.15$ converts temperatures from degrees Fahrenheit F to Kelvin K.

    a. Solve the formula for F.

    b. The freezing point of helium is 0.95 Kelvin. What is this temperature in degrees Fahrenheit?

    c. The temperature of dry ice is $-78.5°C$. Which is colder, dry ice or liquid nitrogen?

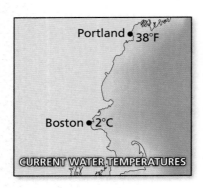

30. **(MP) MODELING REAL LIFE** In which city is the water temperature higher?

31. **GEOMETRY** The volume of a square pyramid with a height of 30 feet is 360 cubic feet. What are the side lengths of the base? Justify your answer.

32. **DIG DEEPER!** The Navy Pier Ferris Wheel in Chicago has a circumference that is 56% of the circumference of the first Ferris wheel built in 1893.

    a. What is the radius of the Navy Pier Ferris Wheel?

    b. What was the radius of the first Ferris wheel?

    c. The first Ferris wheel took 9 minutes to make a complete revolution. How fast was the wheel moving?

C = 439.6 ft

Connecting Concepts

Problem-Solving Strategies

Using an appropriate strategy will help you make sense of problems as you study the mathematics in this course. You can use the following strategies to solve problems that you encounter.

- Use a verbal model.
- Draw a diagram.
- Write an equation.
- Solve a simpler problem.
- Sketch a graph or number line.
- Make a table.
- Make a list.
- Break the problem into parts.

▶ Using the Problem-Solving Plan

1. The battery life of a one-year-old cell phone is 75% of its original battery life. When the battery is charged to 50% of its capacity, it dies after $4\frac{1}{2}$ hours. Find the original battery life of the phone. Justify your answer.

You know how long a cell phone battery lasts when it is charged to 50% of its capacity. You also know that the battery life of the phone is 75% of its original battery life. You are asked to find the original battery life of the phone.

Make a plan.

First, find the battery life of the one-year-old cell phone. Then use this information to write and solve an equation for the original battery life of the phone.

Solve and check.

Use the plan to solve the problem. Then check your solution.

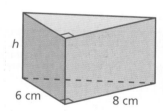

2. The triangular prism shown has a volume of 132 cubic centimeters. Find the height of the prism. Justify your answer.

h

6 cm   8 cm

Performance Task

Target Heart Rates

At the beginning of this chapter, you watched a STEAM Video called "Training for a Half Marathon." You are now ready to complete the performance task related to this video, available at *BigIdeasMath.com*. Be sure to use the problem-solving plan as you work through the performance task.

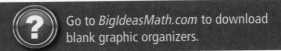

▶ Review Vocabulary

Write the definition and give an example of the vocabulary term.

literal equation, *p. 26*

▶ Graphic Organizers

You can use an **Information Frame** to help organize and remember a concept. Here is an example of an Information Frame for *solving equations with variables on both sides*.

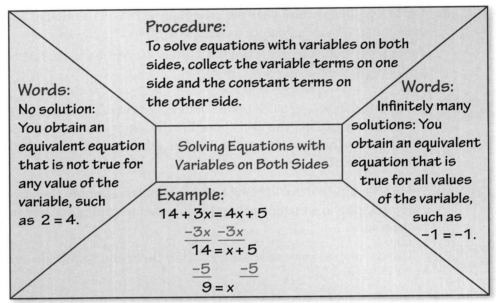

Procedure:
To solve equations with variables on both sides, collect the variable terms on one side and the constant terms on the other side.

Words:
No solution: You obtain an equivalent equation that is not true for any value of the variable, such as $2 = 4$.

Solving Equations with Variables on Both Sides

Words:
Infinitely many solutions: You obtain an equivalent equation that is true for all values of the variable, such as $-1 = -1$.

Example:
$$14 + 3x = 4x + 5$$
$$\underline{-3x \quad -3x}$$
$$14 = x + 5$$
$$\underline{-5 \qquad -5}$$
$$9 = x$$

Choose and complete a graphic organizer to help you study the concept.

1. solving simple equations using addition

2. solving simple equations using subtraction

3. solving simple equations using multiplication

4. solving simple equations using division

5. inverse operations

6. literal equation

Definition: Legendary founders of ancient Rome

Key Words: twins, orphans, wild

Romulus & Remus

Example:

Details: Raised in the wild by a wolf

There's no place like Rome.

"I finished my Information Frame about Romulus and Remus. What did Romulus and Remus say to their mommy?"

Chapter Self-Assessment

As you complete the exercises, use the scale below to rate your understanding of the success criteria in your journal.

1	**2**	**3**	**4**
I do not understand.	I can do it with help.	I can do it on my own.	I can teach someone else.

1.1 Solving Simple Equations *(pp. 3–10)*

Learning Target: Write and solve one-step equations.

Solve the equation. Check your solution.

1. $y + 8 = -11$

2. $3.2 = -0.4n$

3. $-\dfrac{t}{4} = -3\pi$

4. $v - |\,2.4\,| = 5.7$

5. $-6 = -2 + w$

6. $x - \dfrac{2}{3} = -\dfrac{11}{12}$

7. The *boiling point* of a liquid is the temperature at which the liquid becomes a gas. The boiling point of mercury is about $\dfrac{41}{200}$ of the boiling point of lead. Write and solve an equation to find the boiling point of lead.

Boiling point of mercury

8. Write an equation that you can use the Addition Property of Equality to solve.

9. To solve $\dfrac{2}{5}x = 14$, you multiply both sides of the equation by $\dfrac{5}{2}$. Your friend divides both sides of the equation by $\dfrac{2}{5}$. Who is correct? Explain.

10. Write and solve an equation to find the value of x.

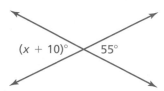

$(x + 10)°$ $55°$

11. The circumference C of a circle is 24π inches. Use the formula $C = 2\pi r$ to find the radius r of the circle.

1.2 Solving Multi-Step Equations (pp. 11–16)

Learning Target: Write and solve multi-step equations.

Solve the equation. Check your solution.

12. $3n + 12 = 30$

13. $2(3 - p) - 17 = 41$

14. $-14x + 28 + 6x = -44$

15. $1.06(12.95 + x) = 31.27$

16. The sum of the angle measures of a quadrilateral is 360°. Find the value of x. Then find the angle measures of the quadrilateral.

17. The equation $P = 2.5m + 35$ represents the price P (in dollars) of a bracelet, where m is the cost of the materials (in dollars). The price of a bracelet is $115. What is the cost of the materials?

18. A 455-foot fence encloses a pasture. What is the length of each side of the pasture?

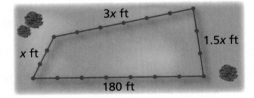

1.3 Solving Equations with Variables on Both Sides (pp. 17–24)

Learning Target: Write and solve equations with variables on both sides.

Solve the equation. Check your solution, if possible.

19. $3(x - 4) = -2(4 - x)$

20. $4 - 5k = -8 - 5k$

21. $5m - 1 = 4m + 5$

22. $3(5p - 3) = 5(p - 1)$

23. $0.4n + 0.1 = 0.5(n + 4)$

24. $7t + 3 = 8 + 7t$

25. $\frac{1}{5}(15b - 7) = 3b - 9$

26. $\frac{1}{6}(12z - 18) = 2z - 3$

27. The side lengths of an isosceles triangle are $(3x + 1)$ inches, $(4x + 5)$ inches, and $(2x + 7)$ inches. Find the perimeters of two possible triangles.

28. A shuttle company charges $3.25 plus $0.55 per mile. A taxi company charges $2.50 plus $0.60 per mile. After how many miles will both companies charge the same amount?

29. You begin the year with $25 in a savings account and $50 in a checking account. Each week you deposit $5 into the savings account and $10 into the checking account. In how many weeks is the amount in the checking account twice the amount in the savings account?

1.4 Rewriting Equations and Formulas *(pp. 25–30)*

Learning Target: Solve literal equations for given variables and convert temperatures.

Solve the equation for y.

30. $6y + x = 8$

31. $10x - \frac{1}{3}y = 15$

32. $20 = 5x + 10y$

33. The formula $F = \frac{9}{5}(K - 273.15) + 32$ converts a temperature from Kelvin K to Fahrenheit F.

  a. Solve the formula for K.

  b. Convert 240°F to Kelvin. Round your answer to the nearest hundredth.

34. Use the trapezoid shown.

  a. Write the formula for the area A of a trapezoid.

  b. Solve the formula for h.

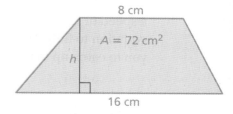

  c. Use the new formula to find the height h of the trapezoid.

35. The equation for a line in slope-intercept form is $y = mx + b$. Solve the equation for x.

36. The formula for the volume of a cylinder is $V = \pi r^2 h$, where r is the radius of the circular base and h is the height of the cylinder.

  a. Solve the formula for h.

  b. Use the new formula to find the height of the cylinder.

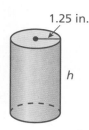

Volume = 6π in.^{3}

Solve the equation. Check your solution, if possible.

1. $4 + y = 9.5$

2. $-\dfrac{x}{9} = -8$

3. $z - \dfrac{2}{3} = \dfrac{1}{8}$

4. $15 = 9 - 3a$

5. $4(b + 5) - 9 = -7$

6. $9j - 8 = 8 + 9j$

7. $3.8n - 13 = 1.4n + 5$

8. $9(8d - 5) + 13 = 12d - 2$

9. $\dfrac{1}{4}t + 4 = \dfrac{3}{4}(t + 8)$

10. The sum of the angle measures of a triangle is $180°$. Find the value of x. Then find the angle measures of the triangle.

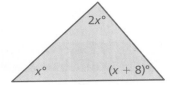

11. A formula for the perimeter of a rectangle is $P = 2\ell + 2w$.

    a. Solve the formula for w.

    b. Use the new formula to find the width w (in meters) of a rectangle with a perimeter of 2 meters and a length of 40 centimeters.

12. Solve $0.5 = 0.4y - 0.25x$ for y.

13. Your basketball team wins a game by 13 points. The opposing team scores 72 points. Explain how to find your team's score.

14. You are biking at a speed of 18 miles per hour. You are 3 miles behind your friend, who is biking at a speed of 12 miles per hour. Write and solve an equation to find the amount of time it takes for you to catch up to your friend.

15. Two scientists are measuring the temperatures of lava. One scientist records a temperature of $1725°F$. The other scientist records a temperature of $950°C$. Which is the greater temperature?

16. Your profit for mowing lawns this week is $24. You are paid $8 per hour and you paid $40 for gas for the lawn mower. How many hours did you work this week?

1. Which value of x makes the equation true?

$$4x = 32$$

A. 8

B. 28

C. 36

D. 128

2. A taxi ride costs \$3 plus \$2 for each mile driven. You spend \$39 on a taxi. This can be modeled by the equation $2m + 3 = 39$, where m represents the number of miles driven. How long was your taxi ride?

F. 18 mi

G. 21 mi

H. 34 mi

I. 72 mi

3. Which of the following equations has exactly one solution?

A. $\frac{2}{3}(x + 6) = \frac{2}{3}x + 4$

B. $\frac{3}{7}y + 13 = 13 - \frac{3}{7}y$

C. $\frac{4}{5}\left(n + \frac{1}{3}\right) = \frac{4}{5}n + \frac{1}{3}$

D. $\frac{7}{8}\left(2t + \frac{1}{8}\right) = \frac{7}{4}t$

4. The perimeter of the square is equal to the perimeter of the triangle. What are the side lengths of the square?

square: $3x + 3$

triangle: $7x - 2$, $7x - 2$, $2x + 4$

5. The formula $d = rt$ relates distance, rate, and time. Solve the formula for t.

F. $t = dr$

G. $t = \dfrac{d}{r}$

H. $t = d - r$

I. $t = \dfrac{r}{d}$

6. What is a possible first step to solve the equation $3x + 5 = 2(x + 7)$?

    A. Combine $3x$ and 5.

    B. Multiply x by 2 and 7 by 2.

    C. Subtract x from $3x$.

    D. Subtract 5 from 7.

7. You work as a sales representative. You earn \$400 per week plus 5% of your total sales for the week.

    Part A Last week, you had total sales of \$5000. Find your total earnings. Show your work.

    Part B One week, you earned \$1350. Let s represent your total sales that week. Write an equation that you can use to find s.

    Part C Using your equation from Part B, find s. Show all steps clearly.

8. In 10 years, your aunt will be 39 years old. Let m represent your aunt's age today. Which equation can you use to find m?

    F. $m = 39 + 10$

    G. $m - 10 = 39$

    H. $m + 10 = 39$

    I. $10m = 39$

9. Which value of y makes the equation $3y + 8 = 7y + 11$ true?

    A. -4.75

    B. -0.75

    C. 0.75

    D. 4.75

10. What is the value of x?

    F. 23

    G. 39

    H. 58

    I. 68

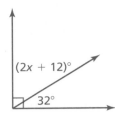

11. You have already saved $35 for a new cell phone. You need $175 to buy the cell phone. You think you can save $10 per week. At this rate, how many more weeks will you need to save money before you can buy the new cell phone?

12. What is the greatest angle measure in the triangle?

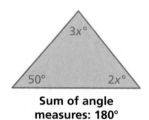

Sum of angle measures: 180°

A. $26°$ **B.** $78°$

C. $108°$ **D.** $138°$

13. Which value of x makes the equation $6(x - 3) = 4x - 7$ true?

F. -5.5 **G.** -2

H. 1.1 **I.** 5.5

14. The drawing below shows equal weights on two sides of a balance scale.

What can you conclude from the drawing?

A. A mug weighs one-third as much as a trophy.

B. A mug weighs one-half as much as a trophy.

C. A mug weighs twice as much as a trophy.

D. A mug weighs three times as much as a trophy.

2 Transformations

Chapter Learning Target:
Understand transformations.

Chapter Success Criteria:
- I can identify a translation.
- I can describe a transformation.
- I can describe a sequence of rigid motions between two congruent figures.
- I can solve real-life problems involving transformations.

STEAM Video: "Shadow Puppets"

STEAM Video

Shadow Puppets

Some puppets are controlled using strings or wires. How else can a puppet be controlled?

Watch the STEAM Video "Shadow Puppets." Then answer the following questions.

1. Tory and Robert are using a light source to display puppets on a screen. Tory wants to show the pig jumping from the floor to the window. Should she use a *translation*, *reflection*, *rotation*, or *dilation*? Explain.

2. How can Tory show the pig getting smaller as it jumps out the window?

Performance Task

Master Puppeteer

After completing this chapter, you will be able to use the concepts you learned to answer the questions in the *STEAM Video Performance Task*. You will be given the coordinates of a kite being used by a puppeteer.

You will be asked to identify transformations for given movements of the kite. When might a puppeteer want to use a reflection?

Getting Ready for Chapter

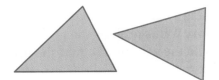

Congruent (same size and shape)

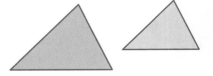

Not Congruent (same shape but not same size)

1. **Work with a partner. Form each triangle on a geoboard.**

- Which of the triangles are congruent to the triangle at the right?

- Measure the sides of each triangle with a ruler. Record your results in a table.

- Write a conclusion about the side lengths of triangles that are congruent.

a.

b.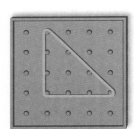

c.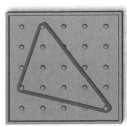

d.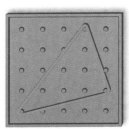

e.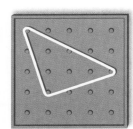

f.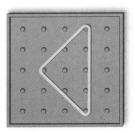

Vocabulary

The following vocabulary terms are defined in this chapter. Think about what the terms might mean and record your thoughts.

translation

rotation

dilation

reflection

rigid motion

similar figures

2.1 Translations

Learning Target: Translate figures in the coordinate plane.

Success Criteria:
• I can identify a translation.
• I can find the coordinates of a translated figure.
• I can use coordinates to translate a figure.

EXPLORATION 1

Sliding Figures

Work with a partner.

a. For each figure below, draw the figure in a coordinate plane. Then copy the figure onto a piece of transparent paper and slide the copy to a new location in the coordinate plane. Describe the location of the copy compared to the location of the original.

• point
• line segment
• line

• triangle
• rectangle

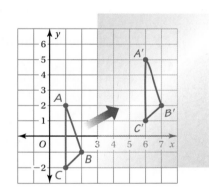

Math Practice

Recognize Usefulness of Tools

How does using transparencies help you compare each figure and its copy?

b. When you slide figures, what do you notice about sides, angles, and parallel lines?

c. Describe the location of each point below compared to the point $A(x, y)$.

$$B(x + 1, y + 2) \qquad C(x - 3, y + 4)$$

$$D(x - 2, y + 3) \qquad E(x + 4, y - 1)$$

d. You copy a point with coordinates (x, y) and slide it horizontally a units and vertically b units. What are the coordinates of the copy?

2.1 Lesson

Key Vocabulary 🔊
transformation, *p. 44*
image, *p. 44*
translation, *p. 44*

A **transformation** changes a figure into another figure. The new figure is called the **image**.

A **translation** is a transformation in which a figure *slides* but does not turn. Every point of the figure moves the same distance and in the same direction.

Slide

EXAMPLE 1   Identifying a Translation

Tell whether the blue figure is a translation of the red figure.

a.

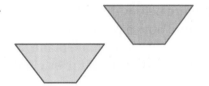

The red figure *slides* to form the blue figure.

▷ So, the blue figure is a translation of the red figure.

b.

The red figure *turns* to form the blue figure.

▷ So, the blue figure is *not* a translation of the red figure.

Try It   **Tell whether the blue figure is a translation of the red figure.**

1.

2.

🔑 Key Idea

Reading 📖

A′ is read "*A* prime." Use *prime* symbols when naming an image.

$A \rightarrow A'$
$B \rightarrow B'$
$C \rightarrow C'$

Translations in the Coordinate Plane

Words   To translate a figure *a* units horizontally and *b* units vertically in a coordinate plane, add *a* to the *x*-coordinates and *b* to the *y*-coordinates of the vertices.

Positive values of *a* and *b* represent translations up and right. Negative values of *a* and *b* represent translations down and left.

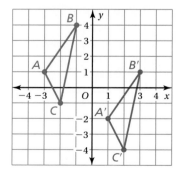

Algebra $(x, y) \rightarrow (x + a, y + b)$

In a translation, the original figure and its image are identical.

EXAMPLE 2 Translating a Figure in the Coordinate Plane

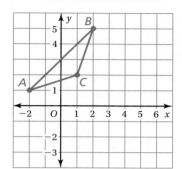

Translate the red triangle 3 units right and 3 units down. What are the coordinates of the image?

Method 1: Use a coordinate plane. Move each vertex 3 units right and 3 units down.

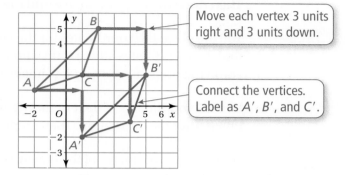

Move each vertex 3 units right and 3 units down.

Connect the vertices. Label as A', B', and C'.

▷ The coordinates of the image are $A'(1, -2)$, $B'(5, 2)$, and $C'(4, -1)$.

Method 2: Use coordinates. Add 3 to the x-coordinates of the vertices and add -3, or subtract 3, from the y-coordinates of the vertices.

$$A(-2, 1) \rightarrow A'(-2 + 3, 1 - 3) \rightarrow A'(1, -2)$$
$$B(2, 5) \longrightarrow B'(2 + 3, 5 - 3) \longrightarrow B'(5, 2)$$
$$C(1, 2) \longrightarrow C'(1 + 3, 2 - 3) \longrightarrow C'(4, -1)$$

▷ The coordinates of the image are $A'(1, -2)$, $B'(5, 2)$, and $C'(4, -1)$.

Try It

3. **WHAT IF?** The red triangle is translated 4 units left and 2 units up. What are the coordinates of the image?

Self-Assessment *for Concepts & Skills*

Solve each exercise. Then rate your understanding of the success criteria in your journal.

IDENTIFYING A TRANSLATION **Tell whether the blue figure is a translation of the red figure.**

4.

5.

6. **TRANSLATING A FIGURE** The vertices of a triangle are $A(-2, -2)$, $B(0, 2)$, and $C(3, 0)$. Translate the triangle 1 unit left and 2 units up. What are the coordinates of the image?

EXAMPLE 3 **Modeling Real Life**

A landscaper represents a park using a coordinate plane. He draws a square with vertices $A(1, -2)$, $B(3, -2)$, $C(3, -4)$, and $D(1, -4)$ to represent the location of a new fountain. City officials want to move the fountain 4 units left and 6 units up. Find the coordinates of the image. Then draw the original figure and the image in a coordinate plane.

 Understand the problem.

You are given the coordinates for the vertices of a fountain. You are asked to find the coordinates after a translation 4 units left and 6 units up, and then graph the original figure and its image in a coordinate plane.

Make a plan.

Use the coordinates of the original figure to calculate the coordinates of the image after the translation. Then graph each figure in a coordinate plane.

Solve and check.

To find the coordinates of the image, subtract 4 from each x-coordinate and add 6 to each y-coordinate.

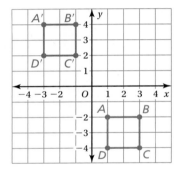

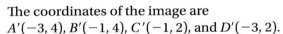
$$(x, y) \longrightarrow (x - 4, y + 6)$$

Check Counting grid lines in the graph shows that each vertex of the image is translated 4 units left and 6 units up. ✓

$A(1, -2) \longrightarrow A'(1 - 4, -2 + 6) \longrightarrow A'(-3, 4)$

$B(3, -2) \longrightarrow B'(3 - 4, -2 + 6) \longrightarrow B'(-1, 4)$

$C(3, -4) \longrightarrow C'(3 - 4, -4 + 6) \longrightarrow C'(-1, 2)$

$D(1, -4) \longrightarrow D'(1 - 4, -4 + 6) \longrightarrow D'(-3, 2)$

The coordinates of the image are $A'(-3, 4)$, $B'(-1, 4)$, $C'(-1, 2)$, and $D'(-3, 2)$.

 Self-Assessment for Problem Solving

Solve each exercise. Then rate your understanding of the success criteria in your journal.

7. A neighborhood planner uses a coordinate plane to design a new neighborhood. The coordinates $A(1, -1)$, $B(1, -2)$, and $C(2, -1)$ represent House A, House B, and House C. The planner decides to place a playground centered at the origin, and moves the houses to make space. House A is now located at $A'(3, -4)$. What are the new coordinates of House B and House C when each house is moved using the same translation? Justify your answer.

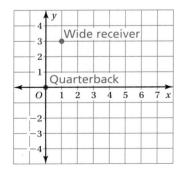

8. The locations of a quarterback and a wide receiver on a football field are represented in a coordinate plane. The quarterback throws the football to the point $(6, -2)$. Use a translation to describe a path the wide receiver can take to catch the pass.

2.1 Practice

Go to *BigIdeasMath.com* to get
HELP with solving the exercises.

▶ Review & Refresh

Solve the equation for y.

1. $6x + y = 12$　　　　**2.** $9 = x + 3y$　　　　**3.** $\frac{1}{3}x + 2y = 8$

4. You put \$550 in an account that earns 4.4% simple interest per year.
How much interest do you earn in 6 months?

　　A. \$1.21　　　　**B.** \$12.10　　　　**C.** \$121.00　　　　**D.** \$145.20

▶ Concepts, Skills, & Problem Solving

DESCRIBING RELATIONSHIPS **For each figure, describe the location of the blue figure
relative to the location of the red figure.** (See Exploration 1, p. 43.)

5. 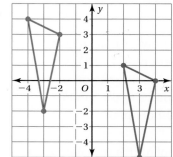　　　　**6.**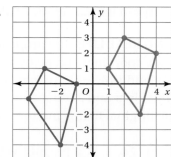

IDENTIFYING A TRANSLATION **Tell whether the blue figure is a translation of the
red figure.**

7. 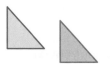　　　　**8.** 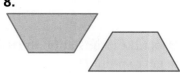　　　　**9.**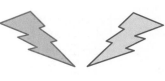

10. 　　　　**11.** 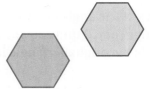　　　　**12.**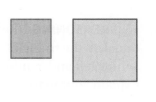

TRANSLATING A FIGURE **The vertices of a triangle are $L(0, 1)$, $M(1, -2)$, and
$N(-2, 1)$. Draw the figure and its image after the translation.**

13. 1 unit left and 6 units up　　　　**14.** 5 units right

15. $(x + 2, y + 3)$　　　　**16.** $(x - 3, y - 4)$

17. **⬤ YOU BE THE TEACHER** Your friend
translates point A 2 units down and 1 unit right.
Is your friend correct? Explain your reasoning.

> $A(3, 1) \rightarrow A'(3 - 2, 1 + 1) \rightarrow A'(1, 2)$
>
> The translated point is $A'(1, 2)$.

18. TRANSLATING A FIGURE
Translate the triangle 4 units right and 3 units down. What are the coordinates of the image?

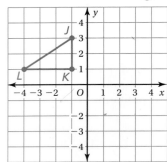

19. TRANSLATING A FIGURE
Translate the figure 2 units left and 4 units down. What are the coordinates of the image?

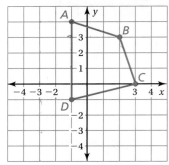

DESCRIBING A TRANSLATION Describe the translation of the point to its image.

20. $(3, -2) \longrightarrow (1, 0)$

21. $(-8, -4) \longrightarrow (-3, 5)$

22. **MP REASONING** You can click and drag an icon on a computer's desktop. Is this an example of a translation? Explain.

23. **MP MODELING REAL LIFE** The proposed location for a new oil platform is represented in a coordinate plane by a rectangle with vertices $A(1, -3)$, $B(1, 4)$, $C(4, 4)$, and $D(4, -3)$. An inspector recommends moving the oil platform 4 units right and 2 units down. Find the coordinates of the image. Then draw the original figure and the image in the coordinate plane.

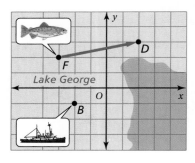

24. **MP PROBLEM SOLVING** A school of fish translates from point F to point D.

    a. Describe the translation of the school of fish.

    b. Can the fishing boat make the same translation? Explain.

    c. Describe a translation the fishing boat could make to get to point D.

25. **MP REASONING** The vertices of a triangle are $A(0, -3)$, $B(2, -1)$, and $C(3, -3)$. You translate the triangle 5 units right and 2 units down. Then you translate the image 3 units left and 8 units down. Is the original triangle identical to the final image? Explain your reasoning.

26. **DIG DEEPER!** In chess, a knight can move only in an L-shaped pattern:
- *two* vertical squares, then *one* horizontal square;
- *two* horizontal squares, then *one* vertical square;
- *one* vertical square, then *two* horizontal squares; or
- *one* horizontal square, then *two* vertical squares.

Write a series of translations to move the knight from g8 to g5.

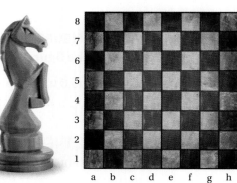

2.2 Reflections

Learning Target: Reflect figures in the coordinate plane.

Success Criteria:
- I can identify a reflection.
- I can find the coordinates of a figure reflected in an axis.
- I can use coordinates to reflect a figure in the *x*- or *y*-axis.

EXPLORATION 1

Reflecting Figures

Work with a partner.

a. For each figure below, draw the figure in the coordinate plane. Then copy the axes and the figure onto a piece of transparent paper. Flip the transparent paper and align the origin and the axes with the coordinate plane. For each pair of figures, describe the line of symmetry.

- point
- line segment
- line

- triangle
- rectangle

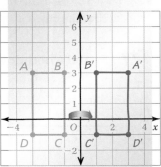

b. When you reflect figures, what do you notice about sides, angles, and parallel lines?

c. Describe the relationship between each point below and the point $A(4, 7)$ in terms of reflections.

$B(-4, 7)$ $C(4, -7)$ $D(-4, -7)$

d. A point with coordinates (x, y) is reflected in the *x*-axis. What are the coordinates of the image?

e. Repeat part (d) when the point is reflected in the *y*-axis.

2.2 Lesson

A **reflection**, or *flip*, is a transformation in which a figure is reflected in a line called the **line of reflection**. A reflection creates a mirror image of the original figure.

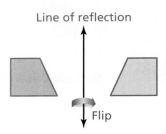

Line of reflection

Flip

EXAMPLE 1 ## Identifying Reflections

Tell whether the blue figure is a reflection of the red figure.

a.

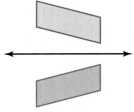

The red figure can be *flipped* to form the blue figure.

▷ So, the blue figure is a reflection of the red figure.

b.

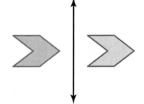

If the red figure were *flipped,* it would point to the left.

▷ So, the blue figure is *not* a reflection of the red figure.

Try It **Tell whether the blue figure is a reflection of the red figure.**

1.

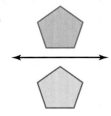

2.

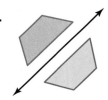

 Key Idea

Reflections in the Coordinate Plane

Words To reflect a figure in the *x*-axis, take the opposite of the *y*-coordinate.

To reflect a figure in the *y*-axis, take the opposite of the *x*-coordinate.

Algebra Reflection in *x*-axis: $(x, y) \rightarrow (x, -y)$

Reflection in *y*-axis: $(x, y) \rightarrow (-x, y)$

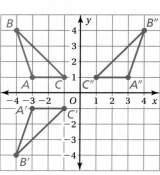

In a reflection, the original figure and its image are identical.

🔊 **Multi-Language Glossary at** *BigIdeasMath.com*

EXAMPLE 2 **Reflecting Figures**

The vertices of a triangle are $A(1, 1)$, $B(1, 4)$, and $C(3, 4)$. Draw the figure and its reflection in (a) the *x*-axis and (b) the *y*-axis. What are the coordinates of the image?

Another Method
Take the opposite of each *y*-coordinate. The *x*-coordinates do not change.

$A(1, 1) \rightarrow A'(1, -1)$

$B(1, 4) \rightarrow B'(1, -4)$

$C(3, 4) \rightarrow C'(3, -4)$ ✓

a. Point *A* is 1 unit above the *x*-axis, so plot A' 1 unit below the *x*-axis. Points *B* and *C* are 4 units above the *x*-axis, so plot B' and C' 4 units below the *x*-axis.

> The coordinates of the image are $A'(1, -1)$, $B'(1, -4)$, and $C'(3, -4)$.

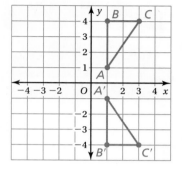

b. Points *A* and *B* are 1 unit to the right of the *y*-axis, so plot A' and B' 1 unit to the left of the *y*-axis. Point *C* is 3 units to the right of the *y*-axis, so plot C' 3 units to the left of the *y*-axis.

> The coordinates of the image are $A'(-1, 1)$, $B'(-1, 4)$, and $C'(-3, 4)$.

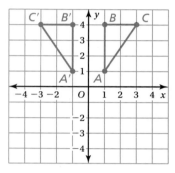

Try It

3. The vertices of a rectangle are $A(-4, -3)$, $B(-4, -1)$, $C(-1, -1)$, and $D(-1, -3)$. Draw the figure and its reflection in (a) the *x*-axis and (b) the *y*-axis.

 Self-Assessment for Concepts & Skills

Solve each exercise. Then rate your understanding of the success criteria in your journal.

4. REFLECTING A FIGURE The vertices of a triangle are $J(-3, -5)$, $K(-2, 2)$, and $L(1, -4)$. Draw the figure and its reflection in (a) the *x*-axis and (b) the *y*-axis.

5. WHICH ONE DOESN'T BELONG? Which transformation does *not* belong with the other three? Explain your reasoning.

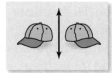 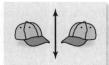 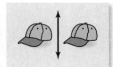 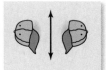

EXAMPLE 3 **Modeling Real Life**

A graphic artist designs a T-shirt using a pentagon with vertices $P(0, 0)$, $Q(-2, 0)$, $R(-1, 3)$, $S(-4, 3)$, and $T(0, 7)$. The artist reflects the pentagon in the y-axis to create the design. Find the coordinates of the reflected image. Then draw the design in the coordinate plane.

The pentagon is reflected in the y-axis. To find the coordinates of the reflected image, take the opposite of each x-coordinate. The y-coordinates do not change.

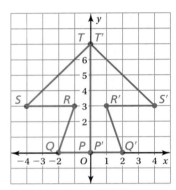

$$(x, y) \longrightarrow (-x, y)$$

$$P(0, 0) \longrightarrow P'(0, 0)$$

$$Q(-2, 0) \longrightarrow Q'(2, 0)$$

$$R(-1, 3) \longrightarrow R'(1, 3)$$

$$S(-4, 3) \longrightarrow S'(4, 3)$$

$$T(0, 7) \longrightarrow T'(0, 7)$$

▷ The coordinates of the reflected image are $P'(0, 0)$, $Q'(2, 0)$, $R'(1, 3)$, $S'(4, 3)$, and $T'(0, 7)$.

Self-Assessment for Problem Solving

Solve each exercise. Then rate your understanding of the success criteria in your journal.

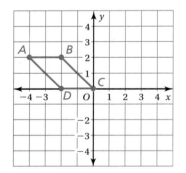

6. You design a logo using the figure shown at the left. You want both the x-axis and the y-axis to be lines of reflection. Describe how to use reflections to complete the design. Then draw the logo in the coordinate plane.

7. **DIG DEEPER!** You hit the golf ball along the path shown, so that its final location is a reflection in the y-axis of its starting location.

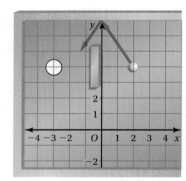

  a. Does the golf ball land in the hole? Explain.

  b. Your friend tries the shot from the same starting location. He bounces the ball off the wall at the point $(-0.5, 7)$ so that its path is a reflection. Does the golf ball land in the hole?

2.2 Practice

 Go to *BigIdeasMath.com* to get HELP with solving the exercises.

▶ Review & Refresh

The vertices of a quadrilateral are $P(-1, -1)$, $Q(0, 4)$, $R(3, 1)$, and $S(1, -2)$. Draw the figure and its image after the translation.

1. 7 units down

2. 3 units left and 2 units up

3. $(x + 4, y - 1)$

4. $(x - 5, y - 6)$

Tell whether the angles are *complementary*, *supplementary*, or *neither*.

5.
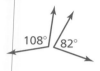
108° 82°

6.

47°
43°

7.

38°
62°

8. 36 is 75% of what number?

   A. 27   **B.** 48   **C.** 54   **D.** 63

▶▶ Concepts, Skills, & Problem Solving

DESCRIBING RELATIONSHIPS Describe the relationship between the given point and the point $A(5, 3)$ in terms of reflections. (See Exploration 1, p. 49.)

9. $B(5, -3)$

10. $C(-5, -3)$

11. $D(-5, 3)$

IDENTIFYING A REFLECTION Tell whether the blue figure is a reflection of the red figure.

12.
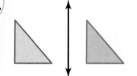

13.

14.
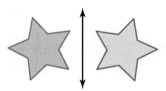

15.
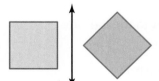

16.
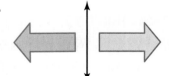

17.

REFLECTING FIGURES Draw the figure and its reflection in the *x*-axis. Identify the coordinates of the image.

18. $A(3, 2)$, $B(4, 4)$, $C(1, 3)$

19. $M(-2, 1)$, $N(0, 3)$, $P(2, 2)$

20. $H(2, -2)$, $J(4, -1)$, $K(6, -3)$, $L(5, -4)$

21. $D(-2, -5)$, $E(0, -1)$, $F(2, -1)$, $G(0, -5)$

REFLECTING FIGURES Draw the figure and its reflection in the y-axis. Identify the coordinates of the image.

22. $Q(-4, 2), R(-2, 4), S(-1, 1)$

23. $T(4, -2), U(4, 2), V(6, -2)$

24. $W(2, -1), X(5, -2), Y(5, -5), Z(2, -4)$

25. $J(2, 2), K(7, 4), L(9, -2), M(3, -1)$

26. **MP REASONING** Which letters look the same when reflected in the line?

A B C D E F G H I J K L M N O P Q R S T U V W X Y Z

MP STRUCTURE The coordinates of a point and its image after a reflection are given. Identify the line of reflection.

27. $(2, -2) \longrightarrow (2, 2)$

28. $(-4, 1) \longrightarrow (4, 1)$

29. $(-2, -5) \longrightarrow (4, -5)$

30. $(-3, -4) \longrightarrow (-3, 0)$

TRANSFORMING FIGURES Find the coordinates of the figure after the transformations.

31. Translate the triangle 1 unit right and 5 units down. Then reflect the image in the y-axis.

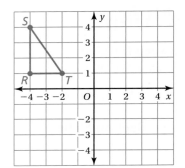

32. Reflect the trapezoid in the x-axis. Then translate the image 2 units left and 3 units up.

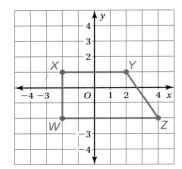

33. **MP REASONING** In Exercises 31 and 32, is the original figure identical to the final image? Explain.

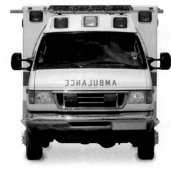

34. **CRITICAL THINKING** Hold a mirror to the left side of the photo of the vehicle.

   a. What word do you see in the mirror?

   b. Why do you think it is written that way on the front of the vehicle?

35. **DIG DEEPER!** Reflect the triangle in the line $y = x$. How are the x- and y-coordinates of the image related to the x- and y-coordinates of the original triangle?

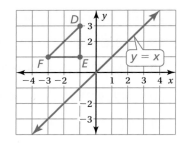

2.3 Rotations

Learning Target: Rotate figures in the coordinate plane.

Success Criteria:
• I can identify a rotation.
• I can find the coordinates of a figure rotated about the origin.
• I can use coordinates to rotate a figure about the origin.

EXPLORATION 1

Rotating Figures

Work with a partner.

Math Practice

Explain the Meaning
What does it mean to rotate a figure about the origin?

a. For each figure below, draw the figure in the coordinate plane. Then copy the axes and the figure onto a piece of transparent paper. Turn the transparent paper and align the origin and the axes with the coordinate plane. For each pair of figures, describe the angle of rotation.

• point
• line segment
• line

• triangle
• rectangle

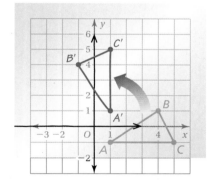

b. When you rotate figures, what do you notice about sides, angles, and parallel lines?

c. Describe the relationship between each point below and the point $A(3, 6)$ in terms of rotations.

$$B(-3, -6) \qquad C(6, -3) \qquad D(-6, 3)$$

d. What are the coordinates of a point $P(x, y)$ after a rotation 90° counterclockwise about the origin? 180°? 270°?

Key Vocabulary 🔊
rotation, *p. 56*
center of rotation, *p. 56*
angle of rotation, *p. 56*

A **rotation**, or *turn*, is a transformation in which a figure is rotated about a point called the **center of rotation**. The number of degrees a figure rotates is the **angle of rotation**.

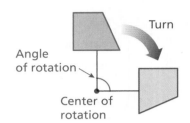

Turn

Angle of rotation

Center of rotation

EXAMPLE 1 **Identifying a Rotation**

You must rotate the puzzle piece 270° clockwise about point *P* to fit it into a puzzle. Which piece fits in the puzzle as shown?

●*P*

A.

B.

C.

D.

Rotate the puzzle piece 270° clockwise about point *P*.

When rotating figures, it may help to sketch the rotation in several steps, as shown in Example 1.

turn 270°

P

▷ So, the correct answer is **C.**

Try It Tell whether the blue figure is a rotation of the red figure about the origin. If so, give the angle and direction of rotation.

1.
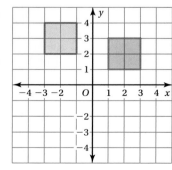

2.

🔊 *Multi-Language Glossary at BigIdeasMath.com*

You can use coordinate rules to find the coordinates of a point after a rotation of 90°, 180°, or 270° about the origin.

 **Key Idea**

Rotations in the Coordinate Plane
When a point (x, y) is rotated counterclockwise about the origin, the following are true.

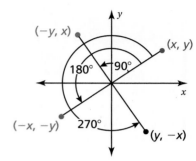

- For a rotation of 90°, $(x, y) \rightarrow (-y, x)$.
- For a rotation of 180°, $(x, y) \rightarrow (-x, -y)$.
- For a rotation of 270°, $(x, y) \rightarrow (y, -x)$.

In a rotation, the original figure and its image are identical.

> A counterclockwise rotation of $n°$ is the same as a clockwise rotation of $(360 - n)°$. Similarly, a clockwise rotation of $n°$ is the same as a counterclockwise rotation of $(360 - n)°$.

EXAMPLE 2 **Rotating a Figure**

Math Practice

Build Arguments
Explain why you do not need to specify direction when rotating a figure 180°.

The vertices of a trapezoid are $W(-4, 2)$, $X(-3, 4)$, $Y(-1, 4)$, and $Z(-1, 2)$. Rotate the trapezoid 180° about the origin. What are the coordinates of the image?

A point (x, y) rotated 180° about the origin results in an image with coordinates $(-x, -y)$.

$$(x, y) \longrightarrow (-x, -y)$$

$$W(-4, 2) \longrightarrow W'(4, -2)$$
$$X(-3, 4) \longrightarrow X'(3, -4)$$
$$Y(-1, 4) \longrightarrow Y'(1, -4)$$
$$Z(-1, 2) \longrightarrow Z'(1, -2)$$

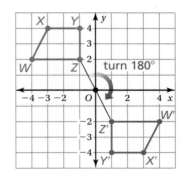

> The coordinates of the image are $W'(4, -2)$, $X'(3, -4)$, $Y'(1, -4)$, and $Z'(1, -2)$.

Try It The vertices of a figure are given. Rotate the figure as described. Find the coordinates of the image.

3. $J(-4, -4)$, $K(-4, 2)$, $L(-1, 0)$, $M(-2, -3)$; 180° about the origin

4. $P(-3, 2)$, $Q(6, 1)$, $R(-1, -5)$; 90° counterclockwise about the origin

5. $A(5, 3)$, $B(4, -1)$, $C(1, -1)$; 90° clockwise about the origin

EXAMPLE 3 **Using More Than One Transformation**

The vertices of a rectangle are $A(-3, -3)$, $B(1, -3)$, $C(1, -5)$, and $D(-3, -5)$. Rotate the rectangle 90° clockwise about the origin, and then reflect it in the *y*-axis. What are the coordinates of the image?

Common Error

Be sure to pay attention to whether a rotation is clockwise or counterclockwise.

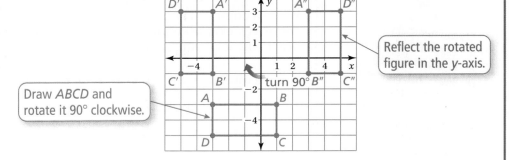

Draw *ABCD* and rotate it 90° clockwise.

Reflect the rotated figure in the *y*-axis.

The coordinates of the image are $A''(3, 3)$, $B''(3, -1)$, $C''(5, -1)$, and $D''(5, 3)$.

Try It

6. The vertices of a triangle are $P(-1, 2)$, $Q(-1, 0)$, and $R(2, 0)$. Rotate the triangle 180° about the origin, and then reflect it in the *x*-axis. What are the coordinates of the image?

Self-Assessment *for Concepts & Skills*

Solve each exercise. Then rate your understanding of the success criteria in your journal.

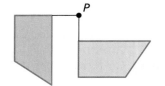

7. **IDENTIFYING A ROTATION** Tell whether the blue figure is a rotation of the red figure about point *P*. If so, give the angle and direction of rotation.

8. **DIFFERENT WORDS, SAME QUESTION** Which is different? Find "both" answers.

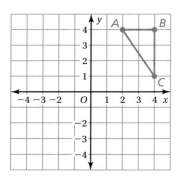

What are the coordinates of the image after a 90° clockwise rotation about the origin?

What are the coordinates of the image after a 270° clockwise rotation about the origin?

What are the coordinates of the image after turning the figure 90° to the right about the origin?

What are the coordinates of the image after a 270° counterclockwise rotation about the origin?

EXAMPLE 4

EXAMPLE 4   **Modeling Real Life**

A carousel is represented in a coordinate plane with the center of the carousel at the origin. You and three friends sit at $A(-4, -4)$, $B(-3, 0)$, $C(-1, -2)$, and $D(-2, -3)$. At the end of the ride, your positions have rotated 270° clockwise about the center of the carousel. What are your locations at the end of the ride?

A rotation of 270° clockwise about the origin is the same as a rotation of 90° counterclockwise about the origin. Use coordinate rules to find the locations after a rotation of 90° counterclockwise about the origin.

A point (x, y) rotated 90° counterclockwise about the origin results in an image with coordinates $(-y, x)$.

$$(x, y) \longrightarrow (-y, x)$$

$$A(-4, -4) \longrightarrow A'(4, -4)$$
$$B(-3, 0) \longrightarrow B'(0, -3)$$
$$C(-1, -2) \longrightarrow C'(2, -1)$$
$$D(-2, -3) \longrightarrow D'(3, -2)$$

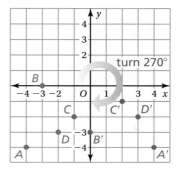

▷ Your locations at the end of the ride are $A'(4, -4)$, $B'(0, -3)$, $C'(2, -1)$, and $D'(3, -2)$.

Self-Assessment for Problem Solving

Solve each exercise. Then rate your understanding of the success criteria in your journal.

9. You move the red game piece to the indicated location using a rotation about the origin, followed by a translation. What are the coordinates of the vertices of the game piece after the rotation? Justify your answer.

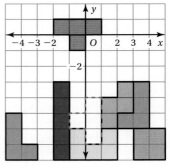

10. **DIG DEEPER!** *Skytyping* is a technique that airplanes use to write messages in the sky. The coordinate plane shows a message typed in the sky over a city, where the positive *y*-axis represents north. What does the message say? How can you transform the message so that it is read from north to south?

Go to *BigIdeasMath.com* to get HELP with solving the exercises.

▶Review & Refresh

Tell whether the blue figure is a reflection of the red figure.

1.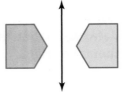

2.

Find the circumference of the object. Use 3.14 or $\frac{22}{7}$ for π.

3.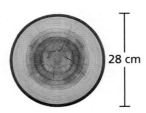
28 cm

4.
11.4 in.

5.
0.5 ft

⏩ Concepts, Skills, & Problem Solving

DESCRIBING RELATIONSHIPS Describe the relationship between the given point and the point $A(2, 7)$ in terms of rotations. (See Exploration 1, p. 55.)

6. $B(7, -2)$

7. $C(-7, 2)$

8. $D(-2, -7)$

IDENTIFYING A ROTATION Tell whether the blue figure is a rotation of the red figure about the origin. If so, give the angle and direction of rotation.

9.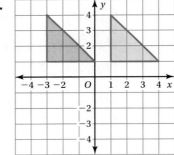

10.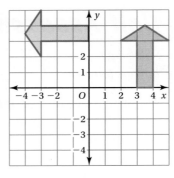

11.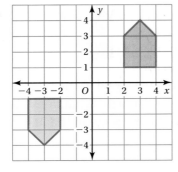

12.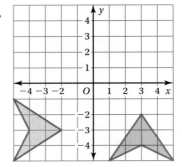

ROTATING A FIGURE The vertices of a figure are given. Rotate the figure as described. Find the coordinates of the image.

13. $A(2, -2)$, $B(4, -1)$, $C(4, -3)$, $D(2, -4)$
    90° counterclockwise about the origin

14. $F(1, 2)$, $G(3, 5)$, $H(3, 2)$
    180° about the origin

15. $J(-4, 1)$, $K(-2, 1)$, $L(-4, -3)$
    90° clockwise about the origin

16. $P(-3, 4)$, $Q(-1, 4)$, $R(-2, 1)$, $S(-4, 1)$
    270° clockwise about the origin

17. $W(-6, -2)$, $X(-2, -2)$, $Y(-2, -6)$, $Z(-5, -6)$
    270° counterclockwise about the origin

18. $A(1, -1)$, $B(5, -6)$, $C(1, -6)$
    90° counterclockwise about the origin

19. **(MP) YOU BE THE TEACHER** The vertices of a triangle are $A(4, 4)$, $B(1, -2)$, and $C(-3, 0)$. Your friend finds the coordinates of the image after a rotation 90° clockwise about the origin. Is your friend correct? Explain your reasoning.

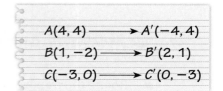

$A(4, 4) \longrightarrow A'(-4, 4)$
$B(1, -2) \longrightarrow B'(2, 1)$
$C(-3, 0) \longrightarrow C'(0, -3)$

20. **(MP) PROBLEM SOLVING** A game show contestant spins the prize wheel shown. The arrow remains in a fixed position while the wheel rotates. The wheel stops spinning, resulting in an image that is a rotation 270° clockwise about the center of the wheel. What is the result?

(MP) PATTERNS A figure has *rotational symmetry* if a rotation of 180° or less produces an image that fits exactly on the original figure. Determine whether the figure has rotational symmetry. Explain your reasoning.

21.

22.

23.

USING MORE THAN ONE TRANSFORMATION The vertices of a figure are given. Find the coordinates of the image after the transformations given.

24. $R(-7, -5)$, $S(-1, -2)$, $T(-1, -5)$
    Rotate 90° counterclockwise about the origin. Then translate 3 units left and 8 units up.

25. $J(-4, 4)$, $K(-3, 4)$, $L(-1, 1)$, $M(-4, 1)$
    Reflect in the x-axis, and then rotate 180° about the origin.

CRITICAL THINKING Describe two different sequences of transformations in which the blue figure is the image of the red figure.

26.

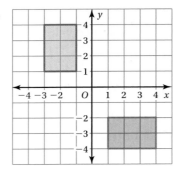

27.

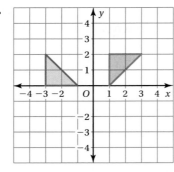

28. **MP** **REASONING** A trapezoid has vertices $A(-6, -2)$, $B(-3, -2)$, $C(-1, -4)$, and $D(-6, -4)$.

    a. Rotate the trapezoid 180° about the origin. What are the coordinates of the image?

    b. Describe a way to obtain the same image without using rotations.

ROTATING A FIGURE The vertices of a figure are given. Rotate the figure as described. Find the coordinates of the image.

29. $D(2, 1)$, $E(2, -2)$, $F(-1, 4)$
    90° counterclockwise about vertex D

30. $L(-4, -3)$, $M(-1, -1)$, $N(2, -2)$
    180° about vertex M

31. $W(-5, 0)$, $X(-1, 4)$, $Y(3, -1)$, $Z(0, -4)$
    270° counterclockwise about vertex W

32. $D(-3, -4)$, $E(-5, 2)$, $F(1, -1)$, $G(3, -7)$
    270° clockwise about vertex E

33. **MP** **LOGIC** You want to find the treasure located on the map at ✕. You are located at ●. The following transformations will lead you to the treasure, but they are not in the correct order. Find the correct order. Use each transformation exactly once.

    • Rotate 180° about the origin.

    • Reflect in the y-axis.

    • Rotate 90° counterclockwise about the origin.

    • Translate 1 unit right and 1 unit up.

34. **DIG DEEPER!** You rotate a triangle 90° counterclockwise about the origin. Then you translate its image 1 unit left and 2 units down. The vertices of the final image are $(-5, 0)$, $(-2, 2)$, and $(-2, -1)$. What are the vertices of the original triangle?

2.4 Congruent Figures

Learning Target: Understand the concept of congruent figures.

Success Criteria:
- I can identify congruent figures.
- I can describe a sequence of rigid motions between two congruent figures.

Transforming Figures

Work with a partner.

a. For each pair of figures whose vertices are given below, draw the figures in a coordinate plane. Then copy one of the figures onto a piece of transparent paper. Use transformations to try to obtain one of the figures from the other figure.

- $A(-5, 1)$, $B(-5, -4)$, $C(-2, -4)$ and $D(1, 4)$, $E(1, -1)$, $F(-2, -1)$

- $G(1, 2)$, $H(2, -6)$, $J(5, 0)$ and $L(-1, -2)$, $M(-2, 6)$, $N(-5, 0)$

- $P(0, 0)$, $Q(2, 2)$, $R(4, -2)$ and $X(0, 0)$, $Y(3, 3)$, $Z(6, -3)$

- $A(0, 4)$, $B(3, 8)$, $C(6, 4)$, $D(3, 0)$ and $F(-4, -3)$, $G(-8, 0)$, $H(-4, 3)$, $J(0, 0)$

- $P(-2, 1)$, $Q(-1, -2)$, $R(1, -2)$, $S(1, 1)$ and $W(7, 1)$, $X(5, -2)$, $Y(3, -2)$, $Z(3, 1)$

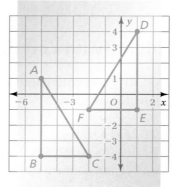

Math Practice

Communicate Precisely

When you can use translations, reflections, and rotations to obtain one figure from another, what do you know about the side lengths and angle measures of the figures?

b. Which pairs of figures in part (a) are identical? Explain your reasoning.

c. Figure A and Figure B are identical. Do you think there must be a sequence of transformations that obtains Figure A from Figure B? Explain your reasoning.

A **rigid motion** is a transformation that preserves length and angle measure. Translations, reflections, and rotations are rigid motions.

Key Idea

Congruent Figures

Two figures are **congruent figures** when one can be obtained from the other by a sequence of rigid motions. Congruent figures have the same size and the same shape. Angles with the same measure are called **congruent angles**. Sides with the same measure are **congruent sides**.

The triangles below are congruent.

Reading

The symbol △ means *triangle*. The symbol ≅ means *is congruent to*. In the Key Idea,

$\triangle ABC \cong \triangle DEF$.

In diagrams, matching arcs indicate congruent angles.

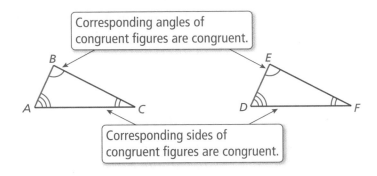

Sides
$\overline{AB} \cong \overline{DE}, \overline{BC} \cong \overline{EF}, \overline{AC} \cong \overline{DF}$

Angles
$\angle A \cong \angle D, \angle B \cong \angle E, \angle C \cong \angle F$

EXAMPLE 1 Identifying Congruent Figures

Common Error

When writing a congruence statement, make sure to list the vertices of the figures in the correct order.

Identify any congruent figures in the coordinate plane.

$\triangle DEF$ is a translation 1 unit left and 5 units down of $\triangle MNP$. So, $\triangle DEF$ and $\triangle MNP$ are congruent.

$\triangle ABC$ is a reflection in the x-axis of $\triangle JKL$. So, $\triangle ABC$ and $\triangle JKL$ are congruent.

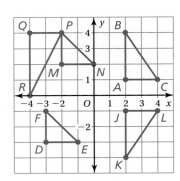

Try It

1. A triangle has vertices $X(0, 4)$, $Y(4, 4)$, and $Z(4, 2)$. Is $\triangle XYZ$ congruent to any of the triangles in Example 1? Explain.

Multi-Language Glossary at *BigIdeasMath.com*

EXAMPLE 2 **Describing a Sequence of Rigid Motions**

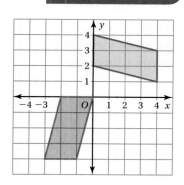

The red figure is congruent to the blue figure. Describe a sequence of rigid motions between the figures.

The orientations of the figures are different. You can rotate the red figure 90° to match the orientation of the blue figure.

After rotating the red figure, you can translate its image to the blue figure.

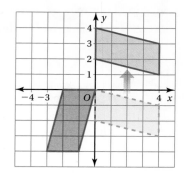

 So, one possible sequence of rigid motions is to rotate the red figure 90° counterclockwise about the origin and then translate the image 4 units up.

Try It

2. Describe a different sequence of rigid motions between the figures.

Self-Assessment for Concepts & Skills

Solve each exercise. Then rate your understanding of the success criteria in your journal.

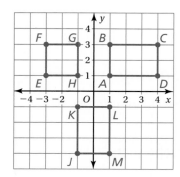

3. **IDENTIFYING CONGRUENT FIGURES** Use the coordinate plane shown.

   a. Identify any congruent figures.

   b. A rectangle has vertices $W(-4, -1)$, $X(-4, 2)$, $Y(-1, 2)$, and $Z(-1, -1)$. Is Rectangle $WXYZ$ congruent to any of the rectangles in the coordinate plane? Explain.

RIGID MOTIONS The red figure is congruent to the blue figure. Describe a sequence of rigid motions between the figures.

4.

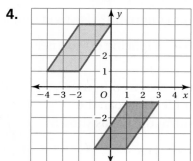

5.

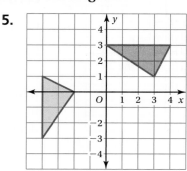

EXAMPLE 3 **Modeling Real Life**

You can use the buttons shown at the left to transform objects in a computer program. You can rotate objects 90° in either direction and reflect objects in a horizontal or vertical line. How can you transform the emoji as shown below?

Original

Image

When you rotate the emoji 90° counterclockwise, the tongue is in the wrong place. Reflect the emoji in a horizontal line to move the tongue to the correct location.

To transform the emoji as shown, you can use a 90° counterclockwise rotation followed by a reflection in a horizontal line.

 Self-Assessment *for Problem Solving*

Solve each exercise. Then rate your understanding of the success criteria in your journal.

6. In the coordinate plane at the left, each grid line represents 50 feet. Each figure represents a pasture.

   a. Are the figures congruent? Use rigid motions to justify your answer.

   b. How many feet of fencing do you need to enclose each pasture?

7. A home decorator uses a computer to design a floor tile. How can the decorator transform the tile as shown?

   Original Image

2.4 Practice

▶ Review & Refresh

The vertices of a figure are given. Rotate the figure as described. Find the coordinates of the image.

1. $A(1, 3)$, $B(2, 5)$, $C(3, 5)$, $D(2, 3)$
90° counterclockwise about the origin

2. $F(-2, 1)$, $G(-1, 3)$, $H(3, 1)$
180° about the origin

Factor the expression using the greatest common factor.

3. $4n - 32$

4. $3w + 66$

5. $2y - 18$

▶ Concepts, Skills, & Problem Solving

TRANSFORMING FIGURES The vertices of a pair of figures are given. Determine whether the figures are identical. (See Exploration 1, p. 63.)

6. $G(0, 0)$, $H(3, 2)$, $J(1, -2)$ and $L(-1, 0)$, $M(2, 2)$, $N(0, -3)$

7. $A(-2, -1)$, $B(-2, 2)$, $C(-1, 1)$, $D(-1, -2)$ and $F(-2, 0)$, $G(-1, 1)$, $H(2, 1)$, $J(1, 0)$

IDENTIFYING CONGRUENT FIGURES Identify any congruent figures in the coordinate plane.

8.
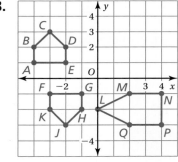

9.
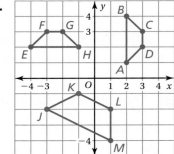

DESCRIBING A SEQUENCE OF RIGID MOTIONS The red figure is congruent to the blue figure. Describe a sequence of rigid motions between the figures.

10.
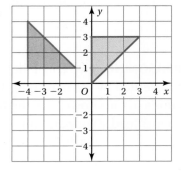

11.
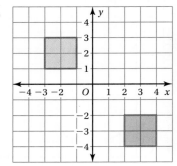

12. **MP YOU BE THE TEACHER** Your friend describes a sequence of rigid motions between the figures. Is your friend correct? Explain your reasoning.

Reflect the red figure in the x-axis, and then translate it left 5 units.

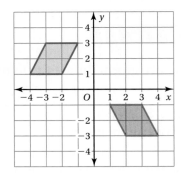

NAMING CORRESPONDING PARTS The figures are congruent. Name the corresponding angles and the corresponding sides.

13.

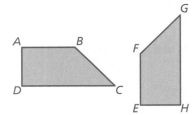

14.

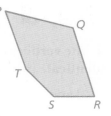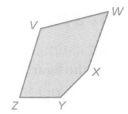

15. **MP MODELING REAL LIFE** You use a computer program to transform an emoji. How can you transform the emoji as shown?

Original   Image

16. **CRITICAL THINKING** Two figures are congruent. Are the areas of the two figures the same? the perimeters? Explain your reasoning.

17. **DIG DEEPER!** The houses are identical.

    a. What is the length of side *LM*?

    b. Which angle of *JKLMN* corresponds to ∠*D*?

    c. Side *AB* is congruent to side *AE*. What is the length of side *AB*? What is the perimeter of *ABCDE*?

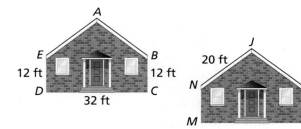

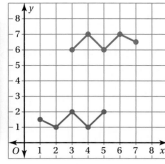

18. **MP REASONING** Two constellations are represented by the figures in the coordinate plane shown. Are the figures congruent? Justify your answer.

2.5 Dilations

Learning Target: Dilate figures in the coordinate plane.

Success Criteria:
- I can identify a dilation.
- I can find the coordinates of a figure dilated with respect to the origin.
- I can use coordinates to dilate a figure with respect to the origin.

The Meaning of a Word ▷ Dilate

When you have your eyes checked, the optometrist sometimes

dilates one or both of the pupils of your eyes.

EXPLORATION 1

Dilating a Polygon

Work with a partner. Use geometry software.

Math Practice

Consider Similar Problems

How does your previous work with scale drawings help you understand the concept of dilations?

a. Draw a polygon in the coordinate plane. Then *dilate* the polygon with respect to the origin. Describe the scale factor of the image.

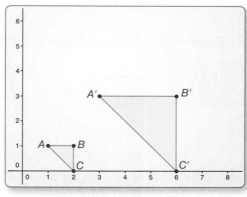

Available at BigIdeasMath.com.

Sample

Points
$A(1, 1)$
$B(2, 1)$
$C(2, 0)$

Segments
$AB = 1$
$BC = 1$
$AC = 1.41$

Angles
$m\angle A = 45°$
$m\angle B = 90°$
$m\angle C = 45°$

b. Compare the image and the original polygon in part (a). What do you notice about the sides? the angles?

c. Describe the relationship between each point below and the point $A(x, y)$ in terms of dilations.

$\qquad B(3x, 3y)$ $\qquad\qquad$ $C(5x, 5y)$ $\qquad\qquad$ $D(0.5x, 0.5y)$

d. What are the coordinates of a point $P(x, y)$ after a dilation with respect to the origin by a scale factor of k?

A scale drawing is an example of a dilation.

A **dilation** is a transformation in which a figure is made larger or smaller with respect to a point called the **center of dilation**. In a dilation, the angles of the image and the original figure are congruent.

Center of dilation

EXAMPLE 1 Identifying a Dilation

Tell whether the blue figure is a dilation of the red figure.

Key Vocabulary
dilation, *p. 70*
center of dilation, *p. 70*
scale factor, *p. 70*

a.

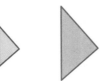

Lines connecting corresponding vertices meet at a point.

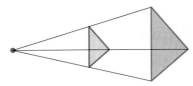

So, the blue figure is a dilation of the red figure.

b.

The figures have the same size and shape. The red figure *slides* to form the blue figure.

So, the blue figure is *not* a dilation of the red figure. It is a translation.

***Try It* Tell whether the blue figure is a dilation of the red figure.**

1.

2.

In a dilation, the value of the ratio of the side lengths of the image to the corresponding side lengths of the original figure is the **scale factor** of the dilation.

🔑 Key Idea

In this course, when the center of dilation is not specified, it is the origin.

Dilations in the Coordinate Plane

Words   To dilate a figure with respect to the origin, multiply the coordinates of each vertex by the scale factor k.

Algebra $(x, y) \longrightarrow (kx, ky)$

- When $k > 1$, the dilation is an enlargement.
- When $k > 0$ and $k < 1$, the dilation is a reduction.

🔊 Multi-Language Glossary at *BigIdeasMath.com*

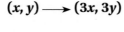 **EXAMPLE 2** **Dilating a Figure**

The vertices of a triangle are $A(1, 3)$, $B(2, 3)$, and $C(2, 1)$. Draw the image after a dilation with a scale factor of 3. Identify the type of dilation.

Multiply each x- and y-coordinate by the scale factor 3.

$$(x, y) \longrightarrow (3x, 3y)$$

$A(1, 3) \longrightarrow A'(3 \cdot 1, 3 \cdot 3) \longrightarrow A'(3, 9)$

$B(2, 3) \longrightarrow B'(3 \cdot 2, 3 \cdot 3) \longrightarrow B'(6, 9)$

$C(2, 1) \longrightarrow C'(3 \cdot 2, 3 \cdot 1) \longrightarrow C'(6, 3)$

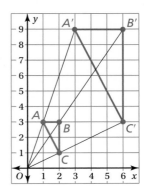

> The image is shown at the right. The dilation is an *enlargement* because the scale factor is greater than 1.

> **Math Practice**
>
> **Use a Graph**
> Check your answer by drawing a line from the origin through each vertex of the original figure. The vertices of the image should lie on these lines.

Try It

3. **WHAT IF?** Triangle ABC is dilated by a scale factor of 2. What are the coordinates of the image?

EXAMPLE 3 **Dilating a Figure**

The vertices of a rectangle are $W(-4, -6)$, $X(-4, 8)$, $Y(4, 8)$, and $Z(4, -6)$. Draw the image after a dilation with a scale factor of 0.5. Identify the type of dilation.

Multiply each x- and y-coordinate by the scale factor 0.5.

$$(x, y) \longrightarrow (0.5x, 0.5y)$$

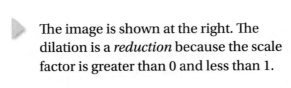

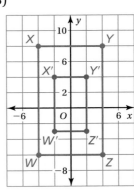

> The image is shown at the right. The dilation is a *reduction* because the scale factor is greater than 0 and less than 1.

Try It

4. **WHAT IF?** Rectangle $WXYZ$ is dilated by a scale factor of $\frac{1}{4}$. What are the coordinates of the image?

EXAMPLE 4 **Using More than One Transformation**

The vertices of a trapezoid are $A(-2, -1)$, $B(-1, 1)$, $C(0, 1)$, and $D(0, -1)$. Dilate the trapezoid using a scale factor of 2. Then translate it 6 units right and 2 units up. What are the coordinates of the image?

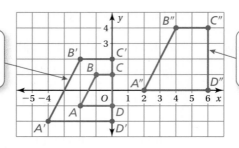

Draw *ABCD*. Then dilate it with respect to the origin using a scale factor of 2.

Translate the dilated figure 6 units right and 2 units up.

▷ The coordinates of the image are $A''(2, 0)$, $B''(4, 4)$, $C''(6, 4)$, and $D''(6, 0)$.

Try It

5. **WHAT IF?** Trapezoid *ABCD* is dilated using a scale factor of 3, and then rotated 180° about the origin. What are the coordinates of the image?

Self-Assessment for Concepts & Skills

Solve each exercise. Then rate your understanding of the success criteria in your journal.

IDENTIFYING A DILATION Tell whether the blue figure is a dilation of the red figure.

6.

7.

8. **DILATING A FIGURE** The vertices of a rectangle are $J(4, 8)$, $K(12, 8)$, $L(12, 4)$, and $M(4, 4)$. Draw the image after a dilation with a scale factor of $\frac{1}{4}$. Identify the type of dilation.

9. **VOCABULARY** How is a dilation different from other transformations?

EXAMPLE 5 **Modeling Real Life**

A wildlife refuge is mapped on a coordinate plane, where each grid line represents 1 mile. The refuge has vertices $J(0, 0)$, $K(1, 3)$, and $L(4, 0)$. An expansion of the refuge can be represented by a dilation with a scale factor of 1.5. How much does the area of the wildlife refuge increase?

Multiply each x- and y-coordinate by the scale factor 1.5. Then find the area of each figure.

$$(x, y) \longrightarrow (1.5x, 1.5y)$$

$$J(0, 0) \longrightarrow J'(1.5 \cdot 0, 1.5 \cdot 0) \longrightarrow J'(0, 0)$$

$$K(1, 3) \longrightarrow K'(1.5 \cdot 1, 1.5 \cdot 3) \longrightarrow K'(1.5, 4.5)$$

$$L(4, 0) \longrightarrow L'(1.5 \cdot 4, 1.5 \cdot 0) \longrightarrow L'(6, 0)$$

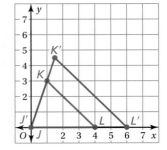

The original figure is a triangle with a base of 4 miles and a height of 3 miles. The image has a base of 6 miles and a height of 4.5 miles. Use the formula for the area of a triangle to find the areas of the original figure and the image.

Original Figure		*Image*
$A = \dfrac{1}{2}bh$	Write the formula.	$A = \dfrac{1}{2}bh$
$= \dfrac{1}{2}(4)(3)$	Substitute for b and h.	$= \dfrac{1}{2}(6)(4.5)$
$= 6$	Simplify.	$= 13.5$

▷ So, the area of the wildlife refuge increases $13.5 - 6 = 7.5$ square miles.

 Self-Assessment for Problem Solving

Solve each exercise. Then rate your understanding of the success criteria in your journal.

10. A photograph is dilated to fit in a frame, so that its area after the dilation is 9 times greater than the area of the original photograph. What is the scale factor of the dilation? Explain.

11. **DIG DEEPER!** The location of a water treatment plant is mapped using a coordinate plane, where each unit represents 1 foot. The plant has vertices $(0, 0)$, $(0, 180)$, $(240, 180)$, and $(240, 0)$. You dilate the figure with a scale factor of $\dfrac{1}{3}$. What are the coordinates of the image? What do you need to change so that the image accurately represents the location of the plant? Explain your reasoning.

2.5 Practice

Go to *BigIdeasMath.com* to get HELP with solving the exercises.

▶ **Review & Refresh**

The red figure is congruent to the blue figure. Describe a sequence of rigid motions between the figures.

1.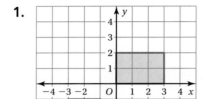

2.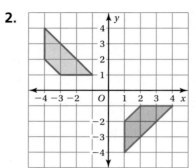

Tell whether the ratios form a proportion.

3. 3 : 5 and 15 : 20

4. 2 to 3 and 12 to 18

5. 7 : 28 and 12 : 48

▶▶ **Concepts, Skills, & Problem Solving**

DESCRIBING RELATIONSHIPS Describe the relationship between the given point and the point A(8, 12) in terms of dilations. (See Exploration 1, p. 69.)

6. B(16, 24)

7. C(2, 3)

8. D(6, 9)

IDENTIFYING A DILATION Tell whether the blue figure is a dilation of the red figure.

9.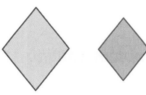

10.

11.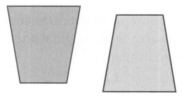

12.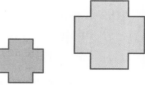

13.

14.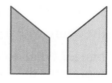

DILATING A FIGURE The vertices of a figure are given. Draw the figure and its image after a dilation with the given scale factor. Identify the type of dilation.

15. $A(1, 1)$, $B(1, 4)$, $C(3, 1)$; $k = 4$

16. $D(0, 2)$, $E(6, 2)$, $F(6, 4)$; $k = 0.5$

17. $G(-2, -2)$, $H(-2, 6)$, $J(2, 6)$; $k = 0.25$

18. $M(2, 3)$, $N(5, 3)$, $P(5, 1)$; $k = 3$

19. $Q(-3, 0)$, $R(-3, 6)$, $T(4, 6)$, $U(4, 0)$; $k = \dfrac{1}{3}$

20. $V(-2, -2)$, $W(-2, 3)$, $X(5, 3)$, $Y(5, -2)$; $k = 5$

21. **MP YOU BE THE TEACHER** Your friend finds the coordinates of the image of $\triangle ABC$ after a dilation with a scale factor of 2. Is your friend correct? Explain your reasoning.

$A(2, 5) \longrightarrow A'(2 \cdot 2, 2 \cdot 5) \longrightarrow A'(4, 10)$
$B(2, 0) \longrightarrow B'(2 \cdot 2, 2 \cdot 0) \longrightarrow B'(4, 0)$
$C(4, 0) \longrightarrow C'(2 \cdot 4, 2 \cdot 0) \longrightarrow C'(8, 0)$

FINDING A SCALE FACTOR The blue figure is a dilation of the red figure. Identify the type of dilation and find the scale factor.

22.
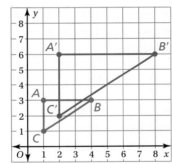

23.
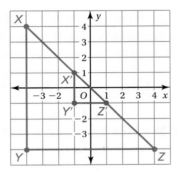

24.
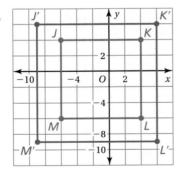

25.
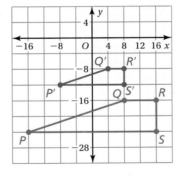

USING MORE THAN ONE TRANSFORMATION The vertices of a figure are given. Find the coordinates of the image after the transformations given.

26. $A(-5, 3)$, $B(-2, 3)$, $C(-2, 1)$, $D(-5, 1)$

Reflect in the y-axis. Then dilate using a scale factor of 2.

27. $F(-9, -9)$, $G(-3, -6)$, $H(-3, -9)$

Dilate using a scale factor of $\dfrac{2}{3}$. Then translate 6 units up.

28. $J(1, 1)$, $K(3, 4)$, $L(5, 1)$

Rotate 90° clockwise about the origin. Then dilate using a scale factor of 3.

29. **MP LOGIC** You can use a flashlight and a shadow puppet (your hands) to project shadows on the wall.

   a. Identify the type of dilation.

   b. What does the flashlight represent?

   c. The length of the ears on the shadow puppet is 3 inches. The length of the ears on the shadow is 4 inches. What is the scale factor?

   d. Describe what happens as the shadow puppet moves closer to the flashlight. How does this affect the scale factor?

30. **MP REASONING** A triangle is dilated using a scale factor of 3. The image is then dilated using a scale factor of $\frac{1}{2}$. What scale factor can you use to dilate the original triangle to obtain the final image? Explain.

CRITICAL THINKING The coordinate notation shows how the coordinates of a figure are related to the coordinates of its image after transformations. What are the transformations? Are the figure and its image congruent? Explain.

31. $(x, y) \rightarrow (2x + 4, 2y - 3)$ 32. $(x, y) \rightarrow (-x - 1, y - 2)$ 33. $(x, y) \rightarrow \left(\frac{1}{3}x, -\frac{1}{3}y\right)$

MP STRUCTURE The blue figure is a transformation of the red figure. Use coordinate notation to describe the transformation. Explain your reasoning.

34.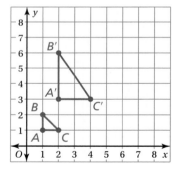

35.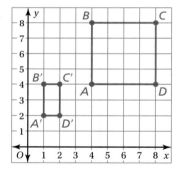

36. **MP NUMBER SENSE** You dilate a figure using a scale factor of 2, and then translate it 3 units right. Your friend translates the same figure 3 units right and then dilates it using a scale factor of 2. Are the images congruent? Explain.

37. **MP PROBLEM SOLVING** The vertices of a trapezoid are $A(-2, 3)$, $B(2, 3)$, $C(5, -2)$, and $D(-2, -2)$. Dilate the trapezoid with respect to vertex A using a scale factor of 2. What are the coordinates of the image? Explain the method you used.

38. **DIG DEEPER!** A figure is dilated using a scale factor of -1. How can you obtain the image without using a dilation? Explain your reasoning.

2.6 Similar Figures

Learning Target: Understand the concept of similar figures.

Success Criteria:
- I can identify similar figures.
- I can describe a similarity transformation between two similar figures.

EXPLORATION 1

Transforming Figures

Work with a partner. Use geometry software.

a. For each pair of figures whose vertices are given below, draw the figures in a coordinate plane. Use dilations and rigid motions to try to obtain one of the figures from the other figure.

- $A(-3, 6)$, $B(0, -3)$, $C(3, 6)$ and $G(-1, 2)$, $H(0, -1)$, $J(1, 2)$

- $D(0, 0)$, $E(3, 0)$, $F(3, 3)$ and $L(0, 0)$, $M(0, 6)$, $N(-6, 6)$

- $P(1, 0)$, $Q(4, 2)$, $R(7, 0)$ and $X(-1, 0)$, $Y(-4, 6)$, $Z(-7, 0)$

- $A(-3, 2)$, $B(-1, 2)$, $C(-1, -1)$, $D(-3, -1)$ and
  $F(6, 4)$, $G(2, 4)$, $H(2, -2)$, $J(6, -2)$

- $P(-2, 2)$, $Q(-1, -1)$, $R(1, -1)$, $S(2, 2)$ and
  $W(2, 8)$, $X(3, 3)$, $Y(7, 3)$, $Z(8, 8)$

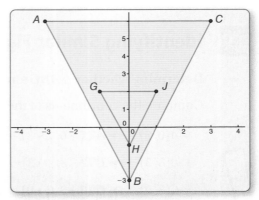

Available at BigIdeasMath.com.

Math Practice

Interpret Results
When you need a dilation to obtain one figure from another, what does it tell you about the side lengths and angle measures of the figures?

b. Is a scale drawing represented by any of the pairs of figures in part (a)? Explain your reasoning.

c. Figure A is a scale drawing of Figure B. Do you think there must be a sequence of transformations that obtains Figure A from Figure B? Explain your reasoning.

2.6 Lesson

Key Vocabulary
similarity
    transformation,
    p. 78
similar figures, p. 78

Dilations do not preserve length, so dilations are not rigid motions. A **similarity transformation** is a dilation or a sequence of dilations and rigid motions.

Key Idea

Similar Figures

Two figures are **similar figures** when one can be obtained from the other by a similarity transformation. Similar figures have the same shape but not necessarily the same size. The triangles below are similar.

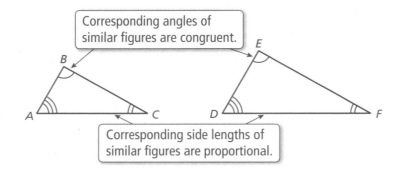

Corresponding angles of similar figures are congruent.

Corresponding side lengths of similar figures are proportional.

Reading

The symbol ~ means *is similar to*.
In the Key Idea,
$\triangle ABC \sim \triangle DEF$.

Side Lengths

$$\frac{AB}{DE} = \frac{BC}{EF} = \frac{AC}{DF}$$

Angles

$$\angle A \cong \angle D, \angle B \cong \angle E, \angle C \cong \angle F$$

EXAMPLE 1 Identifying Similar Figures

Determine whether $\triangle ABC$ and $\triangle JKL$ are similar.

Compare the coordinates of the vertices.

$$A(0, 3) \longrightarrow A'(2 \cdot 0, 2 \cdot 3) \longrightarrow J(0, 6)$$
$$B(3, 3) \longrightarrow B'(2 \cdot 3, 2 \cdot 3) \longrightarrow K(6, 6)$$
$$C(3, 0) \longrightarrow C'(2 \cdot 3, 2 \cdot 0) \longrightarrow L(6, 0)$$

$\triangle JKL$ is a dilation of $\triangle ABC$ using a scale factor of 2.

So, $\triangle ABC$ and $\triangle JKL$ are similar.

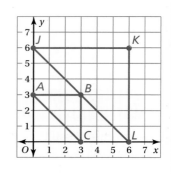

Common Error

When writing a similarity statement, make sure to list the vertices of the figures in the correct order.

Try It

1. A triangle has vertices $D(0, 4)$, $E(5, 4)$, and $F(5, 0)$. Is $\triangle DEF$ similar to $\triangle ABC$ and $\triangle JKL$ in Example 1? Explain.

EXAMPLE 2 **Describing a Similarity Transformation**

The red figure is similar to the blue figure. Describe a similarity transformation between the figures.

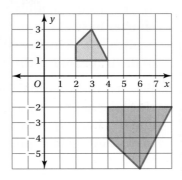

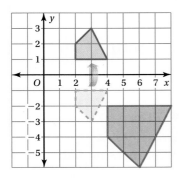

By comparing corresponding side lengths, you can see that the blue figure is one-half the size of the red figure. So, begin by dilating the red figure with respect to the origin using a scale factor of $\frac{1}{2}$.

After dilating the red figure, you need to reflect the figure in the x-axis.

So, one possible similarity transformation is to dilate the red figure with respect to the origin using a scale factor of $\frac{1}{2}$ and then reflect the image in the x-axis.

Try It

2. Can you reflect the red figure first, and then perform the dilation to obtain the blue figure? Explain.

Self-Assessment *for Concepts & Skills*

Solve each exercise. Then rate your understanding of the success criteria in your journal.

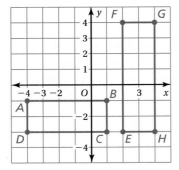

3. **IDENTIFYING SIMILAR FIGURES** In the coordinate plane at the left, determine whether Rectangle *ABCD* is similar to Rectangle *EFGH*. Explain your reasoning.

4. **SIMILARITY TRANSFORMATION** The red triangle is similar to the blue triangle. Describe a similarity transformation between the figures.

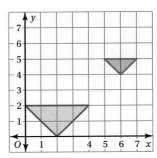

EXAMPLE 3 **Modeling Real Life**

An artist draws a replica of a painting that is on a remaining piece of the Berlin Wall. The painting includes a red trapezoid. The shorter base of the similar trapezoid in the replica is 3.75 inches. What is the height h of the trapezoid in the replica?

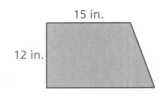

Painting

Because the trapezoids are similar, corresponding side lengths are proportional. So, the ratios 3.75 : 15 and h : 12 are equivalent. Use the values of the ratios to write and solve a proportion to find h.

3.75 in.

h

Replica

$$\frac{3.75}{15} = \frac{h}{12}$$ Write a proportion.

$$12 \cdot \frac{3.75}{15} = 12 \cdot \frac{h}{12}$$ Multiplication Property of Equality

$$3 = h$$ Simplify.

So, the height of the trapezoid in the replica is 3 inches.

Another Method The replica is a scale drawing of the painting with a scale factor of $\frac{3.75}{15} = \frac{1}{4}$. So, the height of the trapezoid in the replica is $\frac{1}{4}$ the height of the trapezoid in the painting, $\frac{1}{4}(12) = 3$ inches. ✓

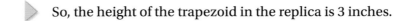

 Self-Assessment for Problem Solving

Solve each exercise. Then rate your understanding of the success criteria in your journal.

5. A medical supplier sells gauze in large and small rectangular sheets. A large sheet has a length of 9 inches and an area of 45 square inches. A small sheet has a length of 4 inches and a width of 3 inches. Are the sheets similar? Justify your answer.

6. The sail on a souvenir boat is similar in shape to the sail on a sailboat. The sail on the sailboat is in the shape of a right triangle with a base of 9 feet and a height of 24 feet. The height of the souvenir's sail is 3 inches. What is the base of the souvenir's sail?

7. **DIG DEEPER!** A coordinate plane is used to represent a cheerleading formation. The vertices of the formation are $A(-4, 4)$, $B(0, 8)$, $C(4, 4)$, and $D(0, 6)$. A choreographer creates a new formation similar to the original formation. Three vertices of the new formation are $J(-2, -2)$, $K(0, -4)$, and $L(2, -2)$. What is the location of the fourth vertex? Explain.

2.6 Practice

? Go to *BigIdeasMath.com* to get HELP with solving the exercises.

▶ Review & Refresh

Tell whether the blue figure is a dilation of the red figure.

1.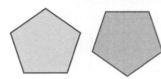

2.

3. You solve the equation $S = \ell w + 2wh$ for w. Which equation is correct?

  A. $w = \dfrac{S - \ell}{2h}$ **B.** $w = \dfrac{S - 2h}{\ell}$

  C. $w = \dfrac{S}{\ell + 2h}$ **D.** $w = S - \ell - 2h$

▶▶ Concepts, Skills, & Problem Solving

TRANSFORMING FIGURES The vertices of a pair of figures are given. Determine whether a scale drawing is represented by the pair of figures. (See Exploration 1, p. 77.)

4. $A(-8, -2)$, $B(-4, 2)$, $C(-4, -2)$ and $G(2, -1)$, $H(4, -1)$, $J(2, -3)$

5. $A(0, 3)$, $B(3, 4)$, $C(5, 3)$, $D(3, 2)$ and $F(-4, 4)$, $G(-1, 5)$, $H(5, 3)$, $J(3, 2)$

IDENTIFYING SIMILAR FIGURES Determine whether the figures are similar. Explain your reasoning.

6.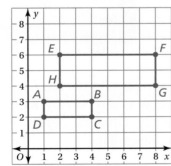

7.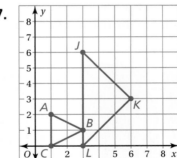

IDENTIFYING SIMILAR FIGURES Draw the figures with the given vertices in a coordinate plane. Which figures are similar? Explain your reasoning.

8. Rectangle A: $(0, 0)$, $(4, 0)$, $(4, 2)$, $(0, 2)$
    Rectangle B: $(0, 0)$, $(-6, 0)$, $(-6, 3)$, $(0, 3)$
    Rectangle C: $(0, 0)$, $(4, 0)$, $(4, 2)$, $(0, 2)$

9. Figure A: $(-4, 2)$, $(-2, 2)$, $(-2, 0)$, $(-4, 0)$
    Figure B: $(1, 4)$, $(4, 4)$, $(4, 1)$, $(1, 1)$
    Figure C: $(2, -1)$, $(5, -1)$, $(5, -3)$, $(2, -3)$

DESCRIBING A SIMILARITY TRANSFORMATION The red figure is similar to the blue figure. Describe a similarity transformation between the figures.

10.

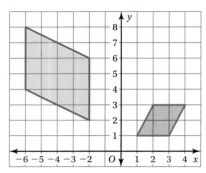

11.

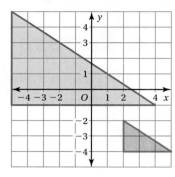

12. **MP** **MODELING REAL LIFE** A barrier in the shape of a rectangle is used to retain oil spills. On a blueprint, a similar barrier is 9 inches long and 2 inches wide. The width of the actual barrier is 1.2 miles. What is the length of the actual barrier?

13. **MP** **LOGIC** Are the following figures *always*, *sometimes*, or *never* similar? Explain.

    a. two triangles   **b.** two squares   **c.** two rectangles

14. **CRITICAL THINKING** Can you draw two quadrilaterals each having two 130° angles and two 50° angles that are *not* similar? Justify your answer.

15. **MP** **REASONING** The sign is rectangular.

    a. You increase each side length by 20%. Is the new sign similar to the original? Explain your reasoning.

    b. You increase each side length by 6 inches. Is the new sign similar to the original? Explain your reasoning.

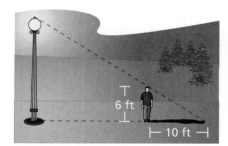

16. **DIG DEEPER!** A person standing 20 feet from a streetlight casts a shadow as shown. How many times taller is the streetlight than the person? Assume the triangles are similar.

17. **GEOMETRY** Use a ruler to draw two different isosceles triangles similar to the one shown. Measure the heights of each triangle.

    a. Are the ratios of the corresponding heights equivalent to the ratios of the corresponding side lengths?

    b. Do you think this is true for all similar triangles? Explain.

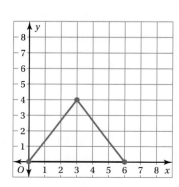

18. **CRITICAL THINKING** Given $\triangle ABC \sim \triangle DEF$ and $\triangle DEF \sim \triangle JKL$, is $\triangle ABC \sim \triangle JKL$? Justify your answer.

2.7 Perimeters and Areas of Similar Figures

Learning Target: Find perimeters and areas of similar figures.

Success Criteria:
- I can use corresponding side lengths to compare perimeters of similar figures.
- I can use corresponding side lengths to compare areas of similar figures.
- I can use similar figures to solve real-life problems involving perimeter and area.

EXPLORATION 1

Comparing Similar Figures

MP CHOOSE TOOLS **Work with a partner. Draw a rectangle in the coordinate plane.**

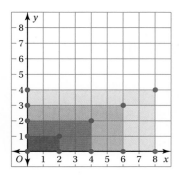

a. Dilate your rectangle using each indicated scale factor k. Then complete the table for the perimeter P of each rectangle. Describe the pattern.

Original Side Lengths	$k = 2$	$k = 3$	$k = 4$	$k = 5$	$k = 6$
$P =$					

b. **MP REPEATED REASONING** Compare the ratios of the perimeters to the ratios of the corresponding side lengths. What do you notice?

c. Repeat part (a) to complete the table for the area A of each rectangle. Describe the pattern.

Original Side Lengths	$k = 2$	$k = 3$	$k = 4$	$k = 5$	$k = 6$
$A =$					

Math Practice

Look for Patterns
How can you use the pattern in part (c) to find the area of the rectangle after a dilation using any scale factor?

d. **MP REPEATED REASONING** Compare the ratios of the areas to the ratios of the corresponding side lengths. What do you notice?

e. The rectangles shown are similar. You know the perimeter and the area of the red rectangle and a pair of corresponding side lengths. How can you find the perimeter of the blue rectangle? the area of the blue rectangle?

Key Idea

Perimeters of Similar Figures

When two figures are similar, the value of the ratio of their perimeters is equal to the value of the ratio of their corresponding side lengths.

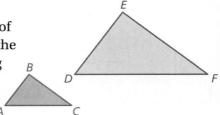

$$\frac{\text{Perimeter of } \triangle ABC}{\text{Perimeter of } \triangle DEF} = \frac{AB}{DE} = \frac{BC}{EF} = \frac{AC}{DF}$$

EXAMPLE 1 **Comparing Perimeters of Similar Figures**

You can think of the red rectangle as a scale drawing of the blue rectangle, where the ratio of the side lengths is the scale, and the value of the ratio is the scale factor.

Find the value of the ratio (red to blue) of the perimeters of the similar rectangles.

$$\frac{\text{Perimeter of red rectangle}}{\text{Perimeter of blue rectangle}} = \frac{4}{6} = \frac{2}{3}$$

▷ The value of the ratio of the perimeters is $\frac{2}{3}$.

Try It

1. The height of Figure A is 9 feet. The height of a similar Figure B is 15 feet. What is the value of the ratio of the perimeter of A to the perimeter of B?

Key Idea

Areas of Similar Figures

When two figures are similar, the value of the ratio of their areas is equal to the *square* of the value of the ratio of their corresponding side lengths.

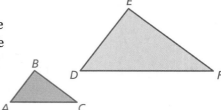

$$\frac{\text{Area of } \triangle ABC}{\text{Area of } \triangle DEF} = \left(\frac{AB}{DE}\right)^2 = \left(\frac{BC}{EF}\right)^2 = \left(\frac{AC}{DF}\right)^2$$

EXAMPLE 2 **Comparing Areas of Similar Figures**

Find the value of the ratio (red to blue) of the areas of the similar triangles.

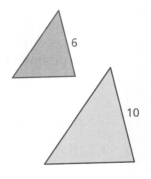

Math Practice

Specify Units
Does the value of the ratio of the areas change when the side lengths are measured in inches? feet? Explain your reasoning.

$$\frac{\text{Area of red triangle}}{\text{Area of blue triangle}} = \left(\frac{6}{10}\right)^2$$

$$= \left(\frac{3}{5}\right)^2$$

$$= \frac{9}{25}$$

▷ The value of the ratio of the areas is $\frac{9}{25}$.

Try It

2. The base of Triangle P is 8 meters. The base of a similar Triangle Q is 7 meters. What is the value of the ratio of the area of P to the area of Q?

 Self-Assessment *for Concepts & Skills*

Solve each exercise. Then rate your understanding of the success criteria in your journal.

COMPARING PERIMETERS OF SIMILAR FIGURES Find the value of the ratio (red to blue) of the perimeters of the similar figures.

3.

4.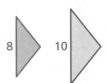

COMPARING AREAS OF SIMILAR FIGURES Find the value of the ratio (red to blue) of the areas of the similar figures.

5.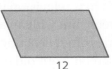

6.

EXAMPLE 3 **Modeling Real Life**

18 yd

10 yd

Area = 200 yd²
Perimeter = 60 yd

A swimming pool is similar in shape to a volleyball court. Find the perimeter *P* and the area *A* of the pool.

The rectangular pool and the court are similar. So, use the ratio of corresponding side lengths to write and solve proportions to find the perimeter and the area of the pool.

Perimeter	*Area*

$$\frac{\text{Perimeter of court}}{\text{Perimeter of pool}} = \frac{\text{Width of court}}{\text{Width of pool}} \qquad \frac{\text{Area of court}}{\text{Area of pool}} = \left(\frac{\text{Width of court}}{\text{Width of pool}}\right)^2$$

$$\frac{60}{P} = \frac{10}{18} \qquad\qquad \frac{200}{A} = \left(\frac{10}{18}\right)^2$$

$$1080 = 10P \qquad\qquad \frac{200}{A} = \frac{100}{324}$$

$$108 = P \qquad\qquad 64{,}800 = 100A$$

$$648 = A$$

So, the perimeter of the pool is 108 yards, and the area is 648 square yards.

Self-Assessment *for Problem Solving*

Solve each exercise. Then rate your understanding of the success criteria in your journal.

7. Two similar triangular regions are prepared for development.

Grassland Perimeter = 240 yd
Grassland Area = 2400 yd²

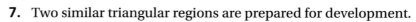

Grassland

60 yd

Forest

45 yd

a. It costs $6 per foot to install fencing. How much does it cost to surround the forest with a fence?

b. The cost to prepare 1 square yard of grassland is $15 and the cost to prepare 1 square yard of forest is $25. Which region costs more to prepare? Justify your answer.

8. **DIG DEEPER!** You buy a new television with a screen similar in shape to your old television screen, but with an area four times greater. The size of a television screen is often described using the distance between opposite corners of the screen. Your old television has a 30-inch screen. What is the size of your new television screen? Explain.

2.7 Practice

 Go to *BigIdeasMath.com* to get HELP with solving the exercises.

▶ Review & Refresh

The red figure is similar to the blue figure. Describe a similarity transformation between the figures.

1.
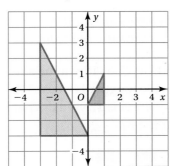

2.
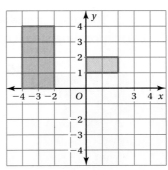

Find the area of the figure.

3.
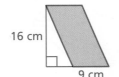
16 cm
9 cm

4.

5 in.
3 in.

5.
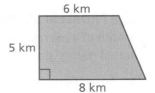
6 km
5 km
8 km

▶▶ Concepts, Skills, & Problem Solving

COMPARING SIMILAR FIGURES Dilate the figure using the indicated scale factor k. What is the value of the ratio (new to original) of the perimeters? the areas? (See Exploration 1, p. 83.)

6. a triangle with vertices $(0, 0)$, $(0, 2)$, and $(2, 0)$; $k = 3$

7. a square with vertices $(0, 0)$, $(0, 4)$, $(4, 4)$, and $(4, 0)$; $k = 0.5$

PERIMETERS AND AREAS OF SIMILAR FIGURES Find the values of the ratios (red to blue) of the perimeters and areas of the similar figures.

8.

11
6

9.

5
8

10.

7
4

11.
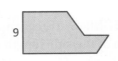
9
14

USING SIMILAR FIGURES The figures are similar. Find *x*.

12. The ratio of the perimeters is 7 : 10.

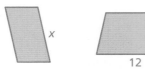

13. The ratio of the perimeters is 8 : 5.

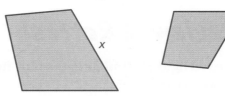

14. **COMPARING AREAS** The playing surfaces of two foosball tables are similar. The ratio of the corresponding side lengths is 10 : 7. What is the ratio of the areas?

21 in.

9 in.

15. **CRITICAL THINKING** The ratio of the side length of Square A to the side length of Square B is 4 : 9. The side length of Square A is 12 yards. What is the perimeter of Square B?

16. **MP MODELING REAL LIFE** The cost of the piece of fabric shown is $1.31. What would you expect to pay for a similar piece of fabric that is 18 inches by 42 inches?

17. **MP PROBLEM SOLVING** A scale model of a merry-go-round and the actual merry-go-round are similar.

a. How many times greater is the base area of the actual merry-go-round than the base area of the scale model? Explain.

b. What is the base area of the actual merry-go-round in square feet?

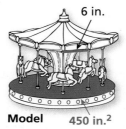

6 in.

Model   450 in.²

10 ft

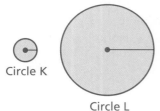

Circle K

Circle L

18. **MP STRUCTURE** The circumference of Circle K is π. The circumference of Circle L is 4π. What is the value of the ratio of their circumferences? of their radii? of their areas?

19. **GEOMETRY** A triangle with an area of 10 square meters has a base of 4 meters. A similar triangle has an area of 90 square meters. What is the height of the larger triangle?

20. **MP PROBLEM SOLVING** You need two bottles of fertilizer to treat the flower garden shown. How many bottles do you need to treat a similar garden with a perimeter of 105 feet?

18 ft

4 ft   5 ft

15 ft

21. **MP REPEATED REASONING** Three square mirrors are used for a light reflection experiment. The ratio of the side length of Mirror A to the side length of Mirror B is 5 : 6. The ratio of the area of Mirror B to the area of Mirror C is 16 : 25. The perimeter of Mirror C is 280 centimeters. What is the area of Mirror A? Justify your answer.

Connecting Concepts

Using the Problem-Solving Plan

1. A scale drawing of a helipad uses a scale of 1 ft : 20 ft. The scale drawing has an area of 6.25 square feet. What is the area of the actual helipad?

 Understand the problem. You know the scale of the drawing and the area of the helipad in the drawing. You are asked to find the area of the actual helipad.

Make a plan. A scale drawing is similar to the actual object. So, use the scale 1 ft : 20 ft and the ratio 6.25 ft^2 : A ft^2 to write and solve a proportion that represents the area A of the actual helipad.

Solve and check. Use the plan to solve the problem. Then check your solution.

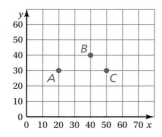

2. The locations of three cargo ships are shown in the coordinate plane. Each ship travels at the same speed in the same direction. After 1 hour, the x- and y-coordinates of Ship A increase 80%. Use a translation to describe the change in the locations of the ships. Then find the new coordinates of each ship.

3. All circles are similar. A circle with a radius of 2 inches is dilated, resulting in a circle with a circumference of 22π inches. What is the scale factor? Justify your answer.

Performance Task

Master Puppeteer

At the beginning of this chapter, you watched a STEAM Video called "Shadow Puppets." You are now ready to complete the performance task related to this video, available at *BigIdeasMath.com*. Be sure to use the problem-solving plan as you work through the performance task.

▶ Review Vocabulary

Write the definition and give an example of each vocabulary term.

transformation, *p. 44*
image, *p. 44*
translation, *p. 44*
reflection, *p. 50*
line of reflection, *p. 50*
rotation, *p. 56*

center of rotation, *p. 56*
angle of rotation, *p. 56*
rigid motion, *p. 64*
congruent figures, *p. 64*
congruent angles, *p. 64*
congruent sides, *p. 64*

dilation, *p. 70*
center of dilation, *p. 70*
scale factor, *p. 70*
similarity transformation, *p. 78*
similar figures, *p. 78*

▶ Graphic Organizers

You can use a **Summary Triangle** to explain a concept. Here is an example of a Summary Triangle for *translating a figure*.

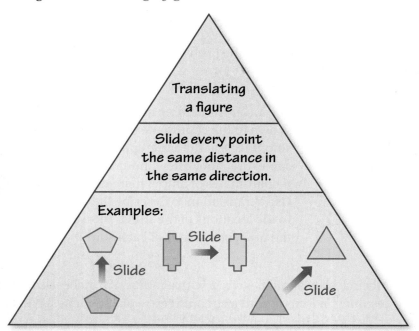

Choose and complete a graphic organizer to help you study the concept.

1. reflecting a figure

2. rotating a figure

3. congruent figures

4. dilating a figure

5. similar figures

6. perimeters of similar figures

7. areas of similar figures

"I hope my owner sees my **Summary Triangle**. I just can't seem to learn 'roll over.' "

Chapter Self-Assessment

As you complete the exercises, use the scale below to rate your understanding of the success criteria in your journal.

1 I do not understand.

2 I can do it with help.

3 I can do it on my own.

4 I can teach someone else.

2.1 Translations *(pp. 43–48)*

Learning Target: Translate figures in the coordinate plane.

Tell whether the blue figure is a translation of the red figure.

1.

2.

3. The vertices of a quadrilateral are $W(1, 2)$, $X(1, 4)$, $Y(4, 4)$, and $Z(4, 2)$. Draw the figure and its image after a translation 3 units left and 2 units down.

4. The vertices of a triangle are $A(-1, -2)$, $B(-2, 2)$, and $C(-3, 0)$. Draw the figure and its image after a translation 5 units right and 1 unit up.

5. Your locker number is 20 and your friend's locker number is 33. Describe the location of your friend's locker relative to the location of your locker.

6. Translate the triangle 4 units left and 1 unit down. What are the coordinates of the image?

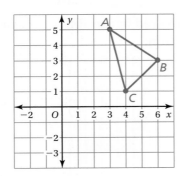

7. Describe a translation of the airplane from point A to point B.

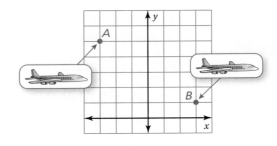

2.2 Reflections *(pp. 49–54)*

Learning Target: Reflect figures in the coordinate plane.

Tell whether the blue figure is a reflection of the red figure.

8. 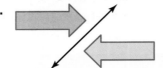   **9.** 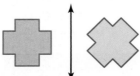   **10.**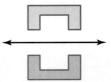

Draw the figure and its reflection in (a) the *x*-axis and (b) the *y*-axis. Identify the coordinates of the image.

11. $A(2, 0)$, $B(1, 5)$, $C(4, 3)$ **12.** $D(-5, -5)$, $E(-5, 0)$, $F(-2, -2)$, $G(-2, -5)$

13. The vertices of a rectangle are $E(-1, 1)$, $F(-1, 3)$, $G(-5, 3)$, and $H(-5, 1)$. Find the coordinates of the figure after reflecting in the *x*-axis, and then translating 3 units right.

The coordinates of a point and its image after a reflection are given. Identify the line of reflection.

14. $(-1, -3) \longrightarrow (1, -3)$ **15.** $(2, 1) \longrightarrow (2, -1)$

16. You perform an experiment involving angles of refraction with a laser pen. You point a laser pen from point L at a mirror along the red path and the image is a reflection in the *y*-axis.

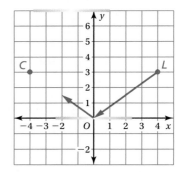

    a. Does the light reach a cat at point C? Explain.

    b. You bounce the light off the top mirror so its path is a reflection. What line of reflection is needed for the light to reach the cat?

2.3 Rotations *(pp. 55–62)*

Learning Target: Rotate figures in the coordinate plane.

Tell whether the blue figure is a rotation of the red figure about the origin. If so, give the angle and the direction of rotation.

17. 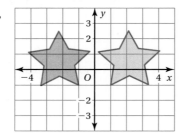   **18.**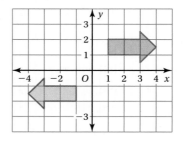

The vertices of a triangle are $A(-4, 2)$, $B(-2, 2)$, and $C(-3, 4)$. Rotate the triangle as described. Find the coordinates of the image.

19. 180° about the origin

20. 270° clockwise about the origin

21. A bicycle wheel is represented in a coordinate plane with the center of the wheel at the origin. Reflectors are placed on the bicycle wheel at points $(7, 4)$ and $(-5, -6)$. After a bike ride, the reflectors have rotated 90° counterclockwise about the origin. What are the locations of the reflectors at the end of the bike ride?

2.4 Congruent Figures (pp. 63–68)

Learning Target: Understand the concept of congruent figures.

Identify any congruent figures in the coordinate plane.

22.

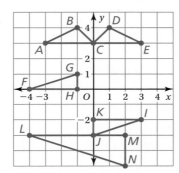

23.

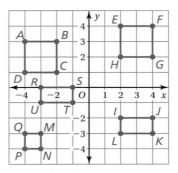

The red figure is congruent to the blue figure. Describe a sequence of rigid motions between the figures.

24.

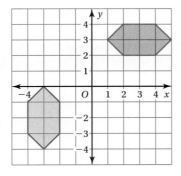

25.

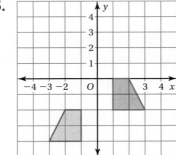

26. The figures are congruent. Name the corresponding angles and the corresponding sides.

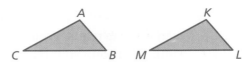

27. Trapezoids *EFGH* and *QRST* are congruent.

    a. What is the length of side *QR*?

    b. Which angle in *QRST* corresponds to $\angle H$?

    c. What is the perimeter of *QRST*?

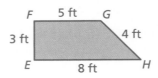
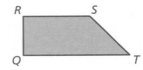

2.5 Dilations *(pp. 69–76)*

Learning Target: Dilate figures in the coordinate plane.

Tell whether the blue figure is a dilation of the red figure.

28.

29.

The vertices of a figure are given. Draw the figure and its image after a dilation with the given scale factor. Identify the type of dilation.

30. $P(-3, -2), Q(-3, 0), R(0, 0); k = 4$

31. $B(3, 3), C(3, 6), D(6, 6), E(6, 3); k = \dfrac{1}{3}$

32. The blue figure is a dilation of the red figure. Identify the type of dilation and find the scale factor.

33. The vertices of a rectangle are $Q(-6, 2), R(6, 2), S(6, -4)$, and $T(-6, -4)$. Dilate the rectangle with respect to the origin using a scale factor of $\dfrac{3}{2}$. Then translate it 5 units right and 1 unit down. What are the coordinates of the image?

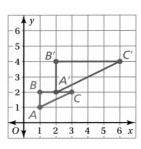

2.6 Similar Figures *(pp. 77–82)*

Learning Target: Understand the concept of similar figures.

34. Determine whether the two figures are similar. Explain your reasoning.

35. Draw figures with the given vertices in a coordinate plane. Which figures are similar? Explain your reasoning.

Triangle A: $(-4, 4), (-2, 4), (-2, 0)$

Triangle B: $(-2, 2), (-1, 2), (-1, 0)$

Triangle C: $(6, 6), (3, 6), (3, 0)$

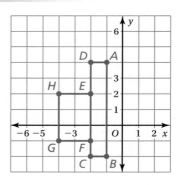

The figures are similar. Find x.

36.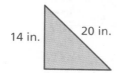

14 in.   20 in.   7 in. x

37.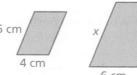

6 cm   4 cm x 6 cm

2.7   Perimeters and Areas of Similar Figures   *(pp. 83–88)*

Learning Target: Find perimeters and areas of similar figures.

Find the values of the ratios (red to blue) of the perimeters and areas of the similar figures.

38.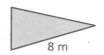

6 m   8 m

39.

16 m   28 m

The figures are similar. Find x.

40. The ratio of the perimeters is $5 : 7$.

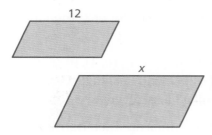

12   x

41. The ratio of the perimeters is $6 : 5$.

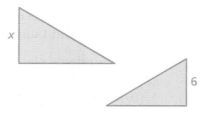

x 6

42. Two photos are similar. The ratio of the corresponding side lengths is $3 : 4$. What is the ratio of the areas?

43. The ratio of side lengths of Square A to Square B is $2 : 3$. The perimeter of Square A is 16 inches. What is the area of Square B?

44. The TV screen is similar to the computer screen. What is the area of the TV screen?

12 in.

20 in.

Area = 108 in.²

Triangles *ABC* and *DEF* are congruent.

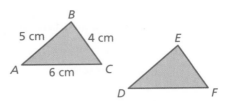

1. Which angle of *DEF* corresponds to ∠*C*?

2. What is the perimeter of *DEF*?

Tell whether the blue figure is a *translation*, *reflection*, *rotation*, or *dilation* of the red figure.

3.

4.

5.

6.

The vertices of a triangle are *A*(2, 5), *B*(1, 2), and *C*(3, 1). Find the coordinates of the image after the transformations given.

7. Reflect in the *y*-axis.

8. Rotate 90° clockwise about the origin.

9. Reflect in the *x*-axis, and then rotate 90° counterclockwise about the origin.

10. Dilate with respect to the origin using a scale factor of 2. Then translate 2 units left and 1 unit up.

11. In a coordinate plane, draw Rectangle A: (−4, 4), (0, 4), (0, 2), (−4, 2); Rectangle B: (−2, 2), (0, 2), (0, 1), (−2, 1); and Rectangle C: (−6, 6), (0, 6), (0, 3), (−6, 3). Which figures are similar? Explain your reasoning.

12. Translate a point (*x*, *y*) 3 units left and 5 units up. Then translate the image 5 units right and 2 units up. What are the coordinates of the point after the translations?

13. The two figures are similar. (a) Find the value of *x*. (b) Find the values of the ratios (red to blue) of the perimeters and of the areas.

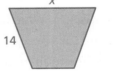

14. A wide-screen television measures 36 inches by 54 inches. A movie theater screen measures 42 feet by 63 feet. Are the screens similar? Explain.

15. You want to use the rectangular piece of fabric shown to make a pair of curtains for your window. Name the types of congruent shapes you can make with one straight cut. Draw an example of each type.

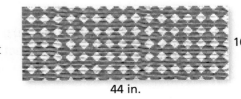

16 in.

44 in.

Cumulative Practice

1. A clockwise rotation of 90° is equivalent to a counterclockwise rotation of how many degrees?

2. The formula $K = C + 273.15$ converts temperatures from degrees Celsius C to Kelvin K. Which of the following formulas is *not* correct?

    A. $K - C = 273.15$

    B. $C = K - 273.15$

    C. $C - K = -273.15$

    D. $C = K + 273.15$

Test-Taking Strategy
After Answering Easy Questions, Relax

What type of transformation is shown?
Ⓐ rotation Ⓑ translation
Ⓒ dilation Ⓓ reflection

Lookin' good!

"After answering the easy questions, relax and try the harder ones. For this, the image is flipped. So, it's D."

3. You want to solve the equation $-3(x + 2) = 12x$. What should you do first?

    F. Subtract 2 from each side.

    H. Multiply each side by -3.

    G. Add 3 to each side.

    I. Divide each side by -3.

4. Which value of x makes the equation $\frac{3}{4}x = 12$ true?

    A. 9

    B. $11\frac{1}{4}$

    C. 16

    D. 48

5. A triangle is graphed in the coordinate plane. What are the coordinates of the image after a translation 3 units right and 2 units down?

    F. $A'(1, 4), B'(1, 1), C'(3, 1)$

    G. $A'(1, 2), B'(1, -1), C'(3, -1)$

    H. $A'(-2, 2), B'(-2, -1), C'(0, -1)$

    I. $A'(0, 1), B'(0, -2), C'(2, -2)$

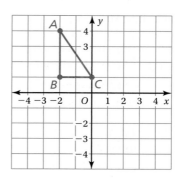

6. Your friend solved the equation in the box shown. What should your friend do to correct the error that he made?

A. Add $\dfrac{2}{5}$ to each side to get $-\dfrac{x}{3} = -\dfrac{1}{15}$.

B. Multiply each side by -3 to get $x + \dfrac{2}{5} = \dfrac{7}{5}$.

C. Multiply each side by -3 to get $x = 2\dfrac{3}{5}$.

D. Subtract $\dfrac{2}{5}$ from each side to get $-\dfrac{x}{3} = -\dfrac{5}{10}$.

$$-\frac{x}{3} + \frac{2}{5} = -\frac{7}{15}$$

$$-\frac{x}{3} + \frac{2}{5} - \frac{2}{5} = -\frac{7}{15} - \frac{2}{5}$$

$$-\frac{x}{3} = -\frac{13}{15}$$

$$3 \cdot \left(-\frac{x}{3}\right) = 3 \cdot \left(-\frac{13}{15}\right)$$

$$x = -2\frac{3}{5}$$

7. Your teacher dilates the rectangle using a scale factor of $\dfrac{1}{2}$.

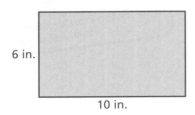

6 in.

10 in.

What is the area of the dilated rectangle in square inches?

8. Your cousin earns \$9.25 an hour at work. Last week she earned \$222.00 How many hours did she work last week?

F. $\dfrac{1}{24}$ hour

G. 22 hours

H. 24 hours

I. 212.75 hours

9. Triangle *EFG* is a dilation of Triangle *HIJ*.

Which proportion is *not* true for Triangle *EFG* and Triangle *HIJ*?

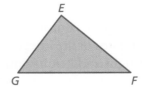

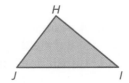

A. $\dfrac{EF}{FG} = \dfrac{HI}{IJ}$

B. $\dfrac{EG}{HI} = \dfrac{FG}{IJ}$

C. $\dfrac{GE}{EF} = \dfrac{JH}{HI}$

D. $\dfrac{EF}{HI} = \dfrac{GE}{JH}$

10. The red figure is congruent to the blue figure. Which of the following is a sequence of rigid motions between the figures?

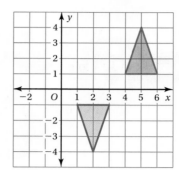

F. Reflect the red triangle in the *x*-axis, and then translate it 3 units left.

G. Reflect the red triangle in the *x*-axis, and then translate it 3 units right.

H. Reflect the red triangle in the *y*-axis, and then translate it 3 units left.

I. Rotate the red triangle 90° clockwise about the origin.

11. Several transformations are used to create the pattern.

Part A   Describe the transformation of Triangle *GLM* to Triangle *DGH*.

Part B   Describe the transformation of Triangle *ALQ* to Triangle *GLM*.

Part C   Triangle *DFN* is a dilation of Triangle *GHM*. Find the scale factor.

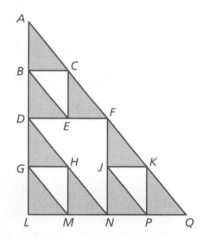

12. A rectangle is graphed in the coordinate plane.

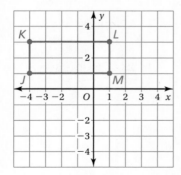

What are the coordinates of the image after a reflection in the *y*-axis?

A. $J'(4, 1), K'(4, 3), L'(-1, 3), M'(-1, 1)$

B. $J'(-4, -1), K'(-4, -3), L'(1, -3), M'(1, -1)$

C. $J'(1, 4), K'(3, 4), L'(3, -1), M'(1, -1)$

D. $J'(-4, 1), K'(-4, 3), L'(1, 3), M'(1, 1)$

3 Angles and Triangles

Chapter Learning Target:
Understand angles.

Chapter Success Criteria:
- I can identify angle relationships.
- I can find angle measurements.
- I can compare angles.
- I can apply angle relationships to solve real-life problems.

STEAM Video: "Honeycombs"

STEAM Video

Honeycombs

Each cell in a honeycomb is in the shape of a regular hexagon. Why might bees use this shape?

Watch the STEAM Video "Honeycombs." Then answer the following questions.

1. Enid and Tony show regular tilings made out of squares, equilateral triangles, and regular hexagons. What is the sum of the interior angle measures of the tiling made from equilateral triangles, outlined below in yellow?

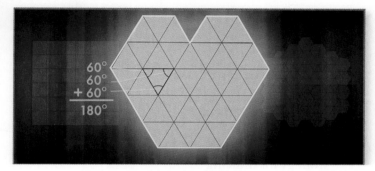

$$\begin{array}{r} 60° \\ 60° \\ + 60° \\ \hline 180° \end{array}$$

2. The cells in a honeycomb use a tiling pattern of the regular hexagon shown. A cell is 10 millimeters deep. About how much honey can one cell hold? Explain.

4 mm

Performance Task

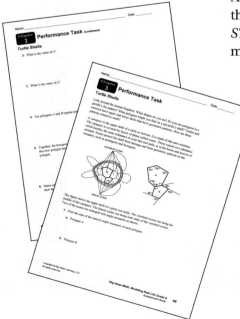

Turtle Shells

After completing this chapter, you will be able to use the concepts you learned to answer the questions in the *STEAM Video Performance Task*. You will be given angle measures of shapes seen on a turtle shell.

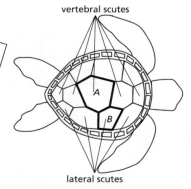

vertebral scutes

lateral scutes

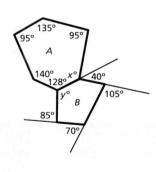

You will be asked to find angle sums and missing angle measures. What other animals have features that resemble geometric shapes?

Getting Ready for Chapter

Chapter Exploration

When an object is **transverse**, it is lying or extending across something. In the drawing, the fallen tree lying across the railroad track is transverse to the track.

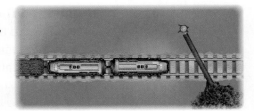

1. **Work with a partner.**

   - Discuss what it means for two lines to be parallel. Decide on a strategy for drawing parallel lines. Then draw two parallel lines.

   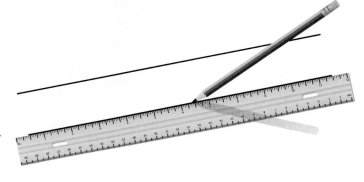

   - Draw a third line that intersects the parallel lines. This line is called a *transversal*.

   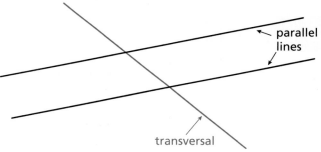

   parallel lines

   transversal

   a. How many angles are formed by the parallel lines and the transversal? Label each angle.

   b. Which of these angles have equal measures? Explain your reasoning.

Vocabulary

The following vocabulary terms are defined in this chapter. Think about what the terms might mean and record your thoughts.

transversal

interior angles of a polygon

exterior angles of a polygon

regular polygon

3.1 Parallel Lines and Transversals

Learning Target: Find missing angle measures created by the intersections of lines.

Success Criteria:
- I can identify congruent angles when a transversal intersects parallel lines.
- I can find angle measures when a transversal intersects parallel lines.

EXPLORATION 1

Exploring Intersections of Lines

Work with a partner. Use geometry software and the lines *A* and *B* shown.

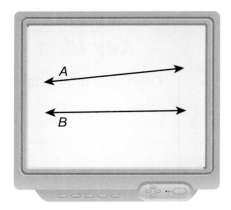

Math Practice

Use Clear Definitions

What does it mean for two lines to be parallel? How does this help you answer the question in part (a)?

a. Are line *A* and line *B* parallel? Explain your reasoning.

b. Draw a line *C* that intersects both line *A* and line *B*. What do you notice about the measures of the angles that are created?

c. Rotate line *A* or line *B* until the angles created by the intersection of line *A* and line *C* are congruent to the angles created by the intersection of line *B* and line *C*. What do you notice about line *A* and line *B*?

d. Rotate line *C* to create different angle measures. Are the angles that were congruent in part (c) still congruent?

e. Make a conjecture about the measures of the angles created when a line intersects two parallel lines.

Lines in the same plane that do not intersect are called *parallel lines*. Lines that intersect at right angles are called *perpendicular lines*.

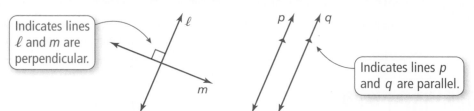

Indicates lines ℓ and *m* are perpendicular.

Indicates lines *p* and *q* are parallel.

A line that intersects two or more lines is called a **transversal**. When parallel lines are cut by a transversal, several pairs of congruent angles are formed.

🗝 Key Idea

Corresponding angles lie on the same side of the transversal in corresponding positions.

Corresponding Angles

When a transversal intersects parallel lines, corresponding angles are congruent.

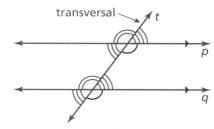

transversal

Corresponding angles

EXAMPLE 1 Finding Angle Measures

Use the figure to find the measures of (a) ∠1 and (b) ∠2.

a. ∠1 and the 110° angle are corresponding angles formed by a transversal intersecting parallel lines. The angles are congruent.

▷ So, the measure of ∠1 is 110°.

b. ∠1 and ∠2 are supplementary.

∠1 + ∠2 = 180°	Definition of supplementary angles
110° + ∠2 = 180°	Substitute 110° for ∠1.
∠2 = 70°	Subtract 110° from each side.

▷ So, the measure of ∠2 is 70°.

Try It **Use the figure to find the measure of the angle. Explain your reasoning.**

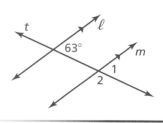

1. ∠1

2. ∠2

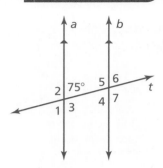

EXAMPLE 2 Using Corresponding Angles

Use the figure to find the measures of the numbered angles.

∠**1:** ∠1 and the 75° angle are vertical angles. They are congruent.

So, the measure of ∠1 is 75°.

∠**2 and** ∠**3:** The 75° angle is supplementary to both ∠2 and ∠3.

$$75° + ∠2 = 180°$$ Definition of supplementary angles

$$∠2 = 105°$$ Subtract 75° from each side.

So, the measures of ∠2 and ∠3 are 105°.

∠**4,** ∠**5,** ∠**6, and** ∠**7:** Corresponding angles are congruent because they are formed by a transversal intersecting parallel lines. So, the measures of ∠4 and ∠6 are 75°, and the measures of ∠5 and ∠7 are 105°.

Try It

3. Use the figure to find the measures of the numbered angles.

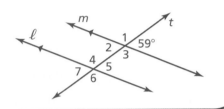

When two parallel lines are cut by a transversal, four **interior angles** are formed on the inside of the parallel lines and four **exterior angles** are formed on the outside of the parallel lines.

∠3, ∠4, ∠5, and ∠6 are interior angles.

∠1, ∠2, ∠7, and ∠8 are exterior angles.

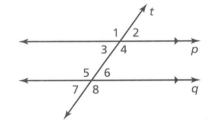

🔑 Key Ideas

Alternate interior angles and alternate exterior angles lie on opposite sides of the transversal.

Alternate Interior Angles and Alternate Exterior Angles

When a transversal intersects parallel lines, alternate interior angles are congruent and alternate exterior angles are congruent.

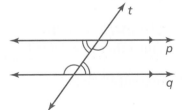

Alternate interior angles

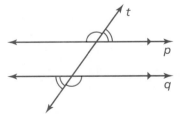

Alternate exterior angles

EXAMPLE 3 **Identifying Angle Relationships**

The photo shows a portion of an airport. Describe the relationship between each pair of angles.

a. ∠3 and ∠6

∠3 and ∠6 are alternate exterior angles formed by a transversal intersecting parallel lines.

▷ So, ∠3 is congruent to ∠6.

b. ∠2 and ∠7

∠2 and ∠7 are alternate interior angles formed by a transversal intersecting parallel lines.

▷ So, ∠2 is congruent to ∠7.

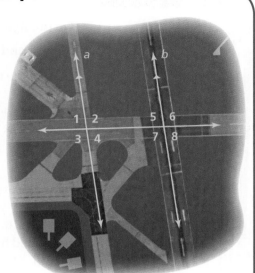

Try It In Example 3, the measure of ∠4 is 84°. Find the measure of the angle. Explain your reasoning.

4. ∠3   **5.** ∠5   **6.** ∠6

Self-Assessment for Concepts & Skills

Solve each exercise. Then rate your understanding of the success criteria in your journal.

FINDING ANGLE MEASURES Use the figure to find the measures of the numbered angles.

7.

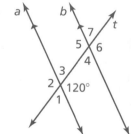

8.

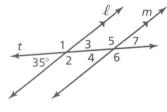

9. WHICH ONE DOESN'T BELONG? Which angle measure does *not* belong with the other three? Explain your reasoning.

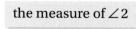

the measure of ∠2	the measure of ∠5
the measure of ∠6	the measure of ∠8

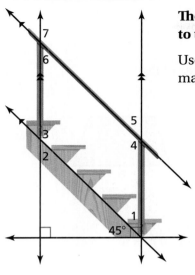

EXAMPLE 4 **Modeling Real Life**

The stairs have a 45° incline. At what angles do you need to attach a rail to two parallel posts so that the rail is parallel to the incline of the steps?

Use angle relationships to find the measures of $\angle 4$, $\angle 5$, $\angle 6$, and $\angle 7$ that make the rail parallel to the incline of the steps.

$\angle 1$: The 45° angle is complementary to $\angle 1$.

$$45° + \angle 1 = 90°$$ Definition of complementary angles

$$\angle 1 = 45°$$ Subtract 45° from each side.

$\angle 5$: $\angle 1$ and $\angle 5$ are congruent because they are corresponding angles formed by a transversal intersecting parallel lines.

So, the measure of $\angle 5$ is 45°.

$\angle 4$: $\angle 4$ and $\angle 5$ are supplementary.

$$\angle 4 + \angle 5 = 180°$$ Definition of supplementary angles

$$\angle 4 + 45° = 180°$$ Substitute 45° for $\angle 5$.

$$\angle 4 = 135°$$ Subtract 45° from each side.

$\angle 6$ and $\angle 7$: Using alternate interior angles, the measure of $\angle 6$ is 45° and the measure of $\angle 7$ is 135°.

▷ You need to attach the rail so that the measures of $\angle 5$ and $\angle 6$ are 45° and the measures of $\angle 4$ and $\angle 7$ are 135°.

Self-Assessment *for Problem Solving*

Solve each exercise. Then rate your understanding of the success criteria in your journal.

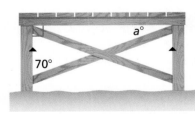

10. A cross section of a pier is shown. Find the value of *a*. Justify your answer.

11. The *head tube angle* of a bike determines how easy the bike is to steer. A bike frame with angle approximations is shown. What is the head tube angle of the bike?

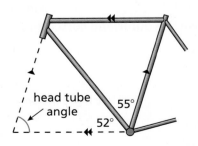

? Go to *BigIdeasMath.com* to get HELP with solving the exercises.

▶ *Review & Refresh*

Find the values of the ratios (red to blue) of the perimeters and areas of the similar figures.

1.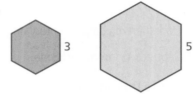

3   5

2.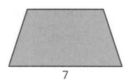

7   6

Evaluate the expression.

3. $4 + 3^2$

4. $5(2)^2 - 6$

5. $11 + (-7)^2 - 9$

▶▶ *Concepts, Skills, & Problem Solving*

MP USING TOOLS Use a protractor to determine whether lines *a* and *b* are parallel. (See Exploration 1, p. 103.)

6.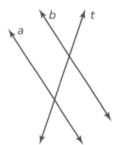

7.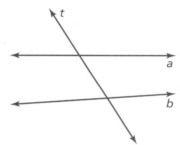

FINDING ANGLE MEASURES Use the figure to find the measures of the numbered angles. Explain your reasoning.

8.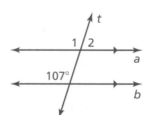

9.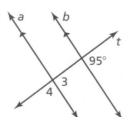

10.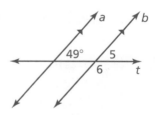

11. MP YOU BE THE TEACHER Your friend describes a relationship between the angles shown. Is your friend correct? Explain your reasoning.

∠5 is congruent to ∠6.

12. **MP PROBLEM SOLVING** The painted lines that separate parking spaces are parallel. The measure of ∠1 is 60°. What is the measure of ∠2? Explain.

13. **OPEN-ENDED** Describe two real-life situations that use parallel lines.

USING CORRESPONDING ANGLES Use the figure to find the measures of the numbered angles.

14.
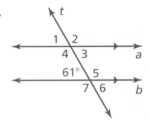

15.
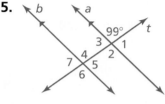

16.
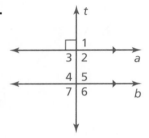

USING CORRESPONDING ANGLES Complete the statement. Explain your reasoning.

17. If the measure of ∠1 = 124°, then the measure of ∠4 = ☐.

18. If the measure of ∠2 = 48°, then the measure of ∠3 = ☐.

19. If the measure of ∠4 = 55°, then the measure of ∠2 = ☐.

20. If the measure of ∠6 = 120°, then the measure of ∠8 = ☐.

21. If the measure of ∠7 = 50.5°, then the measure of ∠6 = ☐.

22. If the measure of ∠3 = 118.7°, then the measure of ∠2 = ☐.

23. **MP MODELING REAL LIFE** A rainbow forms when sunlight reflects off raindrops at different angles. For blue light, the measure of ∠2 is 40°. What is the measure of ∠1?

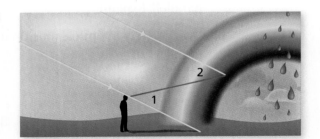

24. **MP REASONING** Is there a relationship between exterior angles that lie on the same side of a transversal? interior angles that lie on the same side of a transversal? Explain.

25. **MP REASONING** When a transversal is perpendicular to two parallel lines, all the angles formed measure 90°. Explain why.

26. **MP REASONING** Two horizontal lines are cut by a transversal. What is the least number of angle measures you need to know to find the measure of every angle? Explain your reasoning.

27. **MP LOGIC** Describe two ways you can show that ∠1 is congruent to ∠7.

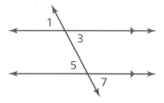

FINDING A VALUE Find the value of *x*.

28.
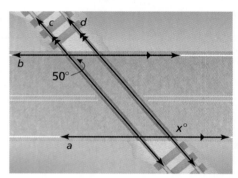

29.
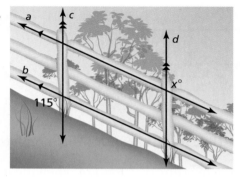

30. **PROJECT** Trace line *p* and line *t* on a piece of paper. Label ∠1. Move the paper so that ∠1 aligns with ∠8. Describe the transformations that you used to show that ∠1 is congruent to ∠8.

31. **OPEN-ENDED** Refer to the figure.

   a. Do the horizontal lines appear to be parallel? Explain.

   b. Draw your own optical illusion using parallel lines.

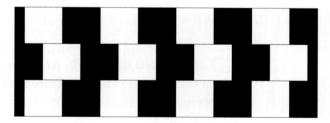

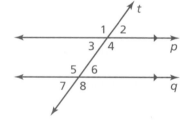

32. **DIG DEEPER!** The figure shows the angles used to make a shot on an air hockey table.

   a. Find the value of *x*.

   b. How does the angle the puck hits the edge of the table relate to the angle it leaves the edge of the table?

3.2 Angles of Triangles

Learning Target: Understand properties of interior and exterior angles of triangles.

Success Criteria:
- I can use equations to find missing angle measures of triangles.
- I can use interior and exterior angles of a triangle to solve real-life problems.

EXPLORATION 1

Exploring Interior and Exterior Angles of Triangles

Work with a partner.

a. Draw several triangles using geometry software. What can you conclude about the sums of the angle measures?

b. You can extend one side of a triangle to form an *exterior angle,* as shown.

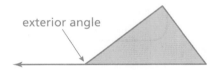

exterior angle

Use geometry software to draw a triangle and an exterior angle. Compare the measure of the exterior angle with the measures of the interior angles. Repeat this process for several different triangles. What can you conclude?

EXPLORATION 2

Using Parallel Lines and Transversals

Work with a partner. Describe what is shown in the figure below. Then use what you know about parallel lines and transversals to justify your conclusions in Exploration 1.

Math Practice

Look for Structure
Which angle labeled in the diagram is an exterior angle of △ABC?

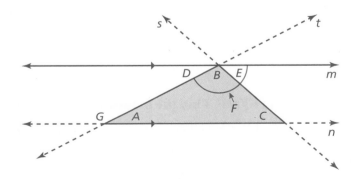

Key Vocabulary 🔊
interior angles of a
polygon, *p. 112*
exterior angles of a
polygon, *p. 112*

The angles inside a polygon are called **interior angles**. When the sides of a polygon are extended, other angles are formed. The angles outside the polygon that are adjacent to the interior angles are called **exterior angles**.

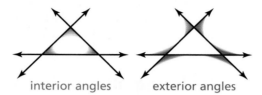

interior angles   exterior angles

🔑 Key Idea

Interior Angle Measures of a Triangle

Words   The sum of the interior angle
measures of a triangle is 180°.

Algebra $x + y + z = 180$

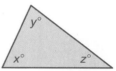

EXAMPLE 1   Using Interior Angle Measures

Find the measures of the interior angles of each triangle.

a.

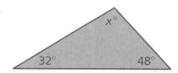

$$x + 32 + 48 = 180$$
$$x + 80 = 180$$
$$x = 100$$

▷ So, the measures of the interior angles are 100°, 48°, and 32°.

b.

$$x + (x + 28) + 90 = 180$$
$$2x + 118 = 180$$
$$2x = 62$$
$$x = 31$$

▷ So, the measures of the interior angles are (31 + 28)° = 59°, 31°, and 90°.

Math Practice

Find Entry Points
Use a relationship between only two angle measures in part (b) to find the interior angle measures.

Try It   **Find the measures of the interior angles of the triangle.**

1.

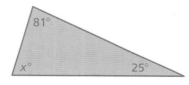

2.

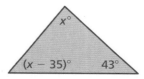

 **Key Idea**

Exterior Angle Measures of a Triangle

Words The measure of an exterior angle of a triangle is equal to the sum of the measures of the two nonadjacent interior angles.

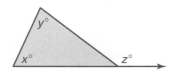

Algebra $z = x + y$

EXAMPLE 2 **Finding Exterior Angle Measures**

Find the measure of the exterior angle.

> Each vertex has a pair of congruent exterior angles. However, it is common to show only one exterior angle at each vertex.

a.

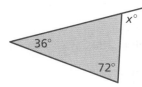

$x = 36 + 72$
$x = 108$

▷ So, the measure of the exterior angle is 108°.

b.

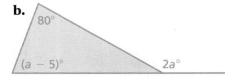

$2a = (a - 5) + 80$
$2a = a + 75$
$a = 75$

▷ So, the measure of the exterior angle is $2(75)° = 150°$.

Try It

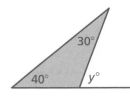

3. Find the measure of the exterior angle of the triangle at the left.

 Self-Assessment *for Concepts & Skills*

Solve each exercise. Then rate your understanding of the success criteria in your journal.

4. VOCABULARY How many exterior angles does a triangle have at each vertex? Explain.

FINDING ANGLE MEASURES Find the value of x.

5.

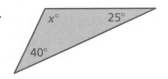

6.

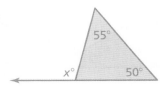

EXAMPLE 3 **Modeling Real Life**

An airplane leaves Miami and travels around the Bermuda Triangle as shown in the diagram. What is the measure of the interior angle at Miami?

 Understand the problem.

You are given expressions representing the interior angle measures of the Bermuda Triangle. You are asked to find the measure of the interior angle at Miami.

Make a plan.

Use what you know about interior angle measures of triangles to write and solve an equation for x.

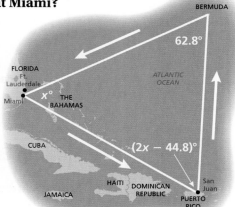

Solve and check.

$$x + (2x - 44.8) + 62.8 = 180 \quad \text{Write an equation.}$$
$$3x + 18 = 180 \quad \text{Combine like terms.}$$
$$3x = 162 \quad \text{Subtract 18 from each side.}$$
$$x = 54 \quad \text{Divide each side by 3.}$$

Check

$$x + (2x - 44.8) + 62.8 = 180$$
$$54 + [2(54) - 44.8] + 62.8 \overset{?}{=} 180$$
$$54 + 63.2 + 62.8 \overset{?}{=} 180$$
$$180 = 180 \checkmark$$

So, the measure of the interior angle at Miami is 54°.

 Self-Assessment for Problem Solving

Solve each exercise. Then rate your understanding of the success criteria in your journal.

7. The *Historic Triangle* in Virginia connects Jamestown, Williamsburg, and Yorktown. The interior angle at Williamsburg is 120°. The interior angle at Jamestown is twice the measure of the interior angle at Yorktown. Find the measures of the interior angles at Jamestown and Yorktown. Explain your reasoning.

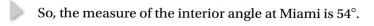

8. A helicopter travels from point C to point A to perform a medical supply drop. The helicopter then needs to land at point B. How many degrees should the helicopter turn at point A to travel towards point B? Justify your answer.

3.2 Practice

 Go to *BigIdeasMath.com* to get HELP with solving the exercises.

▶ Review & Refresh

Use the figure to find the measure of the angle. Explain your reasoning.

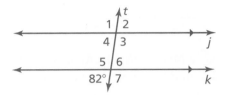

1. $\angle 2$

2. $\angle 6$

3. $\angle 4$

4. $\angle 1$

You spin the spinner shown.

5. What are the favorable outcomes of spinning a number less than 4?

6. In how many ways can spinning an odd number occur?

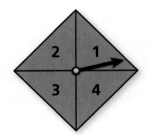

▶▶ Concepts, Skills, & Problem Solving

USING PARALLEL LINES AND TRANSVERSALS **Consider the figure below.** (See Exploration 2, p. 111.)

7. Use a protractor to find the measures of the labeled angles.

8. Is $\angle F$ an exterior angle of Triangle *ABC*? Justify your answer.

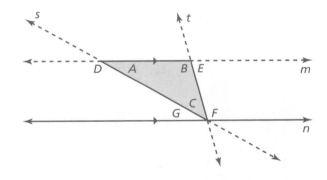

USING INTERIOR ANGLE MEASURES **Find the measures of the interior angles of the triangle.**

9.
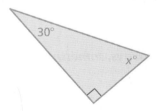

10.
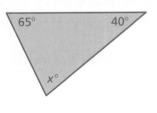

11.
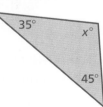

12.
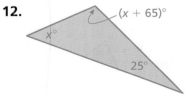

13.
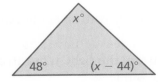

14.
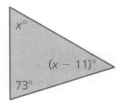

FINDING EXTERIOR ANGLE MEASURES Find the measure of the exterior angle.

15.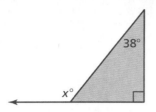

16.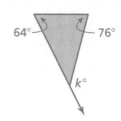

17.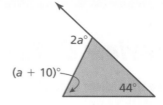

18. 🔵 **MODELING REAL LIFE** A tornado is located between city hall and a cell phone tower and is heading towards the cell phone tower. By what angle does the tornado's direction need to change so that it passes over the radar station instead? Justify your answer.

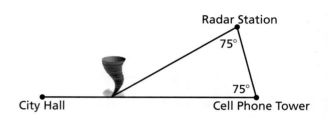

19. 🔵 **YOU BE THE TEACHER** Your friend finds the measure of the exterior angle shown. Is your friend correct? Explain your reasoning.

$$(3x - 6) + x + 30 = 180$$
$$4x + 24 = 180$$
$$x = 39$$
The exterior angle is $(3(39) - 6)° = 111°$.

20. 🔵 **REASONING** The ratio of the interior angle measures of a triangle is $2:3:5$. What are the angle measures?

21. 🔵 **PROBLEM SOLVING** The support for a window air-conditioning unit forms a triangle and an exterior angle. What is the measure of the exterior angle?

22. 🔵 **REASONING** A triangle has an exterior angle with a measure of $120°$. Can you determine the measures of the interior angles? Explain.

ANGLES OF TRIANGLES Determine whether the statement is *always, sometimes,* or *never* true. Explain your reasoning.

23. Given three angle measures, you can construct a triangle.

24. The acute interior angles of a right triangle are complementary.

25. A triangle has more than one vertex with an acute exterior angle.

26. **DIG DEEPER!** Using the figure at the right, write an equation that represents z in terms of x and y.

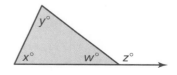

3.3 Angles of Polygons

Learning Target: Find interior angle measures of polygons.

Success Criteria:
- I can explain how to find the sum of the interior angle measures of a polygon.
- I can use an equation to find an interior angle measure of a polygon.
- I can find the interior angle measures of a regular polygon.

EXPLORATION 1

Exploring Interior Angles of Polygons

Work with a partner. In parts (a)–(f), use what you know about the interior angle measures of triangles to find the sum of the interior angle measures of each figure.

Math Practice

View as Components

How does dividing the figure into triangles help you find the sum of the interior angle measures?

a.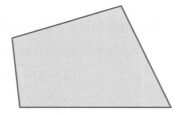

b.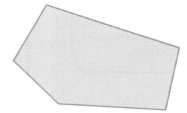

c.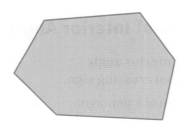

d.

e.

f.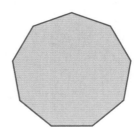

g. **MP REPEATED REASONING** Use your results in parts (a)–(f) to complete the table. Then write an equation that represents the sum S of the interior angle measures of a polygon with n sides.

Number of Sides, n	3	4	5	6	7	8	9
Number of Triangles							
Interior Angle Sum, S							

Key Vocabulary
regular polygon,
   p. 120

A *polygon* is a closed plane figure made up of three or more line segments that intersect only at their endpoints.

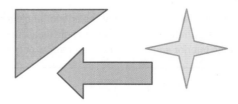

Polygons

Not polygons

Reading

For polygons whose names you have not learned, you can use the phrase "*n*-gon," where *n* is the number of sides. For example, a 15-gon is a polygon with 15 sides.

 Key Idea

Interior Angle Measures of a Polygon

The sum S of the interior angle measures of a polygon with n sides is

$$S = (n - 2) \cdot 180°.$$

EXAMPLE 1 **Finding the Sum of Interior Angle Measures**

Find the sum of the interior angle measures of the school crossing sign.

The sign is in the shape of a pentagon. It has 5 sides.

$S = (n - 2) \cdot 180°$	Write the formula.
$= (5 - 2) \cdot 180°$	Substitute 5 for n.
$= 3 \cdot 180°$	Subtract.
$= 540°$	Multiply.

▷ The sum of the interior angle measures is 540°.

Try It **Find the sum of the interior angle measures of the green polygon.**

1.

2.

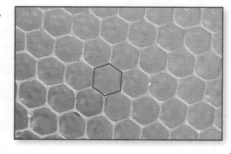

  Multi-Language Glossary at *BigIdeasMath.com*

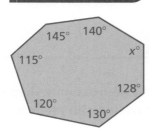

EXAMPLE 2 Finding an Interior Angle Measure of a Polygon

Find the value of x.

Step 1: The polygon has 7 sides. Find the sum of the interior angle measures.

$$S = (n - 2) \cdot 180°$$ Write the formula.

$$= (7 - 2) \cdot 180°$$ Substitute 7 for n.

$$= 900°$$ Simplify. The sum of the interior angle measures is 900°.

Step 2: Write and solve an equation.

$$140 + 145 + 115 + 120 + 130 + 128 + x = 900$$

$$778 + x = 900$$

$$x = 122$$

▷ The value of x is 122.

Try It Find the value of x.

3.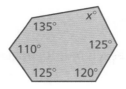

4.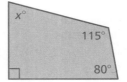

Self-Assessment for Concepts & Skills

Solve each exercise. Then rate your understanding of the success criteria in your journal.

5. **WRITING** Explain how to find the sum of the interior measures of a polygon.

6. **FINDING THE SUM OF INTERIOR ANGLE MEASURES** Find the sum of the interior angle measures of the green polygon.

FINDING AN INTERIOR ANGLE MEASURE Find the value of x.

7.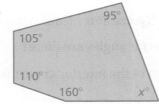

8.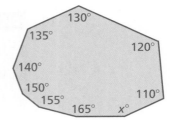

In a **regular polygon**, all the sides are congruent, and all the interior angles are congruent.

Modeling Real Life

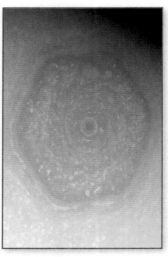

The hexagon is about 15,000 miles across. Approximately four Earths can fit inside it.

A cloud system discovered on Saturn is in the approximate shape of a regular hexagon. Find the measure of each interior angle of the hexagon.

A hexagon has 6 sides. Use the formula to find the sum of the interior angle measures.

$S = (n - 2) \cdot 180°$	Write the formula.
$= (6 - 2) \cdot 180°$	Substitute 6 for n.
$= 720°$	Simplify. The sum of the interior angle measures is 720°.

In a regular polygon, each interior angle is congruent. So, divide the sum of the interior angle measures by the number of interior angles, 6.

$$720° \div 6 = 120°$$

▷ The measure of each interior angle is 120°.

 Self-Assessment for *Problem Solving*

Solve each exercise. Then rate your understanding of the success criteria in your journal.

9. A company installs an octagonal swimming pool.

   a. Find the value of a for the pool shown at the left.

   b. The company installs a different pool that is also in the shape of an octagon. The second pool has twice the length and one-third the width of the first pool. Are the sums of the interior angles of the pools different? Justify your answer.

10. **DIG DEEPER!** A *Bronze Star Medal* is shown.

   a. How many interior angles are there?

   b. What is the sum of the interior angle measures?

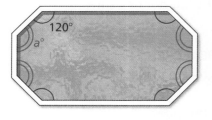

3.3 Practice

? Go to *BigIdeasMath.com* to get HELP with solving the exercises.

▶ Review & Refresh

Find the value of *x*.

1.

2.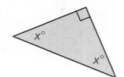

3.

Solve the proportion.

4. $\dfrac{x}{12} = \dfrac{3}{4}$

5. $\dfrac{14}{21} = \dfrac{x}{3}$

6. $\dfrac{9}{x} = \dfrac{6}{2}$

▶▶ Concepts, Skills, & Problem Solving

EXPLORING INTERIOR ANGLES OF POLYGONS Use triangles to find the sum of the interior angle measures of the polygon. (See Exploration 1, p. 117.)

7.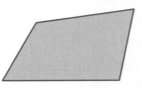

8.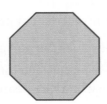

9.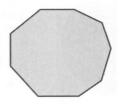

FINDING THE SUM OF INTERIOR ANGLE MEASURES Find the sum of the interior angle measures of the polygon.

10.

11.

12.

13. **MP YOU BE THE TEACHER** Your friend finds the sum of the interior angle measures of a 13-gon. Is your friend correct? Explain your reasoning.

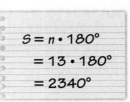

FINDING AN INTERIOR ANGLE MEASURE Find the value of *x*.

14.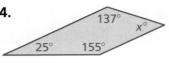

15.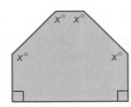

16.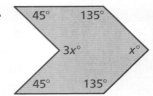

FINDING A MEASURE Find the measure of each interior angle of the regular polygon.

17.

18.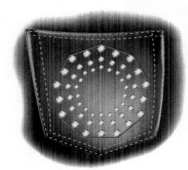

19.

20. **MP YOU BE THE TEACHER** Your friend finds the measure of each interior angle of a regular 20-gon. Is your friend correct? Explain your reasoning.

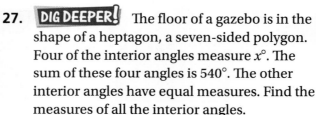

$$S = (n - 2) \cdot 180°$$
$$= (20 - 2) \cdot 180°$$
$$= 18 \cdot 180°$$
$$= 3240°$$
$$3240° \div 18 = 180°$$
The measure of each interior angle is 180°.

21. **MP MODELING REAL LIFE** A fire hydrant bolt is in the shape of a regular pentagon.

   a. What is the measure of each interior angle?

   b. **RESEARCH** Why are fire hydrants made this way?

22. **MP PROBLEM SOLVING** The interior angles of a regular polygon each measure 165°. How many sides does the polygon have?

23. **MP STRUCTURE** A molecule can be represented by a polygon with interior angles that each measure 120°. What polygon represents the molecule? Does the polygon have to be regular? Justify your answers.

24. **MP PROBLEM SOLVING** The border of a Susan B. Anthony dollar is in the shape of a regular polygon.

   a. How many sides does the polygon have?

   b. What is the measure of each interior angle of the border? Round your answer to the nearest degree.

25. **MP REASONING** The center of the stained glass window is in the shape of a regular polygon. What are the measures of the interior angles of the green triangle?

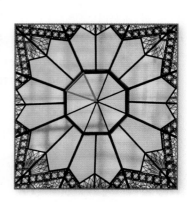

26. **GEOMETRY** Draw a pentagon that has two right interior angles, two 45° interior angles, and one 270° interior angle.

27. **DIG DEEPER!** The floor of a gazebo is in the shape of a heptagon, a seven-sided polygon. Four of the interior angles measure $x°$. The sum of these four angles is 540°. The other interior angles have equal measures. Find the measures of all the interior angles.

3.4 Using Similar Triangles

Learning Target: Use similar triangles to find missing measures.

Success Criteria:
• I can use angle measures to determine whether triangles are similar.
• I can use similar triangles to solve real-life problems.

EXPLORATION 1

Drawing Triangles Given Two Angle Measures

Work with a partner. Use geometry software.

a. Draw a triangle that has a 50° angle and a 30° angle. Then draw a triangle that is either larger or smaller that has the same two angle measures. Are the triangles congruent? similar? Explain your reasoning.

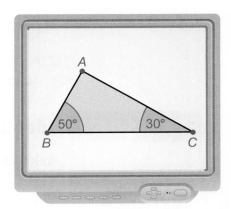

b. Choose any two angle measures whose sum is less than 180°. Repeat part (a) using the angle measures you chose.

c. Compare your results in parts (a) and (b) with other pairs of students. Make a conjecture about two triangles that have two pairs of congruent angles.

EXPLORATION 2

Using Indirect Measurement

Work with a partner. Use the fact that two rays from the Sun are parallel to make a plan for how to find the height of the flagpole. Explain your reasoning.

Math Practice

Make Sense of Quantities

What do you know about the sides of similar triangles?

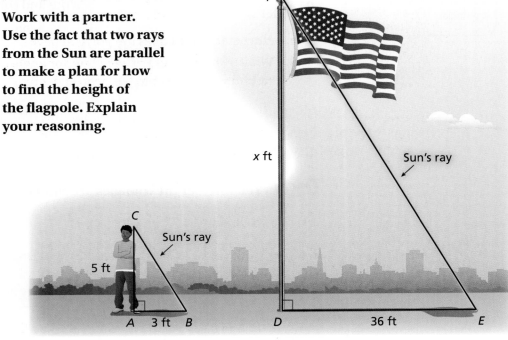

3.4 Lesson

Key Vocabulary 🔊
indirect measurement,
p. 126

 Key Idea

Angles of Similar Triangles

Words When two angles in one triangle are congruent to two angles in another triangle, the third angles are also congruent and the triangles are similar.

Example

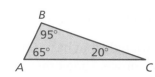 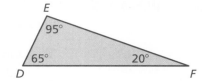

Triangle *ABC* is similar to Triangle *DEF*: △*ABC* ~ △*DEF*.

EXAMPLE 1 ## Identifying Similar Triangles

Tell whether the triangles are similar. Explain.

Math Practice

Build Arguments
Explain why you only need to know that two pairs of angles are congruent to know that two triangles are similar.

a.

The triangles have two pairs of congruent angles.

▷ So, the third angles are congruent, and the triangles are similar.

b.

Write and solve an equation to find *x*.

$$x + 90 + 42 = 180$$
$$x + 132 = 180$$
$$x = 48$$

The triangles do not have two pairs of congruent angles.

▷ So, the triangles are not similar.

Try It **Tell whether the triangles are similar. Explain.**

1.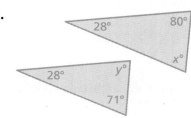

2.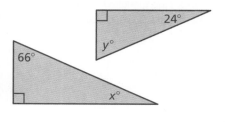

🔊 *Multi-Language Glossary at BigIdeasMath.com*

EXAMPLE 2 **Identifying Similar Triangles**

Can you determine whether △JKL and △JMN are similar? Explain.

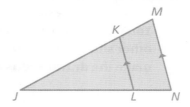

Side *KL* and side *MN* are parallel, and each is intersected by side *JN*. So, ∠*JLK* and ∠*N* are congruent corresponding angles. Each triangle also shares ∠*J*.

You can also use corresponding angles to show that ∠*JKL* is congruent to ∠*M*.

▸ Because two angles in △*JKL* are congruent to two angles in △*JMN*, the third angles are also congruent and the triangles are similar.

Try It

3. Can you determine whether △*PQR* and △*TSR* are similar? Explain.

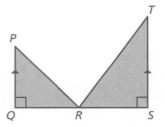

 Self-Assessment *for Concepts & Skills*

Solve each exercise. Then rate your understanding of the success criteria in your journal.

4. **IDENTIFYING SIMILAR TRIANGLES** Tell whether the triangles are similar. Explain.

5. **DIFFERENT WORDS, SAME QUESTION** Which is different? Find "both" answers.

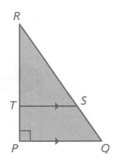

Are △*PQR* and △*TSR* similar?

Are △*PQR* and △*TSR* the same size and shape?

Is △*PQR* a dilation of △*TSR*?

Is △*PQR* a scale drawing of △*TSR*?

Indirect measurement uses similar figures to find a missing measure when it is difficult to find directly.

EXAMPLE 3 **Modeling Real Life**

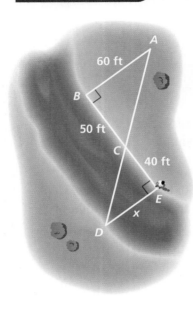

You plan to cross a river and want to know how far it is to the other side. You take measurements on your side of the river and make the drawing shown. What is the distance *x* across the river?

Notice that $\angle B$ and $\angle E$ are right angles, so they are congruent. $\angle ACB$ and $\angle DCE$ are vertical angles, so they are congruent. Because two angles in $\triangle ABC$ are congruent to two angles in $\triangle DEC$, the third angles are also congruent and the triangles are similar.

Ratios of corresponding side lengths in similar triangles are equivalent. So, the ratios $x : 60$ and $40 : 50$ are equivalent. Write and solve a proportion to find x.

$$\frac{x}{60} = \frac{40}{50}$$ Write a proportion.

$$60 \cdot \frac{x}{60} = 60 \cdot \frac{40}{50}$$ Multiplication Property of Equality

$$x = 48$$ Simplify.

▷ So, the distance across the river is 48 feet.

Self-Assessment for Problem Solving

Solve each exercise. Then rate your understanding of the success criteria in your journal.

6. Engineers plan to construct an aqueduct to transport water from the top of a ridge to farmland. A portion of the project is complete. Find the length of the entire aqueduct.

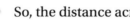

5 km

2.6 km

1 km

2.4 km

7. You want to go on a swamp tour. How long does it take a swamp vehicle that travels at 3.2 miles per hour to travel across the swamp, from point *Z* to point *Y*? Justify your answer.

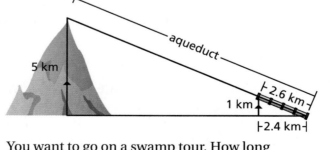

Z   *Y*

3 miles

X

6 miles

V   10 miles   *W*

3.4 Practice

? Go to *BigIdeasMath.com* to get HELP with solving the exercises.

▶ *Review & Refresh*

Find the measure of each interior angle of the regular polygon.

1. octagon

2. decagon

3. 18-gon

Solve the equation. Check your solution.

4. $3.5 + y = -1$

5. $9x = 54$

6. $-4 = \dfrac{2}{7}p$

▶▶ *Concepts, Skills, & Problem Solving*

CREATING SIMILAR TRIANGLES **Draw a triangle that is either larger or smaller than the one given and has two of the same angle measures. Explain why the new triangle is similar to the original triangle.** (See Exploration 1, p. 123.)

7.

8.

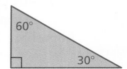

IDENTIFYING SIMILAR TRIANGLES **Tell whether the triangles are similar. Explain.**

9.

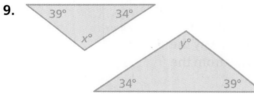

10.

11.

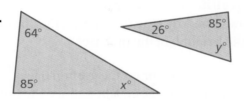

12.

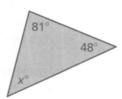

13. GEOMETRY Which of the rulers are similar in shape? Explain.

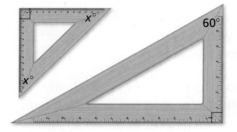
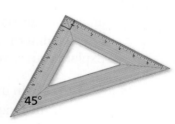

MP STRUCTURE Tell whether the triangles are similar. Explain.

14.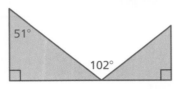
51°
102°

15.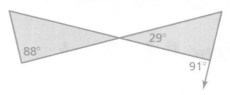
88°
29°
91°

IDENTIFYING SIMILAR TRIANGLES Can you determine whether the triangles are similar? Explain.

16. △PQS and △RQS

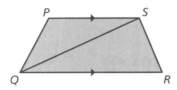
P
S
Q
R

17. △ABC and △EDC

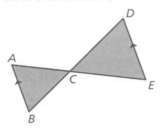
D
A
C
E
B

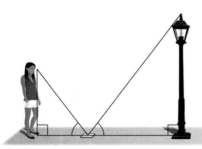
50 ft
5 ft
1.5 ft
d
Not drawn to scale

18. **MP PROBLEM SOLVING** A water sample must be taken from water at least 20 feet deep. Find the depth of the water 50 feet from shore. Is this an appropriate location for a water sample?

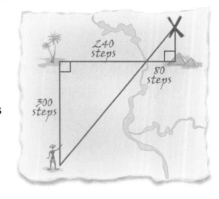
240 steps
80 steps
300 steps

19. **MP MODELING REAL LIFE** A map shows the number of steps you must take to get to a treasure. However, the map is old, and the last dimension is unreadable. Explain why the triangles are similar. How many steps do you take from the pyramids to the treasure?

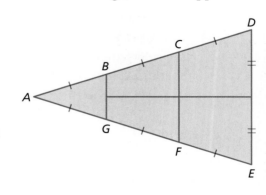

20. **MP PROBLEM SOLVING** A person who is 6 feet tall casts a 3-foot-long shadow. A nearby pine tree casts a 15-foot-long shadow. What is the height h of the pine tree?

21. **OPEN-ENDED** You place a mirror on the ground 6 feet from the lamppost. You move back 3 feet and see the top of the lamppost in the mirror. What is the height of the lamppost?

22. **DIG DEEPER!** In each of two right triangles, one angle measure is two times another angle measure. Can you determine that the triangles are similar? Explain your reasoning.

23. **GEOMETRY** In the diagram, $\overline{BG}$, $\overline{CF}$, and $\overline{DE}$ are parallel. The length of $\overline{BD}$ is 6.32 feet, and the length of $\overline{DE}$ is 6 feet. Name all pairs of similar triangles in the diagram. Then find the lengths of $\overline{BG}$ and $\overline{CF}$.

D
C
B
A
G
F
E

Connecting Concepts

Using the Problem-Solving Plan

1. A dog park is divided into sections for large and small dogs. The ratio of the perimeter of the small dog section to the perimeter of the entire dog park is 7 : 12. Find the area of each section.

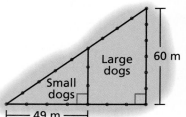

 You know two dimensions of a dog park and the **ratio** of the perimeter of the small dog section to the perimeter of the entire park. You are asked to find the area of each section.

 Verify that the small triangle and the large triangle are similar. Then use the ratio of the perimeters to find the base or the height of each triangle and calculate the areas.

Solve and check. Use the plan to solve the problem. Then check your solution.

2. You rotate lines m and t 180° about point P. The image of line m is parallel to the original line. Use the diagram to show that when a transversal intersects parallel lines, each of the following pairs of angles are congruent. Explain your reasoning.

   a. alternate interior angles

   b. alternate exterior angles

   c. corresponding angles

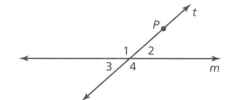

Performance Task

Turtle Shells

At the beginning of this chapter, you watched a STEAM Video called "Honeycombs." You are now ready to complete the performance task related to this video, available at **BigIdeasMath.com**. Be sure to use the problem-solving plan as you work through the performance task.

▶ Review Vocabulary

Write the definition and give an example of each vocabulary term.

transversal, *p. 104*

interior angles, *p. 105*

exterior angles, *p. 105*

interior angles of a polygon, *p. 112*

exterior angles of a polygon, *p. 112*

regular polygon, *p. 120*

indirect measurement, *p. 126*

▶ Graphic Organizers

You can use an **Example and Non-Example Chart** to list examples and non-examples of a concept. Here is an Example and Non-Example Chart for *transversals*.

Transversals

Examples	Non-Examples
line *p*, line *q*, line *r*	line *a*, line *b*, line *c*
line *a*, line *b*, line *c*, line *d*	line *p*, line *t*

Choose and complete a graphic organizer to help you study the concept.

1. interior angles formed by parallel lines and a transversal

2. exterior angles formed by parallel lines and a transversal

3. interior angles of a triangle

4. exterior angles of a triangle

5. polygons

6. similar triangles

"What do you think of my Example & Non-Example Chart for popular cat toys?"

Chapter Self-Assessment

As you complete the exercises, use the scale below to rate your understanding of the success criteria in your journal.

1	**2**	**3**	**4**
I do not understand.	I can do it with help.	I can do it on my own.	I can teach someone else.

3.1 Parallel Lines and Transversals (pp. 103–110)

Learning Target: Find missing angle measures created by the intersections of lines.

Use the figure to find the measure of the angle. Explain your reasoning.

1. ∠8

2. ∠5

3. ∠7

4. ∠2

5. ∠6

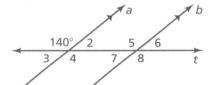

Complete the statement. Explain your reasoning.

6. If the measure of ∠1 = 123°,

   then the measure of ∠7 = ⬜ .

7. If the measure of ∠2 = 58°,

   then the measure of ∠5 = ⬜ .

8. If the measure of ∠5 = 119°, then the measure of ∠3 = ⬜ .

9. If the measure of ∠4 = 60°, then the measure of ∠6 = ⬜ .

10. In Exercises 6–9, describe the relationship between ∠2 and ∠8.

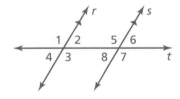

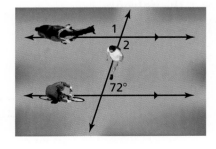

11. In a park, a bike path and a horse riding path are parallel. In one part of the park, a hiking trail intersects the two paths. Find the measures of ∠1 and ∠2. Explain your reasoning.

3.2 Angles of Triangles *(pp. 111–116)*

Learning Target: Understand properties of interior and exterior angles of triangles.

Find the measures of the interior angles of the triangle.

12.

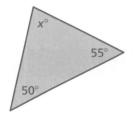

13.

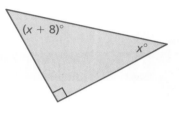

Find the measure of the exterior angle.

14.

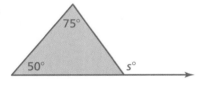

15.

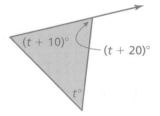

16. What is the measure of each interior angle of an equilateral triangle? Explain.

17. You draw the Leo constellation. You notice that the three stars Denebola, Zosma, and Chertan form a triangle. In your drawing, you find the measure of the interior angle at Denebola is 30° and the measure of the interior angle of the triangle at Zosma is 56°. What is the measure of the interior angle of the triangle at Chertan?

3.3 Angles of Polygons *(pp. 117–122)*

Learning Target: Find interior angle measures of polygons.

Find the sum of the interior angle measures of the polygon.

18.

19.

Find the value of x.

20.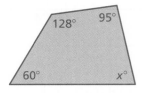

21.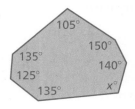

22.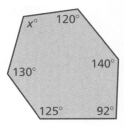

23. Find the measure of each interior angle of the regular polygon.

3.4 Using Similar Triangles *(pp. 123–128)*

Learning Target: Use similar triangles to find missing measures.

Tell whether the triangles are similar. Explain.

24.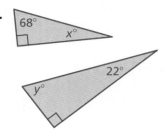

25.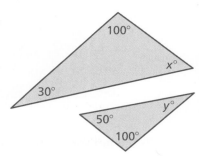

26.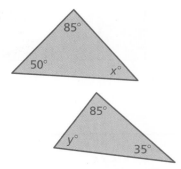

27.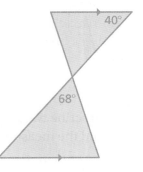

28. A person who is 5 feet tall casts a shadow that is 4 feet long. A nearby building casts a shadow that is 24 feet long. What is the height of the building?

Use the figure to find the measure of the angle. Explain your reasoning.

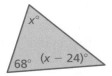

1. ∠7

2. ∠6

3. ∠4

4. ∠5

5. Find the value of x.

6. Find the measures of the interior angles.

7. Find the measure of the exterior angle.

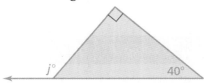

8. Find the sum of the interior angle measures of the border of the coin.

9. Find the value of x.

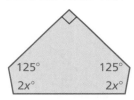

10. Find the measure of each interior angle of the regular polygon.

Tell whether the triangles are similar. Explain.

11.

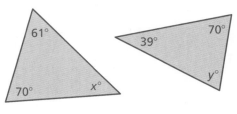

12.

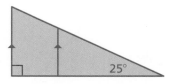

13. Describe two ways you can find the measure of ∠5.

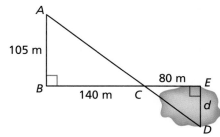

14. You swim 3.6 kilometers per hour. How long (in minutes) will it take you to swim the distance d across the pond?

Cumulative Practice

1. The border of a Canadian one-dollar coin is shaped like an 11-sided regular polygon. The shape was chosen to help visually impaired people identify the coin. How many degrees are in each interior angle along the border? Round your answer to the nearest degree.

2. A public utility charges its residential customers for natural gas based on the number of therms used each month. The formula shows how the monthly cost C in dollars is related to the number t of therms used.

$$C = 11 + 1.6t$$

Solve this formula for t.

   A. $t = \dfrac{C}{12.6}$ **B.** $t = \dfrac{C - 11}{1.6}$

   C. $t = \dfrac{C}{1.6} - 11$ **D.** $t = C - 12.6$

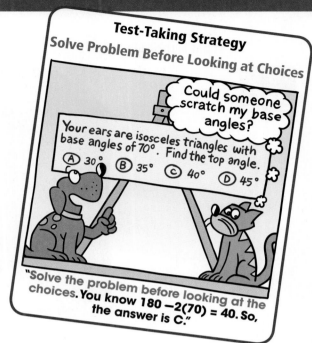

Test-Taking Strategy
Solve Problem Before Looking at Choices

Could someone scratch my base angles?

Your ears are isosceles triangles with base angles of 70°. Find the top angle.
(A) 30° (B) 35° (C) 40° (D) 45°

"Solve the problem before looking at the choices. You know $180 - 2(70) = 40$. So, the answer is C."

3. What is the value of x?

$$5(x - 4) = 3x$$

   F. -10 **G.** 2

   H. $2\dfrac{1}{2}$ **I.** 10

4. In the figures, $\triangle PQR$ is similar to $\triangle STU$. What is the value of x?

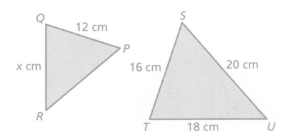

   A. 9.6   **B.** $10\dfrac{2}{3}$

   C. 13.5   **D.** 15

5. What is the value of x?

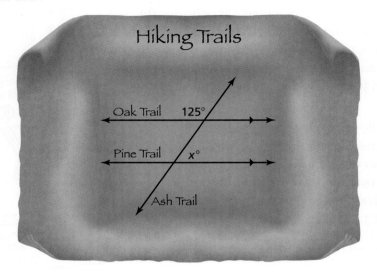

6. Your friend was solving an equation in the box shown.

$$-\frac{2}{5}(10x - 15) = -30$$

$$10x - 15 = -30\left(-\frac{2}{5}\right)$$

$$10x - 15 = 12$$

$$10x - 15 + 15 = 12 + 15$$

$$10x = 27$$

$$\frac{10x}{10} = \frac{27}{10}$$

$$x = \frac{27}{10}$$

What should your friend do to correct the error that she made?

   F. Multiply both sides by $-\frac{5}{2}$ instead of $-\frac{2}{5}$.

   G. Multiply both sides by $\frac{2}{5}$ instead of $-\frac{2}{5}$.

   H. Distribute $-\frac{2}{5}$ to get $-4x - 6$.

   I. Add 15 to -30.

7. In the coordinate plane below, △XYZ is plotted and its vertices are labeled.

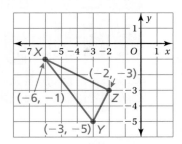

Which of the following shows △X'Y'Z', the image of △XYZ after it is reflected in the y-axis?

A.

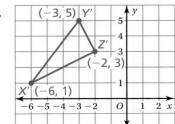

B.

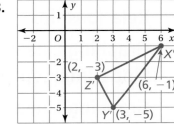

C.

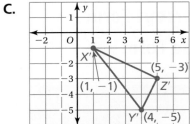

D.

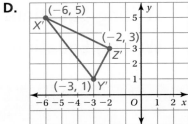

8. The sum S of the interior angle measures of a polygon with n sides can be found by using a formula.

Part A Write the formula.

Part B A quadrilateral has angles measuring 100°, 90°, and 90°. Find the measure of its fourth angle. Show your work and explain your reasoning.

Part C The sum of the measures of the angles of the pentagon shown is 540°. Divide the pentagon into triangles to show why this must be true. Show your work and explain your reasoning.

4 Graphing and Writing Linear Equations

Chapter Learning Target:
Understand graphing linear equations.

Chapter Success Criteria:
- ▪ I can identify key features of a graph.
- ▪ I can explain the meaning of different forms of linear equations.
- ▪ I can interpret the slope and intercepts of a line.
- ▪ I can create graphs of linear equations.

STEAM Video: "Hurricane!"

Wind Speed

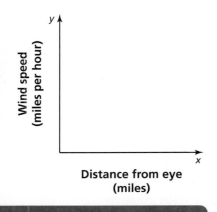

Hurricane!

A hurricane is a storm with violent winds. How can you prepare your home for a hurricane?

Watch the STEAM Video "Hurricane!" Then answer the following questions.

1. Robert says that the closer you are to the eye of a hurricane, the stronger the winds become. The wind speed on an island is 50 miles per hour when the eye of a hurricane is 140 miles away.

   a. Describe the wind speed on the island when the eye of the hurricane is 100 miles away.

   b. Describe the distance of the island from the eye of the hurricane when the wind speed on the island is 25 miles per hour.

   c. Sketch a line that could represent the wind speed y (in miles per hour) on the island when the eye of the hurricane is x miles away from the island.

2. A storm dissipates as it travels over land. What does this mean?

Anatomy of a Hurricane

After completing this chapter, you will be able to use the concepts you learned to answer the questions in the *STEAM Video Performance Task*. You will be given information about the atmospheric pressure inside a hurricane.

Time, x (hours)	Atmospheric Pressure, y (millibars)
18	1008
36	999
84	975

You will be asked to use a model to find the strength of a hurricane after x hours of monitoring. Why is it helpful to predict how strong the winds of a hurricane will become?

Getting Ready for Chapter

Chapter Exploration

1. **Work with a partner.**

    a. Use the equation $y = \frac{1}{2}x + 1$ to complete the table. (Choose any two x-values and find the y-values.)

    b. Write the two ordered pairs given by the table. These are called *solutions* of the equation.

    c. **MP PRECISION** Plot the two solutions. Draw a line *exactly* through the points.

    d. Find a different point on the line. Check that this point is a solution of the equation $y = \frac{1}{2}x + 1$.

    e. **MP LOGIC** Do you think it is true that *any* point on the line is a solution of the equation $y = \frac{1}{2}x + 1$? Explain.

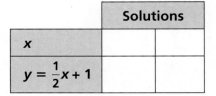

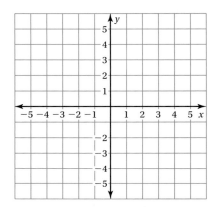

    f. Choose five additional x-values for the table below. (Choose both positive and negative x-values.) Plot the five corresponding solutions. Does each point lie on the line?

	Solutions				
x					
$y = \frac{1}{2}x + 1$					

    g. **MP LOGIC** Do you think it is true that any solution of the equation $y = \frac{1}{2}x + 1$ is a point on the line? Explain.

    h. Why do you think $y = ax + b$ is called a *linear equation*?

Vocabulary

The following vocabulary terms are defined in this chapter. Think about what each term might mean and record your thoughts.

linear equation   slope y-intercept

solution of a linear equation x-intercept

4.1 Graphing Linear Equations

Learning Target: Graph linear equations.

Success Criteria:
- I can create a table of values and write ordered pairs given a linear equation.
- I can plot ordered pairs to create a graph of a linear equation.
- I can use a graph of a linear equation to solve a real-life problem.

EXPLORATION 1

Creating Graphs

Work with a partner. It starts snowing at midnight in Town A and Town B. The snow falls at a rate of 1.5 inches per hour.

a. In Town A, there is no snow on the ground at midnight. How deep is the snow at each hour between midnight and 6 A.M.? Make a graph that represents this situation.

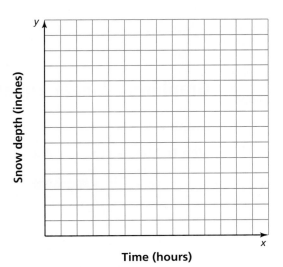

Snow depth (inches)

Time (hours)

b. Repeat part (a) for Town B, which has 4 inches of snow on the ground at midnight.

c. The equations below represent the depth y (in inches) of snow x hours after midnight in Town C and Town D. Graph each equation.

Town C	Town D
$y = 2x + 3$	$y = 8$

d. Use your graphs to compare the snowfall in each town.

Math Practice

Use a Graph
How can you use each graph to find the rate of snowfall? the depth of the snow when it begins to fall?

4.1 Lesson

Key Vocabulary
linear equation, *p. 142*
solution of a linear
equation, *p. 142*

 Key Idea

Linear Equations

A **linear equation** is an equation whose graph is a line. The points on the line are **solutions** of the equation.

You can use a graph to show the solutions of a linear equation. The graph below represents the equation $y = x + 1$.

Remember

An ordered pair (x, y) is used to locate a point in a coordinate plane.

x	y	(x, y)
−1	0	(−1, 0)
0	1	(0, 1)
2	3	(2, 3)

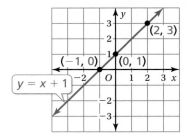

EXAMPLE 1 **Graphing a Linear Equation**

Graph $y = -2x + 1$.

Step 1: Make a table of values.

x	y = −2x + 1	y	(x, y)
−1	$y = -2(-1) + 1$	3	(−1, 3)
0	$y = -2(0) + 1$	1	(0, 1)
2	$y = -2(2) + 1$	−3	(2, −3)

Step 2: Plot the ordered pairs.

Step 3: Draw a line through the points.

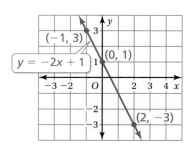

Try It **Graph the linear equation.**

1. $y = 3x$

2. $y = -2x - 1$

3. $y = -\frac{1}{2}x + 2$

Multi-Language Glossary at BigIdeasMath.com

Every point that is a solution of $y = b$ has a y-coordinate of b. These points lie on a horizontal line through $(0, b)$. You can use similar reasoning to understand why the graph of $x = a$ is a vertical line through $(a, 0)$.

 **Key Idea**

Graphing Horizontal and Vertical Lines

The graph of $y = b$ is a horizontal line passing through $(0, b)$.

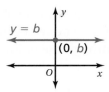

The graph of $x = a$ is a vertical line passing through $(a, 0)$.

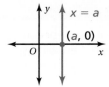

EXAMPLE 2 **Graphing a Horizontal Line and a Vertical Line**

a. **Graph $y = -3$.**

The graph of $y = -3$ is a horizontal line passing through $(0, -3)$. Draw a horizontal line through this point.

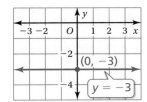

b. **Graph $x = 2$.**

The graph of $x = 2$ is a vertical line passing through $(2, 0)$. Draw a vertical line through this point.

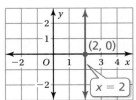

Try It **Graph the linear equation.**

4. $y = 3$ 5. $y = -1.5$ 6. $x = -4$ 7. $x = \dfrac{1}{2}$

 Self-Assessment *for Concepts & Skills*

Solve each exercise. Then rate your understanding of the success criteria in your journal.

GRAPHING A LINEAR EQUATION **Graph the linear equation.**

8. $y = -x + 1$

9. $y = 0.8x - 2$

10. $x = 2.5$

11. $y = \dfrac{2}{3}$

12. **WHICH ONE DOESN'T BELONG?** Which equation does *not* belong with the other three? Explain your reasoning.

| $y = x - 2$ | $4x + 3 = y$ | $y = x^2 + 6$ | $x + 5 = y$ |

EXAMPLE 3 **Modeling Real Life**

A tropical storm becomes a hurricane when wind speeds are at least 74 miles per hour.

The wind speed y (in miles per hour) of a tropical storm is $y = 2x + 66$, where x is the number of hours after the storm enters the Gulf of Mexico. When does the storm become a hurricane?

Use a graph to find the time it takes for the storm to become a hurricane. Make a table of values. Plot the ordered pairs and draw a line through the points.

x	$y = 2x + 66$	y	(x, y)
0	$y = 2(0) + 66$	66	$(0, 66)$
1	$y = 2(1) + 66$	68	$(1, 68)$
2	$y = 2(2) + 66$	70	$(2, 70)$
3	$y = 2(3) + 66$	72	$(3, 72)$

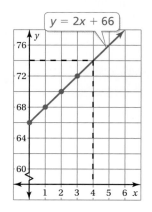

Math Practice

Use Equations
How else can you use the equation $y = 2x + 66$ to help you determine when the storm becomes a hurricane?

From the graph, you can see that $y = 74$ when $x = 4$.

▷ So, the storm becomes a hurricane 4 hours after it enters the Gulf of Mexico.

Self-Assessment for Problem Solving

Solve each exercise. Then rate your understanding of the success criteria in your journal.

13. A game show contestant earns y dollars for completing a puzzle in x minutes. This situation is represented by the equation $y = -250x + 5000$. How long did a contestant who earned $500 take to complete the puzzle? Justify your answer.

14. The total cost y (in dollars) to join a cheerleading team and attend x competitions is represented by the equation $y = 10x + 50$.

   a. Graph the linear equation.

   b. You have $75 to spend. How many competitions can you attend?

15. The seating capacity y for a banquet hall is represented by $y = 8x + 56$, where x is the number of extra tables you need. How many extra tables do you need to double the original seating capacity?

4.1 Practice

? Go to *BigIdeasMath.com* to get HELP with solving the exercises.

▶ Review & Refresh

Tell whether the triangles are similar. Explain.

1.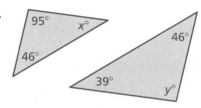

2.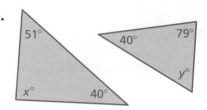

Describe the translation of the point to its image.

3. $(1, -4) \longrightarrow (3, 0)$ **4.** $(6, 4) \longrightarrow (-4, -6)$ **5.** $(4, -2) \longrightarrow (-9, 3)$

▶▶ Concepts, Skills, & Problem Solving

CREATING GRAPHS   Make a graph of the situation. (See Exploration 1, p. 141.)

6. The equation $y = -2x + 8$ represents the amount y (in fluid ounces) of dish detergent in a bottle after x days of use.

7. The equation $y = 15x + 20$ represents the cost y (in dollars) of a gym membership after x months.

MP PRECISION   Copy and complete the table with two solutions. Plot the ordered pairs and draw the graph of the linear equation. Use the graph to find a third solution of the equation.

8.

x		
$y = 3x - 1$		

9.

x		
$y = \frac{1}{3}x + 2$		

GRAPHING A LINEAR EQUATION   Graph the linear equation.

10. $y = -5x$ **11.** $y = 9x$ **12.** $y = 5$ **13.** $x = -6$

14. $y = x - 3$ **15.** $y = -7x - 1$ **16.** $y = -\dfrac{x}{3} + 4$ **17.** $y = 0.75x - 0.5$

18. $y = -\dfrac{2}{3}$ **19.** $y = 6.75$ **20.** $x = -0.5$ **21.** $x = \dfrac{1}{4}$

22. MP YOU BE THE TEACHER Your friend graphs the equation $y = 4$. Is your friend correct? Explain your reasoning.

23. MP MODELING REAL LIFE The equation $y = 20$ represents the cost y (in dollars) for sending x text messages in a month. Graph the linear equation. What does the graph tell you about your texting plan?

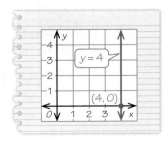

24. **(MP) MODELING REAL LIFE** The equation $y = 2x + 3$ represents the cost y (in dollars) of mailing a package that weighs x pounds.

   a. Use a graph to estimate how much it costs to mail the package.

   b. Use the equation to find exactly how much it costs to mail the package.

SOLVING A LINEAR EQUATION Solve for y. Then graph the linear equation.

25. $y - 3x = 1$

26. $5x + 2y = 4$

27. $-\dfrac{1}{3}y + 4x = 3$

28. $x + 0.5y = 1.5$

29. **(MP) MODELING REAL LIFE** The depth y (in inches) of a lake after x years is represented by the equation $y = 0.2x + 42$. How much does the depth of the lake increase in four years? Use a graph to justify your answer.

30. **(MP) MODELING REAL LIFE** The amount y (in dollars) of money in your savings account after x months is represented by the equation $y = 12.5x + 100$.

   a. Graph the linear equation.

   b. How many months will it take you to save a total of $237.50?

31. **(MP) PROBLEM SOLVING** The radius y (in millimeters) of a chemical spill after x days is represented by the equation $y = 6x + 50$.

   a. Graph the linear equation.

   b. The leak is noticed after two weeks. What is the area of the leak when it is noticed? Justify your answer.

32. **GEOMETRY** The sum S of the interior angle measures of a polygon with n sides is $S = (n - 2) \cdot 180°$.

   a. Plot four points (n, S) that satisfy the equation. Is the equation a linear equation? Explain your reasoning.

   b. Does the value $n = 3.5$ make sense in the context of the problem? Explain your reasoning.

33. **DIG DEEPER!** One second of video on your cell phone uses the same amount of memory as two pictures. Your cell phone can store 2500 pictures.

   a. Create a graph that represents the number y of pictures your cell phone can store when you take x seconds of video.

   b. How many pictures can your cell phone store in addition to a video that is one minute and thirty seconds long?

4.2 Slope of a Line

Learning Target: Find and interpret the slope of a line.

Success Criteria:
- I can explain the meaning of slope.
- I can find the slope of a line.
- I can interpret the slope of a line in a real-life problem.

EXPLORATION 1

Measuring the Steepness of a Line

Work with a partner. Draw any nonvertical line in a coordinate plane.

a. Develop a way to measure the *steepness* of the line. Compare your method with other pairs.

b. Draw a line that is parallel to your line. What can you determine about the steepness of each line? Explain your reasoning.

EXPLORATION 2

Using Right Triangles

Work with a partner. Use the figure shown.

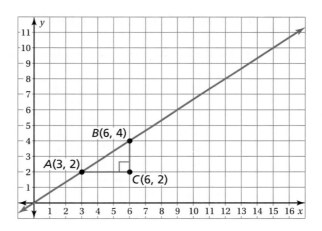

a. $\triangle ABC$ is a right triangle formed by drawing a horizontal line segment from point A and a vertical line segment from point B. Use this method to draw another right triangle, $\triangle DEF$, with its longest side on the line.

Math Practice

Construct Arguments

Do your answers to parts (b) and (c) change when you draw $\triangle DEF$ in a different location in part (a)? Explain.

b. What can you conclude about the two triangles in part (a)? Justify your conclusion. Compare your results with other pairs.

c. Based on your conclusions in part (b), what is true about $\dfrac{BC}{AC}$ and the corresponding measure in $\triangle DEF$? Explain your reasoning. What do these values tell you about the line?

🗝 Key Idea

Slope

The **slope** m of a line is the value of the ratio of the change in y (the **rise**) to the change in x (the **run**) between any two points, (x_1, y_1) and (x_2, y_2), on the line. The slope of a line is a measure of the steepness of the line.

$$m = \frac{\text{rise}}{\text{run}}$$

$$= \frac{\text{change in } y}{\text{change in } x}$$

$$= \frac{y_2 - y_1}{x_2 - x_1}$$

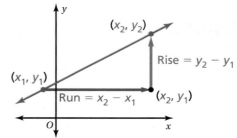

Lines with positive slopes rise from left to right.

Lines with negative slopes fall from left to right.

Reading 📖

In the slope formula, x_1 is read as "x sub one," and y_2 is read as "y sub two." The numbers 1 and 2 in x_1 and y_2 are called *subscripts*.

EXAMPLE 1 **Finding Slopes of Lines**

Describe the slope of each line. Then find each slope.

a.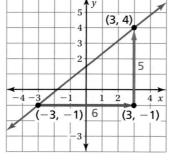

b.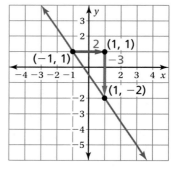

The methods in parts (a) and (b) show that you can find the slope of a line by using the graph or by using a formula.

The line rises from left to right. So, the slope is positive. Use the graph to find the rise and the run of the line.

$$m = \frac{\text{rise}}{\text{run}}$$

$$= \frac{5}{6}$$

The line falls from left to right. So, the slope is negative. Use the coordinates $(x_1, y_1) = (-1, 1)$ and $(x_2, y_2) = (1, -2)$ to find the slope.

$$m = \frac{y_2 - y_1}{x_2 - x_1}$$

$$= \frac{-2 - 1}{1 - (-1)}$$

$$= \frac{-3}{2}, \text{ or } -\frac{3}{2}$$

🔊 Multi-Language Glossary at *BigIdeasMath.com*

Try It **Find the slope of the line.**

1.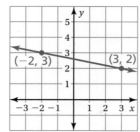

2.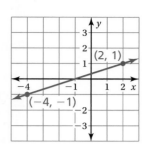

EXAMPLE 2 **Finding Slopes of Horizontal and Vertical Lines**

Find the slope of each line.

a.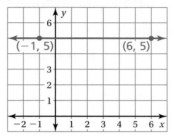

b.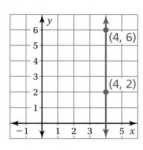

The slope of every horizontal line is 0. The slope of every vertical line is undefined.

a.
$$m = \frac{y_2 - y_1}{x_2 - x_1}$$

$$= \frac{5 - 5}{6 - (-1)}$$

$$= \frac{0}{7}, \text{ or } 0$$

▷ The slope is 0.

b.
$$m = \frac{y_2 - y_1}{x_2 - x_1}$$

$$= \frac{6 - 2}{4 - 4}$$

$$= \frac{4}{0} \quad \textbf{✗}$$

▷ Division by zero is undefined. So, the slope is undefined.

Try It **Find the slope of the line through the given points.**

3. $(1, -2), (7, -2)$

4. $(-3, -3), (-3, -5)$

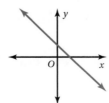 **Summary**

Slope

Positive Slope	*Negative Slope*	*Slope of 0*	*Undefined Slope*
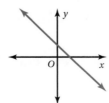	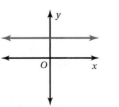		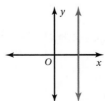
The line rises from left to right.	The line falls from left to right.	The line is horizontal.	The line is vertical.

 **Key Idea**

Parallel Lines and Slope

Lines in the same plane that do not intersect are parallel lines. Nonvertical parallel lines have the same slope.

All vertical lines are parallel.

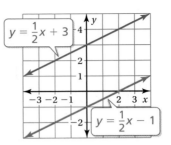

EXAMPLE 3 **Identifying Parallel Lines**

Which lines are parallel? How do you know?

Find the slope of each line.

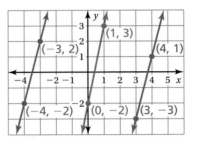

Blue Line	Red Line	Green Line
$m = \dfrac{y_2 - y_1}{x_2 - x_1}$	$m = \dfrac{y_2 - y_1}{x_2 - x_1}$	$m = \dfrac{y_2 - y_1}{x_2 - x_1}$
$= \dfrac{-2 - 2}{-4 - (-3)}$	$= \dfrac{-2 - 3}{0 - 1}$	$= \dfrac{-3 - 1}{3 - 4}$
$= \dfrac{-4}{-1}$, or 4	$= \dfrac{-5}{-1}$, or 5	$= \dfrac{-4}{-1}$, or 4

The slopes of the blue and green lines are 4. The slope of the red line is 5.

▷ The blue and green lines have the same slope, so they are parallel.

Try It

5. **WHAT IF?** The blue line passes through $(-4, -3)$ and $(-3, 2)$. Are any of the lines parallel? Explain.

 Self-Assessment *for Concepts & Skills*

Solve each exercise. Then rate your understanding of the success criteria in your journal.

6. **VOCABULARY** What does it mean for a line to have a slope of 4?

FINDING THE SLOPE OF A LINE **Find the slope of the line through the given points.**

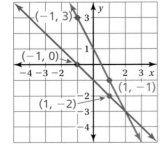

7. $(1, -1), (6, 2)$

8. $(2, -3), (5, -3)$

9. **FINDING SLOPE** Are the lines parallel? Explain your reasoning.

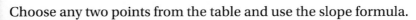

EXAMPLE 4	Modeling Real Life

The table shows the distance y (in miles) of a space probe from a comet x minutes after it begins its approach. The points in the table lie on a line. Find and interpret the slope of the line.

x	1	4	7	10
y	8	6	4	2

© ESA/Rosetta/MPS for OSIRIS TeamMPS/
UPD/LAM/IAA/SSO/INTA/UPM/DASP/IDA

Choose any two points from the table and use the slope formula.

Use the points $(x_1, y_1) = (1, 8)$ and $(x_2, y_2) = (4, 6)$.

$$m = \frac{y_2 - y_1}{x_2 - x_1}$$

$$= \frac{6 - 8}{4 - 1}$$

$$= \frac{-2}{3}, \text{ or } -\frac{2}{3}$$

▷ The slope is $-\frac{2}{3}$. So, the distance between the probe and the comet decreases 2 miles every 3 minutes, or $\frac{2}{3}$ mile every minute.

Check

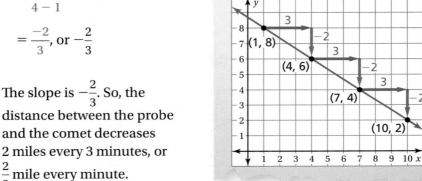

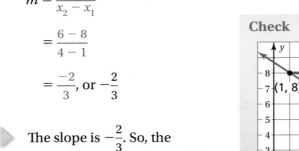

Self-Assessment for Problem Solving

Solve each exercise. Then rate your understanding of the success criteria in your journal.

x	y
1	0.5
2	1
3	1.5
4	2

10. The table shows the lengths y (in inches) of your hair x months after your last haircut. The points in the table lie on a line. Find and interpret the slope of the line. After how many months is your hair 4 inches long?

11. A customer pays an initial fee and a daily fee to rent a snowmobile. The total payment for 3 days is 92 dollars. The total payment for 5 days is 120 dollars. What is the daily fee? Justify your answer.

12. You in-line skate from an elevation of 720 feet to an elevation of 750 feet in 30 minutes. Your friend in-line skates from an elevation of 600 feet to an elevation of 690 feet in one hour. Compare your rates of change in elevation.

Go to *BigIdeasMath.com* to get HELP with solving the exercises.

▶ Review & Refresh

Graph the linear equation.

1. $y = 4x - 3$

2. $x = -3$

3. $y = 2$

4. $y = \dfrac{3}{2}x - \dfrac{1}{2}$

Find the missing values in the ratio table.

5.

Yards	1		5	7
Feet	3	10		

6.

Miles	0.6		1.8	
Hours	1	2		4

▶▶ Concepts, Skills, & Problem Solving

USING RIGHT TRIANGLES Use the figure shown. (See Exploration 2, p. 147.)

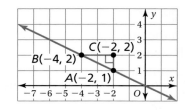

7. Find the slope of the line.

8. Let point D be at $(-4, 1)$. Use the sides of $\triangle BDA$ to find the slope of the line.

FINDING THE SLOPE OF A LINE Find the slope of the line.

9.

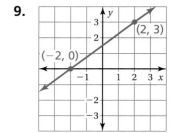

10.

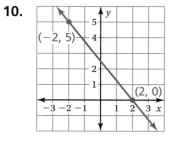

11.

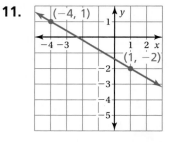

12.

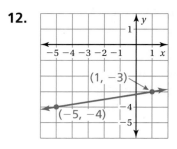

13.

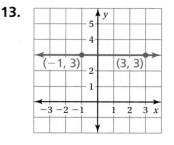

14.

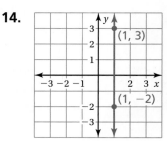

FINDING THE SLOPE OF A LINE Find the slope of the line through the given points.

15. $(4, -1), (-2, -1)$

16. $(5, -3), (5, 8)$

17. $(-7, 0), (-7, -6)$

18. $(-3, 1), (-1, 5)$

19. $(10, 4), (4, 15)$

20. $(-3, 6), (2, 6)$

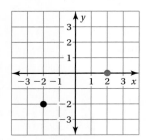

21. **(MP) REASONING** Draw a line through each point using a slope of $m = \dfrac{1}{4}$. Do the lines intersect? Explain.

22. **(MP) YOU BE THE TEACHER** Your friend finds the slope of the line shown. Is your friend correct? Explain your reasoning.

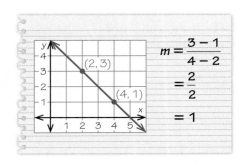

IDENTIFYING PARALLEL LINES Which lines are parallel? How do you know?

23.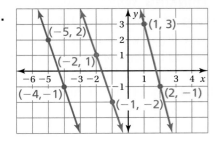

24.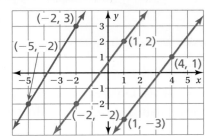

IDENTIFYING PARALLEL LINES Are the given lines parallel? Explain your reasoning.

25. $y = -5, y = 3$

26. $y = 0, x = 0$

27. $x = -4, x = 1$

FINDING SLOPE The points in the table lie on a line. Find the slope of the line.

28.

x	1	3	5	7
y	2	10	18	26

29.

x	-3	2	7	12
y	0	2	4	6

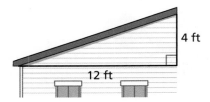

4 ft

12 ft

30. **(MP) MODELING REAL LIFE** Carpenters refer to the slope of a roof as the *pitch* of the roof. Find the pitch of the roof.

31. **PROJECT** The guidelines for a wheelchair ramp suggest that the ratio of the rise to the run be no greater than 1 : 12.

    a. **MP CHOOSE TOOLS** Find a wheelchair ramp in your school or neighborhood. Measure its slope. Does the ramp follow the guidelines?

    b. Design a wheelchair ramp that provides access to a building with a front door that is 2.5 feet above the sidewalk. Illustrate your design.

USING AN EQUATION Use an equation to find the value of k so that the line that passes through the given points has the given slope.

32. $(1, 3), (5, k); m = 2$

33. $(-2, k), (2, 0); m = -1$

34. $(-4, k), (6, -7); m = -\dfrac{1}{5}$

35. $(4, -4), (k, -1); m = \dfrac{3}{4}$

36. **MP MODELING REAL LIFE** The graph shows the numbers of prescriptions filled over time by a pharmacy.

    a. Find the slope of the line.

    b. Explain the meaning of the slope as a rate of change.

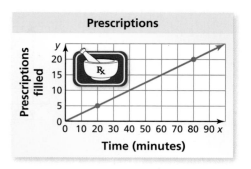

Prescriptions

37. **CRITICAL THINKING** Which is steeper: the boat ramp, or a road with a 12% grade? Explain. (*Note:* Road grade is the vertical increase divided by the horizontal distance.)

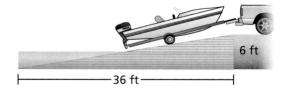

38. **MP REASONING** Do the points $A(-2, -1)$, $B(1, 5)$, and $C(4, 11)$ lie on the same line? Without using a graph, how do you know?

39. **MP PROBLEM SOLVING** A small business earns a profit of $6500 in January and $17,500 in May. What is the rate of change in profit for this time period? Justify your answer.

40. **MP STRUCTURE** Choose two points in the coordinate plane. Use the slope formula to find the slope of the line that passes through the two points. Then find the slope using the formula $\dfrac{y_1 - y_2}{x_1 - x_2}$. Compare your results.

41. **DIG DEEPER!** The top and the bottom of the slide are level with the ground, which has a slope of 0.

    a. What is the slope of the main portion of the slide?

    b. Describe the change in the slope when the bottom of the slide is only 12 inches above the ground. Explain your reasoning.

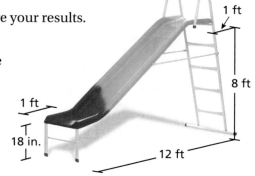

4.3 Graphing Proportional Relationships

Learning Target: Graph proportional relationships.

Success Criteria:
- I can graph an equation that represents a proportional relationship.
- I can write an equation that represents a proportional relationship.
- I can use graphs to compare proportional relationships.

EXPLORATION 1

Using a Ratio Table to Find Slope

Work with a partner. The graph shows amounts of vinegar and water that can be used to make a cleaning product.

a. Use the graph to make a ratio table relating the quantities. Explain how the slope of the line is represented in the table.

b. Make a ratio table that represents a different ratio of vinegar to water. Use the table to describe the slope of the graph of the new relationship.

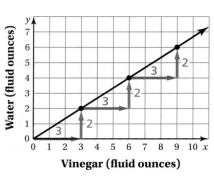

EXPLORATION 2

Deriving an Equation

Work with a partner. Let (x, y) represent any point on the graph of a proportional relationship.

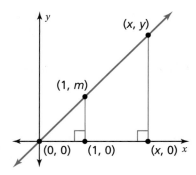

a. Describe the relationship between the corresponding side lengths of the triangles shown in the graph. Explain your reasoning.

b. Use the relationship in part (a) to write an equation relating y, m, and x. Then solve the equation for y.

c. What does your equation in part (b) describe? What does m represent? Explain your reasoning.

 **Key Idea**

Proportional Relationships

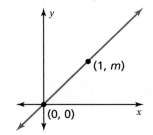

In the equation $y = mx$, m represents the constant of proportionality, the slope, and the unit rate.

Words When two quantities x and y are proportional, the relationship can be represented by the equation $y = mx$, where m is the constant of proportionality.

Graph The graph of $y = mx$ is a line with a slope of m that passes through the origin.

EXAMPLE 1 ## Graphing a Proportional Relationship

The cost y (in dollars) for x ounces of frozen yogurt is represented by $y = 0.5x$. Graph the equation and interpret the slope.

Method 1: Make a table of values.

x	$y = 0.5x$	y	(x, y)
0	$y = 0.5(0)$	0	$(0, 0)$
1	$y = 0.5(1)$	0.5	$(1, 0.5)$
2	$y = 0.5(2)$	1	$(2, 1)$
3	$y = 0.5(3)$	1.5	$(3, 1.5)$

Method 2: Use the slope.

The equation shows that the slope m is 0.5. So, the graph passes through $(0, 0)$ and $(1, 0.5)$.

Plot the ordered pairs and draw a line through the points. Because negative values of x do not make sense in this context, graph in the first quadrant only.

Math Practice

Use a Graph
Why does it make sense to graph the equations in Example 1 in the first quadrant only?

▷ The slope indicates that the unit cost is $0.50 per ounce.

Frozen Yogurt

Try It

1. **WHAT IF?** The cost of frozen yogurt is represented by $y = 0.75x$. Graph the equation and interpret the slope.

EXAMPLE 2 **Writing and Using an Equation**

The weight y of an object on Titan, one of Saturn's moons, is proportional to the weight x of the object on Earth. An object that weighs 105 pounds on Earth would weigh 15 pounds on Titan.

a. Write an equation that represents the situation.

Use the point (105, 15) to find the slope of the line.

$y = mx$	Equation of a proportional relationship
$15 = m(105)$	Substitute 15 for y and 105 for x.
$\dfrac{1}{7} = m$	Simplify.

> So, an equation that represents the situation is $y = \dfrac{1}{7}x$.

Math Practice

Interpret Results
Interpret the slope in the context of the problem.

b. How much would a chunk of ice that weighs 3.5 pounds on Titan weigh on Earth?

$3.5 = \dfrac{1}{7}x$	Substitute 3.5 for y.
$24.5 = x$	Multiply each side by 7.

> So, the chunk of ice would weigh 24.5 pounds on Earth.

Try It

2. How much would a spacecraft that weighs 3500 kilograms on Earth weigh on Titan?

Self-Assessment *for Concepts & Skills*

Solve each exercise. Then rate your understanding of the success criteria in your journal.

GRAPHING A PROPORTIONAL RELATIONSHIP Graph the equation.

3. $y = 4x$ 4. $y = -3x$ 5. $y = 8x$

6. **WRITING AND USING AN EQUATION** The number y of objects a machine produces is proportional to the time x (in minutes) that the machine runs. The machine produces five objects in four minutes.

a. Write an equation that represents the situation.

b. Graph the equation in part (a) and interpret the slope.

c. How many objects does the machine produce in one hour?

EXAMPLE 3 **Modeling Real Life**

The distance y (in meters) that a four-person ski lift travels in x seconds is represented by the equation $y = 2.5x$. The graph shows the distance that a two-person ski lift travels.

Two-Person Lift

a. **Which ski lift is faster?**

Identify the slope of the graph for each lift. Then interpret each slope as a unit rate.

Four-Person Lift

$$y = 2.5x$$

The slope is 2.5.

Two-Person Lift

$$\text{slope} = \frac{\text{change in } y}{\text{change in } x}$$

$$= \frac{8}{4} = 2$$

The four-person lift travels 2.5 meters per second.

The two-person lift travels 2 meters per second.

➤ So, the four-person lift is faster than the two-person lift.

b. **Graph the equation that represents the four-person lift in the same coordinate plane as the two-person lift. Compare and interpret the steepness of each graph.**

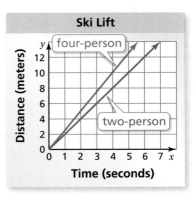

➤ The graph that represents the four-person lift is steeper than the graph that represents the two-person lift. So, the four-person lift is faster.

 Self-Assessment for Problem Solving

Solve each exercise. Then rate your understanding of the success criteria in your journal.

Artificial Waterfall

7. The amount y (in liters) of water that flows over a natural waterfall in x seconds is represented by the equation $y = 500x$. The graph shows the number of liters of water that flow over an artificial waterfall. Which waterfall has a greater flow? Justify your answer.

8. The speed of sound in air is 343 meters per second. You see lightning and hear thunder 12 seconds later.

   a. Is there a proportional relationship between the amount of time that passes and your distance from a lightning strike? Explain.

   b. Estimate your distance from the lightning strike.

4.3 Practice

? Go to *BigIdeasMath.com* to get HELP with solving the exercises.

▶ Review & Refresh

Find the slope of the line.

1.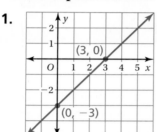

2.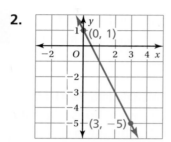

3.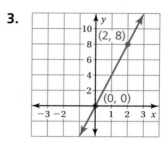

Solve the equation. Check your solution.

4. $2x + 3x = 10$

5. $x + \dfrac{1}{6} = 4 - 2x$

6. $2(1 - x) = 11$

▶ Concepts, Skills, & Problem Solving

USING EQUIVALENT RATIOS **The graph shows amounts of water and flour that can be used to make dough.** (See Exploration 1, p. 155.)

7. Use the graph to make a ratio table relating the quantities. Explain how the slope of the line is represented in the table.

8. Make a ratio table that represents a different ratio of flour to water. Use the table to describe the slope of the graph of the new relationship.

9. **GRAPHING AN EQUATION** The amount y (in dollars) that you raise by selling x fundraiser tickets is represented by the equation $y = 5x$. Graph the equation and interpret the slope.

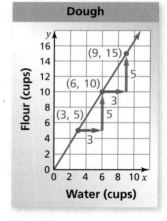

Dough

IDENTIFYING PROPORTIONAL RELATIONSHIPS **Tell whether x and y are in a proportional relationship. Explain your reasoning. If so, write an equation that represents the relationship.**

10.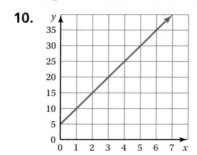

11.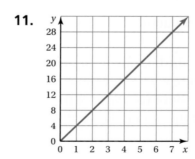

12.
x	3	6	9	12
y	1	2	3	4

13.
x	2	5	8	10
y	4	8	13	23

14. **MP** **MODELING REAL LIFE** The cost y (in dollars) to rent a kayak is proportional to the number x of hours that you rent the kayak. It costs $27 to rent the kayak for 3 hours.

   a. Write an equation that represents the situation.

   b. Interpret the slope of the graph of the equation.

   c. How much does it cost to rent the kayak for 5 hours? Justify your answer.

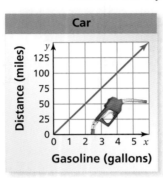

15. **MP** **MODELING REAL LIFE** The distance y (in miles) that a truck travels on x gallons of gasoline is represented by the equation $y = 18x$. The graph shows the distance that a car travels.

   a. Which vehicle gets better gas mileage? Explain how you found your answer.

   b. How much farther can the vehicle you chose in part (a) travel on 8 gallons of gasoline?

16. **MP** **PROBLEM SOLVING** Toenails grow about 13 millimeters per year. The table shows fingernail growth.

Weeks	1	2	3	4
Fingernail Growth (millimeters)	0.7	1.4	2.1	2.8

   a. Do fingernails or toenails grow faster? Explain.

   b. In the same coordinate plane, graph equations that represent the growth rates of toenails and fingernails. Compare and interpret the steepness of each graph.

17. **MP** **REASONING** The quantities x and y are in a proportional relationship. What do you know about the ratio of y to x for any point (x, y) on the graph of x and y?

18. **DIG DEEPER!** The graph relates the temperature change y (in degrees Fahrenheit) to the altitude change x (in thousands of feet).

   a. Is the relationship proportional? Explain.

   b. Write an equation of the line. Interpret the slope.

   c. You are at the bottom of a mountain where the temperature is 74°F. The top of the mountain is 5500 feet above you. What is the temperature at the top of the mountain? Justify your answer.

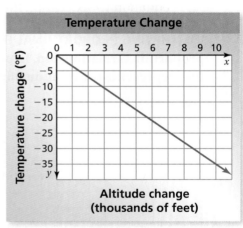

19. **CRITICAL THINKING** Consider the distance equation $d = rt$, where d is the distance (in feet), r is the rate (in feet per second), and t is the time (in seconds). You run for 50 seconds. Are the distance you run and the rate you run at proportional? Use a graph to justify your answer.

4.4 Graphing Linear Equations in Slope-Intercept Form

Learning Target: Graph linear equations in slope-intercept form.

Success Criteria:
- I can identify the slope and y-intercept of a line given an equation.
- I can rewrite a linear equation in slope-intercept form.
- I can use the slope and y-intercept to graph linear equations.

EXPLORATION 1

Deriving an Equation

Work with a partner. In the previous section, you learned that the graph of a proportional relationship can be represented by the equation $y = mx$, where m is the constant of proportionality.

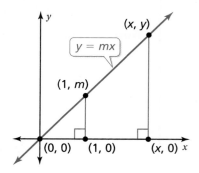

Math Practice

Understand Quantities

How does the meaning of the equation $y = mx$ help you make a conjecture in part (a)?

a. You translate the graph of a proportional relationship 3 units up as shown below. Let (x, y) represent any point on the graph. Make a conjecture about the equation of the line. Explain your reasoning.

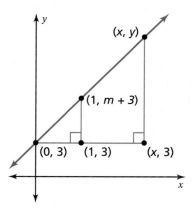

b. Describe the relationship between the corresponding side lengths of the triangles. Explain your reasoning.

c. Use the relationship in part (b) to write an equation relating y, m, and x. Does your equation support your conjecture in part (a)? Explain.

d. You translate the graph of a proportional relationship b units up. Write an equation relating y, m, x, and b. Justify your answer.

Key Vocabulary 🔊
x-intercept, *p. 162*
y-intercept, *p. 162*
slope-intercept form,
   p. 162

🔑 Key Ideas

Intercepts

The **x-intercept** of a line is the *x*-coordinate of the point where the line crosses the *x*-axis. It occurs when $y = 0$.

The **y-intercept** of a line is the *y*-coordinate of the point where the line crosses the *y*-axis. It occurs when $x = 0$.

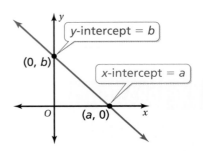

Slope-Intercept Form

Words   A linear equation written in the form $y = mx + b$ is in **slope-intercept form**. The slope of the line is m, and the *y*-intercept of the line is b.

Algebra $y = mx + b$

slope   *y*-intercept

> Linear equations can, but do not always, pass through the origin. So, proportional relationships are a special type of linear equation in which $b = 0$.

EXAMPLE 1   **Identifying Slopes and *y*-Intercepts**

Find the slope and the *y*-intercept of the graph of each linear equation.

a. $y = -4x - 2$

$y = -4x + (-2)$ Write in slope-intercept form.

▷ The slope is -4, and the *y*-intercept is -2.

b. $y - 5 = \dfrac{3}{2}x$

$y = \dfrac{3}{2}x + 5$ Add 5 to each side.

▷ The slope is $\dfrac{3}{2}$, and the *y*-intercept is 5.

Try It   **Find the slope and the *y*-intercept of the graph of the linear equation.**

1. $y = 3x - 7$ **2.** $y - 1 = -\dfrac{2}{3}x$

EXAMPLE 2 **Graphing a Linear Equation in Slope-Intercept Form**

Graph $y = -3x + 3$. Identify the x-intercept.

Step 1: Find the slope and the y-intercept.

$$y = -3x + 3$$

slope ⟶ | | ⟵ y-intercept

Step 2: The y-intercept is 3. So, plot $(0, 3)$.

Step 3: Use the slope to find another point and draw the line.

$$m = \frac{\text{rise}}{\text{run}} = \frac{-3}{1}$$

Plot the point that is 1 unit right and 3 units down from $(0, 3)$. Draw a line through the two points.

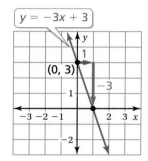

▷ The line crosses the x-axis at $(1, 0)$. So, the x-intercept is 1.

Math Practice

Find General Methods
How can you use substitution to find the x-intercept of a line?

Try It Graph the linear equation. Identify the x-intercept.

3. $y = x - 4$

4. $y = -\frac{1}{2}x + 1$

Self-Assessment for Concepts & Skills

Solve each exercise. Then rate your understanding of the success criteria in your journal.

5. **IN YOUR OWN WORDS** Consider the graph of the equation $y = mx + b$.

   a. How does changing the value of m affect the graph of the equation?

   b. How does changing the value of b affect the graph of the equation?

IDENTIFYING SLOPE AND y-INTERCEPT Find the slope and the y-intercept of the graph of the linear equation.

6. $y = -x + 0.25$

7. $y - 2 = -\frac{3}{4}x$

GRAPHING A LINEAR EQUATION Graph the linear equation. Identify the x-intercept.

8. $y = x - 7$

9. $y = 2x + 8$

 **EXAMPLE 3** **Modeling Real Life**

The cost y (in dollars) of taking a taxi x miles is represented by the equation $y = 2.5x + 2$. Graph the equation. Interpret the y-intercept and the slope.

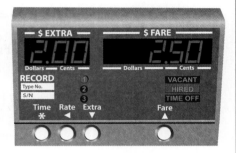

 **Understand the problem.**

You are given an equation that represents the cost of taking a taxi. You are asked to graph the equation and interpret the y-intercept and the slope.

 Make a plan.

Use the equation to identify the slope and the y-intercept. Then graph the equation and interpret the y-intercept and the slope.

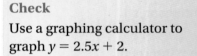 **Solve and check.**

The equation is already written in the form $y = mx + b$. So, the slope is $2.5 = \dfrac{5}{2}$ and the y-intercept is 2. Use the slope and the y-intercept to graph the equation.

Check

Use a graphing calculator to graph $y = 2.5x + 2$.

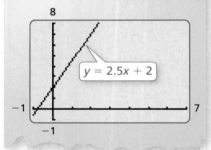

$y = 2.5x + 2$

The y-intercept is 2. So, plot (0, 2).

Use the slope to plot another point, (2, 7). Draw a line through the points.

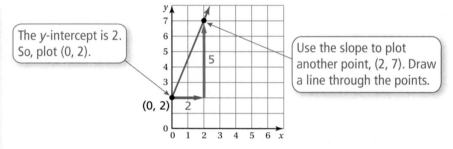

(0, 2)

> The y-intercept is 2. So, there is an initial fee of \$2 to take the taxi. The slope is 2.5. So, the cost per mile is \$2.50.

 Self-Assessment for Problem Solving

Solve each exercise. Then rate your understanding of the success criteria in your journal.

10. The height y (in feet) of a movable bridge after rising for x seconds is represented by the equation $y = 3x + 16$. Graph the equation. Interpret the y-intercept and slope. How many seconds does it take the bridge to reach a height of 76 feet? Justify your answer.

11. The number y of perfume bottles in storage after x months is represented by the equation $y = -20x + 460$. Graph the equation. Interpret the y-intercept and the slope. In how many months will there be no perfume bottles left in storage? Justify your answer.

4.4 Practice

? Go to *BigIdeasMath.com* to get HELP with solving the exercises.

▶ Review & Refresh

Tell whether *x* and *y* are in a proportional relationship. Explain your reasoning. If so, write an equation that represents the relationship.

1.

x	1	2	3	4
y	6	8	10	12

2.

x	−8	−4	4	8
y	4	2	−2	−4

Solve the equation for *y*.

3. $x = 4y - 2$

4. $3y = -6x + 1$

5. $1 + y = -\dfrac{4}{5}x - 2$

6. $2.5y = 5x - 5$

7. $1.3y + 5.2 = -3.9x$

8. $y - \dfrac{2}{3}x = -6$

▶▶ Concepts, Skills, & Problem Solving

GRAPHING A LINEAR EQUATION Graph the equation. (See Exploration 1, p. 161.)

9. The graph of $y = 3.5x$ is translated up 2 units.

10. The graph of $y = -5x$ is translated down 3 units.

MATCHING EQUATIONS AND GRAPHS Match the equation with its graph. Identify the slope and the *y*-intercept.

11. $y = 2x + 1$

12. $y = \dfrac{1}{3}x - 2$

13. $y = -\dfrac{2}{3}x + 1$

A.
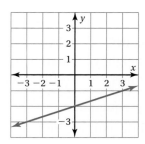

B.
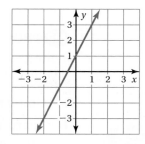

C.
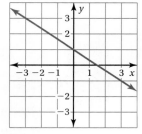

IDENTIFYING SLOPES AND *y*-INTERCEPTS Find the slope and the *y*-intercept of the graph of the linear equation.

14. $y = 4x - 5$

15. $y = -7x + 12$

16. $y = -\dfrac{4}{5}x - 2$

17. $y = 2.25x + 3$

18. $y + 1 = \dfrac{4}{3}x$

19. $y - 6 = \dfrac{3}{8}x$

20. $y - 3.5 = -2x$

21. $y = -5 - \dfrac{1}{2}x$

22. $y = 11 + 1.5x$

23. **(MP) YOU BE THE TEACHER** Your friend finds the slope and *y*-intercept of the graph of the equation $y = 4x - 3$. Is your friend correct? Explain your reasoning.

y = 4x − 3; The slope is 4 and the y-intercept is 3.

24. **(MP) MODELING REAL LIFE** The number y of seasonal allergy shots available at a facility x days after receiving a shipment is represented by $y = -15x + 375$.

   a. Graph the linear equation.

   b. Interpret the slope and the y-intercept.

GRAPHING AN EQUATION Graph the linear equation. Identify the x-intercept.

25. $y = x + 3$

26. $y = 4x - 8$

27. $y = -3x + 9$

28. $y = -5x - 5$

29. $y + 14 = -7x$

30. $y = 8 - 2x$

31. **(MP) PRECISION** You go to a harvest festival and pick apples.

   a. Which equation represents the cost (in dollars) of going to the festival and picking x pounds of apples? Explain.

   $y = 5x + 0.75$ $y = 0.75x + 5$

   b. Graph the equation you chose in part (a).

   You Pick 'Em
   Apples $0.75 per lb
   Admission: $5

32. **(MP) REASONING** Without graphing, identify the equations of the lines that are parallel. Explain your reasoning.

   $y = 2x + 4$ $y = \frac{1}{2}x + 1$ $y = 2x - 3$ $y = 2x + 1$ $y = \frac{1}{2}x + 2$

33. **(MP) PROBLEM SOLVING** A skydiver parachutes to the ground. The height y (in feet) of the skydiver after x seconds is $y = -10x + 3000$.

   a. Graph the linear equation.

   b. Interpret the slope, y-intercept, and x-intercept.

34. **DIG DEEPER!** Six friends create a website. The website earns money by selling banner ads. It costs $120 a month to operate the website.

   a. A banner ad earns $0.005 per click. Write a linear equation that represents the monthly profit after paying operating costs.

   b. Graph the equation in part (a). On the graph, label the number of clicks needed for the friends to start making a profit. Explain.

4.5 Graphing Linear Equations in Standard Form

Learning Target: Graph linear equations in standard form.

Success Criteria:
- I can rewrite the standard form of a linear equation in slope-intercept form.
- I can find intercepts of linear equations written in standard form.
- I can use intercepts to graph linear equations.

EXPLORATION 1

Using Intercepts

Work with a partner. You spend $150 on fruit trays and vegetable trays for a party.

Fruit Tray: $50

Vegetable Tray: $25

a. You buy x fruit trays and y vegetable trays. Complete the verbal model. Then use the verbal model to write an equation that relates x and y.

$$\frac{\boxed{}}{1 \text{ fruit tray}} \cdot \begin{array}{c}\text{Number}\\\text{of fruit}\\\text{trays}\end{array} + \frac{\boxed{}}{1 \text{ vegetable tray}} \cdot \begin{array}{c}\text{Number}\\\text{of vegetable}\\\text{trays}\end{array} = \boxed{}$$

b. What is the greatest number of fruit trays that you can buy? vegetable trays? Can you use these numbers to graph your equation from part (a) in the coordinate plane? Explain.

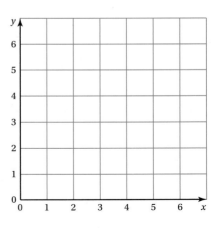

c. Use a graph to determine the different combinations of fruit trays and vegetable trays that you can buy. Justify your answers algebraically.

d. You are given an extra $50 to spend. How does this affect the intercepts of your graph in part (c)? Explain your reasoning.

Math Practice

Make Sense of Quantities

What does the slope of the line represent in this context?

Key Vocabulary 🔊
standard form, *p. 168*

Any linear equation can be written in standard form.

🔑 Key Idea

Standard Form of a Linear Equation

The **standard form** of a linear equation is

$$Ax + By = C$$

where A and B are not both zero.

EXAMPLE 1 **Graphing a Linear Equation in Standard Form**

Graph $-2x + 3y = -6$.

Step 1: Write the equation in slope-intercept form.

$-2x + 3y = -6$ Write the equation.

$3y = 2x - 6$ Add 2*x* to each side.

$y = \dfrac{2}{3}x - 2$ Divide each side by 3.

Step 2: Use the slope and the *y*-intercept to graph the equation.

$$y = \frac{2}{3}x + (-2)$$

slope   *y*-intercept

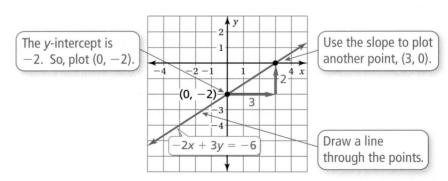

The *y*-intercept is -2. So, plot $(0, -2)$.

Use the slope to plot another point, $(3, 0)$.

$(0, -2)$

$-2x + 3y = -6$

Draw a line through the points.

Try It **Graph the linear equation.**

1. $x + y = -2$

2. $-\dfrac{1}{2}x + 2y = 6$

3. $-\dfrac{2}{3}x + y = 0$

4. $2x + y = 5$

🔊 *Multi-Language Glossary at BigIdeasMath.com*

EXAMPLE 2 **Graphing a Linear Equation in Standard Form**

Graph $x + 3y = -3$ using intercepts.

Step 1: To find the x-intercept, substitute 0 for y.

To find the y-intercept, substitute 0 for x.

$$x + 3y = -3$$
$$x + 3(0) = -3$$
$$x = -3$$

$$x + 3y = -3$$
$$0 + 3y = -3$$
$$y = -1$$

Step 2: Graph the equation.

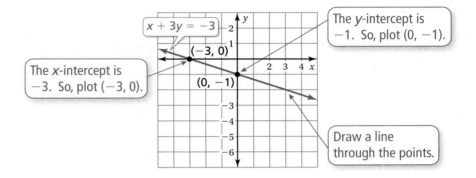

The x-intercept is -3. So, plot $(-3, 0)$.

The y-intercept is -1. So, plot $(0, -1)$.

Draw a line through the points.

Math Practice

Find Entry Points
Given the information in Example 2, how would you write the given equation in slope-intercept form?

Try It Graph the linear equation using intercepts.

5. $2x - y = 8$

6. $x + 3y = 6$

Self-Assessment for Concepts & Skills

Solve each exercise. Then rate your understanding of the success criteria in your journal.

MP **STRUCTURE** Determine whether the equation is in standard form. If not, rewrite the equation in standard form.

7. $y = x - 6$

8. $y - \dfrac{1}{6}x + 5 = 0$

9. $4x + y = 5$

10. **WRITING** Describe two ways to graph the equation $4x + 2y = 6$.

GRAPHING A LINEAR EQUATION Graph the linear equation.

11. $4x + y = 5$

12. $\dfrac{1}{3}x + 2y = 8$

13. $5x - y = 10$

14. $x - 3y = 9$

EXAMPLE 3 **Modeling Real Life**

Bananas
$0.60/pound

Apples
$1.50/pound

You have \$6 to spend on apples and bananas. The equation $1.5x + 0.6y = 6$ represents this situation, where x is the number of pounds of apples and y is the number of pounds of bananas. Graph the equation. Interpret the intercepts.

Find the intercepts. Then use the intercepts to graph the equation and interpret the intercepts.

x-intercept	y-intercept
$1.5x + 0.6y = 6$	$1.5x + 0.6y = 6$
$1.5x + 0.6(0) = 6$	$1.5(0) + 0.6y = 6$
$x = 4$	$y = 10$

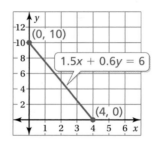

The x-intercept shows that you can buy 4 pounds of apples when you do not buy any bananas. The y-intercept shows that you can buy 10 pounds of bananas when you do not buy any apples.

 Self-Assessment for Problem Solving

Solve each exercise. Then rate your understanding of the success criteria in your journal.

15. You have \$30 to spend on paint and clay. The equation $2x + 6y = 30$ represents this situation, where x is the number of paint bottles and y is the number of tubs of clay. Graph the equation. Interpret the intercepts. How many bottles of paint can you buy if you buy 3 tubs of clay? Justify your answer.

16. You complete two projects for a class in 60 minutes. The equation $x + y = 60$ represents this situation, where x is the time (in minutes) you spend assembling a birdhouse and y is the time (in minutes) you spend writing a paper.

 a. Graph the equation. Interpret the intercepts.

 b. You spend twice as much time assembling the birdhouse as you do writing the paper. How much time do you spend writing the paper? Justify your answer.

4.5 Practice

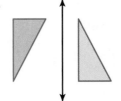

Go to *BigIdeasMath.com* to get HELP with solving the exercises.

▶ Review & Refresh

Find the slope and the *y*-intercept of the graph of the linear equation.

1. $y = x - 1$

2. $y = -2x + 1$

3. $y = \dfrac{8}{9}x - 8$

Tell whether the blue figure is a reflection of the red figure.

4.

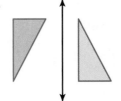

5.

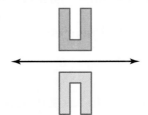

6.

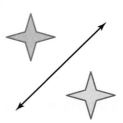

▶▶ Concepts, Skills, & Problem Solving

USING INTERCEPTS **Define two variables for the verbal model. Write an equation in slope-intercept form that relates the variables. Graph the equation using intercepts.** (See Exploration 1, p. 167.)

7. $\dfrac{\$2.00}{\text{pound}} \cdot \text{Pounds of peaches} + \dfrac{\$1.50}{\text{pound}} \cdot \text{Pounds of apples} = \$15$

8. $\dfrac{16 \text{ miles}}{\text{hour}} \cdot \text{Hours biked} + \dfrac{2 \text{ miles}}{\text{hour}} \cdot \text{Hours walked} = 32 \text{ miles}$

REWRITING AN EQUATION **Write the linear equation in slope-intercept form.**

9. $2x + y = 17$

10. $5x - y = \dfrac{1}{4}$

11. $-\dfrac{1}{2}x + y = 10$

GRAPHING AN EQUATION **Graph the linear equation.**

12. $-18x + 9y = 72$

13. $16x - 4y = 2$

14. $\dfrac{1}{4}x + \dfrac{3}{4}y = 1$

MATCHING **Match the equation with its graph.**

15. $15x - 12y = 60$

16. $5x + 4y = 20$

17. $10x + 8y = -40$

A.

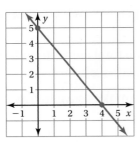

B.

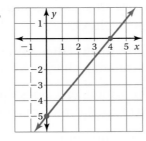

C.

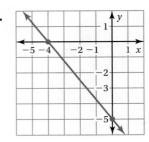

18. **MP YOU BE THE TEACHER** Your friend finds the x-intercept of $-2x + 3y = 12$. Is your friend correct? Explain your reasoning.

$$-2x + 3y = 12$$
$$-2(0) + 3y = 12$$
$$3y = 12$$
$$y = 4$$

19. **MP MODELING REAL LIFE** A charm bracelet costs $65, plus $25 for each charm. The equation $-25x + y = 65$ represents the cost y (in dollars) of the bracelet, where x is the number of charms.

    a. Graph the equation.

    b. How much does a bracelet with three charms cost?

USING INTERCEPTS TO GRAPH Graph the linear equation using intercepts.

20. $3x - 4y = -12$

21. $2x + y = 8$

22. $\frac{1}{3}x - \frac{1}{6}y = -\frac{2}{3}$

23. **MP MODELING REAL LIFE** Your cousin has $90 to spend on video games and movies. The equation $30x + 15y = 90$ represents this situation, where x is the number of video games purchased and y is the number of movies purchased. Graph the equation. Interpret the intercepts.

24. **MP PROBLEM SOLVING** A group of friends go scuba diving. They rent a boat for x days and scuba gear for y people, represented by the equation $250x + 50y = 1000$.

    a. Graph the equation and interpret the intercepts.

    b. How many friends can go scuba diving if they rent the boat for 1 day? 2 days?

    c. How much money is spent in total?

25. **MP MODELING REAL LIFE** You work at a restaurant as a host and a server. You earn $9.45 for each hour you work as a host and $3.78 for each hour you work as a server.

    a. Write an equation in standard form that models your earnings.

    b. Graph the equation.

Basic Information
Number of hours worked as host: x
Number of hours worked as server: y
Earnings for this pay period: $113.40

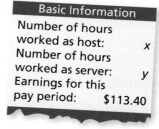

26. **MP LOGIC** Does the graph of every linear equation have an x-intercept? Justify your reasoning.

27. **CRITICAL THINKING** For a house call, a veterinarian charges $70, plus $40 per hour.

    a. Write an equation that represents the total fee y (in dollars) the veterinarian charges for a visit lasting x hours.

    b. Find the x-intercept. Does this value make sense in this context? Explain your reasoning.

    c. Graph the equation.

4.6 Writing Equations in Slope-Intercept Form

Learning Target: Write equations of lines in slope-intercept form.

Success Criteria:
- I can find the slope and the *y*-intercept of a line.
- I can use the slope and the *y*-intercept to write an equation of a line.
- I can write equations in slope-intercept form to solve real-life problems.

EXPLORATION 1

Writing Equations of Lines

Work with a partner. For each part, answer the following questions.

- **What are the slopes and the *y*-intercepts of the lines?**
- **What are equations that represent the lines?**
- **What do the lines have in common?**

Math Practice

Analyze Givens
Why are the slope and *y*-intercept enough information to write an equation for a line?

a.
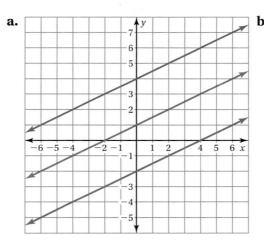

b.
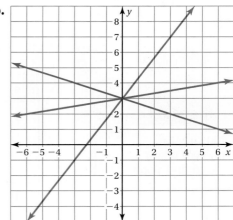

EXPLORATION 2

Interpreting the Slope and the *y*-Intercept

Work with a partner. The graph represents the distance *y* (in miles) of a car from Phoenix after *t* hours of a trip.

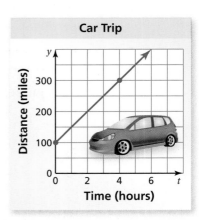

a. Find the slope and the *y*-intercept of the line. What do they represent in this situation?

b. Write an equation that represents the graph.

c. How can you determine the distance of the car from Phoenix after 11 hours?

| EXAMPLE 1 | **Writing Equations in Slope-Intercept Form** |

Write an equation in slope-intercept form of the line that passes through the given points.

a.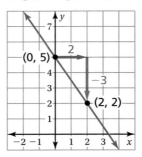

Find the slope and the y-intercept.

$$m = \frac{y_2 - y_1}{x_2 - x_1}$$

$$= \frac{2 - 5}{2 - 0}$$

$$= \frac{-3}{2}, \text{ or } -\frac{3}{2}$$

> After writing an equation, check that the given points are solutions of the equation.

Because the line crosses the y-axis at $(0, 5)$, the y-intercept is 5.

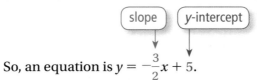

▷ So, an equation is $y = -\dfrac{3}{2}x + 5$.

b.

x	y
0	−3
3	2
6	7
9	12

Find the slope and the y-intercept. Use the points $(0, -3)$ and $(3, 2)$.

$$m = \frac{y_2 - y_1}{x_2 - x_1}$$

$$= \frac{-3 - 2}{0 - 3}$$

$$= \frac{-5}{-3}, \text{ or } \frac{5}{3}$$

> **Remember**
>
> You can use *any* two points on a line to find slope.

Because $y = -3$ when $x = 0$, the y-intercept is -3.

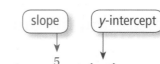
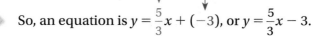

▷ So, an equation is $y = \dfrac{5}{3}x + (-3)$, or $y = \dfrac{5}{3}x - 3$.

Try It **Write an equation in slope-intercept form of the line that passes through the given points.**

1.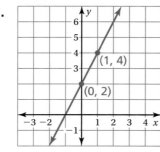

2.

x	y
−3	3
0	−1
3	−5
6	−9

EXAMPLE 2 **Writing an Equation**

Which equation is shown in the graph?

    A. $y = -4$ **B.** $y = -3$

    C. $y = 0$ **D.** $y = -3x$

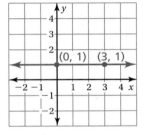

Find the slope and the y-intercept. The line is horizontal, so the change in y is 0.

$$m = \frac{\text{change in } y}{\text{change in } x} = \frac{0}{3} = 0$$

Because the line crosses the y-axis at $(0, -4)$, the y-intercept is -4.

So, the equation is $y = 0x + (-4)$, or $y = -4$.

   ▶ The correct answer is **A**.

> **Remember**
>
>
>
> The graph of $y = a$ is a horizontal line that passes through $(0, a)$.

Try It **Write an equation of the line that passes through the given points.**

3.

x	-4	0	4
y	5	5	5

4.

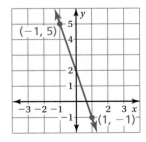

Self-Assessment *for Concepts & Skills*

Solve each exercise. Then rate your understanding of the success criteria in your journal.

WRITING EQUATIONS IN SLOPE-INTERCEPT FORM Write an equation in slope-intercept form of the line that passes through the given points.

5.

x	y
-2	-4
-1	-1
0	2
1	5

6.

7. WRITING AN EQUATION Write an equation of the line that passes through $(0, -5)$ and $(2, -5)$.

EXAMPLE 3 **Modeling Real Life**

Engineers used tunnel boring machines like the ones shown above to dig an extension of the Metro Gold Line in Los Angeles. The tunnels are 1.7 miles long and 21 feet wide.

Engineers are digging a 3500-foot long tunnel at a constant rate. After 4 months, the engineers still need to dig 1500 feet to finish the project. How much time does it take to complete the tunnel from start to finish?

Write an equation of the line that represents the distance y (in feet) remaining after x months.

When the project starts, the engineers still need to dig 3500 feet, represented by $(0, 3500)$. So, the y-intercept is 3500.

After 4 months, the engineers still need to dig 1500 feet, represented by $(4, 1500)$. Use the points $(0, 3500)$ and $(4, 1500)$ to find the slope.

$$m = \frac{\text{change in } y}{\text{change in } x} = \frac{-2000}{4} = -500$$

So, an equation is $y = -500x + 3500$.

The tunnel is complete when the distance remaining is 0 feet. So, find the value of x when $y = 0$.

$y = -500x + 3500$	Write the equation.
$0 = -500x + 3500$	Substitute 0 for y.
$-3500 = -500x$	Subtract 3500 from each side.
$7 = x$	Divide each side by -500.

▷ It takes 7 months to complete the tunnel from start to finish.

Self-Assessment for *Problem Solving*

Solve each exercise. Then rate your understanding of the success criteria in your journal.

8. You load boxes onto an empty truck at a constant rate. After 3 hours, there are 100 boxes on the truck. How much longer do you work if you load a total of 120 boxes? Justify your answer.

9. The table shows the amounts y (in tons) of waste left in a landfill after x months of waste relocation. Interpret the slope and the y-intercept of the line that passes through the given points. How many months does it take to empty the landfill? Justify your answer.

x	0	6	12
y	15	12	9

10. A lifetime subscription to a website costs $250. A monthly subscription to the website costs $10 to join and $15 per month. Write equations to represent the costs of each plan. If you want to be a member for one year, which plan is less expensive? Explain.

4.6 Practice

 Go to *BigIdeasMath.com* to get HELP with solving the exercises.

▶ Review & Refresh

Write the linear equation in slope-intercept form.

1. $4x + y = 1$

2. $x - y = \dfrac{1}{5}$

3. $-\dfrac{2}{3}x + 2y = -7$

Plot the ordered pair in a coordinate plane.

4. $(1, 4)$

5. $(-1, -2)$

6. $(0, 1)$

7. $(2, 7)$

▶▶ Concepts, Skills, & Problem Solving

INTERPRETING THE SLOPE AND THE y-INTERCEPT **The graph represents the cost y (in dollars) to open an online gaming account and buy x games.** (See Exploration 2, p. 173.)

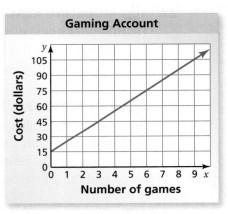

8. Find the slope and the y-intercept of the line. What do they represent in this situation?

9. Write an equation that represents the graph.

10. How can you determine the total cost of opening an account and buying 6 games?

WRITING EQUATIONS IN SLOPE-INTERCEPT FORM **Write an equation in slope-intercept form of the line that passes through the given points.**

11.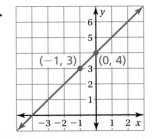

12.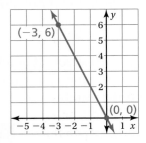

13.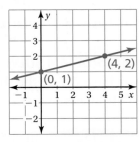

14.

x	y
−2	2
0	1
2	0
4	−1

15.

x	y
−3	−4
0	−3
3	−2
6	−1

16.

x	y
−4	9
−2	4
0	−1
2	−6

WRITING EQUATIONS **Write an equation of the line that passes through the given points.**

17. $(-1, 4), (0, 2)$

18. $(-1, 0), (0, 0)$

19. $(0, 4), (0, -3)$

20. **MP YOU BE THE TEACHER** Your friend writes an equation of the line shown. Is your friend correct? Explain your reasoning.

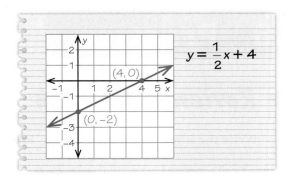

$$y = \frac{1}{2}x + 4$$

$(4, 0)$

$(0, -2)$

21. **MP MODELING REAL LIFE** A boa constrictor is 18 inches long at birth and grows 8 inches per year. Write an equation in slope-intercept form that represents the length y (in feet) of a boa constrictor that is x years old.

22. **MP MODELING REAL LIFE** The table shows the speeds y (in miles per hour) of a car after x seconds of braking. Write an equation of the line that passes through the points in the table. Interpret the slope and the y-intercept of the line.

x	0	1	2	3
y	70	60	50	40

23. **MP MODELING REAL LIFE** A dentist charges a flat fee for an office visit, plus an additional fee for every tooth removed. The graph shows the total cost y (in dollars) for a patient when the dentist removes x teeth. Interpret the slope and the y-intercept.

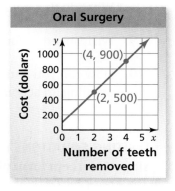

Oral Surgery

Cost (dollars)

$(4, 900)$

$(2, 500)$

Number of teeth removed

24. **MP MODELING REAL LIFE** One of your friends gives you $10 for a charity walkathon. Another friend gives you an amount per mile. After 5 miles, you have raised $13.50 total. Write an equation that represents the amount y of money you have raised after x miles.

25. **MP PROBLEM SOLVING** You have 500 sheets of notebook paper. After 1 week, you have 72% of the sheets left. You use the same number of sheets each week. Write an equation that represents the number y of sheets remaining after x weeks.

26. **DIG DEEPER!** The palm tree on the left is 10 years old. The palm tree on the right is 8 years old. The trees grow at the same rate.

   a. Estimate the height y (in feet) of each tree.

   b. Plot the two points (x, y), where x is the age of each tree and y is the height of each tree.

   c. What is the rate of growth of the trees?

   d. Write an equation that represents the height of a palm tree in terms of its age.

6 ft

4.7 Writing Equations in Point-Slope Form

Learning Target: Write equations of lines in point-slope form.

Success Criteria:
- I can use a point on a line and the slope to write an equation of the line.
- I can use any two points to write an equation of a line.
- I can write equations in point-slope form to solve real-life problems.

EXPLORATION 1

Deriving an Equation

Work with a partner. Let (x_1, y_1) represent a specific point on a line. Let (x, y) represent any other point on the line.

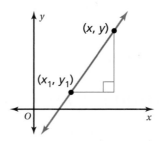

Math Practice

Recognize Usefulness of Tools

How does the graph help you derive an equation?

a. Write an equation that represents the slope m of the line. Explain your reasoning.

b. Multiply each side of your equation in part (a) by the expression in the denominator. What does the resulting equation represent? Explain your reasoning.

EXPLORATION 2

Writing an Equation

Work with a partner.

For 4 months, you saved $25 a month. You now have $175 in your savings account.

a. Draw a graph that shows the balance in your account after t months.

b. Use your result from Exploration 1 to write an equation that represents the balance A after t months.

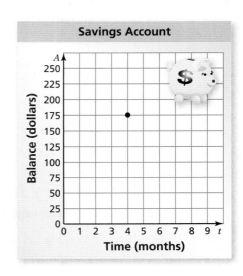

4.7 Lesson

Key Vocabulary 🔊
point-slope form,
p. 180

🔑 Key Idea

Point-Slope Form

Words A linear equation written in the form $y - y_1 = m(x - x_1)$ is in **point-slope form**. The line passes through the point (x_1, y_1), and the slope of the line is m.

Algebra

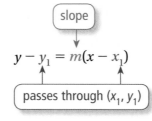

$$y - y_1 = m(x - x_1)$$

passes through (x_1, y_1)

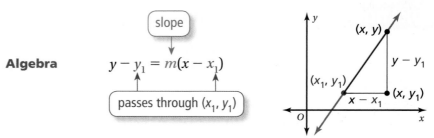

EXAMPLE 1 **Writing an Equation Using a Slope and a Point**

Write an equation in point-slope form of the line that passes through the point $(-6, 1)$ with slope $\frac{2}{3}$.

$y - y_1 = m(x - x_1)$ Write the point-slope form.

$y - 1 = \frac{2}{3}[x - (-6)]$ Substitute $\frac{2}{3}$ for m, -6 for x_1, and 1 for y_1.

$y - 1 = \frac{2}{3}(x + 6)$ Simplify.

▷ So, an equation is $y - 1 = \frac{2}{3}(x + 6)$.

> **Check** Check that $(-6, 1)$ is a solution of the equation.
>
> $y - 1 = \frac{2}{3}(x + 6)$ Write the equation.
>
> $1 - 1 \overset{?}{=} \frac{2}{3}(-6 + 6)$ Substitute.
>
> $0 = 0$ ✓   Simplify.

Try It Write an equation in point-slope form of the line that passes through the given point and has the given slope.

   1. $(1, 2)$; $m = -4$ **2.** $(7, 0)$; $m = 1$ **3.** $(-8, -5)$; $m = -\frac{3}{4}$

EXAMPLE 2 **Writing an Equation Using Two Points**

Write an equation in slope-intercept form of the line that passes through the given points.

x	y
−1	10
2	4
5	−2

Find the slope. Use the points $(2, 4)$ and $(5, -2)$.

$$m = \frac{y_2 - y_1}{x_2 - x_1} = \frac{-2 - 4}{5 - 2} = \frac{-6}{3} = -2$$

Then use the slope $m = -2$ and the point $(2, 4)$ to write an equation of the line.

$y - y_1 = m(x - x_1)$	Write the point-slope form.
$y - 4 = -2(x - 2)$	Substitute -2 for m, 2 for x_1, and 4 for y_1.
$y - 4 = -2x + 4$	Distributive Property
$y = -2x + 8$	Write in slope-intercept form.

Math Practice

Build Arguments
Will you obtain the same equation when you use a different pair of points from the table? Explain why or why not.

Try It Write an equation in slope-intercept form of the line that passes through the given points.

4. $(-2, 1), (3, -4)$

5.
x	−5	−3	−1
y	5	3	1

Self-Assessment for Concepts & Skills

Solve each exercise. Then rate your understanding of the success criteria in your journal.

WRITING AN EQUATION Write an equation in point-slope form of the line that passes through the given point and has the given slope.

6. $(2, 0)$; $m = 1$ 7. $(-3, -1)$; $m = -\frac{1}{3}$ 8. $(5, 4)$; $m = 3$

x	3	5	7
y	1	−2	−5

9. **WRITING AN EQUATION** Write an equation of the line that passes through the points given in the table.

10. **DIFFERENT WORDS, SAME QUESTION** Which is different? Sketch "both" graphs.

What is the graph of the equation $y = 4x + 3$?

Graph the line that passes through the points $(4, 5)$ and $(5, 9)$.

Graph $y = 4x + 3$.

Graph the linear equation $y - 7 = 4(x - 1)$.

EXAMPLE 3 **Modeling Real Life**

10 feet per second

You finish parasailing and are being pulled back to the boat. After 2 seconds, you are 25 feet above the boat. At what height were you parasailing?

You are 25 feet above the boat after 2 seconds, which can be represented by the point (2, 25). You are being pulled down at a rate of 10 feet per second. So, the slope is -10.

Because you know a point and the slope, use point-slope form to write an equation that represents your height y (in feet) above the boat after x seconds.

$y - y_1 = m(x - x_1)$	Write the point-slope form.
$y - 25 = -10(x - 2)$	Substitute for m, x_1, and y_1.
$y - 25 = -10x + 20$	Distributive Property
$y = -10x + 45$	Write in slope-intercept form.

The height at which you were parasailing is represented by the y-intercept.

▷ So, you were parasailing at a height of 45 feet.

Self-Assessment for Problem Solving

Solve each exercise. Then rate your understanding of the success criteria in your journal.

11. A writer finishes a project that a coworker started at a rate of 3 pages per hour. After 3 hours, 25% of the project is complete.

   a. The project is 200 pages long. Write and graph an equation for the total number y of pages that have been finished after the writer works for x hours.

   b. The writer has a total of 45 hours to finish the project. Will the writer meet the deadline? Explain your reasoning.

12. **DIG DEEPER!** You and your friend begin to run along a path at different constant speeds. After 1 minute, your friend is 45 meters ahead of you. After 3 minutes, your friend is 105 meters ahead of you.

   a. Write and graph an equation for the distance y (in meters) your friend is ahead of you after x minutes. Justify your answer.

   b. Did you and your friend start running from the same spot? Explain your reasoning.

4.7 Practice

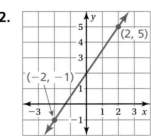

? Go to *BigIdeasMath.com* to get HELP with solving the exercises.

▶ Review & Refresh

Write an equation in slope-intercept form of the line that passes through the given points.

1.

x	−2	0	2
y	4	5	6

2.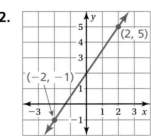

Solve the equation. Check your solution, if possible.

3. $2x + 3 = 2x$

4. $6x - 7 = 1 - 3x$

5. $0.1x - 1 = 1.2x - 5.4$

▶▶ Concepts, Skills, & Problem Solving

WRITING AN EQUATION The value of a new car decreases $4000 each year. After **3 years, the car is worth $18,000.** (See Exploration 2, p. 179.)

6. Draw a graph that shows the value of the car after t years.

7. Write an equation that represents the value V of the car after t years.

WRITING AN EQUATION Write an equation in point-slope form of the line that passes through the given point and has the given slope.

8. $(3, 0)$; $m = -\dfrac{2}{3}$

9. $(4, 8)$; $m = \dfrac{3}{4}$

10. $(1, -3)$; $m = 4$

11. $(7, -5)$; $m = -\dfrac{1}{7}$

12. $(3, 3)$; $m = \dfrac{5}{3}$

13. $(-1, -4)$; $m = -2$

WRITING AN EQUATION Write an equation in slope-intercept form of the line that passes through the given points.

14. $(-1, -1), (1, 5)$

15. $(2, 4), (3, 6)$

16. $(-2, 3), (2, 7)$

17. $(4, 1), (8, 2)$

18. $(-9, 5), (-3, 3)$

19. $(1, 2), (-2, -1)$

20. **MP MODELING REAL LIFE** At 0°C, the volume of a gas is 22 liters. For each degree the temperature T (in degrees Celsius) increases, the volume V (in liters) of the gas increases by $\dfrac{2}{25}$. Write an equation that represents the volume of the gas in terms of the temperature.

WRITING AN EQUATION Write an equation of the line that passes through the given points in any form. Explain your choice of form.

21.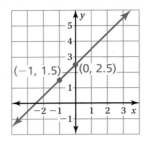

22.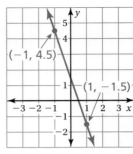

23.

24.

x	y
−1	3.5
1	−0.5
3	−4.5

25.

x	y
−3	−1
0	1
3	3

26.

x	y
−7	6
−3	4
1	2

27. **MP** **REASONING** Write an equation of the line that passes through the point (8, 2) and is parallel to the graph of the equation $y = 4x - 3$.

28. **MP** **MODELING REAL LIFE** The table shows the amount y (in fluid ounces) of carpet cleaner in a tank after x minutes of cleaning.

x	y
5	108
10	88
15	68

   a. Write an equation that represents the amount of cleaner in the tank after x minutes.

   b. How much cleaner is in the tank when the cleaning begins?

   c. After how many minutes is the tank empty? Justify your answer.

29. **DIG DEEPER!** According to Dolbear's law, you can predict the temperature T (in degrees Fahrenheit) by counting the number x of chirps made by a snowy tree cricket in 1 minute. When the temperature is 50°F, a cricket chirps 40 times in 1 minute. For each rise in temperature of 0.25°F, the cricket makes an additional chirp each minute.

   a. You count 100 chirps in 1 minute. What is the temperature?

   b. The temperature is 96°F. How many chirps do you expect the cricket to make? Justify your answer.

Leaning Tower of Pisa

30. **MP** **PROBLEM SOLVING** The Leaning Tower of Pisa in Italy was built between 1173 and 1350.

   a. Write an equation that represents the yellow line.

   b. The tower is 56 meters tall. How far from the center is the top of the tower? Justify your answer.

Connecting Concepts

▷ *Using the Problem-Solving Plan*

1. Every item in a retail store is on sale for 40% off. Write and graph an equation that represents the sale price y of an item that has an original price of x dollars.

 Understand the problem.

You know the percent discount of items in a retail store. You are asked to write and graph an equation that represents the sale price of an item that has an original price of x dollars.

Make a plan.

Selling an item for 40% off is the same as selling an item for 60% of its original price. Use this information to write and graph an equation that represents the situation.

 Solve and check.

Use the plan to solve the problem. Then check your solution.

2. Two supplementary angles have angle measures of $x°$ and $y°$. Write and graph an equation that represents the relationship between the measures of the angles.

3. A mechanic charges a diagnostic fee plus an hourly rate. The table shows the numbers of hours worked and the total costs for three customers. A fourth customer pays $285. Find the number of hours that the mechanic worked for the fourth customer.

Hours, x	1	3	5
Cost, y (dollars)	90	210	330

Performance Task

Anatomy of a Hurricane

At the beginning of this chapter, you watched a STEAM Video called "Hurricane!" You are now ready to complete the performance task related to this video, available at *BigIdeasMath.com*. Be sure to use the problem-solving plan as you work through the performance task.

▶ Review Vocabulary

Write the definition and give an example of each vocabulary term.

linear equation, *p. 142*
solution of a linear equation,
   p. 142
slope, *p. 148*

rise, *p. 148*
run, *p. 148*
x-intercept, *p. 162*
y-intercept, *p. 162*

slope-intercept form,
   p. 162
standard form, *p. 168*
point-slope form, *p. 180*

▶ Graphic Organizers

You can use a **Definition and Example Chart** to organize information about a concept. Here is an example of a Definition and Example Chart for the vocabulary term *linear equation*.

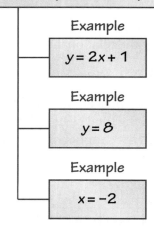

Linear equation: **an equation whose graph is a line**

Example

$y = 2x + 1$

Example

$y = 8$

Example

$x = -2$

Choose and complete a graphic organizer to help you study the concept.

1. slope

2. slope of parallel lines

3. proportional relationship

4. slope-intercept form

5. standard form

6. point-slope form

Weekday: A day of the week other than Saturday or Sunday

EXAMPLE

Wednesday: Woden's day

EXAMPLE

Thursday: Thor's day

I hope catsup wasn't named after cat soup!

"Here is my Definition and Example Chart. Wednesday, Thursday, and Friday (Freya's day) are all named after mythical beings."

▷ Chapter Self-Assessment

As you complete the exercises, use the scale below to rate your understanding of the success criteria in your journal.

1 I do not understand.

2 I can do it with help.

3 I can do it on my own.

4 I can teach someone else.

4.1 Graphing Linear Equations (pp. 141–146)

Learning Target: Graph linear equations.

Graph the linear equation.

1. $y = \dfrac{3}{5}x$

2. $y = -2$

3. $y = 9 - x$

4. $y = -0.25x + 4$

5. $y = \dfrac{2}{3}x + 2$

6. $x = -5$

7. The equation $y = 0.5x + 3$ represents the cost y (in dollars) of riding in a taxi x miles.

   a. Use a graph to estimate how much it costs to ride 5.25 miles in a taxi.

   b. Use the equation to find exactly how much it costs to ride 5.25 miles in a taxi.

8. The equation $y = 9.5x$ represents the earnings y (in dollars) of an aquarium gift shop employee that works x hours.

   a. Graph the linear equation.

   b. How much does the employee earn for working 40 hours?

9. Is $y = x^2$ a linear equation? Explain your reasoning.

10. The sum S of the exterior angle measures of a polygon with n sides is $S = 360°$.

    a. Plot four points (n, S) that satisfy the equation. Is the equation a linear equation? Explain your reasoning.

    b. Does the value $n = 2$ make sense in the context of the problem? Explain your reasoning.

4.2 Slope of a Line (pp. 147–154)

Learning Target: Find and interpret the slope of a line.

Describe the slope of the line. Then find the slope of the line.

11.
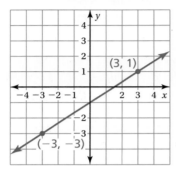

12.
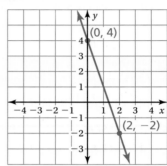

Find the slope of the line through the given points.

13. $(-5, 4), (8, 4)$

14. $(-3, 5), (-3, 1)$

The points in the table lie on a line. Find the slope of the line.

15.

x	0	1	2	3
y	−1	0	1	2

16.

x	−2	0	2	4
y	3	4	5	6

17. How do you know when two lines are parallel? Use an example to justify your answer.

18. Draw a line through the point $(-1, 2)$ that is parallel to the graph of the line in Exercise 11.

4.3 Graphing Proportional Relationships (pp. 155–160)

Learning Target: Graph proportional relationships.

Tell whether *x* and *y* are in a proportional relationship. Explain your reasoning. If so, write an equation that represents the relationship.

19.
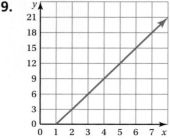

20.
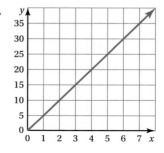

21. The cost y (in dollars) to provide food for guests at a dinner party is proportional to the number x of guests attending the party. It costs \$30 to provide food for 4 guests.

    a. Write an equation that represents the situation.

    b. Interpret the slope of the graph of the equation.

    c. How much does it cost to provide food for 10 guests? Justify your answer.

22. The distance y (in miles) you run after x weeks is represented by the equation $y = 8x$. Graph the equation and interpret the slope.

23. You research that hair grows 15 centimeters per year on average. The table shows your friend's hair growth.

Months	1	2	3	4
Hair Growth (centimeters)	1.5	3	4.5	6

    a. Does your friend's hair grow faster than average? Explain.

    b. In the same coordinate plane, graph the average hair growth and the hair growth of your friend. Compare and interpret the steepness of each of the graphs.

4.4 Graphing Linear Equations in Slope-Intercept Form *(pp. 161–166)*

Learning Target: Graph linear equations in slope-intercept form.

Find the slope and the y-intercept of the graph of the linear equation.

24. $y = -4x + 1$ **25.** $y = \dfrac{2}{3}x - 12$ **26.** $y - 7 = 0.5x$

Graph the linear equation. Identify the x-intercept.

27. $y = 2x - 6$ **28.** $y = -4x + 8$ **29.** $y = -x - 8$

30. The cost y (in dollars) of one person buying admission to a fair and going on x rides is $y = x + 12$.

    a. Graph the equation.

    b. Interpret the y-intercept and the slope.

31. Graph the linear equation with slope -5 and y-intercept 0.

4.5 Graphing Linear Equations in Standard Form *(pp. 167–172)*

Learning Target: Graph linear equations in standard form.

Write the linear equation in slope-intercept form.

32. $4x + 2y = -12$

33. $x - y = \frac{1}{4}$

Graph the linear equation.

34. $\frac{1}{4}x + y = 3$

35. $-4x + 2y = 8$

36. $x + 5y = 10$

37. $-\frac{1}{2}x + \frac{1}{8}y = \frac{3}{4}$

38. A dog kennel charges \$30 per night to board your dog and \$6 for each hour of playtime. The amount of money you spend is given by $30x + 6y = 180$, where x is the number of nights and y is the number of hours of playtime. Graph the equation and interpret the intercepts.

4.6 Writing Equations in Slope-Intercept Form *(pp. 173–178)*

Learning Target: Write equations of lines in slope-intercept form.

Write an equation in slope-intercept form of the line that passes through the given points.

39.

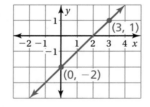

40.

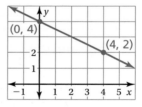

41.

x	y
−2	4
0	1
2	−2
4	−5

42.

x	y
0	−3
1	−1
2	1
3	3

43. Write an equation of the line that passes through $(0, 8)$ and $(6, 8)$.

44. Write an equation of the line that passes through $(0, -5)$ and $(-5, -5)$.

45. A construction crew is extending a highway sound barrier that is 13 miles long. The crew builds $\frac{1}{2}$ of a mile per week. Write an equation in slope-intercept form that represents the length y (in miles) of the barrier after x weeks.

4.7 Writing Equations in Point-Slope Form (pp. 179–184)

Learning Target: Write equations of lines in point-slope form.

Write an equation in point-slope form of the line that passes through the given point and has the given slope.

46. $(4, 4);\ m = 3$

47. $(2, -8);\ m = -\dfrac{2}{3}$

Write an equation in slope-intercept form of the line that passes through the given points.

48. $(-4, 2), (6, -3)$

49.

x	1	2	3
y	−3	1	5

50. The table shows your elevation y (in feet) on a ski slope after x minutes.

x	1	2	3
y	800	600	400

    a. Write an equation that represents your elevation after x minutes.

    b. What is your starting elevation?

    c. After how many minutes do you reach the bottom of the ski slope? Justify your answer.

51. A company offers cable television at $29.95 per month plus a one-time installation fee. The total cost for the first six months of service is $214.70.

    a. Write an equation in point-slope form that represents the total cost you pay for cable television after x months.

    b. How much is the installation fee? Justify your answer.

52. When might it be better to represent an equation in point-slope form rather than slope-intercept form? Use an example to justify your answer.

Practice Test

Find the slope and the y-intercept of the graph of the linear equation.

1. $y = 6x - 5$

2. $y - 1 = 3x + 8.4$

3. $-\dfrac{1}{2}x + 2y = 7$

Graph the linear equation.

4. $y = -\dfrac{1}{2}x - 5$

5. $-3x + 6y = 12$

6. $y = \dfrac{2}{3}x$

7. Which lines are parallel? Explain.

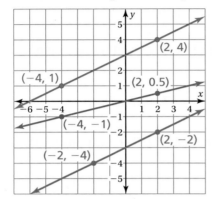

8. The points in the table lie on a line. Find the slope of the line.

x	y
-1	-4
0	-1
1	2
2	5

Write an equation in slope-intercept form of the line that passes through the given points.

9.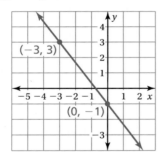

10.

x	y
-2	2
0	2
2	2
4	2

11. Write an equation in point-slope form of the line that passes through $(-4, 1)$ and $(4, 3)$.

12. The number y of new vocabulary words that you learn after x weeks is represented by the equation $y = 15x$.

    a. Graph the equation and interpret the slope.

    b. How many new vocabulary words do you learn after 5 weeks?

    c. How many more vocabulary words do you learn after 6 weeks than after 4 weeks?

13. You used $90 worth of paint for a school float. The amount of money you spend is given by $18x + 15y = 90$, where x is the number of gallons of blue paint and y is the number of gallons of white paint. Graph the equation and interpret the intercepts.

Cumulative Practice

1. Which equation matches the line shown in the graph?

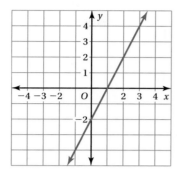

A. $y = 2x - 2$

B. $y = 2x + 1$

C. $y = x - 2$

D. $y = x + 1$

2. Which point lies on the graph of $6x - 5y = 14$?

F. $(-4, -1)$ **G.** $(-2, 4)$

H. $(-1, -4)$ **I.** $(4, -2)$

3. You reflect the triangle in the *x*-axis. What are the coordinates of the image?

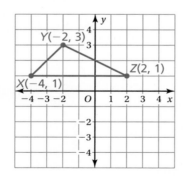

A. $X'(4, 1), Y'(2, 3), Z'(-2, 1)$ **B.** $X'(4, -1), Y'(2, -3), Z'(-2, -1)$

C. $X'(-4, -1), Y'(-2, -3), Z'(2, -1)$ **D.** $X'(1, 4), Y'(3, 2), Z'(1, -2)$

4. Which of the following is the equation of a line parallel to the line shown in the graph?

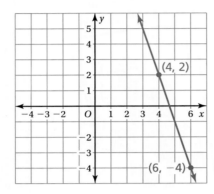

F. $y = 3x - 10$

G. $y = \dfrac{1}{3}x + 12$

H. $y = -3x + 5$

I. $y = -\dfrac{1}{3}x - 18$

5. What is the value of x?

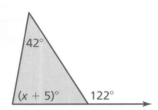

42°

$(x + 5)°$ 122°

6. An emergency plumber charges $49.00 plus $70.00 per hour of the repair. A bill to repair your sink is $241.50. This can be modeled by $70.00h + 49.00 = 241.50$, where h represents the number of hours for the repair. How many hours did it take to repair your sink?

A. 2.75 hours

B. 3.45 hours

C. 4.15 hours

D. 13,475 hours

7. It costs $40 to rent a car for one day. In addition, the rental agency charges you for each mile driven, as shown in the graph.

> Think
> Solve
> Explain

Part A Determine the slope of the line joining the points on the graph.

Part B Explain what the slope represents.

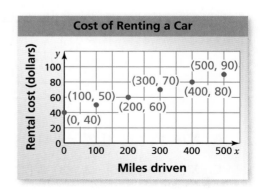

8. What value of x makes the equation true?

$$7 + 2x = 4x - 5$$

9. Trapezoid *KLMN* is graphed in the coordinate plane shown.

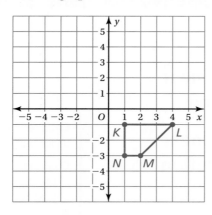

Rotate Trapezoid *KLMN* $90°$ clockwise about the origin. What are the coordinates of point M', the image of point M after the rotation?

F. $(-3, -2)$ **G.** $(-2, -3)$

H. $(-2, 3)$ **I.** $(3, 2)$

10. Solve the formula $K = 3M - 7$ for M.

A. $M = K + 7$ **B.** $M = \dfrac{K + 7}{3}$

C. $M = \dfrac{K}{3} + 7$ **D.** $M = \dfrac{K - 7}{3}$

11. What is the distance d across the canyon?

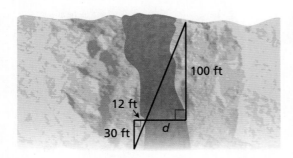

F. 3.6 ft   **G.** 12 ft

H. 40 ft   **I.** 250 ft

5 Systems of Linear Equations

Chapter Learning Target:
Understand systems of linear equations.

Chapter Success Criteria:
- I can identify a linear equation.
- I can describe a system of linear equations.
- I can solve a system of linear equations.
- I can model solving systems with different numbers of solutions.

STEAM Video: "Gold Alloys"

STEAM Video

Gold Alloys

An *alloy* is a mixture of different metals melted together at high temperatures. A dental filling is created using a gold alloy. What are other uses of alloys?

Watch the STEAM Video "Gold Alloys." Then answer the following questions.

1. Enid says that the proportion of gold in an alloy can be measured in *karats*. For example, 24 karats represents 100% gold and 18 karats represents 75% gold.

   a. A dental filling is 9 karats. What percent of the filling is gold?

   b. A watch is 60% gold. How many karats is the watch?

2. What percent gold is each described alloy?

   a. A mixture of 2 grams 10-karat gold and 2 grams 14-karat gold

   b. A mixture of 6 grams 24-karat gold and 4 grams 9-karat gold

Performance Task

Mixing Alloys

After completing this chapter, you will be able to use the concepts you learned to answer the questions in the *STEAM Video Performance Task*. You will be given a list of gold alloys available at a jewelry store.

Alloys at Jewelry Store

    Alloy 1:   **25% gold**

    Alloy 2:   **50% gold**

    Alloy 3:   **82% gold**

You will use a *system of equations* to determine the amounts of the given alloys that a jeweler needs to create a new alloy. Why might a jeweler need to create a mixture with a specific proportion of gold?

Getting Ready for Chapter  5

Chapter Exploration

1. **Work with a partner. Your family starts a bed-and-breakfast. You spend $500 fixing up a bedroom to rent. The cost for food and utilities is $10 per night. Your family charges $60 per night to rent the bedroom.**

   a. Write an equation that represents the costs.

Cost, C (in dollars)	=	$10 per night	·	Number of nights, x	+	$500

   b. Write an equation that represents the revenue (income).

Revenue, R (in dollars)	=	$60 per night	·	Number of nights, x

   c. A set of two (or more) linear equations is called a *system of linear equations.* Write the system of linear equations for this problem.

2. **Work with a partner. Use a graphing calculator to solve the system.**

   $y = 10x + 500$ Equation 1
   $y = 60x$ Equation 2

   a. Enter the equations into your calculator. Then graph the equations. What is an appropriate window?

   b. On your graph, how can you determine which line is the graph of which equation? Label the equations on the graph shown.

   c. Visually estimate the point of intersection of the graphs.

   d. To find the solution, use the *intersect* feature to find the point of intersection.

   The solution is $\left(\rule{1cm}{0.4pt} , \rule{1cm}{0.4pt} \right)$.

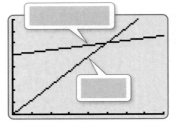

Vocabulary

The following vocabulary terms are defined in this chapter. Think about what each term might mean and record your thoughts.

system of linear equations   solution of a system of linear equations

Learning Target: Understand how to solve systems of linear equations by graphing.

Success Criteria:
- I can graph a linear equation.
- I can find the point where two lines intersect.
- I can solve a system of linear equations by graphing.

EXPLORATION 1

Using a Graph to Solve a Problem

Work with a partner. You charge your headphones and your phone. The equations below represent the battery powers p% of the devices after x minutes of charging.

$$p = \frac{5}{3}x \qquad \text{Headphones}$$

$$p = x + 25 \qquad \text{Phone}$$

a. You check the battery power of each device every 10 minutes. Copy and complete the table. How do the devices' battery powers compare?

x (minutes)	10	20	30	40	50	60
p (headphones)						
p (phone)						

b. After how much time do the devices have the same battery power? What is the battery power at that time? Justify your answer.

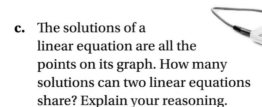

c. The solutions of a linear equation are all the points on its graph. How many solutions can two linear equations share? Explain your reasoning.

Math Practice

Use Technology to Explore

What features of a graphing calculator can you use to check your answers in part (b)?

d. Graph the battery power equations in the same coordinate plane. What do you notice?

e. **MP USING TOOLS** Use a graphing calculator to check your answers in part (b). Explain your method.

Key Vocabulary 🔊

system of linear equations, *p. 200*
solution of a system of linear equations, *p. 200*

A **system of linear equations** is a set of two or more linear equations in the same variables. An example is shown below. A system of linear equations is also called a *linear system*.

$$y = x + 1 \qquad \text{Equation 1}$$
$$y = 2x - 7 \qquad \text{Equation 2}$$

A **solution of a system of linear equations** in two variables is an ordered pair that is a solution of each equation in the system. The solution of a system of linear equations is the point of intersection of the graphs of the equations.

EXAMPLE 1 **Solving a System of Linear Equations by Graphing**

Solve the system by graphing.
$$y = 2x + 5 \qquad \text{Equation 1}$$
$$y = -4x - 1 \qquad \text{Equation 2}$$

Graph each equation.

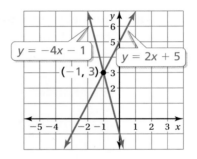

Always check that the estimated intersection point is a solution of each equation.

The graphs appear to intersect at $(-1, 3)$. Check that the point is a solution of each equation.

Equation 1

$$y = 2x + 5$$
$$3 \stackrel{?}{=} 2(-1) + 5$$
$$3 = 3 \quad ✓$$

Equation 2

$$y = -4x - 1$$
$$3 \stackrel{?}{=} -4(-1) - 1$$
$$3 = 3 \quad ✓$$

 The solution is $(-1, 3)$.

Check

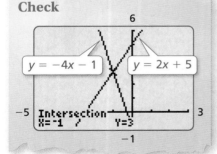

Try It **Solve the system by graphing.**

1. $y = x - 1$
$ y = -x + 3$

2. $y = -5x + 14$
$ y = x - 10$

3. $y = x$
$ y = 2x + 1$

EXAMPLE 2 **Solving a System of Linear Equations by Graphing**

Solve the system by graphing. $y = 2x - 2$ Equation 1

$-x + 2y = -4$ Equation 2

Graph each equation.

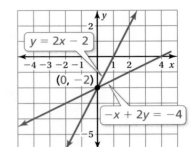

The graphs appear to intersect at $(0, -2)$. Check that the point is a solution of each equation.

Equation 1   Equation 2

$y = 2x - 2$ $-x + 2y = -4$

$-2 \stackrel{?}{=} 2(0) - 2$ $-0 + 2(-2) \stackrel{?}{=} -4$

$-2 = -2$ ✓ $-4 = -4$ ✓

▷ The solution is $(0, -2)$.

Math Practice

Communicate Precisely

Write a system that has the same solution as the system in Example 2. Explain your method to a classmate.

Try It Solve the system by graphing.

4. $y = -4x - 7$ **5.** $x - y = 5$ **6.** $\dfrac{1}{2}x + y = -6$

   $x + y = 2$ $-3x + y = -1$ $6x + 2y = 8$

Self-Assessment *for Concepts & Skills*

Solve each exercise. Then rate your understanding of the success criteria in your journal.

SOLVING A SYSTEM OF LINEAR EQUATIONS Solve the system by graphing.

7. $y = x + 1$ **8.** $3x - y = -1$ **9.** $x + 2y = 3$

   $y = 4x + 7$ $y = -x + 5$ $-x + 3y = 7$

10. WRITING Explain why the solution of a system of linear equations is the point of intersection of their graphs.

11. DIFFERENT WORDS, SAME QUESTION Which is different? Find "both" answers.

$y = -2x + 8$ Equation 1
$y = 4x + 2$ Equation 2

What is the solution of the system?

At what point do the graphs of the equations intersect?

What ordered pair makes both equations true?

What are the solutions of each equation?

EXAMPLE 3 **Modeling Real Life**

In football, each extra point made is 1 point and each field goal made is 3 points. A kicker makes a total of 8 extra points and field goals in a game and scores 12 points. How many field goals did the kicker make?

Use a verbal model to write a system of linear equations. Let x represent the number of extra points and let y represent the number of field goals.

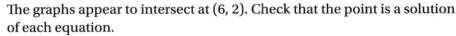

Number of extra points, x	$+$	Number of field goals, y	$=$	Total number of kicks

Points per extra point	$\cdot$	Number of extra points, x	$+$	Points per field goal	$\cdot$	Number of field goals, y	$=$	Total number of points

The system is:

$$x + y = 8 \qquad \text{Equation 1}$$
$$x + 3y = 12 \qquad \text{Equation 2}$$

Graph each equation.

The graphs appear to intersect at $(6, 2)$. Check that the point is a solution of each equation.

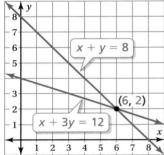

Equation 1	Equation 2
$x + y = 8$	$x + 3y = 12$
$6 + 2 \overset{?}{=} 8$	$6 + 3(2) \overset{?}{=} 12$
$8 = 8 \checkmark$	$12 = 12 \checkmark$

The solution is $(6, 2)$. So, the kicker made 2 field goals.

Self-Assessment for Problem Solving

Solve each exercise. Then rate your understanding of the success criteria in your journal.

12. Your family attends a comic convention. Each autograph costs $20 and each photograph costs $50. Your family buys a total of 5 autographs and photographs for $160. How many photographs does your family buy?

13. **DIG DEEPER!** Two apps on your phone take away points for using your phone at school. You have 140 points on the first app and 80 points on the second app when a school day begins. Each time you check your phone, you lose 10 points on your first app and p points on your second app. After you check your phone ten times, you have the same number of points on each app. Find the value of p.

5.1 Practice

Go to *BigIdeasMath.com* to get
HELP with solving the exercises.

▶ Review & Refresh

Write an equation in point-slope form of the line that passes through the given point and has the given slope.

1. $(3, -4)$; $m = 1$

2. $(5, 6)$; $m = \dfrac{3}{5}$

3. $(1, 0)$; $m = -\dfrac{1}{4}$

Solve the equation. Check your solution.

4. $\dfrac{3}{4}c - \dfrac{1}{4}c + 3 = 7$

5. $5(2 - y) + y = -6$

6. $6x - 3(x + 8) = 9$

▶▶ Concepts, Skills, & Problem Solving

USING A GRAPH TO SOLVE A PROBLEM **The equations below represent the numbers y of tickets sold after x weeks for two different local music festivals.** (See Exploration 1, p. 199.)

$y = 10x + 150$	Country Music Festival
$y = 20x + 115$	Pop Music Festival

7. You check the ticket sales for both festivals each week for 10 weeks. Create a table for the ticket sales each week. How do the festivals' ticket sales compare?

8. After how much time have the same number of tickets been sold for both festivals? What is the number of tickets sold at that time?

SOLVING A SYSTEM OF LINEAR EQUATIONS **Solve the system by graphing.**

9. $y = 2x + 9$
  $y = 6 - x$

10. $y = -x - 4$
  $y = \dfrac{3}{5}x + 4$

11. $y = 2x + 5$
  $y = \dfrac{1}{2}x - 1$

12. $x + y = 27$
  $y = x + 3$

13. $y - x = 17$
  $y = 4x + 2$

14. $x - y = 7$
  $0.5x + y = 5$

USING A GRAPHING CALCULATOR **Use a graphing calculator to solve the system.**

15. $2.2x + y = 12.5$
  $1.4x - 4y = 1$

16. $2.1x + 4.2y = 14.7$
  $-5.7x - 1.9y = -11.4$

17. $-1.1x - 5.5y = -4.4$
  $0.8x - 3.2y = -11.2$

18. **MP YOU BE THE TEACHER** Your friend solves the system of linear equations below. Is your friend correct? Explain your reasoning.

  $y = 0.5x + 1$ Equation 1
  $y = -x + 7$ Equation 2

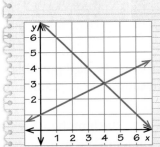

The solution of the linear system is $x = 4$.

19. **MP** **MODELING REAL LIFE** You have a total of 42 math and science problems for homework. You have 10 more math problems than science problems. How many problems do you have in each subject? Use a system of linear equations to justify your answer.

20. **MP** **PROBLEM SOLVING** A generator contains 60 gallons of fuel and uses 2.5 gallons per hour. A more efficient power generator contains 40 gallons of fuel and uses 1.5 gallons per hour. After how many hours do the generators have the same amount of fuel? Which generator runs longer? Justify your answers.

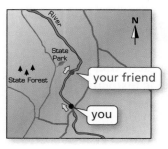

21. **MP** **PROBLEM SOLVING** You and your friend are in a canoe race. Your friend is a half mile in front of you and paddling 3 miles per hour. You are paddling 3.4 miles per hour.

 a. You are 8.5 miles from the finish line. How long will it take you to catch up to your friend?

 b. You both maintain your paddling rates for the remainder of the race. How far ahead of your friend will you be when you cross the finish line?

OPEN-ENDED **Write a system of linear equations that fits the description. Use a graph to justify your answer.**

22. The solution of the system is a point on the line $y = -9x + 1$.

23. The solution of the system is $(3, -1)$.

24. **DIG DEEPER!** A graph of a system of two linear equations is shown. Write the system of linear equations represented by the graph. What is the solution of the system?

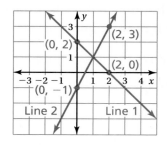

25. **CRITICAL THINKING** Your friend is trying to grow her hair as long as her cousin's hair. The table shows their hair lengths (in inches) in different months.

Month	Friend's Hair (in.)	Cousin's Hair (in.)
March	4	7
August	6.5	9

 a. Write a system of linear equations that represents this situation. Let $x = 1$ represent January.

 b. Will your friend's hair ever be as long as her cousin's hair? If so, in what month?

26. **MP** **REASONING** Is it possible for a system of two linear equations to have multiple solutions? Explain your reasoning.

27. **GEOMETRY** The length of a rectangle is 8 feet more than its width. The perimeter of the rectangle is 72 feet. Find the width of the rectangle.

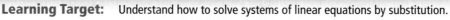

5.2 Solving Systems of Linear Equations by Substitution

Learning Target: Understand how to solve systems of linear equations by substitution.

Success Criteria:
- I can solve a linear equation in two variables for either variable.
- I can solve a system of linear equations by substitution.

EXPLORATION 1

Solving Systems Algebraically

Work with a partner.

a. Find the value of each symbol in the systems below. Compare your solution methods with other pairs of students.

System 1:
$$☽ + ☽ - 1 = ★ \qquad \text{Equation 1}$$
$$☽ + ★ + ★ = 8 \qquad \text{Equation 2}$$

System 2:
$$☼ - ❄ = 3 \qquad \text{Equation 1}$$
$$☼ + ❄ = 1 \qquad \text{Equation 2}$$

Math Practice

Make a Plan
How does your work in part (a) help you make a plan for solving the system in part (b)?

b. Use a method similar to your method in part (a) to solve the system below. Then explain how to solve a system of linear equations in two variables algebraically.

$$3x + y = 1 \qquad \text{Equation 1}$$
$$x - y = -5 \qquad \text{Equation 2}$$

EXPLORATION 2

Writing and Solving Systems of Equations

Work with a partner. Roll two number cubes that are different colors. Then write the ordered pair shown by the number cubes.

a. Write a system of linear equations that has your ordered pair as its solution. Explain how you found your system.

b. Exchange systems with another pair of students. Use a method from Exploration 1 to solve the system.

x-value

y-value

Another way to solve a system of linear equations is to use substitution to obtain an equation in one variable. Then solve the resulting equation and substitute to find the value of the other variable.

EXAMPLE 1 **Solving a System of Linear Equations by Substitution**

Solve the system by substitution.

$$y = 2x - 4 \qquad \text{Equation 1}$$
$$7x - 2y = 5 \qquad \text{Equation 2}$$

Step 1: Notice that Equation 1 is solved for y. So, you can substitute $2x - 4$ for y in Equation 2 to obtain an equation in one variable, x. Then solve the equation to find the value of x.

$7x - 2y = 5$	Equation 2
$7x - 2(2x - 4) = 5$	Substitute $2x - 4$ for y.
$7x - 4x + 8 = 5$	Distributive Property
$3x + 8 = 5$	Combine like terms.
$3x = -3$	Subtract 8 from each side.
$x = -1$	Divide each side by 3.

Step 2: Substitute -1 for x in Equation 1 and solve for y.

$y = 2x - 4$	Equation 1
$= 2(-1) - 4$	Substitute -1 for x.
$= -2 - 4$	Multiply.
$= -6$	Subtract.

▷ The solution is $(-1, -6)$.

You can substitute -1 for x in either equation. Using Equation 2,
$$7(-1) - 2y = 5$$
$$-2y = 12$$
$$y = -6.$$

Check

Equation 1

$$y = 2x - 4$$
$$-6 \overset{?}{=} 2(-1) - 4$$
$$-6 = -6 \checkmark$$

Equation 2

$$7x - 2y = 5$$
$$7(-1) - 2(-6) \overset{?}{=} 5$$
$$5 = 5 \checkmark$$

Try It Solve the system by substitution. Check your solution.

1. $y = 2x + 3$
$ y = 5x$

2. $4x + 2y = 0$
$ y = \dfrac{1}{2}x - 5$

3. $x = 5y + 3$
$ 2x + 4y = -1$

EXAMPLE 2 **Solving a System of Linear Equations**

Solve the system using any method. $2x + 3y = -3$ Equation 1

$2x = y + 5$ Equation 2

Step 1: Both equations have a term of $2x$. So, one solution method is to substitute $y + 5$ for $2x$ in Equation 1 and solve to find the value of y.

$2x + 3y = -3$	Equation 1
$y + 5 + 3y = -3$	Substitute $y + 5$ for $2x$.
$4y + 5 = -3$	Combine like terms.
$4y = -8$	Subtract 5 from each side.
$y = -2$	Divide each side by 4.

Step 2: Substitute -2 for y in Equation 2 and solve for x.

$2x = y + 5$	Equation 2
$2x = -2 + 5$	Substitute -2 for y.
$2x = 3$	Add.
$x = 1.5$	Divide each side by 2.

The solution is $(1.5, -2)$.

Math Practice

Calculate Accurately
Solve the system using a different substitution. Which method do you prefer?

Try It Solve the system. Explain your choice of method.

4. $y = -3x + 2$
   $y = 2$

5. $4y = x$
   $x + 4y = -8$

6. $2x + 2y = 1$
   $-x + 2y = -3$

 Self-Assessment *for Concepts & Skills*

Solve each exercise. Then rate your understanding of the success criteria in your journal.

7. **(MP) REASONING** Does solving a system of linear equations by graphing give the same solution as solving by substitution? Explain.

SOLVING A SYSTEM OF LINEAR EQUATIONS Solve the system by substitution. Check your solution.

8. $y = x - 8$
   $y = 2x - 14$

9. $x = 2y + 2$
   $2x - 5y = 1$

10. $x - 5y = 1$
    $-2x + 9y = -1$

CHOOSING A SOLUTION METHOD Solve the system. Explain your choice of method.

11. $y = -x + 3$
    $y = 2x$

12. $0.5x + y = 2$
    $0.5x = 1 + y$

13. $x = 5y$
    $y = 22 - 2x$

EXAMPLE 3 **Modeling Real Life**

You are planning a birthday party. You buy a total of 50 turkey burgers and veggie burgers for $90.00. You pay $2.00 per turkey burger and $1.50 per veggie burger. How many of each burger do you buy?

Use a verbal model to write a system of linear equations. Let x represent the number of turkey burgers and let y represent the number of veggie burgers.

| Number of turkey burgers, x | + | Number of veggie burgers, y | = | Total number of burgers |

| Cost per turkey burger | · | Number of turkey burgers, x | + | Cost per veggie burger | · | Number of veggie burgers, y | = | Total cost |

The system is: $x + y = 50$ Equation 1
$2x + 1.5y = 90$ Equation 2

Step 1: One solution method is to rewrite Equation 1 as $x = 50 - y$. Then substitute $50 - y$ for x in Equation 2 and solve to find the value of y.

$2x + 1.5y = 90$ Equation 2
$2(50 - y) + 1.5y = 90$ Substitute $50 - y$ for x.
$100 - 2y + 1.5y = 90$ Distributive Property
$-0.5y = -10$ Simplify.
$y = 20$ Divide each side by -0.5.

Check

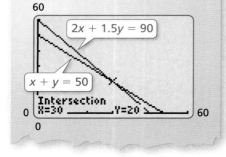

Step 2: Substitute 20 for y in Equation 1 and solve for x.

$x + y = 50$ Equation 1
$x + 20 = 50$ Substitute 20 for y.
$x = 30$ Subtract 20 from each side.

▷ You buy 30 turkey burgers and 20 veggie burgers.

Self-Assessment for Problem Solving

Solve each exercise. Then rate your understanding of the success criteria in your journal.

14. To stock your school store, you buy a total of 25 sweatshirts and hats for $172.50. You pay $8.00 per sweatshirt and $2.50 per hat. How many of each item do you buy?

15. **DIG DEEPER!** The length of a volleyball court is twice its width. The perimeter of the court is 180 feet. Find the area of the volleyball court. Justify your answer.

5.2 Practice

 Go to *BigIdeasMath.com* to get HELP with solving the exercises.

▶ Review & Refresh

Solve the system by graphing.

1. $y = 2x - 3$
   $y = -x + 9$

2. $6x + y = -2$
   $y = -3x + 1$

3. $4x + 2y = 2$
   $3x = 4 - y$

4. Use the figure to find the measure of $\angle 2$.

   A. $17°$ B. $73°$

   C. $83°$ D. $107°$

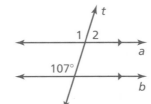

▶▶ Concepts, Skills, & Problem Solving

SOLVING A SYSTEM ALGEBRAICALLY Find the value of each symbol in the system.
(See Exploration 1, p. 205.)

5. $☽ + 1 = ★ + ★$ Equation 1

   $☽ = 3 + ★$ Equation 2

6. $☼ - ❄ = -2$ Equation 1

   $☼ - ❄ = 1 + ❄$ Equation 2

SOLVING A SYSTEM OF LINEAR EQUATIONS Solve the system by substitution. Check your solution.

7. $y = x - 4$
   $y = 4x - 10$

8. $y = 2x + 5$
   $y = 3x - 1$

9. $x = 2y + 7$
   $3x - 2y = 3$

10. $4x - 2y = 14$
    $y = \frac{1}{2}x - 1$

11. $2x = y - 10$
    $2x + 7 = 2y$

12. $8x - \frac{1}{3}y = 0$
    $12x + 3 = y$

13. $y - x = 0$
    $2x - 5y = 9$

14. $x + 4y = 14$
    $3x + 4y = 22$

15. $-2x - 5y = 3$
    $3x + 8y = -6$

16. **(MP) MODELING REAL LIFE** There are a total of 64 students in a filmmaking club and a yearbook club. The filmmaking club has 14 more students than the yearbook club.

    a. Write a system of linear equations that represents this situation.

    b. How many students are in the filmmaking club? the yearbook club?

17. **MP MODELING REAL LIFE** A drama club earns $1040 from a production by selling 64 adult tickets and 132 student tickets. An adult ticket costs twice as much as a student ticket.

    a. Write a system of linear equations that represents this situation.

    b. What is the cost of each ticket?

18. **OPEN-ENDED** Write a system of linear equations that has the ordered pair $(1, 6)$ as its solution.

CHOOSING A SOLUTION METHOD **Solve the system. Explain your choice of method.**

19. $y - x = 4$
    $x + y = 6$

20. $0.5x + y = 4$
    $0.5x - y = -1$

21. $y = 2x + 5$
    $y = -3x$

22. **CRITICAL THINKING** A system consists of two different proportional relationships. What is the solution of the system? Justify your answer.

23. **GEOMETRY** The measure of the obtuse angle in the isosceles triangle is two and a half times the measure of one of the acute angles. Write and solve a system of linear equations to find the measure of each angle.

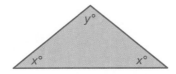

24. **MP NUMBER SENSE** The sum of the digits of a two-digit number is 8. When the digits are reversed, the number increases by 36. Find the original number.

25. **DIG DEEPER!** A hospital employs a total of 77 nurses and doctors. The ratio of nurses to doctors is $9:2$. How many nurses are employed at the hospital? How many doctors are employed at the hospital?

26. **MP REPEATED REASONING** A DJ has a total of 1075 dance, rock, and country songs on her system. The dance selection is three times the rock selection. The country selection has 105 more songs than the rock selection. How many songs on the system are dance? rock? country?

5.3 Solving Systems of Linear Equations by Elimination

Learning Target: Understand how to solve systems of linear equations by elimination.

Success Criteria:
- I can add or subtract equations in a system.
- I can use the Multiplication Property of Equality to produce equivalent equations.
- I can solve a system of linear equations by elimination.

EXPLORATION 1

Solving a System Algebraically

Work with a partner. A student found the value of x in the system using substitution as shown.

$$3x + y = 1 \qquad \text{Equation 1}$$
$$x - y = -5 \qquad \text{Equation 2}$$

Step 1:
$$3x + y = 1 \qquad \text{Equation 1}$$
$$x + 5 = y \qquad \text{Revised Equation 2}$$

Step 2:
$$3x + x + 5 = 1 \qquad \text{Substitute } x + 5 \text{ for } y \text{ in Equation 1.}$$
$$4x + 5 = 1 \qquad \text{Combine like terms.}$$
$$4x = -4 \qquad \text{Subtract 5 from each side.}$$
$$x = -1 \qquad \text{Divide each side by 4.}$$

a. Find another way to obtain the equation $4x = -4$ from the original system. Does your method produce an equation in one variable for any system? Explain.

b. Can you use your method in part (a) to solve each system below? If so, solve the system. If not, replace one of the equations with an equivalent equation that allows you to use your method in part (a). Then solve the system.

System 1:
$$2x + 3y = -4 \qquad \text{Equation 1}$$
$$2x - 3y = 8 \qquad \text{Equation 2}$$

System 2:
$$x + 4y = -5 \qquad \text{Equation 1}$$
$$3x - 2y = 13 \qquad \text{Equation 2}$$

Math Practice

Find Entry Points
What do you look for when deciding how to solve a system of equations?

c. Compare your solution methods in part (b) with other pairs of students.

When the equations in a linear system have a pair of like terms with the same or opposite coefficients, you can add or subtract the equations to *eliminate* one of the variables. Then use the resulting equation to solve the system.

EXAMPLE 1 Solving a System of Linear Equations by Elimination

Solve the system by elimination.

$$x + 3y = -2 \qquad \text{Equation 1}$$
$$x - 3y = 16 \qquad \text{Equation 2}$$

Step 1: Notice that the coefficients of the y-terms are opposites. So, you can add the equations to obtain an equation in one variable, x.

$x + 3y = -2$	Equation 1
$\underline{x - 3y = \ 16}$	Equation 2
$2x \qquad\ = \ 14$	Add the equations.

Because the coefficients of x are the same, you can also subtract the equations in Step 1.

$$x + 3y = -2$$
$$\underline{x - 3y = 16}$$
$$6y = -18$$

So, $y = -3$.

Step 2: Solve for x.

$2x = 14$	Equation from Step 1
$x = 7$	Divide each side by 2.

Step 3: Substitute 7 for x in one of the original equations and solve for y.

$x + 3y = -2$	Equation 1
$7 + 3y = -2$	Substitute 7 for x.
$3y = -9$	Subtract 7 from each side.
$y = -3$	Divide each side by 3.

▷ The solution is $(7, -3)$.

Check

Equation 1

$$x + 3y = -2$$
$$7 + 3(-3) \stackrel{?}{=} -2$$
$$-2 = -2 \ \checkmark$$

Equation 2

$$x - 3y = 16$$
$$7 - 3(-3) \stackrel{?}{=} 16$$
$$16 = 16 \ \checkmark$$

Try It Solve the system by elimination. Check your solution.

1. $2x - y = 9$
$4x + y = 21$

2. $-5x + 2y = 13$
$5x + y = -1$

3. $3x + 4y = -6$
$7x + 4y = -14$

To solve a system by elimination, you may need to multiply one or both equations by a constant so a pair of like terms has the same or opposite coefficients.

EXAMPLE 2 **Solving a System of Linear Equations by Elimination**

Solve the system by elimination. $-6x + 5y = 25$ Equation 1

$-2x - 4y = 14$ Equation 2

Step 1: Notice that no pairs of like terms have the same or opposite coefficients. One way to solve by elimination is to multiply Equation 2 by 3 so that the x-terms have a coefficient of -6.

$-6x + 5y = 25$ $-6x + 5y = 25$ Equation 1

$-2x - 4y = 14$ **Multiply by 3.** $-6x - 12y = 42$ Revised Equation 2

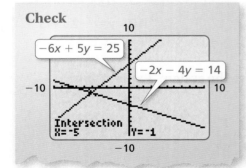

Notice that you can also multiply Equation 2 by -3 and then add the equations.

Step 2: Subtract the equations to obtain an equation in one variable, y.

$-6x + 5y = 25$ Equation 1

$\underline{-6x - 12y = 42}$ Revised Equation 2

$17y = -17$ Subtract the equations.

Step 3: Solve for y.

$17y = -17$ Equation from Step 2

$y = -1$ Divide each side by 17.

Step 4: Substitute -1 for y in one of the original equations and solve for x.

$-2x - 4y = 14$ Equation 2

$-2x - 4(-1) = 14$ Substitute -1 for y.

$-2x + 4 = 14$ Multiply.

$-2x = 10$ Subtract 4 from each side.

$x = -5$ Divide each side by -2.

▷ The solution is $(-5, -1)$.

Check

10

$-6x + 5y = 25$

$-2x - 4y = 14$

-10 10

Intersection
X=-5   Y=-1

-10

Try It Solve the system by elimination. Check your solution.

4. $3x + y = 11$
$6x + 3y = 24$

5. $4x - 5y = -19$
$-x - 2y = 8$

6. $5y = 15 - 5x$
$y = -2x + 3$

EXAMPLE 3 **Choosing a Solution Method**

Which are efficient approaches to solving the system?

$$x - 2y = 6 \qquad \text{Equation 1}$$
$$-x + 4y = 6 \qquad \text{Equation 2}$$

A. Add the equations.

B. Multiply Equation 1 by 2 and subtract the equations.

C. Solve Equation 1 for x and substitute the result in Equation 2.

D. Substitute $-x + 4y$ for 6 in Equation 1.

The methods in Choices A and C result in an equation in one variable, y. You can solve these equations and use the results to find the value of x.

The methods in Choices B and D will not result in an equation in one variable.

 So, Choices A and C are efficient approaches to solving the system.

Try It

7. Change one word in Choice B so that it represents an efficient approach to solving the system.

Self-Assessment for Concepts & Skills

Solve each exercise. Then rate your understanding of the success criteria in your journal.

SOLVING A SYSTEM OF LINEAR EQUATIONS Solve the system by elimination. Check your solution.

8. $2x + y = 4$
$\quad -2x + 2y = 5$

9. $-x + y = 1$
$\quad -3x + y = 7$

10. $y = -2x + 3$
$\quad 4x - 5y = 13$

CHOOSING A SOLUTION METHOD Solve the system. Explain your choice of method.

11. $y = 6x - 1$
$\quad y = 3x - 4$

12. $3x = y + 2$
$\quad 3x + 2y = 5$

13. $2x - y = 7$
$\quad x + y = 5$

14. **WHICH ONE DOESN'T BELONG?** Which system does *not* belong with the other three? Explain your reasoning.

$3x + 3y = 3$	$-2x + y = 6$	$2x + 3y = 11$	$x + y = 5$
$2x - 3y = 7$	$2x - 3y = -10$	$3x - 2y = 10$	$3x - y = 3$

EXAMPLE 4 **Modeling Real Life**

You buy 8 hostas and 15 daylilies for \$193. Your friend buys 3 hostas and 12 daylilies for \$117. Find the cost of each daylily.

Use a verbal model to write a system of linear equations. Let x represent the cost of each hosta and let y represent the cost of each daylily.

Number of hostas	$\cdot$	Cost of each hosta, x	$+$	Number of daylilies	$\cdot$	Cost of each daylily, y	$=$	Total cost

The system is:
$$8x + 15y = 193 \qquad \text{Equation 1 (You)}$$
$$3x + 12y = 117 \qquad \text{Equation 2 (Your friend)}$$

Step 1: One way to find the cost of each daylily is to eliminate the x-terms and solve for y. Multiply Equation 1 by 3 and Equation 2 by 8.

$8x + 15y = 193$ **Multiply by 3.** ➡ $24x + 45y = 579$ Revised Equation 1

$3x + 12y = 117$ **Multiply by 8.** ➡ $24x + 96y = 936$ Revised Equation 2

Step 2: Subtract the revised equations.

$$
\begin{array}{ll}
24x + 45y = 579 & \text{Revised Equation 1} \\
\underline{24x + 96y = 936} & \text{Revised Equation 2} \\
{-51y} = -357 & \text{Subtract the equations.}
\end{array}
$$

Step 3: Solving the equation $-51y = -357$ gives $y = 7$.

▷ So, each daylily costs \$7.

Math Practice

Maintain Oversight

Do you need to find the value of x in Example 4? Explain your reasoning.

Self-Assessment for Problem Solving

Solve each exercise. Then rate your understanding of the success criteria in your journal.

15. A fitness instructor purchases exercise bikes and treadmills for two gyms. For the first gym, 2 exercise bikes and 3 treadmills cost \$2200. For the second gym, 3 exercise bikes and 4 treadmills cost \$3000. How much does a treadmill cost?

16. **DIG DEEPER!** At your school, cooking club members raise \$5 per member for a charity and woodshop club members raise \$10 per member for a different charity. The cooking club has three times as many members as the woodshop club. The difference of the number of members in the two clubs is 12 members. How much does each club raise?

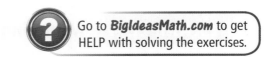

Go to *BigIdeasMath.com* to get HELP with solving the exercises.

▶ Review & Refresh

Solve the system by substitution. Check your solution.

1. $x = 5 - y$
$x - y = 3$

2. $x - 5y = 1$
$-x + y = 7$

3. $x + 6y = -2$
$-x = 3y - 10$

The vertices of a triangle are given. Draw the triangle and its image after a dilation with the given scale factor. Identify the type of dilation.

4. $A(-1, 1), B(1, 3), C(3, 1); k = 2$

5. $D(-8, -4), E(-4, 8), F(0, 0); k = 0.5$

▶▶ Concepts, Skills, & Problem Solving

SOLVING A SYSTEM ALGEBRAICALLY **Explain how to obtain the equation** $3x = 6$ **from the given system.** (See Exploration 1, p. 211.)

6. $2x + y = 5$
$x - y = 1$

7. $5x + 2y = 2$
$x + y = -2$

8. $-x + y = -3$
$6x - 3y = 15$

SOLVING A SYSTEM OF LINEAR EQUATIONS **Solve the system by elimination. Check your solution.**

9. $x + 3y = 5$
$-x - y = -3$

10. $x - 2y = -7$
$3x + 2y = 3$

11. $4x + 3y = -5$
$-x + 3y = -10$

12. $2x + 7y = 1$
$2x - 4y = 12$

13. $2x + 5y = 16$
$3x - 5y = -1$

14. $3x - 2y = 4$
$6x - 2y = -2$

15. (MP) **YOU BE THE TEACHER**
Your friend solves the system. Is your friend correct? Explain your reasoning.

> $5x + 2y = 9$ Equation 1
> $3x - 2y = -1$ Equation 2
> $2x \quad\quad = 10$
> $\quad\quad x = 5$
> The solution is $(5, -8)$.

16. (MP) **MODELING REAL LIFE**
You and your friend are selling raffle tickets for a new laptop. You sell 14 more tickets than your friend sells. Together, you and your friend sell 58 tickets.

   a. Write a system of linear equations that represents this situation.

   b. How many tickets do each of you sell?

17. (MP) **MODELING REAL LIFE** You can jog around your block twice and the park once in 10 minutes. You can jog around your block twice and the park 3 times in 22 minutes. Write a system of linear equations that represents this situation. How long does it take you to jog around the park?

SOLVING A SYSTEM OF LINEAR EQUATIONS Solve the system by elimination. Check your solution.

18. $2x - y = 0$
$3x - 2y = -3$

19. $x + 4y = 1$
$3x + 5y = 10$

20. $-2x + 3y = 7$
$5x + 8y = -2$

21. $3x + 3 = 3y$
$2x - 6y = 2$

22. $2x - 6 = 4y$
$7y = -3x + 9$

23. $5x = 4y + 8$
$3y = 3x - 3$

24. Ⓜ️ **YOU BE THE TEACHER** Your friend solves the system. Is your friend correct? Explain your reasoning.

$x + y = 1$ Equation 1   **Multiply by −5.** $-5x + y = 1$
$5x + 3y = -3$ Equation 2 $\underline{5x + 3y = -3}$
                                                      $4y = -2$
                                                      $y = -0.5$

The solution is $(-0.3, -0.5)$.

CHOOSING A SOLUTION METHOD Solve the system. Explain your choice of method.

25. $x + y = 4$
$x - y = 4$

26. $y = x - 3$
$y = -2x + 3$

27. $x + 2y = 0$
$2x - y = 4$

28. $y + 5x = 1$
$5y - x = 5$

29. $2 = x - 3y$
$-2x + y = 4$

30. $8x + 5y = 6$
$8x = 3 - 2y$

Ⓜ️ **NUMBER SENSE** For what value of a might you choose to solve the system by elimination? Explain.

31. $4x - y = 3$
$ax + 10y = 6$

32. $x - 7y = 6$
$-6x + ay = 9$

CRITICAL THINKING Determine whether the line through the first pair of points intersects the line through the second pair of points. Explain.

33. Line 1: $(-2, 1), (2, 7)$
Line 2: $(-4, -1), (0, 5)$

34. Line 1: $(-2, 8), (0, 2)$
Line 2: $(3, -2), (6, 4)$

35. Ⓜ️ **REASONING** Two airplanes are flying to the same airport. Their positions are shown in the graph. Write a system of linear equations that represents this situation. Solve the system by elimination to justify your answer.

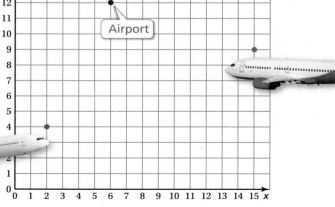

36. **MODELING REAL LIFE** A laboratory uses liquid nitrogen tanks of two different sizes. The combined volume of 3 large tanks and 2 small tanks is 24 liters. The combined volume of 2 large tanks and 3 small tanks is 21 liters. What is the volume of each size of tank? Justify your answer.

37. **PROBLEM SOLVING** The table shows the numbers of correct answers on a practice standardized test. You score 86 points on the test and your friend scores 76 points. How many points is each type of question worth?

	You	Your Friend
Multiple Choice	23	28
Short Response	10	5

38. **LOGIC** You solve a system of equations in which x represents the number of adult memberships sold and y represents the number of student memberships sold. Can $(-6, 24)$ be the solution of the system? Explain your reasoning.

39. **PROBLEM SOLVING** The table shows the activities of two tourists at a vacation resort. You want to go parasailing for 1 hour and horseback riding for 2 hours. How much do you expect to pay?

	Parasailing	Horseback Riding	Total Cost
Tourist 1	2 hours	5 hours	$205
Tourist 2	3 hours	3 hours	$240

40. **REASONING** Write a system of linear equations containing $2x + y = 0$ and that has the solution $(2, -4)$.

41. **REASONING** A metal alloy is a mixture of two or more metals. A jeweler wants to make 8 grams of 18-karat gold, which is 75% gold. The jeweler has an alloy that is 90% gold and an alloy that is 50% gold. How much of each alloy should the jeweler use?

42. **PROBLEM SOLVING** It takes a powerboat traveling with the current 30 minutes to go 10 miles. The return trip takes 50 minutes traveling against the current. What is the speed of the current?

43. **DIG DEEPER!** Solve the system of equations by elimination.

$$2x - y + 3z = -1$$
$$x + 2y - 4z = -1$$
$$y - 2z = 0$$

5.4 Solving Special Systems of Linear Equations

Learning Target: Solve systems with different numbers of solutions.

Success Criteria:
- I can determine the number of solutions of a system.
- I can solve a system of linear equations with any number of solutions.

EXPLORATION 1

Exploring Solutions of Systems

Work with a partner. You spend $50 on a sewing machine to make dog backpacks. Each backpack costs you $15 for materials.

   a. Represent the cost y (in dollars) to make x backpacks in the coordinate plane.

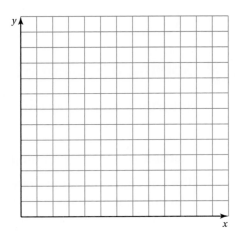

   b. You charge $25 per backpack. How many backpacks do you have to sell to *break even*? Use a graph to justify your answer.

   c. Can you break even when you sell each backpack for $20? $15? Use graphs to justify your answers.

Math Practice

Look for Structure

How can you use slopes and y-intercepts to determine the number of solutions of a system of linear equations?

   d. Explain whether it is possible for a system of linear equations to have the numbers of solutions below.

- no solution
- exactly one solution
- exactly two solutions
- infinitely many solutions

Key Idea

Solutions of Systems of Linear Equations

A system of linear equations can have *one solution, no solution,* or *infinitely many solutions.*

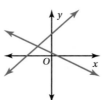 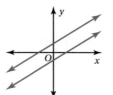 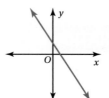

One solution

The lines intersect.
• different slopes

No solution

The lines are parallel.
• same slope
• different y-intercepts

Infinitely many solutions

The lines are the same.
• same slope
• same y-intercept

EXAMPLE 1   **Solving a System with No Solution**

Solve the system using any method.

$y = 3x + 1$ Equation 1
$y = 3x - 3$ Equation 2

Method 1: Solve by graphing.

The lines have the same slope, 3, and different y-intercepts, 1 and -3. So, the lines are parallel. Because parallel lines do not intersect, there is no point that is a solution of both equations.

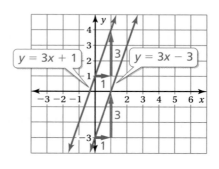

▷ So, the system has no solution.

You can also solve by substituting $3x - 3$ for y in Equation 1.

$3x - 3 = 3x + 1$
$-3 = 1$ ✗

The equation $-3 = 1$ is never true. So, the system has no solution.

Method 2: Solve by inspection.

Notice that you can rewrite the system as

$-3x + y = 1$ Revised Equation 1
$-3x + y = -3$.   Revised Equation 2

▷ The expression $-3x + y$ cannot be equal to 1 and -3 at the same time. So, the system has no solution.

Try It Solve the system. Explain your choice of method.

1. $y = -x + 3$
    $y = -x + 5$

2. $y = -5x - 2$
    $5x + y = 0$

3. $x = 2y + 10$
    $2x + 3y = -1$

EXAMPLE 2 **Solving a System with Infinitely Many Solutions**

Solve the system using any method. $x + 2y = 6$ Equation 1

$3x + 6y = 18$ Equation 2

Method 1: Solve by graphing.

The lines have the same slope, $-\dfrac{1}{2}$, and the same y-intercept, 3.

So, the two equations in the system represent the same line.

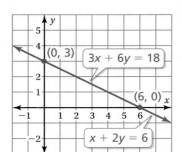

▷ All the points on the line are solutions of the system. So, the system has infinitely many solutions.

Method 2: Solve by elimination.

Multiply Equation 1 by 3 and subtract the equations.

$x + 2y = 6$	**Multiply by 3.**	$3x + 6y = 18$	Revised Equation 1
$3x + 6y = 18$		$\underline{3x + 6y = 18}$	Equation 2
		$0 = 0$	Subtract.

The equation $0 = 0$ is always true. You can also see from Revised Equation 1 that the two equations in the system are equivalent.

▷ All the points on the line are solutions of the system. So, the system has infinitely many solutions.

Try It Solve the system. Explain your choice of method.

4. $x + y = 3$
$x = y - 3$

5. $2x + y = 5$
$4x + 2y = 0$

6. $2x - 4y = 10$
$-12x + 24y = -60$

Self-Assessment for *Concepts & Skills*

Solve each exercise. Then rate your understanding of the success criteria in your journal.

MP **STRUCTURE** **Without graphing or solving, determine the number of solutions of the system. Explain your reasoning.**

7. $y = 5x - 9$
$y = 5x + 9$

8. $y = 6x + 2$
$y = 3x + 1$

9. $y = 8x - 2$
$y - 8x = -2$

CHOOSING A METHOD **Solve the system. Explain your choice of method.**

10. $2x + y = 6$
$x - y = 3$

11. $4y - 4x = 8$
$y = x + 2$

12. $5x - 4y = 12$
$7.5x = 6(y - 1)$

13. $-6x = 9$
$6x - y = 3$

14. $0.5x + 4y = -11$
$-1.5x - 12y = 33$

15. $x = y + 2$
$3x = 6(y + 2)$

EXAMPLE 3 **Modeling Real Life**

You and your friend plant an urban garden. You pay \$15.00 for 6 tomato plants and 6 pepper plants. Your friend pays \$22.50 for 9 tomato plants and 9 pepper plants. How much does each plant cost?

 Understand the problem.

You are given the total costs of two different combinations of tomato plants and pepper plants. You are asked to find the cost of each plant.

 Make a plan.

Use a verbal model to write a system of linear equations. Let x represent the cost of each tomato plant and let y represent the cost of each pepper plant. Then solve the system.

 **Solve and check.**

| Number of tomato plants | $\cdot$ | Cost of each tomato plant, x | $+$ | Number of pepper plants | $\cdot$ | Cost of each pepper plant, y | $=$ | Total cost |

The system is: $\quad 6x + 6y = 15 \qquad$ Equation 1 (You)

$\qquad\qquad\qquad\quad 9x + 9y = 22.5 \qquad$ Equation 2 (Your friend)

One way to solve is to use elimination. Multiply Equation 1 by 1.5 and subtract the equations.

$6x + 6y = 15$ **Multiply by 1.5.** ➡ $9x + 9y = 22.5 \qquad$ Revised Equation 1

$9x + 9y = 22.5 \qquad\qquad\qquad\qquad \underline{9x + 9y = 22.5} \qquad$ Equation 2

$\qquad\qquad\qquad\qquad\qquad\qquad\qquad\qquad\qquad\quad 0 = 0 \qquad$ Subtract.

The equation $0 = 0$ is always true. The system has infinitely many solutions.

> So, there is not enough information to find the cost of each plant.

Look Back Revised Equation 1 shows that the two equations in the system are equivalent.

So, the system has infinitely many solutions. ✓

 Self-Assessment for Problem Solving

Solve each exercise. Then rate your understanding of the success criteria in your journal.

16. Your friend wants to sell painted rocks. He spends \$10.00 on startup costs, and each painted rock costs him \$0.75 to make. A store offers to pay your friend's startup costs and buy his painted rocks for \$0.75 each. How many painted rocks does your friend need to sell to make a profit?

17. **DIG DEEPER!** The difference in age of two orangutans is 6 years. In 4 years, is it possible for the older orangutan to be twice as old as the younger orangutan? three times as old? Justify your answers.

5.4 Practice

 Go to *BigIdeasMath.com* to get HELP with solving the exercises.

▶ Review & Refresh

Solve the system by elimination. Check your solution.

1. $x + 2y = 4$
$-x - y = 2$

2. $2x - y = 1$
$x + 3y - 4 = 0$

3. $3x = -4y + 10$
$4x + 3y = 11$

Write an equation of the line that passes through the given points.

4. $(0, 0), (2, 6)$

5. $(0, -3), (3, 3)$

6. $(-6, 5), (0, 2)$

▶▶ Concepts, Skills, & Problem Solving

EXPLORING SOLUTIONS OF SYSTEMS **Use a graph to determine the number of solutions of the system.** (See Exploration 1, p. 219.)

7. $y = 2x + 1$
$y = 2x + 5$

8. $y + 8 = 0$
$y = -8$

9. $x + y = 2$
$5x + y = 9$

SOLVING A SYSTEM **Solve the system. Explain your choice of method.**

10. $y = 2x - 2$
$y = 2x + 9$

11. $y = 3x + 1$
$-x + 2y = -3$

12. $y = \dfrac{\pi}{3}x + \pi$
$-\pi x + 3y = -6\pi$

13. $y = -\dfrac{1}{6}x + 5$
$x + 6y = 30$

14. $\dfrac{1}{3}x + y = 1$
$2x + 6y = 6$

15. $-2x + y = 1.3$
$2(0.5x - y) = 4.6$

16. $2(x + y) = 9$
$1 = -4(x + y)$

17. $y = 9x$
$x + y = 1$

18. $0.2y = 4.6x + 1.2$
$-2.3x = -0.1y + 0.6$

19. 🔵 **YOU BE THE TEACHER** Your friend finds the number of solutions of the system. Is your friend correct? Explain your reasoning.

> $y = -2x + 4$
> $y = -2x + 6$
> The lines have the same slope, so there are infinitely many solutions.

20. 🔵 **REASONING** In a pig race, your pig has a head start of 3 feet and runs at a rate of 2 feet per second. Your friend's pig also runs at a rate of 2 feet per second. A system of linear equations that represents this situation is $y = 2x + 3$ and $y = 2x$. Does your friend's pig catch up to your pig? Explain.

21. **MP REASONING** One equation in a system of linear equations has a slope of -3. The other equation has a slope of 4. How many solutions does the system have? Explain.

22. **MP LOGIC** How can you use the slopes and the y-intercepts of equations in a system of linear equations to determine whether the system has *one solution, infinitely many solutions,* or *no solution*?

23. **MP PROBLEM SOLVING** You and a friend both work two different jobs. The system of linear equations represents the total earnings (in dollars) for x hours worked at the first job and y hours worked at the second job. Your friend earns twice as much as you.

$$4x + 8y = 64 \qquad \text{You}$$
$$8x + 16y = 128 \qquad \text{Your Friend}$$

   a. One week, both of you work 4 hours at the first job. How many hours do you and your friend work at the second job?

   b. Both of you work the same number of hours at the second job. Compare the numbers of hours you and your friend work at the first job.

24. **MP MODELING REAL LIFE** You download a digital album for $10.00. Then you and your friend each download the same number of individual songs for $0.99 each. Write a system of linear equations that represents this situation. Will you and your friend spend the same amount of money? Explain.

25. **MP MODELING REAL LIFE** The table shows the research activities of two students at an observatory. How much does a student pay to use the telescope for one hour? the supercomputer for one hour?

	Telescope Use	Supercomputer Use	Total Cost
Student 1	5 hours	3 hours	$70.50
Student 2	6 hours	2 hours	$67.00

26. **MP PRECISION** Does the system shown *always, sometimes,* or *never* have a solution when $a = b$? $a \geq b$? $a < b$? Explain your reasoning.

$$y = ax + 1$$
$$y = bx + 4$$

Group	1	2	3
Number of Lift Tickets	36	24	18
Number of Ski Rentals	18	12	18
Total Cost (dollars)	684	456	432

27. **MP LOGIC** The table shows the numbers of lift tickets and ski rentals sold to different groups. Is it possible to determine how much each lift ticket costs using the information for Groups 1 and 2? Groups 1 and 3? Justify your answers.

28. **DIG DEEPER!** Find the values of a and b so the system shown has the solution $(2, 3)$. Does the system have any other solutions for these values of a and b? Explain.

$$12x - 2by = 12$$
$$3ax - by = 6$$

Connecting Concepts

▶ Using the Problem-Solving Plan

1. An animal shelter has a total of 65 cats and dogs. The ratio of cats to dogs is 6 : 7. Find the number of cats and the number of dogs in the shelter.

 You know the total number of cats and dogs in an animal shelter, and the ratio of cats to dogs. You are asked to find the number of cats and the number of dogs in the shelter.

Make a plan. Write a system of equations. Use the total number of cats and dogs to write an equation relating the number x of cats and the number y of dogs. Use the ratio of cats to dogs to write a second equation. Then solve the system.

Solve and check. Use the plan to solve the problem. Then check your solution.

2. The measure of $\angle 1$ is 15 degrees less than two times the measure of $\angle 2$. Find the measure of each of the four angles formed by the intersecting lines. Justify your answer.

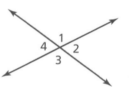

3. A landscaper plants grass seed over the entire area of two parks that are similar in shape. The ratio of the perimeter of Park A to the perimeter of Park B is 2 : 1. The parks have a combined area of 9000 square feet. How many square feet does the landscaper cover with grass seed at Park A? Park B? Justify your answer.

Performance Task

Mixing Alloys

At the beginning of this chapter, you watched a STEAM Video called "Gold Alloys." You are now ready to complete the performance task related to this video, available at *BigIdeasMath.com*. Be sure to use the problem-solving plan as you work through the performance task.

5 Chapter Review

Go to *BigIdeasMath.com* to download blank graphic organizers.

▶ Review Vocabulary

Write the definition and give an example of each vocabulary term.

system of linear equations, *p. 200* solution of a system of linear equations, *p. 200*

▶ Graphic Organizers

You can use a **Four Square** to organize information about a concept. Each of the four squares can be a category, such as definition, vocabulary, example, non-example, words, algebra, table, numbers, visual, graph, or equation. Here is an example of a Four Square for *solving systems of linear equations by graphing*.

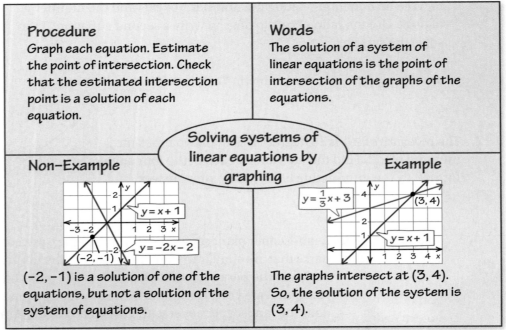

Choose and complete a graphic organizer to help you study the concept.

1. solving systems of linear equations by substitution

2. solving systems of linear equations by elimination

3. systems of linear equations with no solution

4. systems of linear equations with infinitely many solutions

"Here is my **Four Square** about bonsai. This bonsai tree is over 90 years old."

Chapter Self-Assessment

As you complete the exercises, use the scale below to rate your understanding of the success criteria in your journal.

1 I do not understand.

2 I can do it with help.

3 I can do it on my own.

4 I can teach someone else.

5.1 Solving Systems of Linear Equations by Graphing *(pp. 199–204)*

Learning Target: Understand how to solve systems of linear equations by graphing.

Solve the system by graphing.

1. $y = 2x - 3$
$y = x + 2$

2. $y = -x + 4$
$x + 3y = 0$

3. $x - y = -2$
$2x - 3y = -2$

Use a graphing calculator to solve the system.

4. $y = -0.5x$
$y = 0.75x + 1.25$

5. $y = 0.2x - 3$
$10x + 3y = 5$

6. $2.6x + 1.3y = 7.8$
$1.2x - 3.6y = 12$

7. The sum of two numbers is 38. Find each number when one number is 8 more than the other number. Use a system of linear equations to justify your answer.

8. You observe the heights of two plants for an experiment. Plant A has a height of 8 centimeters and grows 1 centimeter each week. Plant B has a height of 4 centimeters and grows 2 centimeters each week.

   a. Write a system of linear equations that represents this situation.

   b. Will the plants ever have the same height? If so, what is the height?

9. Write a system of linear equations containing the equation $y = -3x + 2$ and that has a solution of $(-1, 5)$. Use a graph to justify your answer.

5.2 Solving Systems of Linear Equations by Substitution (pp. 205–210)

Learning Target: Understand how to solve systems of linear equations by substitution.

Solve the system by substitution. Check your solution.

10. $y = -3x - 7$

$y = x + 9$

11. $\frac{1}{2}x + y = -4$

$y = 2x + 16$

12. $-x + 5y = 28$

$x + 3y = 20$

13. Zoo admission costs $6 for children and $9 for adults. On Monday, 2200 people visit the zoo and the zoo collects $14,850 in admissions.

    a. Write a system of linear equations that represents this situation.

    b. How many zoo visitors are children? adults?

Solve the system. Explain your choice of method.

14. $y = x - 2$

$y = -2x + 1$

15. $3y + 9 = 3x$

$y = -\frac{1}{3}x + 1$

16. $-x + 2y = -4$

$4y = x$

17. The measure of an acute angle in a right triangle is one-fourth the measure of the other acute angle. Write a system of linear equations that represents this situation and use it to find the measures of the acute angles of the triangle.

5.3 Solving Systems of Linear Equations by Elimination (pp. 211–218)

Learning Target: Understand how to solve systems of linear equations by elimination.

Solve the system by elimination. Check your solution.

18. $2x + 5y = 60$

$2x - 5y = -20$

19. $4x - 3y = 15$

$2x + y = -5$

20. A gift basket that contains jars of jam and packages of bread mix costs $45. There are 8 items in the basket. Jars of jam cost $6 each, and packages of bread mix cost $5 each. Write and solve a system of linear equations to find the number of each item in the gift basket.

21. When might it be easier to solve a system by elimination instead of graphing?

22. You have a total of 10 coins consisting of nickels and dimes in your pocket. The value of the coins is $0.70. Write and solve a system of linear equations to find the numbers of nickels and dimes in your pocket.

5.4 Solving Special Systems of Linear Equations *(pp. 219–224)*

Learning Target: Solve systems with different numbers of solutions.

Solve the system. Explain your choice of method.

23. $x + 2y = -5$
$x - 2y = -5$

24. $3x - 2y = 1$
$9x - 6y = 3$

25. $8x - 2y = 16$
$-4x + y = 8$

26. $4y = x - 8$
$-\dfrac{1}{4}x + y = -1$

27. $-2x + y = -2$
$3x + y = 3$

28. $3x = \dfrac{1}{3}y + 2$
$9x - y = -6$

29. You have $50 in your savings account and plan to deposit $10 each week. Your friend has $25 in her savings account and plans to also deposit $10 each week.

   a. Write a system of linear equations that represents this situation.

   b. Will your friend's account ever have the same amount of money as your account? Explain.

Write a system of linear equations that fits the description. Use a graph to justify your answer.

30. The system has no solution.

31. The system has infinitely many solutions.

32. The system has one solution.

33. Solve the system by graphing, by substitution, and by elimination. Which method do you prefer? Explain your reasoning.

$$5x + y = 8$$
$$2y = -10x + 8$$

34. Your friend chooses to solve the system of equations by graphing. Would you choose the same method? Why or why not?

$$5x + 2y = 12$$
$$y = x - 8$$

1. Solve the system by graphing.

$$y = \frac{1}{2}x + 10$$

$$y = 4x - 4$$

2. Solve the system by substitution. Check your solution.

$$-3x + y = 2$$

$$-x + y - 4 = 0$$

3. Solve the system by elimination. Check your solution.

$$x + y = 12$$
$$3x = 2y + 6$$

4. Solve the system. Explain your choice of method.

$$-2x + y + 3 = 0$$
$$3x + 4y = -1$$

Without graphing or solving, determine whether the system of linear equations has *one solution*, *infinitely many solutions*, or *no solution*. Explain your reasoning.

5. $y = 4x + 8$
   $y = 5x + 1$

6. $2y = 16x - 2$
   $y = 8x - 1$

7. $y = -3x + 2$
   $6x + 2y = 10$

8. In the diagram, the measure of $\angle 1$ is three times the measure of $\angle 2$. Find the measure of each angle.

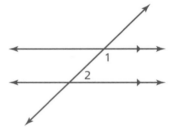

9. The price of 2 pears and 6 apples is $14. The price of 3 pears and 9 apples is $21. Can you determine the unit prices for pears and apples? Explain.

10. A bouquet of lilies and tulips has 12 flowers. Lilies cost $3 each, and tulips cost $2 each. The bouquet costs $32. Write and solve a system of linear equations to find the numbers of lilies and tulips in the bouquet.

GUEST CHECK

4 Specials
2 Glasses of milk

$28.00

GUEST CHECK

3 Specials
4 Glasses of milk

$26.25

11. How much does it cost for 2 specials and 2 glasses of milk?

Cumulative Practice

1. What is the solution of the system of equations?

$$y = -\frac{2}{3}x - 1$$
$$4x + 6y = -6$$

A. $\left(-\frac{3}{2}, 0\right)$ **B.** $(0, -1)$

C. no solution

D. infinitely many solutions

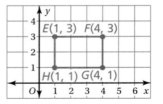

Test-Taking Strategy
Read Question Before Answering

I buy 2 toys and 1 new leash for $7. You buy 3 toys and 1 new leash for $9. How much is a new leash?

Ⓐ $2   Ⓑ $3   Ⓒ $4   Ⓓ $5

A leash? Me? I don't think so!

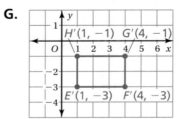

"Take your time and read the question carefully before choosing your answer."

2. What is the value of x?

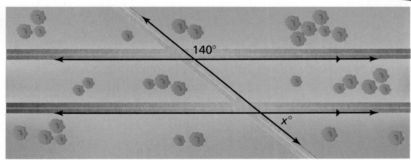

140°

$x°$

3. Which of the following shows Rectangle $E'F'G'H'$, the image of Rectangle $EFGH$ after it is translated 4 units down?

[Graph showing Rectangle EFGH with vertices E(1, 3), F(4, 3), H(1, 1), G(4, 1)]

F.

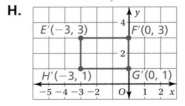

[Graph with E'(1, −1), F'(4, −1), H'(1, −3), G'(4, −3)]

G.

[Graph with H'(1, −1), G'(4, −1), E'(1, −3), F'(4, −3)]

H.

[Graph with E'(−3, 3), F'(0, 3), H'(−3, 1), G'(0, 1)]

I.

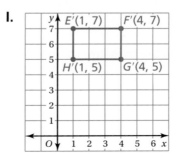

[Graph with E'(1, 7), F'(4, 7), H'(1, 5), G'(4, 5)]

4. Which point is a solution of the system of equations?

$$x + 3y = 10$$
$$x = 2y - 5$$

A. $(1, 3)$

B. $(3, 1)$

C. $(55, -15)$

D. $(-35, -15)$

5. The graph of a system of two linear equations is shown. Which point is the solution of the system?

F. $(-1, 2)$

G. $(0, 4)$

H. $(2, -1)$

I. $(0, 0)$

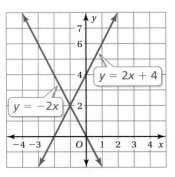

6. A scenic train ride has one price for adults and one price for children. One family of two adults and two children pays $62 for the train ride. Another family of one adult and four children pays $70. Which system of linear equations can you use to find the price x for an adult and the price y for a child?

A. $2x + 2y = 70$
$x + 4y = 62$

B. $x + y = 62$
$x + y = 70$

C. $2x + 2y = 62$
$4x + y = 70$

D. $2x + 2y = 62$
$x + 4y = 70$

7. Which of the following is true about the graph of the linear equation $y = -7x + 5$?

F. The slope is 5, and the y-intercept is -7.

G. The slope is -5, and the y-intercept is -7.

H. The slope is -7, and the y-intercept is -5.

I. The slope is -7, and the y-intercept is 5.

8. What is the measure (in degrees) of the exterior angle of the triangle?

9. The graph of which equation is parallel to the line that passes through the points $(-1, 5)$ and $(4, 7)$?

    A. $y = \dfrac{2}{3}x + 6$ **B.** $y = -\dfrac{5}{2}x + 4$

    C. $y = \dfrac{2}{5}x + 1$ **D.** $y = \dfrac{5}{2}x - 1$

10. You buy 3 T-shirts and 2 pairs of shorts for $42.50. Your friend buys 5 T-shirts and 3 pairs of shorts for $67.50. Use a system of linear equations to find the cost of each T-shirt. Show your work and explain your reasoning.

11. The red figure is congruent to the blue figure. Which of the following is a sequence of rigid motions between the figures?

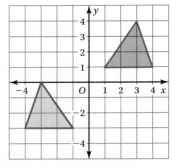

    F. Translate the red triangle 6 units left and then 4 units down.

    G. Reflect the red triangle in the x-axis, and then translate 4 units down.

    H. Reflect the red triangle in the y-axis, and then translate 4 units down.

    I. Rotate the red triangle 180° clockwise about the origin.

12. Which of the following is true about the graph of the linear equation $y = 2$?

    A. The graph is a vertical line that passes through $(2, 0)$.

    B. The graph is a vertical line that passes through $(0, 2)$.

    C. The graph is a horizontal line that passes through $(2, 0)$.

    D. The graph is a horizontal line that passes through $(0, 2)$.

13. The sum of one-third of a number and 10 is equal to 13. What is the number?

    F. $\dfrac{8}{3}$ **G.** 9   **H.** 29   **I.** 69

14. Solve the equation $4x + 7y = 16$ for x.

    A. $x = 4 + \dfrac{7}{4}y$ **B.** $x = 4 - \dfrac{7}{4}y$

    C. $x = 4 + \dfrac{4}{7}y$ **D.** $x = 16 - 7y$

6 Data Analysis and Displays

- **6.1** Scatter Plots
- **6.2** Lines of Fit
- **6.3** Two-Way Tables
- **6.4** Choosing a Data Display

Chapter Learning Target:
Understand data displays.

Chapter Success Criteria:
- ☐ I can identify a data set.
- ☐ I can use appropriate data displays to represent a situation.
- ☒ I can interpret a data set.
- ☒ I can compare different data sets.

STEAM Video: "Fuel Economy"

Fuel Economy

The *fuel economy* of a vehicle is a measure of the efficiency of the vehicle's engine. What are the benefits of using a car with high fuel economy?

Watch the STEAM Video "Fuel Economy." Then answer the following questions.

1. Tory says that the *footprint* of a vehicle is the area of the rectangle formed by the wheel base and the track width. What is the footprint of a car with a wheel base of 106 inches and a track width of 61 inches?

2. The graph shows the relationship between the fuel economy and the footprint for four vehicles.

   a. What happens to the fuel economy as the footprint increases?

   b. Plot the point (50, 40) on the graph. What does this point represent? Does the point fit in with the other points? Explain.

Performance Task

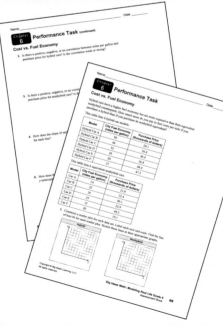

Cost vs. Fuel Economy

After completing this chapter, you will be able to use the concepts you learned to answer the questions in the *STEAM Video Performance Task*. You will be given fuel economies and purchase prices of hybrid and nonhybrid car models.

Model	City Fuel Economy (miles per gallon)	Purchase Price (thousands of dollars)
Car A	24	21.8
Car B	22	22.4
Car C	18	40.1

You will be asked to create graphs to compare car models. Why might you want to know the relationship between the fuel economy and the purchase price of a vehicle?

Getting Ready for Chapter 6

Chapter Exploration

1. **Work with a partner. The table shows the number of absences and the final grade for each student in a sample.**

Absences	Final Grade
0	95
3	88
2	90
5	83
7	79
9	70
4	85
1	94
10	65
8	75

   a. Write the ordered pairs from the table. Then plot them in a coordinate plane.

   b. Describe the relationship between absences and final grade.

   c. **MODELING** A student has been absent 6 days. Use the data to predict the student's final grade. Explain how you found your answer.

2. **Work with a partner. Match the data sets with the most appropriate scatter plot. Explain your reasoning.**

   a. month of birth and birth weight for infants at a day care

   b. quiz score and test score of each student in a class

   c. age and value of laptop computers

   i. 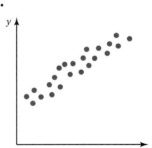   **ii.** 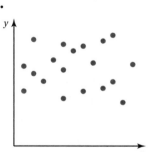   **iii.**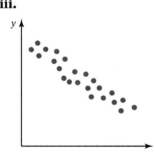

Vocabulary

The following vocabulary terms are defined in this chapter. Think about what each term might mean and record your thoughts.

scatter plot   two-way table
line of fit   joint frequency

6.1 Scatter Plots

Learning Target: Use scatter plots to describe patterns and relationships between two quantities.

Success Criteria:
- I can make a scatter plot.
- I can identify outliers, gaps, and clusters in a scatter plot.
- I can use scatter plots to describe relationships between data.

EXPLORATION 1

Finding Relationships Between Data

Work with a partner. The weights and circumferences of several sports balls are shown.

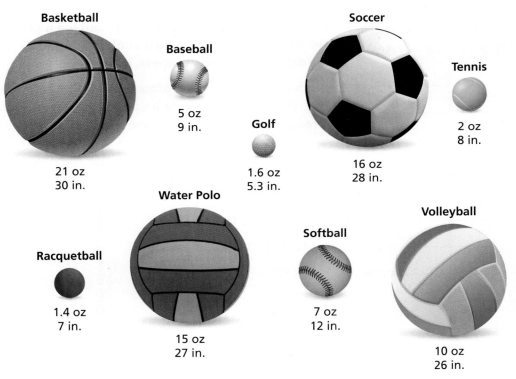

Basketball
21 oz
30 in.

Baseball
5 oz
9 in.

Golf
1.6 oz
5.3 in.

Soccer
16 oz
28 in.

Tennis
2 oz
8 in.

Racquetball
1.4 oz
7 in.

Water Polo
15 oz
27 in.

Softball
7 oz
12 in.

Volleyball
10 oz
26 in.

Math Practice

Label Axes
Can you graph the data with circumference on the *x*-axis and weight on the *y*-axis? Explain.

a. Represent the data in the coordinate plane. Explain your method.

b. Is there a relationship between the size and the weight of a sports ball? Explain your reasoning.

c. Is it reasonable to use the graph to predict the weights of the sports balls below? Explain your reasoning.

- **Kickball:** circumference = 26 in.
- **Bowling ball:** circumference = 27 in.

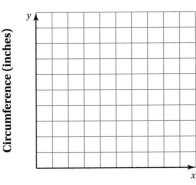

 **Key Idea**

Scatter Plot

A **scatter plot** is a graph that shows the relationship between two data sets. The two sets of data are graphed as ordered pairs in a coordinate plane.

EXAMPLE 1 **Making a Scatter Plot**

Age (years)	Data Used (gigabytes)
37	3.2
30	3.3
32	3.1
65	0.9
53	1.8
25	3.5
59	1.3
30	1.8
50	1.9
34	3.3

The table shows the ages of 10 adults and the numbers of gigabytes of cell phone data used by each adult in 1 month. Make a scatter plot of the data. Identify any outliers, gaps, or clusters.

Use ordered pairs (x, y) to represent the data, where x represents age (in years) and y represents data used (in gigabytes). Then plot the ordered pairs in a coordinate plane and analyze the scatter plot.

(37, 3.2) (25, 3.5)

(30, 3.3) (59, 1.3)

(32, 3.1) (30, 1.8)

(65, 0.9) (50, 1.9)

(53, 1.8) (34, 3.3)

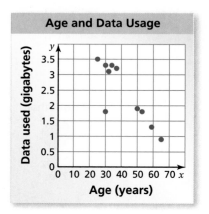

There appears to be an outlier at (30, 1.8). There is a cluster of data from 25 years old to 37 years old and a gap in the data from 37 years old to 50 years old.

Try It

1. Make a scatter plot of the data. Identify any outliers, gaps, or clusters.

Study Time (min), x	30	20	80	90	45	10	30	75	120	80
Test Score, y	80	74	95	97	85	62	83	90	70	91

A scatter plot can show relationships between two data sets.

Positive Linear Relationship

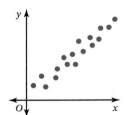

The points lie close to a line. As *x* increases, *y* increases.

Negative Linear Relationship

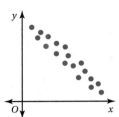

The points lie close to a line. As *x* increases, *y* decreases.

Nonlinear Relationship

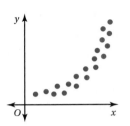

The points lie in the shape of a curve.

No Relationship

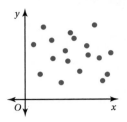

The points show no pattern.

EXAMPLE 2 **Identifying Relationships**

Describe the relationship between the data in the scatter plot.

The points appear to lie close to a line with a positive slope. As *x* increases, *y* increases.

▷ So, the scatter plot shows a positive linear relationship.

The closer the points are to a line, the stronger the linear relationship. This scatter plot shows a strong linear relationship.

Television Size and Price

Price (dollars) vs Television size (inches)

Try It

2. Describe the relationship between the data in Example 1.

Self-Assessment for Concepts & Skills

Solve each exercise. Then rate your understanding of the success criteria in your journal.

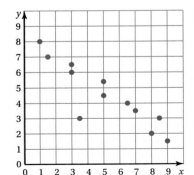

3. **SCATTER PLOT** Make a scatter plot of the data. Identify any outliers, gaps, or clusters. Then describe the relationship between the data.

Phone Age (months), *x*	3	22	23	22	8	12	24	4	23
Start-up Time (sec), *y*	24	34	34	33	36	29	34	27	33

4. **WHICH ONE DOESN'T BELONG?** Using the scatter plot, which point does *not* belong with the other three? Explain your reasoning.

(1, 8)   (3, 6.5)   (3.5, 3)   (8, 2)

EXAMPLE 3 **Modeling Real Life**

Fat (grams)	Calories
17	400
12	470
29	540
26	510
10	420
42	740
30	600
33	640
44	790
22	510
39	610
28	510

The table shows the amounts of fat and the numbers of calories in 12 restaurant sandwiches. How many grams of fat do you expect in a sandwich that contains 650 calories?

Use a scatter plot to determine whether a relationship exists between the data. If so, use the data to make a prediction.

Use ordered pairs (x, y), where x represents grams of fat and y represents the number of calories.

(17, 400)	(30, 600)
(12, 470)	(33, 640)
(29, 540)	(44, 790)
(26, 510)	(22, 510)
(10, 420)	(39, 610)
(42, 740)	(28, 510)

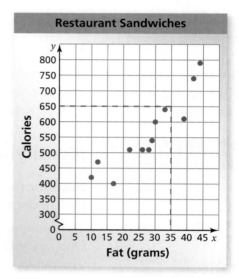

The points appear to lie close to a line with a positive slope. As x increases, y increases. So, the scatter plot shows a positive linear relationship.

▷ Looking at the graph, you can expect a sandwich that contains 650 calories to have about 35 grams of fat.

 Self-Assessment *for Problem Solving*

Solve each exercise. Then rate your understanding of the success criteria in your journal.

5. The table shows the high school and college grade point averages (GPAs) of 10 students. What college GPA do you expect for a high school student with a GPA of 2.7?

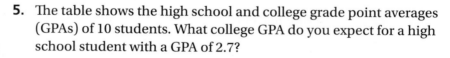

High School	2.6	2.8	3.2	4.0	3.8	3.7	3.5	3.5	3.4	1.4
College	2.4	2.5	3.0	3.6	3.5	3.6	3.6	3.4	3.2	0.5

6. The scatter plot shows the ages of 12 people and the numbers of pets each person owns. Identify any outliers, gaps, or clusters. Then describe the relationship between the data.

6.1 Practice

Go to *BigIdeasMath.com* to get
HELP with solving the exercises.

▶ Review & Refresh

Solve the system. Check your solution.

1. $y = -5x + 1$
$y = -5x - 2$

2. $2x + 2y = 9$
$x = 4.5 - y$

3. $y = -x$
$6x + y = 4$

4. When graphing a proportional relationship represented by $y = mx$, which point is not on the graph?

A. $(0, 0)$ **B.** $(0, m)$ **C.** $(1, m)$ **D.** $(2, 2m)$

▶▶ Concepts, Skills, & Problem Solving

USING A SCATTER PLOT The table shows the average prices (in dollars) of jeans sold at different stores and the numbers of pairs of jeans sold at each store in one month. (See Exploration 1, p. 237.)

5. Represent the data in a coordinate plane.

Average Price (dollars)	22	40	28	35	46
Number Sold	152	94	134	110	81

6. Is there a relationship between the average price and the number sold? Explain your reasoning.

MAKING A SCATTER PLOT Make a scatter plot of the data. Identify any outliers, gaps, or clusters.

7.

Temperature (°F), x	82	32	40	44	86	84	83	89	102	43
Number of Tourists, y	102	22	38	41	100	98	97	110	63	40

8.

Social Media (hours), x	0	1.5	2.5	5.5	2	1.5	1.5	2	4.5	5
Homework (hours), y	5.5	2	1	0.5	1	1	2	1.5	1	0.5

IDENTIFYING RELATIONSHIPS Describe the relationship between the data. Identify any outliers, gaps, or clusters.

9.
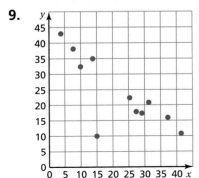

10.
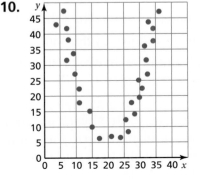

11.
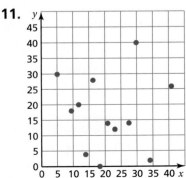

12. **CRITICAL THINKING** The table shows the average price per pound for honey at a store from 2014 to 2017. Describe the relationship between the data.

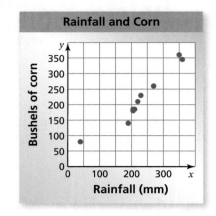

Year, x	2014	2015	2016	2017
Average Price per Pound, y	$4.65	$5.90	$6.50	$7.70

13. **MP MODELING REAL LIFE** The scatter plot shows the amount of rainfall and the amount of corn produced by a farm over the last 10 years. Describe the relationship between the amount of rainfall and the amount of corn produced.

Rainfall and Corn

14. **OPEN-ENDED** Describe a set of real-life data that has a negative linear relationship.

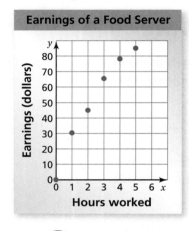

Earnings of a Food Server

15. **MP MODELING REAL LIFE** The scatter plot shows the total earnings (wages and tips) of a food server during one day.

   a. About how many hours must the server work to earn $70?

   b. About how much does the server earn for 5 hours of work?

   c. Describe the relationship shown by the data.

16. **MP PROBLEM SOLVING** The table shows the memory capacities (in gigabytes) and prices (in dollars) of tablet computers. (a) Make a scatter plot of the data. Then describe the relationship between the data. (b) Identify any outliers, gaps, or clusters. Explain why they might exist.

Memory (GB), x	128	16	64	32	64	16	64	32	16	128	16	128
Price (dollars), y	320	50	250	230	260	200	270	250	180	300	210	280

17. **MP PATTERNS** The scatter plot shows the numbers of drifting scooters sold by a company.

   a. In what year were 1000 scooters sold?

   b. About how many scooters were sold in 2015?

   c. Describe the relationship shown by the data.

   d. Assuming this trend continues, in what year are about 500 drifting scooters sold?

Drifting Scooter Sales

18. **DIG DEEPER!** Sales of sunglasses and beach towels at a store show a positive linear relationship in the summer. Does this mean that the sales of one item *cause* the sales of the other item to increase? Explain.

6.2 Lines of Fit

Learning Target: Use lines of fit to model data.

Success Criteria:
- I can write and interpret an equation of a line of fit.
- I can find an equation of a line of best fit.
- I can use a line of fit to make predictions.

EXPLORATION 1

Representing Data by a Linear Equation

Work with a partner. You have been working on a science project for 8 months. Each month, you measured the length of a baby alligator.

The table shows your measurements.

September ↓   April ↓

Month, x	0	1	2	3	4	5	6	7
Length (in.), y	22.0	22.5	23.5	25.0	26.0	27.5	28.5	29.5

Math Practice

Find General Methods

How can you draw a line that "fits" the data? How should the line be positioned with respect to the points?

a. Use a scatter plot to draw a line that you think best describes the relationship between the data.

b. Write an equation for your line in part (a).

c. MODELING Use your equation in part (b) to predict the length of the baby alligator next September.

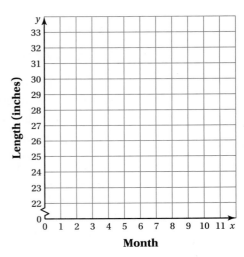

Key Vocabulary
line of fit, *p. 244*
line of best fit,
    p. 245

A **line of fit** is a line drawn on a scatter plot close to most of the data points. It can be used to estimate data on a graph.

EXAMPLE 1 Finding a Line of Fit

Absences, x	Final Exam Score, y
0	97
3	88
2	93
5	83
7	73
9	70
5	88
1	94
9	65
8	73

The table shows the number of absences in a school year and the final exam scores for several students. **(a) Make a scatter plot of the data and draw a line of fit. (b) Write an equation of the line of fit. (c) Interpret the slope and the y-intercept of the line of fit.**

a. Plot the points in a coordinate plane. The scatter plot shows a negative linear relationship. Draw a line that is close to the data points. Try to have as many points above the line as below it.

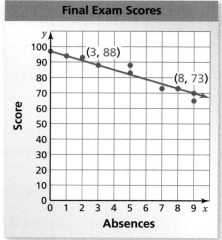

b. The line passes through (3, 88) and (8, 73).

$$\text{slope} = \frac{\text{rise}}{\text{run}} = \frac{-15}{5} = -3$$

You can use the slope -3 and the point (3, 88) to determine that the y-intercept is 97.

So, an equation of the line of fit is $y = -3x + 97$.

c. The slope is -3 and the y-intercept is 97. So, a student with 0 absences is expected to earn a 97 on the exam, and the score decreases by about 3 points per absence.

> A line of fit does not need to pass through any of the data points.

Try It

1. The table shows the numbers of people who attend a festival over an eight-year period. (a) Make a scatter plot of the data and draw a line of fit. (b) Write an equation of the line of fit. (c) Interpret the slope and the y-intercept of the line of fit.

Year, x	1	2	3	4	5	6	7	8
Attendance, y	420	500	650	900	1100	1500	1750	2400

◀)) Multi-Language Glossary at *BigIdeasMath.com*

Graphing calculators use *linear regression* to find a **line of best fit**. Calculators often give a value *r* called the *correlation coefficient*. Values of *r* range from −1 to 1, with values close to −1 indicating a strong negative correlation, values close to 1 indicating a strong positive correlation, and values close to 0 indicating no correlation.

EXAMPLE 2 **Identifying Relationships**

Goals, x	Games Won, y
219	39
249	50
215	36
183	28
282	55
241	41
263	50
256	48

The table shows the numbers of goals scored and games won by 8 hockey teams. Use a graphing calculator to find an equation of the line of best fit. Identify and interpret the correlation coefficient.

Step 1: Enter the data from the table into your calculator.

L1	L2	L3	1
219	39	------	
249	50		
215	36		
183	28		
282	55		
241	41		
263	50		

L1(1)=219

Step 2: Use the *linear regression* feature.

LinReg
y=ax+b
a=.2777857968 ← slope
b=-22.87691253 ← y-intercept
r²=.9548537904
r=.9771662041 ← correlation coefficient

▷ An equation of the line of best fit is $y = 0.3x − 23$. The correlation coefficient is about 0.977. This means that the relationship between goals scored and games won is a strong positive correlation and the equation closely models the data.

Try It

2. Find an equation of the line of best fit for the data in Example 1. Identify and interpret the correlation coefficient.

Self-Assessment for Concepts & Skills

Solve each exercise. Then rate your understanding of the success criteria in your journal.

Days Training, x	Race Time (minutes), y
2	25.45
14	22.30
7	23.85
5	24.10
21	20.90
18	21.20

3. **FINDING A LINE OF FIT** The table shows the numbers of days spent training and the race times for several people in a race.

  a. Make a scatter plot of the data and draw a line of fit.

  b. Write an equation of the line of fit.

  c. Interpret the slope and the *y*-intercept of the line of fit.

4. **IDENTIFYING RELATIONSHIPS** Find an equation of the line of best fit for the data at the left. Identify and interpret the correlation coefficient.

 **EXAMPLE 3** **Modeling Real Life**

The table shows the number of bats in a cave each year from 2010 to 2017, where $x = 0$ represents the year 2010. Assuming this trend continues, in what year will there be 65,000 bats in the cave?

Year, x	Bats (thousands), y
0	327
1	306
2	299
3	270
4	254
5	232
6	215
7	197

 Understand the problem.

You are given the number of bats in a cave each year from 2010 to 2017. You are asked to predict in which year there will be 65,000 bats in the cave.

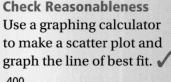 **Make a plan.**

Use a graphing calculator to find an equation of the line of best fit. Then solve the equation for x when $y = 65$.

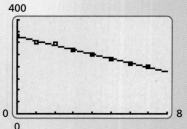 **Solve and check.**

Enter the data from the table into your calculator and use the *linear regression* feature.

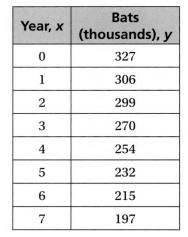
```
LinReg
y=ax+b
a=-18.83333333
b=328.4166667
r²=.9938069824
r=-.9968986821
```

Check Reasonableness
Use a graphing calculator to make a scatter plot and graph the line of best fit. ✓

An equation of the line of best fit is $y = -18.8x + 328$. Solve the equation for x when $y = 65$.

$$y = -18.8x + 328 \qquad \text{Write the equation.}$$
$$65 = -18.8x + 328 \qquad \text{Substitute 65 for } y.$$
$$-263 = -18.8x \qquad \text{Subtract 328 from each side.}$$
$$14 \approx x \qquad \text{Divide each side by } -18.8.$$

▷ There should be 65,000 bats in the cave in 2024.

 ## *Self-Assessment* for Problem Solving

Solve each exercise. Then rate your understanding of the success criteria in your journal.

Height (ft), x	Completions, y
4	27
4.2	22
4.4	18
4.5	16
4.6	11
4.7	8

5. The ordered pairs show amounts y (in inches) of rainfall equivalent to x inches of snow. About how many inches of rainfall are equivalent to 6 inches of snow? Justify your answer.

(16, 1.5)   (12, 1.3)   (18, 1.8)   (15, 1.5)   (20, 2.1)   (23, 2.4)

6. The table shows the heights (in feet) of a high jump bar and the number of people who successfully complete each jump. Identify and interpret the correlation coefficient.

6.2 Practice

Go to *BigIdeasMath.com* to get HELP with solving the exercises.

▶ Review & Refresh

Describe the relationship between the data. Identify any outliers, gaps, or clusters.

1.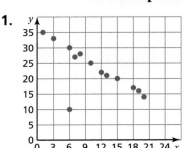

2.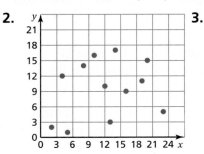

3.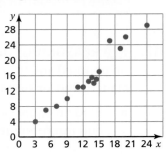

Write the fraction as a decimal and a percent.

4. $\dfrac{29}{100}$

5. $\dfrac{7}{25}$

6. $\dfrac{33}{50}$

▶▶ Concepts, Skills, & Problem Solving

REPRESENTING DATA BY A LINEAR EQUATION Use a scatter plot to draw a line that you think best describes the relationship between the data. (See Exploration 1, p. 243.)

7.

Blueberries (pints), *x*	0	1	2	3	4	5
Weight (pounds), *y*	0	0.8	1.50	2.20	3.0	3.75

8.

Age (years), *x*	0	2	4	6	8	10
Value (dollars), *y*	91	82	74	65	55	43

9. FINDING A LINE OF FIT The table shows the daily high temperatures (°F) and the numbers of hot chocolates sold at a coffee shop for eight randomly selected days.

Temperature (°F), *x*	30	36	44	51	60	68	75	82
Hot Chocolates, *y*	45	43	36	35	30	27	23	17

   a. Make a scatter plot of the data and draw a line of fit.

   b. Write an equation of the line of fit.

   c. Interpret the slope and the *y*-intercept of the line of fit.

10. MP NUMBER SENSE Which correlation coefficient indicates a stronger relationship: -0.98 or 0.91? Explain.

11. **IDENTIFYING RELATIONSHIPS** The table shows the admission costs (in dollars) and the average number of daily visitors at an amusement park each year for the past 8 years. Find an equation of the line of best fit. Identify and interpret the correlation coefficient.

Cost (dollars), x	20	21	22	24	25	27	28	30
Daily Attendance, y	940	935	940	925	920	905	910	890

12. **MP REASONING** The table shows the weights (in pounds) and the prescribed dosages (in milligrams) of medicine for six patients.

   a. Find an equation of the line of best fit. Identify and interpret the correlation coefficient.

   b. Interpret the slope of the line of best fit.

   c. A patient who weighs 140 pounds is prescribed 135 milligrams of medicine. How does this affect the line of best fit?

Weight (lb), x	Dosage (mg), y
94	72
119	90
135	103
150	115
185	140
202	156

Population (millions), x	Electoral Votes, y
4.4	8
0.7	3
20.6	29
6.6	11
8.9	14
8.4	13
27.9	38
39.3	55

13. **MP MODELING REAL LIFE** The table shows the populations (in millions) and the numbers of electoral votes assigned for eight states in the 2016 presidential election.

   a. Find an equation of the line of best fit. Identify and interpret the correlation coefficient.

   b. Interpret the slope of the line of best fit.

   c. Interpret the y-intercept of the line of best fit.

   d. **RESEARCH** Research the Electoral College to explain the meaning of your answer in part (c).

14. **MP MODELING REAL LIFE** The table shows the numbers (in millions) of active accounts for two social media websites over the past five years. Assuming this trend continues, how many active accounts will Website B have when Website A has 280 million active accounts? Justify your answer.

Website A, x	Website B, y
312	188
306	215
300	235
299	236
293	253

Seconds, x	Height (feet), y
0	3
0.5	39
1	67
1.5	87
2	99

15. **DIG DEEPER!** The table shows the heights y (in feet) of a baseball x seconds after it was hit.

   a. Predict the height after 5 seconds.

   b. The actual height after 5 seconds is about 3 feet. Why might this be different from your prediction?

6.3 Two-Way Tables

Learning Target: Use two-way tables to represent data.

Success Criteria:
- I can read a two-way table.
- I can make a two-way table.
- I can use a two-way table to describe relationships between data.

EXPLORATION 1

Analyzing Data

Work with a partner. You are the manager of a sports shop. The table shows the numbers of soccer T-shirts that your shop has left in stock at the end of a soccer season.

		T-Shirt Size					
		S	M	L	XL	XXL	Total
Color	Blue/White	5	4	1	0	2	
	Blue/Gold	3	6	5	2	0	
	Red/White	4	2	4	1	3	
	Black/White	3	4	1	2	1	
	Black/Gold	5	2	3	0	2	
	Total						65

a. Complete the table.

b. Are there any black-and-gold XL T-shirts in stock? Justify your answer.

c. The numbers of T-shirts you ordered at the beginning of the soccer season are shown below. Complete the table.

		T-Shirt Size					
		S	M	L	XL	XXL	Total
Color	Blue/White	5	6	7	6	5	
	Blue/Gold	5	6	7	6	5	
	Red/White	5	6	7	6	5	
	Black/White	5	6	7	6	5	
	Black/Gold	5	6	7	6	5	
	Total						

Math Practice

Listen and Ask Questions

Listen to another pair explain their answer in part (d). Ask any questions you have about their reasoning.

d. **MP REASONING** How would you alter the numbers of T-shirts you order for the next soccer season?

Key Vocabulary 🔊
two-way table, *p. 250*
joint frequency, *p. 250*
marginal frequency,
    p. 250

A **two-way table** displays two categories of data collected from the same source.

You randomly survey students about their grades on a test and whether they studied for the test. The two-way table shows the results. Each entry in the table is called a **joint frequency**.

		Student	
		Studied	**Did Not Study**
Grade	**Passed**	21	2
	Failed	1	6

joint frequency

EXAMPLE 1 Reading a Two-Way Table

How many students in the survey above studied for the test and passed?

The entry in the "Studied" column and "Passed" row is 21.

▷ So, 21 of the students in the survey studied for the test and passed.

Try It

1. How many students in the survey above studied for the test and failed?

The sums of the rows and columns in a two-way table are called **marginal frequencies**.

EXAMPLE 2 Finding Marginal Frequencies

Find and interpret the marginal frequencies for the survey above.

Create a new column and a new row for the sums. Then add the entries.

		Student		
		Studied	**Did Not Study**	**Total**
Grade	**Passed**	21	2	23
	Failed	1	6	7
	Total	22	8	30

23 students passed.
7 students failed.
30 students were surveyed.
22 students studied.
8 students did not study.

Try It

		Football Game	
		Attend	**Not Attend**
Dance	**Attend**	35	5
	Not Attend	16	20

2. You randomly survey students in a cafeteria about their plans for a football game and a school dance. The two-way table shows the results. Find and interpret the marginal frequencies for the survey.

EXAMPLE 3 **Making a Two-Way Table**

Rides Bus

Age	Tally
12-13	卌 卌 卌 卌 llll
14-15	卌 卌 ll
16-17	卌 卌 llll

Does Not Ride Bus

Age	Tally
12-13	卌 卌 卌 l
14-15	卌 卌 lll
16-17	卌 卌 卌 卌 l

You randomly survey students between the ages of 12 and 17 about whether they ride the bus to school. The results are shown in the tally sheets. Make a two-way table that includes the marginal frequencies.

The two categories for the table are the ages and whether or not students ride the bus. Use the tally sheets to calculate each joint frequency. Then add to find each marginal frequency.

		Age			
		12–13	**14–15**	**16–17**	**Total**
Student	**Rides Bus**	24	12	14	50
	Does Not Ride Bus	16	13	21	50
	Total	40	25	35	100

Try It

3. You randomly survey students about whether they buy a school lunch or pack a lunch. The results are shown. Make a two-way table that includes the marginal frequencies.

Grade 6 Students	Grade 7 Students	Grade 8 Students
11 pack lunch, 9 buy school lunch	23 pack lunch, 27 buy school lunch	16 pack lunch, 14 buy school lunch

Self-Assessment *for Concepts & Skills*

Solve each exercise. Then rate your understanding of the success criteria in your journal.

Zoo

Gender	Tally
Male	卌 卌 卌 lll
Female	卌 卌 卌 卌 l

Museum

Gender	Tally
Male	卌 卌 ll
Female	卌 卌 llll

4. **READING A TWO-WAY TABLE** The results of a music survey are shown in the two-way table. How many students dislike both country and jazz? How many students like country but dislike jazz?

		Jazz	
		Likes	**Dislikes**
Country	**Likes**	26	14
	Dislikes	17	8

5. **MAKING A TWO-WAY TABLE** You randomly survey students about their preference for a class field trip. The results are shown in the tally sheets. Make a two-way table that includes the marginal frequencies.

EXAMPLE 4 **Modeling Real Life**

For each age group in Example 3, what percent of the students ride the bus? do not ride the bus? Determine whether there is a relationship between age and riding the bus to school.

Divide each joint frequency by the total number of students in the corresponding age group. Organize the results in a two-way table.

		Age		
		12–13	**14–15**	**16–17**
Student	**Rides Bus**	$\frac{24}{40} = 60\%$	$\frac{12}{25} = 48\%$	$\frac{14}{35} = 40\%$
	Does Not Ride Bus	$\frac{16}{40} = 40\%$	$\frac{13}{25} = 52\%$	$\frac{21}{35} = 60\%$

Check
The percents in each column of the table should sum to 100%.

$60\% + 40\% = 100\%$
$48\% + 52\% = 100\%$
$40\% + 60\% = 100\%$ ✓

Each age group increase corresponds with a decrease in the percent of students who ride the bus and an increase in the percent of students who do not ride the bus.

▷ So, the table shows that as age increases, students are less likely to ride the bus to school.

Self-Assessment for *Problem Solving*

Solve each exercise. Then rate your understanding of the success criteria in your journal.

		Voter's Age		
		18–34	**35–64**	**65+**
Candidate	**A**	36	25	6
	B	12	32	24

6. The results of a voting survey are shown in the two-way table. For each age group, what percent of voters prefer Candidate A? Candidate B? Determine whether there is a relationship between age and candidate preference.

7. You randomly survey 40 students about whether they play an instrument. You find that 8 males play an instrument and 13 females do not play an instrument. A total of 17 students in the survey play an instrument. Make a two-way table that includes the marginal frequencies.

8. Collect data from each student in your math class about whether they like math and whether they like science. Is there a relationship between liking math and liking science? Justify your answer.

Go to *BigIdeasMath.com* to get HELP with solving the exercises.

Review & Refresh

Find an equation of the line of best fit for the data.

1.

x	0	1	2	3	4
y	75	91	101	109	129

2.

x	7	8	10	13	15
y	25	29	41	48	57

The vertices of a triangle are $A(1, 2)$, $B(3, 1)$, and $C(1, -1)$. Draw the figure and its image after the translation.

3. 4 units left

4. 2 units down

5. $(x - 2, y + 3)$

Concepts, Skills, & Problem Solving

ANALYZING DATA **In Exploration 1, determine how many of the indicated T-shirt are in stock at the end of the soccer season.** (See Exploration 1, p. 249.)

6. black-and-white M

7. blue-and-gold XXL

8. blue-and-white L

READING A TWO-WAY TABLE **You randomly survey students about participating in a yearly fundraiser. The two-way table shows the results.**

9. How many female students participate in the fundraiser?

10. How many male students do *not* participate in the fundraiser?

		Fundraiser	
		No	Yes
Gender	Female	22	51
	Male	30	29

FINDING MARGINAL FREQUENCIES **Find and interpret the marginal frequencies.**

11.

		School Play	
		Attend	Not Attend
Class	Junior	41	30
	Senior	52	23

12.

		Cell Phone Company	
		A	B
Data Plan	Limited	78	94
	Unlimited	175	135

Treatment
Improved: 34
Did not improve: 10

No Treatment
Improved: 12
Did not improve: 29

13. **MAKING A TWO-WAY TABLE** A researcher randomly surveys people with a medical condition about whether they received a treatment and whether their condition improved. The results are shown. Make a two-way table that includes the marginal frequencies.

14. **MP MODELING REAL LIFE** You randomly survey students in your school about the color of their eyes. The results are shown in the tables.

Eye Color of Males Surveyed		
Green	Blue	Brown
5	16	27

Eye Color of Females Surveyed		
Green	Blue	Brown
3	19	18

a. Make a two-way table.

b. Find and interpret the marginal frequencies for the survey.

c. For each eye color, what percent of the students in the survey are male? female? Organize the results in a two-way table.

15. **MP REASONING** Use the information from Exercise 14. For each gender, what percent of the students in the survey have green eyes? blue eyes? brown eyes? Organize the results in a two-way table.

16. **CRITICAL THINKING** What percent of students in the survey in Exercise 14 are either female or have green eyes? What percent of students in the survey are males who do not have green eyes? Find and explain the sum of these two percents.

17. **MP MODELING REAL LIFE** You randomly survey people in your neighborhood about whether they have at least $1000 in savings. The results are shown in the tally sheets. For each age group, what percent of the people have at least $1000 in savings? do not have at least $1000 in savings? Determine whether there is a relationship between age and having at least $1000 in savings.

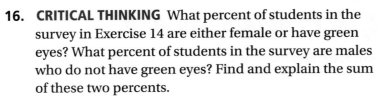

Have at Least $1000 in Savings

Age	Tally
20-29	卌 卌 IIII
30-39	卌 卌 卌 卌 卌 II
40-49	卌 卌 卌 卌 卌

Don't Have at Least $1000 in Savings

Age	Tally
20-29	卌 卌 卌 卌 卌 卌 卌 I
30-39	卌 卌 卌 卌 卌 卌 III
40-49	卌 卌 卌

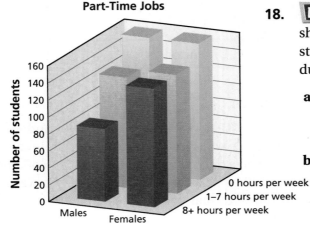

Part-Time Jobs

18. **DIG DEEPER!** The three-dimensional bar graph shows information about the numbers of hours students at a high school work at part-time jobs during the school year.

a. Make a two-way table that represents the data. Use estimation to find the entries in your table.

b. A newspaper article claims that more males than females drop out of high school to work full-time. Do the data support this claim? Explain your reasoning.

6.4 Choosing a Data Display

Learning Target: Use appropriate data displays to represent situations.

Success Criteria:
- I can choose appropriate data displays for situations.
- I can identify misleading data displays.
- I can analyze a variety of data displays.

EXPLORATION 1

Displaying Data

Work with a partner. Analyze and display each data set in a way that best describes the data. Explain your choice of display.

MOOSE XING

a. **NEW ENGLAND ROADKILL** A group of schools in New England participated in a two-month study. They reported 3962 dead animals.

Birds: 307   Mammals: 2746
Amphibians: 145   Reptiles: 75
Unknown: 689

b. **BLACK BEAR ROADKILL** The data below show the numbers of black bears killed on a state's roads each year for 20 years.

Year 1:	30	Year 8:	47	Year 15:	99
Year 2:	37	Year 9:	49	Year 16:	129
Year 3:	46	Year 10:	61	Year 17:	111
Year 4:	33	Year 11:	74	Year 18:	127
Year 5:	43	Year 12:	88	Year 19:	141
Year 6:	35	Year 13:	82	Year 20:	135
Year 7:	43	Year 14:	109		

Math Practice

Choose Tools

For each set of data, is there more than one way that you can accurately display the data?

c. **RACCOON ROADKILL** A one-week study along a four-mile section of road found the following weights (in pounds) of raccoons that had been killed by vehicles.

13.4	14.8	17.0	12.9
21.3	21.5	16.8	14.8
15.2	18.7	18.6	17.2
18.5	9.4	19.4	15.7
14.5	9.5	25.4	21.5
17.3	19.1	11.0	12.4
20.4	13.6	17.5	18.5
21.5	14.0	13.9	19.0

d. What can be done to minimize the number of animals killed by vehicles?

Key Idea

Data Display	What does it do?	
Pictograph	shows data using pictures	
Bar Graph	shows data in specific categories	
Circle Graph	shows data as parts of a whole	
Line Graph	shows how data change over time	
Histogram	shows frequencies of data values in intervals of the same size	
Stem-and-Leaf Plot	orders numerical data and shows how they are distributed	
Box-and-Whisker Plot	shows the variability of a data set by using quartiles	
Dot Plot	shows the number of times each value occurs in a data set	
Scatter Plot	shows the relationship between two data sets by using ordered pairs in a coordinate plane	

EXAMPLE 1 **Choosing an Appropriate Data Display**

Choose an appropriate data display for the situation. Explain your reasoning.

a. the number of students in a marching band each year

> A line graph shows change over time. So, a line graph is an appropriate data display.

b. a comparison of people's shoe sizes and their heights

> You want to compare two different data sets. So, a scatter plot is an appropriate data display.

Try It **Choose an appropriate data display for the situation. Explain your reasoning.**

1. the population of the United States divided into age groups

2. the number of students in your school who play basketball, football, soccer, or lacrosse

EXAMPLE 2 **Identifying an Appropriate Data Display**

You record the number of hits for your school's new website for 5 months. Tell whether each data display is appropriate for representing how the number of hits changed during the 5 months. Explain your reasoning.

Month	Hits
August	250
September	320
October	485
November	650
December	925

a.

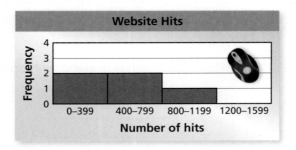

▶ The bar graph shows the number of hits for each month. So, it is an appropriate data display.

b.

Website Hits

▶ The histogram does not show the number of hits for each month or how the number of hits changes over time. So, it is *not* an appropriate data display.

Math Practice

Maintain Oversight

What can you look for in the data displays to determine whether they show data changing over time?

c.

▶ The line graph shows how the number of hits changes over time. So, it is an appropriate data display.

Try It Tell whether the data display is appropriate for representing the data in Example 2. Explain your reasoning.

3. dot plot   **4.** circle graph   **5.** stem-and-leaf plot

EXAMPLE 3 **Identifying a Misleading Data Display**

Which line graph is misleading? Explain.

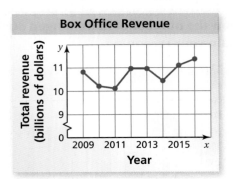

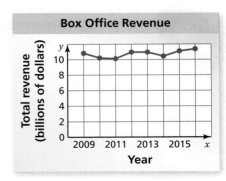

The vertical axis of the line graph on the left has a break (⌇) and begins at 9. This graph makes it appear that the total revenue fluctuated drastically from 2009 to 2016. The graph on the right has an unbroken axis. It is more honest and shows that the total revenue changed much less from 2009 to 2016.

▷ So, the graph on the left is misleading.

Try It

6. Which bar graph is misleading? Explain.

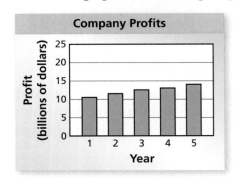

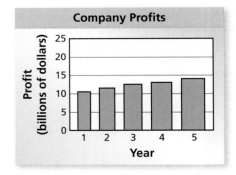

 Self-Assessment *for Concepts & Skills*

Solve each exercise. Then rate your understanding of the success criteria in your journal.

CHOOSING A DATA DISPLAY **Choose an appropriate data display for the situation. Explain your reasoning.**

7. the percent of band students playing each instrument

8. a comparison of the amount of time spent using a tablet computer and the remaining battery life

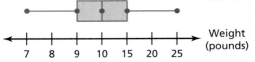

9. **IDENTIFYING A MISLEADING DISPLAY** Is the box-and-whisker plot misleading? Explain.

EXAMPLE 4 **Modeling Real Life**

Food Drive Donation Totals

Canned food
Boxed food
Juice

= 20 cans = 20 boxes = 20 bottles

The organizer of a food drive creates the pictograph shown. (a) A volunteer concludes that the numbers of cans of food and boxes of food donated were about the same. Determine whether this conclusion is accurate. (b) Estimate the number of each item that has been donated.

a. Each icon represents the same number of items. Because the box icon is larger than the can icon, it looks like the number of boxes is about the same as the number of cans. The number of boxes is actually about half of the number of cans.

▷ So, the conclusion is not accurate.

b. Each icon represents 20 items. Multiply each number of icons by 20.

$11 \times 20 = 220$ cans

$6 \times 20 = 120$ boxes

$2\frac{1}{2} \times 20 = 50$ bottles

▷ So, about 220 cans, 120 boxes, and 50 bottles have been donated.

Self-Assessment for Problem Solving

Solve each exercise. Then rate your understanding of the success criteria in your journal.

Employee Salary

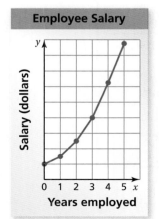

Salary (dollars)

0 1 2 3 4 5 *x*

Years employed

10. An employee at an animal shelter creates the histogram shown. A visitor concludes that the number of 7-year-old to 9-year-old dogs is triple the number of 1-year-old to 3-year-old dogs. Determine whether this conclusion is accurate. Explain.

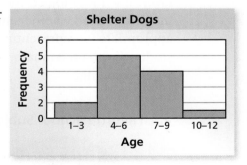

Shelter Dogs

Frequency

1–3 4–6 7–9 10–12

Age

11. **DIG DEEPER!** A business manager creates the line graph shown. (a) How do the data *appear* to change over time? Explain why this conclusion may not be accurate. (b) Why might the business manager want to use this line graph?

Go to *BigIdeasMath.com* to get HELP with solving the exercises.

▶ Review & Refresh

You randomly survey students about whether they recycle. The two-way table shows the results.

		Recycle	
		Yes	No
Gender	Female	28	9
	Male	24	14

1. How many male students recycle? How many female students do *not* recycle?

2. Find and interpret the marginal frequencies.

Find the slope and the *y*-intercept of the graph of the linear equation.

3. $y = 4x + 10$
4. $y = -3.5x - 2$
5. $y - 8 = -x$

▶▶ Concepts, Skills, & Problem Solving

6. **DISPLAYING DATA** Analyze and display the data in a way that best describes the data. Explain your choice of display. (See Exploration 1, p. 255.)

Notebooks Sold in One Week		
192 red	170 green	203 black
183 pink	230 blue	165 yellow
210 purple	250 orange	179 white

CHOOSING A DATA DISPLAY Choose an appropriate data display for the situation. Explain your reasoning.

7. a student's test scores and how the scores are spread out

8. the prices of different televisions and the numbers of televisions sold

9. the outcome of rolling a number cube

10. the distance a person drives each month

11. **IDENTIFYING AN APPROPRIATE DISPLAY**
A survey asked 800 students to choose their favorite school subject. The results are shown in the table. Tell whether each data display is appropriate for representing the portion of students who prefer math. Explain your reasoning.

Favorite School Subject	
Subject	Number of Students
Science	224
Math	176
Literature	240
Social studies	160

a. **Favorite School Subject**

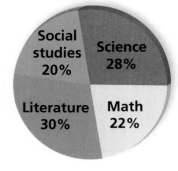

b.

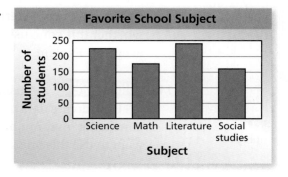

12. IDENTIFYING AN APPROPRIATE DISPLAY The table shows how many hours you worked as a lifeguard from May to August. Tell whether each data display is appropriate for representing how the number of hours worked changed during the 4 months. Explain your reasoning.

Lifeguard Schedule	
Month	**Hours Worked**
May	40
June	80
July	160
August	120

a.

Key: = 20 hours

b.

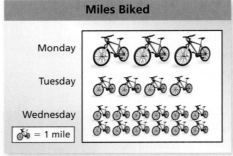

13. WRITING When should you use a histogram instead of a bar graph to display data? Use an example to support your answer.

IDENTIFYING MISLEADING DISPLAYS Which data display is misleading? Explain.

14.

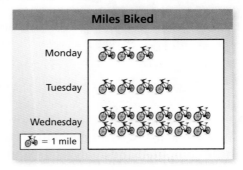

15.

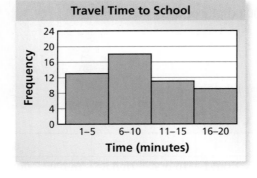

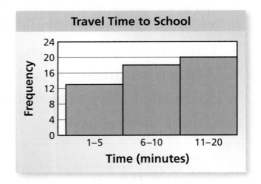

16. **MP** **REASONING** What type of data display is appropriate for showing the mode of a data set?

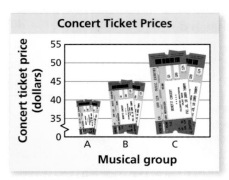
Concert Ticket Prices

17. **CRITICAL THINKING** The director of a music festival creates the data display shown. A customer concludes that the ticket price for Group C is more than double the ticket price for Group A. Determine whether this conclusion is accurate. Explain.

18. **MP** **PATTERNS** A scientist gathers data about a decaying chemical compound and creates the scatter plot shown.

   a. The scientist concludes that there is a negative linear relationship between the data. Determine whether this conclusion is accurate. Explain.

   b. Estimate the amount of the compound remaining after 1 hour, 3 hours, 5 hours, and 7 hours.

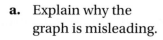

Decaying Chemical Compound

19. **MP** **REASONING** A survey asks 100 students to choose their favorite sports. The results are shown in the circle graph.

   a. Explain why the graph is misleading.

   b. What type of data display is more appropriate for the data? Explain.

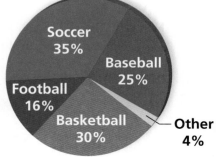
Favorite Sports

20. **MP** **STRUCTURE** With the help of computers, mathematicians have computed and analyzed trillions of digits of the irrational number π. One of the things they analyze is the frequency of each of the numbers 0 through 9. The table shows the frequency of each number in the first 100,000 digits of π.

   a. Display the data in a bar graph.

   b. Display the data in a circle graph.

   c. Which data display is more appropriate? Explain.

   d. Describe the distribution.

Number	0	1	2	3	4	5	6	7	8	9
Frequency	9999	10,137	9908	10,025	9971	10,026	10,029	10,025	9978	9902

6 Connecting Concepts

▶ Using the Problem-Solving Plan

1. You randomly survey middle school students about whether they prefer action, comedy, or animation movies. The two-way table shows the results. Estimate the probability that a randomly selected middle school student prefers action movies.

		Grade		
		6	**7**	**8**
Genre	**Action**	12	18	10
	Comedy	8	6	3
	Animation	9	11	14

You know the results of a survey about movie preference. You are asked to estimate the probability that a randomly selected middle school student prefers action movies.

Find the marginal frequencies for the data. Then use the marginal frequencies to find the probability that a randomly selected middle school student prefers action movies.

Use the plan to solve the problem. Then check your solution.

2. An equation of the line of best fit for a data set is $y = -0.68x + 2.35$. Describe what happens to the slope and the y-intercept of the line when each y-value in the data set increases by 7.

3. On a school field trip, there must be 1 adult chaperone for every 16 students. There are 8 adults who are willing to be a chaperone for the trip, but only the number of chaperones that are necessary will attend. In a class of 124 students, 80 attend the trip. Make a two-way table that represents the data.

Performance Task

Cost vs. Fuel Economy

At the beginning of this chapter, you watched a STEAM Video called "Fuel Economy." You are now ready to complete the performance task related to this video, available at *BigIdeasMath.com*. Be sure to use the problem-solving plan as you work through the performance task.

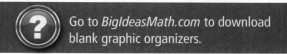
Go to *BigIdeasMath.com* to download blank graphic organizers.

▶ Review Vocabulary

Write the definition and give an example of each vocabulary term.

scatter plot, *p. 238*

line of fit, *p. 244*

line of best fit, *p. 245*

two-way table, *p. 250*

joint frequency, *p. 250*

marginal frequency, *p. 250*

▶ Graphic Organizers

You can use an **Information Frame** to help organize and remember a concept. Here is an example of an Information Frame for *scatter plots*.

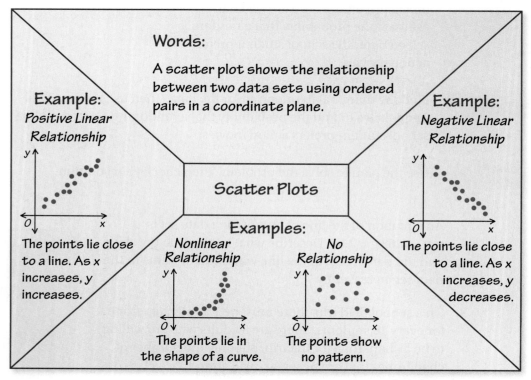

Words:

A scatter plot shows the relationship between two data sets using ordered pairs in a coordinate plane.

Example: *Positive Linear Relationship*

The points lie close to a line. As x increases, y increases.

Scatter Plots

Example: *Negative Linear Relationship*

The points lie close to a line. As x increases, y decreases.

Examples:

Nonlinear Relationship

The points lie in the shape of a curve.

No Relationship

The points show no pattern.

Choose and complete a graphic organizer to help you study the concept.

1. lines of fit

2. two-way tables

3. data displays

$A = \pi r^2$

$d = 2r$ Circle $C = \pi d$

Shape of flea collar

One too many regions to fill, huh?

"Dear Teacher, I am emailing my **Information Frame** showing the characteristics of circles."

Chapter Self-Assessment

As you complete the exercises, use the scale below to rate your understanding of the success criteria in your journal.

1	2	3	4
I do not understand.	I can do it with help.	I can do it on my own.	I can teach someone else.

6.1 Scatter Plots (pp. 237–242)

Learning Target: Use scatter plots to describe patterns and relationships between two quantities.

1. Make a scatter plot of the data. Identify any outliers, gaps, or clusters.

Age (years), x	15	3	14	12	8	11	9	4	13	10
Height (inches), y	67	38	65	70	50	58	53	41	63	56

Describe the relationship between the data. Identify any outliers, gaps, or clusters.

2.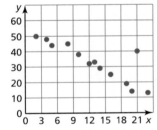

3.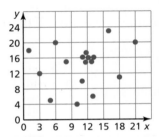

4.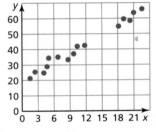

5. Your school is ordering custom T-shirts. The scatter plot shows the numbers of T-shirts ordered and the cost per shirt. Describe the relationship between the numbers of T-shirts ordered and the cost per T-shirt.

6. Describe a set of real-life data that has each relationship.

   a. positive linear relationship

   b. no relationship

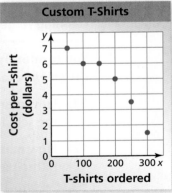

7. The table shows the numbers of hours a waitress works and the amounts she earns in tips. How many hours do you expect the waitress to work when she earns $42 in tips?

Hours Worked, x	2	5.5	1	7	2.5	8	3	5
Tips (dollars), y	15	40	7	50	18	55	20	36

6.2 Lines of Fit (pp. 243–248)

Learning Target: Use lines of fit to model data.

8. The table shows the numbers of students at a middle school over a 10-year period.

   a. Make a scatter plot of the data and draw a line of fit.

   b. Write an equation of the line of fit.

   c. Interpret the slope and the y-intercept of the line of fit.

   d. Predict the number of students in year 11.

Year, x	Number of Students, y
1	492
2	507
3	520
4	535
5	550
6	562
7	577
8	591
9	604
10	618

9. Find an equation of the line of best fit for the data in Exercise 8. Identify and interpret the correlation coefficient.

10. The table shows the revenue (in millions of dollars) for a company over an eight-year period. Assuming this trend continues, how much revenue will there be in year 9?

Year, x	1	2	3	4	5	6	7	8
Revenue (millions of dollars), y	20	35	46	56	68	82	92	108

6.3 Two-Way Tables (pp. 249–254)

Learning Target: Use two-way tables to represent data.

You randomly survey students about participating in the science fair. The two-way table shows the results.

11. How many male students participate in the science fair?

12. How many female students *do not* participate in the science fair?

		Science Fair	
		No	Yes
Gender	Female	15	22
	Male	12	32

13. You randomly survey students in your school about whether they liked a recent school play. The two-way table shows the results. Find and interpret the marginal frequencies.

		Student	
		Liked	Did Not Like
Gender	Male	48	12
	Female	56	14

You randomly survey people at a mall about whether they like the new food court. The results are shown.

14. Make a two-way table that includes the marginal frequencies.

15. For each group, what percent of the people surveyed like the food court? dislike the food court? Organize your results in a two-way table.

16. Does your table in Exercise 15 show a relationship between age and whether people like the food court?

> **Teenagers**
> 96 likes, 4 dislikes
>
> **Adults**
> 21 likes, 79 dislikes
>
> **Senior Citizens**
> 18 likes, 82 dislikes

6.4 Choosing a Data Display *(pp. 255–262)*

Learning Target: Use appropriate data displays to represent situations.

Choose an appropriate data display for the situation. Explain your reasoning.

17. the numbers of pairs of shoes sold by a store each week

18. the percent of votes that each candidate received in an election

19. *Bird banding* is attaching a tag to a bird's wing or leg to track the movement of the bird. This provides information about the bird's migration patterns and feeding behaviors. The table shows the numbers of robins banded in Pennsylvania over 5 years. Tell whether each data display is appropriate for representing how the number of bandings changed during the 5 years. Explain your reasoning.

Year	Number of Bandings
2012	168
2013	142
2014	355
2015	330
2016	345

a.
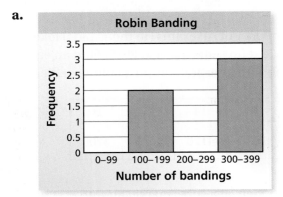

b.
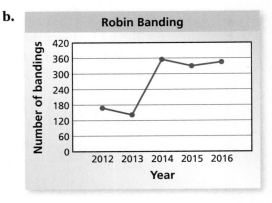

20. Give an example of a bar graph that is misleading. Explain your reasoning.

21. Give an example of a situation where a dot plot is an appropriate data display. Explain your reasoning.

6 Practice Test

1. The graph shows the population (in millions) of the United States from 1960 to 2010.

   a. In what year was the population of the United States about 180 million?

   b. What was the approximate population of the United States in 1990?

   c. Describe the relationship shown by the data.

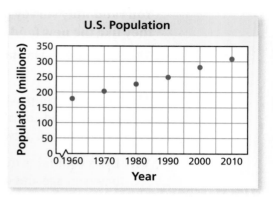

2. The table shows the weight of a baby over several months.

   a. Make a scatter plot of the data and draw a line of fit.

   b. Write an equation of the line of fit.

   c. Interpret the slope and the *y*-intercept of the line of fit.

   d. Predict how much the baby will weigh at 7 months.

Age (months)	Weight (pounds)
1	8
2	9.25
3	11.75
4	13
5	14.5
6	16

	Nonfiction	
	Likes	Dislikes
Fiction Likes	26	20
Dislikes	22	2

3. You randomly survey students at your school about what type of books they like to read. The two-way table shows your results. Find and interpret the marginal frequencies.

Choose an appropriate data display for the situation. Explain your reasoning.

4. magazine sales grouped by price range

5. the distance a person hikes each week

6. The table shows the numbers *y* of AP exams (in thousands) taken from 2012 to 2016, where $x = 12$ represents the year 2012. Find an equation of the line of best fit. Identify and interpret the correlation coefficient.

Year, *x*	12	13	14	15	16
Number of AP Exams, *y*	3698	3938	4176	4479	4705

7. You randomly survey shoppers at a supermarket about whether they use reusable bags. Of 60 male shoppers, 15 use reusable bags. Of 110 female shoppers, 60 use reusable bags. Organize your results in a two-way table. Include the marginal frequencies. Estimate the probability that a randomly selected male shopper uses reusable bags.

6 Cumulative Practice

1. What is the solution of the system of linear equations?

$$y = 2x - 1$$
$$y = 3x + 5$$

   A. $(-13, -6)$

   B. $(-6, -13)$

   C. $(-13, 6)$

   D. $(-6, 13)$

2. The diagram shows parallel lines cut by a transversal. Which angle is the corresponding angle for $\angle 6$?

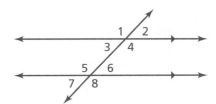

   F. $\angle 2$ G. $\angle 3$

   H. $\angle 4$ I. $\angle 8$

3. You randomly survey students in your school. You ask whether they have jobs. You display your results in the two-way table. How many male students do *not* have a job?

		Job	
		Yes	**No**
Gender	**Male**	27	12
	Female	31	17

4. Which scatter plot shows a negative relationship between x and y?

A.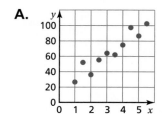

B.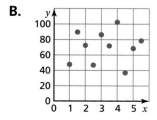

C.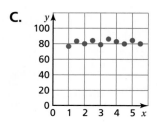

D.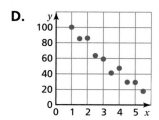

5. A system of two linear equations has no solution. What can you conclude about the graphs of the two equations?

    F. The lines have the same slope and the same y-intercept.

    G. The lines have the same slope and different y-intercepts.

    H. The lines have different slopes and the same y-intercept.

    I. The lines have different slopes and different y-intercepts.

6. What is the solution of the equation?

$$0.22(x + 6) = 0.2x + 1.8$$

    A. $x = 2.4$ **B.** $x = 15.6$

    C. $x = 24$ **D.** $x = 156$

7. A person who is $5\frac{1}{2}$ feet tall casts a $3\frac{1}{2}$-foot-long shadow. A nearby flagpole casts a 28-foot-long shadow. What is the height (in feet) of the flagpole?

8. A store records total sales (in dollars) each month for three years. Which type of graph can best show how sales increase over this time period?

   F. circle graph

   G. line graph

   H. histogram

   I. stem-and-leaf plot

9. Trapezoid *KLMN* is graphed in the coordinate plane shown.

   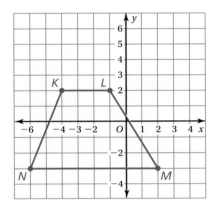

   Rotate Trapezoid *KLMN* 90° clockwise about the origin. What are the coordinates of point *M′*, the image of point *M* after the rotation?

   A. $(-3, -2)$

   B. $(-2, -3)$

   C. $(-2, 3)$

   D. $(3, 2)$

10. The table shows the numbers of hours students spent watching television from Monday through Friday for one week and their scores on a test that Friday.

Hours of Television, *x*	5	2	10	15	3	4	8	2	12	9
Test Score, *y*	92	98	79	66	97	88	82	95	72	81

   Part A   Make a scatter plot of the data.

   Part B   Describe the relationship between the hours of television watched and the test scores.

   Part C   Explain how to justify your answer in Part B using the *linear regression* feature of a graphing calculator.

7 Functions

Chapter Learning Target:
Understand functions.

Chapter Success Criteria:
- I can identify functions.
- I can represent functions in a variety of ways.
- I can evaluate functions.
- I can solve problems using function rules.

STEAM Video: "Apparent Temperature"

STEAM Video

Apparent Temperature

Sometimes it feels hotter or colder outside than the actual temperature. How hot or cold it feels is called the *apparent temperature.* What weather factors might contribute to the apparent temperature?

**Watch the STEAM Video "Apparent Temperature."
Then answer the following questions.**

1. Robert says that the Wet-Bulb Globe Temperature (WBGT) index is used as a measure of apparent temperature.

$$WBGT = 0.7T_W + 0.2T_G + 0.1T_D$$

In the formula, T_W is the natural wet-bulb temperature, T_G is the black-globe temperature, and T_D is the dry-bulb temperature. Find *WBGT* when $T_W = 75°F$, $T_G = 100°F$, and $T_D = 84°F$.

WBGT Categories

Category	WBGT, °F	Flag Color
1	< 82	White
2	82–84.9	Green
3	85–87.9	Yellow
4	88–89.9	Red
5	≥ 90	Black

2. Different categories of Wet-Bulb Globe Temperatures are shown in the chart. Each category can be represented by a different-colored flag. Which flag color is displayed when *WGBT* = 87.5°F?

Performance Task

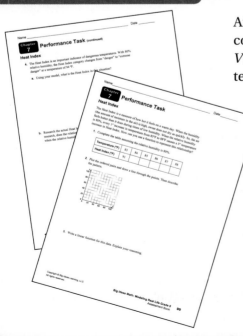

Heat Index

After completing this chapter, you will be able to use the concepts you learned to answer the questions in the *STEAM Video Performance Task.* You will be given information about temperature and the *heat index.*

Temperature (°F)	83	84	85	86	87	88
Heat Index (°F)	91					

You will be asked to create a graph of the temperatures and heat indices. Why is it useful to know the heat index?

Getting Ready for Chapter

Chapter Exploration

Work with a partner. Copy and complete the diagram.

1. Area *A*

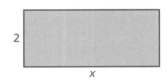

2. Perimeter *P*

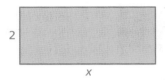

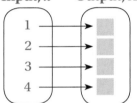

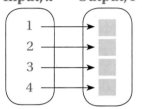

3. Circumference *C*

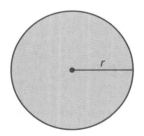

4. Volume *V*

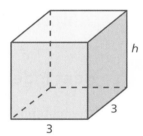

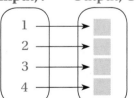

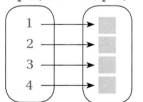

Vocabulary

The following vocabulary terms are defined in this chapter. Think about what each term might mean and record your thoughts.

input   mapping diagram   nonlinear function

output   linear function

7.1 Relations and Functions

Learning Target: Understand the concept of a function.

Success Criteria:
- I can represent a relation as a set of ordered pairs.
- I can determine whether a relation is a function.
- I can use functions to solve real-life problems.

EXPLORATION 1

Interpreting Diagrams

Work with a partner. Describe the relationship between the *inputs* and *outputs* in each diagram. Then complete each diagram. Is there more than one possible answer? Explain your reasoning.

a.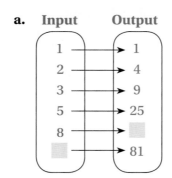

b.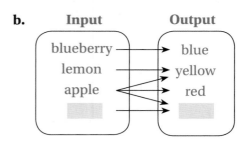

EXPLORATION 2

Describing Relationships Between Quantities

Work with a partner. The diagrams show the numbers of tickets bought by customers for two different plays and the total costs (in dollars).

Math Practice

Analyze Relationships

Is it possible for one person to pay $16 for 2 tickets to Play B and another person to pay $8 for 2 tickets to Play B? Explain.

Play A

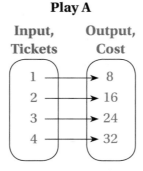

Play B

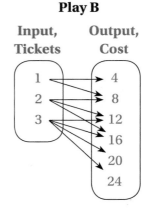

a. For each diagram, how many outputs does each input have?

b. Describe the prices of tickets for each play.

c. A person buys 4 tickets for each play. Can you determine the total cost of all 8 tickets? Explain.

Key Vocabulary 🔊

input, *p. 276*
output, *p. 276*
relation, *p. 276*
mapping diagram,
   p. 276
function, *p. 277*

Ordered pairs can be used to show **inputs** and **outputs**.

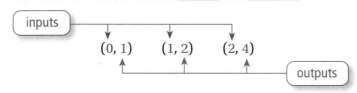

🔑 Key Ideas

Relations and Mapping Diagrams

A **relation** pairs inputs with outputs. A relation can be represented by ordered pairs or a **mapping diagram**.

Ordered Pairs

(0, 1)

(1, 2)

(2, 4)

Mapping Diagram

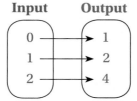

EXAMPLE 1 **Listing Ordered Pairs of Relations**

List the ordered pairs shown in each mapping diagram.

a. Input   Output

```
1 ────▶ 3
2 ────▶ 6
3 ────▶ 9
4 ────▶ 12
```

b. Input   Output

```
0 ────▶ 1
2 ────▶ 0
4 ────▶ −2
       ────▶ −3
```

▷ The ordered pairs are (1, 3), (2, 6), (3, 9), and (4, 12).

▷ The ordered pairs are (0, 0), (2, 1), (2, −2), and (4, −3).

Try It List the ordered pairs shown in the mapping diagram.

1. Input   Output

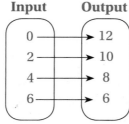

2. Input   Output

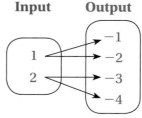

🔊 Multi-Language Glossary at *BigIdeasMath.com*

A relation that pairs each input with *exactly one* output is a **function**.

EXAMPLE 2 **Determining Whether Relations Are Functions**

Determine whether each relation is a function.

a.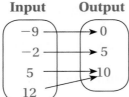

b.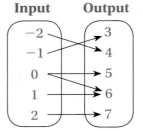

▷ Each input has exactly one output. So, the relation is a function.

▷ The input 0 has two outputs, 5 and 6. So, the relation is *not* a function.

Try It Determine whether the relation is a function.

3.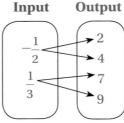

4.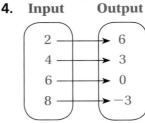

 Self-Assessment for Concepts & Skills

Solve each exercise. Then rate your understanding of the success criteria in your journal.

5. **MP PRECISION** Describe how relations and functions are different.

IDENTIFYING FUNCTIONS List the ordered pairs shown in the mapping diagram. Then determine whether the relation is a function.

6.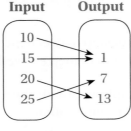

7.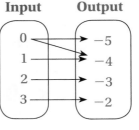

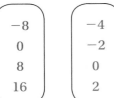

8. **OPEN-ENDED** Copy and complete the mapping diagram at the left to represent a relation that is a function. Then describe how you can modify the mapping diagram so that the relation is *not* a function.

EXAMPLE 3 **Modeling Real Life**

The mapping diagram represents the prices of one-way subway tickets to different zones of a city.

Input, Zone	Output, Price
0	→$2.00
1	→$3.50
2	→$5.00
3	→$6.50

a. Is the price of a subway ticket a function of the zone number?

Each input has exactly one output.

▷   So, the price of a subway ticket is a function of the zone number.

b. Describe the relationship between the price and the zone number.

Identify the relationship between the inputs and the outputs.

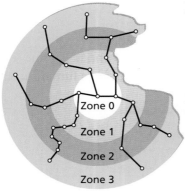

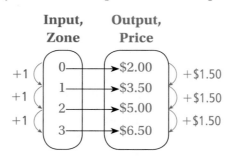

As each input increases by 1, the output increases by $1.50.

▷   So, the price of a one-way subway ticket increases by $1.50 for each additional zone traveled.

 Self-Assessment for *Problem Solving*

Solve each exercise. Then rate your understanding of the success criteria in your journal.

9. The mapping diagram represents the costs of reserving a hotel room for different numbers of nights.

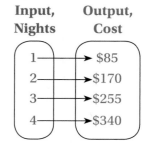

  a. Is the cost a function of the number of nights reserved?

  b. Describe the relationship between the cost and the number of nights reserved.

10. **DIG DEEPER!** The graph represents the number of contestants in each round of a talent competition.

  a. Is the number of contestants a function of the round number?

  b. Predict the number of contestants in the talent competition during Round 7. Explain your reasoning.

Talent Competition Contestants

7.1 Practice

? Go to **BigIdeasMath.com** to get HELP with solving the exercises.

▶ Review & Refresh

Choose an appropriate data display for the situation. Explain your reasoning.

1. the number of runners in each age group at a marathon

2. the high temperature and the attendance at a water park each day

Graph the linear equation.

3. $y = 2x - 3$

4. $y = -0.5x$

5. $y = -3x + 4$

6. Which word best describes two figures that have the same size and the same shape?

    A. congruent   **B.** adjacent   **C.** parallel   **D.** similar

▶▶ Concepts, Skills, & Problem Solving

INTERPRETING DIAGRAMS **Describe the relationship between the *inputs* and *outputs* in the diagram. Then complete the diagram. Is there more than one possible answer? Explain your reasoning.** (See Exploration 1, p. 275.)

7.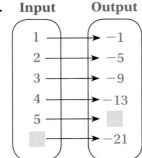

8.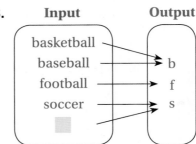

LISTING ORDERED PAIRS **List the ordered pairs shown in the mapping diagram.**

9.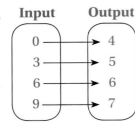

10.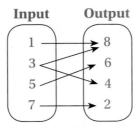

11.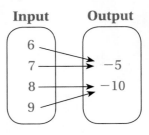

IDENTIFYING FUNCTIONS **Determine whether the relation is a function.**

12.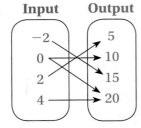

13.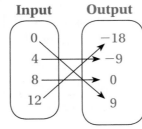

14.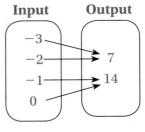

15. **MP** **YOU BE THE TEACHER** Your friend determines whether the relation shown in the mapping diagram is a function. Is your friend correct? Explain your reasoning.

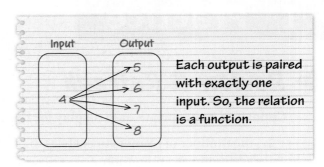

Input   Output

Each output is paired with exactly one input. So, the relation is a function.

MP **REASONING** Draw a mapping diagram that represents the relation. Then determine whether the relation is a function. Explain.

16.
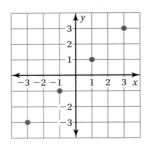

17.
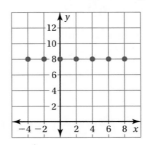

18.
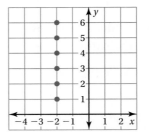

19. **MP** **MODELING REAL LIFE** The normal pressure at sea level is 1 atmosphere of pressure (1 ATM). As you dive below sea level, the pressure changes. The mapping diagram represents the pressures at different depths.

    a. Complete the mapping diagram.

    b. Is pressure a function of depth?

    c. Describe the relationship between pressure and depth.

    d. List the ordered pairs. Then plot the ordered pairs in a coordinate plane. What do you notice about the points?

    e. **RESEARCH** What are common depths for beginner scuba divers? What are common depths for experienced scuba divers?

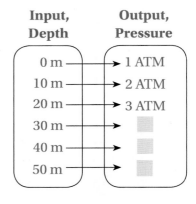

Input, Depth	Output, Pressure
0 m	1 ATM
10 m	2 ATM
20 m	3 ATM
30 m	▮
40 m	▮
50 m	▮

20. **DIG DEEPER!** The table shows the cost of purchasing 1, 2, 3, or 4 T-shirts from a souvenir shop.

    a. Is the cost a function of the number of T-shirts purchased?

    b. Describe the relationship between the cost and the number of T-shirts purchased. How does the *cost per T-shirt* change as you purchase more T-shirts?

T-Shirts	Cost
1	$10
2	$18
3	$24
4	$28

21. **MP** **REPEATED REASONING** The table shows the outputs for several inputs. Use two methods to predict the output for an input of 200.

Input, x	0	1	2	3	4
Output, y	25	30	35	40	45

7.2 Representations of Functions

Learning Target: Represent functions in a variety of ways.

Success Criteria:
- I can write a function rule that describes a relationship.
- I can evaluate functions for given inputs.
- I can represent functions using tables and graphs.

EXPLORATION 1

Using a Table to Describe Relationships

Work with a partner. Make a table that shows the relationship between the figure number x and the area A of each figure. Then use an equation to find which figure has an area of 81 square units when the pattern continues.

1 square unit

a.

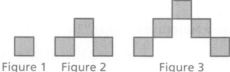

Figure 1   Figure 2   Figure 3   Figure 4

b.

Figure 1   Figure 2   Figure 3   Figure 4

EXPLORATION 2

Using a Graph

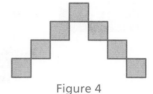

Work with a partner. Use a graph to test the truth of each statement. If the statement is true, write an equation that shows how to obtain one measurement from the other.

Math Practice

Construct Arguments

How does the graph help you determine whether the statement is true?

a. "You can find the horsepower of a race-car engine if you know its volume in cubic inches."

Volume (cubic inches), x	200	350	350	500
Horsepower, y	375	650	250	600

b. "You can find the volume of a race-car engine in cubic centimeters if you know its volume in cubic inches."

Volume (cubic inches), x	100	200	300
Volume (cubic centimeters), y	1640	3280	4920

Remember

An independent variable represents a quantity that can change freely. A dependent variable depends on the independent variable.

Key Idea

Functions as Equations

A **function rule** is an equation that describes the relationship between inputs (independent variable) and outputs (dependent variable).

Input $\xrightarrow{-2}$ Function Rule: $y = 3x$ $\xrightarrow{-6}$ Output

EXAMPLE 1 **Writing Function Rules**

a. Write a function rule for "The output is five less than the input."

Words The output is five less than the input.

Equation $y \quad = \quad x - 5$

▷ A function rule is $y = x - 5$.

b. Write a function rule for "The output is the square of the input."

Words The output is the square of the input.

Equation $y \quad = \quad x^2$

▷ A function rule is $y = x^2$.

Try It

1. Write a function rule for "The output is one-fourth of the input."

EXAMPLE 2 **Evaluating a Function**

What is the value of $y = 2x + 5$ when $x = 3$?

$y = 2x + 5$ Write the equation.

$= 2(3) + 5$ Substitute 3 for *x*.

$= 11$ Simplify.

Try It   Find the value of *y* when $x = 5$.

2. $y = 4x - 1$ 3. $y = 10x$ 4. $y = 7 - 3x$

 **Key Idea**

Functions as Tables and Graphs

A function can be represented by an input-output table and by a graph.
The table and graph below represent the function $y = x + 2$.

Input, x	Output, y	Ordered Pair, (x, y)
1	3	(1, 3)
2	4	(2, 4)
3	5	(3, 5)

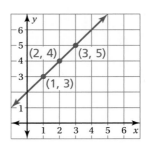

By drawing a line through the points, you graph *all* of the solutions
of the function $y = x + 2$.

EXAMPLE 3 **Graphing a Function**

Graph the function $y = -2x + 1$.

Make an input-output table using inputs of -1, 0, 1, and 2.

Input, x	−2x + 1	Output, y	Ordered Pair, (x, y)
−1	−2(−1) + 1	3	(−1, 3)
0	−2(0) + 1	1	(0, 1)
1	−2(1) + 1	−1	(1, −1)
2	−2(2) + 1	−3	(2, −3)

Plot the ordered pairs and draw a line through the points.

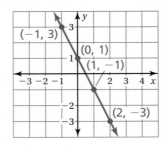

Try It **Graph the function.**

5. $y = x + 1$ **6.** $y = -3x$ **7.** $y = 3x + 2$

 **Summary**

Representations of Functions

Words The output is 2 more than the input.

Equation $y = x + 2$

Input-Output Table

Input, x	Output, y
−1	1
0	2
1	3
2	4

Mapping Diagram

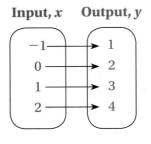

Graph

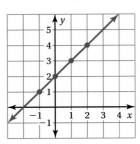

Self-Assessment *for Concepts & Skills*

Solve each exercise. Then rate your understanding of the success criteria in your journal.

WRITING FUNCTION RULES **Write a function rule for the statement.**

8. The output is three times the input.

9. The output is eight more than one-seventh of the input.

EVALUATING A FUNCTION **Find the value of y when $x = -5$.**

10. $y = 6x$

11. $y = 11 - x$

12. $y = \dfrac{1}{5}x + 1$

GRAPHING A FUNCTION **Graph the function.**

13. $y = -2x$

14. $y = x - 3$

15. $y = 9 - 3x$

16. **DIFFERENT WORDS, SAME QUESTION** Which is different? Find "both" answers.

What output is 4 more than twice the input 3?	What output is twice the sum of the input 3 and 4?
What output is the sum of 2 times the input 3 and 4?	What output is 4 increased by twice the input 3?

EXAMPLE 4 **Modeling Real Life**

A car produces 20 pounds of carbon dioxide for every gallon of gasoline burned. Write and graph a function that describes the relationship.

Use a verbal model to write a function rule.

| Verbal Model | Carbon dioxide (pounds) | = | Pounds per gallon | · | Gasoline used (gallons) |

Variable Let p represent the number of pounds of carbon dioxide, and let g represent the number of gallons of gasoline used.

Equation $p = 20 \cdot g$

Make an input-output table that represents the function $p = 20g$.

Math Practice

Analyze Relationships
Which variable is the independent variable? the dependent variable? Explain.

Input, g	$20g$	Output, p	Ordered Pair, (g, p)
1	$20(1)$	20	$(1, 20)$
2	$20(2)$	40	$(2, 40)$
3	$20(3)$	60	$(3, 60)$

Plot the ordered pairs and draw a line through the points.

Because you cannot burn a negative number of gallons of gasoline, use only positive values of g.

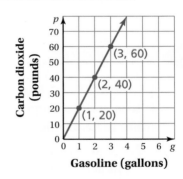

 Self-Assessment for Problem Solving

Solve each exercise. Then rate your understanding of the success criteria in your journal.

17. The World Health Organization (WHO) suggests having 23 health-care workers for every 10,000 people. How many health-care workers are needed to meet the WHO suggestion for a population of 250,000 people? Justify your answer using a graph.

18. **DIG DEEPER!** A truck produces 22 pounds of carbon dioxide for every gallon of diesel fuel burned. The fuel economy of the truck is 18 miles per gallon. Write and graph a function that describes the relationship between carbon dioxide produced and distance traveled.

7.2 Practice

? Go to *BigIdeasMath.com* to get HELP with solving the exercises.

▶ Review & Refresh

Determine whether the relation is a function.

1. Input Output

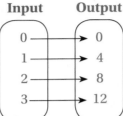

2. Input Output

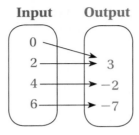

3. Input Output

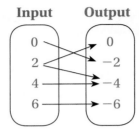

Find the slope of the line.

4.

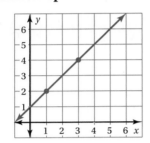

5.

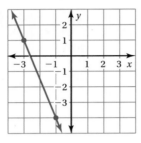

6.

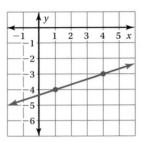

▶▶ Concepts, Skills, & Problem Solving

USING A GRAPH Use a graph to test the truth of the statement. If the statement is true, write an equation that shows how to obtain one measurement from the other measurement. (See Exploration 2, p. 281.)

7. "You can find the weight of a cell phone in ounces if you know its screen size in inches."

Screen Size (inches), x	4	4.7	5	5.5
Weight (ounces), y	4	4.8	4.8	6.4

8. "You can find the age of a child in years if you know the age of the child in months."

Age (months), x	9	12	15	24
Age (years), y	0.75	1	1.25	2

WRITING FUNCTION RULES Write a function rule for the statement.

9. The output is half of the input.

10. The output is eleven more than the input.

11. The output is three less than the input.

12. The output is the cube of the input.

13. The output is six times the input.

14. The output is one more than twice the input.

EVALUATING A FUNCTION Find the value of y for the given value of x.

15. $y = x + 5$; $x = 3$

16. $y = 7x$; $x = -5$

17. $y = 1 - 2x$; $x = 9$

18. $y = 3x + 2$; $x = 0.5$

19. $y = 2x^3$; $x = 3$

20. $y = \dfrac{x}{2} + 9$; $x = -12$

GRAPHING A FUNCTION Graph the function.

21. $y = x + 4$

22. $y = 2x$

23. $y = -5x + 3$

24. $y = \dfrac{x}{4}$

25. $y = \dfrac{3}{2}x + 1$

26. $y = 1 + 0.5x$

MATCHING Match the graph with the function it represents.

27.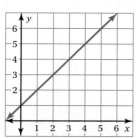

28.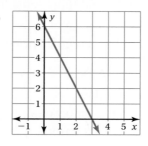

29.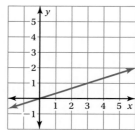

A. $y = \dfrac{x}{3}$

B. $y = x + 1$

C. $y = -2x + 6$

30. **MP YOU BE THE TEACHER** Your friend graphs the function represented by the input-output table. Is your friend correct? Explain your reasoning.

Input, x	−4	−2	0	2
Output, y	−1	1	3	5

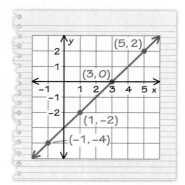

31. **MODELING REAL LIFE** A dolphin eats 30 pounds of fish per day.

   a. Write and graph a function that relates the number p of pounds of fish that a dolphin eats in d days.

   b. How many total pounds of fish does a dolphin eat in 30 days?

32. **MP MODELING REAL LIFE** You fill a fish tank with 55 gallons of water on Saturday. The water evaporates at a rate of 1.5 gallons per day. You plan to add water when the tank reaches 49 gallons. When will you add water? Justify your answer.

USING AN EQUATION Find the value of x for the given value of y.

33. $y = 5x - 7$; $y = -22$

34. $y = 9 - 7x$; $y = 37$

35. $y = \dfrac{x}{4} - 7$; $y = 2$

36. **MP PROBLEM SOLVING** You decide to make and sell bracelets. The cost of your materials is $84.00. You charge $3.50 for each bracelet.

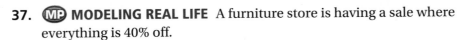

   a. Write a function that represents the profit *P* for selling *b* bracelets.

   b. Which variable is independent? dependent? Explain.

   c. You will *break even* when the cost of your materials equals your income. How many bracelets must you sell to break even?

37. **MP MODELING REAL LIFE** A furniture store is having a sale where everything is 40% off.

   a. Write and graph a function that represents the amount of discount on an item at regular price.

   b. You buy a bookshelf that has a regular price of $85. What is the sale price of the bookshelf?

38. **MP REASONING** You want to take a two-hour airboat tour. Which is a better deal, Snake Tours or Gator Tours? Use functions to justify your answer.

39. **MP REASONING** The graph of a function is a line that passes through the points (3, 2), (5, 8), and (8, *y*). What is the value of *y*?

40. **CRITICAL THINKING** Make a table where the independent variable is the side length of a square and the dependent variable is the *perimeter*. Make a second table where the independent variable is the side length of a square and the dependent variable is the *area*. Graph both functions in the same coordinate plane. Compare the functions.

41. **PUZZLE** The blocks that form the diagonals of each square are shaded. Each block has an area of one square unit. Find the "green area" of Square 20. Find the "green area" of Square 21. Explain your reasoning.

Square 1

Square 2

Square 3

Square 4

Square 5

7.3 Linear Functions

Learning Target: Use functions to model linear relationships.

Success Criteria:
• I can write linear functions to model relationships.
• I can interpret linear functions in real-life situations.

EXPLORATION 1

Writing and Graphing Functions

Work with a partner. Each table shows a familiar pattern from geometry.

• Determine what the variables x and y represent. Then write a function rule that relates y to x.

• Is the function a *linear function*? Explain your reasoning.

Math Practice

Interpret Results
How can you determine whether a function is a linear function using a graph? an equation?

a.

x	1	2	3	4
y	10	12	14	16

b.

x	1	2	3	4
y	π	4π	9π	16π

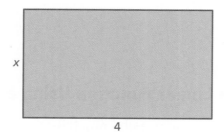

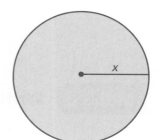

c.

x	1	2	3	4
y	5	6	7	8

d.

x	1	2	3	4
y	28	40	52	64

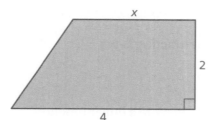

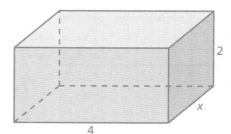

Key Vocabulary 🔊
linear function, *p. 290*

A **linear function** is a function whose graph is a nonvertical line. A linear function can be written in the form $y = mx + b$, where m is the slope and b is the y-intercept.

EXAMPLE 1 **Writing a Linear Function Using a Graph**

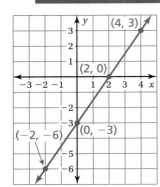

Use the graph to write a linear function that relates y to x.

Find the slope of the line using the points $(2, 0)$ and $(4, 3)$.

$$m = \frac{\text{change in } y}{\text{change in } x} = \frac{3 - 0}{4 - 2} = \frac{3}{2}$$

Because the line crosses the y-axis at $(0, -3)$, the y-intercept is -3.

▷ So, the linear function is $y = \frac{3}{2}x - 3$.

Try It

1. Use the graph to write a linear function that relates y to x.

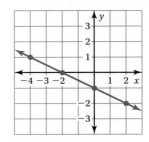

EXAMPLE 2 **Writing a Linear Function Using a Table**

Use the table to write a linear function that relates y to x.

x	−3	−2	−1	0
y	9	7	5	3

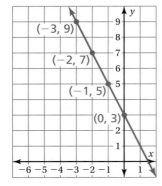

Plot the points in the table. Draw a line through the points.

Find the slope of the line using the points $(-2, 7)$ and $(-3, 9)$.

$$m = \frac{\text{change in } y}{\text{change in } x} = \frac{9 - 7}{-3 - (-2)} = \frac{2}{-1} = -2$$

Because the line crosses the y-axis at $(0, 3)$, the y-intercept is 3.

▷ So, the linear function is $y = -2x + 3$.

Try It

2. Use the table to write a linear function that relates y to x.

x	−2	−1	0	1
y	2	2	2	2

EXAMPLE 3 **Interpreting a Linear Function**

An unmanned aerial vehicle (UAV) is used for surveillance. The table shows the height y (in thousands of feet) of the UAV x minutes after it begins to descend from cruising altitude.

Minutes, x	Height (thousands of feet), y
0	65
10	60
20	55

a. **Write and graph a linear function that relates y to x.**

The table shows a constant rate of change, so you can write a linear function that relates the dependent variable y to the independent variable x.

The point $(0, 65)$ indicates that the y-intercept is 65. Use the points $(0, 65)$ and $(10, 60)$ to find the slope.

$$m = \frac{\text{change in } y}{\text{change in } x} = \frac{60 - 65}{10 - 0} = \frac{-5}{10} = -0.5$$

So, the linear function is $y = -0.5x + 65$. Plot the points in the table and draw a line through the points.

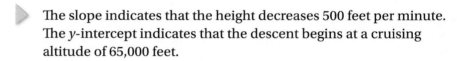

UAV Flight

$y = -0.5x + 65$

Height (thousands of feet) / Minutes

b. **Interpret the slope and the y-intercept.**

The slope indicates that the height decreases 500 feet per minute. The y-intercept indicates that the descent begins at a cruising altitude of 65,000 feet.

Try It

3. **WHAT IF?** The rate of descent doubles. Repeat parts (a) and (b).

Self-Assessment for Concepts & Skills

Solve each exercise. Then rate your understanding of the success criteria in your journal.

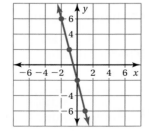

4. **WRITING A LINEAR FUNCTION** Use the graph to write a linear function that relates y to x.

5. **INTERPRETING A LINEAR FUNCTION** The table shows the revenue R (in millions of dollars) of a company when it spends A (in millions of dollars) on advertising.

Advertising, A	0	2	4	6	8
Revenue, R	2	6	10	14	18

a. Write and graph a linear function that relates R to A.

b. Interpret the slope and the y-intercept.

EXAMPLE 4 **Modeling Real Life**

The cost y (in dollars) of buying x cubic yards of mulch from Company A, including a one-time shipping fee, is represented by the linear function $y = 29x + 30$. The table shows the cost, including a one-time shipping fee, of buying mulch from Company B. Which company charges more per cubic yard of mulch? How much more?

Mulch (cubic yards), x	Cost (dollars), y
1	48.50
2	82.00
3	115.50

 Understand the problem.

You are given functions that represent the costs of buying mulch from two different companies. You are asked to determine which company charges more per cubic yard of mulch and how much more it charges.

 **Make a plan.**

The table shows a constant rate of change, so the relationship is linear. The cost per cubic yard of mulch for each company is represented by the slope of the graph of each function. Find and compare the slopes.

 Solve and check.

Company A

$y = 29x + 30$

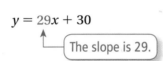 The slope is 29.

Company A charges $29.00 per cubic yard.

Company B

$$\frac{\text{change in cost}}{\text{change in amount of mulch}} = \frac{82 - 48.50}{2 - 1}$$

$$= 33.5$$

Company B charges $33.50 per cubic yard.

> So, Company B charges $33.50 - 29.00 = \$4.50$ more per cubic yard of mulch.

Check Reasonableness
For Company B, use the points (2, 82) and (3, 115.50) to find the slope.

$$\text{slope} = \frac{115.50 - 82.00}{3 - 2}$$

$$= 33.5 \checkmark$$

 Self-Assessment *for Problem Solving*

Solve each exercise. Then rate your understanding of the success criteria in your journal.

Earnings of Manager B

(3, 75)

6. Manager A earns $15 per hour and receives a $50 bonus. The graph shows the earnings of Manager B. (a) Which manager has a greater hourly wage? (b) After how many hours does Manager B earn more money than Manager A?

7. Each month, you start with 2 gigabytes of data and use 0.08 gigabyte per day. The table shows the amount y (in gigabytes) of data that your friend has left x days after the start of each month. Who runs out of data first? Justify your answer.

Day, x	Data (gigabytes), y
0	3
7	2.3
14	1.6

7.3 Practice

Go to *BigIdeasMath.com* to get
HELP with solving the exercises.

▶ Review & Refresh

Write a function rule for the statement. Then graph the function.

1. The output is ten less than the input.   **2.** The output is one-third of the input.

Solve the system.

3. $y = x + 5$
$\quad y = -3x + 1$

4. $x + y = -4$
$\quad 6x + 2y = 4$

5. $-4x + 3y = 14$
$\quad y = 2x + 8$

▶▶ Concepts, Skills, & Problem Solving

WRITING AND GRAPHING FUNCTIONS The table shows a familiar pattern from geometry. **(a)** Determine what the variables x and y represent. Then write a function rule that relates y to x. **(b)** Is the function a *linear function*? Explain your reasoning. (See Exploration 1, p. 289.)

6.

x	1	2	3	4	5
y	2	4	6	8	10

7.

x	1	2	3	4	5
y	π	2π	3π	4π	5π

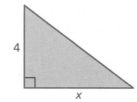

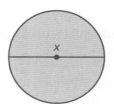

WRITING LINEAR FUNCTIONS Use the graph or table to write a linear function that relates y to x.

8.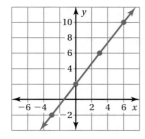

9.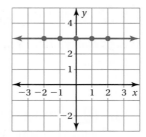

10.

x	−8	−4	0	4
y	2	1	0	−1

11.

x	−3	0	3	6
y	3	5	7	9

12. INTERPRETING A LINEAR FUNCTION The table shows the length y (in inches) of a person's hair after x months.

    a. Write and graph a linear function that relates y to x.

    b. Interpret the slope and the y-intercept.

Months, x	Hair Length, y
0	11.0
3	12.5
6	14.0

13. **INTERPRETING A LINEAR FUNCTION** The table shows the percent y (in decimal form) of battery power remaining x hours after you turn on a laptop computer.

Hours, x	0	2	4
Power Remaining, y	1.0	0.6	0.2

   a. Write and graph a linear function that relates y to x.

   b. Interpret the slope, the x-intercept, and the y-intercept.

   c. After how many hours is the battery power at 75%?

14. **MP MODELING REAL LIFE** The number y of calories burned after x minutes of kayaking is represented by the linear function $y = 4.5x$. The graph shows the number of calories burned by hiking.

   a. Which activity burns more calories per minute?

   b. You perform each activity for 45 minutes. How many total calories do you burn? Justify your answer.

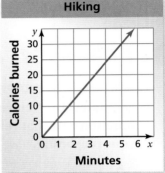

Hiking

15. **DIG DEEPER!** You and a friend race each other. You give your friend a 50-foot head start. The distance y (in feet) your friend runs after x seconds is represented by the linear function $y = 14x + 50$. A 10-second race ends in a tie. Write an equation for the distance y (in feet) you run after x seconds. When do you win the race? Explain your reasoning.

16. **MP REASONING** You and your friend are saving money to buy bicycles that cost $175 each. You have $45 to start and save an additional $5 each week. The graph shows the amount y (in dollars) that your friend has after x weeks. Who can buy a bicycle first? Justify your answer.

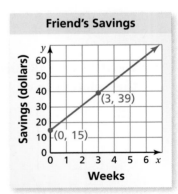

Friend's Savings

17. **CRITICAL THINKING** Is every linear equation a linear function? Explain your reasoning.

18. **MP PROBLEM SOLVING** The heat index is calculated using the relative humidity and the temperature. For every 1 degree increase in the temperature from 94°F to 97°F at 75% relative humidity, the heat index rises 4°F. On a summer day, the relative humidity is 75%, the temperature is 94°F, and the heat index is 124°F. Estimate the heat index when the relative humidity is 75% and the temperature is 100°F. Use a function to justify your answer.

7.4 Comparing Linear and Nonlinear Functions

Learning Target: Understand differences between linear and nonlinear functions.

Success Criteria:
- I can recognize linear functions represented as tables, equations, and graphs.
- I can compare linear and nonlinear functions.

EXPLORATION 1

Comparing Functions

Work with a partner. Each equation represents the height h (in feet) of a falling object after t seconds.

- **MP** **CHOOSE TOOLS** Graph each equation. Explain your method.

- Decide whether each graph represents a *linear* or *nonlinear* function.

- Compare the falling objects.

a. Skydiver

$$h = 300 - 15t$$

b. Bowling ball

$$h = 300 - 16t^2$$

Skydiver

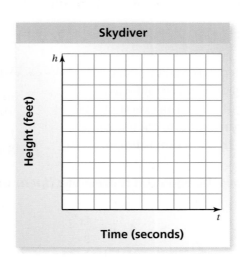

Height (feet) — h / Time (seconds) — t

Bowling Ball

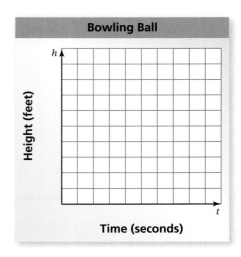

Height (feet) — h / Time (seconds) — t

The graph of a linear function shows a constant rate of change. A **nonlinear function** does not have a constant rate of change. So, its graph is *not* a line.

EXAMPLE 1 Identifying Functions from Tables

Does each table represent a *linear* or *nonlinear* function? Explain.

a.

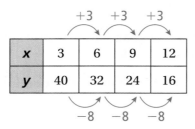

b.

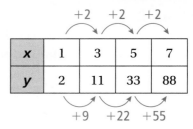

▷ As x increases by 3, y decreases by 8. The rate of change is constant. So, the function is linear.

▷ As x increases by 2, y increases by different amounts. The rate of change is *not* constant. So, the function is nonlinear.

Try It **Does the table represent a *linear* or *nonlinear* function? Explain.**

1.

x	2	4	6	8
y	−8	−4	0	4

2.

x	0	3	7	12
y	25	20	15	10

EXAMPLE 2 Identifying Functions from Equations

Does each equation represent a *linear* or *nonlinear* function? Explain.

a. $y = 4(x − 1)$

b. $y = \dfrac{4}{x}$

▷ You can rewrite $y = 4(x − 1)$ in slope-intercept form as $y = 4x − 4$. The function has a constant rate of change. So, the function is linear.

▷ You cannot rewrite $y = \dfrac{4}{x}$ in slope-intercept form. The function does not have a constant rate of change. So, the function is nonlinear.

Try It **Does the equation represent a *linear* or *nonlinear* function? Explain.**

3. $y = x + 5$

4. $y = \dfrac{4x}{3}$

5. $y = 1 − x^2$

◀)) Multi-Language Glossary at *BigIdeasMath.com*

EXAMPLE 3 Identifying Functions from Graphs

Does each graph represent a *linear* or *nonlinear* function? Explain.

a.
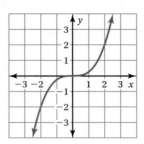

b.
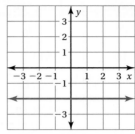

▷ The graph is *not* a line. So, the function is nonlinear.

▷ The graph is a line. So, the function is linear.

Try It Does the graph represent a *linear* or *nonlinear* function? Explain.

6.
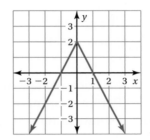

7.
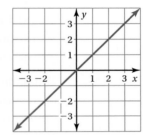

Self-Assessment *for Concepts & Skills*

Solve each exercise. Then rate your understanding of the success criteria in your journal.

IDENTIFYING FUNCTIONS Does the table or graph represent a *linear* or *nonlinear* function? Explain.

8.

x	3	−1	−5	−9
y	0	2	4	6

9.
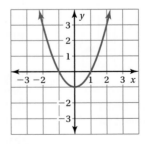

10. **WHICH ONE DOESN'T BELONG?** Which equation does *not* belong with the other three? Explain your reasoning.

$$15y = 6x$$

$$y = \frac{2}{5}x$$

$$10y = 4x$$

$$5xy = 2$$

EXAMPLE 4 **Modeling Real Life**

Year, *t*	Account A Balance	Account B Balance
0	$100	$100
1	$110	$110
2	$120	$121
3	$130	$133.10
4	$140	$146.41
5	$150	$161.05

Two accounts earn different types of interest. The table shows the balances of each account for five years. Graph the data and compare the balances of the accounts over time.

Plot the points in the table for each account.

The points for Account A lie on a line. Draw a line through the points.

The points for Account B do not lie on a line. Draw a *curve* through the points.

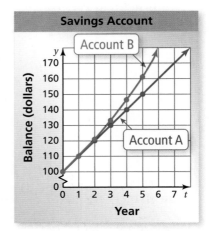

The graphs show that both balances are positive and increasing. The graphs also show that the balance of Account B grows faster.

The balance of Account A has a constant rate of change of $10. The balance of Account B increases by different amounts each year. So, Account A shows linear growth and Account B shows nonlinear growth.

Self-Assessment for *Problem Solving*

Solve each exercise. Then rate your understanding of the success criteria in your journal.

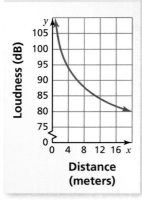

11. The loudness of sound is measured in *decibels* (dB). The graph shows the loudness *y* of a sound (in decibels) *x* meters from the source of the sound. Is the relationship between loudness and distance *linear* or *nonlinear*? Approximate the loudness of the sound 12 meters from the source.

12. **DIG DEEPER!** A *video blogger* is someone who records a video diary. A new website currently hosts 90 video bloggers and projects a gain of 10 video bloggers per month. The table below shows the actual numbers of video bloggers. How does the projection differ from the actual change?

Month	0	1	2	3	4	5
Video Bloggers	90	97	110	128	153	190

7.4 Practice

? Go to **BigIdeasMath.com** to get HELP with solving the exercises.

▶ Review & Refresh

Write a linear function that relates *y* to *x*.

1.

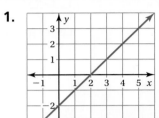

2.

x	0	1.5	3	4.5
y	5	4	3	2

The vertices of a figure are given. Draw the figure and its image after a dilation with the given scale factor. Identify the type of dilation.

3. $A(-3, 1)$, $B(-1, 3)$, $C(-1, 1)$; $k = 3$ **4.** $J(2, 4)$, $K(6, 10)$, $L(8, 10)$, $M(8, 4)$; $k = \frac{1}{4}$

▶▶ Concepts, Skills, & Problem Solving

COMPARING FUNCTIONS **Graph each equation. Decide whether each graph represents a *linear* or *nonlinear* function.** (See Exploration 1, p. 295.)

5. $h = 5 + 6t$ Equation 1

     $h = 5 + 6t^2$ Equation 2

6. $y = -\dfrac{x}{3}$ Equation 1

     $y = -\dfrac{3}{x}$ Equation 2

IDENTIFYING FUNCTIONS FROM TABLES **Does the table represent a *linear* or *nonlinear* function? Explain.**

7.

x	0	1	2	3
y	4	8	12	16

8.

x	6	5	4	3
y	21	15	10	6

IDENTIFYING FUNCTIONS FROM EQUATIONS **Does the equation represent a *linear* or *nonlinear* function? Explain.**

9. $2x + 3y = 7$ **10.** $y + x = 4x + 5$ **11.** $y = \dfrac{8}{x^2}$

IDENTIFYING FUNCTIONS FROM GRAPHS **Does the graph represent a *linear* or *nonlinear* function? Explain.**

12.

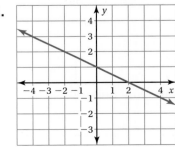

13.

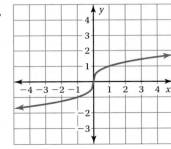

14. **IDENTIFYING A FUNCTION** The graph shows the volume V (in cubic feet) of a cube with an edge length of x feet. Does the graph represent a *linear* or *nonlinear* function? Explain.

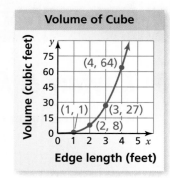

Volume of Cube

15. **MP MODELING REAL LIFE** The frequency y (in terahertz) of a light wave is a function of its wavelength x (in nanometers). Is the function relating the wavelength of light to its frequency *linear* or *nonlinear*?

Color	Red	Yellow	Green	Blue	Violet
Wavelength, x	660	595	530	465	400
Frequency, y	454	504	566	645	749

16. **DIG DEEPER!** The table shows the cost y (in dollars) of x pounds of sunflower seeds.

Pounds, x	Cost, y
2	2.80
3	?
4	5.60

a. What is the missing y-value that makes the table represent a linear function?

b. Write a linear function that represents the cost y of x pounds of seeds. Interpret the slope.

c. Does the function have a maximum value? Explain your reasoning.

17. **MP MODELING REAL LIFE** A birch tree is 9 feet tall and grows at a rate of 2 feet per year. The table shows the height h (in feet) of a willow tree after x years.

Years, x	Height, h
0	5
1	11
4	17
9	23

a. Does the table represent a *linear* or *nonlinear* function? Explain.

b. Which tree is taller after 10 years? Explain.

18. **CRITICAL THINKING** In their first year, Show A has 7 million viewers and Show B has 5 million viewers. Each year, Show A has 90% of the viewers it had in the previous year. Show B loses 200,000 viewers each year.

a. Determine whether the function relating the year to the number of viewers is *linear* or *nonlinear* for each show.

b. Which show has more viewers in its sixth year?

19. **MP PATTERNS** The ordered pairs represent a function.

$$(0, -1), (1, 0), (2, 3), (3, 8), \text{ and } (4, 15)$$

a. Graph the ordered pairs and describe the pattern. Is the function *linear* or *nonlinear*?

b. Write an equation that represents the function.

7.5 Analyzing and Sketching Graphs

Learning Target: Use graphs of functions to describe relationships between quantities.

Success Criteria:
- I can describe relationships between quantities in graphs.
- I can sketch graphs given verbal descriptions of relationships.

EXPLORATION 1

Matching Situations to Graphs

Work with a partner. Each graph shows your speed during a bike ride. Match each situation with its graph. Explain your reasoning.

A.
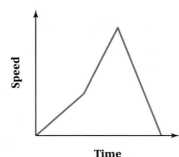

B.
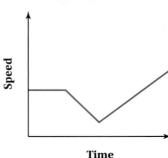

C.
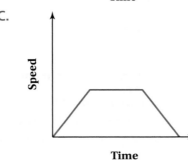

D.
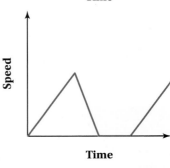

Math Practice

Analyze Relationships
A graph relating distance and time shows a positive linear relationship. Describe a graph relating speed and time in this situation.

a. You increase your speed, then ride at a constant speed along a bike path. You then slow down until you reach your friend's house.

b. You increase your speed, then go down a hill. You then quickly come to a stop at an intersection.

c. You increase your speed, then stop at a store for a couple of minutes. You then continue to ride, increasing your speed.

d. You ride at a constant speed, then go up a hill. Once on top of the hill, you increase your speed.

EXPLORATION 2

Interpreting a Graph

Work with a partner. Write a short paragraph that describes how the height changes over time in the graph shown. What situation can this graph represent?

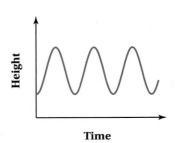

7.5 Lesson

Graphs can show the relationship between quantities without using specific numbers on the axes.

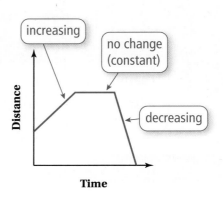

EXAMPLE 1 **Analyzing Graphs**

The graphs show the temperatures throughout the day in two cities.

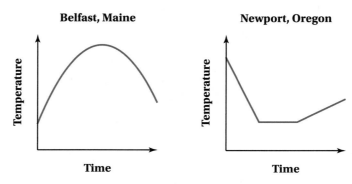

a. **Describe the change in temperature in each city.**

Belfast: The temperature increases at the beginning of the day. The rate of increase slows until the temperature begins to decrease. Then the temperature decreases at a faster and faster rate for the rest of the day.

Newport: The temperature decreases at a constant rate at the beginning of the day. Then the temperature stays the same for a while before increasing at a constant rate for the rest of the day.

b. **Write an explanation for the decrease in temperature and the increase in temperature in Newport, Oregon.**

A storm moves through the city in the morning, causing the temperature to drop. When the storm ends, the temperature increases at a constant rate.

Math Practice

Make Sense of Quantities
Are there other possible explanations for the changes in temperature in Example 1(b)? Explain.

Try It

1. The graph shows the location of a pelican relative to your location.

    a. Describe the path of the pelican.

    b. Write an explanation for the decrease in the vertical distance of the pelican.

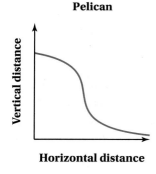

You can sketch graphs showing relationships between quantities that are described verbally.

EXAMPLE 2 **Sketching Graphs**

A stopped subway train gains speed at a constant rate until it reaches its maximum speed. It travels at this speed for a while, and then slows down at a constant rate until coming to a stop at the next station. Sketch a graph that represents this situation.

Draw the axes. Label the vertical axis "Speed" and the horizontal axis "Time." Then sketch the graph.

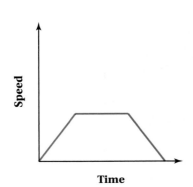

Words	Graph
A stopped subway train gains speed at a constant rate . . .	increasing line segment starting at the origin
until it reaches its maximum speed. It travels at this speed for a while, . . .	horizontal line segment
and then slows down at a constant rate until coming to a stop at the next station.	decreasing line segment ending at the horizontal axis

Try It

2. A fully-charged battery loses its charge at a constant rate until it has no charge left. You plug it in, and it fully recharges at a constant rate. Then it loses its charge at a constant rate until it has no charge left. Sketch a graph that represents this situation.

Self-Assessment *for Concepts & Skills*

Solve each exercise. Then rate your understanding of the success criteria in your journal.

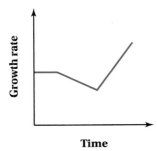

3. **ANALYZING GRAPHS** The graph shows the growth rate of a plant over time.

   a. Describe the change in growth rate.

   b. Write an explanation for the decrease in growth rate and the increase in growth rate.

4. **SKETCHING GRAPHS** As you snowboard down a hill, you gain speed at a constant rate. You come to a steep section of the hill and gain speed at a greater constant rate. You then slow down at a constant rate until you come to a stop. Sketch a graph that represents this situation.

EXAMPLE 3 **Modeling Real Life**

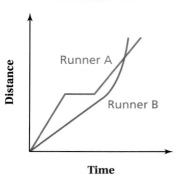

The graph shows the distances traveled by two runners in a race from start to finish. Describe the speed of each runner throughout the race. Then determine who finishes first.

Runner A

The red line increases at a constant rate at the beginning of the race, stays horizontal for a short time in the middle, and then increases at a constant rate at the end of the race.

So, Runner A starts running at a constant speed, stops to rest, and then continues to run at a constant speed.

Runner B

The blue line increases at a constant rate for most of the race, and then increases at a faster and faster rate at the end of the race.

So, Runner B starts running at a constant speed and continues to run that speed for most of the race. Near the end of the race, Runner B accelerates through the finish line.

▷ The graph shows that Runner B travels the same distance as Runner A, but in a shorter amount of time. So, Runner B wins the race.

 Self-Assessment *for Problem Solving*

Solve each exercise. Then rate your understanding of the success criteria in your journal.

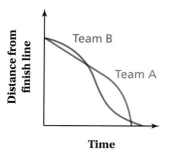

5. Two rowing teams are in a race. The graph shows their distances from the finish line over time. Describe the speed of each team throughout the race. Then determine which team finishes first.

6. **DIG DEEPER!** The graphs show the movements of two airplanes over time. Describe the movement of each airplane.

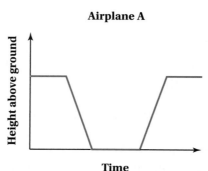

Airplane A

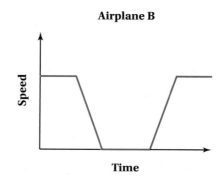

Airplane B

Go to *BigIdeasMath.com* to get HELP with solving the exercises.

▶ Review & Refresh

Does the table or equation represent a *linear* or *nonlinear* function? Explain.

1.

x	−5	−1	3	7
y	14	12	10	8

2. $y = x^2 + 8$

Graph the linear equation.

3. $-4x + y = -1$

4. $2x - 3y = 12$

5. $5x + 10y = 30$

▶▶ Concepts, Skills, & Problem Solving

MATCHING DESCRIPTIONS WITH GRAPHS The graph shows your speed during a run. **Match the verbal description with the part of the graph it describes.** (See Exploration 1, p. 301.)

6. You run at a constant speed.

7. You slow down at a constant rate.

8. You increase your speed at a constant rate.

9. You increase your speed at a faster and faster rate.

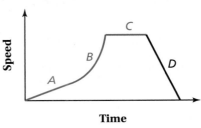

ANALYZING GRAPHS **Describe the relationship between the two quantities.**

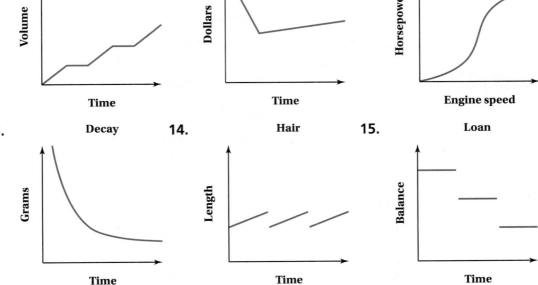

10. Balloon

11. Sales

12. Engine Power

13. Decay

14. Hair

15. Loan

16. **ANALYZING GRAPHS** Write an explanation for the relationship shown in the graph in Exercise 10.

17. **MP MODELING REAL LIFE** The graph shows the natural gas usage for a house.

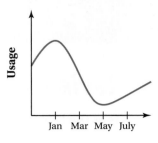

   a. Describe the change in usage from January to March.

   b. Describe the change in usage from March to May.

SKETCHING GRAPHS **Sketch a graph that represents the situation.**

18. The value of a television decreases at a constant rate, and then remains constant.

19. The distance from the ground changes as your friend swings on a swing.

20. The value of a rare coin increases at a faster and faster rate.

21. You are typing at a constant rate. You pause to think about your next paragraph, and then you resume typing at the same constant rate.

22. **CRITICAL THINKING** The graph shows the speed of an object over time.

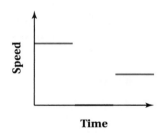

   a. Sketch a graph that shows the distance traveled by the object over time.

   b. Describe a possible situation represented by the graphs.

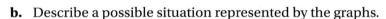

23. **MP MODELING REAL LIFE** The graph shows the average scores of two bowlers from the start of a season to the end of the season.

   a. Describe each bowler's performance.

   b. Who had a greater average score most of the season? Who had a greater average score at the end of the season?

   c. Write an explanation for the change in each bowler's average score throughout the bowling season.

24. **DIG DEEPER!** You can use a *supply and demand model* to understand how the price of a product changes in a market. The *supply curve* of a particular product represents the quantity suppliers will produce at various prices. The *demand curve* for the product represents the quantity consumers are willing to buy at various prices.

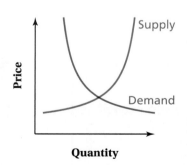

   a. Describe and interpret each curve.

   b. Which part of the graph represents a surplus? a shortage? Explain your reasoning.

   c. The curves intersect at the *equilibrium point*, which is where the quantity produced equals the quantity demanded. Suppose that demand for a product suddenly increases, causing the entire demand curve to shift to the right. What happens to the equilibrium point?

Connecting Concepts

▷ *Using the Problem-Solving Plan*

Length, x	Weight, y
19.2	6.9
19.3	7.3
18.9	6.5
19.4	7.2
19.7	7.6
19.2	7.0
19.5	7.6

1. The table shows the lengths x (in inches) and weights y (in pounds) of several infants born at a hospital. Determine whether weight is a function of length. Then estimate the weight of an infant that is 20 inches long.

Understand the problem.

You know the lengths and weights of several infants. You are asked to determine whether weight is a function of length and to estimate the weight of a 20-inch-long infant.

Make a plan.

Determine whether any of the lengths are paired with more than one weight. Then use a graphing calculator to find an equation that represents the data. Evaluate the equation when $x = 20$ to estimate the weight of a 20-inch-long infant.

Solve and check.

Use the plan to solve the problem. Then check your solution.

2. Each mapping diagram represents a linear function. At what point do the graphs of the functions intersect? Justify your answer.

Function 1

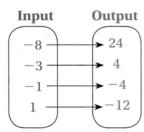

Function 2

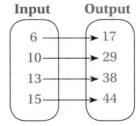

Performance Task

Heat Index

At the beginning of this chapter, you watched a STEAM Video called "Apparent Temperature." You are now ready to complete the performance task related to this video, available at *BigIdeasMath.com*. Be sure to use the problem-solving plan as you work through the performance task.

Go to *BigIdeasMath.com* to download blank graphic organizers.

▶ Review Vocabulary

Write the definition and give an example of each vocabulary term.

input, *p. 276*   mapping diagram, *p. 276*   linear function, *p. 290*

output, *p. 276*   function, *p. 277*   nonlinear function, *p. 296*

relation, *p. 276*   function rule, *p. 282*

▶ Graphic Organizers

You can use an **Example and Non-Example Chart** to list examples and non-examples of a concept. Here is an Example and Non-Example Chart for *functions*.

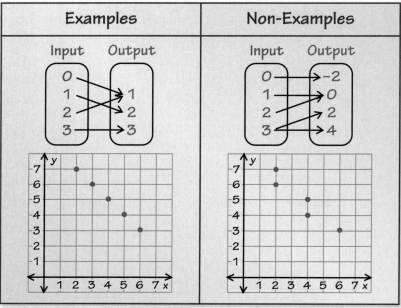

Functions

Choose and complete a graphic organizer to help you study the concept.

1. linear functions

2. nonlinear functions

3. linear functions with positive slope

4. linear functions with negative slope

"I finished my **Example and Non-Example Chart** about animals living in the Grand Canyon."

Chapter Self-Assessment

As you complete the exercises, use the scale below to rate your understanding of the success criteria in your journal.

1	2	3	4
I do not understand.	I can do it with help.	I can do it on my own.	I can teach someone else.

7.1 Relations and Functions *(pp. 275–280)*

Learning Target: Understand the concept of a function.

List the ordered pairs shown in the mapping diagram. Then determine whether the relation is a function.

1.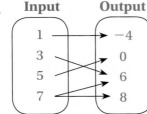

2.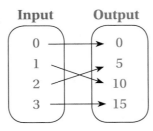

3.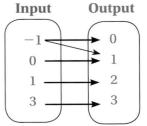

4. For ordered pairs that represent relations, which coordinate represents the input? the output?

5. Draw a mapping diagram that represents the relation shown in the graph. Then determine whether the relation is a function. Explain.

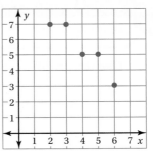

6. The mapping diagram represents the lengths (in centimeters) of a rubber band when different amounts of force (in Newtons) are applied.

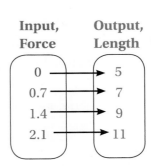

    a. Is the length of a rubber band a function of the force applied to the rubber band?

    b. Describe the relationship between the length of a rubber band and the force applied to the rubber band.

7.2 Representations of Functions *(pp. 281–288)*

Learning Target: Represent functions in a variety of ways.

Write a function rule for the statement.

7. The output is two less than the input.

8. The output is two more than one-fourth of the input.

Find the value of y for the given value of x.

9. $y = 2x - 3$; $x = -4$ **10.** $y = 2 - 9x$; $x = \dfrac{2}{3}$ **11.** $y = \dfrac{x}{3} + 5$; $x = 6$

Graph the function.

12. $y = x + 3$ **13.** $y = -5x$ **14.** $y = 3 - 3x$

15. An online music store sells songs for $0.90 each.

    a. Write a function that you can use to find the cost C of buying s songs.

    b. What is the cost of buying 5 songs?

7.3 Linear Functions *(pp. 289–294)*

Learning Target: Use functions to model linear relationships.

Use the graph or table to write a linear function that relates y to x.

16.

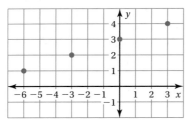

17.

x	-2	0	2	4
y	-7	-7	-7	-7

18. The table shows the age x (in weeks) of a puppy and its weight y (in pounds).

Age, x	6	8	10	12
Weight, y	12	15	18	21

    a. Write and graph a linear function that relates y to x.

    b. Interpret the slope and the y-intercept.

    c. After how many weeks will the puppy weigh 33 pounds?

7.4 Comparing Linear and Nonlinear Functions (pp. 295–300)

Learning Target: Understand differences between linear and nonlinear functions.

Does the table represent a *linear* or *nonlinear* function? Explain.

19.

x	3	6	9	12
y	1	10	19	28

20.

x	1	3	5	7
y	3	1	1	3

21. Does the graph represent a *linear* or *nonlinear* function? Explain.

22. Does the equation $y = 2.3x$ represent a *linear* or *nonlinear* function? Explain.

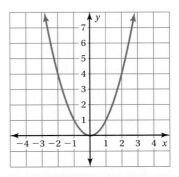

7.5 Analyzing and Sketching Graphs (pp. 301–306)

Learning Target: Use graphs of functions to describe relationships between quantities.

23. Describe the relationship between the two quantities in the graph.

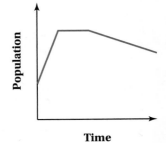

City Population

Sketch a graph that represents the situation.

24. You climb a climbing wall. You climb halfway up the wall at a constant rate, then stop and take a break. You then climb to the top of the wall at a greater constant rate.

25. The price of a stock increases at a constant rate for several months before the stock market crashes. The price then quickly decreases at a constant rate.

26. The graph shows the sales of two companies during a particular year.

   a. Describe the sales of each company.

   b. Which company has greater total sales for the year?

   c. Give a possible explanation for the change in each company's sales throughout the year.

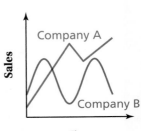

1. List the ordered pairs shown in the mapping diagram. Then determine whether the relation is a function.

Input   Output

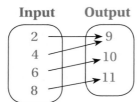

2. Draw a mapping diagram that represents the relation. Then determine whether the relation is a function. Explain.

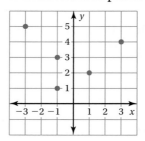

3. Write a function rule for "The output is twice the input."

4. Graph the function $y = 1 - 3x$.

5. Use the graph to write a linear function that relates y to x.

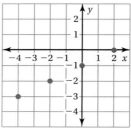

6. Does the table represent a *linear* or *nonlinear* function? Explain.

x	0	2	4	6
y	8	0	-8	-16

7. The table shows the number of meters y a water-skier travels in x minutes.

Minutes, x	1	2	3	4	5
Meters, y	600	1200	1800	2400	3000

    a. Write a function that relates y to x.

    b. Graph the linear function.

    c. At this rate, how many kilometers will the water-skier travel in 12 minutes?

    d. Another water-skier travels at the same rate but starts a minute after the first water-skier. Will this water-skier catch up to the first water-skier? Explain.

8. The graph shows the prices of two stocks during one day.

    a. Describe the changes in the price of each stock.

    b. Which stock has a greater price at the end of the day?

    c. Give a possible explanation for the change in the price of Stock B throughout the day.

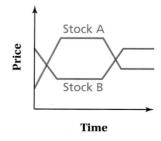

9. You are competing in a footrace. You begin the race by increasing your speed at a constant rate. You then run at a constant speed until you get a cramp and have to stop. You wait until your cramp goes away before you start increasing your speed again at a constant rate. Sketch a graph that represents the situation.

1. What is the slope of the line?

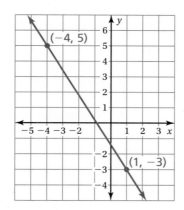

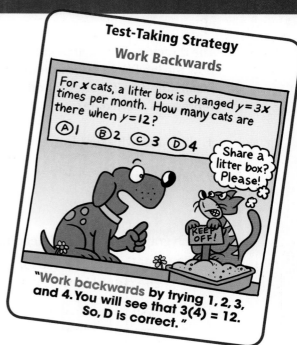

A. $-\dfrac{8}{3}$ **B.** $-\dfrac{8}{5}$

C. $-\dfrac{2}{3}$ **D.** $-\dfrac{2}{5}$

2. Which value of a makes the equation $24 = \dfrac{a}{3} - 9$ true?

F. 5   **G.** 11

H. 45   **I.** 99

3. A mapping diagram is shown.

What number belongs in the box so that the equation describes the function represented by the mapping diagram?

$$y = \boxed{}\, x + 5$$

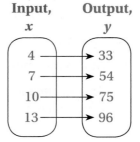

Input, x	Output, y
4	33
7	54
10	75
13	96

4. What is the solution of the system of linear equations?

$$3x + 2y = 5$$
$$x = y + 5$$

A. $(3, -2)$ **B.** $(-2, 3)$

C. $(-1, 4)$ **D.** $(1, -4)$

5. The director of a research lab wants to present data to donors. The data show how the lab uses a large amount of donated money for research and only a small amount of money for other expenses. Which type of display best represents these data?

   F. box-and-whisker plot   **G.** circle graph

   H. line graph   **I.** scatter plot

6. Which graph shows a nonlinear function?

   A.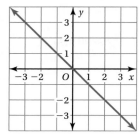

   B.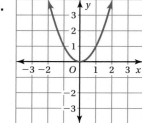

   C.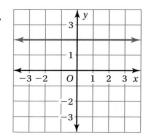

   D.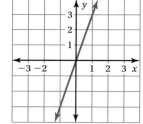

7. Which equation of a line passes through the point $(-2, 3)$ and has a slope of $\frac{3}{4}$?

   F. $y - 3 = \frac{3}{4}(x + 2)$

   G. $y + 3 = \frac{3}{4}(x - 2)$

   H. $y + 2 = \frac{3}{4}(x - 3)$

   I. $y = \frac{3}{4}(x + 2)$

8. The tables show the sales (in millions of dollars) for two companies over a five-year period.

Year	1	2	3	4	5
Sales	2	4	6	8	10

Year	1	2	3	4	5
Sales	1	1	2	3	5

Part A   Does the first table show a linear function? Explain your reasoning.

Part B   Does the second table show a linear function? Explain your reasoning.

9. The equations $y = -x + 4$ and $y = \frac{1}{2}x - 8$ form a system of linear equations. The table shows the values of y for given values of x.

x	0	2	4	6	8	10
$y = -x + 4$	4	2	0	−2	−4	−6
$y = \frac{1}{2}x - 8$	−8	−7	−6	−5	−4	−3

What can you conclude from the table?

A. The system has one solution, when $x = 0$.

B. The system has one solution, when $x = 4$.

C. The system has one solution, when $x = 8$.

D. The system has no solution.

10. The vertices of a triangle are $A(-1, 3)$, $B(1, 2)$, and $C(-1, -1)$. Dilate the triangle using a scale factor of 2. What is the y-coordinate of the image of B?

8 Exponents and Scientific Notation

Chapter Learning Target:
Understand exponents and scientific notation.

Chapter Success Criteria:
- ☐ I can write products using exponents.
- ☐ I can describe the value of powers.
- ■ I can evaluate expressions.
- ■ I can compare quantities using scientific notation.

STEAM Video: "Carbon Atoms"

Carbon Atoms

Carbon is one of the four main elements of life. The number of carbon atoms in a compound can be represented using exponents. In what other real-life situations are exponents used?

Watch the STEAM Video "Carbon Atoms." Then answer the following questions.

1. The table shows the percents carbon by weight for humans and plants. How many pounds of carbon are in a 130-pound person? a 25-pound plant?

	Percent Carbon by Weight
Human	18%
Plant	45%

2. Steven says 5×10^{22}, or 50,000,000,000,000,000,000,000, carbon atoms are in 1 gram of carbon. How many carbon atoms are in 3 grams of carbon?

Elements in the Universe

After completing this chapter, you will be able to use the concepts you learned to answer the questions in the *STEAM Video Performance Task*. You will be given information about the *atomic masses* of the four most common elements in the universe: oxygen, hydrogen, helium, and carbon.

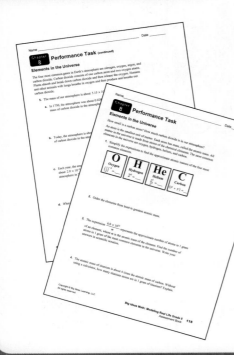

O Oxygen $\left(\frac{1}{2}\right)^{-4} =$ ____

H Hydrogen $2^0 =$ ____

He Helium $\dfrac{2^5}{2^3} =$ ____

C Carbon $(3^2 + 3^1) =$ ____

You will be asked to solve problems about the amounts of carbon dioxide in Earth's atmosphere for several years. What might cause the amount of carbon dioxide in the atmosphere to increase over time?

Getting Ready for Chapter 8

Chapter Exploration

1. Work with a partner. Write each distance as a whole number. Which numbers do you know how to write in words? For instance, in words, 10^2 is equal to *one hundred*.

a. 10^{27} meters: diameter of the observable universe

b. 10^{21} meters: diameter of the Milky Way galaxy

c. 10^{16} meters: diameter of the solar system

d. 10^7 meters: diameter of Earth

e. 10^4 meters: diameter of Halley's Comet

f. 10^3 meters: diameter of a meteor crater

2. Work with a partner. Write the numbers of wives, sacks, cats, and kits as powers.

As I was going to St. Ives
I met a man with seven wives
Each wife had seven sacks
Each sack had seven cats
Each cat had seven kits
Kits, cats, sacks, wives
How many were going to St. Ives?

Nursery Rhyme, 1730

Vocabulary

The following vocabulary terms are defined in this chapter. Think about what each term might mean and record your thoughts.

power

base of a power

exponent of a power

scientific notation

8.1 Exponents

Learning Target: Use exponents to write and evaluate expressions.

Success Criteria:
- I can write products using exponents.
- I can evaluate expressions involving powers.
- I can use exponents to solve real-life problems.

The expression 3^5 is called a *power*. The *base* is 3. The *exponent* is 5.

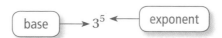

base $\longrightarrow 3^5 \longleftarrow$ exponent

EXPLORATION 1

Using Exponent Notation

Work with a partner.

a. Copy and complete the table.

Power	Repeated Multiplication Form	Value
$(-3)^1$	-3	-3
$(-3)^2$	$(-3) \cdot (-3)$	9
$(-3)^3$		
$(-3)^4$		
$(-3)^5$		
$(-3)^6$		
$(-3)^7$		

Math Practice

Build Arguments

When is the value of $(-3)^n$ positive? negative?

b. Describe what is meant by the expression $(-3)^n$. How can you find the value of $(-3)^n$?

EXPLORATION 2

Using Exponent Notation

Work with a partner. On a game show, each small cube is worth $3. The small cubes are arranged to form a large cube. Show how you can use a power to find the total value of the large cube. Then write an explanation to convince a friend that your answer is correct.

8.1 Lesson

Key Vocabulary 🔊
power, *p. 320*
base, *p. 320*
exponent, *p. 320*

A **power** is a product of repeated factors. The **base** of a power is the repeated factor. The **exponent** of a power indicates the number of times the base is used as a factor.

base — exponent

$$\left(\frac{1}{2}\right)^5 = \underbrace{\frac{1}{2} \cdot \frac{1}{2} \cdot \frac{1}{2} \cdot \frac{1}{2} \cdot \frac{1}{2}}$$

power $\frac{1}{2}$ is used as a factor 5 times.

EXAMPLE 1 Writing Expressions Using Exponents

Write each product using exponents.

a. $(-7) \cdot (-7) \cdot (-7)$

Because -7 is used as a factor 3 times, its exponent is 3.

▶ So, $(-7) \cdot (-7) \cdot (-7) = (-7)^3$.

b. $\pi \cdot \pi \cdot r \cdot r \cdot r$

Because π is used as a factor 2 times, its exponent is 2. Because r is used as a factor 3 times, its exponent is 3.

▶ So, $\pi \cdot \pi \cdot r \cdot r \cdot r = \pi^2 r^3$.

Math Practice

Communicate Precisely
Explain why you need to use parentheses to write powers when the base is negative.

Try It Write the product using exponents.

1. $\dfrac{1}{4} \cdot \dfrac{1}{4} \cdot \dfrac{1}{4} \cdot \dfrac{1}{4} \cdot \dfrac{1}{4}$

2. $0.3 \cdot 0.3 \cdot 0.3 \cdot 0.3 \cdot x \cdot x$

EXAMPLE 2 Evaluating Expressions

Evaluate each expression.

a. $(-2)^4$

$(-2)^4 = (-2) \cdot (-2) \cdot (-2) \cdot (-2)$	Write as repeated multiplication.
$= 16$	Simplify.

The base is -2.

b. -2^4

$-2^4 = -(2 \cdot 2 \cdot 2 \cdot 2)$	Write as repeated multiplication.
$= -16$	Simplify.

The base is 2.

Try It Evaluate the expression.

3. 12^2

4. $(-2)^6$

5. -5^4

6. $\left(-\dfrac{1}{6}\right)^3$

EXAMPLE 3 **Using Order of Operations**

Evaluate each expression.

a. $3 + 2 \cdot 3^4 = 3 + 2 \cdot 81$ Evaluate the power.

$ = 3 + 162$ Multiply.

$ = 165$ Add.

b. $3^3 - 8^2 \div 2 = 27 - 64 \div 2$ Evaluate the powers.

$ = 27 - 32$ Divide.

$ = -5$ Subtract.

c. $-3 \cdot (-10^2 + 70) = -3 \cdot (-100 + 70)$ Evaluate the power.

$ = -3 \cdot (-30)$ Perform operation in parentheses.

$ = 90$ Multiply.

Math Practice

Look for Structure
Can you use the Distributive Property to evaluate the expression in part (c)? Explain.

Try It Evaluate the expression.

7. $9 - 2^5 \cdot 0.5$ **8.** $\left| -3^3 \div 27 \right|$ **9.** $(7 \cdot 4 - 4^3) \div 6$

Self-Assessment for Concepts & Skills

Solve each exercise. Then rate your understanding of the success criteria in your journal.

WRITING EXPRESSIONS USING EXPONENTS Write the product using exponents.

10. $(-0.9) \cdot (-0.9) \cdot (-0.9)$ **11.** $\frac{1}{8} \cdot \frac{1}{8} \cdot y \cdot y \cdot y$

EVALUATING EXPRESSIONS Evaluate the expression.

12. 11^2 **13.** -6^3 **14.** $(-0.3)^4$

USING ORDER OF OPERATIONS Evaluate the expression.

15. $\left| -24 \div 2^2 \right|$ **16.** $(3^3 - 6 \cdot 8) \div 7$

17. WHICH ONE DOESN'T BELONG? Which expression does *not* belong with the other three? Explain your reasoning.

$(-2)^6$ -8^2

8^2 2^6

EXAMPLE 4 Modeling Real Life

The annual profit P (in thousands of dollars) earned by a technology company x years after opening is represented by the equation $P = 0.1x^3 + 3$. How much more profit is earned in year 5 than in year 4?

Use the equation to find the profits earned in year 4 and year 5. Then subtract the profit in year 4 from the profit in year 5 to determine how much more profit is earned in year 5.

Year 4		**Year 5**
$P = 0.1x^3 + 3$	Write the equation.	$P = 0.1x^3 + 3$
$= 0.1(4)^3 + 3$	Substitute.	$= 0.1(5)^3 + 3$
$= 0.1(64) + 3$	Evaluate the power.	$= 0.1(125) + 3$
$= 9.4$	Simplify.	$= 15.5$

▷ So, the company earns $15.5 - 9.4 = 6.1$, or $6100 more profit in year 5 than in year 4.

Self-Assessment for Problem Solving

Solve each exercise. Then rate your understanding of the success criteria in your journal.

18. **DIG DEEPER!** Consider the diameters of three planets.

   Planet A: 10^9 m **Planet B:** 10^7 m **Planet C:** 10^8 m

   a. Write each diameter as a whole number.

   b. A dwarf planet is discovered with a radius that is $\dfrac{1}{100}$ the radius of Planet C. Write the diameter of the dwarf planet as a power.

19. A fish jumps out of the water at a speed of 12 feet per second. The height y (in feet) of the fish above the surface of the water is represented by the equation $y = -16x^2 + 12x$, where x is the time (in seconds) since the jump began. The fish reaches its highest point above the surface of the water after 0.375 second. How far above the surface is the fish at this time?

8.1 Practice

? Go to *BigIdeasMath.com* to get HELP with solving the exercises.

Review & Refresh

Sketch a graph that represents the situation.

1. A trading card becomes more valuable over time. The value increases at a constant rate, and then at a faster and faster rate.

2. The water level of a river remains constant, and then decreases at a constant rate.

The vertices of a figure are given. Rotate the figure as described. Find the coordinates of the image.

3. $A(0, -4)$, $B(0, -1)$, $C(2, -1)$
   90° clockwise about the origin

4. $E(1, 2)$, $F(1, 3)$, $G(4, 3)$, $H(4, 2)$
   180° about the origin

Concepts, Skills, & Problem Solving

USING EXPONENT NOTATION **Write the power in repeated multiplication form. Then find the value of the power.** (See Exploration 1, p. 319.)

5. 4^4

6. $(-8)^2$

7. $(-2)^3$

WRITING EXPRESSIONS USING EXPONENTS **Write the product using exponents.**

8. $3 \cdot 3 \cdot 3 \cdot 3$

9. $(-6) \cdot (-6)$

10. $\left(-\frac{1}{2}\right) \cdot \left(-\frac{1}{2}\right) \cdot \left(-\frac{1}{2}\right)$

11. $\frac{1}{3} \cdot \frac{1}{3} \cdot \frac{1}{3}$

12. $\pi \cdot \pi \cdot \pi \cdot x \cdot x \cdot x \cdot x$

13. $(-4) \cdot (-4) \cdot (-4) \cdot y \cdot y$

14. $6.4 \cdot 6.4 \cdot 6.4 \cdot 6.4 \cdot b \cdot b \cdot b$

15. $(-t) \cdot (-t) \cdot (-t) \cdot (-t) \cdot (-t)$

16. $-(7 \cdot 7 \cdot 7 \cdot 7 \cdot 7)$

17. $-\left(\frac{1}{4} \cdot \frac{1}{4} \cdot \frac{1}{4} \cdot \frac{1}{4}\right)$

EVALUATING EXPRESSIONS **Evaluate the expression.**

18. 5^2

19. -11^3

20. $(-1)^6$

21. $\left(\frac{1}{2}\right)^6$

22. $\left(-\frac{1}{12}\right)^2$

23. $-\left(\frac{1}{9}\right)^3$

24. **MP YOU BE THE TEACHER** Your friend evaluates the power -6^2. Is your friend correct? Explain your reasoning.

$$-6^2 = (-6) \cdot (-6) = 36$$

MP STRUCTURE Write the prime factorization of the number using exponents.

25. 675

26. 280

27. 363

28. **MP PATTERNS** The largest doll is 12 inches tall. The height of each of the other dolls is $\frac{7}{10}$ the height of the next larger doll. Write an expression involving a power that represents the height of the smallest doll. What is the height of the smallest doll?

USING ORDER OF OPERATIONS Evaluate the expression.

29. $5 + 3 \cdot 2^3$

30. $2 + 7 \cdot (-3)^2$

31. $(13^2 - 12^2) \div 5$

32. $\frac{1}{2}(4^3 - 6 \cdot 3^2)$

33. $\left| \frac{1}{2}(7 + 5^3) \right|$

34. $\left| \left(-\frac{1}{2} \right)^3 \div \left(\frac{1}{4} \right)^2 \right|$

35. $(9^2 - 15 \cdot 2) \div 17$

36. $-6 \cdot (-5^2 + 20)$

37. $(-4 + 12 - 6^2) \div 7$

38. **MP STRUCTURE** Copy and complete the table. Compare the values of $2^h - 1$ with the values of 2^{h-1}. When are the values the same?

h	1	2	3	4	5
$2^h - 1$					
2^{h-1}					

39. **MP MODELING REAL LIFE** Scientists use carbon-14 dating to determine the age of a sample of organic material.

    a. The amount C (in grams) of carbon-14 remaining after t years of a sample of organic material is represented by the equation $C = 100(0.99988)^t$. Find the amount of carbon-14 remaining after 4 years.

    b. What percent of the carbon-14 remains after 4 years?

40. **DIG DEEPER!** The frequency (in vibrations per second) of a note on a piano is represented by the equation $F = 440(1.0595)^n$, where n is the number of notes above A440. Each black or white key represents one note. Use the frequencies of A and A440 to make a conjecture about frequencies of notes on a piano. Explain your reasoning.

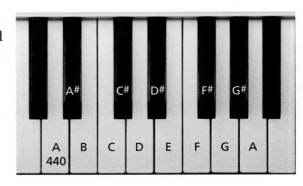

8.2 Product of Powers Property

Learning Target: Generate equivalent expressions involving products of powers.

Success Criteria:
- I can find products of powers that have the same base.
- I can find powers of powers.
- I can find powers of products.

EXPLORATION 1

Finding Products of Powers

Work with a partner.

a. Copy and complete the table. Use your results to write a *general rule* for finding $a^m \cdot a^n$, a product of two powers with the same base.

Product	Repeated Multiplication Form	Power
$2^2 \cdot 2^4$		
$(-3)^2 \cdot (-3)^4$		
$7^3 \cdot 7^2$		
$5.1^1 \cdot 5.1^6$		
$(-4)^2 \cdot (-4)^2$		
$10^3 \cdot 10^5$		
$\left(\dfrac{1}{2}\right)^5 \cdot \left(\dfrac{1}{2}\right)^5$		

Math Practice

Consider Similar Problems

How are the expressions in part (b) similar to the expressions in part (a)?

b. Show how to use your rule in part (a) to write each expression below as a single power. Then write a *general rule* for finding $(a^m)^n$, a power of a power.

$$(7^3)^2 \qquad (6^2)^2 \qquad (3^2)^3 \qquad (2^2)^4 \qquad \left(\left(\dfrac{1}{2}\right)^2\right)^5$$

EXPLORATION 2

Finding Powers of Products

Work with a partner. Copy and complete the table. Use your results to write a *general rule* for finding $(ab)^m$, a power of a product.

Power	Repeated Multiplication Form	Product of Powers
$(2 \cdot 3)^3$		
$(2 \cdot 5)^2$		
$(5 \cdot 4)^3$		
$(-2 \cdot 4)^2$		
$(-3 \cdot 2)^4$		

Key Ideas

Common Error

When multiplying powers, do not multiply the bases.

$4^2 \cdot 4^3 = 4^5$, not 16^5.

Product of Powers Property

Words To multiply powers with the same base, add their exponents.

Numbers $4^2 \cdot 4^3 = 4^{2+3} = 4^5$

Algebra $a^m \cdot a^n = a^{m+n}$

Power of a Power Property

Words To find a power of a power, multiply the exponents.

Numbers $(4^6)^3 = 4^{6 \cdot 3} = 4^{18}$

Algebra $(a^m)^n = a^{mn}$

Power of a Product Property

Words To find a power of a product, find the power of each factor and multiply.

Numbers $(3 \cdot 2)^5 = 3^5 \cdot 2^5$

Algebra $(ab)^m = a^m b^m$

EXAMPLE 1 **Multiplying Powers with the Same Base**

a. $2^4 \cdot 2^5 = 2^{4+5}$ Product of Powers Property

$= 2^9$ Simplify.

b. $-5 \cdot (-5)^6 = (-5)^1 \cdot (-5)^6$ Rewrite -5 as $(-5)^1$.

$= (-5)^{1+6}$ Product of Powers Property

$= (-5)^7$ Simplify.

When a number is written without an exponent, its exponent is 1.

c. $x^3 \cdot x^7 = x^{3+7}$ Product of Powers Property

$= x^{10}$ Simplify.

Try It Simplify the expression. Write your answer as a power.

1. $6^2 \cdot 6^4$ **2.** $\left(-\dfrac{1}{2}\right)^3 \cdot \left(-\dfrac{1}{2}\right)^6$ **3.** $z \cdot z^{12}$

EXAMPLE 2 **Finding a Power of a Power**

a. $(3^4)^3 = 3^{4 \cdot 3}$ Power of a Power Property

       $= 3^{12}$ Simplify.

b. $(w^5)^4 = w^{5 \cdot 4}$ Power of a Power Property

       $= w^{20}$ Simplify.

Try It **Simplify the expression. Write your answer as a power.**

4. $(4^3)^5$ **5.** $(y^2)^4$ **6.** $\left((-4)^3\right)^2$

EXAMPLE 3 **Finding a Power of a Product**

a. $(2x)^3 = 2^3 \cdot x^3$ Power of a Product Property

       $= 8x^3$ Simplify.

b. $(3xy)^2 = 3^2 \cdot x^2 \cdot y^2$ Power of a Product Property

       $= 9x^2y^2$ Simplify.

Try It **Simplify the expression.**

7. $(5y)^4$ **8.** $(ab)^5$ **9.** $(0.5mn)^2$

Self-Assessment for Concepts & Skills

Solve each exercise. Then rate your understanding of the success criteria in your journal.

FINDING POWERS **Simplify the expression. Write your answer as a power.**

10. $4^7 \cdot 4^4$ **11.** $(g^6)^3$ **12.** $\left(-\dfrac{1}{3}\right)^5 \cdot \left(-\dfrac{1}{3}\right)^7$

FINDING A POWER OF A PRODUCT **Simplify the expression.**

13. $(8t)^4$ **14.** $(yz)^6$ **15.** $\left(\dfrac{1}{4}gh\right)^3$

16. CRITICAL THINKING Can you use the Product of Powers Property to simplify $5^2 \cdot 6^4$? Explain.

17. OPEN-ENDED Write an expression that simplifies to x^{12} using the Product of Powers Property.

EXAMPLE 4 Modeling Real Life

Details ⊗

Local Disk (C:)
Local Disk

Free Space: 16 GB

Total Space: 64 GB

One gigabyte (GB) of computer storage space is 2^{30} bytes. The storage details of a computer are shown. How many bytes of total storage space does the computer have?

The computer has 64 gigabytes of total storage space. Notice that you can write 64 as a power, 2^6.

Use a verbal model to solve the problem.

$$\boxed{\text{Total number of bytes}} = \boxed{\substack{\text{Number of} \\ \text{bytes in a} \\ \text{gigabyte}}} \cdot \boxed{\substack{\text{Number of} \\ \text{gigabytes}}}$$

$= 2^{30} \cdot 2^6$ Substitute.

$= 2^{30+6}$ Product of Powers Property

$= 2^{36}$ Simplify.

▷ So, the computer has 2^{36} bytes of total storage space.

Self-Assessment for Problem Solving

Solve each exercise. Then rate your understanding of the success criteria in your journal.

18. A newborn blue whale weighs 3^7 kilograms. An adult blue whale weighs 81 times the weight of the newborn. How many kilograms does the adult blue whale weigh?

19. One megabyte of cell phone storage space is 2^{20} bytes. An app uses 4^4 megabytes of storage space. How many bytes of storage space does the app use?

20. **DIG DEEPER!** The diagram shows the area of a small circular rug. The radius of a large circular rug is 3 times the radius of the small rug. Write an expression for the area of the large rug in terms of x. Justify your answer.

$A = \frac{1}{4}\pi x^2$

8.2 Practice

▶ Review & Refresh

Write the product using exponents.

1. $11 \cdot 11 \cdot 11 \cdot 11 \cdot 11$

2. $(-6) \cdot (-6) \cdot (-6) \cdot z \cdot z$

Find the value of y for the given value of x.

3. $y = -4x; \ x = 7$

4. $y = 5x + 6; \ x = -2$

5. $y = 10 - 3x; \ x = 3$

6. What is the measure of each interior angle of the regular polygon?

   A. $45°$

   B. $135°$

   C. $1080°$

   D. $1440°$

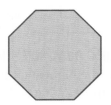

▶ Concepts, Skills, & Problem Solving

FINDING PRODUCTS OF POWERS Write the expression in repeated multiplication form. Then write the expression as a power. (See Exploration 1, p. 325.)

7. $5^6 \cdot 5^3$

8. $(6^4)^2$

9. $(-8)^3 \cdot (-8)^4$

FINDING POWERS Simplify the expression. Write your answer as a power.

10. $3^2 \cdot 3^2$

11. $8^{10} \cdot 8^4$

12. $(5^4)^3$

13. $\left((-3)^2\right)^4$

14. $(-4)^5 \cdot (-4)^7$

15. $h^6 \cdot h$

16. $(b^{12})^3$

17. $\left(\dfrac{2}{3}\right)^2 \cdot \left(\dfrac{2}{3}\right)^6$

18. $(3.8^3)^4$

19. $(n^3)^5$

20. $\left(\left(-\dfrac{3}{4}\right)^5\right)^2$

21. $\left(-\dfrac{5}{7}\right)^8 \cdot \left(-\dfrac{5}{7}\right)^9$

(MP) YOU BE THE TEACHER Your friend simplifies the expression. Is your friend correct? Explain your reasoning.

22.
$$5^2 \cdot 5^9 = (5 \cdot 5)^{2+9}$$
$$= 25^{11}$$

23.
$$(r^6)^4 = r^{6+4}$$
$$= r^{10}$$

FINDING A POWER OF A PRODUCT Simplify the expression.

24. $(6g)^3$

25. $(-3v)^5$

26. $\left(\dfrac{1}{5}k\right)^2$

27. $(1.2m)^4$

28. $(rt)^{12}$

29. $\left(-\dfrac{3}{4}p\right)^3$

w in.

w in.

30. **MP PRECISION** Is $3^2 + 3^3$ equal to 3^5? Explain.

31. **MP PROBLEM SOLVING** A display case for the artifact shown is in the shape of a cube. Each side of the display case is three times longer than the width w of the artifact.

   a. Write a power that represents the volume of the case.

   b. Simplify your expression in part (a).

32. **MP LOGIC** Show that $(3 \cdot 8 \cdot x)^7 = 6^7 \cdot 4^7 \cdot x^7$.

33. **MP MODELING REAL LIFE** The lowest altitude of an altocumulus cloud is about 3^8 feet. The highest altitude of an altocumulus cloud is about 3 times the lowest altitude. What is the highest altitude of an altocumulus cloud? Write your answer as a power.

34. **GEOMETRY** A square pyramid has a height h and a base with side length s. The side lengths of the base increase by 50%. Write a formula for the volume of the new pyramid in terms of s and h.

35. **MP MODELING REAL LIFE** The United States Postal Service delivers about $2^4 \cdot 3 \cdot 5^3$ pieces of mail each second. There are $2^8 \cdot 3^4 \cdot 5^2$ seconds in 6 days. How many pieces of mail does the United States Postal Service deliver in 6 days? Write your answer as an expression involving three powers.

36. **MP REASONING** The row numbers y and column numbers x of a chessboard are shown. Each position on the chessboard has a stack of pennies. (Only the first row is shown.) The number of pennies in each stack is $2^x \cdot 2^y$.

   a. Which locations have 32 pennies in their stacks?

   b. How much money (in dollars) is in the location with the tallest stack?

   c. A penny is about 0.06 inch thick. About how tall is the tallest stack?

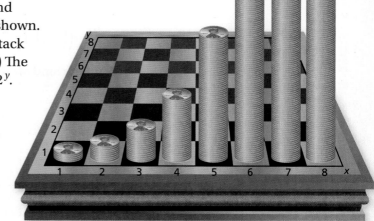

37. **CRITICAL THINKING** Find the value of x in the equation without evaluating the power.

   a. $2^5 \cdot 2^x = 256$

   b. $\left(\dfrac{1}{3}\right)^2 \cdot \left(\dfrac{1}{3}\right)^x = \dfrac{1}{729}$

8.3 Quotient of Powers Property

Learning Target: Generate equivalent expressions involving quotients of powers.

Success Criteria:
- I can find quotients of powers that have the same base.
- I can simplify expressions using the Quotient of Powers Property.
- I can solve real-life problems involving quotients of powers.

EXPLORATION 1

Finding Quotients of Powers

Work with a partner.

a. Copy and complete the table. Use your results to write a *general rule* for finding $\dfrac{a^m}{a^n}$, a quotient of two powers with the same base.

Math Practice

Find General Methods

How does writing the expanded form of each expression help you find a general rule?

Quotient	Repeated Multiplication Form	Power
$\dfrac{2^4}{2^2}$	$\dfrac{2 \cdot 2 \cdot 2 \cdot 2}{2 \cdot 2}$	
$\dfrac{(-4)^5}{(-4)^2}$		
$\dfrac{7^7}{7^3}$		
$\dfrac{8.5^9}{8.5^6}$		
$\dfrac{10^8}{10^5}$		
$\dfrac{3^{12}}{3^4}$		
$\dfrac{(-5)^7}{(-5)^5}$		
$\dfrac{11^4}{11^1}$		
$\dfrac{x^6}{x^2}$		

b. Use your rule in part (a) to simplify the quotients in the first column of the table above. Does your rule give the results in the third column?

Key Idea

Quotient of Powers Property

Words To divide powers with the same base, subtract their exponents.

Numbers $\dfrac{4^5}{4^2} = 4^{5-2} = 4^3$ **Algebra** $\dfrac{a^m}{a^n} = a^{m-n}$, where $a \neq 0$

EXAMPLE 1 **Dividing Powers with the Same Base**

a. $\dfrac{2^6}{2^4} = 2^{6-4}$ Quotient of Powers Property

$= 2^2$ Simplify.

b. $\dfrac{(-7)^9}{(-7)^3} = (-7)^{9-3}$ Quotient of Powers Property

$= (-7)^6$ Simplify.

c. $\dfrac{h^7}{h^6} = h^{7-6}$ Quotient of Powers Property

$= h^1 = h$ Simplify.

Common Error

When dividing powers, do not divide the bases.
$\dfrac{2^6}{2^4} = 2^2$, not 1^2.

Try It **Simplify the expression. Write your answer as a power.**

1. $\dfrac{9^7}{9^4}$ **2.** $\dfrac{4.2^6}{4.2^5}$ **3.** $\dfrac{(-8)^8}{(-8)^4}$ **4.** $\dfrac{x^8}{x^3}$

EXAMPLE 2 **Simplifying an Expression**

Simplify $\dfrac{3^4 \cdot 3^2}{3^3}$. Write your answer as a power.

The numerator is a product of powers. Add the exponents in the numerator.

$\dfrac{3^4 \cdot 3^2}{3^3} = \dfrac{3^{4+2}}{3^3}$ Product of Powers Property

$= \dfrac{3^6}{3^3}$ Simplify.

$= 3^{6-3}$ Quotient of Powers Property

$= 3^3$ Simplify.

Try It **Simplify the expression. Write your answer as a power.**

5. $\dfrac{6^7 \cdot 6^3}{6^5}$ **6.** $\dfrac{2^{15}}{2^3 \cdot 2^5}$ **7.** $\dfrac{m^8 \cdot m^6}{m^5}$

EXAMPLE 3 **Simplifying Expressions**

a. $\dfrac{(-4)^9}{(-4)^5} \cdot \dfrac{(-4)^8}{(-4)^2} = (-4)^{9-5} \cdot (-4)^{8-2}$ Quotient of Powers Property

$\qquad\qquad\qquad\qquad = (-4)^4 \cdot (-4)^6$ Simplify.

$\qquad\qquad\qquad\qquad = (-4)^{4+6}$ Product of Powers Property

$\qquad\qquad\qquad\qquad = (-4)^{10}$ Simplify.

Math Practice

Look for Structure
Show how you can simplify the expression in part (b) by first multiplying the numerators and then multiplying the denominators.

b. $\dfrac{a^{10}}{a^6} \cdot \dfrac{a^7}{a^4} = a^{10-6} \cdot a^{7-4}$ Quotient of Powers Property

$\qquad\qquad\quad = a^4 \cdot a^3$ Simplify.

$\qquad\qquad\quad = a^{4+3}$ Product of Powers Property

$\qquad\qquad\quad = a^7$ Simplify.

Try It **Simplify the expression. Write your answer as a power.**

8. $\dfrac{(-5)^7 \cdot (-5)^6}{(-5)^5 \cdot (-5)^2}$ 9. $\dfrac{d^5}{d} \cdot \dfrac{d^9}{d^8}$ 10. $\dfrac{p^3 \cdot p^6}{p^2} \cdot \dfrac{p^4}{p}$

Self-Assessment for Concepts & Skills

Solve each exercise. Then rate your understanding of the success criteria in your journal.

SIMPLIFYING EXPRESSIONS **Simplify the expression. Write your answer as a power.**

11. $\dfrac{(-3)^9}{(-3)^2}$ 12. $\dfrac{8^6 \cdot 8^2}{8^5}$ 13. $\dfrac{x^{11}}{x^4 \cdot x^6}$

14. $\dfrac{5^6}{5} \cdot \dfrac{5^3}{5^2}$ 15. $\dfrac{(-2)^9 \cdot (-2)^4}{(-2)^4 \cdot (-2)^4}$ 16. $\dfrac{b^{10} \cdot b^3}{b^2} \cdot \dfrac{b^5}{b^3}$

17. **WHICH ONE DOESN'T BELONG?** Which quotient does *not* belong with the other three? Explain your reasoning.

$$\dfrac{(-10)^7}{(-10)^2} \qquad \dfrac{6^3}{6^2}$$

$$\dfrac{(-4)^8}{(-3)^4} \qquad \dfrac{5^6}{5^3}$$

EXAMPLE 4 **Modeling Real Life** ————————————

Land area:
about 5.9^6 mi^2

The projected population of Tennessee in 2030 is about $5 \cdot 5.9^8$. Predict the average number of people per square mile in Tennessee in 2030.

You can find the average number of people per square mile in 2030 by dividing the projected population of Tennessee in 2030 by the land area.

$$\text{People per square mile} = \frac{\text{Population in 2030}}{\text{Land area}}$$

$$= \frac{5 \cdot 5.9^8}{5.9^6} \qquad \text{Substitute.}$$

$$= 5 \cdot \frac{5.9^8}{5.9^6} \qquad \text{Rewrite.}$$

$$= 5 \cdot 5.9^2 \qquad \text{Quotient of Powers Property}$$

$$= 174.05 \qquad \text{Evaluate.}$$

▷ So, you can predict that there will be about 174 people per square mile in Tennessee in 2030.

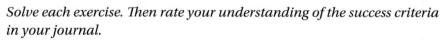

Self-Assessment for Problem Solving

Solve each exercise. Then rate your understanding of the success criteria in your journal.

18. You want to purchase a cat tracker. Tracker A detects your cat within a radius of $4 \cdot 10^2$ feet of your home. Tracker B detects your cat within a radius of 10^4 feet of your home. Which tracker has a greater radius? How many times greater?

19. **DIG DEEPER!** An earthquake of magnitude 3.0 is 10^2 times stronger than an earthquake of magnitude 1.0. An earthquake of magnitude 8.0 is 10^7 times stronger than an earthquake of magnitude 1.0. How many times stronger is an earthquake of magnitude 8.0 than an earthquake of magnitude 3.0?

20. The edge length of a cube-shaped crate is the square of the edge length of a cube-shaped box. Write an expression for the number of boxes that can fit in the crate. Justify your answer.

8.3 Practice

? Go to *BigIdeasMath.com* to get
HELP with solving the exercises.

▶ Review & Refresh

Simplify the expression. Write your answer as a power.

1. $4^2 \cdot 4^3$

2. $\left(a^5\right)^5$

3. $(xy)^7$

The red figure is similar to the blue figure. Describe a similarity transformation between the figures.

4.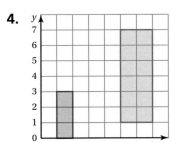

5.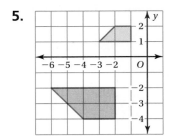

▶▶ Concepts, Skills, & Problem Solving

FINDING QUOTIENTS OF POWERS **Write the quotient as repeated multiplication. Then write the quotient as a power.** (See Exploration 1, p. 331.)

6. $\dfrac{7^9}{7^6}$

7. $\dfrac{(-4.5)^6}{(-4.5)^2}$

8. $\dfrac{m^{10}}{m^5}$

DIVIDING POWERS WITH THE SAME BASE **Simplify the expression. Write your answer as a power.**

9. $\dfrac{6^{10}}{6^4}$

10. $\dfrac{8^9}{8^7}$

11. $\dfrac{(-3)^4}{(-3)^1}$

12. $\dfrac{4.5^5}{4.5^3}$

13. $\dfrac{64^4}{64^3}$

14. $\dfrac{(-17)^5}{(-17)^2}$

15. $\dfrac{(-6.4)^8}{(-6.4)^6}$

16. $\dfrac{\pi^{11}}{\pi^7}$

17. **MP** **YOU BE THE TEACHER** Your friend simplifies the quotient. Is your friend correct? Explain your reasoning.

$$\frac{6^{15}}{6^5} = 6^{15/5}$$
$$= 6^3$$

SIMPLIFYING AN EXPRESSION **Simplify the expression. Write your answer as a power.**

18. $\dfrac{7^5 \cdot 7^3}{7^2}$

19. $\dfrac{6^{13}}{6^4 \cdot 6^2}$

20. $\dfrac{(-6.1)^{11}}{(-6.1)^7 \cdot (-6.1)^2}$

21. $\dfrac{\pi^{30}}{\pi^{18} \cdot \pi^4}$

22. $\dfrac{c^{22}}{c^8 \cdot c^9}$

23. $\dfrac{z^8 \cdot z^6}{z^8}$

24. **MP MODELING REAL LIFE** The sound intensity of a normal conversation is 10^6 times greater than the quietest noise a person can hear. The sound intensity of a jet at takeoff is 10^{14} times greater than the quietest noise a person can hear. How many times more intense is the sound of a jet at takeoff than the sound of a normal conversation?

SIMPLIFYING AN EXPRESSION Simplify the expression. Write your answer as a power.

25. $\dfrac{(-4)^8 \cdot (-4)^3}{(-4)^4 \cdot (-4)^2}$

26. $\dfrac{6^2}{6} \cdot \dfrac{6^{12}}{6^8}$

27. $\dfrac{3^2 \cdot 3^6}{3^2} \cdot \dfrac{3^5}{3}$

28. $\dfrac{z^7 \cdot z^6}{z \cdot z^2}$

29. $\dfrac{x^5}{x^4} \cdot \dfrac{x^{13}}{x^8}$

30. $\dfrac{y^8 \cdot y^2}{y^7} \cdot \dfrac{y^4}{y} \cdot \dfrac{y^7}{y^2}$

Device	Storage (GB)	Price
A	2^5	$30
B	2^6	$50
C	2^7	$70
D	2^8	$90
E	2^9	$110

31. **MP REASONING** The storage capacities and prices of five devices are shown in the table.

    a. How many times more storage does Device D have than Device B?

    b. Do storage and price have a linear relationship? Explain.

32. **DIG DEEPER!** Consider the equation $\dfrac{9^m}{9^n} = 9^{2n}$.

    a. Find two numbers m and n that satisfy the equation.

    b. Describe the number of solutions that satisfy the equation. Explain your reasoning.

Milky Way galaxy:
$10 \cdot 10^{10}$ stars

33. **MP MODELING REAL LIFE** A scientist estimates that there are about 10^{24} stars in the universe and that each galaxy has, on average, approximately the same number of stars as the Milky Way galaxy. About how many galaxies are in the universe?

34. **MP NUMBER SENSE** Find the value of x that makes $\dfrac{8^{3x}}{8^{2x+1}} = 8^9$ true. Explain how you found your answer.

8.4 Zero and Negative Exponents

Learning Target: Understand the concepts of zero and negative exponents.

Success Criteria:
- I can explain the meanings of zero and negative exponents.
- I can evaluate numerical expressions involving zero and negative exponents.
- I can simplify algebraic expressions involving zero and negative exponents.

EXPLORATION 1

Understanding Zero Exponents

Work with a partner.

a. Copy and complete the table.

Quotient	Quotient of Powers Property	Power
$\dfrac{5^3}{5^3}$		
$\dfrac{6^2}{6^2}$		
$\dfrac{(-3)^4}{(-3)^4}$		
$\dfrac{(-4)^5}{(-4)^5}$		

Math Practice

Find Entry Points

How can you use what you know about division to evaluate the expressions in the table?

b. Evaluate each expression in the first column of the table in part (a). How can you use these results to define a^0, where $a \neq 0$?

EXPLORATION 2

Understanding Negative Exponents

Work with a partner.

a. Copy and complete the table.

Product	Product of Powers Property	Power	Value
$5^{-3} \cdot 5^3$			
$6^2 \cdot 6^{-2}$			
$(-3)^4 \cdot (-3)^{-4}$			
$(-4)^{-5} \cdot (-4)^5$			

b. How can you use the Multiplicative Inverse Property to rewrite the powers containing negative exponents in the first column of the table?

c. Use your results in parts (a) and (b) to define a^{-n}, where $a \neq 0$ and n is an integer.

 **Key Ideas**

Zero Exponents

Words For any nonzero number a, $a^0 = 1$. The power 0^0 is *undefined*.

Numbers $4^0 = 1$ **Algebra** $a^0 = 1$, where $a \neq 0$

Negative Exponents

Words For any integer n and any nonzero number a, a^{-n} is the reciprocal of a^n.

Numbers $4^{-2} = \dfrac{1}{4^2}$ **Algebra** $a^{-n} = \dfrac{1}{a^n}$, where $a \neq 0$

EXAMPLE 1 **Evaluating Expressions**

a. $3^{-4} = \dfrac{1}{3^4}$ Definition of a negative exponent

$\phantom{3^{-4}} = \dfrac{1}{81}$ Evaluate the power.

b. $(-8.5)^{-4} \cdot (-8.5)^4 = (-8.5)^{-4+4}$ Product of Powers Property

$\phantom{(-8.5)^{-4} \cdot (-8.5)^4} = (-8.5)^0$ Simplify.

$\phantom{(-8.5)^{-4} \cdot (-8.5)^4} = 1$ Definition of a zero exponent

c. $\dfrac{2^6}{2^8} = 2^{6-8}$ Quotient of Powers Property

$\phantom{\dfrac{2^6}{2^8}} = 2^{-2}$ Simplify.

$\phantom{\dfrac{2^6}{2^8}} = \dfrac{1}{2^2}$ Definition of a negative exponent

$\phantom{\dfrac{2^6}{2^8}} = \dfrac{1}{4}$ Evaluate the power.

Try It **Evaluate the expression.**

1. 4^{-2} **2.** $(-2)^{-5}$ **3.** $6^{-8} \cdot 6^8$

4. $\dfrac{(-3)^5}{(-3)^6}$ **5.** $\dfrac{1}{5^7} \cdot \dfrac{1}{5^{-4}}$ **6.** $\dfrac{4^5 \cdot 4^{-3}}{4^2}$

EXAMPLE 2 **Simplifying Expressions**

a. $-5x^0 = -5(1)$ Definition of a zero exponent

        $= -5$ Multiply.

b. $\dfrac{9y^{-3}}{y^5} = 9y^{-3-5}$ Quotient of Powers Property

        $= 9y^{-8}$ Simplify.

        $= \dfrac{9}{y^8}$ Definition of a negative exponent

c. $\dfrac{n^4 \cdot n^{-7}}{6} = \dfrac{n^{4+(-7)}}{6}$ Product of Powers Property

        $= \dfrac{n^{-3}}{6}$ Simplify.

        $= \dfrac{1}{6n^3}$ Definition of a negative exponent

Try It **Simplify. Write the expression using only positive exponents.**

7. $8x^{-2}$ **8.** $b^0 \cdot b^{-10}$ **9.** $\dfrac{z^6}{15z^9}$

Self-Assessment *for Concepts & Skills*

Solve each exercise. Then rate your understanding of the success criteria in your journal.

EVALUATING EXPRESSIONS **Evaluate the expression.**

10. 7^{-2} **11.** $4^{-3} \cdot 4^0$ **12.** $\dfrac{(-9)^5}{(-9)^7}$

SIMPLIFYING EXPRESSIONS **Simplify. Write the expression using only positive exponents.**

13. $10t^{-5}$ **14.** $w^3 \cdot w^{-9}$ **15.** $\dfrac{r^8 \cdot r^{-8}}{4}$

16. **DIFFERENT WORDS, SAME QUESTION** Which is different? Find "both" answers.

Write $\dfrac{1}{3 \cdot 3 \cdot 3}$ using a negative exponent.

Write 3 to the negative third.

Write $\dfrac{1}{3}$ cubed as a power with an integer base.

Write $(-3) \cdot (-3) \cdot (-3)$ as a power with an integer base.

EXAMPLE 3 **Modeling Real Life**

One drop of water leaks from a faucet every second. How many liters of water leak from the faucet in 1 hour?

Because you know how much water leaks per second, convert 1 hour to seconds.

$$1 \cancel{h} \times \frac{60 \cancel{\text{min}}}{1 \cancel{h}} \times \frac{60 \text{ sec}}{1 \cancel{\text{min}}} = 3600 \text{ sec}$$

Multiply the rate that water leaks by 3600 seconds.

$3600 \cancel{\text{sec}} \cdot \dfrac{50^{-2} \text{ L}}{1 \cancel{\text{sec}}} = 3600 \cdot \dfrac{1}{50^2} \text{ L}$	Definition of a negative exponent
$= 3600 \cdot \dfrac{1}{2500} \text{ L}$	Evaluate the power.
$= \dfrac{3600}{2500} \text{ L}$	Multiply.
$= 1\dfrac{11}{25}, \text{ or } 1.44 \text{ L}$	Simplify.

Drop of water: 50^{-2} liter

▷ So, 1.44 liters of water leak from the faucet in 1 hour.

 Self-Assessment *for Problem Solving*

Solve each exercise. Then rate your understanding of the success criteria in your journal.

17. The mass of a grain of sand is about 10^{-3} gram. About how many grains of sand are in a 10-kilogram bag of sand?

18. A one-celled, aquatic organism called a *dinoflagellate* is 1000 micrometers long. A microscope magnifies the dinoflagellate 100 times. What is the magnified length of the dinoflagellate in meters? (1 micrometer is 10^{-6} meter.)

19. **DIG DEEPER!** A garden is 12 yards long. Assuming the snail moves at a constant speed, how many minutes does it take the snail to travel the length of the garden? Justify your answer.

Speed: 5^{-2} foot per second

8.4 Practice

 Go to *BigIdeasMath.com* to get HELP with solving the exercises.

▶ Review & Refresh

Simplify the expression. Write your answer as a power.

1. $\dfrac{10^8}{10^4}$

2. $\dfrac{y^9}{y^7}$

3. $\dfrac{(-3)^8 \cdot (-3)^3}{(-3)^2}$

Tell whether the triangles are similar. Explain.

4.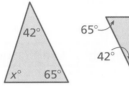

5.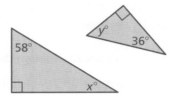

6. Which data display best orders numerical data and shows how they are distributed?

   A. bar graph

   B. line graph

   C. scatter plot

   D. stem-and-leaf plot

▶▶ Concepts, Skills, & Problem Solving

UNDERSTANDING NEGATIVE EXPONENTS **Copy and complete the table.** (See Exploration 2, p. 337.)

	Product	Product of Powers Property	Power	Value
7.	$7^{-4} \cdot 7^4$			
8.	$(-2)^5 \cdot (-2)^{-5}$			

EVALUATING EXPRESSIONS **Evaluate the expression.**

9. $\dfrac{8^7}{8^7}$

10. $5^0 \cdot 5^3$

11. $(-2)^{-8} \cdot (-2)^8$

12. $9^4 \cdot 9^{-4}$

13. 6^{-2}

14. 158^0

15. $\dfrac{4^3}{4^5}$

16. $\dfrac{-3}{(-3)^2}$

17. $2^2 \cdot 2^{-4}$

18. $3^{-3} \cdot 3^{-2}$

19. $\dfrac{1}{5^{-3}} \cdot \dfrac{1}{5^6}$

20. $\dfrac{(1.5)^2}{(1.5)^{-2} \cdot (1.5)^4}$

21. **MP YOU BE THE TEACHER** Your friend evaluates 4^{-3}. Is your friend correct? Explain your reasoning.

$$4^{-3} = (-4)(-4)(-4)$$
$$= -64$$

22. **CRITICAL THINKING** How can you write the number 1 as a power with base 2? a power with base 10?

23. **(MP) NUMBER SENSE** Without evaluating, order 5^0, 5^4, and 5^{-5} from least to greatest. Explain your reasoning.

SIMPLIFYING EXPRESSIONS Simplify. Write the expression using only positive exponents.

24. $6y^{-4}$

25. $8^{-2} \cdot a^7$

26. $\dfrac{9c^3}{c^{-4}}$

27. $\dfrac{5b^{-2}}{b^{-3}}$

28. $\dfrac{8x^3}{2x^9}$

29. $3d^{-4} \cdot 4d^4$

30. $m^{-2} \cdot n^3$

31. $\dfrac{3^{-2} \cdot k^0 \cdot w^0}{w^{-6}}$

32. **OPEN-ENDED** Write two different powers with negative exponents that have the same value. Justify your answer.

(MP) REASONING In Exercises 33–36, use the table.

33. How many millimeters are in a decimeter?

34. How many micrometers are in a centimeter?

35. How many nanometers are in a millimeter?

36. How many micrometers are in a meter?

Unit of Length	Length (meter)
Decimeter	10^{-1}
Centimeter	10^{-2}
Millimeter	10^{-3}
Micrometer	10^{-6}
Nanometer	10^{-9}

37. **(MP) MODELING REAL LIFE** A bacterium is 100 micrometers long. A virus is 1000 times smaller than the bacterium.

   a. Using the table above, find the length of the virus in meters.

   b. Is the answer to part (a) *less than*, *greater than*, or *equal to* 1 micrometer?

38. **DIG DEEPER!** Every 2 seconds, someone in the United States needs blood. A sample blood donation is shown.

   a. One cubic millimeter of blood contains about 10^4 white blood cells. How many white blood cells are in the donation? ($1\ mm^3 = 10^{-3}\ mL$)

   b. One cubic millimeter of blood contains about 5×10^6 red blood cells. How many red blood cells are in the donation?

   c. Compare your answers for parts (a) and (b).

39. **(MP) PRECISION** Describe how to rewrite a power with a positive exponent as a fraction with a power in the denominator. Use the definition of negative exponents to justify your reasoning.

40. **(MP) REASONING** The definition of a negative exponent states that $a^{-n} = \dfrac{1}{a^n}$. Explain why this rule does not apply when $a = 0$.

8.5 Estimating Quantities

Learning Target:	Round numbers and write the results as the product of a single digit and a power of 10.
Success Criteria:	• I can round very large and very small numbers.
	• I can write a multiple of 10 as a power.
	• I can compare very large or very small quantities.

EXPLORATION 1

Using Powers of 10

Work with a partner. Match each picture with the most appropriate distance. Explain your reasoning.

6×10^3 m	1×10^1 m	2×10^{-1} m	6×10^{-2} m

a.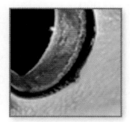

b.

c.

d.

EXPLORATION 2

Approximating Numbers

Work with a partner. Match each number in List 1 with its closest approximation in List 2. Explain your method.

	List 1		List 2
a.	180,000,000,000,000	**A.**	3×10^{11}
b.	0.0000000011	**B.**	1×10^{-5}
c.	302,000,000,000	**C.**	2×10^{14}
d.	0.00000028	**D.**	3×10^{13}
e.	0.0000097	**E.**	3×10^{-7}
f.	330,000,000,000,000	**F.**	1×10^{-9}
g.	26,000,000,000,000	**G.**	2×10^{-5}
h.	0.000023	**H.**	3×10^{14}

Math Practice

Look for Patterns
How can you use the number of zeros to determine the value of the exponent for each number in List 1?

Round the number so that it contains exactly one nonzero digit.

One way to approximate a very large or a very small number is to round the number and write the result as the product of a single digit and a power of 10.

EXAMPLE 1 **Approximating a Large Number**

Round the volume of water on Earth. Write the result as the product of a single digit and a power of 10.

$332,500,000 \approx 300,000,000$	Round to the nearest 100,000,000.
$= 3 \times 100,000,000$	Factor out 3.
$= 3 \times 10^8$	Write 100,000,000 as a power of 10.

▷ Earth contains about 3×10^8 cubic miles of water.

Earth contains about 332,500,000 cubic miles of water. The blue sphere represents all of the water on Earth, relative to the size of the planet.

Try It **Round the number. Write the result as the product of a single digit and a power of 10.**

1. 8,031,426,100   **2.** 98,247,836,218

EXAMPLE 2 **Approximating a Small Number**

A blood vessel has a diameter of 0.0000924 meter. Round the diameter of the blood vessel. Write the result as the product of a single digit and a power of 10.

$0.0000924 \approx 0.00009$	Round to the nearest 0.00001.
$= 9 \times 0.00001$	Factor out 9.
$= 9 \times 10^{-5}$	Write 0.00001 as a power of 10.

▷ The diameter of the blood vessel is about 9×10^{-5} meter.

Try It **Round the number. Write the result as the product of a single digit and a power of 10.**

3. 0.000384509   **4.** 0.00000726

EXAMPLE 3 **Approximating a Quantity**

The distance from Saturn to Neptune is about 1,911,674,960 miles. The distance from Mercury to Neptune is about 1.5 times this distance. What is the approximate distance from Mercury to Neptune?

A. 2×10^9 miles   **B.** 3×10^9 miles

C. 2×10^{10} miles   **D.** 3×10^{10} miles

Round the distance from Saturn to Neptune. Write the result as the product of a single digit and a power of 10.

$$1,911,674,960 \approx 2,000,000,000 \qquad \text{Round to the nearest 1,000,000,000.}$$
$$= 2 \times 1,000,000,000 \qquad \text{Factor out 2.}$$
$$= 2 \times 10^9 \qquad \text{Write 1,000,000,000 as a power of 10.}$$

The distance from Mercury to Neptune is about 1.5 times the distance from Saturn to Neptune. So, the distance from Mercury to Neptune is about $1.5(2 \times 10^9)$, or 3×10^9, miles.

 The correct answer is **B**.

Math Practice

Justify Conclusions
Explain to a classmate why you do not use the Distributive Property to multiply 1.5 and (2×10^9).

Try It

5. The distance from Mercury to Mars is about 105,651,744 miles. The distance from Saturn to Jupiter is about 4 times this distance. What is the approximate distance from Saturn to Jupiter?

Self-Assessment for Concepts & Skills

Solve each exercise. Then rate your understanding of the success criteria in your journal.

APPROXIMATING A NUMBER **Round the number. Write the result as the product of a single digit and a power of 10.**

6. 899,032,878,300   7. 62,322,118,987

8. 0.00000278101   9. 0.000013094

10. **APPROXIMATING A QUANTITY** Lake A has a volume of 21,150,427,000 cubic meters. Lake B has a volume that is 2.5 times the volume of Lake A. What is the approximate volume of Lake B?

EXAMPLE 4 **Modeling Real Life**

The population of the Philippines is about 104,260,000 and the population of India is about 1,282,000,000. Approximately how many times greater is the population of India than the population of the Philippines?

 **Understand the problem.**
You are given the populations of the Philippines and India. You are asked to approximate the number of times greater the population of India is than the population of the Philippines.

 **Make a plan.**
Round each number. Write each result as the product of a single digit and a power of 10. Then divide the population of India by the population of the Philippines.

 **Solve and check.**

Philippines	*India*
$104{,}260{,}000 \approx 100{,}000{,}000$	$1{,}282{,}000{,}000 \approx 1{,}000{,}000{,}000$
$= 1 \times 100{,}000{,}000$	$= 1 \times 1{,}000{,}000{,}000$
$= 1 \times 10^{8}$	$= 1 \times 10^{9}$

Divide the population of India by the population of the Philippines.

$$\frac{1 \times 10^{9}}{1 \times 10^{8}} = \frac{10^{9}}{10^{8}} \qquad \text{Multiplication Property of One}$$

$$= 10^{9-8} \qquad \text{Quotient of Powers Property}$$

$$= 10^{1} \qquad \text{Simplify.}$$

Check Use a calculator to divide the numbers.

$$\frac{1{,}282{,}000{,}000}{104{,}260{,}000} \approx 12.3 \approx 10 \checkmark$$

So, the population of India is about 10 times greater than the population of the Philippines.

 Self-Assessment for Problem Solving

Solve each exercise. Then rate your understanding of the success criteria in your journal.

11. On average, a small dog's heart beats about 530,000,000 times during its lifetime, and a large dog's heart beats about 1.4 times this amount. What is the approximate number of heartbeats in the lifetime of a large dog?

12. **DIG DEEPER!** A physicist observes a gamma ray with a wavelength of 0.00000000135 millimeter and an X-ray with a wavelength of 0.00000012 millimeter. (a) About how many times shorter is the wavelength of the gamma ray than the wavelength of the X-ray? (b) The diagram shows wavelengths of visible light. Which ray has a wavelength closer to the wavelength of dark blue light?

Visible Light

4×10^{-4} 7×10^{-4}

Wavelength (millimeters)

8.5 Practice

? Go to *BigIdeasMath.com* to get HELP with solving the exercises.

▷ Review & Refresh

Simplify. Write the expression using only positive exponents.

1. $3x^{-5}$

2. $d^0 \cdot d^{-4}$

3. $\dfrac{a^6}{2a^{11}}$

Write an equation in point-slope form of the line that passes through the given point and has the given slope.

4. $(-1, 2)$; $m = -\dfrac{1}{3}$

5. $(3, 4)$; $m = \dfrac{3}{4}$

6. $(1, -4)$; $m = -2$

▷▷ Concepts, Skills, & Problem Solving

APPROXIMATING NUMBERS Match the number with its closest approximation. (See Exploration 2, p. 343.)

7. 0.000618

8. 7,257,993,201

9. 0.0006781004

10. 782,309,441

A. 8×10^8

B. 6×10^{-4}

C. 7×10^{-4}

D. 7×10^9

APPROXIMATING A LARGE NUMBER Round the number. Write the result as a product of a single digit and a power of 10.

11. 414,148,636,008

12. 231,210

13. 28,007,806,203

14. 38,108,996,999

15. 1,003,111,391,008

16. 627,638,538

17. **APPROXIMATING A LARGE NUMBER** A company earns $518,204,500. Round the number. Write the result as a product of a single digit and a power of 10.

APPROXIMATING A SMALL NUMBER Round the number. Write the result as a product of a single digit and a power of 10.

18. 0.00000124

19. 0.00003946

20. 0.00001726

21. 0.00063718

22. 0.00000000305

23. 0.000000000994

24. **MP YOU BE THE TEACHER** Your friend rounds 0.000468 to the nearest ten thousandth and writes the result as a product of a single digit and a power of 10. Is your friend correct? Explain your reasoning.

$$0.000468 \approx 0.0005$$
$$= 5 \times 0.0001$$
$$= 5 \times 10^{-4}$$

25. **APPROXIMATING A QUANTITY** A series of mystery books contains 2,029,242 words. A series of science fiction books contains about 3.5 times the number of words as the mystery book series. What is the approximate number of words in the science fiction book series?

26. **APPROXIMATING A QUANTITY** A volcanic eruption ejects about 43,600,000,000 cubic feet of volcanic rock. A smaller volcanic eruption ejects about 75% of this amount. What is the approximate amount of volcanic rock that the smaller volcanic eruption ejects?

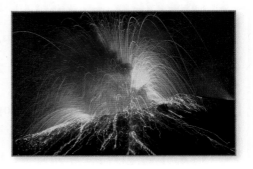

27. **(MP) STRUCTURE** Find a number that is approximately 1.5 times 61,040,000,100. Write the result as the product of a single digit and a power of 10.

Mitochondrion

28. **APPROXIMATING A QUANTITY** A mitochondrion has a diameter of about 0.00000031 meter. The diameter of a chloroplast is about 3 times that of the mitochondrion. What is the approximate diameter of the chloroplast?

29. **(MP) MODELING REAL LIFE** A photo taken with a smartphone has 1,227,104 pixels. A photo taken with a camera has 11,943,936 pixels. Approximately how many times more pixels are in the photo taken with the camera?

30. **(MP) MODELING REAL LIFE** A star has a core temperature of about 115,000,000°F. The temperature of a lightning strike is about 10,300°F. Approximately how many times hotter is the core temperature of the star than the temperature of the lightning strike?

31. **(MP) REASONING** The table shows the diameters of five types of animal hairs.

Animal	Buffalo	Rat	Camel	Cow	Donkey
Diameter (meter)	0.00011	0.00004	0.00008	0.00016	0.00005

    a. Order the hair types from greatest to least diameter.

    b. What unit should be used to represent these data? Explain your reasoning.

32. **(MP) PROBLEM SOLVING** The distance between New York City and Princeton is about 68,500 meters. The distance between New York City and San Antonio is about 40 times this distance. What is the approximate distance between New York City and San Antonio? Write the result as the product of a single digit and a power of 10.

33. **(MP) REASONING** Is 5×10^6 a better approximation of 5,447,040 or 5,305,004? Explain.

34. **(MP) NUMBER SENSE** A proton weighs 0.00000000000167 nanogram. About how much do 8 protons weigh? Write the result as the product of a single digit and a power of 10. Is your answer an overestimate or an underestimate?

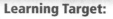

8.6 Scientific Notation

Learning Target: Understand the concept of scientific notation.

Success Criteria:
- I can convert between scientific notation and standard form.
- I can choose appropriate units to represent quantities.
- I can use scientific notation to solve real-life problems.

EXPLORATION 1

Using a Graphing Calculator

Work with a partner. Use a graphing calculator.

a. Experiment with multiplying very large numbers until your calculator displays an answer that is *not* in standard form. What do you think the answer means?

b. Enter the function $y = 10^x$ into your graphing calculator. Use the *table* feature to evaluate the function for positive integer values of x until the calculator displays a y-value that is not in standard form. Do the results support your answer in part (a)? Explain.

```
Plot1 Plot2 Plot3
\Y1◘10^X
\Y2=
\Y3=
\Y4=
\Y5=
\Y6=
\Y7=
```

X	Y₁
1	10
2	100
3	1000
4	10000
5	100000
6	1E6
7	1E7

X=6

c. Repeat part (a) with very small numbers.

Math Practice

Make Sense of Quantities
How can writing $\frac{1}{10}$ as a power of 10 help you understand the calculator display?

d. Enter the function $y = \left(\frac{1}{10}\right)^x$ into your graphing calculator. Use the *table* feature to evaluate the function for positive integer values of x until the calculator displays a y-value that is not in standard form. Do the results support your answer in part (c)? Explain.

```
Plot1 Plot2 Plot3
\Y1◘(1/10)^X
\Y2=
\Y3=
\Y4=
\Y5=
\Y6=
\Y7=
```

X	Y₁
1	.1
2	.01
3	.001
4	1E⁻4
5	1E⁻5
6	1E⁻6
7	1E⁻7

X=6

A number is written in **scientific notation** when it is represented as the product of a factor and a power of 10. The factor must be greater than or equal to 1 and less than 10.

> The factor is greater than or equal to 1 and less than 10. → 8.3×10^{-7} ← The power of 10 has an integer exponent.

 Key Idea

Writing Numbers in Scientific Notation

Move the decimal point so it is located to the right of the leading nonzero digit. The number of places you moved the decimal point indicates the exponent of the power of 10, as shown below.

> If the number is greater than or equal to 10, then the exponent is positive. If the number is between 0 and 1, then the exponent is negative.

Number Greater Than or Equal to 10

Use a positive exponent when you move the decimal point to the left.

$$8600 = 8.6 \times 10^3$$
       3

Number Between 0 and 1

Use a negative exponent when you move the decimal point to the right.

$$0.0024 = 2.4 \times 10^{-3}$$
        3

EXAMPLE 1 **Writing Numbers in Scientific Notation**

a. Write 173,000,000 in scientific notation.

> Move the decimal point 8 places to the left. → $173{,}000{,}000 = 1.73 \times 10^8$ ← The number is greater than 10. So, the exponent is positive.
> 8

b. Write 0.0000032 in scientific notation.

> Move the decimal point 6 places to the right. → $0.0000032 = 3.2 \times 10^{-6}$ ← The number is between 0 and 1. So, the exponent is negative.
> 6

Try It **Write the number in scientific notation.**

1. 50,000   **2.** 25,000,000   **3.** 683

4. 0.005   **5.** 0.00000033   **6.** 0.000506

 **Key Idea**

Writing Numbers in Standard Form

The absolute value of the exponent indicates how many places to move the decimal point.

- If the exponent is negative, move the decimal point to the left.
- If the exponent is positive, move the decimal point to the right.

EXAMPLE 2 **Writing Numbers in Standard Form**

a. Write 3.22×10^{-4} in standard form.

$3.22 \times 10^{-4} = 0.000322$ Move the decimal point $|-4| = 4$ places to the left.

b. Write 7.9×10^{5} in standard form.

$7.9 \times 10^{5} = 790,000$ Move the decimal point $|5| = 5$ places to the right.

Try It Write the number in standard form.

7. 6×10^{7}

8. 9.9×10^{-5}

9. 1.285×10^{4}

 Self-Assessment for Concepts & Skills

Solve each exercise. Then rate your understanding of the success criteria in your journal.

WRITING NUMBERS IN SCIENTIFIC NOTATION Write the number in scientific notation.

10. 675,000,000

11. 0.000000084

12. 0.000012001

WRITING NUMBERS IN STANDARD FORM Write the number in standard form.

13. 8×10^{-7}

14. 3.876×10^{7}

15. 1.11×10^{-5}

16. **WHICH ONE DOESN'T BELONG?** Which number does *not* belong with the other three? Explain.

| 2.8×10^{15} | 4.3×10^{-30} | 1.05×10^{28} | 10×9.2^{-13} |

EXAMPLE 3 | **Modeling Real Life**

A dog has 100 female fleas. What is the total amount of blood consumed by the fleas each day? Express your answer using more-appropriate units.

Write 1.4×10^{-5} in standard form. Then multiply the number by 100 to determine the amount of blood that 100 female fleas consume each day.

$1.4 \times 10^{-5} = 0.000014$ Move the decimal point $|-5| = 5$ places to the left.

So, 100 female fleas consume about $100(0.000014) = 0.0014$ liter of blood per day. You can use milliliters to express this quantity using more-appropriate units.

$$0.0014 \text{ L} = 0.0014\ \cancel{L} \times \frac{1000 \text{ mL}}{1\ \cancel{L}} = 1.4 \text{ mL}$$

▷ The fleas consume about 0.0014 liter, or 1.4 milliliters, of blood each day.

A female flea consumes about 1.4×10^{-5} liter of blood each day.

Self-Assessment *for Problem Solving*

Solve each exercise. Then rate your understanding of the success criteria in your journal.

17. A series of movies is about 3.285×10^4 seconds long. How long does it take to watch the series twice? Express your answer using more-appropriate units.

18. The total power of a space shuttle during launch is the sum of the power from its solid rocket boosters and the power from its main engines. The power from the solid rocket boosters is 9,750,000,000 watts. What is the power from the main engines?

Total Power = 1.174×10^{10} watts

19. The area of a trampoline is about 1.8×10^4 square inches. Write this number in standard form. Then represent the area of the trampoline using more-appropriate units.

20. **DIG DEEPER!** The *epidermis, dermis,* and *hypodermis* are layers of your skin. The dermis is about 3.5 millimeters thick. The epidermis is about 1.25×10^{-3} meter thick. The hypodermis is about 0.15 centimeter thick. What is the difference in thickness of the thickest layer and the thinnest layer? Justify your answer.

Go to *BigIdeasMath.com* to get
HELP with solving the exercises.

▶ Review & Refresh

Round the number. Write the result as the product of a single digit and a power of 10.

1. 0.00000129

2. 4,241,933,200

3. 0.0000001801

4. 879,679,466

Write the product using exponents.

5. $4 \cdot 4 \cdot 4 \cdot 4 \cdot 4$

6. $3 \cdot 3 \cdot 3 \cdot y \cdot y \cdot y$

7. $(-2) \cdot (-2) \cdot (-2)$

▶▶ Concepts, Skills, & Problem Solving

MP USING TOOLS Use a graphing calculator to evaluate the function when $x = 10$. Write the number in standard form. (See Exploration 1, p. 349.)

8. $y = \left(\dfrac{1}{10}\right)^x$

9. $y = 20^x$

WRITING NUMBERS IN SCIENTIFIC NOTATION Write the number in scientific notation.

10. 0.0021

11. 5,430,000

12. 321,000,000

13. 0.00000625

14. 0.00004

15. 10,700,000

16. 45,600,000,000

17. 0.000000000009256

18. 840,000

WRITING NUMBERS IN STANDARD FORM Write the number in standard form.

19. 7×10^7

20. 8×10^{-3}

21. 5×10^2

22. 2.7×10^{-4}

23. 4.4×10^{-5}

24. 2.1×10^3

25. 1.66×10^9

26. 3.85×10^{-8}

27. 9.725×10^6

28. **MP MODELING REAL LIFE** The U.S. Brig *Niagara*, a warship from the Battle of Lake Erie in 1813, uses about 28,300 feet of rope to operate its sails and spars. Write this number in scientific notation.

29. **MP MODELING REAL LIFE** The radius of a fishing line is 2.5×10^{-4} feet. Write this number in standard form. Then write your answer using inches.

Blood: 2.7×10^8 platelets per milliliter

30. (MP) **MODELING REAL LIFE** Platelets are cell-like particles in the blood that help form blood clots.

　　a. How many platelets are in 3 milliliters of blood? Write your answer in standard form.

　　b. An adult human body contains about 5 liters of blood. How many platelets are in an adult human body?

CHOOSING APPROPRIATE UNITS Match each value with the most appropriate unit of measurement.

31. height of a skyscraper: 2.6×10^2

32. distance between two asteroids: 2.5×10^5

33. depth of a bathtub: 1.6×10^1

34. length of memory chip: 7.8×10^0

　　A. inches

　　B. millimeters

　　C. miles

　　D. meters

35. (MP) **NUMBER SENSE** Describe how the value of a number written in scientific notation changes when you increase the exponent by 1.

36. (MP) **PROBLEM SOLVING** The area of the Florida Keys National Marine Sanctuary is about 9600 square kilometers. The area of the Florida Reef Tract is about 16.2% of the area of the sanctuary. What is the area of the Florida Reef Tract? Write your answer in scientific notation.

37. (MP) **REASONING** A gigameter is 1.0×10^6 kilometers. How many square kilometers are in 5 square gigameters?

38. (MP) **PROBLEM SOLVING** There are about 1.4×10^9 cubic kilometers of water on Earth. About 2.5% of the water is freshwater. How much freshwater is on Earth?

39. **CRITICAL THINKING** The table shows the speed of light through each of five media. Determine in which media light travels the fastest and the slowest.

Medium	Speed
Air	6.7×10^8 mi/h
Glass	6.6×10^8 ft/sec
Ice	2.3×10^5 km/sec
Vacuum	3.0×10^8 m/sec
Water	2.3×10^{10} cm/sec

Equivalent to 1 Atomic Mass Unit
8.3×10^{-24} carat
1.66×10^{-21} milligram

40. (MP) **STRUCTURE** The mass of an atom or molecule is measured in atomic mass units. Which is greater, a *carat* or a *milligram*? Explain.

8.7 Operations in Scientific Notation

Learning Target: Perform operations with numbers written in scientific notation.

Success Criteria:
- I can explain how to add and subtract numbers in scientific notation.
- I can explain how to multiply and divide numbers in scientific notation.
- I can use operations in scientific notation to solve real-life problems.

EXPLORATION 1

Adding and Subtracting in Scientific Notation

Work with a partner.

a. Complete the table by finding the sum and the difference of Expression 1 and Expression 2. Write your answers in scientific notation. Explain your method.

Expression 1	Expression 2	Sum	Difference
3×10^4	1×10^4		
4×10^{-3}	2×10^{-3}		
4.1×10^{-7}	1.5×10^{-7}		
8.3×10^6	1.5×10^6		

Math Practice

Look for Structure
How might you find the sum or difference of two expressions in scientific notation that contain different powers of 10?

b. Use your results in part (a) to explain how to find $(a \times 10^n) + (b \times 10^n)$ and $(a \times 10^n) - (b \times 10^n)$.

EXPLORATION 2

Multiplying and Dividing in Scientific Notation

Work with a partner.

a. Complete the table by finding the product and the quotient of Expression 1 and Expression 2. Write your answers in scientific notation. Explain your method.

Expression 1	Expression 2	Product	Quotient
3×10^4	1×10^4		
4×10^3	2×10^2		
7.7×10^{-2}	1.1×10^{-3}		
4.5×10^5	3×10^{-1}		

b. Use your results in part (a) to explain how to find $(a \times 10^n) \times (b \times 10^m)$ and $(a \times 10^n) \div (b \times 10^m)$. Describe any properties that you use.

To add or subtract numbers written in scientific notation with the same power of 10, add or subtract the factors. When the numbers have different powers of 10, first rewrite the numbers so they have the same power of 10.

EXAMPLE 1 **Adding and Subtracting in Scientific Notation**

Find the sum or difference.

a. $(4.6 \times 10^3) + (8.72 \times 10^3)$

$\qquad = (4.6 + 8.72) \times 10^3$ Distributive Property

$\qquad = 13.32 \times 10^3$ Add.

$\qquad = (1.332 \times 10^1) \times 10^3$ Write 13.32 in scientific notation.

$\qquad = 1.332 \times 10^4$ Product of Powers Property

b. $(3.5 \times 10^{-2}) - (6.6 \times 10^{-3})$

Rewrite 6.6×10^{-3} so that it has the same power of 10 as 3.5×10^{-2}.

$6.6 \times 10^{-3} = 6.6 \times 10^{-1} \times 10^{-2}$ Rewrite 10^{-3} as $10^{-1} \times 10^{-2}$.

$\qquad\qquad\quad = 0.66 \times 10^{-2}$ Rewrite 6.6×10^{-1} as 0.66.

Subtract the factors.

$(3.5 \times 10^{-2}) - (0.66 \times 10^{-2})$

$\qquad = (3.5 - 0.66) \times 10^{-2}$ Distributive Property

$\qquad = 2.84 \times 10^{-2}$ Subtract.

> **Math Practice**
>
> **Look for Structure**
> Solve Example 1(b) by rewriting 3.5×10^{-2} as 35×10^{-3}.

Try It **Find the sum or difference.**

1. $(8.2 \times 10^2) + (3.41 \times 10^{-1})$ 2. $(7.8 \times 10^{-5}) - (4.5 \times 10^{-5})$

To multiply or divide numbers written in scientific notation, multiply or divide the factors and powers of 10 separately.

EXAMPLE 2 **Multiplying in Scientific Notation**

Find $(3 \times 10^{-5}) \times (5 \times 10^{-2})$.

$(3 \times 10^{-5}) \times (5 \times 10^{-2})$

$\qquad = 3 \times 5 \times 10^{-5} \times 10^{-2}$ Commutative Property of Multiplication

$\qquad = (3 \times 5) \times (10^{-5} \times 10^{-2})$ Associative Property of Multiplication

$\qquad = 15 \times 10^{-7}$ Simplify.

$\qquad = (1.5 \times 10^1) \times 10^{-7}$ Write 15 in scientific notation.

$\qquad = 1.5 \times 10^{-6}$ Product of Powers Property

> **Check**
> Use standard form to check your answer.
>
> (3×10^{-5})
> $\times (5 \times 10^{-2})$
> $= 0.00003 \times 0.05$
> $= 0.0000015$
> $= 1.5 \times 10^{-6}$ ✓

Try It **Find the product.**

3. $6 \times (8 \times 10^{-5})$

4. $(7 \times 10^2) \times (3 \times 10^5)$

5. $(2 \times 10^4) \times (6 \times 10^{-7})$

6. $(3 \times 10^8) \times (9 \times 10^3)$

EXAMPLE 3 **Dividing in Scientific Notation**

Find $\dfrac{1.5 \times 10^{-8}}{6 \times 10^7}$.

$$\frac{1.5 \times 10^{-8}}{6 \times 10^7} = \frac{1.5}{6} \times \frac{10^{-8}}{10^7}$$ Rewrite as a product of fractions.

$$= 0.25 \times \frac{10^{-8}}{10^7}$$ Divide 1.5 by 6.

$$= 0.25 \times 10^{-15}$$ Quotient of Powers Property

$$= (2.5 \times 10^{-1}) \times 10^{-15}$$ Write 0.25 in scientific notation.

$$= 2.5 \times 10^{-16}$$ Product of Powers Property

Try It **Find the quotient.**

7. $(9.2 \times 10^{12}) \div 4.6$

8. $(1.5 \times 10^{-3}) \div (7.5 \times 10^2)$

9. $(3.75 \times 10^{-8}) \div (1.25 \times 10^{-7})$

10. $(9.2 \times 10^6) \div (2.3 \times 10^{12})$

 Self-Assessment *for Concepts & Skills*

Solve each exercise. Then rate your understanding of the success criteria in your journal.

11. **WRITING** Describe how to add or subtract two numbers written in scientific notation with the same power of 10.

12. **MP NUMBER SENSE** Two numbers written in scientific notation have different powers of 10. Do you have to rewrite the numbers so they have the same power of 10 before multiplying or dividing? Explain.

OPERATIONS IN SCIENTIFIC NOTATION **Evaluate the expression. Write your answer in scientific notation.**

13. $(7.26 \times 10^4) + (3.4 \times 10^4)$

14. $(2.8 \times 10^{-5}) - (1.6 \times 10^{-6})$

15. $(2.4 \times 10^4) \times (3.8 \times 10^{-6})$

16. $(5.2 \times 10^{-3}) \div (1.3 \times 10^{-12})$

EXAMPLE 4 **Modeling Real Life**

Diameter ≈ 1,400,000,000 m

An aluminum ion has a diameter of about 5×10^{-11} meter. How many times greater is the diameter of the Sun than the diameter of the ion?

Write the diameter of the Sun in scientific notation.

$$1,400,000,000 = 1.4 \times 10^9$$
$$9$$

Divide the diameter of the Sun by the diameter of the aluminum ion.

$$\frac{1.4 \times 10^9}{5 \times 10^{-11}} = \frac{1.4}{5} \times \frac{10^9}{10^{-11}} \qquad \text{Rewrite as a product of fractions.}$$

$$= 0.28 \times \frac{10^9}{10^{-11}} \qquad \text{Divide 1.4 by 5.}$$

$$= 0.28 \times 10^{20} \qquad \text{Quotient of Powers Property}$$

$$= (2.8 \times 10^{-1}) \times 10^{20} \qquad \text{Write 0.28 in scientific notation.}$$

$$= 2.8 \times 10^{19} \qquad \text{Product of Powers Property}$$

▷ The diameter of the Sun is about 2.8×10^{19} times greater than the diameter of the aluminum ion.

Check
Use a calculator to check your answer.

```
(1.4E9)/(5E-11)
            2.8E19
```
✔

Self-Assessment for *Problem Solving*

Solve each exercise. Then rate your understanding of the success criteria in your journal.

17. It takes the Sun about 2.3×10^8 years to orbit the center of the Milky Way. It takes Pluto about 2.5×10^2 years to orbit the Sun. How many times does Pluto orbit the Sun while the Sun completes one orbit around the Milky Way?

18. A person typically breathes about 8.64×10^3 liters of air per day. The life expectancy of a person in the United States at birth is about 29,200 days. Estimate the total amount of air a person born in the United States breathes over a lifetime.

19. **DIG DEEPER!** In one week, about 4100 movie theaters each sold an average of 2200 tickets for Movie A. About 3.6×10^7 total tickets were sold at the theaters during the week. An article claims that about 25% of all tickets sold during the week were for Movie A. Is this claim accurate? Justify your answer.

8.7 Practice

Go to *BigIdeasMath.com* to get HELP with solving the exercises.

▶ Review & Refresh

Write the number in scientific notation.

1. 0.0038

2. 74,000,000

3. 0.0000475

Find the values of the ratios (red to blue) of the perimeters and areas of the similar figures.

4.

5.

▶▶ Concepts, Skills, & Problem Solving

OPERATIONS IN SCIENTIFIC NOTATION Find the sum, difference, product, and quotient of Expression 1 and Expression 2. Write your answers in scientific notation. (See Explorations 1 and 2, p. 355.)

6. 3×10^3 Expression 1

    2×10^3 Expression 2

7. 6×10^{-4} Expression 1

    1.5×10^{-4} Expression 2

ADDING AND SUBTRACTING IN SCIENTIFIC NOTATION Find the sum or difference. Write your answer in scientific notation.

8. $(2 \times 10^5) + (3.8 \times 10^5)$

9. $(6.33 \times 10^{-9}) - (4.5 \times 10^{-9})$

10. $(9.2 \times 10^8) - (4 \times 10^8)$

11. $(7.2 \times 10^{-6}) + (5.44 \times 10^{-6})$

12. $(7.8 \times 10^7) - (2.45 \times 10^6)$

13. $(5 \times 10^{-5}) + (2.46 \times 10^{-3})$

14. $(9.7 \times 10^6) + (6.7 \times 10^5)$

15. $(2.4 \times 10^{-1}) - (5.5 \times 10^{-2})$

16. **MP YOU BE THE TEACHER**
Your friend adds 2.5×10^9 and 5.3×10^8. Is your friend correct? Explain your reasoning.

$$(2.5 \times 10^9) + (5.3 \times 10^8) = (2.5 \times 10^9) + (0.53 \times 10^9)$$
$$= (2.5 + 0.53) \times 10^9$$
$$= 3.03 \times 10^9$$

MULTIPLYING AND DIVIDING IN SCIENTIFIC NOTATION Find the product or quotient. Write your answer in scientific notation.

17. $5 \times (7 \times 10^7)$

18. $(5.8 \times 10^{-6}) \div (2 \times 10^{-3})$

19. $(1.2 \times 10^{-5}) \div 4$

20. $(5 \times 10^{-7}) \times (3 \times 10^6)$

21. $(3.6 \times 10^7) \div (7.2 \times 10^7)$

22. $(7.2 \times 10^{-1}) \times (4 \times 10^{-7})$

23. $(6.5 \times 10^8) \times (1.4 \times 10^{-5})$

24. $(2.8 \times 10^4) \div (2.5 \times 10^6)$

MATCHING You use technology to find four sums. Match the sum with its standard form.

25. 4.3E8

26. 4.3E−8

27. 4.3E10

28. 4.3E−10

A. 0.00000000043

B. 0.000000043

C. 430,000,000

D. 43,000,000,000

29. **MP MODELING REAL LIFE** How many times greater is the thickness of a dime than the thickness of a dollar bill?

Thickness = 0.135 cm

Thickness = 1.0922×10^{-2} cm

30. **MULTIPLE CHOICE** On a social media website, Celebrity A has about 8.6×10^7 followers and Celebrity B has about 4.1×10^6 followers. Determine which of the following is the best estimate for the number of followers for Celebrity A compared to the number of followers for Celebrity B.

A. more than 2 times greater

B. less than 2 times greater

C. more than 20 times greater

D. less than 20 times greater

MP REASONING Evaluate the expression. Write your answer in scientific notation.

31. $5,200,000 \times (8.3 \times 10^2) - (3.1 \times 10^8)$

32. $(9 \times 10^{-3}) + (2.4 \times 10^{-5}) \div 0.0012$

33. **GEOMETRY** Find the perimeter of the rectangle at the right.

Area = 5.612×10^{14} cm²

9.2×10^7 cm   *Not drawn to scale*

34. **DIG DEEPER!** A human heart pumps about 7×10^{-2} liter of blood per heartbeat. The average human heart beats about 72 times per minute. How many liters of blood does a heart pump in 1 year? 70 years?

35. **MP MODELING REAL LIFE** Use the Internet or another reference to find the populations and areas (in square miles) of India, China, Argentina, the United States, and Egypt. Round each population to the nearest million and each area to the nearest thousand square miles.

a. Write each population and area in scientific notation.

b. Use your answers to part (a) to find and order the population densities (people per square mile) of each country from least to greatest.

Connecting Concepts

▶ Using the Problem-Solving Plan

1. Atoms are made of protons, neutrons, and electrons. The table shows the numbers of protons and the masses of several atoms. Use a line of best fit to estimate the mass (in grams) of an atom that has 29 protons.

Protons, x	Mass (gram), y
1	1.67×10^{-24}
5	1.79×10^{-23}
53	2.11×10^{-22}
20	6.65×10^{-23}
14	4.66×10^{-23}
3	1.15×10^{-23}
40	1.51×10^{-22}
16	5.32×10^{-23}

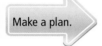

You know the numbers of protons and the masses of several atoms. You are asked to use the line of best fit to estimate the mass of an atom that has 29 protons.

Use a graphing calculator to find an equation of the line of best fit. Then evaluate the equation when $x = 29$.

Solve and check. Use the plan to solve the problem. Then check your solution.

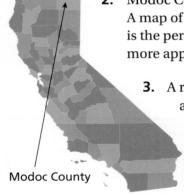

Modoc County

2. Modoc County, California, is 74.9 miles long and 56.2 miles wide. A map of the county is drawn using a scale factor of 2.11×10^{-6}. What is the perimeter of the county on the map? Express your answer using more appropriate units.

3. A research company estimates that in the United States, about 8.37×10^7 adult males and 6.59×10^7 adult females watch NFL football, while 3.13×10^7 adult males and 5.41×10^7 adult females do *not* watch NFL football. Organize the results in a two-way table. Include the marginal frequencies.

Performance Task

Elements in the Universe

At the beginning of this chapter, you watched a STEAM Video called "Carbon Atoms." You are now ready to complete the performance task related to this video, available at **BigIdeasMath.com**. Be sure to use the problem-solving plan as you work through the performance task.

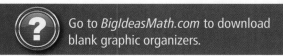
▶ Review Vocabulary

Write the definition and give an example of each vocabulary term.

power, *p. 320*   exponent, *p. 320*
base, *p. 320*   scientific notation, *p. 350*

▶ Graphic Organizers

You can use a **Definition and Example Chart** to organize information about a concept. Here is an example of a Definition and Example Chart for the vocabulary term *power*.

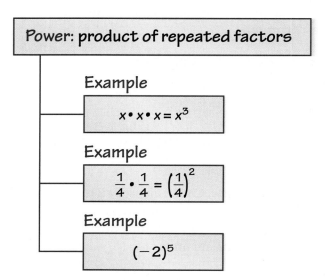

Power: product of repeated factors

Example
$$x \cdot x \cdot x = x^3$$

Example
$$\frac{1}{4} \cdot \frac{1}{4} = \left(\frac{1}{4}\right)^2$$

Example
$$(-2)^5$$

Choose and complete a graphic organizer to help you study the concept.

1. Product of Powers Property

2. Power of a Power Property

3. Power of a Product Property

4. Quotient of Powers Property

5. negative exponents

6. scientific notation

7. adding and subtracting numbers in scientific notation

8. multiplying and dividing numbers in scientific notation

"Here is my Definition and Example Chart. I'm going to take a selfie from the top of the pyramid. Do you want to hold the camera?"

▶ Chapter Self-Assessment

As you complete the exercises, use the scale below to rate your understanding of the success criteria in your journal.

1	**2**	**3**	**4**
I do not understand.	I can do it with help.	I can do it on my own.	I can teach someone else.

8.1 Exponents (pp. 319–324)

Learning Target: Use exponents to write and evaluate expressions.

Write the product using exponents.

1. $(-9) \cdot (-9) \cdot (-9) \cdot (-9) \cdot (-9)$

2. $2 \cdot 2 \cdot 2 \cdot n \cdot n$

Evaluate the expression.

3. 11^3

4. $-\left(\dfrac{1}{2}\right)^4$

5. $\left| \dfrac{1}{2}(16 - 6^3) \right|$

6. The profit P (in dollars) earned by a local merchant selling x items is represented by the equation $P = 0.2x^3 - 10$. How much more profit does he earn selling 15 items than 5 items?

8.2 Product of Powers Property (pp. 325–330)

Learning Target: Generate equivalent expressions involving products of powers.

Simplify the expression. Write your answer as a power.

7. $p^5 \cdot p^2$

8. $(n^{11})^2$

9. $\left(-\dfrac{2}{5}\right)^3 \cdot \left(-\dfrac{2}{5}\right)^2$

10. Simplify $(-2k)^4$.

11. Write an expression that simplifies to x^{24} using the Power of a Power Property.

12. You send an email with a file size of 4 kilobytes. One kilobyte is 2^{10} bytes. What is the file size of your email in bytes?

13. Explain how to use properties of exponents to simplify the expression $27 \cdot 3^2$.

8.3 Quotient of Powers Property (pp. 331–336)

Learning Target: Generate equivalent expressions involving quotients of powers.

Simplify the expression. Write your answer as a power.

14. $\dfrac{8^8}{8^3}$

15. $\dfrac{5^2 \cdot 5^9}{5}$

16. $\dfrac{w^8}{w^7} \cdot \dfrac{w^5}{w^2}$

17. $\dfrac{m^8}{m^6} \cdot \dfrac{m^{10} \cdot m^2}{m^9}$

18. Write an expression that simplifies to x^3 using the Quotient of Powers Property.

19. At the end of a fiscal year, a company has made 1.62×7^7 dollars in profit. The company employs 7^3 people. How much will each person receive if the company divides the profit equally among its employees?

8.4 Zero and Negative Exponents (pp. 337–342)

Learning Target: Understand the concepts of zero and negative exponents.

Evaluate the expression.

20. 2^{-4}

21. 95^0

22. $\dfrac{8^2}{8^4}$

23. $(-12)^{-7} \cdot (-12)^7$

24. $\dfrac{1}{7^9} \cdot \dfrac{1}{7^{-6}}$

25. $\dfrac{9^4 \cdot 9^{-2}}{9^2}$

Simplify. Write the expression using only positive exponents.

26. $x^{-2} \cdot x^0$

27. $y^{-8} y^3$

28. $\dfrac{3^{-1} \cdot z^5}{z^{-2}}$

29. Write an expression that simplifies to x^{-4}.

30. Water flows from a showerhead at a rate of 24^{-1} gallon per second. How many gallons do you use when taking a 15-minute shower? a 20-minute shower?

31. Explain two different methods for simplifying $w^{-2} \cdot w^5$.

8.5 Estimating Quantities (pp. 343–348)

Learning Target: Round numbers and write the results as the product of a single digit and a power of 10.

Round the number. Write the result as a product of a single digit and a power of 10.

32. 29,197,543

33. 0.000000647

34. The speed of light is 299,792,458 meters per second. About how far can a light beam travel in 3 seconds? Write your answer as a product of a single digit and a power of 10.

35. The population of Albany, New York is about 98,989 and the population of Moscow, Russia is about 12,235,448. Approximately how many times greater is the population of Moscow than the population of Albany?

8.6 Scientific Notation (pp. 349–354)

Learning Target: Understand the concept of scientific notation.

Write the number in scientific notation.

36. 0.00036

37. 800,000

38. 79,200,000

Write the number in standard form.

39. 2×10^7

40. 4.8×10^{-3}

41. 6.25×10^5

42. The mass of a single dust particle is 7.52×10^{-10} kilogram. What is the mass of a dust ball made of 100 dust particles? Express your answer using more-appropriate units.

8.7 Operations in Scientific Notation (pp. 355–360)

Learning Target: Perform operations with numbers written in scientific notation.

Evaluate the expression. Write your answer in scientific notation.

43. $(4.2 \times 10^8) + (5.9 \times 10^9)$

44. $(5.9 \times 10^{-4}) - (1.8 \times 10^{-4})$

45. $(7.7 \times 10^8) \times (4.9 \times 10^{-5})$

46. $(3.6 \times 10^5) \div (1.8 \times 10^9)$

Diameter $\approx 8 \times 10^{-6}$ m

47. A white blood cell has a diameter of about 0.000012 meter. How many times greater is the diameter of a white blood cell than the diameter of a red blood cell?

Write the product using exponents.

1. $(-15) \cdot (-15) \cdot (-15)$

2. $4 \cdot 4 \cdot x \cdot x \cdot x$

Evaluate the expression.

3. $10 + 3^3 \div 9$

4. $\dfrac{-2 \cdot (-2)^{-4}}{(-2)^{-2}}$

Simplify the expression. Write your answer as a power.

5. $9^{10} \cdot 9$

6. $(6^6)^5$

7. $\dfrac{(-3.5)^{13} \cdot (-3.5)^2}{(-3.5)^9}$

8. Simplify $(2y)^7$.

Round the number. Write the result as a product of a single digit and a power of 10.

9. 4,610,428,970

10. 0.00000572

Write the number in standard form.

11. 3×10^7

12. 9.05×10^{-3}

Evaluate the expression. Write your answer in scientific notation.

13. $(7.8 \times 10^7) + (9.9 \times 10^7)$

14. $(6.4 \times 10^5) - (5.4 \times 10^4)$

15. $(3.1 \times 10^6) \times (2.7 \times 10^{-2})$

16. $(9.6 \times 10^7) \div (1.2 \times 10^{-4})$

17. Is $(xy^2)^3$ the same as $(xy^3)^2$? Explain.

18. One scoop of rice weighs about 3^9 milligrams.

   a. Write a linear function that relates the weight of rice to the number of scoops. What is the weight of 5 scoops of rice?

   b. A grain of rice weighs about 3^3 milligrams. About how many grains of rice are in 1 scoop?

19. There are about 10,000 taste buds on a human tongue. Write this number in scientific notation.

20. From 1978 to 2008, the amount of lead allowed in the air in the United States was 1.5×10^{-6} gram per cubic meter. In 2008, the amount allowed was reduced by 90%. What is the new amount of lead allowed in the air?

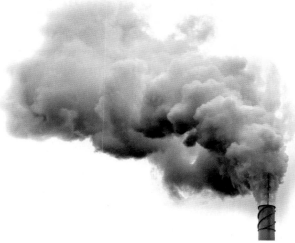

1. Mercury's distance from the Sun is approximately 5.79×10^7 kilometers. What is this distance in standard form?

   A. 5,790,000 km   **B.** 57,900,000 km

   C. 579,000,000 km   **D.** 5,790,000,000 km

Test-Taking Strategy

Use Intelligent Guessing

Cats were first tamed $3 \cdot 2^{10}$ years ago in Egypt. How long ago was that?

ⓐ 3000 ⓑ 3072 ⓒ 5000 ⓓ 40

Who says I am tame? Growl. Hiss.

"It can't be 40 or 5000 because they aren't divisible by 3. So, you can intelligently guess between 3000 and 3072."

2. Your friend solves the problem. What should your friend change to correctly answer the question?

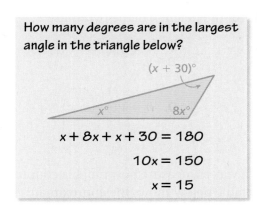

How many degrees are in the largest angle in the triangle below?

$(x + 30)°$

$x°$ $8x°$

$x + 8x + x + 30 = 180$

$10x = 150$

$x = 15$

   F. The left side of the equation should equal 360° instead of 180°.

   G. The sum of the acute angles should equal 90°.

   H. Evaluate the smallest angle when $x = 15$.

   I. Evaluate the largest angle when $x = 15$.

3. Which expression is equivalent to the expression $2^4 2^3$?

   A. 2^{12} **B.** 4^7

   C. 48   **D.** 128

4. You randomly survey students in your school about whether they have a pet. You display your results in the two-way table. How many female students took the survey?

		Pet	
		Yes	No
Gender	Male	33	8
	Female	35	11

5. A bank account pays interest so that the amount in the account doubles every 10 years. The account started with $5,000 in 1940. Which expression represents the amount (in dollars) in the account n decades later?

   F. $2^n \cdot 5000$ **G.** $5000(n + 1)$

   H. 5000^n **I.** $2^n + 5000$

6. The formula for the volume V of a pyramid is $V = \frac{1}{3}Bh$.

Which equation represents a formula for the height h of the pyramid?

   A. $h = \frac{1}{3}VB$ **B.** $h = \frac{3V}{B}$

   C. $h = \frac{V}{3B}$ **D.** $h = V - \frac{1}{3}B$

7. The gross domestic product (GDP) is a way to measure how much a country produces economically in a year. The table below shows the approximate population and GDP for the United States.

United States, 2016	
Population	324,000,000
GDP	$18,600,000,000,000

   Part A Write the population and the GDP using scientific notation.

   Part B Find the GDP per person for the United States using your answers from *Part A*. Write your answer in scientific notation. Show your work and explain your reasoning.

8. What is the equation of the line shown in the graph?

   F. $y = -\frac{1}{3}x + 3$ **G.** $y = \frac{1}{3}x + 1$

   H. $y = -3x + 3$ **I.** $y = 3x - \frac{1}{3}$

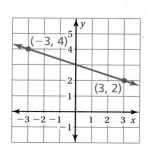

9. Which graph represents a linear function?

A.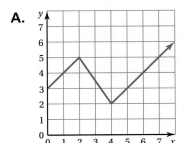

B.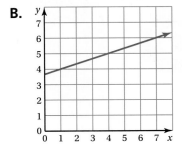

C.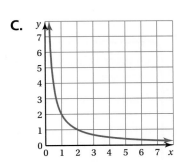

D.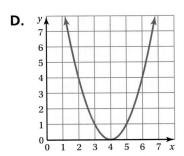

10. Find $(-2.5)^{-2}$.

11. Two lines have the same y-intercept. The slope of one line is 1, and the slope of the other line is -1. What can you conclude?

   F. The lines are parallel.

   G. The lines meet at exactly one point.

   H. The lines meet at more than one point.

   I. The situation described is impossible.

12. Which list of ordered pairs represents the mapping diagram?

   A. $(1, 2), (2, 0), (3, -2)$

   B. $(1, 0), (2, 2), (3, -2)$

   C. $(1, 0), (2, 2), (2, -2), (3, -2)$

   D. $(0, 1), (2, 2), (-2, 2), (-2, 3)$

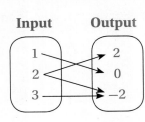

9 Real Numbers and the Pythagorean Theorem

Chapter Learning Target:
Understand square roots.

Chapter Success Criteria:
- ▪ I can describe a square root.
- ▪ I can find the square root(s) of a number.
- ▪ I can approximate the value of the square root of a number.
- ▪ I can explain the Pythagorean Theorem.

STEAM Video: "Metronome Design"

Metronome Design

A *metronome* is a device that ticks at a constant rate. A metronome includes a pendulum, which swings back and forth in a precise time called a *period*. Why do musicians use metronomes?

Watch the STEAM Video "Metronome Design." Then answer the following questions. The equation $T = 0.2\sqrt{L}$ relates the period T (in seconds) and the length L (in centimeters) of a pendulum, where $\sqrt{L}$ is the *square root* of L.

1. The table shows the square roots of several values of L. Use the pattern to find the values of $\sqrt{36}$, $\sqrt{49}$, and $\sqrt{64}$.

L	1	4	9	16	25
$\sqrt{L}$	1	2	3	4	5

2. What is the period of a pendulum that is 100 centimeters long? Justify your answer.

Performance Task

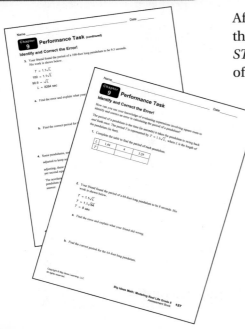

Identify and Correct the Error!

After completing this chapter, you will be able to use the concepts you learned to answer the questions in the *STEAM Video Performance Task*. You will be given the lengths of several pendulums.

Length (feet)	1.44	4	5.29
Period (seconds)			

You will be asked to identify and correct errors in calculations of periods. Why is it important to pay attention to units when substituting values into a formula?

Getting Ready for Chapter

When you multiply a number by itself, you square the number.

> Symbol for squaring is the exponent 2.

$4^2 = 4 \cdot 4$

$= 16$ 4 squared is 16.

To "undo" this, take the *square root* of the number.

> Symbol for square root is a *radical sign*, $\sqrt{}$.

$\sqrt{16} = \sqrt{4^2} = 4$ The square root of 16 is 4.

1. Work with a partner. Find the radius of each circle.

a.

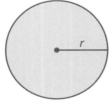

Area = 36π in.^{2}

b.

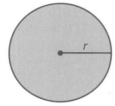

Area = π yd^2

c.

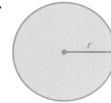

Area = 0.25π ft^2

d.

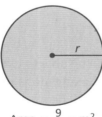

Area = $\frac{9}{16}\pi$ m^2

e.

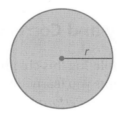

Area = 0.49π cm^2

f.

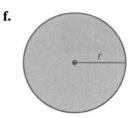

Area = 1.44π in.^{2}

2. WRITING GUIDELINES Work with a partner. Explain how you can find the radius and diameter of a circular object when you are given its area. Justify your answer using an example that is different from those in Exercise 1.

Vocabulary

The following vocabulary terms are defined in this chapter. Think about what the terms might mean and record your thoughts.

square root   cube root   irrational number

perfect square   perfect cube

9.1 Finding Square Roots

Learning Target: Understand the concept of a square root of a number.

Success Criteria:
- I can find square roots of numbers.
- I can evaluate expressions involving square roots.
- I can use square roots to solve equations.

EXPLORATION 1

Finding Side Lengths

Work with a partner. Find the side length s of each square. Explain your method.

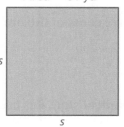

Area = 81 yd²

s

s

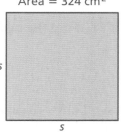

Area = 324 cm²

s

s

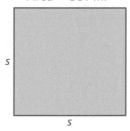

Area = 361 mi²

s

s

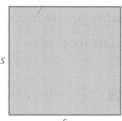

Area = 225 mi²

s

s

Area = 2.89 in.²

s

s

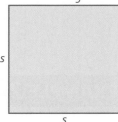

Area = $\frac{4}{9}$ ft²

s

s

EXPLORATION 2

Finding Solutions of Equations

Work with a partner. Use mental math to solve each equation. How many solutions are there for each equation? Explain your reasoning.

Math Practice

Use Operations

How do the sign rules for multiplying integers help you find the solution(s) of each equation?

$x^2 = 0$

$x^2 = 1$

$x^2 = 4$

$x^2 = 9$

$x^2 = 16$

$x^2 = 25$

9.1 Lesson

Key Vocabulary 🔊
square root, *p. 374*
perfect square, *p. 374*
radical sign, *p. 374*
radicand, *p. 374*

A **square root** of a number p is a number whose square is equal to p. So, a square root of a number p is a solution of the equation $x^2 = p$. Every positive number has a positive *and* a negative square root. A **perfect square** is a number with integers as its square roots.

EXAMPLE 1 Finding Square Roots of a Perfect Square

Math Practice

Use Definitions
Explain why 0 only has one square root.

Find the two square roots of 49.

$$7^2 = 49 \text{ and } (-7)^2 = 49$$

▷ So, the square roots of 49 are 7 and −7.

Try It **Find the two square roots of the number.**

1. 36   **2.** 100   **3.** 121

The symbol $\sqrt{}$ is called a **radical sign**. It is used to represent a square root. The number under the radical sign is called the **radicand**.

- $\sqrt{p}$ represents the *positive* square root of p.
- $-\sqrt{p}$ represents the *negative* square root of p.
- $\pm\sqrt{p}$ represents *both* square roots of p.

EXAMPLE 2 Finding Square Roots

Find the square root(s).

a. $\sqrt{25}$

> $\sqrt{25}$ represents the *positive* square root.

▷ Because $5^2 = 25$, $\sqrt{25} = 5$.

b. $-\sqrt{49}$

> $-\sqrt{49}$ represents the *negative* square root.

▷ Because $7^2 = 49$, $-\sqrt{49} = -7$.

c. $\pm\sqrt{16}$

> $\pm\sqrt{16}$ represents both the *positive* and the *negative* square roots.

▷ Because $4^2 = 16$, $\pm\sqrt{16} = -4$ and 4.

Try It **Find the square root(s).**

4. $\sqrt{4}$ **5.** $-\sqrt{81}$ **6.** $\pm\sqrt{64}$

EXAMPLE 3 **Finding Square Roots**

Find the square root(s).

a. $\sqrt{\dfrac{9}{16}}$

▷ Because $\left(\dfrac{3}{4}\right)^2 = \dfrac{9}{16}$, $\sqrt{\dfrac{9}{16}} = \dfrac{3}{4}$.

b. $\pm\sqrt{2.25}$

▷ Because $1.5^2 = 2.25$, $\pm\sqrt{2.25} = -1.5$ and 1.5.

Try It Find the square root(s).

7. $-\sqrt{\dfrac{1}{100}}$ 8. $\pm\sqrt{\dfrac{4}{25}}$ 9. $\sqrt{12.25}$

Squaring a number and finding a square root "undo" each other. So, they are inverse operations. For example,

$$\sqrt{4^2} = \sqrt{16} = 4 \text{ and } \left(\sqrt{4}\right)^2 = 2^2 = 4.$$

You can use this relationship to evaluate expressions.

EXAMPLE 4 **Evaluating Expressions Involving Square Roots**

Evaluate each expression.

a. $5\sqrt{36} + 7 = 5(6) + 7$ Evaluate the square root.

$\phantom{5\sqrt{36} + 7} = 30 + 7$ Multiply.

$\phantom{5\sqrt{36} + 7} = 37$ Add.

b. $\dfrac{1}{4} + \sqrt{\dfrac{18}{2}} = \dfrac{1}{4} + \sqrt{9}$ Simplify.

$\phantom{\dfrac{1}{4} + \sqrt{\dfrac{18}{2}}} = \dfrac{1}{4} + 3$ Evaluate the square root.

$\phantom{\dfrac{1}{4} + \sqrt{\dfrac{18}{2}}} = 3\dfrac{1}{4}$ Add.

c. $\left(\sqrt{81}\right)^2 - 5 = 81 - 5$ Evaluate the power using inverse operations.

$\phantom{\left(\sqrt{81}\right)^2 - 5} = 76$ Subtract.

Try It Evaluate the expression.

10. $12 - 3\sqrt{25}$ 11. $\sqrt{\dfrac{28}{7}} + 2.4$ 12. $15 - \left(\sqrt{4}\right)^2$

Because squaring a number and taking the square root are inverse operations, you can solve an equation of the form $x^2 = p$ by taking the square root of each side.

EXAMPLE 5 **Solving Equations Using Square Roots**

Solve each equation.

a. $x^2 = 81$

$$x^2 = 81 \qquad \text{Write the equation.}$$
$$x = \pm\sqrt{81} \qquad \text{Take the square root of each side.}$$
$$x = \pm 9 \qquad \text{Simplify.}$$

 The solutions are $x = -9$ and $x = 9$.

When solving an equation by taking square roots, take both the positive and the negative square roots.

b. $3a^2 = 48$

$$3a^2 = 48 \qquad \text{Write the equation.}$$
$$a^2 = 16 \qquad \text{Divide each side by 3.}$$
$$a = \pm\sqrt{16} \qquad \text{Take the square root of each side.}$$
$$a = \pm 4 \qquad \text{Simplify.}$$

 The solutions are $a = -4$ and $a = 4$.

Try It Solve the equation.

13. $k^2 = 169$ **14.** $7n^2 = 175$ **15.** $190 = 4b^2 - 6$

 Self-Assessment for *Concepts & Skills*

Solve each exercise. Then rate your understanding of the success criteria in your journal.

FINDING SQUARE ROOTS Find the square root(s).

16. $\sqrt{256}$ **17.** $-\sqrt{\dfrac{1}{9}}$ **18.** $\pm\sqrt{1.44}$

EVALUATING EXPRESSIONS Evaluate the expression.

19. $\sqrt{\dfrac{81}{9}} - 7$ **20.** $-1 - \sqrt{121}$ **21.** $5 + \left(\sqrt{6}\right)^2$

SOLVING EQUATIONS Solve the equation.

22. $2r^2 = 162$ **23.** $d^2 + 5 = 41$ **24.** $-42 = 7b^2 - 385$

EXAMPLE 6 **Modeling Real Life**

The area of a crop circle is 45,216 square feet. What is the radius of the crop circle?

Understand the problem.

You are given the area of a crop circle. You are asked to find the radius of the crop circle.

Make a plan.

Use the formula for the area of a circle. Substitute 45,216 for the area and 3.14 for π. Then solve for the radius.

Solve and check.

$$A = \pi r^2$$ Write the formula for the area of a circle.

$$45{,}216 \approx 3.14 r^2$$ Substitute 45,216 for A and 3.14 for π.

$$14{,}400 = r^2$$ Divide each side by 3.14.

$$\sqrt{14{,}400} = r$$ Take the positive square root of each side.

$$120 = r$$ Simplify.

The radius of a circle cannot be negative, so you do not need to take the negative square root.

The radius of the crop circle is about 120 feet.

Check Find the area of a circle with a radius of 120 feet.

$$A = \pi r^2 = \pi (120)^2 = 14{,}400\pi \approx 45{,}216 \text{ ft}^2 \checkmark$$

 Self-Assessment for *Problem Solving*

Solve each exercise. Then rate your understanding of the success criteria in your journal.

25. Your distance d (in miles) from the horizon can be approximated by $d = 1.22\sqrt{h}$, where h is your eye level (in feet above ground level). What is your eye level when you are 9.76 miles from the horizon?

26. **DIG DEEPER!** The speed s (in meters per second) of a tsunami can be modeled by the function $s = \sqrt{9.8d}$, where d is the water depth (in meters).

    a. What is the speed of the tsunami when the water depth is 500 meters?

    b. What happens to the speed of the tsunami as the depth decreases? Explain.

▶ Review & Refresh

Evaluate the expression. Write your answer in scientific notation.

1. $(4.3 \times 10^3) + (2.4 \times 10^3)$

2. $(1.5 \times 10^{-2}) - (3.5 \times 10^{-3})$

3. $9 \times (7 \times 10^{-2})$

4. $(6.6 \times 10^{-5}) \div (1.1 \times 10^4)$

Make a scatter plot of the data. Identify any outliers, gaps, or clusters.

5.

Length (meters), x	1	8	3.5	2	2.5	3	2.5	2.5	3	9
Weight (pounds), y	4	33	17	8	9	9	8	8.5	11	36

6.

Volume (gallons), x	0.25	1	1	0.5	0.125	1	0.5	1
Cost (dollars), y	0.99	3.95	3.99	5.50	0.50	4.05	2.00	4.00

▶▶ Concepts, Skills, & Problem Solving

FINDING SIDE LENGTHS **Find the side length *s* of the square.** (See Exploration 1, p. 373.)

7. Area = 441 cm²

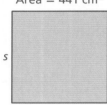

8. Area = 1.69 km²

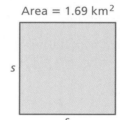

9. Area = $\frac{36}{49}$ yd²

FINDING SQUARE ROOTS OF A PERFECT SQUARE **Find the two square roots of the number.**

10. 9

11. 64

12. 4

13. 144

FINDING SQUARE ROOTS **Find the square root(s).**

14. $\sqrt{625}$

15. $\pm\sqrt{196}$

16. $-\sqrt{1600}$

17. $\pm\sqrt{2500}$

18. $\sqrt{\dfrac{1}{16}}$

19. $\sqrt{\dfrac{49}{576}}$

20. $\pm\sqrt{\dfrac{1}{961}}$

21. $-\sqrt{\dfrac{9}{100}}$

22. $\pm\sqrt{4.84}$

23. $\sqrt{7.29}$

24. $-\sqrt{361}$

25. $-\sqrt{2.25}$

26. 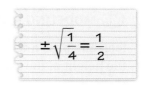 **YOU BE THE TEACHER** Your friend finds $\pm\sqrt{\frac{1}{4}}$. Is your friend correct? Explain your reasoning.

$$\pm\sqrt{\frac{1}{4}} = \frac{1}{2}$$

27.  **MODELING REAL LIFE** The area of a square patch of fabric is 2.25 square inches. What is the side length of the patch?

28. **CRITICAL THINKING** There are two square roots of 25. Why is there only one answer for the radius of the button?

$A = 25\pi \text{ mm}^2$

MP NUMBER SENSE Copy and complete the statement with <, >, or =.

29. $\sqrt{81}$ ___ 8

30. 0.5 ___ $\sqrt{0.25}$

31. $\frac{3}{2}$ ___ $\sqrt{\frac{25}{4}}$

EVALUATING EXPRESSIONS Evaluate the expression.

32. $\left(\sqrt{9}\right)^2 + 5$

33. $28 - \left(\sqrt{144}\right)^2$

34. $3\sqrt{16} - 5$

35. $10 - 4\sqrt{\frac{1}{16}}$

36. $\sqrt{6.76} + 5.4$

37. $8\sqrt{8.41} + 1.8$

38. $2\left(\sqrt{\frac{80}{5}} - 5\right)$

39. $4\left(\sqrt{\frac{147}{3}} + 3\right)$

40. **MP NUMBER SENSE** Without calculating, describe how the value of $\sqrt{\frac{1}{a}}$ changes as a increases. Assume $a > 0$.

SOLVING EQUATIONS Solve the equation.

41. $x^2 = 100$

42. $42 = d^2 - 22$

43. $4z^2 = 144$

44. $\sqrt{\frac{36}{9}} = \frac{1}{3}m^2 - 10$

45. $0.25r^2 = 49$

46. $3h^2 = h^2 + 18$

47. 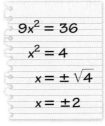 **YOU BE THE TEACHER** Your friend solves the equation $9x^2 = 36$. Is your friend correct? Explain your reasoning.

$9x^2 = 36$
$x^2 = 4$
$x = \pm\sqrt{4}$
$x = \pm 2$

48. **MP PROBLEM SOLVING** The *period* of a pendulum is the time the pendulum takes to complete one back-and-forth swing. The period T (in seconds) can be modeled by the function $T = 1.1\sqrt{L}$, where L is the length (in feet) of the pendulum. Estimate the length of a pendulum with a period of 1.65 seconds.

49.  **MP MODELING REAL LIFE** The area of a sail is $40\frac{1}{2}$ square feet. The base and the height of the sail are equal. What is the height of the sail?

50. **MP REPEATED RASONING** Find several products of perfect squares. What do you notice? Is this true for all products of perfect squares? Explain.

51. **MP PROBLEM SOLVING** The kinetic energy K (in joules) of a falling apple is represented by $K = \frac{v^2}{2}$, where v is the speed of the apple (in meters per second). How fast is the apple traveling when the kinetic energy is 32 joules?

Area $= 4\pi$ cm^2

52. **MP PRECISION** The areas of the two watch faces have a ratio of $16:25$.

    a. What is the ratio of the radius of the smaller watch face to the radius of the larger watch face?

    b. What is the radius of the larger watch face?

53. **MP PROBLEM SOLVING** The cost C (in dollars) of making a square window with a side length of n inches is represented by $C = \frac{n^2}{5} + 175$. A window costs \$355. What is the side length (in feet) of the window? Justify your answer.

54. **DIG DEEPER!** Albert Einstein's most famous equation is $E = mc^2$, where E is the energy of an object (in joules), m is the mass of the object (in kilograms), and c is the speed of light (in meters per second). A hydrogen atom has 15.066×10^{-11} joule of energy and a mass of 1.674×10^{-27} kilogram. What is the speed of light? Write your answer in scientific notation.

55. **MP GEOMETRY** The area of the triangle is represented by the formula $A = \sqrt{s(s - 21)(s - 17)(s - 10)}$, where s is equal to half the perimeter. What is the height of the triangle?

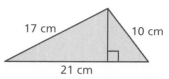

17 cm   10 cm   21 cm

56. **WRITING** Can you find the square root of a negative number? Explain.

MP REASONING Without solving, determine the number of solutions of the equation.

57. $x^2 = 1$ 58. $b^2 = -\sqrt{\dfrac{1}{9}}$ 59. $z = \sqrt{-144}$

9.2 The Pythagorean Theorem

Learning Target: Understand the Pythagorean Theorem.

Success Criteria:
- I can explain the Pythagorean Theorem.
- I can use the Pythagorean Theorem to find unknown side lengths of triangles.
- I can use the Pythagorean Theorem to find distances between points in a coordinate plane.

Pythagoras was a Greek mathematician and philosopher who proved one of the most famous rules in mathematics. In mathematics, a rule is called a **theorem**. So, the rule that Pythagoras proved is called the *Pythagorean Theorem*.

Pythagoras
(c. 570–c. 490 B.C.)

EXPLORATION 1

Discovering the Pythagorean Theorem

Work with a partner.

- **On grid paper, draw a right triangle with one horizontal side and one vertical side.**

- **Label the lengths of the two shorter sides a and b. Label the length of the longest side c.**

- **Draw three squares that each share a side with your triangle. Label the areas of the squares a^2, b^2, and c^2.**

- **Cut out each square. Then make eight copies of the right triangle and cut them out.**

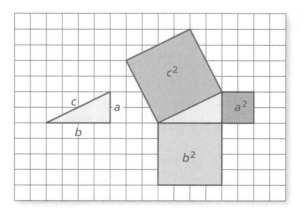

Math Practice

Construct Arguments

Is the relationship among a^2, b^2, and c^2 true for all right triangles? Explain.

a. Arrange the figures to show how a^2 and b^2 relate to c^2. Use an equation to represent this relationship.

b. Estimate the side length c of your triangle. Then use the relationship in part (a) to find c. Compare the values.

Key Vocabulary
theorem, *p. 381*
legs, *p. 382*
hypotenuse, *p. 382*
Pythagorean
   Theorem, *p. 382*

 Key Ideas

Sides of a Right Triangle

The sides of a right triangle have special names.

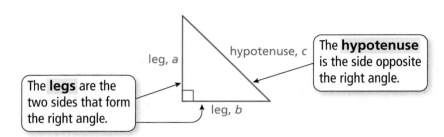

The **legs** are the two sides that form the right angle.

leg, *a*

hypotenuse, *c*

leg, *b*

The **hypotenuse** is the side opposite the right angle.

In a right triangle, the legs are the shorter sides and the hypotenuse is always the longest side.

The Pythagorean Theorem

Words In any right triangle, the sum of the squares of the lengths of the legs is equal to the square of the length of the hypotenuse.

Algebra $a^2 + b^2 = c^2$

EXAMPLE 1 ### Finding the Length of a Hypotenuse

Find the length of the hypotenuse of the triangle.

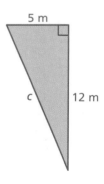

5 m

c

12 m

$a^2 + b^2 = c^2$	Write the Pythagorean Theorem.
$5^2 + 12^2 = c^2$	Substitute 5 for *a* and 12 for *b*.
$25 + 144 = c^2$	Evaluate the powers.
$169 = c^2$	Add.
$13 = c$	Take the positive square root of each side.

▷ The length of the hypotenuse is 13 meters.

Try It **Find the length of the hypotenuse of the triangle.**

1.

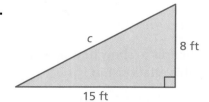

c

8 ft

15 ft

2.

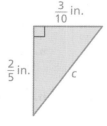

$\frac{3}{10}$ in.

$\frac{2}{5}$ in.

c

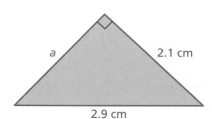

EXAMPLE 2 **Finding the Length of a Leg**

Find the missing length of the triangle.

$$a^2 + b^2 = c^2$$ Write the Pythagorean Theorem.

$$a^2 + 2.1^2 = 2.9^2$$ Substitute 2.1 for b and 2.9 for c.

$$a^2 + 4.41 = 8.41$$ Evaluate the powers.

$$a^2 = 4$$ Subtract 4.41 from each side.

$$a = 2$$ Take the positive square root of each side.

▷ The missing length is 2 centimeters.

Try It **Find the missing length of the triangle.**

3.

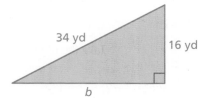

4.

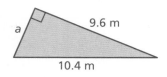

You can use right triangles and the Pythagorean Theorem to find lengths of three-dimensional figures.

EXAMPLE 3 **Finding a Length of a Three-Dimensional Figure**

Find the slant height of the square pyramid.

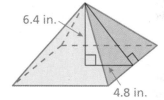

$$a^2 + b^2 = c^2$$ Write the Pythagorean Theorem.

$$6.4^2 + 4.8^2 = c^2$$ Substitute 6.4 for a and 4.8 for b.

$$40.96 + 23.04 = c^2$$ Evaluate the powers.

$$64 = c^2$$ Add.

$$8 = c$$ Take the positive square root of each side.

▷ The slant height is 8 inches.

Try It **Find x.**

5.

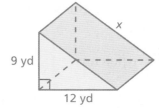

6.

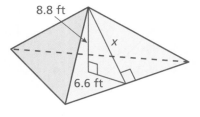

You can use right triangles and the Pythagorean Theorem to find distances between points in a coordinate plane.

EXAMPLE 4 **Finding a Distance in a Coordinate Plane**

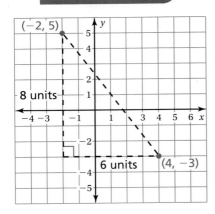

Find the distance between $(-2, 5)$ and $(4, -3)$.

Plot the points in a coordinate plane. Then draw a right triangle with a hypotenuse that represents the distance between the points.

Use the Pythagorean Theorem to find the length of the hypotenuse.

$a^2 + b^2 = c^2$	Write the Pythagorean Theorem.
$8^2 + 6^2 = c^2$	Substitute 8 for a and 6 for b.
$64 + 36 = c^2$	Evaluate the powers.
$100 = c^2$	Add.
$10 = c$	Take the positive square root of each side.

▶ The distance between $(-2, 5)$ and $(4, -3)$ is 10 units.

Try It **Find the distance between the points.**

7. $(3, 6)$ and $(7, 9)$ **8.** $(-3, -4)$ and $(2, 8)$

Self-Assessment *for Concepts & Skills*

Solve each exercise. Then rate your understanding of the success criteria in your journal.

FINDING A MISSING LENGTH Find x.

9.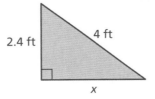

10.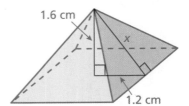

11. **FINDING A DISTANCE** Find the distance between $(-5, 2)$ and $(7, -7)$.

12. **DIFFERENT WORDS, SAME QUESTION** Which is different? Find "both" answers.

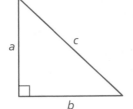

Which side is the hypotenuse?	Which side is the longest?
Which side is a leg?	Which side is opposite the right angle?

EXAMPLE 5 **Modeling Real Life**

You play capture the flag. You are 50 yards north and 20 yards east of your team's base. The other team's base is 80 yards north and 60 yards east of your base. How far are you from the other team's base?

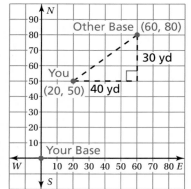

Step 1: Draw the situation in a coordinate plane. Let the origin represent your team's base. From the descriptions, you are at (20, 50) and the other team's base is at (60, 80).

Step 2: Draw a right triangle with a hypotenuse that represents the distance between you and the other team's base. The lengths of the legs are 30 yards and 40 yards.

Step 3: Use the Pythagorean Theorem to find the length of the hypotenuse.

$$a^2 + b^2 = c^2 \qquad \text{Write the Pythagorean Theorem.}$$
$$30^2 + 40^2 = c^2 \qquad \text{Substitute 30 for } a \text{ and 40 for } b.$$
$$900 + 1600 = c^2 \qquad \text{Evaluate the powers.}$$
$$2500 = c^2 \qquad \text{Add.}$$
$$50 = c \qquad \text{Take the positive square root of each side.}$$

So, you are 50 yards from the other team's base.

 Self-Assessment for *Problem Solving*

Solve each exercise. Then rate your understanding of the success criteria in your journal.

13. A zookeeper knows that an escaped red panda is hiding somewhere in the triangular region shown. What is the area (in square miles) that the zookeeper needs to search? Explain.

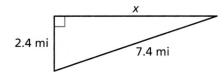

14. **DIG DEEPER!** Objects detected by radar are plotted in a coordinate plane where each unit represents 15 miles. The point (0, 0) represents the location of a shipyard. A cargo ship is traveling at a constant speed and in a constant direction parallel to the coastline. At 9 A.M., the radar shows the cargo ship at (0, 9). At 10 A.M., the radar shows the cargo ship at (1, 9). At what time will the cargo ship be 225 miles from the shipyard? Explain.

▶ *Review & Refresh*

Solve the equation.

1. $7z^2 = 252$

2. $0.75q^2 = 108$

3. $\sqrt{\dfrac{1000}{10}} = n^2 - 54$

4. What is the solution of the system of linear equations $y = 4x + 1$ and $2x + y = 13$?

   A. $(1, 5)$ **B.** $(5, 3)$ **C.** $(2, 9)$ **D.** $(9, 2)$

▶▶ *Concepts, Skills, & Problem Solving*

USING GRID PAPER Find c. (See Exploration 1, p. 381.)

5.
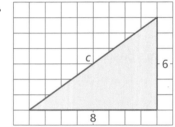

6.
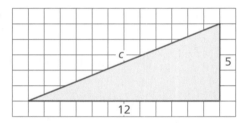

FINDING A MISSING LENGTH Find the missing length of the triangle.

7.
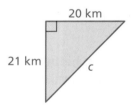

8.
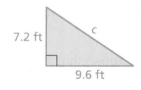

9.

10.
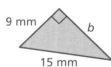

11.
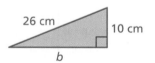

12.
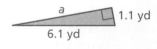

13. **MP** **YOU BE THE TEACHER** Your friend finds the missing length of the triangle. Is your friend correct? Explain your reasoning.

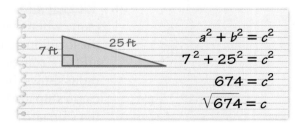

FINDING LENGTHS OF THREE-DIMENSIONAL FIGURES Find x.

14.

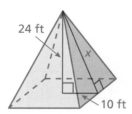

24 ft

x

10 ft

15.

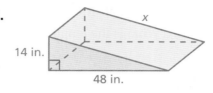

x

14 in.

48 in.

16.

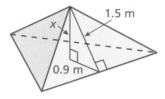

1.5 m

x

0.9 m

17.

6.5 cm

x

2.5 cm

FINDING DISTANCES IN THE COORDINATE PLANE Find the distance between the points.

18. $(0, 0), (9, 12)$

19. $(1, 2), (-3, 5)$

20. $(-18, 9), (22, 0)$

21. $(-7, -2), (13, -23)$

22. $(15, -17), (-20, -5)$

23. $(-13, -3.5), (17, 2)$

FINDING A MISSING LENGTH Find x.

24.

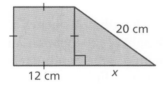

20 cm

12 cm x

25.

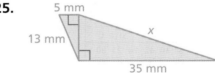

5 mm

13 mm x

35 mm

26. **MP MODELING REAL LIFE** The figure shows the location of a golf ball after a tee shot. How many feet from the hole is the ball?

27. **MP MODELING REAL LIFE** A tennis player asks the referee a question. The sound of the player's voice travels 30 feet. Can the referee hear the question? Explain.

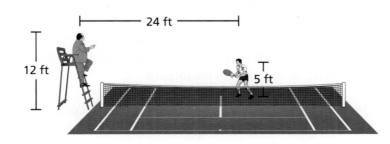

24 ft

12 ft

5 ft

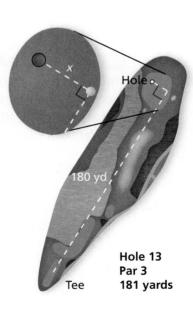

x

Hole

180 yd

Hole 13
Par 3
Tee   181 yards

28. **(MP) PROBLEM SOLVING** You are cutting a rectangular piece of fabric in half along a diagonal. The fabric measures 28 inches wide and $1\frac{1}{4}$ yards long. What is the length (in inches) of the diagonal?

29. **PROJECT** Measure the length, width, and height of a rectangular room. Use the Pythagorean Theorem to find the distance from B to C and the distance from A to B.

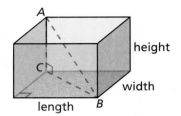

30. **(MP) STRUCTURE** The legs of a right triangle have lengths of 28 meters and 21 meters. The hypotenuse has a length of $5x$ meters. What is the value of x?

31. **(MP) PRECISION** You and a friend stand back-to-back. You run 20 feet forward, then 15 feet to your right. At the same time, your friend runs 16 feet forward, then 12 feet to her right. She stops and hits you with a snowball.

    a. Draw the situation in a coordinate plane.

    b. How far does your friend throw the snowball?

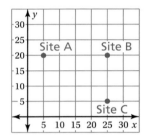

32. **(MP) MODELING REAL LIFE** The coordinate plane shows dig sites for archaeological research. Each unit on the grid represents 1 square foot. What is the distance from Site A to Site C?

33. **(MP) PRECISION** A box has a length of 30 inches, a width of 40 inches, and a height of 120 inches. Can a cylindrical rod with a length of 342.9 centimeters fit in the box? Explain your reasoning.

34. **(MP) MODELING REAL LIFE** A *green roof* is like a traditional roof but covered with plants. Plants used for a green roof cost $0.75 per square foot. The roof at the right is 40 feet long. How much does it cost to cover both sides of the roof? Justify your answer.

35. **CRITICAL THINKING** A triangle has coordinates $A(2, 1)$, $B(2, 4)$, and $C(5, 1)$. Write an expression for the length of $\overline{BC}$. Use a calculator to find the length of $\overline{BC}$ to the nearest hundredth.

36. **DIG DEEPER!** Write an equation for the distance d between the points (x_1, y_1) and (x_2, y_2). Explain how you found the equation.

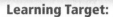

9.3 Finding Cube Roots

Learning Target: Understand the concept of a cube root of a number.

Success Criteria:
- I can find cube roots of numbers.
- I can evaluate expressions involving cube roots.
- I can use cube roots to solve equations.

EXPLORATION 1

Finding Edge Lengths

Work with a partner. Find the edge length s of each cube. Explain your method.

Math Practice

Consider Similar Problems

How is finding the edge length of a cube with a given volume similar to finding the side length of a square with a given area?

Volume = 8 cm³

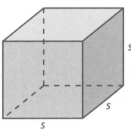

Volume = 27 ft³

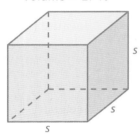

Volume = 125 m³

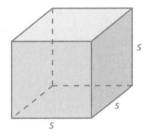

Volume = 343 in.³

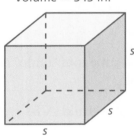

Volume = 0.001 cm³

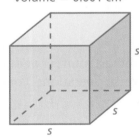

Volume = $\frac{1}{8}$ yd³

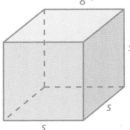

EXPLORATION 2

Finding Solutions of Equations

Work with a partner. Use mental math to solve each equation. How many solutions are there for each equation? Explain your reasoning.

$$x^3 = -27$$

$$x^3 = -8$$

$$x^3 = -1$$

$$x^3 = 1$$

$$x^3 = 8$$

$$x^3 = 27$$

Key Vocabulary 🔊
cube root, *p. 390*
perfect cube, *p. 390*

A **cube root** of a number p is a number whose cube is equal to p. So, a cube root of a number p is a solution of the equation $x^3 = p$. The symbol $\sqrt[3]{}$ is used to represent a cube root. A **perfect cube** is a number that can be written as the cube of an integer.

EXAMPLE 1 **Finding Cube Roots**

Find each cube root.

a. $\sqrt[3]{8}$

▷ Because $2^3 = 8$, $\sqrt[3]{8} = 2$.

b. $\sqrt[3]{-27}$

▷ Because $(-3)^3 = -27$, $\sqrt[3]{-27} = -3$.

c. $\sqrt[3]{\dfrac{1}{64}}$

▷ Because $\left(\dfrac{1}{4}\right)^3 = \dfrac{1}{64}$, $\sqrt[3]{\dfrac{1}{64}} = \dfrac{1}{4}$.

Try It **Find the cube root.**

1. $\sqrt[3]{1}$ **2.** $\sqrt[3]{-343}$ **3.** $\sqrt[3]{-\dfrac{27}{1000}}$

Cubing a number and finding a cube root "undo" each other. So, they are inverse operations. For example,

$$\sqrt[3]{8^3} = \sqrt[3]{512} = 8 \text{ and } \left(\sqrt[3]{8}\right)^3 = 2^3 = 8.$$

You can use this relationship to evaluate expressions.

EXAMPLE 2 **Evaluating Expressions Involving Cube Roots**

Evaluate each expression.

a. $2\sqrt[3]{-216} = 2(-6)$ Evaluate the cube root.

$\qquad\qquad\quad = -12$ Multiply.

b. $\left(\sqrt[3]{125}\right)^3 + 21 = 125 + 21$ Evaluate the power using inverse operations.

$\qquad\qquad\qquad\quad = 146$ Add.

Try It **Evaluate the expression.**

4. $18 - 4\sqrt[3]{8}$ **5.** $\left(\sqrt[3]{-64}\right)^3 + 43$ **6.** $5\sqrt[3]{512} - 19$

Because cubing a number and taking the cube root are inverse operations, you can solve equations of the form $x^3 = p$ by taking the cube root of each side.

EXAMPLE 3 **Solving Equations Using Cube Roots**

Solve each equation.

a. $x^3 = 216$

Check

$x^3 = 216$

$6^3 \stackrel{?}{=} 216$

$216 = 216$ ✓

$x^3 = 216$	Write the equation.
$\sqrt[3]{x^3} = \sqrt[3]{216}$	Take the cube root of each side.
$x = 6$	Simplify.

 The solution is $x = 6$.

b. $-\dfrac{1}{4}n^3 = 2$

Check

$-\dfrac{1}{4}n^3 = 2$

$-\dfrac{1}{4}(-2)^3 \stackrel{?}{=} 2$

$-\dfrac{1}{4}(-8) \stackrel{?}{=} 2$

$2 = 2$ ✓

$-\dfrac{1}{4}n^3 = 2$	Write the equation.
$n^3 = -8$	Multiply each side by -4.
$\sqrt[3]{n^3} = \sqrt[3]{-8}$	Take the cube root of each side.
$n = -2$	Simplify.

 The solution is $n = -2$.

Try It Solve the equation.

7. $z^3 = -1000$ **8.** $3b^3 = 1029$ **9.** $33 = -\dfrac{1}{5}m^3 + 8$

 Self-Assessment for Concepts & Skills

Solve each exercise. Then rate your understanding of the success criteria in your journal.

FINDING CUBE ROOTS Find the cube root.

10. $\sqrt[3]{64}$ **11.** $\sqrt[3]{-216}$ **12.** $\sqrt[3]{-\dfrac{343}{1000}}$

EVALUATING EXPRESSIONS Evaluate the expression.

13. $\left(\sqrt[3]{-27}\right)^3 + 61$ **14.** $15 + 3\sqrt[3]{125}$ **15.** $2\sqrt[3]{-729} - 5$

SOLVING EQUATIONS Solve the equation.

16. $d^3 = 512$ **17.** $w^3 - 12 = -76$ **18.** $-\dfrac{1}{3}m^3 + 13 = 4$

EXAMPLE 4 Modeling Real Life

The baseball display case is made of plastic. How many square inches of plastic are used to make the case?

Volume = 125 in.^{3}

The case is in the shape of a cube. Use the formula for the volume of a cube to find the edge length s.

$V = s^3$	Write the formula for volume.
$125 = s^3$	Substitute 125 for V.
$\sqrt[3]{125} = \sqrt[3]{s^3}$	Take the cube root of each side.
$5 = s$	Simplify.

The edge length is 5 inches. Use a formula to find the surface area of the cube.

$S = 6s^2$	Write the formula for surface area.
$= 6(5)^2$	Substitute 5 for s.
$= 150$	Simplify.

▷ So, 150 square inches of plastic are used to make the case.

Self-Assessment for Problem Solving

Solve each exercise. Then rate your understanding of the success criteria in your journal.

19. You have 275 square inches of wrapping paper. Do you have enough wrapping paper to wrap the gift box shown? Explain.

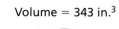

Volume = 343 in.^{3}

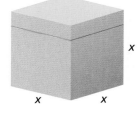

Area = 6400 cm^2

20. A cube-shaped end table has a volume of 216,000 cubic centimeters. Does the end table fit in the corner shown? Justify your answer.

21. **DIG DEEPER!** The relationship between the volumes and the lengths of two cereal boxes is represented by

$$\frac{\text{Volume of Box A}}{\text{Volume of Box B}} = \left(\frac{\text{Length of Box A}}{\text{Length of Box B}}\right)^3.$$

Box A has a volume of 192 cubic inches and a length of 8 inches. Box B has a volume of 375 cubic inches. What is the length of Box B? Justify your answer.

9.3 Practice

Go to *BigIdeasMath.com* to get HELP with solving the exercises.

▶ Review & Refresh

Find the missing length of the triangle.

1.
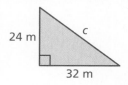
24 m
c
32 m

2.
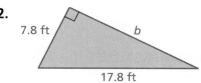
7.8 ft
b
17.8 ft

3. Which linear function is shown by the table?

A. $y = \frac{1}{3}x + 1$ **B.** $y = 4x$

C. $y = 3x + 1$ **D.** $y = \frac{1}{4}x$

x	1	2	3	4
y	4	7	10	13

▶▶ Concepts, Skills, & Problem Solving

FINDING EDGE LENGTHS Find the edge length *s* of the cube. (See Exploration 1, p. 389.)

4. Volume = 216 in.³
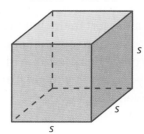
s
s
s

5. Volume = $\frac{1}{27}$ ft³
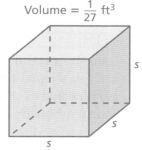
s
s
s

6. Volume = 0.064 m³
s
s
s

FINDING CUBE ROOTS Find the cube root.

7. $\sqrt[3]{729}$

8. $\sqrt[3]{-125}$

9. $\sqrt[3]{-1000}$

10. $\sqrt[3]{1728}$

11. $\sqrt[3]{-\dfrac{1}{512}}$

12. $\sqrt[3]{\dfrac{343}{64}}$

EVALUATING EXPRESSIONS Evaluate the expression.

13. $18 - \left(\sqrt[3]{27}\right)^3$

14. $\left(\sqrt[3]{-\dfrac{1}{8}}\right)^3 + 3\dfrac{3}{4}$

15. $5\sqrt[3]{729} - 24$

16. $\dfrac{1}{4} - 2\sqrt[3]{-\dfrac{1}{216}}$

17. $54 + \sqrt[3]{-4096}$

18. $4\sqrt[3]{8000} - 6$

EVALUATING EXPRESSIONS Evaluate the expression for the given value of the variable.

19. $\sqrt[3]{\dfrac{n}{4}} + \dfrac{n}{10}, n = 500$

20. $\sqrt[3]{6w} - w, w = 288$

21. $2d + \sqrt[3]{-45d}, d = 75$

SOLVING EQUATIONS Solve the equation.

22. $x^3 = 8$

23. $t^3 = -343$

24. $-75 = y^3 + 50$

25. $-\dfrac{1}{2}z^3 = -108$

26. $2h^3 - 11 = 43$

27. $-600 = \dfrac{2}{5}k^3 + 750$

28. **MP MODELING REAL LIFE** The volume of a cube-shaped compost bin is 27 cubic feet. What is the edge length of the compost bin?

29. **MP MODELING REAL LIFE** The volume of a cube of ice for an ice sculpture is 64,000 cubic inches.

    a. What is the edge length of the cube of ice?

    b. What is the surface area of the cube of ice?

30. **MP NUMBER SENSE** There are three numbers that are their own cube roots. What are the numbers?

MP REASONING Copy and complete the statement with <, >, or =.

31. $-\dfrac{1}{4}$ ▢ $\sqrt[3]{-\dfrac{8}{125}}$

32. $\sqrt[3]{0.001}$ ▢ 0.01

33. $\sqrt[3]{64}$ ▢ $\sqrt{64}$

Area of square base = 64 in.²

34. **DIG DEEPER!** You bake a dessert in the baking pan shown. You cut the dessert into cube-shaped pieces of equal size. Each piece has a volume of 8 cubic inches. How many pieces do you get from one pan? Justify your answer.

35. **MP LOGIC** Determine whether each statement is true for square roots. Then determine whether each statement is true for cube roots. Explain your reasoning.

    a. You cannot find the square root of a negative number.

    b. Every positive number has a positive square root and a negative square root.

36. **GEOMETRY** The pyramid has a volume of 972 cubic inches. What are the dimensions of the pyramid?

37. **MP REASONING** The ratio $125 : x$ is equivalent to the ratio $x^2 : 125$. What is the value of x?

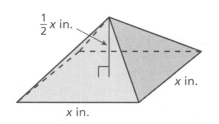

$\frac{1}{2}x$ in.

x in.

x in.

CRITICAL THINKING Solve the equation.

38. $(3x + 4)^3 = 2197$

39. $(8x^3 - 9)^3 = 5832$

40. $\left((5x - 16)^3 - 4\right)^3 = 216,000$

9.4 Rational Numbers

Learning Target: Convert between different forms of rational numbers.

Success Criteria:
- I can explain the meaning of rational numbers.
- I can write fractions and mixed numbers as decimals.
- I can write repeating decimals as fractions or mixed numbers.

Writing Repeating Decimals as Fractions

Work with a partner.

a. Complete the table.

x	$10x$
$x = 0.333\ldots$	$10x = 3.333\ldots$
$x = 0.666\ldots$	
$x = 0.111\ldots$	
$x = 0.2444\ldots$	

Math Practice

Look for Structure
Why was it helpful to multiply each side of the equation $x = d$ by 10 in part (a)?

b. For each row of the table, use the two equations and what you know about solving systems of equations to write a third equation that does not involve a repeating decimal. Then solve the equation. What does your solution represent?

Calculator

$1 \div 3$
$= 0.3333333333$

C	÷	×	⊗
7	8	9	−
4	5	6	+
1	2	3	( )
0	.	+/−	=

c. Write each repeating decimal below as a fraction. How is your procedure similar to parts (a) and (b)? How is it different?

$x = 0.\overline{12}$ $x = 0.\overline{45}$

$x = 0.\overline{27}$ $x = 0.9\overline{40}$

d. Explain how to write a repeating decimal with n repeating digits as a fraction.

9.4 Lesson

You can think of a terminating decimal as a decimal that has repeating zeros at the end.

Recall that a *rational number* is a number that can be written as $\frac{a}{b}$, where a and b are integers and $b \neq 0$. Every rational number can be written as a decimal that will either *terminate* or *repeat*.

Terminating Decimals	Repeating Decimals
$0.25, 4.736, -1.03$	$5.222\ldots, -4.\overline{38}, 12.\overline{015}$

A rational number that can be written as $\frac{a}{b}$, where a is an integer and b is a power of 10, has a decimal form that terminates.

EXAMPLE 1 Writing Fractions and Mixed Numbers as Decimals

a. Write $1\frac{4}{25}$ as a decimal.

Notice that $1\frac{4}{25} = \frac{29}{25}$. Because $\frac{29}{25}$ can be written as $\frac{a}{b}$, where a is an integer and b is a power of 10, the decimal form of the number terminates.

$$\frac{29}{25} = \frac{29 \times 4}{25 \times 4} = \frac{116}{100} = 1.16$$

▷ So, $1\frac{4}{25} = 1.16$.

b. Write $\frac{5}{33}$ as a decimal.

Because $\frac{5}{33}$ cannot be written as $\frac{a}{b}$, where a is an integer and b is a power of 10, the decimal form of the number does not terminate.

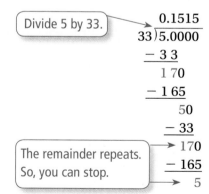

Use long division to divide 5 by 33.

Divide 5 by 33.

```
       0.1515
33)5.0000
  -3 3
    1 70
  - 1 65
       50
     - 33
      170
    - 165
        5
```

The remainder repeats. So, you can stop.

▷ So, $\frac{5}{33} = 0.\overline{15}$.

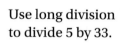

Try It **Write the fraction or mixed number as a decimal.**

1. $\frac{3}{15}$ **2.** $-\frac{2}{9}$ **3.** $4\frac{3}{8}$ **4.** $2\frac{6}{11}$

All terminating decimals and all repeating decimals are rational numbers, so you can write them as fractions.

You have previously written terminating decimals as fractions. To write a repeating decimal d as a fraction, subtract the equation $x = d$ from the equation $10^n x = 10^n d$, where n is the number of repeating digits. Then solve for x.

EXAMPLE 2 **Writing a Repeating Decimal as a Fraction**

Write $1.\overline{25}$ as a mixed number.

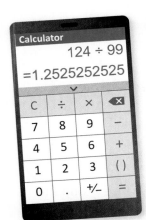

Let $x = 1.\overline{25}$.

$x = 1.\overline{25}$	Write the equation.
$100 \cdot x = 100 \cdot 1.\overline{25}$	There are 2 repeating digits, so multiply each side by $10^2 = 100$.
$100x = 125.\overline{25}$	Simplify.
$-(x = \quad 1.\overline{25})$	Subtract the original equation.
$99x = 124$	Simplify.
$x = \dfrac{124}{99}$	Solve for x.

▷ So, $1.\overline{25} = \dfrac{124}{99} = 1\dfrac{25}{99}$.

Try It Write the decimal as a fraction or a mixed number.

5. $0.888\ldots$ **6.** $2.0\overline{6}$ **7.** $0.\overline{64}$ **8.** $-4.\overline{50}$

Self-Assessment *for Concepts & Skills*

Solve each exercise. Then rate your understanding of the success criteria in your journal.

9. VOCABULARY How can you identify a *rational number*?

WRITING FRACTIONS OR MIXED NUMBERS AS DECIMALS Write the fraction or mixed number as a decimal.

10. $\dfrac{9}{50}$ **11.** $-\dfrac{7}{18}$ **12.** $3\dfrac{4}{9}$ **13.** $-12\dfrac{1}{6}$

WRITING A REPEATING DECIMAL AS A FRACTION Write the repeating decimal as a fraction or a mixed number.

14. $-1.\overline{7}$ **15.** $0.\overline{2}$ **16.** $8.\overline{93}$ **17.** $-6.2\overline{35}$

EXAMPLE 3 **Modeling Real Life**

The weight of an object on the moon is about 0.1$\overline{6}$ times its weight on Earth. An astronaut weighs 192 pounds on Earth. How much does the astronaut weigh on the moon?

Write 0.1$\overline{6}$ as a fraction. Then use the fraction to find the astronaut's weight on the moon.

Let $x = 0.1\overline{6}$.

$x = 0.1\overline{6}$	Write the equation.
$10 \cdot x = 10 \cdot (0.1\overline{6})$	There is 1 repeating digit, so multiply each side by $10^1 = 10$.
$10x = 1.\overline{6}$	Simplify.
$-\,(x = 0.1\overline{6})$	Subtract the original equation.
$9x = 1.5$	Simplify.
$x = \dfrac{1.5}{9}$	Solve for x.

The weight of an object on the moon is about $\dfrac{1.5}{9} = \dfrac{15}{90} = \dfrac{1}{6}$ times its weight on Earth.

▷ So, an astronaut who weighs 192 pounds on Earth weighs about $\dfrac{1}{6} \cdot 192 = 32$ pounds on the moon.

Self-Assessment for Problem Solving

Solve each exercise. Then rate your understanding of the success criteria in your journal.

18. A fun house mirror distorts the image it reflects. Objects reflected in the mirror appear 1.$\overline{3}$ times taller. When a five-foot-tall person looks in the mirror, how tall does he appear?

19. An *exchange rate* represents the value of one currency relative to another. Your friend visits a country that uses a local currency with an exchange rate of 1.2$\overline{65}$ units of the local currency to \$1. If a bank charges \$2 to change currency, how many units of the local currency does your friend receive when she gives the bank \$200?

20. **DIG DEEPER!** A low fuel warning appears when a particular car has 0.014$\overline{6}$ of a tank of gas remaining. The car holds 18.5 gallons of gas and can travel 36 miles for each gallon used. How many miles can the car travel after the low fuel warning appears?

9.4 Practice

? Go to *BigIdeasMath.com* to get
HELP with solving the exercises.

▶ Review & Refresh

Evaluate the expression.

1. $2 + \sqrt[3]{27}$

2. $1 - \sqrt[3]{8}$

3. $7\sqrt[3]{125} - 12$

Find the measures of the interior angles of the triangle.

4.

5.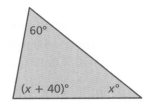

6.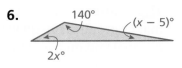

▶▶ Concepts, Skills, & Problem Solving

WRITING REPEATING DECIMALS AS FRACTIONS **Write the repeating decimal as a fraction.** (See Exploration 1, p. 395.)

7. $0.777\ldots$

8. $0.858585\ldots$

9. $0.232323\ldots$

WRITING FRACTIONS OR MIXED NUMBERS AS DECIMALS **Write the fraction or mixed number as a decimal.**

10. $-\dfrac{3}{20}$

11. $9\dfrac{1}{12}$

12. $\dfrac{5}{36}$

13. $6\dfrac{1}{40}$

14. $\dfrac{11}{75}$

15. $-2\dfrac{7}{18}$

16. **MP PRECISION** Your hair is $\dfrac{5}{16}$ inch long. Write this length as a decimal.

WRITING A REPEATING DECIMAL AS A FRACTION **Write the repeating decimal as a fraction or a mixed number.**

17. $-0.\overline{5}$

18. $4.\overline{1}$

19. $-0.3\overline{56}$

20. $6.0\overline{89}$

21. $0.18\overline{72}$

22. $11.5\overline{10}$

23. **MP STRUCTURE** A *forecast cone* defines the probable path of a tropical cyclone. The probability that the center of a particular tropical cyclone remains within the forecast cone is $0.\overline{8}$. Write this probability as a fraction.

24. **⬥ STRUCTURE** Describe how to write a decimal with 12 repeating digits as a fraction.

25. **⬥ STRUCTURE** An approximation for the value of π is $\frac{22}{7}$. Write this number as a repeating decimal.

26. **⬥ MODELING REAL LIFE** The density of iodine is about $6.28\overline{1}$ times the density of acetone. The density of acetone is about 785 kilograms per cubic meter. What is the density of iodine? Write your answer as a repeating decimal.

27. **⬥ MODELING REAL LIFE** A disinfectant manufacturer suggests that its product kills $99.9\overline{8}\%$ of germs. Write this percent as a repeating decimal and then as a fraction. How many germs would survive when the disinfectant is applied to an object with 18,000 germs?

28. **⬥ MODELING REAL LIFE** You and your friend are making pear tarts for a bake sale. Your recipe uses $\frac{7}{6}$ times the weight of the diced pears used in your friend's recipe. Your friend's recipe calls for 0.3 pound of diced pears. How many pounds of pears should you buy to have enough for both recipes?

29. **⬥ PROBLEM SOLVING** The table shows the principal and interest earned per year for each of three savings accounts with simple annual interest. Which account has the greatest interest rate? Justify your answer.

	Principal	Interest Earned
Account A	$90.00	$4.00
Account B	$120.00	$5.50
Account C	$100.00	$4.80

30. **DIG DEEPER!** The probability that an athlete makes a half-court basketball shot is 22 times the probability that the athlete makes a three-quarter-court shot. The probability that the athlete makes a three-quarter-court shot is $0.00\overline{9}$. What is the probability that the athlete makes a half-court shot? Write your answer as a percent.

⬥ NUMBER SENSE Determine whether the numbers are equal. Justify your answer.

31. $\frac{9}{22}$ and $0.4\overline{09}$

32. $\frac{1}{999}$ and 0

33. $\frac{135}{90}$ and 1.5

ADDING AND SUBTRACTING RATIONAL NUMBERS Add or subtract.

34. $0.4\overline{09} + 0.6\overline{81}$

35. $-0.\overline{63} + \frac{5}{99}$

36. $\frac{11}{6} - 0.\overline{27}$

37. $0.\overline{03} - 0.\overline{04}$

38. **⬥ STRUCTURE** Write a repeating decimal that is between $\frac{9}{7}$ and $\frac{10}{7}$. Justify your answer.

9.5 Irrational Numbers

Learning Target: Understand the concept of irrational numbers.

Success Criteria:
- I can classify real numbers as rational or irrational.
- I can approximate irrational numbers.
- I can solve real-life problems involving irrational numbers.

EXPLORATION 1

Approximating Square Roots

Work with a partner. Use the square shown.

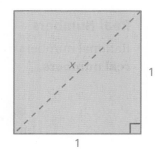

Math Practice

Communicate Precisely

How does the prefix "*ir-*" help you understand the term *irrational number*?

a. Find the exact length x of the diagonal. Is this number a *rational number* or an *irrational number*? Explain.

b. The value of x is between which two whole numbers? Explain your reasoning.

c. Use the diagram below to approximate the length of the diagonal to the nearest tenth. Explain your method.

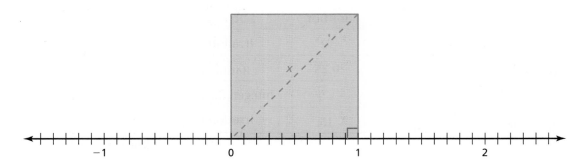

d. Which of the following is the closest approximation of the length of the diagonal? Justify your answer using inverse operations.

1.412	1.413	1.414	1.415

Key Vocabulary
irrational number,
  p. 402
real numbers, p. 402

An **irrational number** is a number that is not rational. So, an irrational number *cannot* be written as $\frac{a}{b}$, where a and b are integers and $b \neq 0$.

- The square root of any whole number that is not a perfect square is irrational. The cube root of any integer that is not a perfect cube is irrational. Another example of an irrational number is π.

- Every number can be written as a decimal. The decimal form of an irrational number neither terminates nor repeats.

Key Idea

Real Numbers

Rational numbers and irrational numbers together form the set of **real numbers**.

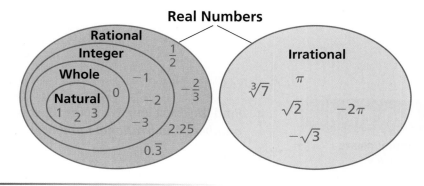

Remember

The decimal form of a rational number either terminates or repeats.

EXAMPLE 1 Classifying Real Numbers

Classify each real number.

When classifying a real number, list all the subsets in which the number belongs.

	Number	Subset(s)	Reasoning
a.	$\sqrt{12}$	Irrational	12 is not a perfect square.
b.	$-0.\overline{25}$	Rational	$-0.\overline{25}$ is a repeating decimal.
c.	$-\sqrt{9}$	Integer, Rational	$-\sqrt{9}$ is equal to -3.
d.	$\sqrt[3]{15}$	Irrational	15 is not a perfect cube.
e.	π	Irrational	The decimal form of π neither terminates nor repeats.

Try It Classify the real number.

1. $0.121221222\ldots$ **2.** $-\sqrt{196}$ **3.** $\sqrt[3]{2}$

EXAMPLE 2 **Approximating an Irrational Number**

Approximate $\sqrt{71}$ to the nearest (a) integer and (b) tenth.

Number	Square of Number
7	49
8	64
9	81
10	100

a. Make a table of numbers whose squares are close to 71.

The table shows that 71 is between the perfect squares 64 and 81. Because 71 is closer to 64 than to 81, $\sqrt{71}$ is closer to 8 than to 9.

So, $\sqrt{71} \approx 8$.

Number	Square of Number
8.3	68.89
8.4	70.56
8.5	72.25
8.6	73.96

b. Make a table of numbers between 8 and 9 whose squares are close to 71. Because 71 is closer to 70.56 than to 72.25, $\sqrt{71}$ is closer to 8.4 than to 8.5.

So, $\sqrt{71} \approx 8.4$.

Try It Approximate the number to the nearest (a) integer and (b) tenth.

4. $\sqrt{8}$ **5.** $-\sqrt{13}$ **6.** $-\sqrt{24}$ **7.** $\sqrt{20}$

EXAMPLE 3 **Comparing Irrational Numbers**

You can use the same procedure to approximate cube roots as you used for square roots.

Which is greater, $\sqrt{35}$ or $\sqrt[3]{80}$?

Approximate $\sqrt{35}$.

Notice that 35 is between $5^2 = 25$ and $6^2 = 36$. Because 35 is closer to 36 than to 25, $\sqrt{35}$ is a little less than 6.

Approximate $\sqrt[3]{80}$.

Notice that 80 is between $4^3 = 64$ and $5^3 = 125$. Because 80 is closer to 64 than to 125, $\sqrt[3]{80}$ is a little greater than 4.

So, $\sqrt{35} > \sqrt[3]{80}$.

Try It Which number is greater? Explain.

8. $\sqrt{8}, \pi$ **9.** $\sqrt[3]{65}, \sqrt{26}$ **10.** $-\sqrt{2}, -\sqrt[3]{10}$

EXAMPLE 4 **Using the Pythagorean Theorem**

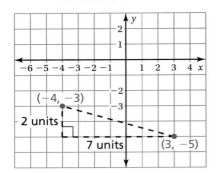

Approximate the distance between $(-4, -3)$ and $(3, -5)$ to the nearest tenth.

Plot the points in a coordinate plane. Then draw a right triangle with a hypotenuse that represents the distance between the points.

Use the Pythagorean Theorem to find the length of the hypotenuse.

$a^2 + b^2 = c^2$	Write the Pythagorean Theorem.
$2^2 + 7^2 = c^2$	Substitute 2 for a and 7 for b.
$4 + 49 = c^2$	Evaluate the powers.
$53 = c^2$	Add.
$\sqrt{53} = c$	Take the positive square root of each side.

 The distance between $(-4, -3)$ and $(3, -5)$ is $\sqrt{53} \approx 7.3$ units.

Try It **Approximate the distance between the points to the nearest tenth.**

11. $(-3, -1)$ and $(-2, -2)$

12. $(1, -1)$ and $(5, 4)$

13. $(5, 4)$ and $(9, 8)$

14. $(-7, 10)$ and $(3, -5)$

Self-Assessment *for Concepts & Skills*

Solve each exercise. Then rate your understanding of the success criteria in your journal.

15. VOCABULARY How are rational numbers and irrational numbers different?

CLASSIFYING REAL NUMBERS **Classify the real number.**

16. $\dfrac{48}{16}$

17. $-\sqrt{76}$

18. $\sqrt[3]{-216}$

APPROXIMATING AN IRRATIONAL NUMBER **Approximate the number to the nearest (a) integer and (b) tenth.**

19. $\sqrt{51}$

20. $-\sqrt{87}$

21. $\sqrt[3]{60}$

22. WHICH ONE DOESN'T BELONG? Which number does *not* belong with the other three? Explain your reasoning.

$$-\dfrac{11}{12} \qquad 25.075 \qquad \sqrt{8} \qquad -3.\overline{3}$$

EXAMPLE 5 **Modeling Real Life**

The equation $d^2 = 1.37h$ represents the relationship between the distance d (in nautical miles) you can see with a periscope and the height h (in feet) of the periscope above the water. About how far can you see when the periscope is 3 feet above the water?

Use the equation to find d when $h = 3$.

$$d^2 = 1.37h \qquad \text{Write the equation.}$$

$$d^2 = 1.37(3) \qquad \text{Substitute 3 for } h.$$

$$d^2 = 4.11 \qquad \text{Multiply.}$$

$$d = \sqrt{4.11} \qquad \text{Take the positive square root of each side.}$$

To approximate d, notice that 4.11 is between the perfect squares 4 and 9. Because 4.11 is close to 4, $\sqrt{4.11}$ is close to 2.

> So, you can see about 2 nautical miles when the periscope is 3 feet above the water.

Check
Use a calculator to approximate $\sqrt{4.11}$.

```
√(4.11)
        2.027313493
```
✓

 Self-Assessment for Problem Solving

Solve each exercise. Then rate your understanding of the success criteria in your journal.

23. The equation $3600b^2 = hw$ represents the relationship among the body surface area b (in square meters), height h (in centimeters), and weight w (in kilograms) of a person. To the nearest tenth, approximate the body surface area of a person who is 168 centimeters tall and weighs 60 kilograms.

24. Which plane is closer to the base of the airport tower? Justify your answer.

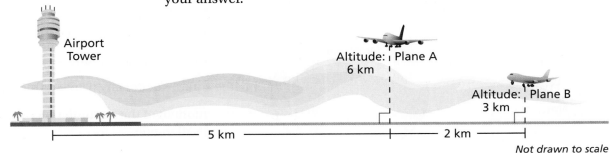

Airport Tower

Altitude: Plane A
6 km

Altitude: Plane B
3 km

5 km   2 km

Not drawn to scale

9.5 Practice

 Go to *BigIdeasMath.com* to get HELP with solving the exercises.

▶ Review & Refresh

Write the repeating decimal as a fraction or a mixed number.

1. $0.\overline{4}$　　　**2.** $1.0\overline{3}$　　　**3.** $0.\overline{75}$　　　**4.** $2.\overline{36}$

Simplify the expression. Write your answer as a power.

5. $(5^4)^2$　　　**6.** $(-9)^4 \cdot (-9)^7$　　　**7.** $a^8 \cdot a$　　　**8.** $(y^3)^6$

▶▶ Concepts, Skills, & Problem Solving

APPROXIMATING SQUARE ROOTS Find the exact length x of the diagonal of the square or rectangle. The value of x is between which two whole numbers? (See Exploration 1, p. 401.)

9.
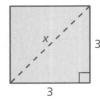

10.
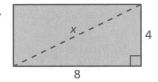

CLASSIFYING REAL NUMBERS Classify the real number.

11. 0　　　**12.** $\sqrt[3]{343}$　　　**13.** $\dfrac{\pi}{6}$　　　**14.** $-\sqrt{81}$

15. -1.125　　　**16.** $\dfrac{52}{13}$　　　**17.** $\sqrt[3]{-49}$　　　**18.** $\sqrt{15}$

19. **(MP) YOU BE THE TEACHER** Your friend classifies $\sqrt{144}$. Is your friend correct? Explain your reasoning.

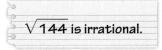 $\sqrt{144}$ is irrational.

20. **(MP) MODELING REAL LIFE** You cut a photograph into a right triangle for a scrapbook. The lengths of the legs of the triangle are 4 inches and 6 inches. Is the length of the hypotenuse a rational number? Explain.

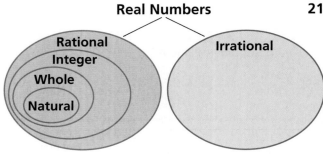

21. **(MP) REASONING** Place each number in the correct area of the Venn diagram.

　a. the last digit of your phone number

　b. the square root of any prime number

　c. the quotient of the circumference of a circle and its diameter

APPROXIMATING AN IRRATIONAL NUMBER Approximate the number to the nearest (a) integer and (b) tenth.

22. $\sqrt{46}$

23. $-\sqrt{105}$

24. $\sqrt[3]{-12}$

25. $\sqrt[3]{310}$

26. $\sqrt{\dfrac{27}{4}}$

27. $-\sqrt{\dfrac{335}{2}}$

COMPARING IRRATIONAL NUMBERS Which number is greater? Explain.

28. $\sqrt{125}, \sqrt{135}$

29. $\sqrt{22}, \sqrt[3]{34}$

30. $-\sqrt[3]{100}, -\sqrt{42}$

31. $\sqrt{5}, \pi$

32. $\sqrt[3]{130}, \sqrt{28}$

33. $-\sqrt{38}, \sqrt[3]{-250}$

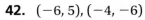

```
√(10)
        3.16227766
√(14)
        3.741657387
```

MP USING TOOLS Use the graphing calculator screen to determine whether the statement is *true* or *false*.

34. To the nearest tenth, $\sqrt{10} = 3.1$.

35. The value of $\sqrt{14}$ is between 3.74 and 3.75.

36. $\sqrt{10}$ lies between 3.1 and 3.16 on a number line.

USING THE PYTHAGOREAN THEOREM Approximate the distance between the points to the nearest tenth.

37. $(1, 2), (7, 6)$

38. $(2, 4), (7, 2)$

39. $(-1, -3), (1, 3)$

40. $(-6, -7), (0, 0)$

41. $(-1, 1), (7, 4)$

42. $(-6, 5), (-4, -6)$

43. **MP MODELING REAL LIFE** The locations of several sites in a forest are shown in the coordinate plane. Approximate each distance to the nearest tenth.

    a. How far is the cabin from the peak?

    b. How far is the fire tower from the lake?

    c. How far is the lake from the peak?

    d. You are standing at $(-5, -6)$. How far are you from the lake?

44. **WRITING** Explain how to continue the method in Example 2 to approximate $\sqrt{71}$ to the nearest hundredth.

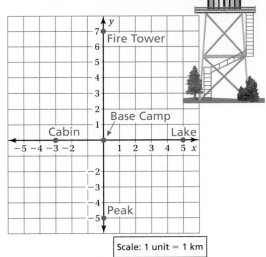

Scale: 1 unit = 1 km

45. **MP MODELING REAL LIFE** The area of a four square court is 66 square feet. Approximate the side length s of the four square court to the nearest whole number.

46. **MP MODELING REAL LIFE** A checkerboard is 8 squares long and 8 squares wide. The area of each square is 14 square centimeters. Approximate the perimeter (in centimeters) of the checkerboard to the nearest tenth.

47. GEOMETRY The cube has a volume of 340 cubic inches. Approximate the length d of the diagonal to the nearest whole number. Justify your answer.

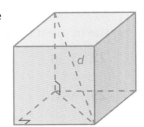

48. CRITICAL THINKING On a number line, π is between 3 and 4.

   a. Use this information to draw a number line and shade a region that represents the location of π^2. Explain your reasoning.

   b. Repeat part (a) using the fact that π is between 3.1 and 3.2.

   c. Repeat part (a) using the fact that π is between 3.14 and 3.15.

MP NUMBER SENSE **Approximate the square root to the nearest tenth.**

49. $\sqrt{0.39}$ **50.** $\sqrt{1.19}$ **51.** $\sqrt{1.52}$

52. MP STRUCTURE Is $\sqrt{\dfrac{1}{4}}$ a rational number? Is $\sqrt{\dfrac{3}{16}}$ a rational number? Explain.

$r = 16.764$ m

53. MP MODELING REAL LIFE The equation $s^2 = 54r$ represents the relationship between the speed s (in meters per second) of a roller-coaster car and the radius r (in meters) of the loop. Approximate the speed of a roller-coaster car going around the loop shown to the nearest tenth.

54. OPEN-ENDED Find two numbers a and b that satisfy the diagram.

               9    $\sqrt{a}$ $\sqrt{b}$ 10

55. **DIG DEEPER!** The equation $d^3 = t^2$ represents the relationship between the mean distance d (in astronomical units) of a planet from the Sun and the time t (in years) it takes the planet to orbit the Sun.

   a. Jupiter takes about 11.9 years to orbit the Sun. Approximate the mean distance of Jupiter from the Sun to the nearest tenth.

   b. The mean distance of Saturn from the Sun is about 9.5 astronomical units. Approximate the time it takes Saturn to orbit the Sun to the nearest tenth.

56. MP MODELING REAL LIFE The equation $h = -16t^2 + 26$ represents the height h (in feet) of a water balloon t seconds after it is dropped. Approximate the time it takes the water balloon to reach the ground to the nearest tenth. Justify your answer.

57. MP NUMBER SENSE Determine whether the statement is *sometimes*, *always*, or *never* true. Explain your reasoning.

   a. A rational number multiplied by a rational number is rational.

   b. A rational number multiplied by an irrational number is rational.

   c. An irrational number multiplied by an irrational number is rational.

9.6 The Converse of the Pythagorean Theorem

Learning Target: Understand the converse of the Pythagorean Theorem.

Success Criteria:
- I can explain the converse of the Pythagorean Theorem.
- I can identify right triangles given three side lengths.
- I can identify right triangles in a coordinate plane.

The *converse* of a statement switches the hypothesis and the conclusion.

Statement:	Converse of the statement:
If p, then q.	If q, then p.

EXPLORATION 1

Analyzing the Converse of a Statement

Work with a partner.

a. Write the converse of each statement. Then determine whether each statement and its converse are *true* or *false*. Explain.

- If I live in California, then I live in the United States.

- If my heart is beating, then I am alive.

- If one figure is a translation of another figure, then the figures are congruent.

b. Write your own statement whose converse is true. Then write your own statement whose converse is false.

> **Math Practice**
>
> **Use Counterexamples**
>
> Is the converse of a false statement always false?

EXPLORATION 2

The Converse of the Pythagorean Theorem

Work with a partner.

a. Write the converse of the Pythagorean Theorem. Do you think the converse is *true* or *false*?

b. Consider $\triangle DEF$ with side lengths a, b, and c such that $a^2 + b^2 = c^2$. Also consider $\triangle JKL$ with leg lengths a and b, where the measure of $\angle K$ is $90°$. Use the two triangles and the Pythagorean Theorem to show that the converse of the Pythagorean Theorem is true.

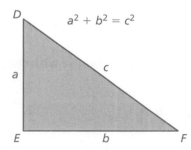
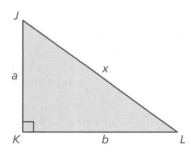

Key Idea

Converse of the Pythagorean Theorem
If the equation $a^2 + b^2 = c^2$ is true for the side lengths of a triangle, then the triangle is a right triangle.

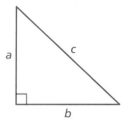

EXAMPLE 1 **Identifying Right Triangles**

Tell whether each triangle is a right triangle.

A *Pythagorean triple* is a set of three positive integers a, b, and c, where $a^2 + b^2 = c^2$.

a.

41 cm
9 cm
40 cm

$$a^2 + b^2 = c^2$$ Write the Pythagorean Theorem.

$$9^2 + 40^2 \stackrel{?}{=} 41^2$$ Substitute 9 for a, 40 for b, and 41 for c.

$$81 + 1600 \stackrel{?}{=} 1681$$ Evaluate the powers.

$$1681 = 1681 \ \checkmark$$ Add.

▷ The triangle *is* a right triangle.

b.

18 ft   12 ft
24 ft

Common Error

When using the converse of the Pythagorean Theorem, always substitute the length of the longest side for c.

$$a^2 + b^2 = c^2$$ Write the Pythagorean Theorem.

$$12^2 + 18^2 \stackrel{?}{=} 24^2$$ Substitute 12 for a, 18 for b, and 24 for c.

$$144 + 324 \stackrel{?}{=} 576$$ Evaluate the powers.

$$468 \neq 576 \ \text{✗}$$ Add.

▷ The triangle is *not* a right triangle.

Try It Tell whether the triangle with the given side lengths is a right triangle.

1. 28 in., 21 in., 20 in.

2. 1.25 mm, 1 mm, 0.75 mm

EXAMPLE 2 **Identifying a Right Triangle**

Tell whether the points $A(1, 1)$, $B(3, 5)$, and $C(3, 0)$ form a right triangle.

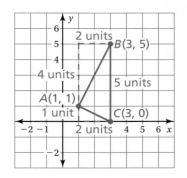

Plot the points in a coordinate plane. The distance between points B and C is 5 units. Use the Pythagorean Theorem to find the distance d_1 between points A and B and the distance d_2 between points A and C.

Distance between Points A and B	*Distance between Points A and C*
$d_1^2 = 4^2 + 2^2$	$d_2^2 = 1^2 + 2^2$
$d_1^2 = 20$	$d_2^2 = 5$
$d_1 = \sqrt{20}$	$d_2 = \sqrt{5}$

Use the converse of the Pythagorean Theorem to determine whether sides with lengths 5, $\sqrt{20}$, and $\sqrt{5}$ form a right triangle.

$$(\sqrt{20})^2 + (\sqrt{5})^2 \stackrel{?}{=} 5^2$$
$$20 + 5 \stackrel{?}{=} 25$$
$$25 = 25 \checkmark$$

▷ So, the points form a right triangle.

Try It **Tell whether the points form a right triangle.**

3. $D(-4, 0)$, $E(-2, 3)$, $F(1, 0)$ **4.** $J(4, 1)$, $K(1, -3)$, $L(-3, 0)$

Self-Assessment for Concepts & Skills

Solve each exercise. Then rate your understanding of the success criteria in your journal.

5. WRITING Explain the converse of the Pythagorean Theorem.

6. IDENTIFYING A RIGHT TRIANGLE Is a triangle with side lengths of 2 millimeters, 2.5 millimeters, and 3 millimeters a right triangle?

7. IDENTIFYING A RIGHT TRIANGLE Do the points $(-1, 1)$, $(-3, 5)$, and $(0, 8)$ form a right triangle?

8. WHICH ONE DOESN'T BELONG? Which set of numbers does *not* belong with the other three? Explain your reasoning.

| 3, 6, 8 | 6, 8, 10 | 5, 12, 13 | 7, 24, 25 |

EXAMPLE 3 **Modeling Real Life**

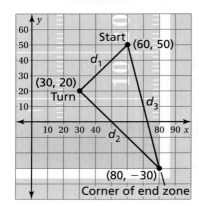

You design a football play in which a player runs down the field, makes a 90° turn, and runs to the corner of the end zone. Your friend ran the play as shown, where each grid line represents 10 feet. Did your friend run the play correctly?

Your friend ended in the corner of the end zone as planned. Determine whether your friend made a 90° turn.

The start, turn, and end locations form a triangle. Use the Pythagorean Theorem to find the side lengths of the triangle.

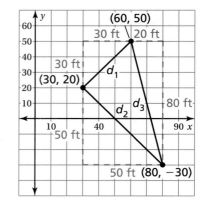

$$d_1 = \sqrt{30^2 + 30^2} = \sqrt{1800} \text{ feet}$$

$$d_2 = \sqrt{50^2 + 50^2} = \sqrt{5000} \text{ feet}$$

$$d_3 = \sqrt{20^2 + 80^2} = \sqrt{6800} \text{ feet}$$

Use the converse of the Pythagorean Theorem to determine whether the sides form a right triangle.

$$\left(\sqrt{1800}\right)^2 + \left(\sqrt{5000}\right)^2 \overset{?}{=} \left(\sqrt{6800}\right)^2$$

$$1800 + 5000 \overset{?}{=} 6800$$

$$6800 = 6800 \checkmark$$

The sides form a right triangle. So, your friend made a 90° turn.

▷ Your friend ran the play correctly.

 Self-Assessment for Problem Solving

Solve each exercise. Then rate your understanding of the success criteria in your journal.

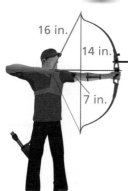

9. You practice archery as shown. Determine whether the arrow is perpendicular to the vertical support. Justify your answer.

10. **DIG DEEPER!** Three fire hydrants in a neighborhood are represented on a map. The coordinates of the fire hydrants are $(0, 0)$, $(2, 5)$, and $(7, y)$. The fire hydrants are arranged in a right triangle, where y is a natural number less than 10. Find y.

Go to *BigIdeasMath.com* to get
HELP with solving the exercises.

▶ Review & Refresh

Approximate the number to the nearest (a) integer and (b) tenth.

1. $\sqrt{31}$ **2.** $-\sqrt{7}$ **3.** $\sqrt[3]{25}$

The figures are similar. Find x.

4. The ratio of the perimeters is $2:5$.

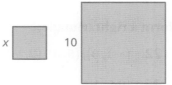

5. The ratio of the perimeters is $4:3$.

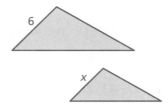

▶▶ Concepts, Skills, & Problem Solving

ANALYZING THE CONVERSE OF A STATEMENT **Write the converse of the statement. Then determine whether the statement and its converse are *true* or *false*. Explain.** (See Exploration 1, p. 409.)

6. If a is an odd number, then a^2 is odd.

7. If $ABCD$ is a square, then $ABCD$ is a parallelogram.

IDENTIFYING A RIGHT TRIANGLE **Tell whether the triangle with the given side lengths is a right triangle.**

8.

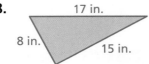

9.

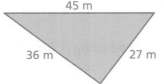

10.

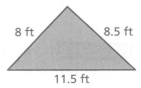

11. 14 mm, 19 mm, 23 mm **12.** $\frac{9}{10}$ mi, $1\frac{1}{5}$ mi, $1\frac{1}{2}$ mi **13.** 1.4 m, 4.8 m, 5 m

14. **MP** **MODELING REAL LIFE** A post-and-beam frame for a shed is shown in the diagram. Does the brace form a right triangle with the post and beam? Explain.

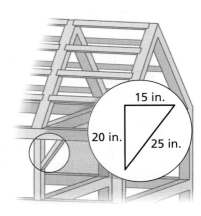

15. **MP** **MODELING REAL LIFE** A traffic sign has side lengths of 12.6 inches, 12.6 inches, and 12.6 inches. Is the sign a right triangle? Explain.

IDENTIFYING A RIGHT TRIANGLE Tell whether a triangle with the given side lengths is a right triangle.

16. $\sqrt{63}, 9, 12$ **17.** $4, \sqrt{15}, 6$ **18.** $\sqrt{18}, \sqrt{24}, \sqrt{42}$

19. **MP** **YOU BE THE TEACHER** Your friend determines whether a triangle with side lengths of $3, \sqrt{58}$, and 7 is a right triangle. Is your friend correct? Explain your reasoning.

$$a^2 + b^2 = c^2$$
$$3^2 + (\sqrt{58})^2 \overset{?}{=} 7^2$$
$$9 + 58 \neq 49$$

The triangle is not a right triangle.

IDENTIFYING A RIGHT TRIANGLE Tell whether the points form a right triangle.

20. $(0, 0), (0, 5), (2, 0)$ **21.** $(0, 8), (2, 2), (11, 6)$ **22.** $(-1, 0), (5, 0), (2, -3)$

23. $(-1, -2), (2, 6), (4, -1)$ **24.** $(-8, 6), (7, 9), (0, -13)$ **25.** $(0.5, 1.5), (7.5, 5.5), (9.5, 0.5)$

26. **MP** **LOGIC** The equation $a^2 + b^2 = c^2$ is *not* true for a particular triangle with side lengths of a, b, and c. What can you conclude about the type of triangle?

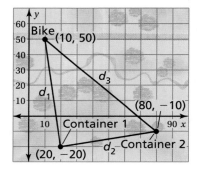

27. **MP** **MODELING REAL LIFE** You spend the day looking for hidden containers in a wooded area using a Global Positioning System (GPS). You park your bike on the side of the road, and then locate Container 1 and Container 2 before going back to your bike. Does your path form a right triangle? Explain. Each grid line represents 10 yards.

28. **DIG DEEPER!** The locations of a fishing boat, buoy, and kayak are represented by the points $(0, 0), (16, 12)$, and $(10, -5)$. Each unit represents 1 nautical mile.

   a. Do the boat, kayak, and buoy form a right triangle?

   b. The boat travels at 8 nautical miles per hour. How long does the boat take to reach the buoy if the boat travels directly toward it?

29. **MP** **STRUCTURE** The vertices of a quadrilateral are $(1, 2), (5, 4), (6, 2)$, and $(2, 0)$. Use the converse of the Pythagorean Theorem to determine whether the quadrilateral is a rectangle.

Connecting Concepts

▶ Using the Problem-Solving Plan

1. The scale drawing of a baseball field has a scale factor of $\frac{1}{270}$. Approximate the distance from home plate to second base on the actual baseball field to the nearest tenth.

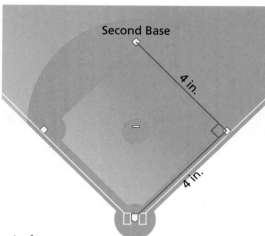

Second Base

4 in.

4 in.

Home Plate

Understand the problem.

You know several measurements and the scale factor in a scale drawing of a baseball field. You are asked to approximate the distance from home plate to second base on the actual baseball field.

Make a plan.

The distance from home plate to second base is the hypotenuse of a right triangle. Approximate the distance in the scale drawing to the nearest tenth. Then use the scale factor to approximate the distance on the actual field.

Solve and check.

Use the plan to solve the problem. Then check your solution.

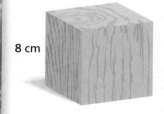

8 cm

2. You cut the wood cube shown into two identical triangular prisms. Approximate the surface area of each triangular prism to the nearest tenth. Justify your answer.

3. Complete the mapping diagram representing the relationship between the lengths of the hypotenuse and the legs of an isosceles right triangle. Is the relationship linear? Explain.

Hypotenuse   **Legs**

$\sqrt{2}$

$\sqrt{32}$

$\sqrt{98}$

$\sqrt{200}$

Performance Task

Identify and Correct the Error!

At the beginning of this chapter, you watched a STEAM Video called "Metronome Design." You are now ready to complete the performance task related to this video, available at *BigIdeasMath.com*. Be sure to use the problem-solving plan as you work through the performance task.

▶ Review Vocabulary

Write the definition and give an example of each vocabulary term.

square root, *p. 374*

perfect square, *p. 374*

radical sign, *p. 374*

radicand, *p. 374*

theorem, *p. 381*

legs, *p. 382*

hypotenuse, *p. 382*

Pythagorean Theorem, *p. 382*

cube root, *p. 390*

perfect cube, *p. 390*

irrational number, *p. 402*

real numbers, *p. 402*

▶ Graphic Organizers

You can use a **Four Square** to organize information about a concept. Each of the four squares can be a category, such as definition, vocabulary, example, non-example, words, algebra, table, numbers, visual, graph, or equation. Here is an example of a Four Square for *Pythagorean Theorem*.

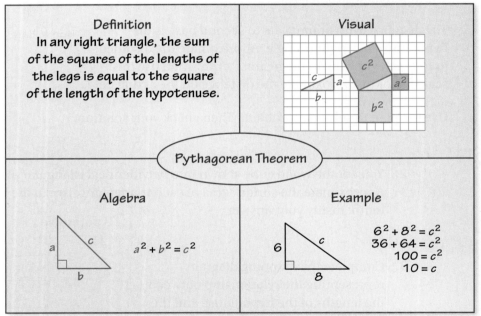

Choose and complete a graphic organizer to help you study the concept.

1. square roots

2. cube roots

3. rational numbers

4. irrational numbers

5. real numbers

6. converse of the Pythagorean Theorem

"I'm taking a survey for my Four Square. How many fleas do you have?"

▶ Chapter Self-Assessment

As you complete the exercises, use the scale below to rate your understanding of the success criteria in your journal.

1	**2**	**3**	**4**
I do not understand.	I can do it with help.	I can do it on my own.	I can teach someone else.

9.1 Finding Square Roots (pp. 373–380)

Learning Target: Understand the concept of a square root of a number.

Find the square root(s).

1. $\sqrt{1}$

2. $-\sqrt{\dfrac{9}{25}}$

3. $\pm\sqrt{1.69}$

Evaluate the expression.

4. $15 - 4\sqrt{36}$

5. $\sqrt{\dfrac{54}{6}} + \dfrac{2}{3}$

6. $(\sqrt{9})^2 - 12$

7. The total area of a checkerboard is 256 square inches. What is the side length (in inches) of one of the small squares?

9.2 The Pythagorean Theorem (pp. 381–388)

Learning Target: Understand the Pythagorean Theorem.

Find the missing length of the triangle.

8.

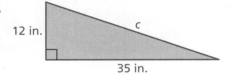

9.

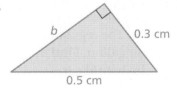

10. You lean a 13-foot ladder on a house so the bottom of the ladder is 5 feet from the house. From the top of the ladder, you can safely reach another 4 feet higher. Can you reach a window that is located 13 feet above the ground? Explain.

11. Find the distance between $(-6, 8)$ and $(10, -4)$.

9.3 Finding Cube Roots (pp. 389–394)

Learning Target: Understand the concept of a cube root of a number.

Find the cube root.

12. $\sqrt[3]{-2197}$

13. $\sqrt[3]{\dfrac{64}{343}}$

14. $\sqrt[3]{-\dfrac{8}{27}}$

15. Evaluate the expression $25 + 2\sqrt[3]{-64}$.

16. Solve the equation $-55 = \dfrac{1}{4}x^3 + 73$.

17. You are shipping a puzzle cube to your friend using the cube-shaped box shown. What is the difference between the height of the puzzle cube and the top of the box when you place the cube in the box?

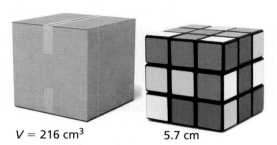

$V = 216$ cm³   5.7 cm

9.4 Rational Numbers (pp. 395–400)

Learning Target: Convert between different forms of rational numbers.

Write the fraction or mixed number as a decimal.

18. $-2\dfrac{5}{6}$

19. $\dfrac{27}{80}$

20. $3\dfrac{8}{9}$

21. Write $1.\overline{36}$ as a mixed number.

22. The gas mileage of a hybrid car is $3.0\overline{3}$ times the gas mileage of a regular car. The regular car averages 24 miles per gallon. Find the gas mileage of the hybrid car.

23. Your friend's cat weighs $0.8\overline{3}$ times the weight of your cat. Your friend's cat weighs 10 pounds. How much more does your cat weigh than your friend's cat?

24. An apple dessert recipe makes $2.\overline{3}$ pounds of dessert and serves 6 people. What is the serving size (in pounds)?

9.5 Irrational Numbers *(pp. 401–408)*

Learning Target: Understand the concept of irrational numbers.

Classify the real number.

25. $0.81\overline{5}$ **26.** $\sqrt{101}$ **27.** $\sqrt{4}$

Approximate the number to the nearest (a) integer and (b) tenth.

28. $\sqrt{14}$ **29.** $\sqrt{90}$ **30.** $\sqrt{175}$

31. Which is greater, $\sqrt{48}$ or $\sqrt[3]{127}$? Explain.

32. Approximate the distance between $(-2, -5)$ and $(3, 5)$ to the nearest tenth.

33. The equation $d = \dfrac{v^2}{15.68}$ represents the relationship between the distance d (in meters) needed to stop a vehicle and the velocity v (in meters per second) of the vehicle. Approximate the velocity of the vehicle when it takes 40 meters to stop.

9.6 The Converse of the Pythagorean Theorem *(pp. 409–414)*

Learning Target: Understand the converse of the Pythagorean Theorem.

Tell whether the triangle with the given side lengths is a right triangle.

34.

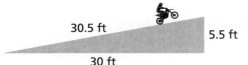

35.

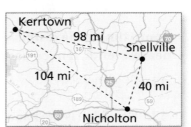

36. Tell whether the points $A(1, -1)$, $B(3, -4)$, and $C(4, 1)$ form a right triangle.

37. You want to make a wooden border around a flower bed in the shape of a right triangle. You have three pieces of wood that measure 3.5 meters, 1.2 meters, and 3.9 meters. Do these pieces of wood form a right triangle? If not, explain how you can cut the longest piece of wood to make a right triangle.

1. Find $-\sqrt{1600}$.

2. Find $\sqrt[3]{-\dfrac{729}{64}}$.

Evaluate the expression.

3. $12 + 8\sqrt{16}$

4. $\left(\sqrt[3]{-125}\right)^3 + 75$

5. Find the missing length of the triangle.

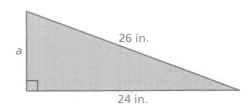

26 in.

a

24 in.

Classify the real number.

6. 16π

7. $-\sqrt{49}$

8. Approximate $\sqrt{83}$ to the nearest (a) integer and (b) tenth.

9. Write $1.\overline{24}$ as a mixed number.

10. Tell whether the triangle is a right triangle.

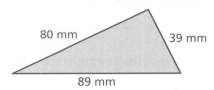

80 mm

39 mm

89 mm

Approximate the distance between the points to the nearest tenth, if necessary.

11. $(-2, 3), (6, 9)$

12. $(0, -5), (4, 1)$

13. How high is the hand of the superhero balloon above the ground?

61 ft

x

11 ft

6 ft

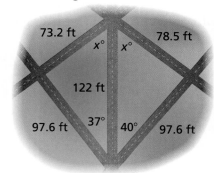

73.2 ft

$x°$ $x°$

78.5 ft

122 ft

97.6 ft

37° 40°

97.6 ft

14. The area of a circular pool cover is 314 square feet. Write and solve an equation to find the diameter of the pool cover. Use 3.14 for π.

15. Five roads form two triangles. What is the value of x? Justify your answer.

1. The period T of a pendulum is the time (in seconds) it takes the pendulum to swing back and forth once. The period can be found using the formula $T = 1.1\sqrt{L}$, where L is the length (in feet) of the pendulum. A pendulum has a length of 4 feet. What is the period of the pendulum?

   A. 2.2 sec

   B. 3.1 sec

   C. 4.4 sec

   D. 5.1 sec

Test-Taking Strategy

Answer Easy Questions First

There are $\sqrt{4}$ different tongue prints on the butter. How many cats licked the butter?

Ⓐ 1   Ⓑ 2   Ⓒ -2   Ⓓ 4

Was Fluffy in our kitchen?

"Scan the test and answer the easy questions first. You know the square root of 4 is 2."

2. What is the value of $y = 5 - 2x$ when $x = -3$?

   F. -1

   G. 1

   H. 4

   I. 11

3. Which graph represents the linear equation $3x + 2y = 12$?

   A.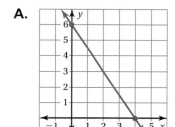

   B.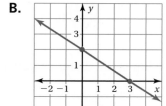

   C.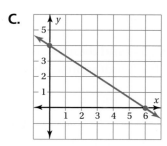

   D.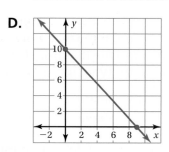

4. Which expression is equivalent to $\dfrac{(-3)^{12}}{(-3)^3}$?

   F. $(-3)^4$

   G. $(-3)^9$

   H. 0^9

   I. 1^9

5. A football field is 40 yards wide and 120 yards long. Approximate the distance between opposite corners of the football field to the nearest tenth. Show your work and explain your reasoning.

Think
Solve
Explain

6. A computer consultant charges $50 plus $40 for each hour she works. The consultant charged $650 for one job. This can be represented by the equation below, where h represents the number of hours worked.

$$40h + 50 = 650$$

How many hours did the consultant work?

7. Which triangle is *not* a right triangle?

A.
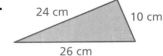
24 cm
10 cm
26 cm

B.
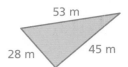
53 m
28 m
45 m

C.
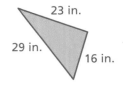
23 in.
29 in.
16 in.

D.
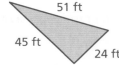
51 ft
45 ft
24 ft

8. What is the distance between $(-3, -1)$ and $(-1, -5)$?

   F. $\sqrt{12}$ **G.** $\sqrt{20}$

   H. $\sqrt{40}$ **I.** $\sqrt{52}$

9. An airplane flies from City 1 at $(0, 0)$ to City 2 at $(33, 56)$ and then to City 3 at $(23, 32)$. What is the total number of miles it flies? Each unit represents 1 mile.

10. The national debt of Country A is $398,038,013,519. The national debt of Country B is $2,137,348,918. Approximately how many times greater is the debt of Country A than the debt of Country B?

   A. 2 times greater   **B.** 20 times greater

   C. 133 times greater   **D.** 200 times greater

11. What is the solution of the system?

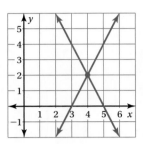

F. $(2, 4)$

G. $(3, 0)$

H. $(4, 2)$

I. $(5, 0)$

12. In the diagram, lines ℓ and m are parallel. Which angle has the same measure as $\angle 1$?

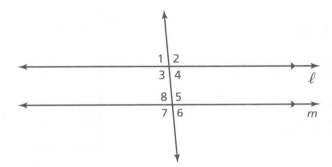

A. $\angle 2$ **B.** $\angle 5$

C. $\angle 7$ **D.** $\angle 8$

13. Which graph represents the linear equation $y = -2x - 2$?

F.
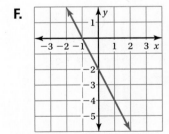

G.
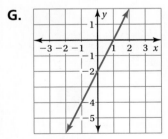

H.
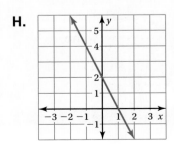

I.
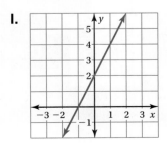

10 Volume and Similar Solids

10.1 **Volumes of Cylinders**

10.2 **Volumes of Cones**

10.3 **Volumes of Spheres**

10.4 **Surface Areas and Volumes of Similar Solids**

Chapter Learning Target:
Understand volume.

Chapter Success Criteria:
- I can explain how to find the volumes of cylinders, cones, and spheres.
- I can use formulas to find volumes of solids.
- I can find missing dimensions of solids.
- I can find surface areas and volumes of similar solids.

STEAM Video: "Canning Salsa"

Canning Salsa

You can estimate the volumes of ingredients to predict the total volume of a finished recipe. In what other real-life situations is it helpful to know the volumes of objects?

Watch the STEAM Video "Canning Salsa." Then answer the following questions.

1. You can approximate the volumes of foods by comparing them to common solids. A cube of cheese has side lengths of 3 centimeters. What is the volume of the cheese?

2. The table shows the amounts x (in cubic inches) of tomato used to make y cubic inches of salsa.

Tomato, x	1	2	3	4
Salsa, y	3	6	9	12

    a. Is there a proportional relationship between x and y? Justify your answer.

    b. How much tomato do you need to make 15 cubic inches of salsa?

Packaging Salsa

After completing this chapter, you will be able to use the concepts you learned to answer the questions in the *STEAM Video Performance Task*. You will be given the dimensions of a jar and a shipping box.

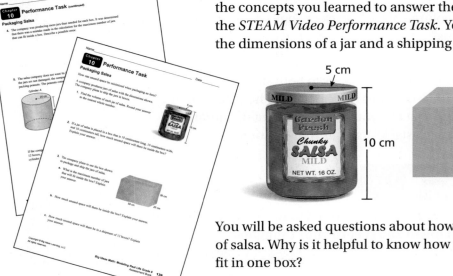

You will be asked questions about how to package jars of salsa. Why is it helpful to know how many jars of salsa fit in one box?

Getting Ready for Chapter

Chapter Exploration

1. Work with a partner.

a. How does the volume of the stack of dimes compare to the volume of a single dime?

b. How does the volume of the stack of nickels compare to the volume of the stack of dimes? Explain your reasoning. (The height of each stack is identical.)

c. How does the volume of each stack change when you double the number of coins?

d. **MP LOGIC** Your friend adds coins to both stacks so that the volume of the stack of dimes is greater than the volume of the stack of nickels. What can you conclude about the number of coins added to each stack? Explain your reasoning.

Vocabulary

The following vocabulary terms are defined in this chapter. Think about what each term might mean and record your thoughts.

cone   hemisphere
sphere   similar solids

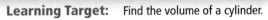

10.1 Volumes of Cylinders

Learning Target: Find the volume of a cylinder.

Success Criteria:
- I can use a formula to find the volume of a cylinder.
- I can use the formula for the volume of a cylinder to find a missing dimension.

Exploring Volume

Work with a partner.

a. Each prism shown has a height of h units and bases with areas of B square units. Write a formula that you can use to find the volume of each prism.

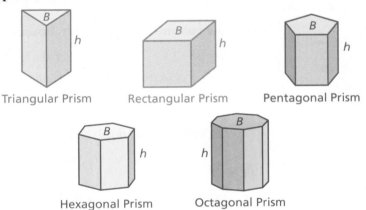

Triangular Prism   Rectangular Prism   Pentagonal Prism

Hexagonal Prism   Octagonal Prism

Math Practice

Find Entry Points
What does a regular polygon with an area of B square units start to look like as you increase the number of sides?

b. How can you find the volume of a prism with bases that each have 100 sides?

c. Make a conjecture about how to find the volume of a cylinder. Explain your reasoning.

Finding Volume Experimentally

Work with a partner. Draw a net for a cylinder. Then cut out the net and use tape to form an open cylinder. Repeat this process to form an open cube. The edge length of the cube should be greater than the diameter and the height of the cylinder.

a. Use your conjecture in Exploration 1 to find the volume of the cylinder.

b. Fill the cylinder with rice. Then pour the rice into the open cube. Find the volume of rice in the cube. Does this support your answer in part (a)? Explain your reasoning.

Remember

The slanted figure is called an *oblique solid*. Volumes of oblique solids are calculated in the same way as volumes of right solids.

Key Idea

Volume of a Cylinder

Words The volume V of a cylinder is the product of the area of the base and the height of the cylinder.

Algebra $V = Bh$

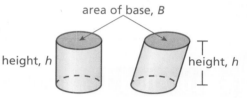

area of base, B

height, h height, h

EXAMPLE 1 Finding the Volume of a Cylinder

Because $B = \pi r^2$, you can use $V = \pi r^2 h$ to find the volume of a cylinder.

Find the volume of the cylinder. Round your answer to the nearest tenth.

$$V = Bh \qquad \text{Write the formula for volume.}$$
$$= \pi(3)^2(6) \qquad \text{Substitute.}$$
$$= 54\pi \approx 169.6 \qquad \text{Use a calculator.}$$

▷ The volume is about 169.6 cubic meters.

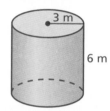

3 m

6 m

Try It

1. Find the volume of a cylinder with a radius of 4 feet and a height of 15 feet. Round your answer to the nearest tenth.

EXAMPLE 2 Finding the Height of a Cylinder

Find the height of the cylinder. Round your answer to the nearest whole number.

The diameter is 10 inches. So, the radius is 5 inches.

$$V = Bh \qquad \text{Write the formula for volume.}$$
$$314 = \pi(5)^2(h) \qquad \text{Substitute.}$$
$$314 = 25\pi h \qquad \text{Simplify.}$$
$$4 \approx h \qquad \text{Divide each side by } 25\pi.$$

▷ The height is about 4 inches.

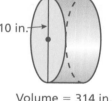

h

10 in.

Volume = 314 in.^{3}

Try It

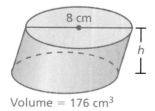

8 cm

h

Volume = 176 cm^3

2. Find the height of the cylinder at the left. Round your answer to the nearest tenth.

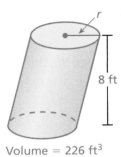

EXAMPLE 3 **Finding the Radius of a Cylinder**

Find the radius of the cylinder. Round your answer to the nearest whole number.

$$V = Bh$$ Write the formula for volume.

$$226 = \pi r^2(8)$$ Substitute.

$$\frac{226}{8\pi} = r^2$$ Divide each side by 8π.

$$\sqrt{\frac{226}{8\pi}} = r$$ Take the positive square root of each side.

$$3 \approx r$$ Use a calculator.

8 ft

Volume = 226 ft³

▷ The radius is about 3 feet.

Try It **Find the radius of the cylinder. Round your answer to the nearest tenth.**

3.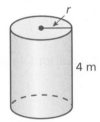

4 m

Volume = 28 m³

4.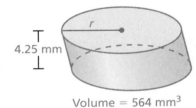

4.25 mm

Volume = 564 mm³

 Self-Assessment *for Concepts & Skills*

Solve each exercise. Then rate your understanding of the success criteria in your journal.

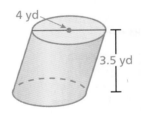

4 yd

3.5 yd

5. **FINDING THE VOLUME OF A CYLINDER** Find the volume of the cylinder at the left. Round your answer to the nearest tenth.

6. **FINDING THE HEIGHT OF A CYLINDER** Find the height of the cylinder at the right. Round your answer to the nearest tenth.

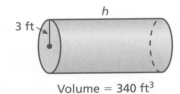

h

3 ft

Volume = 340 ft³

7. **DIFFERENT WORDS, SAME QUESTION** Which is different? Find "both" answers.

How much does it take to fill the cylinder?

What is the capacity of the cylinder?

How much does it take to cover the cylinder?

How much does the cylinder contain?

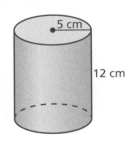

5 cm

12 cm

EXAMPLE 4 **Modeling Real Life**

2.3 ft

1.8 ft

You use the cylindrical barrel shown to collect and study rainwater. About how many gallons of water can the barrel hold? (1 ft³ ≈ 7.5 gal)

Find the volume of the cylinder. The diameter is 1.8 feet. So, the radius is 0.9 foot.

$V = Bh$	Write the formula for volume.
$= \pi(0.9)^2(2.3)$	Substitute.
$= 1.863\pi$	Simplify.

So, the barrel can hold 1.863π cubic feet of water. To find the number of gallons it can hold, multiply the volume by the conversion factor $\dfrac{7.5 \text{ gal}}{1 \text{ ft}^3}$.

$$1.863\pi \text{ ft}^3 \times \frac{7.5 \text{ gal}}{1 \text{ ft}^3} \approx 44 \text{ gal}$$

▷ So, the barrel can hold about 44 gallons of water.

Self-Assessment for Problem Solving

Solve each exercise. Then rate your understanding of the success criteria in your journal.

8. How much salsa is missing from the jar? Explain your reasoning.

5 cm

10 cm

4 cm

9. A cylindrical swimming pool has a circumference of 18π feet and a height of 4 feet. About how many liters of water are needed to fill the swimming pool to 85% of its total volume? Justify your answer. $(1 \text{ ft}^3 \approx 28.3 \text{ L})$

10. **DIG DEEPER!** A company creates two designs for a cylindrical soup can. Can A has a diameter of 3.5 inches and a height of 3.6 inches. Can B has a height of 4.9 inches. Each can holds the same amount of soup. Which can requires less material to make? Explain your reasoning.

10.1 Practice

Go to *BigIdeasMath.com* to get
HELP with solving the exercises.

▶ Review & Refresh

Tell whether the triangle with the given side lengths is a right triangle.

1. 20 m, 21 m, 29 m

2. 1 in., 2.4 in., 2.6 in.

3. 5.6 ft, 8 ft, 10.6 ft

Write the number in standard form.

4. 3.9×10^6

5. 6.7×10^{-5}

6. 6.24×10^{10}

7. Which ordered pair is the solution of the linear system $3x + 4y = -10$ and $2x - 4y = 0$?

   A. $(-6, 2)$ **B.** $(2, -6)$ **C.** $(-2, -1)$ **D.** $(-1, -2)$

▶▶ Concepts, Skills, & Problem Solving

FINDING VOLUME The height h and the base area B of a cylinder are given. Find the volume of the cylinder. Write your answer in terms of π. (See Explorations 1 and 2, p. 427.)

8. $h = 5$ units
   $B = 4\pi$ square units

9. $h = 2$ units
   $B = 25\pi$ square units

10. $h = 4.5$ units
    $B = 16\pi$ square units

FINDING THE VOLUME OF A CYLINDER Find the volume of the cylinder. Round your answer to the nearest tenth.

11.
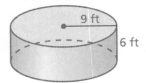
9 ft
6 ft

12.
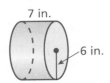
7 in.
6 in.

13.
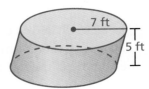
7 ft
5 ft

14.
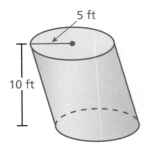
5 ft
10 ft

15.
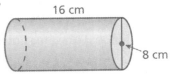
16 cm
8 cm

16.
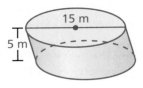
15 m
5 m

17. **MP REASONING** Without calculating, which of the solids has the greater volume? Explain.

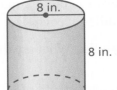
8 in.
8 in.

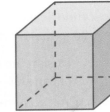
8 in.
8 in.
8 in.

FINDING A MISSING DIMENSION Find the missing dimension of the cylinder. Round your answer to the nearest whole number.

18. Volume $= 10,000\pi$ in.^{3}

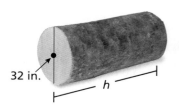

32 in.

h

19. Volume $= 3785$ cm^3

r

19 cm

20. Volume $= 600,000$ cm^3

r

76 cm

21. **MP MODELING REAL LIFE** A cylindrical hazardous waste container has a diameter of 1.5 feet and a height of 1.6 feet. About how many gallons of hazardous waste can the container hold? (1 ft^3 ≈ 7.5 gal)

22. **CRITICAL THINKING** How does the volume of a cylinder change when its diameter is halved? Explain.

5 ft

4 ft

Round Hay Bale

23. **MP PROBLEM SOLVING** A traditional "square" bale of hay is actually in the shape of a rectangular prism. Its dimensions are 2 feet by 2 feet by 4 feet. How many square bales contain the same amount of hay as one large "round" bale?

24. **MP MODELING REAL LIFE** A tank on a road roller is filled with water to make the roller heavy. The tank is a cylinder that has a height of 6 feet and a radius of 2 feet. About how many pounds of water can the tank hold? (One cubic foot of water weighs about 62.5 pounds.)

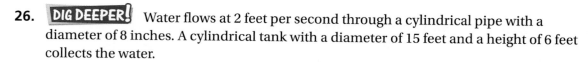

25. **MP REASONING** A cylinder has a surface area of 1850 square meters and a radius of 9 meters. Estimate the volume of the cylinder to the nearest whole number.

26. **DIG DEEPER!** Water flows at 2 feet per second through a cylindrical pipe with a diameter of 8 inches. A cylindrical tank with a diameter of 15 feet and a height of 6 feet collects the water.

  a. What is the volume (in cubic inches) of water flowing out of the pipe every second?

  b. What is the height (in inches) of the water in the tank after 5 minutes?

  c. How many minutes will it take to fill 75% of the tank?

27. **PROJECT** You want to make and sell three different sizes of cylindrical candles. You buy 1 cubic foot of candle wax for $20 to make 8 candles of each size.

  a. Design the candles. What are the dimensions of each size of candle?

  b. You want to make a profit of $100. Decide on a price for each size of candle. Explain how you set your prices.

10.2 Volumes of Cones

Learning Target: Find the volume of a cone.

Success Criteria:
- I can use a formula to find the volume of a cone.
- I can use the formula for the volume of a cone to find a missing dimension.

You already learned how the volume of a pyramid relates to the volume of a prism. In this exploration, you will discover how the volume of a *cone* relates to the volume of a cylinder.

A **cone** is a solid that has one circular base and one vertex.

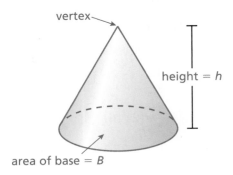

vertex

height = h

area of base = B

EXPLORATION 1

Finding a Formula Experimentally

Work with a partner. Use a paper cup that is shaped like a cone. Measure the height of the cup and the diameter of the circular base. Use these measurements to draw a net for a cylinder with the same base and height as the paper cup. Then cut out the net and use tape to form an open cylinder.

a. Find the volume of the cylinder.

Math Practice

Analyze Relationships
How does the volume of a cone relate to the volume of a cylinder?

b. Fill the paper cup with rice. Then pour the rice into the cylinder. Repeat this until the cylinder is full. How many cones does it take to fill the cylinder?

c. Use your result to write a formula for the volume of a cone.

d. Use your formula in part (c) to find the volume of the cone. How can you tell whether your answer is correct?

e. Do you think your formula for the volume of a cone is also true for *oblique* cones? Explain your reasoning.

Key Vocabulary 🔊
cone, *p. 433*

🔑 **Key Idea**

Volume of a Cone

Words The volume V of a cone is one-third the product of the area of the base and the height of the cone.

Algebra $V = \dfrac{1}{3}Bh$

Right Cone **Oblique Cone**
height, h
area of base, B

EXAMPLE 1 **Finding the Volume of a Cone**

Find the volume of the cone. Round your answer to the nearest tenth.

The diameter is 4 meters. So, the radius is 2 meters.

$V = \dfrac{1}{3}Bh$ Write the formula for volume.

$= \dfrac{1}{3}\pi(2)^2(6)$ Substitute.

$= 8\pi \approx 25.1$ Use a calculator.

▷ The volume is about 25.1 cubic meters.

> Because $B = \pi r^2$, you can use $V = \dfrac{1}{3}\pi r^2 h$ to find the volume of a cone.

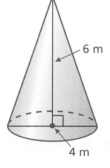

6 m

4 m

Try It

1. Find the volume of a cone with a radius of 6 centimeters and a height of 15 centimeters. Round your answer to the nearest tenth.

EXAMPLE 2 **Finding the Height of a Cone**

Find the height of the cone. Round your answer to the nearest tenth.

$V = \dfrac{1}{3}Bh$ Write the formula for volume.

$956 = \dfrac{1}{3}\pi(9)^2(h)$ Substitute.

$956 = 27\pi h$ Simplify.

$11.3 \approx h$ Divide each side by 27π.

▷ The height is about 11.3 feet.

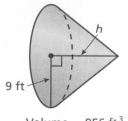

h

9 ft

Volume = 956 ft³

Try It

2. Find the height of the cone at the left. Round your answer to the nearest tenth.

Volume = 7200 yd³

h

15 yd

EXAMPLE 3 **Finding the Radius of a Cone**

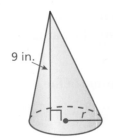

9 in.

Volume = 80 in.³

Find the radius of the cone. Round your answer to the nearest tenth.

$V = \dfrac{1}{3}Bh$	Write the formula for volume.
$80 = \dfrac{1}{3}\pi r^2(9)$	Substitute.
$80 = 3\pi r^2$	Simplify.
$\dfrac{80}{3\pi} = r^2$	Divide each side by 3π.
$\sqrt{\dfrac{80}{3\pi}} = r$	Take the positive square root of each side.
$2.9 \approx r$	Use a calculator.

▷ The radius is about 2.9 inches.

Try It **Find the radius of the cone. Round your answer to the nearest whole number.**

3.

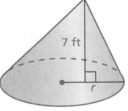

7 ft

r

Volume = 183 ft³

4.

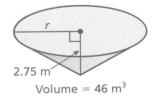

r

2.75 m

Volume = 46 m³

Self-Assessment for Concepts & Skills

Solve each exercise. Then rate your understanding of the success criteria in your journal.

5. **FINDING THE VOLUME OF A CONE** Find the volume of a cone with a diameter of 10 yards and a height of 12 yards. Round your answer to the nearest tenth.

FINDING A MISSING DIMENSION OF A CONE **Find the missing dimension of the cone. Round your answer to the nearest tenth.**

6.

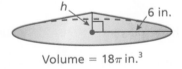

h

6 in.

Volume = 18π in.³

7.

5 cm

r cm

Volume = 16.5 cm³

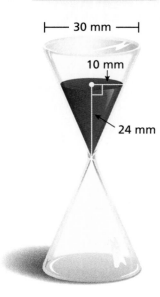

├── 30 mm ──┤

10 mm

24 mm

EXAMPLE 4 **Modeling Real Life**

You must answer a trivia question before the sand in the timer falls to the bottom. Each second, 50 cubic millimeters of sand fall. How much time do you have to answer the question?

Use the formula for the volume of a cone to find the volume of the sand in the timer.

$$V = \frac{1}{3}Bh \qquad \text{Write the formula for volume.}$$

$$= \frac{1}{3}\pi(10)^2(24) \qquad \text{Substitute.}$$

$$= 800\pi \qquad \text{Simplify.}$$

The volume of the sand is 800π cubic millimeters. Use the rate at which the sand falls to determine how much time you have to answer the question.

$$800\pi \ \text{mm}^3 \times \frac{1 \ \text{sec}}{50 \ \text{mm}^3} \approx 50.27 \ \text{sec}$$

▷ So, you have about 50 seconds to answer the question.

Self-Assessment for Problem Solving

Solve each exercise. Then rate your understanding of the success criteria in your journal.

8. A *stalactite* is a mineral formation that hangs from the ceiling of a cave. A cone-shaped stalactite has a height of 48 centimeters and a base circumference of 3.5π centimeters. What is the volume of the stalactite?

9. A store sells two cone-shaped funnels. What is the height of each funnel? ($1 \ \text{pt} = 28.875 \ \text{in.}^3$)

4.5 in.

Volume: 0.5 pint

6 in.

Volume: 1 pint

10. You fill cone-shaped pastry bags with icing to a height of 1 foot and a diameter of 3.5 inches. You use about 1.35 cubic inches of icing per cupcake. About how many cupcakes can you decorate with 2 bags of icing?

10.2 Practice

Go to *BigIdeasMath.com* to get HELP with solving the exercises.

▶ Review & Refresh

Find the volume of the cylinder. Round your answer to the nearest tenth.

1.

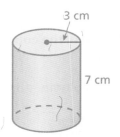

3 cm

7 cm

2.

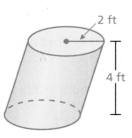

2 ft

4 ft

3.

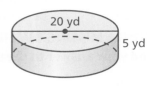

20 yd

5 yd

Solve the equation.

4. $x^3 = 27$

5. $-6 = y^3 + 2$

6. $2h^3 - 33 = 95$

▶▶ Concepts, Skills, & Problem Solving

FINDING A VOLUME The height h and the base area B of a cone are given. Find the volume of the cone. Write your answer in terms of π. (See Exploration 1, p. 433.)

7. $h = 6$ units
$B = 4\pi$ square units

8. $h = 9$ units
$B = 5\pi$ square units

FINDING THE VOLUME OF A CONE Find the volume of the cone. Round your answer to the nearest tenth.

9.

4 in.

2 in.

10.

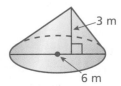

3 m

6 m

11.

10 mm

5 mm

12.

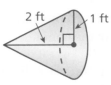

2 ft   1 ft

13.

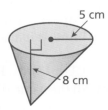

5 cm

8 cm

14.

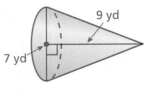

9 yd

7 yd

15.

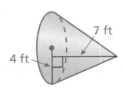

7 ft

4 ft

16.

10 in.

5 in.

17.

4 cm

8 cm

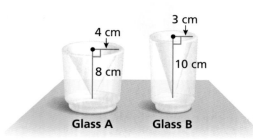

3 cm
4 cm
8 cm
10 cm

Glass A   Glass B

18. **MP STRUCTURE** The inside of each glass is shaped like a cone. Which glass can hold more liquid? How much more?

FINDING A MISSING DIMENSION OF A CONE Find the missing dimension of the cone. Round your answer to the nearest tenth.

19. Volume $= \frac{1}{18}\pi$ ft^3

h

$\frac{1}{3}$ ft

20. Volume $= 225$ cm^3

h

$\vdash$ 10 cm $\dashv$

21. Volume $= 3.6$ in.^{3}

r

4.2 in.

22. **FINDING A MISSING DIMENSION OF A CONE** The volume of a cone with a height of 10 meters is 20π cubic meters. What is the diameter of the cone?

23. **MP MODELING REAL LIFE** Water leaks from a crack in a cone-shaped vase at a rate of 0.5 cubic inch per minute. The vase has a height of 10 inches and a diameter of 4.8 inches. How long does it take for 20% of the water to leak from the vase when it is full of water?

24. **DIG DEEPER!** You have 10 gallons of lemonade to sell. (1 gal ≈ 3785 cm^3)

   a. Each customer uses 1 paper cup. The cups are sold in packages of 50. How many packages should you buy?

   b. How many cups will be left over if you sell 80% of the lemonade?

$\vdash$ 8 cm $\dashv$

11 cm

25. **MP STRUCTURE** The cylinder and the cone have the same volume. What is the height of the cone?

x

y

?

$2x$

26. **CRITICAL THINKING** In Example 4, you use a different timer with the same dimensions. The sand in this timer has a height of 30 millimeters. How much time do you have to answer the question?

27. **MP REASONING** A *vapor cone* is a cloud of condensed water that forms when an aircraft breaks the sound barrier. How does doubling both the diameter and the height affect the volume of the vapor cone?

10.3 Volumes of Spheres

Learning Target: Find the volume of a sphere.

Success Criteria:
- I can use a formula to find the volume of a sphere.
- I can use the formula for the volume of a sphere to find the radius.
- I can find volumes of composite solids.

A **sphere** is the set of all points in space that are the same distance from a point called the *center*. The *radius r* is the distance from the center to any point on the sphere. A sphere is different from the other solids you have studied so far because it does not have a base.

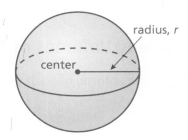

radius, *r*

center

EXPLORATION 1

Finding a Formula Experimentally

Work with a partner. Use a plastic ball similar to the one shown. Draw a net for a cylinder with a diameter and a height equal to the diameter of the ball. Then cut out the net and use tape to form an open cylinder.

a. How is the height *h* of the cylinder related to the radius *r* of the ball?

b. Cover the ball with aluminum foil or tape. Leave one hole open. Fill the ball with rice. Then pour the rice into the cylinder. What fraction of the cylinder is filled with rice?

Math Practice

Look for Structure

Why is it convenient for the height of the cylinder to be equal to the diameter of the sphere?

c. Use your result in part (b) and the formula for the volume of a cylinder to write a formula for the volume of a sphere. Explain your reasoning.

Key Vocabulary
sphere, *p. 439*
hemisphere, *p. 442*

Key Idea

Volume of a Sphere

Words The volume V of a sphere is the product of $\frac{4}{3}\pi$ and the cube of the radius of the sphere.

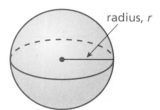
radius, r

Algebra $V = \frac{4}{3}\pi r^3$

EXAMPLE 1 **Finding Volumes of Spheres**

Find the volume of each sphere. Round your answer to the nearest tenth.

a.

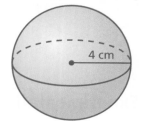
4 cm

b.

10 ft

$V = \frac{4}{3}\pi r^3$	Write the formula for volume.	$V = \frac{4}{3}\pi r^3$
$= \frac{4}{3}\pi(4)^3$	Substitute for r.	$= \frac{4}{3}\pi(5)^3$
$= \frac{256}{3}\pi$	Simplify.	$= \frac{500}{3}\pi$
≈ 268.1	Use a calculator.	≈ 523.6

▷ The volume is about 268.1 cubic centimeters.

▷ The volume is about 523.6 cubic feet.

Try It **Find the volume of the sphere. Round your answer to the nearest tenth.**

1.

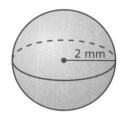
2 mm

2.

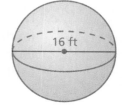
16 ft

◀)) Multi-Language Glossary at *BigIdeasMath.com*

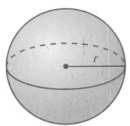

Volume = 288π in.³

EXAMPLE 2 **Finding the Radius of a Sphere**

Find the radius of the sphere.

$$V = \frac{4}{3}\pi r^3$$ Write the formula for volume.

$$288\pi = \frac{4}{3}\pi r^3$$ Substitute 288π for V.

$$288\pi = \frac{4\pi}{3}r^3$$ Multiply.

$$\frac{3}{4\pi} \cdot 288\pi = \frac{3}{4\pi} \cdot \frac{4\pi}{3}r^3$$ Multiplication Property of Equality

$$216 = r^3$$ Simplify.

$$\sqrt[3]{216} = \sqrt[3]{r^3}$$ Take the cube root of each side.

$$6 = r$$ Simplify.

▷ The radius is 6 inches.

Math Practice

Use Expressions
Show that $\frac{3}{4\pi} \cdot 288\pi$ is equal to 216.

Try It **Find the radius of the sphere. Round your answer to the nearest tenth if necessary.**

3.
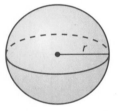

Volume = 36π m³

4.
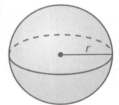

Volume = 14 in.³

Self-Assessment for Concepts & Skills

Solve each exercise. Then rate your understanding of the success criteria in your journal.

32 cm

5. **FINDING THE VOLUME OF A SPHERE** Find the volume of the sphere. Round your answer to the nearest tenth.

6. **FINDING THE RADIUS OF A SPHERE** Find the radius of a sphere with a volume of 4500π cubic yards.

7. **WHICH ONE DOESN'T BELONG?** Which figure does not belong with the other three? Explain your reasoning.

 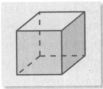 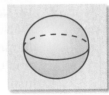 

EXAMPLE 3 **Modeling Real Life**

A hemisphere is one-half of a sphere. The top of the silo is a hemisphere with a radius of 12 feet. What is the volume of the silo? Round your answer to the nearest thousand.

52 ft

Understand the problem.

You are given the dimensions of a silo that is made up of a cylinder and a hemisphere. You are asked to find the volume of the silo.

Make a plan.

Break the problem into parts. Find the volume of the cylinder and the volume of the hemisphere. Then add the volumes to find the total volume of the silo.

Solve and check.

The radius of the hemisphere is 12 feet. So, the cylinder has a height of $52 - 12 = 40$ feet.

A *composite solid* is a solid made up of two or more three-dimensional figures.

Cylinder

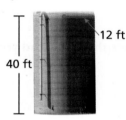

40 ft

12 ft

$V = Bh$

$= \pi(12)^2(40)$

$= 5760\pi$

Hemisphere

12 ft

$V = \frac{1}{2} \cdot \frac{4}{3}\pi r^3$

$= \frac{1}{2} \cdot \frac{4}{3}\pi(12)^3$

$= 1152\pi$

Check Reasonableness
The volume of the silo is less than the volume of a cylinder with a height of 52 feet and a radius of 12 feet.

$V = \pi(12)^2(52)$

$\approx 24{,}000 \text{ ft}^3$ ✓

▷ So, the volume is $5760\pi + 1152\pi = 6912\pi$, or about 22,000 cubic feet.

Self-Assessment *for Problem Solving*

Solve each exercise. Then rate your understanding of the success criteria in your journal.

8. In sphering, a person is secured inside a small, hollow sphere that is surrounded by a larger sphere. The space between the spheres is inflated with air. What is the volume of the inflated space? Explain.

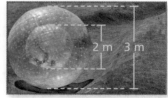

2 m   3 m

├─ 6 cm ─┤

$1.50 each!

12 cm

9. **DIG DEEPER!** A vendor sells cones filled with frozen yogurt, as shown. The vendor has 4 cylindrical containers of frozen yogurt, each with a diameter of 18 centimeters and a height of 15 centimeters. About how much money will the vendor make when all of the frozen yogurt is sold? Justify your answer.

10.3 Practice

? Go to *BigIdeasMath.com* to get HELP with solving the exercises.

▶ Review & Refresh

Find the volume of the cone. Round your answer to the nearest tenth.

1.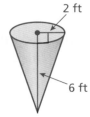
2 ft
6 ft

2.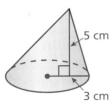
5 cm
3 cm

3.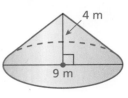
4 m
9 m

Evaluate the expression. Write your answer in scientific notation.

4. $(4.6 \times 10^9) + (3.9 \times 10^9)$

5. $(1.4 \times 10^{-4}) \div (2.8 \times 10^6)$

6. A person who is 5 feet tall casts a 6-foot-long shadow. A nearby flagpole casts a 30-foot-long shadow. What is the height of the flagpole?

   A. 25 ft   **B.** 29 ft   **C.** 36 ft   **D.** 40 ft

▶▶ Concepts, Skills, & Problem Solving

FINDING VOLUME The radius r of a sphere is given. Find the volume of the sphere. **Write your answer in terms of π.** (See Exploration 1, p. 439.)

7. $r = 6$ units

8. $r = 12$ units

9. $r = 10$ units

FINDING THE VOLUME OF A SPHERE Find the volume of the sphere. Round your answer to the nearest tenth.

10.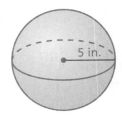
5 in.

11.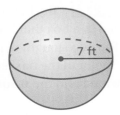
7 ft

12.
18 mm

13.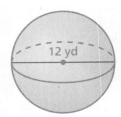
12 yd

14.
3 cm

15.
28 m

FINDING THE RADIUS OF A SPHERE Find the radius of a sphere with the given volume. Round your answer to the nearest tenth if necessary.

16. Volume $= 972\pi \, \text{mm}^3$

17. Volume $= 4.5\pi \, \text{cm}^3$

18. Volume $= 180 \, \text{ft}^3$

19. **MP MODELING REAL LIFE** The globe of the moon has a radius of 13 centimeters. Find the volume of the globe. Round your answer to the nearest whole number.

20. **MP MODELING REAL LIFE** A softball has a volume of about 29 cubic inches. Find the radius of the softball. Round your answer to the nearest tenth.

21. **MP REASONING** A sphere and a right cylinder have the same radius and volume. Find the radius r in terms of the height h of the cylinder.

FINDING VOLUME Find the volume of the composite solid. Round your answer to the nearest tenth.

22.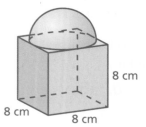
8 cm
8 cm
8 cm

23.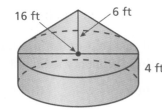
16 ft
6 ft
4 ft

24.
6 in.
11 in.

25. **MP PROBLEM SOLVING** A cylindrical container of three rubber balls has a height of 18 centimeters and a diameter of 6 centimeters. Each ball in the container has a radius of 3 centimeters. Find the amount of space in the container that is not occupied by rubber balls. Round your answer to the nearest whole number.

Volume = 121.5π in.^{3}

26. **DIG DEEPER!** The basketball shown is packaged in a box that is in the shape of a cube. The edge length of the box is equal to the diameter of the basketball. What are the surface area and the volume of the box?

27. **MP PROBLEM SOLVING** The inner core of Earth begins about 3200 miles below the surface of Earth and has a volume of about $581,000,000\pi$ cubic miles. Approximate the radius of Earth. Justify your answer.

Inner Core

28. **MP LOGIC** Your friend says that the volume of a sphere with radius r is four times the volume of a cone with radius r. When is this true? Justify your answer.

10.4 Surface Areas and Volumes of Similar Solids

Learning Target: Find the surface areas and volumes of similar solids.

Success Criteria:
- I can use corresponding dimensions to determine whether solids are similar.
- I can use corresponding dimensions to find missing measures in similar solids.
- I can use linear measures to find surface areas and volumes of similar solids.

EXPLORATION 1

Comparing Similar Solids

Work with a partner.

a. You multiply the dimensions of the smallest cylinder by different factors to create the other four cylinders. Complete the table. Compare the surface area and volume of each cylinder with the surface area and volume of the smallest cylinder.

Math Practice

Use Technology to Explore

How can you use technology to efficiently calculate the missing values in the table?

Radius	1	2	3	4	5
Height	1	2	3	4	5
Surface Area					
Volume					

b. Repeat part (a) using the square pyramids and table below.

Math Practice

Maintain Oversight

When the dimensions of a solid are multiplied by a factor of k, how many times greater is the surface area? the volume?

Base Side	6	12	18	24	30
Height	4	8	12	16	20
Slant Height	5	10	15	20	25
Surface Area					
Volume					

Key Vocabulary ◀))
similar solids, *p. 446*

Similar solids are solids that have the same shape and proportional corresponding dimensions.

EXAMPLE 1 **Identifying Similar Solids**

Cylinder B

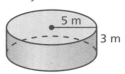
5 m
3 m

Cylinder C

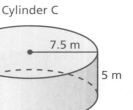
7.5 m
5 m

Which cylinder is similar to Cylinder A?

Check to see if corresponding dimensions are proportional.

Cylinder A

6 m
4 m

Cylinder A and Cylinder B

$\dfrac{\text{Height of A}}{\text{Height of B}} = \dfrac{4}{3}$ $\dfrac{\text{Radius of A}}{\text{Radius of B}} = \dfrac{6}{5}$ Not proportional

Cylinder A and Cylinder C

$\dfrac{\text{Height of A}}{\text{Height of C}} = \dfrac{4}{5}$ $\dfrac{\text{Radius of A}}{\text{Radius of C}} = \dfrac{6}{7.5} = \dfrac{4}{5}$ Proportional

▷ So, Cylinder C is similar to Cylinder A.

Try It

1. Cylinder D has a radius of 7.5 meters and a height of 4.5 meters. Which cylinder in Example 1 is similar to Cylinder D?

EXAMPLE 2 **Finding Missing Measures in Similar Solids**

Cone X

13 yd
5 yd

Cone Y

ℓ
7 yd

The cones are similar. Find the missing slant height ℓ.

$\dfrac{\text{Radius of X}}{\text{Radius of Y}} = \dfrac{\text{Slant height of X}}{\text{Slant height of Y}}$

$\dfrac{5}{7} = \dfrac{13}{\ell}$ Substitute.

$5\ell = 91$ Cross Products Property

$\ell = 18.2$ Divide each side by 5.

▷ The slant height is 18.2 yards.

Try It

2. The prisms at the right are similar. Find the missing width and length.

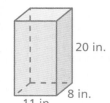
20 in.
8 in.
11 in.

8 in.
ℓ
w

 **Key Ideas**

Linear Measures

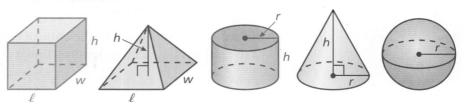

Surface Areas of Similar Solids

When two solids are similar, the value of the ratio of their surface areas is equal to the square of the value of the ratio of their corresponding linear measures.

$$\frac{\text{Surface area of A}}{\text{Surface area of B}} = \left(\frac{a}{b}\right)^2$$

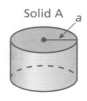

Solid A

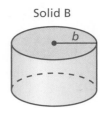

Solid B

EXAMPLE 3 **Finding Surface Area**

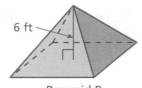

Pyramid A

6 ft

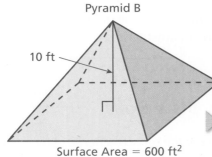

Pyramid B

10 ft

Surface Area = 600 ft²

The pyramids are similar. What is the surface area of Pyramid A?

$$\frac{\text{Surface area of A}}{\text{Surface area of B}} = \left(\frac{\text{Height of A}}{\text{Height of B}}\right)^2$$

$$\frac{S}{600} = \left(\frac{6}{10}\right)^2 \qquad \text{Substitute.}$$

$$\frac{S}{600} = \frac{36}{100} \qquad \text{Evaluate.}$$

$$S = 216 \qquad \text{Multiply each side by 600.}$$

▷ The surface area of Pyramid A is 216 square feet.

Try It **The solids are similar. Find the surface area of the red solid. Round your answer to the nearest tenth.**

3.

8 m

5 m

Surface Area = 608 m²

4.

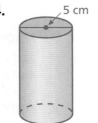

5 cm

4 cm

Surface Area = 110 cm²

 **Key Idea**

Volumes of Similar Solids

When two solids are similar, the value of the ratio of their volumes is equal to the cube of the value of the ratio of their corresponding linear measures.

$$\frac{\text{Volume of A}}{\text{Volume of B}} = \left(\frac{a}{b}\right)^3$$

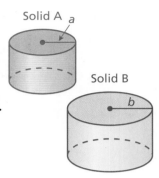

Solid A a

Solid B

b

EXAMPLE 4 **Finding Volume**

The cones are similar. What is the volume of Cone A? Round your answer to the nearest tenth.

$$\frac{\text{Volume of A}}{\text{Volume of B}} = \left(\frac{\text{Height of A}}{\text{Height of B}}\right)^3$$

$$\frac{V}{288} = \left(\frac{5}{12}\right)^3 \qquad \text{Substitute.}$$

$$\frac{V}{288} = \frac{125}{1728} \qquad \text{Evaluate.}$$

$$V \approx 20.8 \qquad \text{Multiply each side by 288.}$$

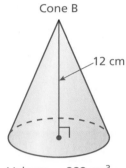

Cone B

Cone A

5 cm

12 cm

Volume = 288 cm³

▷ The volume of Cone A is about 20.8 cubic centimeters.

Try It

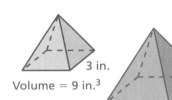

3 in.

Volume = 9 in.³

4 in.

5. The pyramids at the left are similar. Find the volume of the red pyramid. Round your answer to the nearest tenth.

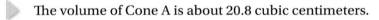

 Self-Assessment for Concepts & Skills

Solve each exercise. Then rate your understanding of the success criteria in your journal.

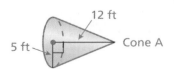

12 ft

5 ft

Cone A

6. **IDENTIFYING SIMILAR SOLIDS** Cone A and Cone B are right cones. Cone B has a radius of 1.25 feet and a height of 3 feet. Are the cones similar?

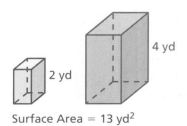

4 yd

2 yd

Surface Area = 13 yd²
Volume = 3 yd³

7. **FINDING A MISSING MEASURE** A cylinder with a radius of 4 inches and a height of 6 inches is similar to a cylinder with a radius of r inches and a height of 9 inches. What is the value of r?

8. **FINDING SURFACE AREA AND VOLUME** The rectangular prisms shown are similar. Find the surface area and volume of the red rectangular prism.

EXAMPLE 5 Modeling Real Life

Original Tank

Volume = 2000 ft³

The dimensions of the touch tank at an aquarium are doubled. How many pounds of water are contained in the new tank? (One cubic foot of water weighs about 62.5 pounds.)

The dimensions are doubled, so the ratio of the dimensions of the original tank to the dimensions of the new tank is 1 : 2.

$$\frac{\text{Original volume}}{\text{New volume}} = \left(\frac{\text{Original dimension}}{\text{New dimension}}\right)^3$$

$$\frac{2000}{V} = \left(\frac{1}{2}\right)^3 \qquad \text{Substitute.}$$

$$\frac{2000}{V} = \frac{1}{8} \qquad \text{Evaluate.}$$

$$16{,}000 = V \qquad \text{Cross Products Property}$$

> When the dimensions of a solid are multiplied by k, the surface area is multiplied by k^2 and the volume is multiplied by k^3.

The new tank holds 16,000 cubic feet of water. To find the weight of the water in the tank, multiply by $\frac{62.5 \text{ lb}}{1 \text{ ft}^3}$.

$$16{,}000 \, \text{ft}^3 \times \frac{62.5 \text{ lb}}{1 \text{ ft}^3} = 1{,}000{,}000 \text{ lb}$$

▷ So, the new tank contains about 1,000,000 pounds of water.

Self-Assessment for Problem Solving

Solve each exercise. Then rate your understanding of the success criteria in your journal.

9. Two snails have shells that are similar in shape. The younger snail has a shell with a height of 3.9 centimeters and a volume of 3 cubic centimeters. The older snail has a shell with a volume of 10 cubic centimeters. Estimate the height of the older snail's shell.

10. Two barrels filled with sand are similar in shape. The smaller barrel has a height of 4 feet and a volume of 4.5 cubic feet. The larger barrel has a height of 6 feet. What is the weight of the sand in the larger barrel? Round your answer to the nearest tenth. (One cubic foot of sand weighs about 110 pounds.)

11. Two trunks are similar in shape. The larger trunk has a length of 6 feet and a surface area of 164.25 square feet. The smaller trunk has a length of 4 feet. The materials needed to manufacture each trunk cost $0.60 per square foot. What is the total cost of the materials needed to manufacture the smaller trunk?

10.4 Practice

Go to *BigIdeasMath.com* to get HELP with solving the exercises.

▶ Review & Refresh

Find the volume of the sphere. Round your answer to the nearest tenth.

1.
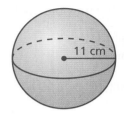
11 cm

2.

4.5 ft

3.

12 mm

4. Which system of linear equations has no solution?

A. $y = 4x + 1$
   $y = -4x + 1$

B. $y = 2x - 7$
   $y = 2x + 7$

C. $3x + y = 1$
   $6x + 2y = 2$

D. $5x + y = 3$
   $x + 5y = 15$

▶▶ Concepts, Skills, & Problem Solving

COMPARING SIMILAR SOLIDS **All of the dimensions of the solid are multiplied by a factor of k. How many times greater is the surface area of the new solid? How many times greater is the volume of the new solid?** (See Exploration 1, p. 445.)

5. $k = 5$

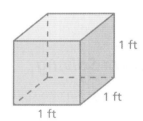
1 ft
1 ft
1 ft

6. $k = 10$

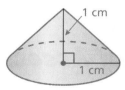
1 cm
1 cm

IDENTIFYING SIMILAR SOLIDS **Determine whether the solids are similar.**

7.
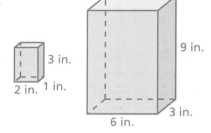
3 in.
2 in. 1 in.
9 in.
3 in.
6 in.

8.
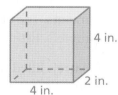
4 in.
4 in.
2 in.

4 in.
2 in. 1 in.

9.
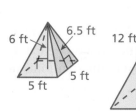
6 ft 6.5 ft
5 ft
5 ft
12 ft
13 ft
10 ft
10 ft

10.
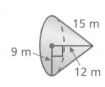
9 m
15 m
12 m
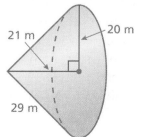
21 m
20 m
29 m

FINDING MISSING MEASURES IN SIMILAR SOLIDS The solids are similar. Find the missing measure(s).

11.

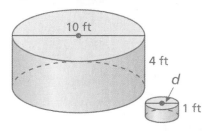

12.

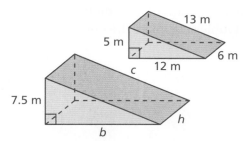

13.

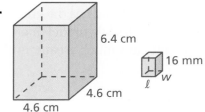

14.

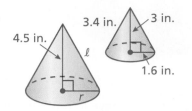

FINDING SURFACE AREA The solids are similar. Find the surface area of the red solid. Round your answer to the nearest tenth if necessary.

15.

4 m
Surface Area = 40 m²

6 m

16.

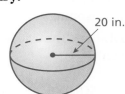

20 in.　15 in.

Surface Area ≈ 5027 in.²

17. FINDING SURFACE AREA The ratio of the corresponding linear measures of two similar cans is 4 to 7. The smaller can has a surface area of 220 square centimeters. Find the surface area of the larger can.

FINDING VOLUME The solids are similar. Find the volume of the red solid.

18.

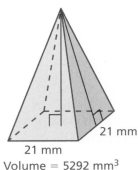

21 mm
21 mm
Volume = 5292 mm³

7 mm
7 mm

19.

10 ft　12 ft

Volume = 7850 ft³

20. **MP** **YOU BE THE TEACHER** The ratio of the corresponding linear measures of two similar solids is 3 : 5. The volume of the smaller solid is 108 cubic inches. Your friend finds the volume of the larger solid. Is your friend correct? Explain your reasoning.

$$\frac{108}{V} = \left(\frac{3}{5}\right)^2$$

$$\frac{108}{V} = \frac{9}{25}$$

$$300 = V$$

The volume of the larger solid is 300 cubic inches.

21. **MP MODELING REAL LIFE** A hemisphere-shaped mole has a diameter of 5.7 millimeters and a surface area of about 51 square millimeters. The radius of the mole doubles. Estimate the new surface area of the mole.

22. **MP REASONING** The volume of a 1968 Ford Mustang GT engine is 390 cubic inches. Which scale model of the Mustang has the greater engine volume, a 1 : 18 scale model or a 1 : 24 scale model? How much greater is it?

23. **DIG DEEPER!** You have a small marble statue of Wolfgang Mozart. It is 10 inches tall and weighs 16 pounds. The original marble statue is 7 feet tall.

   a. Estimate the weight of the original statue. Explain your reasoning.

   b. If the original statue were 20 feet tall, how much would it weigh?

24. **MP REPEATED REASONING** The nesting dolls are similar. The largest doll is 7 inches tall. Each of the other dolls is 1 inch shorter than the next larger doll. Make a table that compares the surface areas and the volumes of the seven dolls.

Wolfgang Mozart

25. **MP PRECISION** You and a friend make paper cones to collect beach glass. You cut out the largest possible three-fourths circle from each piece of paper.

   a. Are the cones similar? Explain your reasoning.

   b. Your friend says that because your sheet of paper is twice as large, your cone will hold exactly twice the volume of beach glass. Is this true? Explain your reasoning.

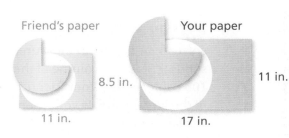

Connecting Concepts

▶ *Using the Problem-Solving Plan*

1. A *yurt* is a dwelling traditionally used in Mongolia and surrounding regions. The yurt shown is made of a cylinder and a cone. What is the volume of the yurt?

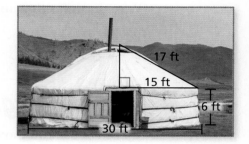

 You know that the yurt is made of a cylinder and a cone. You also know several dimensions. You are asked to find the volume of the yurt.

 Use the Pythagorean Theorem to find the height of the cone. Then use the formulas for the volume of a cylinder and the volume of a cone to find the volume of the yurt.

 Use the plan to solve the problem. Then check your solution.

2. A spherical *supervoid*, a region in space that is unusually empty, has a diameter of 1.8×10^9 light-years. What is the volume of the supervoid? Use 3.14 for π. Write your answer in scientific notation.

3. The cylinders are similar. The volume of Cylinder A is $\dfrac{8}{27}$ times the volume of Cylinder B. Find the volume of each cylinder. Round your answers to the nearest tenth.

Cylinder A
4 cm

Cylinder B
9 cm

Performance Task

Packaging Salsa

At the beginning of this chapter, you watched a STEAM Video called "Canning Salsa." You are now ready to complete the performance task related to this video, available at *BigIdeasMath.com*. Be sure to use the problem-solving plan as you work through the performance task.

▶ Review Vocabulary

Write the definition and give an example of each vocabulary term.

cone, *p. 433*

sphere, *p. 439*

hemisphere, *p. 442*

similar solids, *p. 446*

▶ Graphic Organizers

You can use a **Summary Triangle** to explain a concept. Here is an example of a Summary Triangle for *volume of a cylinder*.

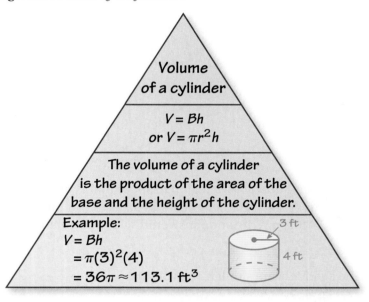

Volume of a cylinder

$V = Bh$
or $V = \pi r^2 h$

The volume of a cylinder is the product of the area of the base and the height of the cylinder.

Example:
$V = Bh$
$\;\;= \pi(3)^2(4)$
$\;\;= 36\pi \approx 113.1\ \text{ft}^3$

3 ft

4 ft

Choose and complete a graphic organizer to help you study the concept.

1. volume of a cone

2. volume of a sphere

3. volume of a composite solid

4. surface areas of similar solids

5. volumes of similar solids

Strike

Knocking all 10 pins down

Points: 10, plus points from the next 2 balls

Rolling 3 strikes in a row is called a turkey.

I thought 3 strikes and you are out.

"I finished my Summary Triangle about rolling a strike in bowling."

▶ Chapter Self-Assessment

As you complete the exercises, use the scale below to rate your understanding of the success criteria in your journal.

1	**2**	**3**	**4**
I do not understand.	I can do it with help.	I can do it on my own.	I can teach someone else.

10.1 Volumes of Cylinders *(pp. 427–432)*

Learning Target: Find the volume of a cylinder.

Find the volume of the cylinder. Round your answer to the nearest tenth.

1.

15 ft

7 ft

2.

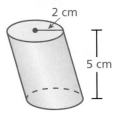

2 cm

5 cm

Find the missing dimension of the cylinder. Round your answer to the nearest whole number.

3. Volume = 28 in.³

3 in.

h

4. Volume = 7599 m³

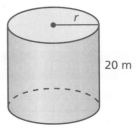

r

20 m

5. You are buying two cylindrical cans of juice. Each can holds the same amount of juice.

   a. What is the height of Can B?

   b. About how many cups of juice does each can hold? (1 in.³ ≈ 0.07 cup)

6. You triple the radius of a cylinder. How many times greater is the volume of the new cylinder? Explain.

4 in.

6 in.

h

6 in.

Can A   Can B

10.2 Volumes of Cones *(pp. 433–438)*

Learning Target: Find the volume of a cone.

Find the volume of the cone. Round your answer to the nearest tenth.

7.
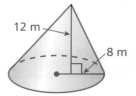
12 m
8 m

8.

4 cm
10 cm

Find the missing dimension of the cone. Round your answer to the nearest tenth.

9.
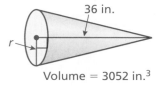
36 in.
r
Volume = 3052 in.³

10.
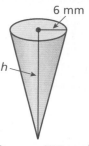
6 mm
h
Volume = 900 mm³

6 cm
h

11. The paper cup can hold 84.78 cubic centimeters of water. What is the height of the cup?

10.3 Volumes of Spheres *(pp. 439–444)*

Learning Target: Find the volume of a sphere.

Find the volume of the sphere. Round your answer to the nearest tenth.

12.

12 ft

13.

22 cm

14. The volume of a *water walking ball* is $\frac{4}{3}\pi$ cubic meters. Find the diameter of the water walking ball.

Find the volume of the composite solid. Round your answer to the nearest tenth if necessary.

15.

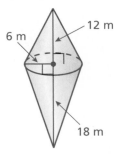

6 m
12 m
18 m

16.

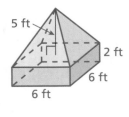

5 ft
2 ft
6 ft
6 ft

17.

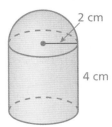

2 cm
4 cm

18. The volume of water that a submerged object displaces is equal to the volume of the object. Find the radius of the sphere. Round your answer to the nearest tenth. ($1 \text{ mL} = 1 \text{ cm}^3$)

Before

After

10.4 Surface Areas and Volumes of Similar Solids *(pp. 445–452)*

Learning Target: Find the surface areas and volumes of similar solids.

19. Determine whether the solids are similar.

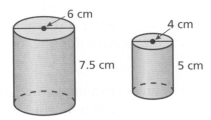

6 cm
7.5 cm
4 cm
5 cm

20. The prisms are similar. Find the missing measures.

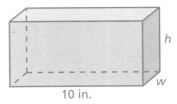

h
10 in.
w

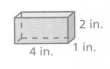

2 in.
4 in.
1 in.

21. The prisms are similar. Find the surface area of the red prism. Round your answer to the nearest tenth.

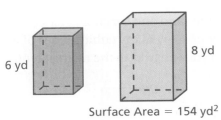

6 yd
8 yd

Surface Area = 154 yd²

22. The pyramids are similar. Find the volume of the red pyramid.

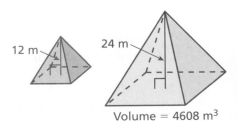

12 m
24 m

Volume = 4608 m³

23. The ratio of the corresponding linear measures of two similar jewelry boxes is 2 to 3. The larger jewelry box has a volume of 162 cubic inches. Find the volume of the smaller jewelry box.

10 Practice Test

Find the volume of the solid. Round your answer to the nearest tenth.

1.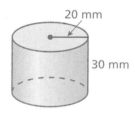
20 mm
30 mm

2.
6 cm
3 cm

3.
26 ft

4.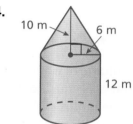
10 m   6 m
12 m

5. The pyramids are similar.

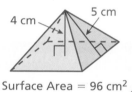 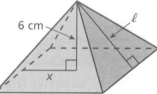

4 cm   5 cm
6 cm   ℓ
Surface Area = 96 cm²   x

    a. Find the missing measures.

    b. Find the surface area of the red pyramid.

5 in.   3 in.
5 in.   5.5 in.

6. You are making smoothies. You will use either the cone-shaped glass or the cylindrical glass. Which glass holds more? About how much more?

7. The ratio of the corresponding linear measures of two similar waffle cones is 3 to 4. The smaller cone has a volume of about 18 cubic inches. Find the volume of the larger cone. Round your answer to the nearest tenth.

8. Draw two different composite solids that have the same volume but different surface areas. Explain your reasoning.

1.5 in.

9. There are 13.5π cubic inches of blue sand and 9π cubic inches of red sand in the cylindrical container. How many cubic inches of white sand are in the container? Round your answer to the nearest tenth.

16 in.

10. Without calculating, determine which solid has the greater volume. Explain your reasoning.

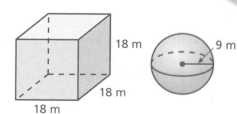
18 m   9 m
18 m
18 m

1. What is the value of $14 - 2\sqrt[3]{64}$?

   A. -50

   B. -2

   C. 6

   D. 48

2. What is the volume of the cone? $\left(\text{Use } \dfrac{22}{7} \text{ for } \pi.\right)$

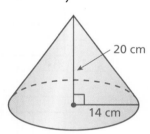
20 cm
14 cm

   F. $1026\dfrac{2}{3}$ cm^3 **G.** 3080 cm^3

   H. $4106\dfrac{2}{3}$ cm^3 **I.** 12,320 cm^3

Test-Taking Strategy

After Answering Easy Questions, Relax

How much catnip fits in a cylinder whose radius is 1 inch and height is 2 inches?
(A) 2π in.^{3} (B) 4π in.^{3} (C) 8π in.^{3} (D) 2 in.^{3}

Catnip pie, yummy for me!

"After answering the easy questions, relax and try the harder ones. For this, $\pi r^2 h = 2\pi$. So, it's A."

3. The cylinders are similar. What is the volume of the red cylinder?

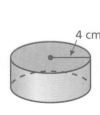
4 cm

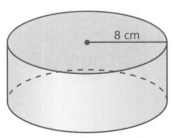
8 cm
Volume = 1206 cm^3

   A. 6 cm   **B.** 150.75 cm^3

   C. 301.5 cm^3 **D.** 603 cm^3

4. A rectangle is graphed in the coordinate plane.

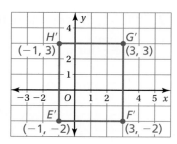

Which of the following shows Rectangle $E'F'G'H'$, the image of Rectangle $EFGH$, after it is reflected in the x-axis?

F.

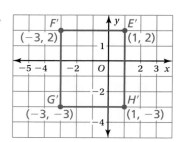

G.

H.

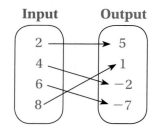

I.

5. What are the ordered pairs shown in the mapping diagram?

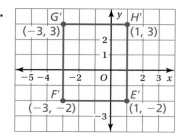

A. $(2, 5), (4, -2), (6, -7), (8, 1)$

B. $(2, -7), (4, -2), (6, 1), (8, 5)$

C. $(2, 5), (4, 1), (6, -2), (8, -7)$

D. $(5, 2), (-2, 4), (-7, 6), (1, 8)$

6. What is $0.\overline{75}$ written as a fraction?

7. Solve the formula $A = P + PI$ for I.

F. $I = A - 2P$

G. $I = \dfrac{A}{P} - P$

H. $I = A - 1$

I. $I = \dfrac{A - P}{P}$

8. A cylinder has a volume of 1296 cubic inches. If you divide the radius of the cylinder by 12, what is the volume (in cubic inches) of the smaller cylinder?

9. The cost y (in dollars) for x pounds of grapes is represented by $y = 2x$. Which graph represents the equation?

A.

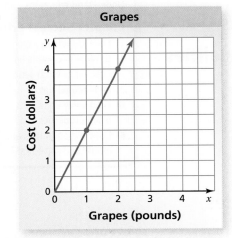

B.

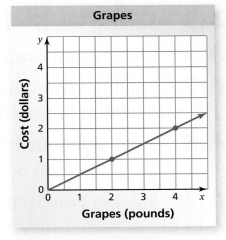

C.

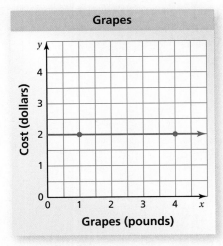

D.

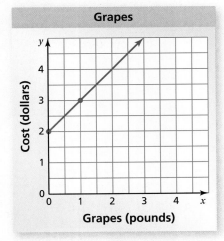

10. You are making a giant crayon.

Think
Solve
Explain

What is the volume (in cubic centimeters) of the entire crayon? Show your work and explain your reasoning. (Use 3.14 for π.)

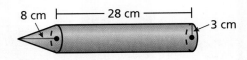

A Equations and Inequalities

Chapter Learning Target:
Understand equations and inequalities.

Chapter Success Criteria:
- ■ I can identify key words and phrases to write equations and inequalities.
- ■ I can write word sentences as equations and inequalities.
- ■ I can solve equations and inequalities using properties.
- ■ I can use equations and inequalities to model and solve real-life problems.

STEAM Video: "Space Cadets"

STEAM Video

Space Cadets

Inequalities can be used to help determine whether someone is qualified to be an astronaut. Can you think of any other real-life situations where inequalities are useful?

Watch the STEAM Video "Space Cadets." Then answer the following questions. Tori and Robert use the inequalities below to represent requirements for applying to be an astronaut, where height is measured in inches and age is measured in years.

$h \geq 62$ $\qquad$ $h \leq 72$ $\qquad$ $Q \geq G + 3$ $\qquad$ $Q \geq V + 1$

h: height $\qquad$ Q: current age $\qquad$ G: college graduation age

V: age when vision corrected

1. Can you use equations to correctly describe the requirements? Explain your reasoning.

2. The graph shows when a person who recently had vision correction surgery can apply to be an astronaut. Explain how you can determine when they had the surgery.

Months

Performance Task

Distance and Brightness of the Stars

After completing this chapter, you will be able to use the concepts you learned to answer the questions in the *STEAM Video Performance Task*. You will be given information about the celestial bodies below.

Sirius	**Earth**
Centauri	**Sun**

You will use inequalities to calculate the distances of stars from Earth and to calculate the brightnesses, or *apparent magnitudes*, of several stars. How do you think you can use one value to describe the brightnesses of all the stars that can be seen from Earth? Explain your reasoning.

Getting Ready for Chapter

Chapter Exploration

$\boxed{+} = +1$

$\boxed{-} = -1$

$\boxed{\ +\ } = x$

1. Work with a partner. Use algebra tiles to model and solve each equation.

a. $x + 4 = -2$

$\boxed{\ +\ }\ \boxed{+}\boxed{+}\boxed{+}\boxed{+} = \boxed{-}\boxed{-}$ Model the equation $x + 4 = -2$.

$\boxed{\ +\ }\ \begin{matrix}\boxed{+}\boxed{+}\boxed{+}\boxed{+}\\\boxed{-}\boxed{-}\boxed{-}\boxed{-}\end{matrix} = \begin{matrix}\boxed{-}\boxed{-}\boxed{-}\\\boxed{-}\boxed{-}\boxed{-}\end{matrix}$ Add four -1 tiles to each side.

$\boxed{\ +\ } = \begin{matrix}\boxed{-}\boxed{-}\boxed{-}\\\boxed{-}\boxed{-}\boxed{-}\end{matrix}$ Remove the zero pairs from the left side.

$\boxed{\ +\ } = \boxed{}$ Write the solution of the equation.

b. $-3 = x - 4$

$\boxed{-}\boxed{-}\boxed{-} = \boxed{\ +\ }\ \boxed{-}\boxed{-}\boxed{-}\boxed{-}$ Model the equation $-3 = x - 4$.

$\begin{matrix}\boxed{-}\boxed{-}\boxed{-}\\\boxed{+}\boxed{+}\boxed{+}\boxed{+}\end{matrix} = \boxed{\ +\ }\ \begin{matrix}\boxed{-}\boxed{-}\boxed{-}\boxed{-}\\\boxed{+}\boxed{+}\boxed{+}\boxed{+}\end{matrix}$ Add four $+1$ tiles to each side.

$\boxed{+} = \boxed{\ +\ }$ Remove the zero pairs from each side.

$\boxed{} = \boxed{\ +\ }$ Write the solution of the equation.

c. $x - 6 = 2$ **d.** $x - 7 = -3$ **e.** $-15 = x - 5$

f. $x + 3 = -5$ **g.** $7 + x = -1$ **h.** $-5 = x - 3$

2. WRITE GUIDELINES Work with a partner. Use your models in Exercise 1 to summarize the algebraic steps that you use to solve an equation.

Vocabulary

The following vocabulary terms are defined in this chapter. Think about what each term might mean and record your thoughts.

equivalent equations   inequality   solution set

A.1 Solving Equations Using Addition or Subtraction

Learning Target: Write and solve equations using addition or subtraction.

Success Criteria:
- I can apply the Addition and Subtraction Properties of Equality to produce equivalent equations.
- I can solve equations using addition or subtraction.
- I can apply equations involving addition or subtraction to solve real-life problems.

EXPLORATION 1

Using Algebra Tiles to Solve Equations

Work with a partner.

a. Use the examples to explain the meaning of each property.

$$\textbf{Addition Property of Equality:} \qquad x + 2 = 1$$
$$x + 2 + 5 = 1 + 5$$

$$\textbf{Subtraction Property of Equality:} \qquad x + 2 = 1$$
$$x + 2 - 1 = 1 - 1$$

Are these properties true for equations involving negative numbers? Explain your reasoning.

b. Write the four equations modeled by the algebra tiles. Explain how you can use algebra tiles to solve each equation. Then find the solutions.

$$[+]\ [-]\ [-]\ [-] = \begin{matrix}[-]\ [-]\\ [-]\ [-]\end{matrix}$$

$$\begin{matrix}[-]\ [-]\ [-]\\ [-]\ [-]\end{matrix} = [+]\ \begin{matrix}[+]\\ [+]\end{matrix}$$

$$[+]\ \begin{matrix}[-]\ [-]\\ [-]\end{matrix} = \begin{matrix}[+]\ [+]\\ [+]\end{matrix}$$

$$\begin{matrix}[+]\ [+]\ [+]\\ [+]\ [+]\end{matrix} = [+]\ \begin{matrix}[-]\\ [-]\end{matrix}$$

Math Practice

Analyze Relationships

How can you use the relationship between addition and subtraction to solve $x + 3 = -5$?

c. How can you solve each equation in part (b) without using algebra tiles?

Two equations are **equivalent equations** when they have the same solutions. The Addition and Subtraction Properties of Equality can be used to produce equivalent equations.

Key Ideas

Addition Property of Equality

Words Adding the same number to each side of an equation produces an equivalent equation.

Algebra If $a = b$, then $a + c = b + c$.

Subtraction Property of Equality

Words Subtracting the same number from each side of an equation produces an equivalent equation.

Algebra If $a = b$, then $a - c = b - c$.

Remember

Addition and subtraction are inverse operations.

EXAMPLE 1 **Solving Equations**

a. Solve $x - 5 = -1$.

$$x - 5 = -1 \qquad \text{Write the equation.}$$

Undo the subtraction. $\longrightarrow \underline{+5 \quad +5} \qquad$ Addition Property of Equality

$$x = 4 \qquad \text{Simplify.}$$

▶ The solution is $x = 4$.

Check

$$x - 5 = -1$$
$$4 - 5 \stackrel{?}{=} -1$$
$$-1 = -1 \checkmark$$

b. Solve $z + \dfrac{3}{2} = \dfrac{1}{2}$.

$$z + \frac{3}{2} = \frac{1}{2} \qquad \text{Write the equation.}$$

Undo the addition. $\longrightarrow \underline{-\dfrac{3}{2} \quad -\dfrac{3}{2}} \qquad$ Subtraction Property of Equality

$$z = -1 \qquad \text{Simplify.}$$

▶ The solution is $z = -1$.

Check

$$z + \frac{3}{2} = \frac{1}{2}$$
$$-1 + \frac{3}{2} \stackrel{?}{=} \frac{1}{2}$$
$$\frac{1}{2} = \frac{1}{2} \checkmark$$

Try It Solve the equation. Check your solution.

1. $p - 5 = -2$ **2.** $w + 13.2 = 10.4$ **3.** $x - \dfrac{5}{6} = -\dfrac{1}{6}$

EXAMPLE 2 **Writing an Equation**

A skydiving company has a profit of $750 this week. This profit is $900 more than the profit P last week. Which equation can be used to find P?

- **A.** $750 = 900 - P$
- **B.** $750 = P + 900$
- **C.** $900 = P - 750$
- **D.** $900 = P + 750$

Write an equation by rewriting the given information.

Words	The profit this week	is	$900	more than	the profit last week.
Equation	750	=	P	+	900

 The equation is $750 = P + 900$. The correct answer is **B**.

Try It

4. A bakery has a profit of $120.50 today. This profit is $145.25 less than the profit P yesterday. Write an equation that can be used to find P.

 Self-Assessment for Concepts & Skills

Solve each exercise. Then rate your understanding of the success criteria in your journal.

SOLVING AN EQUATION Solve the equation. Check your solution.

5. $c - 12 = -4$ 6. $k + 8.4 = -6.3$ 7. $-\dfrac{2}{3} = w - \dfrac{7}{3}$

8. **WRITING** Are the equations $m + 3 = -5$ and $m - 4 = -12$ equivalent? Explain.

9. **WHICH ONE DOESN'T BELONG?** Which equation does *not* belong with the other three? Explain your reasoning.

$$x + 3 = -1 \qquad x + 1 = -5$$

$$x - 2 = -6 \qquad x - 9 = -13$$

EXAMPLE 3 **Modeling Real Life**

You and your friend play a video game. The line graph shows both of your scores after each level. What is your score after Level 4?

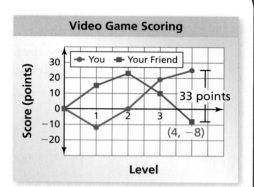

Understand the problem.

You are given a line graph that shows that after Level 4, your friend's score of -8 is 33 points less than your score. You are asked to find your score after Level 4.

Make a plan.

Use the information to write and solve an equation to find your score after Level 4.

Solve and check.

| **Words** | Your friend's score is 33 points less than your score. |

Variable Let s be your score after Level 4.

Equation

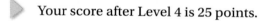

$$-8 \quad = \quad s \quad - \quad 33$$

$$-8 = s - 33 \qquad \text{Write equation.}$$
$$\underline{+\ 33} \quad \underline{+\ 33} \qquad \text{Addition Property of Equality}$$
$$25 = s \qquad \text{Simplify.}$$

▷ Your score after Level 4 is 25 points.

> **Another Method** After Level 4, your score is 33 points greater than your friend's score. So, your score is $-8 + 33 = 25$. ✔

Self-Assessment for Problem Solving

Solve each exercise. Then rate your understanding of the success criteria in your journal.

10. You have $512.50. You earn additional money by shoveling snow. Then you purchase a new cell phone for $249.95 and have $482.55 left. How much money do you earn shoveling snow?

11. **DIG DEEPER!** You swim 4 lengths of a pool and break a record by 0.72 second. The table shows your time for each length compared to the previous record holder. How much faster or slower is your third length than the previous record holder?

Length	Time (seconds)
1	−0.23
2	0.11
3	?
4	−0.42

A.1 Practice

 Go to *BigIdeasMath.com* to get HELP with solving the exercises.

▶ Review & Refresh

Factor out the coefficient of the variable term.

1. $4x - 20$ **2.** $-6y - 18$ **3.** $-\dfrac{2}{5}w + \dfrac{4}{5}$ **4.** $0.75z - 6.75$

Multiply or divide.

5. -7×8 **6.** $6 \times (-12)$ **7.** $18 \div (-2)$ **8.** $-26 \div 4$

9. A class of 144 students voted for a class president. Three-fourths of the students voted for you. Of the students who voted for you, $\dfrac{5}{9}$ are female. How many female students voted for you?

     A. 50   **B.** 60   **C.** 80   **D.** 108

▶▶ Concepts, Skills, & Problem Solving

USING ALGEBRA TILES **Solve the equation using algebra tiles. Explain your reasoning.** (See Exploration 1, p. 465.)

10. $6 + x = 4$ **11.** $x - 3 = -5$ **12.** $-7 + x = -9$

SOLVING AN EQUATION **Solve the equation. Check your solution.**

13. $a - 6 = 13$ **14.** $-3 = z - 8$ **15.** $-14 = k + 6$

16. $x + 4 = -14$ **17.** $g - 9 = -19$ **18.** $c - 7.6 = -4$

19. $-10.1 = w + 5.3$ **20.** $\dfrac{1}{2} = q + \dfrac{2}{3}$ **21.** $p - 3\dfrac{1}{6} = -2\dfrac{1}{2}$

22. $-9.3 = d - 3.4$ **23.** $4.58 + y = 2.5$ **24.** $x - 5.2 = -18.73$

25. $q + \dfrac{5}{9} = \dfrac{5}{6}$ **26.** $-2\dfrac{1}{4} = r - \dfrac{4}{5}$ **27.** $w + 3\dfrac{3}{8} = 1\dfrac{5}{6}$

28. **MP YOU BE THE TEACHER** Your friend solves the equation $x + 8 = -10$. Is your friend correct? Explain your reasoning.

$$x + 8 = -10$$
$$\underline{-8 \quad\quad -8}$$
$$x = -18$$

WRITING AND SOLVING AN EQUATION **Write the word sentence as an equation. Then solve the equation.**

29. 4 less than a number n is -15.   **30.** 10 more than a number c is 3.

31. The sum of a number y and -3 is -8.

32. The difference of a number p and 6 is -14.

33. **(MP) MODELING REAL LIFE** The temperature of dry ice is $-109.3°F$. This is $184.9°F$ less than the outside temperature. Write and solve an equation to find the outside temperature.

34. **(MP) MODELING REAL LIFE** A company makes a profit of $1.38 million. This is $2.54 million more than last year. What was the profit last year? Justify your answer.

35. **(MP) MODELING REAL LIFE** The difference in elevation of a helicopter and a submarine is $18\frac{1}{2}$ meters. The elevation of the submarine is $-7\frac{3}{4}$ meters. What is the elevation of the helicopter? Justify your answer.

GEOMETRY What is the unknown side length?

36. Perimeter = 12 cm

37. Perimeter = 24.2 in.

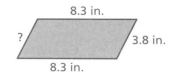

38. Perimeter = 34.6 ft

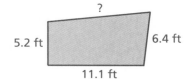

39. **(MP) MODELING REAL LIFE** The total height of the Statue of Liberty and its pedestal is 153 feet more than the height of the statue. What is the height of the statue? Justify your answer.

40. **(MP) PROBLEM SOLVING** When bungee jumping, you reach a positive elevation on your first jump that is $50\frac{1}{6}$ feet greater than the elevation you reach on your second jump. Your change in elevation on the first jump is $-200\frac{2}{3}$ feet. What is your change in elevation on the second jump?

305 ft

41. **(MP) MODELING REAL LIFE** Boatesville is a $65\frac{3}{5}$-kilometer drive from Stanton. A bus traveling from Stanton to Boatesville is $24\frac{1}{3}$ kilometers from Boatesville. How far has the bus traveled? Justify your answer.

42. **GEOMETRY** The sum of the measures of the angles of a triangle equals 180°. What is the missing angle measure?

43. **DIG DEEPER!** The table shows your scores in a skateboarding competition. The first-place finisher scores 311.62 total points, which is 4.72 more points than you score. What is your score in the fourth round?

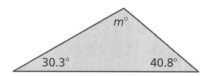

Round	1	2	3	4
Points	63.43	87.15	81.96	?

44. **CRITICAL THINKING** Find the value of $2x - 1$ when $x + 6 = -2$.

CRITICAL THINKING Solve the equation.

45. $|x| = 2$

46. $|x| - 2 = -2$

47. $|x| + 5 = 18$

A.2 Solving Equations Using Multiplication or Division

Learning Target: Write and solve equations using multiplication or division.

Success Criteria:
- I can apply the Multiplication and Division Properties of Equality to produce equivalent equations.
- I can solve equations using multiplication or division.
- I can apply equations involving multiplication or division to solve real-life problems.

EXPLORATION 1 | Using Algebra Tiles to Solve Equations

Work with a partner.

a. Use the examples to explain the meaning of each property.

Multiplication Property of Equality:
$$3x = 1$$
$$2 \cdot 3x = 2 \cdot 1$$

Division Property of Equality:
$$3x = 1$$
$$\frac{3x}{4} = \frac{1}{4}$$

Are these properties true for equations involving negative numbers? Explain your reasoning.

b. Write the three equations modeled by the algebra tiles. Explain how you can use algebra tiles to solve each equation. Then find the solutions.

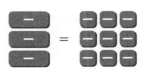

Math Practice

Find General Methods

How can you use properties of equality to solve equations of the form $ax = b$?

c. How can you solve each equation in part (b) without using algebra tiles?

Key Ideas

Multiplication Property of Equality

Words Multiplying each side of an equation by the same number produces an equivalent equation.

Algebra If $a = b$, then $a \cdot c = b \cdot c$.

Division Property of Equality

Words Dividing each side of an equation by the same number produces an equivalent equation.

Algebra If $a = b$, then $a \div c = b \div c$, $c \neq 0$.

> **Remember**
>
> Multiplication and division are inverse operations.

EXAMPLE 1 **Solving Equations**

a. Solve $\dfrac{x}{3} = -6$.

$$\dfrac{x}{3} = -6 \qquad \text{Write the equation.}$$

Undo the division. → $$3 \cdot \dfrac{x}{3} = 3 \cdot (-6) \qquad \text{Multiplication Property of Equality}$$

$$x = -18 \qquad \text{Simplify.}$$

▷ The solution is $x = -18$.

Check

$$\dfrac{x}{3} = -6$$

$$\dfrac{-18}{3} \overset{?}{=} -6$$

$$-6 = -6 \ \checkmark$$

b. Solve $18 = -4y$.

$$18 = -4y \qquad \text{Write the equation.}$$

Undo the multiplication. → $$\dfrac{18}{-4} = \dfrac{-4y}{-4} \qquad \text{Division Property of Equality}$$

$$-4.5 = y \qquad \text{Simplify.}$$

▷ The solution is $y = -4.5$.

Check

$$18 = -4y$$

$$18 \overset{?}{=} -4(-4.5)$$

$$18 = 18 \ \checkmark$$

Try It **Solve the equation. Check your solution.**

1. $\dfrac{x}{5} = -2$ **2.** $-a = -24$ **3.** $3 = -1.5n$

EXAMPLE 2 **Solving Equations Using Reciprocals**

a. Solve $-\dfrac{4}{5}x = -8.$

$$-\dfrac{4}{5}x = -8 \qquad \text{Write the equation.}$$

Multiply each side by $-\dfrac{5}{4}$, the reciprocal of $-\dfrac{4}{5}$.

$$-\dfrac{5}{4} \cdot \left(-\dfrac{4}{5}x\right) = -\dfrac{5}{4} \cdot (-8) \qquad \text{Multiplication Property of Equality}$$

$$x = 10 \qquad \text{Simplify.}$$

▷ The solution is $x = 10$.

b. Solve $-6 = \dfrac{3}{2}z.$

$$-6 = \dfrac{3}{2}z \qquad \text{Write the equation.}$$

Multiply each side by $\dfrac{2}{3}$, the reciprocal of $\dfrac{3}{2}$.

$$\dfrac{2}{3} \cdot (-6) = \dfrac{2}{3} \cdot \dfrac{3}{2}z \qquad \text{Multiplication Property of Equality}$$

$$-4 = z \qquad \text{Simplify.}$$

▷ The solution is $z = -4$.

Try It Solve the equation. Check your solution.

4. $-\dfrac{8}{5}b = 5$ **5.** $\dfrac{3}{8}h = -9$ **6.** $-14 = \dfrac{2}{3}x$

Self-Assessment for Concepts & Skills

Solve each exercise. Then rate your understanding of the success criteria in your journal.

SOLVING AN EQUATION Solve the equation. Check your solution.

7. $6d = 24$ **8.** $\dfrac{t}{3} = -4$ **9.** $-\dfrac{2}{5}p = -6$

10. WRITING Explain why you can use multiplication to solve equations involving division.

11. **MP** **STRUCTURE** Are the equations $\dfrac{2}{3}m = -4$ and $-4m = 24$ equivalent? Explain.

MP **REASONING** Describe the inverse operation that will undo the given operation.

12. subtracting 12 **13.** multiplying by $-\dfrac{1}{8}$ **14.** adding -6

EXAMPLE 3 **Modeling Real Life**

The temperature at midnight is shown at the left. The temperature decreases 4.5°F each hour. When will the temperature be 32°F?

The temperature at midnight is 56°F. To determine when the temperature will reach 32°F, find how long it will take the temperature to decrease 56°F − 32°F = 24°F. Write and solve an equation to find the time.

Verbal Model

Change in temperature (°F)	=	Hourly change in temperature (°F per hour)	•	Time (hours)

Variable   Let t be the time for the temperature to decrease 24°F.

> The changes in temperature are negative because they are decreasing.

Equation -24 $=$ -4.5 • t

$$-24 = -4.5t \qquad \text{Write equation.}$$

$$\frac{-24}{-4.5} = \frac{-4.5t}{-4.5} \qquad \text{Division Property of Equality}$$

$$5.\overline{3} = t \qquad \text{Simplify.}$$

Math Practice

Understand Quantities
Describe a procedure you can use to find the number of minutes in $\frac{1}{3}$ hour.

The temperature will be 32°F at $5\frac{1}{3}$ hours after midnight, or 5 hours and 20 minutes after midnight.

▷   So, the temperature will be 32°F at 5:20 A.M.

Self-Assessment for Problem Solving

Solve each exercise. Then rate your understanding of the success criteria in your journal.

15. The elevation of the surface of a lake is 315 feet. During a drought, the water level of the lake changes $-3\frac{1}{5}$ feet per week.

Find how long it takes for the surface of the lake to reach an elevation of 299 feet. Justify your answer.

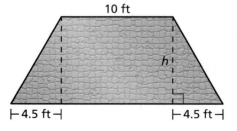

10 ft

h

⊢ 4.5 ft ⊣   ⊢ 4.5 ft ⊣

16.   **DIG DEEPER!**   The patio shown has an area of 116 square feet. What is the value of h? Justify your answer.

A.2 Practice

▶ Review & Refresh

Solve the equation. Check your solution.

1. $n - 9 = -12$

2. $-\dfrac{1}{2} = m - \dfrac{7}{4}$

3. $-6.4 = h + 8.7$

Find the difference.

4. $5 - 12$

5. $-7 - 2$

6. $4 - (-8)$

7. $-14 - (-5)$

8. Of the 120 apartments in a building, 75 have been scheduled to receive new carpet. What percent of the apartments have not been scheduled to receive new carpet?

    A. 25%   **B.** 37.5%   **C.** 62.5%   **D.** 75%

▶▶ Concepts, Skills, & Problem Solving

USING ALGEBRA TILES Solve the equation using algebra tiles. Explain your reasoning. (See Exploration 1, p. 471.)

9. $4x = -16$

10. $2x = -6$

11. $-5x = -20$

SOLVING AN EQUATION Solve the equation. Check your solution.

12. $3h = 15$

13. $-5t = -45$

14. $\dfrac{n}{2} = -7$

15. $\dfrac{k}{-3} = 9$

16. $5m = -10$

17. $8t = -32$

18. $-0.2x = 1.6$

19. $-10 = -\dfrac{b}{4}$

20. $-6p = 48$

21. $-72 = 8d$

22. $\dfrac{n}{1.6} = 5$

23. $-14.4 = -0.6p$

24. $\dfrac{3}{4}g = -12$

25. $8 = -\dfrac{2}{5}c$

26. $-\dfrac{4}{9}f = -3$

27. $26 = -\dfrac{8}{5}y$

28. **MP YOU BE THE TEACHER** Your friend solves the equation $-4.2x = 21$. Is your friend correct? Explain your reasoning.

$$-4.2x = 21$$
$$\dfrac{-4.2x}{4.2} = \dfrac{21}{4.2}$$
$$x = 5$$

WRITING AND SOLVING AN EQUATION Write the word sentence as an equation. Then solve the equation.

29. A number divided by -9 is -16.

30. A number multiplied by $\dfrac{2}{5}$ is $\dfrac{3}{20}$.

31. The product of 15 and a number is -75.

32. The quotient of a number and -1.5 is 21.

33. **MP MODELING REAL LIFE** You make a profit of $0.75 for every bracelet you sell. Write and solve an equation to determine how many bracelets you must sell to earn enough money to buy the soccer cleats shown.

Soccer Cleats $36

34. **MP MODELING REAL LIFE** A rock climber averages $12\frac{3}{5}$ feet climbed per minute. How many feet does the rock climber climb in 30 minutes? Justify your answer.

OPEN-ENDED Write (a) a multiplication equation and (b) a division equation that has the given solution.

35. -3 36. -2.2 37. $-\frac{1}{2}$ 38. $-1\frac{1}{4}$

39. **MP REASONING** Which method(s) can you use to solve $-\frac{2}{3}c = 16$?

> Multiply each side by $-\frac{2}{3}$.

> Multiply each side by $-\frac{3}{2}$.

> Divide each side by $-\frac{2}{3}$.

> Multiply each side by 3, then divide each side by -2.

40. **MP MODELING REAL LIFE** A stock has a return of $-\$1.26$ per day. Find the number of days until the total return is $-\$10.08$. Justify your answer.

41. **MP PROBLEM SOLVING** In a school election, $\frac{3}{4}$ of the students vote. There are 1464 votes. Find the number of students. Justify your answer.

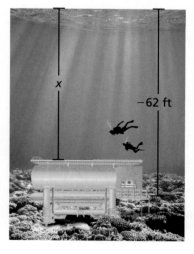

x

-62 ft

42. **DIG DEEPER!** The diagram shows Aquarius, an underwater ocean laboratory located in the Florida Keys National Marine Sanctuary. The equation $\frac{31}{25}x = -62$ can be used to calculate the depth of Aquarius. Interpret the equation. Then find the depth of Aquarius. Justify your answer.

43. **MP PROBLEM SOLVING** The price of a bike at Store A is $\frac{5}{6}$ the price at Store B. The price at Store A is $150.60. Find how much you save by buying the bike at Store A. Justify your answer.

44. **CRITICAL THINKING** Solve $-2|m| = -10$.

45. **MP NUMBER SENSE** In 4 days, your family drives $\frac{5}{7}$ of the total distance of a trip. The total distance is 1250 miles. At this rate, how many more days will it take to reach your destination? Justify your answer.

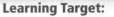

A.3 Solving Two-Step Equations

Learning Target: Write and solve two-step equations.

Success Criteria:
- I can apply properties of equality to produce equivalent equations.
- I can solve two-step equations using the basic operations.
- I can apply two-step equations to solve real-life problems.

EXPLORATION 1

Using Algebra Tiles to Solve Equations

Work with a partner.

a. What is being modeled by the algebra tiles below? What is the solution?

b. Use properties of equality to solve the original equation in part (a). How do your steps compare to the steps performed with algebra tiles?

c. Write the three equations modeled by the algebra tiles below. Then solve each equation using algebra tiles. Check your answers using properties of equality.

Math Practice

Use Operations
In part (c), what operations are you performing first? Why?

d. Explain how to solve an equation of the form $ax + b = c$ for x.

EXAMPLE 1 **Solving a Two-Step Equation**

Solve $-3x + 5 = 2$.

$-3x + 5 = 2$	Write the equation.
Undo the addition. → $\underline{\; -5 \quad -5}$	Subtraction Property of Equality
$-3x = -3$	Simplify.
Undo the multiplication. → $\dfrac{-3x}{-3} = \dfrac{-3}{-3}$	Division Property of Equality
$x = 1$	Simplify.

▷ The solution is $x = 1$.

Check

$-3x + 5 = 2$

$-3(1) + 5 \overset{?}{=} 2$

$-3 + 5 \overset{?}{=} 2$

$2 = 2$ ✓

Try It Solve the equation. Check your solution.

1. $2x + 12 = 4$ **2.** $-5c + 9 = -16$ **3.** $9 = 3x - 12$

EXAMPLE 2 **Solving a Two-Step Equation**

Solve $\dfrac{x}{8} - \dfrac{1}{2} = -\dfrac{7}{2}$.

Math Practice

Consider Simpler Forms

Can you solve the original equation by first multiplying each side by 8? Explain your reasoning.

$\dfrac{x}{8} - \dfrac{1}{2} = -\dfrac{7}{2}$	Write the equation.
$\underline{ +\dfrac{1}{2} \qquad +\dfrac{1}{2}}$	Addition Property of Equality
$\dfrac{x}{8} = -3$	Simplify.
$8 \cdot \dfrac{x}{8} = 8 \cdot (-3)$	Multiplication Property of Equality
$x = -24$	Simplify.

▷ The solution is $x = -24$.

Check

$\dfrac{x}{8} - \dfrac{1}{2} = -\dfrac{7}{2}$

$\dfrac{-24}{8} - \dfrac{1}{2} \overset{?}{=} -\dfrac{7}{2}$

$-3 - \dfrac{1}{2} \overset{?}{=} -\dfrac{7}{2}$

$-\dfrac{7}{2} = -\dfrac{7}{2}$ ✓

Try It Solve the equation. Check your solution.

4. $\dfrac{m}{2} + 6 = 10$ **5.** $-\dfrac{z}{3} + 5 = 9$ **6.** $\dfrac{2}{5} + 4a = -\dfrac{6}{5}$

EXAMPLE 3 **Combining Like Terms Before Solving**

a. Solve $3y - 8y = 25$.

$3y - 8y = 25$	Write the equation.
$-5y = 25$	Combine like terms.
$y = -5$	Divide each side by -5.

 The solution is $y = -5$.

b. Solve $-6 = \dfrac{1}{4}w - \dfrac{1}{2}w$.

$-6 = \dfrac{1}{4}w - \dfrac{1}{2}w$	Write the equation.
$-6 = -\dfrac{1}{4}w$	Combine like terms.
$24 = w$	Multiply each side by -4.

 The solution is $w = 24$.

Try It Solve the equation. Check your solution.

7. $4 - 2y + 3 = -9$ **8.** $7x - 10x = 15$ **9.** $-8 = 1.3m - 2.1m$

Self-Assessment for *Concepts & Skills*

Solve each exercise. Then rate your understanding of the success criteria in your journal.

MATCHING Match the equation with the step(s) to solve it.

10. $4 + 4n = 12$ **11.** $4n = 12$ **12.** $\dfrac{n}{4} = 12$ **13.** $\dfrac{n}{4} - 4 = 12$

A. Add 4 to each side. Then multiply each side by 4.

B. Subtract 4 from each side. Then divide each side by 4.

C. Multiply each side by 4.

D. Divide each side by 4.

SOLVING AN EQUATION Solve the equation. Check your solution.

14. $4p + 5 = 3$ **15.** $-\dfrac{d}{5} - 1 = -6$ **16.** $3.6g = 21.6$

17. WRITING Are the equations $3x + 12 = 6$ and $-2 = 4 - 3x$ equivalent? Explain.

EXAMPLE 4 **Modeling Real Life**

You install 500 feet of invisible fencing along the perimeter of a rectangular yard. The width of the yard is 100 feet. What is the length of the yard?

You are given that the perimeter of a rectangular yard is 500 feet and the width is 100 feet. You are asked to find the length of the yard.

Draw a diagram of the yard. Then use the formula for the perimeter of a rectangle to write and solve an equation to find the length of the yard.

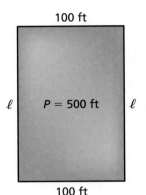

$P = 2\ell + 2w$	Perimeter of a rectangle
$500 = 2\ell + 2(100)$	Substitute for P and w.
$500 = 2\ell + 200$	Multiply.
$300 = 2\ell$	Subtract 200 from each side.
$150 = \ell$	Divide each side by 2.

➤ So, the length of the yard is 150 feet.

Another Method Use a different form of the formula for the perimeter of a rectangle, $P = 2(\ell + w)$.

$500 = 2(\ell + 100)$	Substitute for P and w.
$250 = \ell + 100$	Divide each side by 2.
$150 = \ell$	Subtract 100 from each side.

So, the length of the yard is 150 feet. ✔

Self-Assessment for Problem Solving

Solve each exercise. Then rate your understanding of the success criteria in your journal.

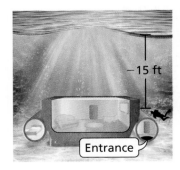

18. You must scuba dive to the entrance of your room at Jules' Undersea Lodge in Key Largo, Florida. The diver is 1 foot deeper than $\frac{2}{3}$ of the elevation of the entrance. What is the elevation of the entrance?

19. **DIG DEEPER!** A car drives east along a road at a constant speed of 46 miles per hour. At 4:00 P.M., a truck is 264 miles away, driving west along the same road at a constant speed. The vehicles pass each other at 7:00 P.M. What is the speed of the truck?

A.3 Practice

Go to *BigIdeasMath.com* to get
HELP with solving the exercises.

▶ Review & Refresh

Solve the equation.

1. $3z = 18$ 2. $-8p = 40$ 3. $-\dfrac{m}{4} = 5$ 4. $\dfrac{5}{6}k = -10$

Multiply or divide.

5. -6.2×5.6 6. $\dfrac{8}{3} \times \left(-2\dfrac{1}{2}\right)$ 7. $\dfrac{5}{2} \div \left(-\dfrac{4}{5}\right)$ 8. $-18.6 \div (-3)$

9. Which fraction is *not* equivalent to 0.75?

    A. $\dfrac{15}{20}$ **B.** $\dfrac{9}{12}$ **C.** $\dfrac{6}{9}$ **D.** $\dfrac{3}{4}$

▶ Concepts, Skills, & Problem Solving

USING ALGEBRA TILES Write the equation modeled by the algebra tiles. Then solve the equation using algebra tiles. Check your answer using properties of equality. (See Exploration 1, p. 477.)

10.

11.

SOLVING AN EQUATION Solve the equation. Check your solution.

12. $2v + 7 = 3$ 13. $4b + 3 = -9$ 14. $17 = 5k - 2$

15. $-6t - 7 = 17$ 16. $8n + 16.2 = 1.6$ 17. $-5g + 2.3 = -18.8$

18. $2t + 8 = -10$ 19. $-4p + 9 = -5$ 20. $15 = -5x + 10$

21. $10.35 + 2.3h = -9.2$ 22. $-4.8f + 6.4 = -8.48$ 23. $7.3y - 5.18 = -51.9$

MP YOU BE THE TEACHER Your friend solves the equation. Is your friend correct? Explain your reasoning.

24.
$$-6 + 2x = -10$$
$$-6 + \dfrac{2x}{2} = -\dfrac{10}{2}$$
$$-6 + x = -5$$
$$x = 1$$

25.
$$-3(x + 6) = 12$$
$$-3x = 6$$
$$\dfrac{-3x}{-3} = \dfrac{6}{-3}$$
$$x = -2$$

SOLVING AN EQUATION Solve the equation. Check your solution.

26. $\dfrac{3}{5}g - \dfrac{1}{3} = -\dfrac{10}{3}$ 27. $\dfrac{a}{4} - \dfrac{5}{6} = -\dfrac{1}{2}$ 28. $-\dfrac{1}{3}(4 + z) = -\dfrac{5}{6}$

29. $2 - \dfrac{b}{3} = -\dfrac{5}{2}$ 30. $-\dfrac{2}{3}\left(x + \dfrac{3}{5}\right) = \dfrac{1}{2}$ 31. $-\dfrac{9}{4}v + \dfrac{4}{5} = \dfrac{7}{8}$

Temperature
at 1:00 P.M.

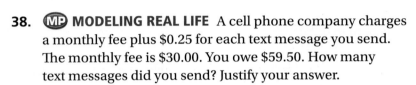

35°F

32. **MP** **PRECISION** Starting at 1:00 P.M., the temperature changes −4°F per hour. Write and solve an equation to determine how long it will take for the temperature to reach −1°F.

COMBINING LIKE TERMS Solve the equation. Check your solution.

33. $3v - 9v = 30$

34. $12t - 8t = -52$

35. $-8d - 5d + 7d = 72$

36. $-3.8g + 5 + 2.7g = 12.7$

37. **MP** **MODELING REAL LIFE** You have $9.25. How many games can you bowl if you rent bowling shoes? Justify your answer.

38. **MP** **MODELING REAL LIFE** A cell phone company charges a monthly fee plus $0.25 for each text message you send. The monthly fee is $30.00. You owe $59.50. How many text messages did you send? Justify your answer.

Shoe Rentals: $2.50

Bowling: $2.25 per game

39. **MP** **PROBLEM SOLVING** The height at the top of a roller coaster hill is 10 times the height h of the starting point. The height decreases 100 feet from the top to the bottom of the hill. The height at the bottom of the hill is −10 feet. Find h.

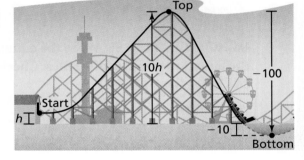

40. **MP** **MODELING REAL LIFE** On a given day, the coldest surface temperature on the Moon, −280°F, is 53.6°F colder than twice the coldest surface temperature on Earth. What is the coldest surface temperature on Earth that day? Justify your answer.

41. **DIG DEEPER!** On Saturday, you catch insects for your science class. Five of the insects escape. The remaining insects are divided into three groups to share in class. Each group has nine insects.

  a. Write and solve an equation to find the number of insects you catch on Saturday.

  b. Find the number of insects you catch on Saturday without using an equation. Compare the steps used to solve the equation in part (a) with the steps used to solve the problem in part (b).

  c. Describe a problem that is more convenient to solve using an equation. Then describe a problem that is more convenient to solve without using an equation.

12 cm

25 cm

42. **GEOMETRY** How can you change the dimensions of the rectangle so that the ratio of the length to the width stays the same, but the perimeter is 185 centimeters? Write an equation that shows how you found your answer.

A.4 Writing and Graphing Inequalities

Learning Target: Write inequalities and represent solutions of inequalities on number lines.

Success Criteria:
- I can write word sentences as inequalities.
- I can determine whether a value is a solution of an inequality.
- I can graph the solutions of inequalities.

EXPLORATION 1

Understanding Inequality Statements

Work with a partner. Create a number line on the floor with both positive and negative numbers.

a. For each statement, stand at a number on your number line that could represent the situation. On what other numbers can you stand?

- At least 3 students from our school are in a chess tournament.

- Your ring size is less than 7.5.

- The temperature is no more than −1 degree Fahrenheit.

- The elevation of a frogfish is greater than $-8\frac{1}{2}$ meters.

Math Practice

State the Meaning of Symbols

What do the symbols $<$, $>$, $\le$, and $\ge$ mean?

b. How can you represent all of the solutions for each statement in part (a) on a number line?

Key Vocabulary

inequality, *p. 484*
solution of an
  inequality, *p. 484*
solution set, *p. 484*
graph of an
  inequality, *p. 486*

An **inequality** is a mathematical sentence that compares expressions. It contains the symbols <, >, ≤, or ≥. To write a word sentence as an inequality, look for the following phrases to determine where to place the inequality symbol.

Inequality Symbols				
Symbol	<	>	≤	≥
Key Phrases	• is less than • is fewer than	• is greater than • is more than	• is less than or equal to • is at most • is no more than	• is greater than or equal to • is at least • is no less than

EXAMPLE 1   Writing an Inequality

A number q plus 5 is less than or equal to -7.9. Write this word sentence as an inequality.

A number q plus 5 is less than or equal to -7.9.

$q + 5$ ≤ -7.9

▷ An inequality is $q + 5 \leq -7.9$.

Try It Write the word sentence as an inequality.

1. A number x is at least -10.   **2.** Twice a number y is more than $-\dfrac{5}{2}$.

A **solution of an inequality** is a value that makes the inequality true. An inequality can have more than one solution. The set of all solutions of an inequality is called the **solution set**.

Reading

The symbol ≰ means *is not less than or equal to.*

Value of x	$x + 2 \leq -1$	Is the inequality true?
-2	$-2 + 2 \overset{?}{\leq} -1$ $0 \nleq -1$ ✗	no
-3	$-3 + 2 \overset{?}{\leq} -1$ $-1 \leq -1$ ✓	yes
-4	$-4 + 2 \overset{?}{\leq} -1$ $-2 \leq -1$ ✓	yes

🔊 *Multi-Language Glossary at BigIdeasMath.com*

EXAMPLE 2 **Checking Solutions**

a. Tell whether -2 is a solution of $y - 5 \geq -6$.

$$y - 5 \geq -6 \qquad \text{Write the inequality.}$$
$$-2 - 5 \overset{?}{\geq} -6 \qquad \text{Substitute } -2 \text{ for } y.$$
$$-7 \ngeq -6 \quad \text{✗} \qquad \text{Simplify.}$$

So, -2 is *not* a solution of the inequality.

b. Tell whether -2 is a solution of $-5.5y < 14$.

$$-5.5y < 14 \qquad \text{Write the inequality.}$$
$$-5.5(-2) \overset{?}{<} 14 \qquad \text{Substitute } -2 \text{ for } y.$$
$$11 < 14 \quad \text{✓} \qquad \text{Simplify.}$$

So, -2 is a solution of the inequality.

Try It Tell whether -5 is a solution of the inequality.

3. $x + 12 > 7$ 4. $1 - 2p \leq -9$ 5. $n \div 2.5 \geq -3$

Self-Assessment for Concepts & Skills

Solve each exercise. Then rate your understanding of the success criteria in your journal.

6. **MP REASONING** Do $x < 5$ and $5 < x$ represent the same inequality? Explain.

7. **DIFFERENT WORDS, SAME QUESTION** Which is different? Write "both" inequalities.

> A number k is less than or equal to -3.

> A number k is at least -3.   A number k is at most -3.

> A number k is no more than -3.

CHECKING SOLUTIONS Tell whether -4 is a solution of the inequality.

8. $c + 6 \leq 3$ 9. $6 > p \div (-0.5)$ 10. $-7 < 2g + 1$

The **graph of an inequality** shows all the solutions of the inequality on a number line. An open circle ○ is used when a number is *not* a solution. A closed circle ● is used when a number is a solution. An arrow to the left or right shows that the graph continues in that direction.

EXAMPLE 3 **Modeling Real Life**

A rock climber's sleeping bag is recommended for temperatures no less than −15°C. Write and graph an inequality that represents the recommended temperatures for the sleeping bag.

Words	temperatures	no less than	−15°C
Variable	Let t be the recommended temperatures.		
Inequality	t	$\geq$	-15

An inequality is $t \geq -15$. Graph the inequality.

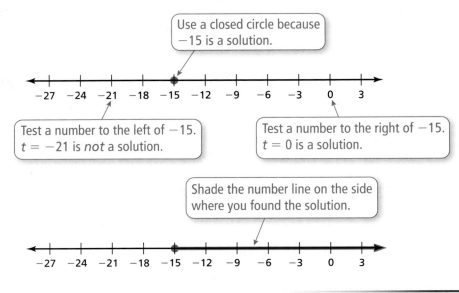

Use a closed circle because −15 is a solution.

Test a number to the left of −15.
$t = -21$ is *not* a solution.

Test a number to the right of −15.
$t = 0$ is a solution.

Shade the number line on the side where you found the solution.

The graph in Example 3 shows that the inequality has *infinitely many* solutions.

Self-Assessment for Problem Solving

Solve each exercise. Then rate your understanding of the success criteria in your journal.

Fitness Test
- Jog at least 2 kilometers
- Perform 25 or more push-ups
- Perform at least 10 pull-ups

11. The three requirements to pass a fitness test are shown. Write and graph three inequalities that represent the requirements. Then give a set of possible values for a person who passes the test.

12. To set a depth record, a submersible vehicle must reach a water depth less than −715 feet. A vehicle breaks the record by more than 10 feet. Write and graph an inequality that represents the possible depths reached by the vehicle.

A.4 Practice

Go to *BigIdeasMath.com* to get HELP with solving the exercises.

▶ Review & Refresh

Solve the equation. Check your solution.

1. $p - 8 = 3$

2. $8.7 + w = 5.1$

3. $x - 2 = -9$

4. $8v + 5 = 1$

5. $\dfrac{7}{8} - \dfrac{1}{4}n = -\dfrac{3}{8}$

6. $1.8 = 2.1h - 5.7 - 4.6h$

7. Which expression has a value less than -5?

   A. $5 + 8$ **B.** $-9 + 5$ **C.** $1 + (-8)$ **D.** $7 + (-2)$

▶▶ Concepts, Skills, & Problem Solving

UNDERSTANDING INEQUALITY STATEMENTS **Choose a number that could represent the situation. What other numbers could represent the situation?**
(See Exploration 1, p. 483.)

8. Visibility in an airplane is greater than 6.5 miles.

9. You must sell no fewer than 20 raffle tickets for a fundraiser.

10. You consume at most 1800 calories per day.

11. The elevation of the Dead Sea is less than -400 meters.

WRITING AN INEQUALITY **Write the word sentence as an inequality.**

12. A number y is no more than -8.

13. A number w added to 2.3 is more than 18.

14. A number t multiplied by -4 is at least $-\dfrac{2}{5}$.

15. A number b minus 4.2 is less than -7.5.

16. $-\dfrac{5}{9}$ is no less than 5 times a number k.

17. **(MP)** **YOU BE THE TEACHER** Your friend writes the word sentence as an inequality. Is your friend correct? Explain your reasoning.

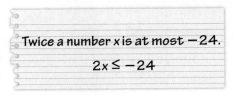

Twice a number x is at most -24.

$2x \leq -24$

CHECKING SOLUTIONS **Tell whether the given value is a solution of the inequality.**

18. $n + 8 \leq 13; n = 4$

19. $-15 < 5h; h = -5$

20. $p + 1.4 \leq 0.5; p = 0.1$

21. $\dfrac{a}{6} > -4; a = -18$

22. $6 \geq -\dfrac{2}{3}s; s = -9$

23. $\dfrac{7}{8} - 3k < -\dfrac{1}{2}; k = \dfrac{1}{4}$

GRAPHING AN INEQUALITY Graph the inequality on a number line.

24. $r \leq -9$ **25.** $g > 2.75$ **26.** $x \geq -3\frac{1}{2}$ **27.** $1\frac{1}{4} > z$

28. **MP MODELING REAL LIFE** Each day at lunchtime, at least 53 people buy food from a food truck. Write and graph an inequality that represents this situation.

CHECKING SOLUTIONS Tell whether the given value is a solution of the inequality.

29. $4k < k + 8$; $k = 3$ **30.** $\frac{w}{3} \geq w - 12$; $w = 15$

31. $7 - 2y > 3y + 13$; $y = -1$ **32.** $\frac{3}{4}b - 2 \leq 2b + 8$; $b = -4$

33. **MP PROBLEM SOLVING** A single subway ride for a student costs $1.25. A monthly pass costs $35.

   a. Write an inequality that represents the numbers of times you can ride the subway each month for the monthly pass to be a better deal.

   b. You ride the subway about 45 times per month. Should you buy the monthly pass? Explain.

34. **MP LOGIC** Consider the inequality $b > -2$.

   a. Describe the values of b that are solutions of the inequality.

   b. Describe the values of b that are *not* solutions of the inequality. Write an inequality that represents these values.

   c. What do all the values in parts (a) and (b) represent? Is this true for any similar pair of inequalities? Explain your reasoning.

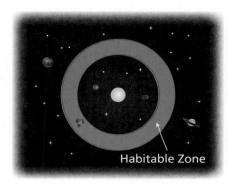

Habitable Zone

35. **MP MODELING REAL LIFE** A planet orbiting a star at a distance such that its temperatures are right for liquid water is said to be in the star's *habitable zone*. The habitable zone of a particular star is at least 0.023 AU and at most 0.054 AU from the star (1 AU is equal to the distance between Earth and the Sun). Draw a graph that represents the habitable zone.

36. **DIG DEEPER!** The *girth* of a package is the distance around the perimeter of a face that does not include the length as a side. A postal service says that a rectangular package can have a maximum combined length and girth of 108 inches.

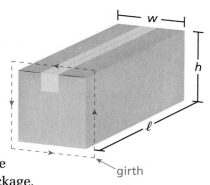

   a. Write an inequality that represents the allowable dimensions for the package.

   b. Find three different sets of allowable dimensions that are reasonable for the package. Find the volume of each package.

Learning Target: Write and solve inequalities using addition or subtraction.

Success Criteria:
- I can apply the Addition and Subtraction Properties of Inequality to produce equivalent inequalities.
- I can solve inequalities using addition or subtraction.
- I can apply inequalities involving addition or subtraction to solve real-life problems.

EXPLORATION 1

Writing Inequalities

Work with a partner. Use two number cubes on which the odd numbers are negative on one of the number cubes and the even numbers are negative on the other number cube.

- Roll the number cubes. Write an inequality that compares the numbers.

- Roll one of the number cubes. Add the number to each side of the inequality and record your result.

- Repeat the previous two steps five more times.

a. When you add the same number to each side of an inequality, does the inequality remain true? Explain your reasoning.

b. When you subtract the same number from each side of an inequality, does the inequality remain true? Use inequalities generated by number cubes to justify your answer.

c. Use your results in parts (a) and (b) to make a conjecture about how to solve an inequality of the form $x + a < b$ for x.

Math Practice

Analyze Conjectures

Use your conjecture to solve $x + 3 < 1$. Does the solution make sense?

A.5 Lesson

You can solve inequalities in the same way you solve equations. Use inverse operations to get the variable by itself.

🔑 Key Ideas

Addition Property of Inequality

Words When you add the same number to each side of an inequality, the inequality remains true.

Numbers

$$-4 < 3$$
$$\underline{+2 \quad +2}$$
$$-2 < 5$$

Algebra If $a < b$, then $a + c < b + c$.

If $a > b$, then $a + c > b + c$.

Subtraction Property of Inequality

Words When you subtract the same number from each side of an inequality, the inequality remains true.

Numbers

$$-2 < 2$$
$$\underline{-3 \quad -3}$$
$$-5 < -1$$

Algebra If $a < b$, then $a - c < b - c$.

If $a > b$, then $a - c > b - c$.

These properties are also true for $\leq$ and $\geq$.

EXAMPLE 1 Solving an Inequality Using Addition

Solve $x - 5 < -3$. Graph the solution.

$x - 5 < -3$	Write the inequality.
Undo the subtraction. → $\underline{+5 \quad +5}$	Addition Property of Inequality
$x < 2$	Simplify.

Check:

$x = 0$: $0 - 5 \overset{?}{<} -3$

$-5 < -3$ ✓

$x = 5$: $5 - 5 \overset{?}{<} -3$

$0 \not< -3$ ✗

The solution is $x < 2$.

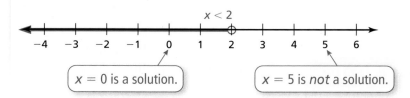

$x = 0$ is a solution. $x = 5$ is *not* a solution.

Try It **Solve the inequality. Graph the solution.**

1. $y - 6 > -7$ **2.** $b - 3.8 \leq 1.7$ **3.** $-\dfrac{1}{2} > z - \dfrac{1}{4}$

 **EXAMPLE 2** **Solving an Inequality Using Subtraction**

Solve $13 \leq x + 14$. Graph the solution.

$$13 \leq x + 14 \qquad \text{Write the inequality.}$$

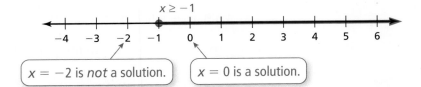

Undo the addition. → $\underline{-14 \qquad -14}$ Subtraction Property of Inequality

$$-1 \leq x \qquad \text{Simplify.}$$

Reading

The inequality $-1 \leq x$ is the same as $x \geq -1$.

▷ The solution is $x \geq -1$.

$$x \geq -1$$

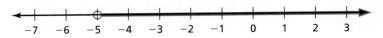

$x = -2$ is *not* a solution. $x = 0$ is a solution.

Try It Solve the inequality. Graph the solution.

4. $w + 3 \leq -1$ **5.** $8.5 \geq d + 10$ **6.** $x + \dfrac{3}{4} > 1\dfrac{1}{2}$

Self-Assessment for Concepts & Skills

Solve each exercise. Then rate your understanding of the success criteria in your journal.

7. WRITING Are the inequalities $c + 3 > 5$ and $c - 1 > 1$ equivalent? Explain.

8. WHICH ONE DOESN'T BELONG? Which inequality does *not* belong with the other three? Explain your reasoning.

$$w + \dfrac{7}{4} < \dfrac{3}{4} \qquad\qquad w - \dfrac{3}{4} > -\dfrac{7}{4}$$

$$w + \dfrac{7}{4} > \dfrac{3}{4} \qquad\qquad -\dfrac{7}{4} < w - \dfrac{3}{4}$$

SOLVING AN INEQUALITY Solve the inequality. Graph the solution.

9. $x - 4 > -6$ **10.** $z + 4.5 \leq 3.25$ **11.** $\dfrac{7}{10} > \dfrac{4}{5} + g$

12. OPEN-ENDED Write two different inequalities that can be represented using the graph. Justify your answers.

EXAMPLE 3 **Modeling Real Life**

To become an astronaut pilot for NASA, a person can be no taller than 6.25 feet. Your friend is 5 feet 9 inches tall. How much can your friend grow and still meet the requirement?

Because the height requirement is given in feet and your friend's height is given in feet and inches, rewrite your friend's height in feet.

$$9 \text{ in.} = 9 \text{ in.} \times \frac{1 \text{ ft}}{12 \text{ in.}} = \frac{9}{12} \text{ ft} = 0.75 \text{ ft}$$

$$5 \text{ ft } 9 \text{ in.} = 5 \text{ ft} + 0.75 \text{ ft} = 5.75 \text{ ft}$$

Use a verbal model to write an inequality that represents the situation.

Verbal Model	Current height (feet)	+	Amount your friend can grow (feet)	≤	Height limit (feet)

Variable   Let h be the possible amounts (in feet) your friend can grow.

Inequality   5.75   + h ≤   6.25

$$
\begin{array}{lll}
5.75 + h \leq & 6.25 & \text{Write the inequality.} \\
\underline{-5.75} & \underline{-5.75} & \text{Subtraction Property of Inequality} \\
h \leq & 0.5 & \text{Simplify.}
\end{array}
$$

▷ So, your friend can grow no more than 0.5 foot, or 6 inches.

 Self-Assessment for *Problem Solving*

Solve each exercise. Then rate your understanding of the success criteria in your journal.

13. **DIG DEEPER!** A volcanologist rappels 1200 feet into a volcano. He wants to climb out of the volcano in less than 4 hours. He climbs the first 535 feet in 100 minutes. Graph an inequality that represents the average rates at which he can climb the remaining distance and meet his goal. Justify your answer.

14. You install a mailbox by burying a post as shown. According to postal service guidelines, the bottom of the box must be at least 41 inches, but no more than 45 inches, above the road. Write and interpret two inequalities that describe the possible lengths of the post.

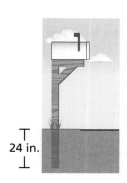

24 in.

A.5 Practice

? Go to **BigIdeasMath.com** to get HELP with solving the exercises.

▶ Review & Refresh

Write the word sentence as an inequality.

1. A number p is greater than 5.

2. A number z times 3 is at most -4.8.

3. The sum of a number n and $\frac{2}{3}$ is no less than $5\frac{1}{3}$.

Solve the equation. Check your solution.

4. $4x = 36$

5. $\frac{w}{3} = -9$

6. $-2b = 44$

7. $60 = \frac{3}{4}h$

8. Which fraction is equivalent to -2.4?

   A. $-\frac{12}{5}$

   B. $-\frac{51}{25}$

   C. $-\frac{8}{5}$

   D. $-\frac{6}{25}$

▶▶ Concepts, Skills, & Problem Solving

WRITING AN INEQUALITY Write an inequality that compares the given numbers. Does the inequality remain true when you add 2 to each side? Justify your answer. (See Exploration 1, p. 489.)

9. $-1; 4$

10. $-3; -6$

11. $-4; -1$

SOLVING AN INEQUALITY Solve the inequality. Graph the solution.

12. $x + 7 \geq 18$

13. $a - 2 > 4$

14. $3 \leq 7 + g$

15. $8 + k \leq -3$

16. $-12 < y - 6$

17. $n - 4 < 5$

18. $t - 5 \leq -7$

19. $p + \frac{1}{4} \geq 2$

20. $\frac{2}{7} > b + \frac{5}{7}$

21. $z - 4.7 \geq -1.6$

22. $-9.1 < d - 6.3$

23. $\frac{8}{5} > s + \frac{12}{5}$

24. $-\frac{7}{8} \geq m - \frac{13}{8}$

25. $r + 0.2 < -0.7$

26. $h - 6 \leq -8.4$

MP YOU BE THE TEACHER Your friend solves the inequality and graphs the solution. Is your friend correct? Explain your reasoning.

27.
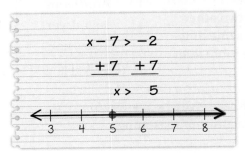

28.
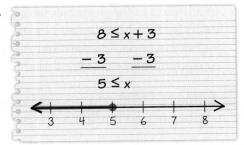

29. **MP MODELING REAL LIFE** A small airplane can hold 44 passengers. Fifteen passengers board the plane.

   a. Write and solve an inequality that represents the additional numbers of passengers that can board the plane.

   b. Can 30 more passengers board the plane? Explain.

GEOMETRY Find the possible values of x.

30. The perimeter is less than 28 feet.

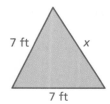

7 ft x

7 ft

31. The base is greater than the height.

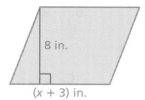

8 in.

$(x + 3)$ in.

32. The perimeter is less than or equal to 51 meters.

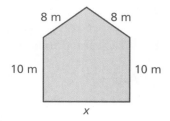

8 m   8 m

10 m   10 m

x

33. **MP REASONING** The inequality $d + s > -3$ is equivalent to $d > -7$. What is the value of s?

34. **MP LOGIC** You can spend up to $35 on a shopping trip.

   a. You want to buy a shirt that costs $14. Write and solve an inequality that represents the remaining amounts of money you can spend if you buy the shirt.

   b. You notice that the shirt is on sale for 30% off. How does this change your inequality in part (a)?

35. **DIG DEEPER!** If items plugged into a circuit use more than 2400 watts of electricity, the circuit overloads. A portable heater that uses 1050 watts of electricity is plugged into the circuit.

   a. Find the additional numbers of watts you can plug in without overloading the circuit.

   b. In addition to the portable heater, what two other items in the table can you plug in at the same time without overloading the circuit? Is there more than one possibility? Explain.

Item	Watts
Aquarium	200
Hair dryer	1200
Television	150
Vacuum cleaner	1100

36. **MP NUMBER SENSE** The possible values of x are given by $x + 8 \leq 6$. What is the greatest possible value of $7x$? Explain your reasoning.

A.6 Solving Inequalities Using Multiplication or Division

Learning Target: Write and solve inequalities using multiplication or division.

Success Criteria:
- I can apply the Multiplication and Division Properties of Inequality to produce equivalent inequalities.
- I can solve inequalities using multiplication or division.
- I can apply inequalities involving multiplication or division to solve real-life problems.

EXPLORATION 1

Writing Inequalities

Work with a partner. Use two number cubes on which the odd numbers are negative on one of the number cubes and the even numbers are negative on the other number cube.

- Roll the number cubes. Write an inequality that compares the numbers.

- Roll one of the number cubes. Multiply each side of the inequality by the number and record your result.

- Repeat the previous two steps nine more times.

a. When you multiply each side of an inequality by the same number, does the inequality remain true? Explain your reasoning.

b. When you divide each side of an inequality by the same number, does the inequality remain true? Use inequalities generated by number cubes to justify your answer.

c. Use your results in parts (a) and (b) to make a conjecture about how to solve an inequality of the form $ax < b$ for x when $a > 0$ and when $a < 0$.

Math Practice

Use Counterexamples

Use a counterexample to show that $2a \geq a$ is not true for every value of a.

 **Key Idea**

Multiplication and Division Properties of Inequality (Case 1)

Words When you multiply or divide each side of an inequality by the same *positive* number, the inequality remains true.

Numbers $\quad\quad -4 < 6$ $\quad\quad\quad\quad\quad\quad\quad\quad 4 > -6$

$\quad\quad\quad\quad 2 \cdot (-4) < 2 \cdot 6 \quad\quad\quad\quad\quad\quad \dfrac{4}{2} > \dfrac{-6}{2}$

$\quad\quad\quad\quad\quad\quad -8 < 12 \quad\quad\quad\quad\quad\quad\quad 2 > -3$

Algebra If $a < b$ and c is positive, then

$$a \cdot c < b \cdot c \quad\quad \text{and} \quad\quad \dfrac{a}{c} < \dfrac{b}{c}.$$

If $a > b$ and c is positive, then

$$a \cdot c > b \cdot c \quad\quad \text{and} \quad\quad \dfrac{a}{c} > \dfrac{b}{c}.$$

These properties are also true for $\le$ and $\ge$.

EXAMPLE 1 **Solving an Inequality Using Multiplication**

Solve $\dfrac{x}{5} \le -3$. Graph the solution.

$\dfrac{x}{5} \le -3$ $\quad\quad\quad\quad\quad$ Write the inequality.

> Undo the division. $\quad\longrightarrow\quad 5 \cdot \dfrac{x}{5} \le 5 \cdot (-3)$ $\quad\quad\quad\quad$ Multiplication Property of Inequality

$x \le -15$ $\quad\quad\quad\quad\quad$ Simplify.

▷ The solution is $x \le -15$.

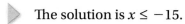

$$x \le -15$$

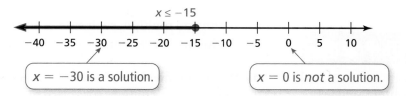

x = −30 is a solution. $\quad\quad\quad\quad\quad\quad\quad\quad$ *x* = 0 is *not* a solution.

Try It **Solve the inequality. Graph the solution.**

1. $n \div 3 < 1$ $\quad\quad\quad\quad$ **2.** $-0.5 \le \dfrac{m}{10}$ $\quad\quad\quad\quad$ **3.** $-3 > \dfrac{2}{3}p$

EXAMPLE 2 **Solving an Inequality Using Division**

Solve $6x > -18$. Graph the solution.

$6x > -18$	Write the inequality.

Undo the multiplication. ⟶ $\dfrac{6x}{6} > \dfrac{-18}{6}$ Division Property of Inequality

$x > -3$ Simplify.

▷ The solution is $x > -3$.

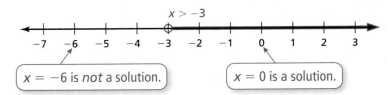

$x > -3$

$x = -6$ is *not* a solution.

$x = 0$ is a solution.

Try It Solve the inequality. Graph the solution.

4. $4b \geq 2$ **5.** $12k \leq -24$ **6.** $-15 < 2.5q$

🔑 Key Idea

Multiplication and Division Properties of Inequality (Case 2)

Words When you multiply or divide each side of an inequality by the same *negative* number, the direction of the inequality symbol must be reversed for the inequality to remain true.

Numbers $-4 < 6$ $4 > -6$

$-2 \cdot (-4) > -2 \cdot 6$ $\dfrac{4}{-2} < \dfrac{-6}{-2}$

$8 > -12$ $-2 < 3$

Algebra If $a < b$ and c is negative, then

$$a \cdot c > b \cdot c \qquad \text{and} \qquad \frac{a}{c} > \frac{b}{c}.$$

If $a > b$ and c is negative, then

$$a \cdot c < b \cdot c \qquad \text{and} \qquad \frac{a}{c} < \frac{b}{c}.$$

These properties are also true for $\leq$ and $\geq$.

Common Error

A negative sign in an inequality does not necessarily mean you must reverse the inequality symbol.

Only reverse the inequality symbol when you multiply or divide each side by a negative number.

EXAMPLE 3	Solving an Inequality Using Multiplication

Solve $-\dfrac{3}{2}n \le 6$. Graph the solution.

$$-\frac{3}{2}n \le 6$$ Write the inequality.

$$-\frac{2}{3} \cdot \left(-\frac{3}{2}n\right) \ge -\frac{2}{3} \cdot 6$$ Use the Multiplication Property of Inequality. Reverse the inequality symbol.

$$n \ge -4$$ Simplify.

Math Practice

Look for Structure
Why do you reverse the inequality symbol when solving in Example 3, but not when solving in Examples 1 and 2?

The solution is $n \ge -4$.

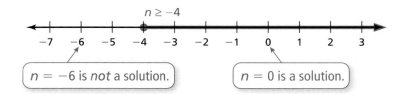

$n \ge -4$

$n = -6$ is *not* a solution.

$n = 0$ is a solution.

Try It Solve the inequality. Graph the solution.

7. $\dfrac{x}{-3} > -4$

8. $0.5 \le -\dfrac{y}{2}$

9. $-12 \ge \dfrac{6}{5}m$

10. $-\dfrac{2}{5}h \le -8$

Self-Assessment for Concepts & Skills

Solve each exercise. Then rate your understanding of the success criteria in your journal.

11. **OPEN-ENDED** Write an inequality that you can solve using the Division Property of Inequality where the direction of the inequality symbol must be reversed.

12. **MP PRECISION** Explain how solving $4x < -16$ is different from solving $-4x < 16$.

SOLVING AN INEQUALITY Solve the inequality. Graph the solution.

13. $6n < -42$

14. $4 \ge -\dfrac{g}{8}$

15. **WRITING** Are the inequalities $12c > -15$ and $4c < -5$ equivalent? Explain.

EXAMPLE 4 **Modeling Real Life**

A submersible descends 37.5 meters per minute from sea level to explore a recent shipwreck. The shipwreck rests on the ocean floor at an elevation deeper than −3810 meters, the elevation of the Titanic shipwreck. How long does it take the submersible to reach the shipwreck?

The submersible begins at sea level, where the elevation is 0 feet. Write and solve an inequality to find how long it takes to reach elevations below −3810 meters.

| **Verbal Model** | Change in elevation (meters per minute) | • | Time (minutes) | < | Elevation of Titanic (meters) |

Variable Let t be the time (in minutes) that the submersible descends.

Inequality $\qquad -37.5 \qquad \bullet \qquad t \qquad < \qquad -3810$

> The change in elevation is negative because the submersible is descending.

$$-37.5t < -3810 \qquad \text{Write the inequality.}$$

$$\frac{-37.5t}{-37.5} > \frac{-3810}{-37.5} \qquad \text{Division Property of Inequality}$$

$$t > 101.6 \qquad \text{Simplify.}$$

▷ So, the submersible takes more than 101.6 minutes, or 1 hour, 41 minutes, and 36 seconds, to reach the shipwreck.

Self-Assessment for Problem Solving

Solve each exercise. Then rate your understanding of the success criteria in your journal.

16. You want to put up a fence that encloses a triangular region with an area greater than or equal to 60 square feet. Describe the possible values of c.

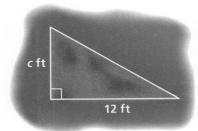

c ft

12 ft

17. A motorcycle rider travels at an average speed greater than 50 miles per hour. Write and solve an inequality to determine how long it will take the motorcycle rider to travel 375 miles. Explain your reasoning.

A.6 Practice

? Go to *BigIdeasMath.com* to get HELP with solving the exercises.

▶ Review & Refresh

Solve the inequality. Graph the solution.

1. $h + 4 < 6$

2. $c - 5 \geq 4$

3. $\dfrac{7}{10} \leq n + \dfrac{4}{5}$

Solve the equation. Check your solution.

4. $-2w + 4 = -12$

5. $\dfrac{v}{5} - 6 = 3$

6. $3(x - 1) = 18$

7. $\dfrac{m}{4} + 50 = 51$

8. What is the value of $\dfrac{2}{3} + \left(-\dfrac{5}{7}\right)$?

     A. $-\dfrac{3}{4}$ **B.** $-\dfrac{1}{21}$ **C.** $\dfrac{7}{10}$ **D.** $1\dfrac{8}{21}$

▶▶ Concepts, Skills, & Problem Solving

WRITING AN INEQUALITY Write an inequality that compares the given numbers. Does the inequality remain true when you multiply each number in the inequality by 2? by -2? Justify your answers. (See Exploration 1, p. 495.)

9. $-2; 5$

10. $4; -1$

11. $6; -3$

SOLVING AN INEQUALITY Solve the inequality. Graph the solution.

12. $2n > 20$

13. $\dfrac{c}{9} \leq -4$

14. $2.2m < 11$

15. $-16 > x \div 2$

16. $\dfrac{1}{6}w \geq 2.5$

17. $7 < 3.5k$

18. $3x \leq -\dfrac{5}{4}$

19. $4.2y \leq -12.6$

20. $11.3 > \dfrac{b}{4.3}$

21. **MP MODELING REAL LIFE** You earn $9.20 per hour at your summer job. Write and solve an inequality that represents the numbers of hours you can work to earn enough money to buy a smart phone that costs $299.

22. **DIG DEEPER!** You have $5.60 to buy avocados for a guacamole recipe. Avocados cost $1.40 each.

     a. Write and solve an inequality that represents the numbers of avocados you can buy.

     b. Are there infinitely many solutions in this context? Explain.

SOLVING AN INEQUALITY Solve the inequality. Graph the solution.

23. $-5n \leq 15$

24. $7w > -49$

25. $-\frac{1}{3}h \geq 8$

26. $-9 < -\frac{1}{5}x$

27. $-3y < -14$

28. $-2d \geq 26$

29. $-4.5 > \dfrac{m}{6}$

30. $\dfrac{k}{-0.25} \leq 36$

31. $-2.4 > \dfrac{b}{-2.5}$

MP YOU BE THE TEACHER Your friend solves the inequality. Is your friend correct? Explain your reasoning.

32.

$$\frac{x}{3} < -9$$
$$3 \cdot \frac{x}{3} > 3 \cdot (-9)$$
$$x > -27$$

33.

$$-3m \geq 9$$
$$\underline{+3m \quad +3m}$$
$$0 \geq 9 + 3m$$
$$\underline{-9 \quad -9}$$
$$-9 \geq 3m$$
$$\frac{-9}{3} \geq \frac{3m}{3}$$
$$-3 \geq m$$

WRITING AND SOLVING AN INEQUALITY Write the word sentence as an inequality. Then solve the inequality.

34. The quotient of a number g and -4 is at most 5.

35. A number p divided by 7 is less than -3.

36. Six times a number w is at least -24.

37. The product of -2 and a number x is greater than 30.

38. $\frac{3}{4}$ is greater than or equal to a number k divided by -8.

39. **MP MODELING REAL LIFE** A *cryotherapy* chamber uses extreme cold to reduce muscle soreness. A chamber is currently 0°F. The temperature in the chamber is dropping 2.5°F every second. Write and solve an inequality that represents the numbers of seconds that can pass for the temperature to drop below −20°F.

40. **MP MODELING REAL LIFE** You are moving some of your belongings into a storage facility.

a. Write and solve an inequality that represents the numbers of boxes that you can stack vertically in the storage unit.

b. Can you stack 6 boxes vertically in the storage unit? Explain.

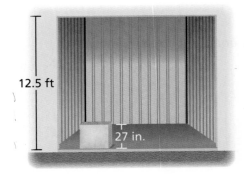

12.5 ft

27 in.

GEOMETRY Write and solve an inequality that represents *x*.

41. Area ≥ 120 cm²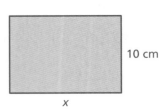

10 cm

x

42. Area < 20 ft²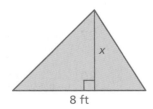

x

8 ft

43. **MP** **MODELING REAL LIFE** A device extracts no more than 37 liters of water per day from the air. How long does it take to collect at least 185 liters of water? Explain your reasoning.

44. **MP** **REASONING** Students in a science class are divided into 6 equal groups with at least 4 students in each group for a project. Describe the possible numbers of students in the class.

45. **PROJECT** Choose two novels to research.

  a. Use the Internet to complete the table below.

  b. Use the table to find and compare the average number of copies sold per month for each novel. Which novel do you consider to be the most successful? Explain.

  c. Assume each novel continues to sell at the average rate. For what numbers of months will the total number of copies sold exceed twice the current number sold for each novel?

	Author	Name of Novel	Release Date	Current Number of Copies Sold
1.				
2.				

46. **MP** **LOGIC** When you multiply or divide each side of an inequality by the same negative number, you must reverse the direction of the inequality symbol. Explain why.

MP **NUMBER SENSE** Describe all numbers that satisfy *both* inequalities. Include a graph with your description.

47. $4m > -4$ and $3m < 15$

48. $\dfrac{n}{3} \geq -4$ and $\dfrac{n}{-5} \geq 1$

49. $2x \geq -6$ and $2x \geq 6$

50. $-\dfrac{1}{2}s > -7$ and $\dfrac{1}{3}s < 12$

A.7 Solving Two-Step Inequalities

Learning Target: Write and solve two-step inequalities.

Success Criteria:
- I can apply properties of inequality to generate equivalent inequalities.
- I can solve two-step inequalities using the basic operations.
- I can apply two-step inequalities to solve real-life problems.

EXPLORATION 1

Using Algebra Tiles to Solve Inequalities

Work with a partner.

a. What is being modeled by the algebra tiles below? What is the solution?

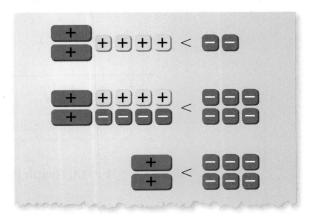

b. Use properties of inequality to solve the original inequality in part (a). How do your steps compare to the steps performed with algebra tiles?

c. Write the three inequalities modeled by the algebra tiles below. Then solve each inequality using algebra tiles. Check your answer using properties of inequality.

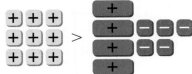

Math Practice

Consider Similar Problems

How is using algebra tiles to solve inequalities similar to using algebra tiles to solve equations?

d. Explain how solving a two-step inequality is similar to solving a two-step equation.

You can solve two-step inequalities in the same way you solve two-step equations.

EXAMPLE 1 **Solving Two-Step Inequalities**

a. **Solve $5x - 4 \geq 11$. Graph the solution.**

$5x - 4 \geq \quad 11$	Write the inequality.
Step 1: Undo the subtraction. $\rightarrow \quad \underline{+4 \quad +4}$	Addition Property of Inequality
$5x \geq \quad 15$	Simplify.
Step 2: Undo the multiplication. $\rightarrow \quad \dfrac{5x}{5} \geq \dfrac{15}{5}$	Division Property of Inequality
$x \geq 3$	Simplify.

▶ The solution is $x \geq 3$.

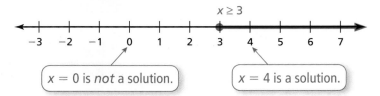

$x = 0$ is *not* a solution. $x = 4$ is a solution.

b. **Solve $\dfrac{b}{-3} + 4 < 13$. Graph the solution.**

$\dfrac{b}{-3} + 4 < \quad 13$	Write the inequality.
Step 1: Undo the addition. $\rightarrow \quad \underline{-4 \quad -4}$	Subtraction Property of Inequality
$\dfrac{b}{-3} < \quad 9$	Simplify.
Step 2: Undo the division. $\rightarrow \quad -3 \cdot \dfrac{b}{-3} > -3 \cdot 9$	Use the Multiplication Property of Inequality. Reverse the inequality symbol.
$b > -27$	Simplify.

▶ The solution is $b > -27$.

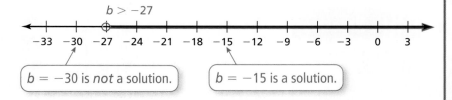

$b = -30$ is *not* a solution. $b = -15$ is a solution.

Try It **Solve the inequality. Graph the solution.**

1. $6y - 7 > 5$ **2.** $4 - 3d \geq 19$ **3.** $\dfrac{w}{-4} + 8 > 9$

EXAMPLE 2 **Graphing an Inequality**

Which graph represents the solution of $-7(x + 3) \leq 28$?

A.
```
←———+——+——+——●——+——+——+——→
  -10  -9  -8  -7  -6  -5  -4
```

B.
```
←——+——+——+——●━━+━━+━━+━━→
  -10  -9  -8  -7  -6  -5  -4
```

C.
```
←━━+━━+━━+━━●——+——+——+——→
    4   5   6   7   8   9   10
```

D.
```
←——+——+——+——●━━+━━+━━+━━→
    4   5   6   7   8   9   10
```

$-7(x + 3) \leq \quad 28$	Write the inequality.
$-7x - 21 \leq \quad 28$	Distributive Property
Step 1: Undo the subtraction. → $\quad +21 \quad +21$	Addition Property of Inequality
$-7x \leq 49$	Simplify.
Step 2: Undo the multiplication. → $\dfrac{-7x}{-7} \geq \dfrac{49}{-7}$	Use the Division Property of Inequality. Reverse the inequality symbol.
$x \geq -7$	Simplify.

▷ The correct answer is **B**.

Try It Solve the inequality. Graph the solution.

4. $2(k - 5) < 6$ **5.** $-4(n - 10) < 32$ **6.** $-3 \leq 0.5(8 + y)$

Self-Assessment for Concepts & Skills

Solve each exercise. Then rate your understanding of the success criteria in your journal.

SOLVING AN INEQUALITY Solve the inequality. Graph the solution.

7. $3d - 7 \geq 8$ **8.** $-6 > \dfrac{z}{-2} + 1$ **9.** $-6(g + 4) \leq 12$

10. **MP STRUCTURE** Describe two different ways to solve the inequality $3(a + 5) < 9$.

11. **WRITING** Are the inequalities $-6x + 18 \leq 12$ and $2x - 4 \leq -2$ equivalent? Explain.

12. **OPEN-ENDED** Write a two-step inequality that can be represented by the graph. Justify your answer.

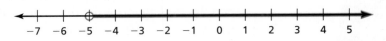
```
←——+——+——○——+——+——+——+——+——+——+——+——+——→
  -7  -6  -5  -4  -3  -2  -1   0   1   2   3   4   5
```

EXAMPLE 3 **Modeling Real Life**

A football team orders the sweatshirts shown. The price per sweatshirt decreases $0.05 for each sweatshirt that is ordered. How many sweatshirts should the team order for the price per sweatshirt to be no greater than $32.50?

Write and solve an inequality to determine how many sweatshirts the team should order for the price per sweatshirt to be no greater than $32.50.

Verbal Model	Base price (dollars)	−	Price decrease (dollars)	•	Number of sweatshirts ordered	≤	Desired price (dollars)

Variable Let n be the number of sweatshirts ordered.

Inequality	40	−	0.05	•	n	≤	32.50

$$40 - 0.05n \leq 32.50 \qquad \text{Write the inequality.}$$
$$\underline{-40} \qquad\qquad \underline{-40} \qquad \text{Subtraction Property of Inequality}$$
$$-0.05n \leq -7.50 \qquad \text{Simplify.}$$
$$\frac{-0.05n}{-0.05} \geq \frac{-7.50}{-0.05} \qquad \text{Use the Division Property of Inequality. Reverse the inequality symbol.}$$
$$n \geq 150 \qquad \text{Simplify.}$$

So, the team should order at least 150 sweatshirts for the price per sweatshirt to be no greater than $32.50.

 Self-Assessment for *Problem Solving*

Solve each exercise. Then rate your understanding of the success criteria in your journal.

13. A fair rents a thrill ride for $3000. It costs $4 to purchase a token for the ride. Write and solve an inequality to determine the numbers of ride tokens that can be sold for the fair to make a profit of at least $750.

14. **DIG DEEPER!** A theater manager predicts that 1000 tickets to a play will be sold if each ticket costs $60. The manager predicts that 20 less tickets will be sold for every $1 increase in price. For what prices can the manager predict that at least 800 tickets will be sold? Use an inequality to justify your answer.

A.7 Practice

 Go to *BigIdeasMath.com* to get HELP with solving the exercises.

▶ Review & Refresh

Solve the inequality. Graph the solution.

1. $-3x \geq 18$

2. $\frac{2}{3}d > 8$

3. $2 \geq \frac{g}{-4}$

Find the missing values in the ratio table. Then write the equivalent ratios.

4.

Flutes	7		28
Clarinets	4	12	

5.

Boys	6	3	
Girls	10		50

6. What is the volume of the cube?

A. 8 ft^3

B. 16 ft^3

C. 24 ft^3

D. 32 ft^3

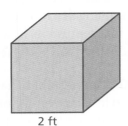

2 ft

▶▶ Concepts, Skills, & Problem Solving

USING ALGEBRA TILES Write the inequality modeled by the algebra tiles. Then solve the inequality using algebra tiles. Check your answer using properties of inequality. (See Exploration 1, p. 503.)

7.
$$\boxed{+}\ \boxed{+}\ \boxed{+} \\ \boxed{+}\ \boxed{+}\ \boxed{+} \geq \boxed{-}\ \boxed{-}\ \boxed{-} \\ \boxed{-}\ \boxed{-}\ \boxed{-}$$

8.
$$\boxed{-}\ \boxed{+} \\ \boxed{-}\ \boxed{+} > \boxed{+}\ \boxed{+}\ \boxed{+} \\ \boxed{+}\ \boxed{+}\ \boxed{+}$$

SOLVING A TWO-STEP INEQUALITY Solve the inequality. Graph the solution.

9. $8y - 5 < 3$

10. $3p + 2 \geq -10$

11. $2 > 8 - \frac{4}{3}h$

12. $-2 > \frac{m}{6} - 7$

13. $-1.2b - 5.3 \geq 1.9$

14. $-1.3 \geq 2.9 - 0.6r$

15. $5(g + 4) > 15$

16. $4(w - 6) \leq -12$

17. $-8 \leq \frac{2}{5}(k - 2)$

18. $-\frac{1}{4}(d + 1) < 2$

19. $7.2 > 0.9(n + 8.6)$

20. $20 \geq -3.2(c - 4.3)$

MP YOU BE THE TEACHER Your friend solves the inequality. Is your friend correct? Explain your reasoning.

21.

$$\frac{x}{3} + 4 < 6$$
$$x + 4 < 18$$
$$x < 14$$

22.

$$3(w - 2) \geq 10$$
$$3w \geq 12$$
$$w \geq 4$$

23. **(MP) MODELING REAL LIFE** The first jump in a unicycle high-jump contest is shown. The bar is raised 2 centimeters after each jump. Solve the inequality $2n + 10 \geq 26$ to find the numbers of additional jumps needed to meet or exceed the goal of clearing a height of 26 centimeters.

10 cm

SOLVING AN INEQUALITY Solve the inequality. Graph the solution.

24. $9x - 4x + 4 \geq 36 - 12$

25. $3d - 7d + 2.8 < 5.8 - 27$

26. **(MP) MODELING REAL LIFE** A cave explorer is at an elevation of -38 feet. The explorer starts moving at a rate of -12 feet per minute. Write and solve an inequality that represents how long it will take the explorer to reach an elevation deeper than -200 feet.

27. **CRITICAL THINKING** A contestant in a weight-loss competition wants to lose an average of at least 8 pounds per month during a five-month period. Based on the progress report, how many pounds must the contestant lose in the fifth month to meet the goal?

Progress Report	
Month	Pounds Lost
1	12
2	9
3	5
4	8

28. **(MP) REASONING** A student theater charges $8.50 per ticket.

 a. The theater has already sold 70 tickets. How many more tickets does the theater need to sell to earn at least $750?

 b. The theater increases the ticket price by $1. Without solving an inequality, describe how this affects the total number of tickets needed to earn at least $750. Explain your reasoning.

29. **DIG DEEPER!** A zoo does not have room to add any more tigers to an enclosure. According to regulations, the area of the enclosure must increase by 150 square feet for each tiger that is added. The zoo is able to enlarge the 450 square foot enclosure for a total area no greater than 1000 square feet.

 a. Write and solve an inequality that represents this situation.

 b. Describe the possible numbers of tigers that can be added to the enclosure. Explain your reasoning.

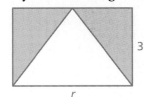

30. **GEOMETRY** For what values of r will the area of the shaded region be greater than or equal to 12 square units?

Using the Problem-Solving Plan

1. Fencing costs $7 per foot. You install x feet of the fencing along one side of a property, as shown. The property has an area of 15,750 square feet. What is the total cost of the fence?

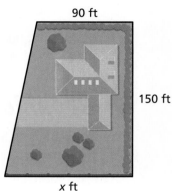

90 ft

150 ft

x ft

Understand the problem.

You know the area, height, and one base length of the trapezoid-shaped property. You are asked to find the cost of x feet of fencing, given that the fencing costs $7 per foot.

Make a plan.

Use the formula for the area of a trapezoid to find the length of fencing that you buy. Then multiply the length of fencing by $7 to find the total cost.

Solve and check.

Use the plan to solve the problem. Then check your solution.

2. A pool is in the shape of a rectangular prism with a length of 15 feet, a width of 10 feet, and a depth of 4 feet. The pool is filled with water at a rate no faster than 3 cubic feet per minute. How long does it take to fill the pool?

3. The table shows your scores on 9 out of 10 quizzes that are each worth 20 points. What score do you need on the final quiz to have a mean score of at least 17 points?

Quiz Scores				
15	14	16	19	18
19	20	15	16	?

Performance Task

Distance and Brightness of the Stars

At the beginning of this chapter, you watched a STEAM Video called "Space Cadets." You are now ready to complete the performance task related to this video, available at *BigIdeasMath.com*. Be sure to use the problem-solving plan as you work through the performance task.

▶ Review Vocabulary

Write the definition and give an example of each vocabulary term.

equivalent equations, *p. 466*   solution of an inequality,   solution set, *p. 484*
inequality, *p. 484*   *p. 484*   graph of an inequality, *p. 486*

▶ Graphic Organizers

You can use a **Summary Triangle** to explain a concept. Here is an example of a Summary Triangle for *Addition Property of Equality*.

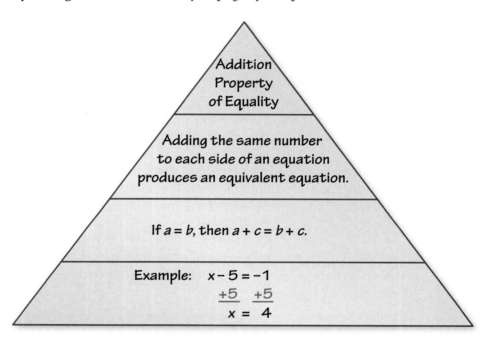

Choose and complete a graphic organizer to help you study the concept.

1. equivalent equations

2. Subtraction Property of Equality

3. Multiplication Property of Equality

4. Division Property of Equality

5. graphing inequalities

6. Addition and Subtraction Properties of Inequality

7. Multiplication and Division Properties of Inequality

"I finished my Summary Triangle about characteristics of hyenas."

▶ Chapter Self-Assessment

As you complete the exercises, use the scale below to rate your understanding of the success criteria in your journal.

1	**2**	**3**	**4**
I do not understand.	I can do it with help.	I can do it on my own.	I can teach someone else.

A.1 Solving Equations Using Addition or Subtraction *(pp. 465–470)*

Learning Target: Write and solve equations using addition or subtraction.

Solve the equation. Check your solution.

1. $p - 3 = -4$
2. $6 + q = 1$
3. $-2 + j = -22$
4. $b - 19 = -11$
5. $n + \dfrac{3}{4} = \dfrac{1}{4}$
6. $v - \dfrac{5}{6} = -\dfrac{7}{8}$
7. $t - 3.7 = 1.2$
8. $\ell + 15.2 = -4.5$

9. Write the word sentence as an equation. Then solve the equation.

   5 more than a number x is -4.

10. The perimeter of the trapezoid-shaped window frame is 23.59 feet. Write and solve an equation to find the unknown side length (in feet).

11. You are 5 years older than your cousin. How old is your cousin when you are 12 years old? Justify your answer.

A.2 Solving Equations Using Multiplication or Division *(pp. 471–476)*

Learning Target: Write and solve equations using multiplication or division.

Solve the equation. Check your solution.

12. $\dfrac{x}{3} = -8$
13. $-7 = \dfrac{y}{7}$
14. $-\dfrac{z}{4} = -\dfrac{3}{4}$
15. $-\dfrac{w}{20} = -2.5$
16. $4x = -8$
17. $-10 = 2y$
18. $-5.4z = -32.4$
19. $-6.8w = 3.4$

20. Write "3 times a number y is -42" as an equation. Then solve the equation.

21. The mean temperature change is $-3.2°F$ per day for 5 days. Write and solve an equation to find the total change over the 5-day period.

22. Describe a real-life situation that can be modeled by $7x = 1.75$.

A.3 Solving Two-Step Equations (pp. 477–482)

Learning Target: Write and solve two-step equations.

Solve the equation. Check your solution.

23. $-2c + 6 = -8$

24. $5 - 4t = 6$

25. $-3x - 4.6 = 5.9$

26. $\dfrac{w}{6} + \dfrac{5}{8} = -1\dfrac{3}{8}$

27. $3(3w - 4) = -20$

28. $-6y + 8y = -24$

29. The floor of a canyon has an elevation of -14.5 feet. Erosion causes the elevation to change by -1.5 feet per year. How many years will it take for the canyon floor to reach an elevation of -31 feet? Justify your solution.

A.4 Writing and Graphing Inequalities (pp. 483–488)

Learning Target: Write inequalities and represent solutions of inequalities on number lines.

Write the word sentence as an inequality.

30. A number w is greater than -3.

31. A number y minus $\dfrac{1}{2}$ is no more than $-\dfrac{3}{2}$.

Tell whether the given value is a solution of the inequality.

32. $5 + j > 8; j = 7$

33. $6 \div n \le -5; n = -3$

34. $7p \ge p - 12; p = -2$

Graph the inequality on a number line.

35. $q > -1.3$

36. $s < 1\dfrac{3}{4}$

37. The Enhanced Fujita scale rates the intensity of tornadoes based on wind speed and damage caused. An EF5 tornado is estimated to have wind speeds greater than 200 miles per hour. Write and graph an inequality that represents this situation.

A.5 Solving Inequalities Using Addition or Subtraction (pp. 489–494)

Learning Target: Write and solve inequalities using addition or subtraction.

Solve the inequality. Graph the solution.

38. $d + 12 < 19$

39. $t - 4 \le -14$

40. $-8 \le z + 6.4$

41. A small cruise ship can hold up to 500 people. There are 115 crew members on board the ship.

    a. Write and solve an inequality that represents the additional numbers of people that can board the ship.

    b. Can 385 more people board the ship? Explain.

42. Write an inequality that can be solved using the Subtraction Property of Inequality and has a solution of all numbers less than -3.

A.6 Solving Inequalities Using Multiplication or Division *(pp. 495–502)*

Learning Target: Write and solve inequalities using multiplication or division.

Solve the inequality. Graph the solution.

43. $6q < -18$

44. $-\dfrac{r}{3} \le 6$

45. $-4 > -\dfrac{4}{3}s$

46. Write the word sentence as an inequality. Then solve the inequality.

    The product of -3 and a number p is greater than 21.

47. You are organizing books on a shelf. Each book has a width of $\dfrac{3}{4}$ inch. Write and solve an inequality for the numbers of books b that can fit on the shelf.

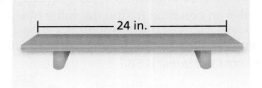

24 in.

A.7 Solving Two-Step Inequalities *(pp. 503–508)*

Learning Target: Write and solve two-step inequalities.

Solve the inequality. Graph the solution.

48. $3x + 4 > 16$

49. $\dfrac{z}{-2} - 6 \le -2$

50. $-2t - 5 < 9$

51. $7(q + 2) < -77$

52. $-\dfrac{1}{3}(p + 9) \le 4$

53. $1.2(j + 3.5) \ge 4.8$

54. Your goal is to raise at least $50 in a charity fundraiser. You earn $3.50 for each candle sold. You also receive a $15 donation. Write and solve an inequality that represents the numbers of candles you must sell to reach your goal.

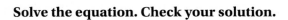

A Practice Test

Solve the equation. Check your solution.

1. $7x = -3$

2. $2(x + 1) = -2$

3. $\frac{2}{9}g = -8$

4. $z + 14.5 = 5.4$

5. $-14 = c - 10$

6. $\frac{2}{7}k - \frac{3}{8} = -\frac{19}{8}$

Write the word sentence as an inequality.

7. A number k plus 19.5 is less than or equal to 40.

8. A number q multiplied by $\frac{1}{4}$ is greater than -16.

Tell whether the given value is a solution of the inequality.

9. $n - 3 \leq 4; n = 7$

10. $-\frac{3}{7}m < 1 + m; m = -7$

Solve the inequality. Graph the solution.

11. $x - 4 > -6$

12. $-\frac{2}{9} + y \leq \frac{5}{9}$

13. $-6z \geq 36$

14. $-5.2 \geq \frac{p}{4}$

15. $4k - 8 \geq 20$

16. $-0.6 > -0.3(d + 6)$

17. You lose 0.3 point for stepping out of bounds during a gymnastics floor routine. Your final score is 9.124. Write and solve an equation to find your score without the penalty.

18. Half the area of the rectangle shown is 24 square inches. Write and solve an equation to find the value of x.

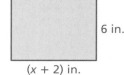

6 in.

$(x + 2)$ in.

19. You can spend no more than $100 on a party you are hosting. The cost per guest is $8.

    a. Write and solve an inequality that represents the numbers of guests you can invite to the party.

    b. What is the greatest number of guests that you can invite to the party? Explain your reasoning.

20. You have $30 to buy baseball cards. Each pack of cards costs $5. Write and solve an inequality that represents the numbers of packs of baseball cards you can buy and still have at least $10 left.

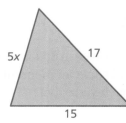

5x

17

15

21. The sum of the lengths of any two sides of a triangle is greater than the length of the third side.

    a. Write and solve three inequalities for the previous statement using the triangle shown.

    b. What values for x make sense?

1. Which equation represents the word sentence?

> The quotient of a number b and 0.3 equals negative 10.

A. $0.3b = 10$

B. $\dfrac{b}{0.3} = -10$

C. $\dfrac{0.3}{b} = -10$

D. $\dfrac{b}{0.3} = 10$

2. What is the value of the expression?

$$-\dfrac{3}{8} \cdot \dfrac{2}{5}$$

F. $-\dfrac{20}{3}$

G. $-\dfrac{16}{15}$

H. $-\dfrac{15}{16}$

I. $-\dfrac{3}{20}$

3. Which graph represents the inequality?

$$\dfrac{x}{-4} - 8 \geq -9$$

A.

B.

C.

D.

4. Which equation is equivalent to $-\dfrac{3}{4}x + \dfrac{1}{8} = -\dfrac{3}{8}$?

F. $-\dfrac{3}{4}x = -\dfrac{3}{8} - \dfrac{1}{8}$

G. $-\dfrac{3}{4}x = -\dfrac{3}{8} + \dfrac{1}{8}$

H. $x + \dfrac{1}{8} = -\dfrac{3}{8} \cdot \left(-\dfrac{4}{3}\right)$

I. $x + \dfrac{1}{8} = -\dfrac{3}{8} \cdot \left(-\dfrac{3}{4}\right)$

5. What is the decimal form of $2\dfrac{5}{8}$?

6. What is the value of the expression when $x = -5$, $y = 3$, and $z = -1$?

$$\frac{x^2 - 3y}{z}$$

A. -34 **B.** -16

C. 16 **D.** 34

7. Which expression is equivalent to $9h - 6 + 7h - 5$?

F. $3h + 2$ **G.** $16h + 1$

H. $2h - 1$ **I.** $16h - 11$

8. Your friend solved the equation $-96 = -6(x - 15)$.

$$-96 = -6(x - 15)$$
$$-96 = -6x - 90$$
$$-96 + 90 = -6x - 90 + 90$$
$$-6 = -6x$$
$$\frac{-6}{-6} = \frac{-6x}{-6}$$
$$1 = x$$

What should your friend do to correct her error?

A. First add 6 to both sides of the equation.

B. First subtract x from both sides of the equation.

C. Distribute the -6 to get $6x - 90$.

D. Distribute the -6 to get $-6x + 90$.

9. Which expression does *not* represent the perimeter of the rectangle?

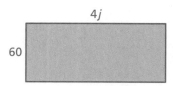

F. $4j(60)$ **G.** $8j + 120$

H. $2(4j + 60)$ **I.** $8(j + 15)$

10. What is the value of the expression?

$$\frac{5}{12} - \frac{7}{8}$$

11. You are selling T-shirts to raise money for a charity. You sell the T-shirts for $10 each.

Part A   You have already sold 2 T-shirts. How many more T-shirts must you sell to raise at least $500? Explain.

Part B   Your friend is raising money for the same charity and has not sold any T-shirts previously. He sells the T-shirts for $8 each. What are the total numbers of T-shirts he can sell to raise at least $500? Explain.

Part C   Who has to sell more T-shirts in total? How many more? Explain.

12. Which expression has the same value as $-\frac{2}{3} - \left(-\frac{4}{9}\right)$?

A. $-\frac{1}{3} + \frac{1}{9}$ **B.** $-\frac{2}{3} \times \left(-\frac{1}{3}\right)$

C. $-\frac{1}{3} - \frac{7}{9}$ **D.** $\frac{3}{2} \div \left(-\frac{1}{3}\right)$

13. You recycle $(6c + 10)$ water bottles. Your friend recycles twice as many water bottles as you recycle. Which expression represents the amount of water bottles your friend recycles?

F. $3c + 5$ **G.** $12c + 10$

H. $12c + 20$ **I.** $6c + 12$

14. What is the value of the expression?

$$-\frac{4}{5} + \left(-\frac{2}{3}\right)$$

A. $-\frac{22}{15}$ **B.** $-\frac{2}{15}$

C. $\frac{2}{15}$ **D.** $\frac{8}{15}$

B Probability

Chapter Learning Target:
Understand probability.

Chapter Success Criteria:
- ☐ I can identify the possible outcomes of a situation.
- ☐ I can explain the meaning of experimental and theoretical probability.
- ■ I can make predictions using probabilities.
- ■ I can solve real-life problems using probability.

THROW!

STEAM Video: "Massively Multiplayer Rock Paper Scissors"

Massively Multiplayer Rock Paper Scissors

You can use *experimental probability* to describe the percent of times that you win, lose, or tie in Rock Paper Scissors. Describe a real-life situation where it is helpful to describe the percent of times that a particular outcome occurs.

Watch the STEAM Video "Massively Multiplayer Rock Paper Scissors." Then answer the following questions.

Rock

Paper

Scissors

1. The table shows the ways that you can win, lose, or tie in Rock Paper Scissors. You and your opponent throw the signs for rock, paper, or scissors at random. What percent of the time do you expect to win? lose? tie?

		Your Throw		
		Rock	**Paper**	**Scissors**
Opponent's Throw	**Rock**	tie	win	lose
	Paper	lose	tie	win
	Scissors	win	lose	tie

2. You play Rock Paper Scissors 15 times. About how many times do you expect to win? Explain your reasoning.

Fair and Unfair Carnival Games

After completing this chapter, you will be able to use the concepts you learned to answer the questions in the *STEAM Video Performance Task.*

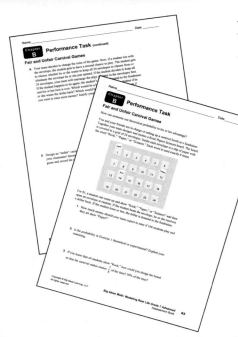

You will be given information about a version of Rock Paper Scissors used at a carnival. Then you will be asked to design your own "unfair" carnival game using a spinner or a number cube, and test your game with a classmate.

In what ways can a game of chance be considered fair? unfair? Explain your reasoning.

Getting Ready for Chapter

Chapter Exploration

Work with a partner.

1. Play Rock Paper Scissors 30 times. Tally your results in the table.

2. How many possible results are there?

3. Of the possible results, in how many ways can Player A win? In how many ways can Player B win? In how many ways can there be a tie?

4. Is one of the players more likely to win than the other player? Explain your reasoning.

GAME RULES
Rock **breaks** scissors.
Paper **covers** rock.
Scissors **cut** paper.

		Player A		
		Rock	Paper	Scissors
Player B	Rock			
	Paper			
	Scissors			

Vocabulary

The following vocabulary terms are defined in this chapter. Think about what each term might mean and record your thoughts.

probability	theoretical probability	simulation
relative frequency	sample space	
experimental probability	compound event	

B.1 Probability

Learning Target: Understand how the probability of an event indicates its likelihood.

Success Criteria:
- I can identify possible outcomes of an experiment.
- I can use probability and relative frequency to describe the likelihood of an event.
- I can use relative frequency to make predictions.

EXPLORATION 1

Determining Likelihood

Work with a partner. Use the spinners shown.

Spinner 1   Spinner 2

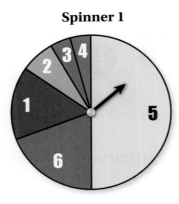 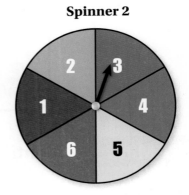

a. For each spinner, determine which numbers you are more likely to spin and which numbers you are less likely to spin. Explain your reasoning.

b. Spin each spinner 20 times and record your results in two tables. Do the data support your answers in part (a)? Explain why or why not.

Math Practice

Recognize Usefulness of Tools

How does organizing the data in tables help you to interpret the results?

Spinner 1	
Number	Frequency
1	
2	
3	
4	
5	
6	

Spinner 2	
Number	Frequency
1	
2	
3	
4	
5	
6	

c. How can you use percents to describe the likelihood of spinning each number? Explain.

Key Vocabulary 🔊
experiment, *p. 522*
outcomes, *p. 522*
event, *p. 522*
favorable outcomes,
    p. 522
probability, *p. 523*
relative frequency,
    p. 524

🔑 *Key Idea*

Outcomes and Events

An **experiment** is an investigation or a procedure that has varying results. The possible results of an experiment are called **outcomes**. A collection of one or more outcomes is an **event**. The outcomes of a specific event are called **favorable outcomes**.

For example, randomly choosing a marble from a group of marbles is an experiment. Each marble in the group is an outcome. Selecting a green marble from the group is an event.

Possible outcomes

Event: Choosing a green marble
Number of favorable outcomes: 2

EXAMPLE 1 **Identifying Outcomes**

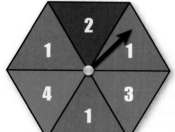

You spin the spinner.

a. **How many possible outcomes are there?**

The possible outcomes are spinning a 1, 2, 1, 3, 1, or 4. So, there are six possible outcomes.

b. **What are the favorable outcomes of spinning an even number?**

The favorable outcomes of spinning an even number are 2 and 4.

even	*not* even
2, 4	1, 1, 3, 1

c. **In how many ways can spinning a number less than 2 occur?**

The possible outcomes of spinning a number less than 2 are 1, 1, and 1. So, spinning a number less than 2 can occur in 3 ways.

less than 2	*not* less than 2
1, 1, 1	2, 3, 4

Try It

1. You randomly choose one of the tiles shown from a hat.

   a. How many possible outcomes are there?

   b. What are the favorable outcomes of choosing a vowel?

   c. In how many ways can choosing a consonant occur?

 **Key Idea**

Probability

The **probability** of an event is a number that represents the likelihood that the event will occur. Probabilities are between 0 and 1, including 0 and 1. The diagram relates likelihoods (above the diagram) and probabilities (below the diagram).

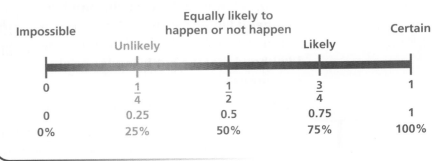

> Probabilities can be written as fractions, decimals, or percents.

EXAMPLE 2 **Describing Likelihood**

There is an 80% chance of rain, a 50% chance of thunderstorms, and a 15% chance of hail tomorrow. Describe the likelihood of each event.

a. **There is rain tomorrow.**

  The probability of rain tomorrow is 80%.

  ▶ Because 80% is close to 75%, it is *likely* that there will be rain tomorrow.

b. **There are thunderstorms tomorrow.**

  The probability of thunderstorms tomorrow is 50%.

  ▶ Because the probability is 50%, thunderstorms are *equally likely to happen or not happen*.

c. **There is hail tomorrow.**

  The probability of hail tomorrow is 15%.

  ▶ Because 15% is between 0% and 25%, it is *unlikely* that there will be hail tomorrow.

Try It **Describe the likelihood of the event given its probability.**

  2. The probability that you land a jump on a snowboard is $\frac{1}{10}$.

  3. There is a 100% chance that the temperature will be less than 120°F tomorrow.

Relative frequency is a measure of probability.

When you conduct an experiment, the **relative frequency** of an event is the fraction or percent of the time that the event occurs.

$$\text{relative frequency} = \frac{\text{number of times the event occurs}}{\text{total number of times you conduct the experiment}}$$

EXAMPLE 3 **Using Relative Frequencies**

You flip a bottle and record the number of times it lands upright and the number of times it lands on its side. Describe the likelihood that the bottle lands upright on your next flip.

Upright	||
Side	JHT JHT JHT JHT III

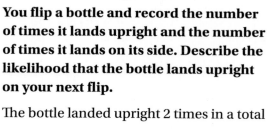

The bottle landed upright 2 times in a total of 25 flips.

$$\text{relative frequency} = \frac{\text{number of times the event occurs}}{\text{total number of times you conduct the experiment}}$$

$$= \frac{2}{25}$$

The bottle landed upright 2 times.

There was a total of 25 flips.

▷ The relative frequency is $\frac{2}{25}$, or 8%. So, it is unlikely that the bottle lands upright.

Try It

Shots Made	JHT IIII
Shots Missed	JHT I

4. You attempt three-point shots on a basketball court and record the number of made and missed shots. Describe the likelihood of each event.

   a. You make your next shot.   b. You miss your next shot.

 Self-Assessment for Concepts & Skills

Solve each exercise. Then rate your understanding of the success criteria in your journal.

5. **IDENTIFYING OUTCOMES** You roll a number cube. What are the possible outcomes?

6. **USING RELATIVE FREQUENCIES** A bag contains only red marbles and blue marbles. You randomly draw a marble from the bag and replace it. The table shows the results of repeating this experiment. Find the likelihood of each event.

Red	JHT JHT JHT JHT I
Blue	JHT JHT JHT JHT I

   a. The next marble you choose is red.

   b. The next marble you choose is neither red nor blue.

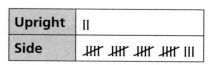

EXAMPLE 4 **Modeling Real Life**

Each turn in a game, you randomly draw a token from a bag and replace it. The table shows the number of times you draw each type of token. How many times can you expect to draw a positive point value in 35 turns?

Token	Frequency
+3 points	卌 卌
+1 point	卌 II
−2 points	III

Understand the problem.

You are given the number of times that you draw each type of token from a bag. You are asked to determine the number of times you can expect to draw a positive point value in 35 turns.

Make a plan.

Find the relative frequency of drawing a positive point value. Then use the relative frequency and the percent equation to answer the question.

Solve and check.

The favorable outcomes of drawing a positive point value are drawing a +3 token or a +1 token. So, the relative frequency of drawing a positive point value is $\frac{10 + 7}{20} = \frac{17}{20}$, or 85%.

Check Reasonableness
The table shows that positive point values are drawn 17 of 20 times. So, in 35 turns, you can expect to draw positive point values less than $17 \times 2 = 34$ times. ✓

To determine the number of times you can expect to draw a positive point value, answer the question "What is 85% of 35?"

$a = p\% \cdot w$ Write percent equation.

$= 0.85 \cdot 35$ Substitute 0.85 for $p\%$ and 35 for w.

$= 29.75$ Multiply.

You can expect to draw a positive point value about 30 times.

 Self-Assessment *for Problem Solving*

Solve each exercise. Then rate your understanding of the success criteria in your journal.

7. The table shows the number of days you have a pop quiz and the number of days you do not have a pop quiz in three weeks of school. How many days can you expect to have a pop quiz during a 180-day school year? Explain.

Pop Quiz	No Pop Quiz
II	卌 卌 III

8. In a football game, the teams pass the ball on 40% of the plays. Of the passes thrown, greater than 75% are completed. You watch the film of a randomly chosen play. Describe the likelihood that the play results in a complete pass. Explain your reasoning.

B.1 Practice

Go to *BigIdeasMath.com* to get HELP with solving the exercises.

▶ Review & Refresh

An account earns simple interest. Find the interest earned.

1. $700 at 3% for 4 years
2. $650 at 2% for 6 years
3. $480 at 1.5% for 5 years
4. $1200 at 2.8% for 30 months

Write the indicated ratio. Then find and interpret the value of the ratio.

5. rolled oats : chopped peanuts
6. sunflower seeds to pumpkin seeds
7. pumpkin seeds : rolled oats

Granola	
(dry ingredients)	
rolled oats	2 cups
chopped peanuts	1/2 cup
sunflower seeds	1/3 cup
pumpkin seeds	1/4 cup

Solve the inequality. Graph the solution.

8. $x + 5 < 9$
9. $b - 2 \geq -7$
10. $1 > -\dfrac{w}{3}$
11. $6 \leq -2g$

▶▶ Concepts, Skills, & Problem Solving

DETERMINING LIKELIHOOD Determine which numbers you are more likely to spin and which numbers you are less likely to spin. Explain your reasoning. (See Exploration 1, p. 521.)

12.
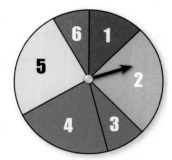

13.
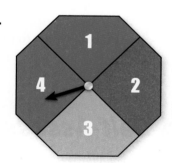

IDENTIFYING OUTCOMES You spin the spinner shown.

14. How many possible outcomes are there?

15. What are the favorable outcomes of spinning a number no greater than 3?

16. In how many ways can spinning an even number occur?

17. In how many ways can spinning a prime number occur?

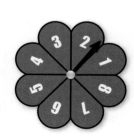

IDENTIFYING OUTCOMES You randomly choose one marble from the bag. (a) Find the number of ways the event can occur. (b) Find the favorable outcomes of the event.

18. Choosing blue

19. Choosing green

20. Choosing purple

21. Choosing yellow

22. Choosing *not* red

23. Choosing *not* blue

24. **MP** **YOU BE THE TEACHER** Your friend finds the number of ways that choosing *not* purple can occur. Is your friend correct? Explain your reasoning.

purple	*not* purple
purple	red, blue, green, yellow

Choosing not purple can occur in 4 ways.

CRITICAL THINKING Tell whether the statement is *true* or *false*. If it is false, change the italicized word to make the statement true.

25. Spinning blue and spinning *green* have the same number of favorable outcomes on Spinner A.

26. There are *three* possible outcomes of spinning Spinner A.

27. Spinning *red* can occur in four ways on Spinner B.

28. Spinning not green can occur in *three* ways on Spinner B.

Spinner A

Spinner B

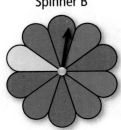

DESCRIBING LIKELIHOOD Describe the likelihood of the event given its probability.

29. Your soccer team wins $\frac{3}{4}$ of the time.

30. There is a 0% chance that you will grow 12 feet.

31. The probability that the sun rises tomorrow is 1.

32. It rains on $\frac{1}{5}$ of the days in June.

33. **MP** **MODELING REAL LIFE** You have a 50% chance of being chosen to explain a math problem in front of the class. Describe the likelihood that you are chosen.

34. **MP** **MODELING REAL LIFE** You roll a number cube and record the number of times you roll an even number and the number of times you roll an odd number. Describe the likelihood of each event.

Even	ЖЖ ЖЖ ЖЖ ЖЖ ЖЖ I
Odd	ЖЖ ЖЖ ЖЖ ЖЖ IIII

a. You roll an even number on your next roll.

b. You roll an odd number on your next roll.

35. MP REASONING You want to determine whether a coin is *fair*. You flip the coin and record the number of times you flip heads and the number of times you flip tails.

Heads	⊮ ⊮ ⊮ ⊮ II
Tails	III

   a. Describe the likelihood that you flip heads on your next flip.

   b. Describe the likelihood that you flip tails on your next flip.

   c. Do you think the coin is a *fair* coin? Explain.

Win	⊮ I
Lose	⊮ ⊮ ⊮
Free Turn	IIII

36. MP LOGIC At a carnival, each guest randomly chooses 1 of 50 rubber ducks and then replaces it. The table shows the numbers of each type of duck that have been drawn so far. Out of 150 draws, how many can you expect to *not* be a losing duck? Justify your answer.

37. CRITICAL THINKING A dodecahedron has twelve sides numbered 1 through 12. Describe the likelihood that each event will occur when you roll the dodecahedron. Explain your reasoning.

   a. rolling a 1

   b. rolling a multiple of 3

   c. rolling a number greater than 6

38. DIG DEEPER! A bargain bin contains classical CDs and rock CDs. There are 60 CDs in the bin. Choosing a rock CD and *not* choosing a rock CD have the same number of favorable outcomes. How many rock CDs are in the bin?

39. MP REASONING You randomly choose one of the cards and set it aside. Then you randomly choose a second card. Describe how the number of possible outcomes changes after the first card is chosen.

MP STRUCTURE A Punnett square is a grid used to show possible gene combinations for the offspring of two parents. In the Punnett square shown, a boy is represented by *XY*. A girl is represented by *XX*.

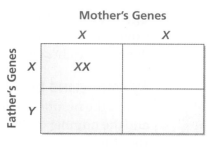

40. Complete the Punnett square. Explain why the events "having a boy" and "having a girl" are equally likely.

41. Two parents each have the gene combination *Cs*. The gene *C* is for curly hair. The gene *s* is for straight hair. Any gene combination that includes a *C* results in curly hair. When all outcomes are equally likely, what is the probability of a child having curly hair?

B.2 Experimental and Theoretical Probability

Learning Target: Develop probability models using experimental and theoretical probability.

Success Criteria:
- I can explain the meanings of experimental probability and theoretical probability.
- I can find experimental and theoretical probabilities.
- I can use probability to make predictions.

EXPLORATION 1

Conducting Experiments

Work with a partner. Conduct the following experiments and find the relative frequencies.

Experiment 1

- Flip a quarter 25 times and record whether each flip lands heads up or tails up.

Experiment 2

- Toss a thumbtack onto a table 25 times and record whether each toss lands point up or on its side.

a. Combine your results with those of your classmates. Do the relative frequencies change? What do you notice?

b. Everyone in your school conducts each experiment and you combine the results. How do you expect the relative frequencies to change? Explain.

c. How many times in 1000 flips do you expect a quarter to land heads up? How many times in 1000 tosses do you expect a thumbtack to land point up? Explain your reasoning.

d. In a *uniform probability model,* each outcome is equally likely to occur. Can you use a uniform probability model to describe either experiment? Explain.

Math Practice

Use Definitions
You know the number of possible outcomes in a uniform probability model. Can you find the probability of each outcome? Explain your reasoning.

Key Vocabulary
experimental
   probability, p. 530
theoretical
   probability, p. 530

Key Idea

Experimental Probability

Probability that is based on repeated trials of an experiment is called **experimental probability**.

$$P(\text{event}) = \frac{\text{number of times the event occurs}}{\text{total number of trials}}$$

EXAMPLE 1 **Finding an Experimental Probability**

Heads	Tails
6	19

The table shows the results of spinning a penny 25 times. What is the experimental probability of spinning heads?

Heads was spun 6 times in a total of $6 + 19 = 25$ spins.

$$P(\text{event}) = \frac{\text{number of times the event occurs}}{\text{total number of trials}}$$

Experimental probabilities are found the same way as relative frequencies.

$$P(\text{heads}) = \frac{6}{25}$$
Heads was spun 6 times.
There was a total of 25 spins.

▶ The experimental probability is $\frac{6}{25}$, 0.24, or 24%.

Try It The table shows the results of rolling a number cube 50 times. Find the experimental probability of the event.

Number Rolled	1	2	3	4	5	6
Frequency	10	4	8	11	11	6

1. rolling a 3   **2.** rolling an odd number

 Key Idea

Theoretical Probability

When all possible outcomes are equally likely, the **theoretical probability** of an event is the quotient of the number of favorable outcomes and the number of possible outcomes.

$$P(\text{event}) = \frac{\text{number of favorable outcomes}}{\text{number of possible outcomes}}$$

EXAMPLE 2 **Finding a Theoretical Probability**

You randomly choose one of the letters shown. What is the theoretical probability of choosing a vowel?

$$P(\text{vowel}) = \frac{\text{number of favorable outcomes}}{\text{number of possible outcomes}} = \frac{3}{7}$$

There are 3 vowels.

There is a total of 7 letters.

▷ The probability of choosing a vowel is $\frac{3}{7}$, or about 43%.

Try It

3. What is the theoretical probability of randomly choosing an X?

EXAMPLE 3 **Comparing Probabilities**

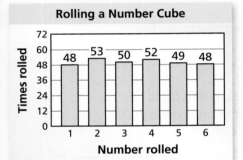

Rolling a Number Cube

The bar graph shows the results of rolling a number cube 300 times. How does the experimental probability of rolling an odd number compare with the theoretical probability?

Step 1: Find the experimental probability of rolling an odd number.

The bar graph shows 48 ones, 50 threes, and 49 fives. So, an odd number was rolled $48 + 50 + 49 = 147$ times in a total of 300 rolls.

$$P(\text{odd}) = \frac{\text{number of times an odd number was rolled}}{\text{total number of rolls}}$$

$$= \frac{147}{300}$$

$$= \frac{49}{100}, \text{ or } 49\%$$

In general, as the number of trials increases, the experimental probability gets closer to the theoretical probability.

Step 2: Find the theoretical probability of rolling an odd number.

$$P(\text{odd}) = \frac{\text{number of favorable outcomes}}{\text{number of possible outcomes}} = \frac{3}{6} = \frac{1}{2}, \text{ or } 50\%$$

▷ The experimental probability of rolling an odd number is 49%, which is close to the theoretical probability of 50%.

Try It

4. How does the experimental probability of rolling a number greater than 1 compare with the theoretical probability?

EXAMPLE 4 **Using an Experimental Probability**

Color	Frequency
Blue	3
Green	12
Red	9
Yellow	6

A bag contains 50 marbles. You randomly draw a marble from the bag, record its color, and then replace it. The table shows the results after 30 draws. Predict the number of red marbles in the bag.

Find the experimental probability of drawing a red marble.

$$P(\text{event}) = \frac{\text{number of times the event occurs}}{\text{total number of trials}}$$

$$P(\text{red}) = \frac{9}{30} = \frac{3}{10}$$

> You draw red 9 times.

> You draw a total of 30 marbles.

To make a prediction, multiply the probability of drawing red by the total number of marbles in the bag.

$$\frac{3}{10} \cdot 50 = 15$$

▷ So, you can predict that there are 15 red marbles in the bag.

Try It

5. An inspector randomly selects 200 pairs of jeans and finds 5 defective pairs. About how many pairs of jeans do you expect to be defective in a shipment of 5000?

Self-Assessment for Concepts & Skills

Solve each exercise. Then rate your understanding of the success criteria in your journal.

6. VOCABULARY Explain what it means for an event to have a theoretical probability of 0.25 and an experimental probability of 0.3.

7. DIFFERENT WORDS, SAME QUESTION You flip a coin and record the results in the table. Which is different? Find "both" answers.

Heads	Tails
32	28

> What is the experimental probability of flipping heads?

> What fraction of the flips can you expect a result of heads?

> What percent of the flips result in heads?

> What is the relative frequency of flipping heads?

532   Chapter B   Probability

EXAMPLE 5 **Modeling Real Life**

The theoretical probability of winning a bobblehead when spinning a prize wheel is $\frac{1}{6}$. The wheel has 18 sections.

a. How many sections have a bobblehead as a prize?

Use the equation for theoretical probability.

$$P(\text{bobblehead}) = \frac{\text{number of bobblehead sections}}{\text{total number of sections}}$$

$\frac{1}{6} = \frac{s}{18}$ Substitute. Let s be the number of bobblehead sections.

$3 = s$ Multiply each side by 18.

▷ So, 3 sections have a bobblehead as a prize.

b. The prize wheel is spun 540 times. About how many bobbleheads do you expect to be won?

To make a prediction, multiply the probability of winning a bobblehead by the total number of times the wheel is spun.

$\frac{1}{6} \cdot 540 = 90$

▷ So, you can predict about 90 bobbleheads will be won.

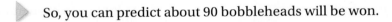

Self-Assessment for Problem Solving

Solve each exercise. Then rate your understanding of the success criteria in your journal.

Ticket	Frequency
Win	2
Lose	29
Draw again	9

8. Contestants randomly draw a ticket from a hat and replace it. The table shows the results after 40 draws. There are 7 winning tickets in the hat. Predict the total number of tickets in the hat. Explain.

9. **DIG DEEPER!** You randomly choose two different songs on a music playlist that has 80 songs. The probability that the first song is a hip-hop song is 45%. The first song you choose is a hip-hop song. What is the probability that the second song is also a hip-hop song? Explain your reasoning.

B.2 Practice

Go to *BigIdeasMath.com* to get HELP with solving the exercises.

▶ Review & Refresh

Describe the likelihood of the event given its probability.

1. You randomly guess the correct answer of a multiple choice question $\frac{1}{4}$ of the time.

2. There is a 95% chance that school will *not* be cancelled tomorrow.

Find the annual interest rate.

3. $I = \$16$, $P = \$200$, $t = 2$ years

4. $I = \$26.25$, $P = \$500$, $t = 18$ months

Tell whether x and y are proportional.

5.

x	1	3	9
y	8	24	75

6.

x	0.75	1.5	2.25
y	0.3	0.6	0.9

▶▶ Concepts, Skills, & Problem Solving

CONDUCTING AN EXPERIMENT Use the bar graph below to find the relative frequency of the event. (See Exploration 1, p. 529.)

7. spinning a 6

8. spinning an even number

FINDING AN EXPERIMENTAL PROBABILITY
Use the bar graph to find the experimental probability of the event.

9. spinning a number less than 3

10. *not* spinning a 1

11. spinning a 1 or a 3

12. spinning a 7

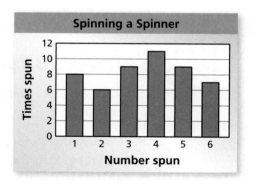

There are 6 possible outcomes. So, the experimental probability of spinning a 4 is $\frac{1}{6}$.

13. **MP YOU BE THE TEACHER** Your friend uses the bar graph above to find the experimental probability of spinning a 4. Is your friend correct? Explain your reasoning.

14. **MP MODELING REAL LIFE** You check 20 laser pointers at random. Three of the laser pointers are defective. What is the experimental probability that a laser pointer is defective?

FINDING A THEORETICAL PROBABILITY **Use the spinner to find the theoretical probability of the event.**

15. spinning red

16. spinning a 1

17. spinning an odd number

18. spinning a multiple of 2

19. spinning a number less than 7

20. spinning a 9

21. **(MP) REASONING** Each letter of the alphabet is printed on an index card. What is the theoretical probability of randomly choosing any letter except Z?

COMPARING PROBABILITIES **The bar graph shows the results of spinning the spinner below 200 times. Compare the theoretical and experimental probabilities of the event.**

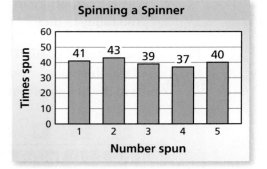

22. spinning a 4

23. spinning a 3

24. spinning a number greater than 4

25. spinning an odd number

26. **(MP) REASONING** Should you use *theoretical* or *experimental* probability to predict the number of times you will spin a 3 in 10,000 spins? Explain.

27. **(MP) MODELING REAL LIFE** A board game uses a bag of 105 lettered tiles. You randomly choose a tile and then return it to the bag. The table shows the number of vowels and the number of consonants after 50 draws. Predict the number of vowels in the bag.

Vowel	Consonant
卌 卌 卌 III	卌 卌 卌 卌 卌 卌 II

28. **(MP) MODELING REAL LIFE** On a game show, a contestant randomly draws a chip from a bag and replaces it. Each chip says either *win* or *lose*. The theoretical probability of drawing a winning chip is $\frac{3}{10}$. The bag contains 9 winning chips.

    a. How many chips are in the bag?

    b. Out of 20 contestants, how many do you expect to draw a winning chip?

29. **(MP) PROBLEM SOLVING** There are 8 females and 10 males in a class.

    a. What is the theoretical probability that a randomly chosen student is female?

    b. One week later, there are 27 students in the class. The theoretical probability that a randomly chosen student is a female is the same as last week. How many males joined the class?

30. **MP NUMBER SENSE** The table at the right shows the results of flipping two coins 12 times each.

HH	HT	TH	TT
2	6	3	1

    a. What is the experimental probability of flipping two tails? Using this probability, how many times can you expect to flip two tails in 600 trials?

HH	HT	TH	TT
23	29	26	22

    b. The table at the left shows the results of flipping the same two coins 100 times each. What is the experimental probability of flipping two tails? Using this probability, how many times can you expect to flip two tails in 600 trials?

    c. Why is it important to use a large number of trials when using experimental probability to predict results?

31. **COMPARING PROBABILITIES** The table shows the possible outcomes of rolling a pair of number cubes. You roll a pair of number cubes 60 times and record your results in the bar graph shown.

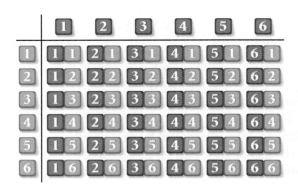

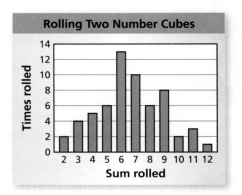

    a. Compare the theoretical and experimental probabilities of rolling each sum.

    b. Which sum do you expect to be most likely after 500 trials? 1000 trials? Explain your reasoning.

    c. Predict the experimental probability of rolling each sum after 10,000 trials. Explain your reasoning.

32. **PROJECT** When you toss a paper cup into the air, there are three ways for the cup to land: *open-end up, open-end down,* or *on its side.*

    a. Toss a paper cup 100 times and record your results. Do the outcomes for tossing the cup appear to be equally likely? Explain.

    b. Predict the number of times each outcome will occur in 1000 tosses. Explain your reasoning.

    c. Suppose you tape a quarter to the bottom of the cup. Do you think the cup will be *more likely* or *less likely* to land open-end up? Justify your answer.

B.3 Compound Events

Learning Target: Find sample spaces and probabilities of compound events.

Success Criteria:
- I can find the sample space of two or more events.
- I can find the total number of possible outcomes of two or more events.
- I can find probabilities of compound events.

EXPLORATION 1

Comparing Combination Locks

Work with a partner. You are buying a combination lock. You have three choices.

a. One lock has 3 wheels. Each wheel is numbered from 0 to 9. How many possible outcomes are there for each wheel? How many possible combinations are there?

b. How can you use the number of possible outcomes on each wheel to determine the number of possible combinations?

c. Another lock has one wheel numbered from 0 to 39. Each combination uses a sequence of three numbers. How many possible combinations are there?

Math Practice

View as Components

What is the number of possible outcomes for each wheel of the lock? Explain.

d. Another lock has 4 wheels as described. How many possible combinations are there?

Wheel 1: 0–9
Wheel 2: A–J
Wheel 3: K–T
Wheel 4: 0–9

e. For which lock are you least likely to guess the combination? Why?

The set of all possible outcomes of one or more events is called the **sample space**. You can use tables and tree diagrams to find the sample space of two or more events.

EXAMPLE 1 **Finding a Sample Space**

Key Vocabulary 🔊
sample space, *p. 538*
Fundamental
  Counting Principle,
  p. 538
compound event,
  p. 540

You randomly choose a bread and type of sandwich. Find the sample space. How many different sandwiches are possible?

Use a tree diagram to find the sample space.

Bread	Type	Outcome
Wheat	Ham	Wheat Ham
	Turkey	Wheat Turkey
	Steak	Wheat Steak
	Chicken	Wheat Chicken
Sourdough	Ham	Sourdough Ham
	Turkey	Sourdough Turkey
	Steak	Sourdough Steak
	Chicken	Sourdough Chicken

Bread
• Wheat
• Sourdough

Type
• Ham
• Turkey
• Steak
• Chicken

> There are 8 different outcomes in the sample space. So, there are 8 different sandwiches possible.

Try It

1. **WHAT IF?** The sandwich shop adds a multi-grain bread. Find the sample space. How many sandwiches are possible?

You can use the sample space or the **Fundamental Counting Principle** to find the total number of possible outcomes of two or more events.

The Fundamental Counting Principle can be extended to more than two events.

 Key Idea

Fundamental Counting Principle

An event M has m possible outcomes. An event N has n possible outcomes. The total number of outcomes of event M followed by event N is $m \times n$.

🔊 Multi-Language Glossary at *BigIdeasMath.com*

EXAMPLE 2 **Finding the Total Number of Possible Outcomes**

Find the total number of possible outcomes of rolling a number cube and flipping a coin.

Method 1: Use a table to find the sample space. Let H = heads and T = tails.

	1	2	3	4	5	6
(coin heads)	1H	2H	3H	4H	5H	6H
(coin tails)	1T	2T	3T	4T	5T	6T

▷ There are 12 possible outcomes.

Method 2: Use the Fundamental Counting Principle. Identify the number of possible outcomes of each event.

Event 1: Rolling a number cube has 6 possible outcomes.

Event 2: Flipping a coin has 2 possible outcomes.

$$6 \times 2 = 12 \qquad \text{Fundamental Counting Principle}$$

▷ There are 12 possible outcomes.

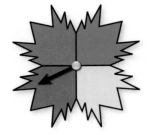

Try It

2. Find the total number of possible outcomes of spinning the spinner and randomly choosing a number from 1 to 5.

EXAMPLE 3 **Finding the Total Number of Possible Outcomes**

How many different outfits can you make from the T-shirts, jeans, and shoes in the closet?

Use the Fundamental Counting Principle. Identify the number of possible outcomes for each event.

Event 1: Choosing a T-shirt has 7 possible outcomes.

Event 2: Choosing jeans has 4 possible outcomes.

Event 3: Choosing shoes has 3 possible outcomes.

$$7 \times 4 \times 3 = 84 \qquad \text{Fundamental Counting Principle}$$

▷ So, you can make 84 different outfits.

Try It

3. How many different outfits can you make from 4 T-shirts, 5 pairs of jeans, and 5 pairs of shoes?

A **compound event** consists of two or more events. As with a single event, the probability of a compound event is the quotient of the number of favorable outcomes and the number of possible outcomes.

EXAMPLE 4 **Finding the Probability of a Compound Event**

In Example 2, what is the probability of rolling a number greater than 4 and flipping tails?

There are two favorable outcomes in the sample space for rolling a number greater than 4 and flipping tails: 5T and 6T.

$$P(\text{event}) = \frac{\text{number of favorable outcomes}}{\text{number of possible outcomes}}$$

$$P(\text{greater than 4 and tails}) = \frac{2}{12} \qquad \text{Substitute.}$$

$$= \frac{1}{6} \qquad \text{Simplify.}$$

The probability is $\frac{1}{6}$, or $16\frac{2}{3}\%$.

Try It

4. In Example 2, what is the probability of rolling at most 4 and flipping heads?

Self-Assessment for Concepts & Skills

Solve each exercise. Then rate your understanding of the success criteria in your journal.

Flower
- Daffodil
- Hyacinth
- Tulip

Ornament
- Figurine
- Trophy

5. **FINDING THE SAMPLE SPACE** You randomly choose a flower and ornament for a display case. Find the sample space. How many different displays are possible?

6. **FINDING THE TOTAL NUMBER OF POSSIBLE OUTCOMES** You randomly choose a number from 1 to 5 and a letter from A to D. Find the total number of possible outcomes.

7. **WHICH ONE DOESN'T BELONG?** You roll a number cube and flip a coin. Which probability does *not* belong with the other three? Explain your reasoning.

$P(\text{less than 2 and heads})$ $P(\text{greater than 2 and tails})$

$P(\text{less than 2 and tails})$ $P(\text{greater than 5 and heads})$

EXAMPLE 5 Modeling Real Life

On a game show, you choose one box from each pair of boxes shown. In each pair, one box contains a prize and the other does not. What is the probability of winning at least one prize?

Choice 1

Use a tree diagram to find the sample space. Let P = prize and N = no prize. Circle the outcomes in which you win 1, 2, or 3 prizes.

Choice 2

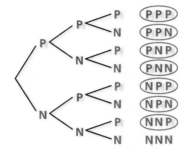

Choice 3

There are seven favorable outcomes in the sample space for winning at least one prize.

$$P(\text{event}) = \frac{\text{number of favorable outcomes}}{\text{number of possible outcomes}}$$

$P(\text{at least one prize}) = \dfrac{7}{8}$ \qquad Substitute.

▷ The probability of winning at least one prize is $\dfrac{7}{8}$, or 87.5%.

 Self-Assessment for Problem Solving

Solve each exercise. Then rate your understanding of the success criteria in your journal.

8. A tour guide organizes vacation packages at a beachside town. There are 7 hotels, 5 cabins, 4 meal plans, 3 escape rooms, and 2 amusement parks. The tour guide chooses either a hotel or a cabin and then selects one of each of the remaining options. Find the total number of possible vacation packages.

9. **DIG DEEPER!** A fitness club with 100 members offers one free training session per member in either running, swimming, or weightlifting. Thirty of the fitness center members sign up for the free session. The running and swimming sessions are each twice as popular as the weightlifting session. What is the probability that a randomly chosen fitness club member signs up for a free running session?

Go to *BigIdeasMath.com* to get HELP with solving the exercises.

▶ Review & Refresh

Use the bar graph to find the experimental probability of the event.

1. rolling a 5

2. rolling a 2 or 6

3. rolling at least a 3

4. rolling a number less than or equal to 4

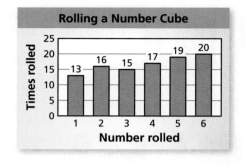

Find the product.

5. $3 \cdot 2$

6. $5(-3)$

7. $-6(-2)$

▶▶ Concepts, Skills, & Problem Solving

COMPARING PASSWORDS Determine which password is less likely to be guessed. (See Exploration 1, p. 537.)

8. a password with 3 numbers or a password with 3 capital letters

9. a password with 6 numbers or a password with 4 capital letters

USING A TREE DIAGRAM Use a tree diagram to find the sample space and the total number of possible outcomes.

10.

Birthday Party	
Activity	Miniature golf, Laser tag, Roller skating
Time	1:00 P.M.–3:00 P.M., 6:00 P.M.–8:00 P.M.

11.

New School Mascot	
Type	Lion, Bear, Hawk, Dragon
Style	Realistic, Cartoon

12.

Party Favor	
Item	Keychain, Magnet
Color	Blue, Green , Red

13.

Fidget Toy	
Type	Cube, Necklace, Spinner
Frame	Metal, Plastic, Rubber

14. **⟨MP⟩ YOU BE THE TEACHER** Your friend finds the total number of ways that you can answer a quiz with five true-false questions. Is your friend correct? Explain your reasoning.

> $2 + 2 + 2 + 2 + 2 = 10$
>
> You can answer the quiz in 10 different ways.

USING THE FUNDAMENTAL COUNTING PRINCIPLE Use the Fundamental
Counting Principle to find the total number of possible outcomes.

15.

Beverage	
Size	Small, Medium, Large
Flavor	Orange juice, Apple juice, Lemonade, Milk

16.

Fitness Tracker	
Battery	1 day, 3 days, 5 days, 7 days
Color	Silver, Green, Blue, Pink, Black

17.

Clown	
Suit	Dotted, Striped, Checkered
Wig	Single color, Multicolor
Talent	Balloon animals, Juggling, Unicycle, Magic

18.

Meal	
Appetizer	Soup, Spinach dip, Salad
Entrée	Chicken, Beef, Spaghetti, Fish
Dessert	Yogurt, Fruit, Rice pudding

19. **(MP) CHOOSE TOOLS** You randomly choose one of
the marbles. Without replacing the first marble, you
choose a second marble.

 a. Name two ways you can find the total number of
 possible outcomes.

 b. Find the total number of possible outcomes.

20. **FINDING A PROBABILITY** You roll two number cubes. What is the probability
 of rolling double threes?

FINDING THE PROBABILITY OF A COMPOUND EVENT You spin the spinner and
flip a coin. Find the probability of the compound event.

21. spinning a 1 and flipping heads

22. spinning an even number and flipping heads

23. spinning a number less than 3 and flipping tails

24. spinning a 6 and flipping tails

25. *not* spinning a 5 and flipping heads

26. spinning a prime number and *not* flipping heads

FINDING THE PROBABILITY OF A COMPOUND EVENT You spin the spinner, flip a coin,
and then spin the spinner again. Find the probability of the compound event.

27. spinning blue, flipping heads, then spinning a 1

28. spinning an odd number, flipping heads, then spinning yellow

29. spinning an even number, flipping tails, then spinning
 an odd number

30. *not* spinning red, flipping tails, then *not* spinning an even number

31. **MP REASONING** You randomly guess the answers to two questions on a multiple-choice test. Each question has three choices: A, B, and C.

    a. What is the probability that you guess the correct answers to both questions?

    b. Suppose you can eliminate one of the choices for each question. How does this change the probability that both of your guesses are correct?

32. **MP REASONING** You forget the last two digits of your cell phone password.

    a. What is the probability that you randomly choose the correct digits?

    b. Suppose you remember that both digits are even. How does this change the probability that you choose the correct digits?

33. **MP MODELING REAL LIFE** A combination lock has 3 wheels, each numbered from 0 to 9. You try to guess the combination by writing five different numbers from 0 to 999 on a piece of paper. Find the probability that the correct combination is written on the paper.

34. **MP MODELING REAL LIFE** A train has one engine and six train cars. Find the total number of ways an engineer can arrange the train. (The engine must be first.)

35. **MP REPEATED REASONING** You have been assigned a nine-digit identification number.

    a. Should you use the Fundamental Counting Principle or a tree diagram to find the total number of possible identification numbers? Explain.

    b. How many identification numbers are possible?

    c. **RESEARCH** Use the Internet to find out why the possible number of Social Security numbers is not the same as your answer to part (b).

36. **DIG DEEPER!** A social media account password includes a number from 0 to 9, an uppercase letter, a lowercase letter, and a special character, in that order.

    a. There are 223,080 password combinations. How many special characters are there?

    b. What is the probability of guessing the account password if you know the number and uppercase letter, but forget the rest?

37. **MP PROBLEM SOLVING** From a group of 5 scientists, an environmental committee of 3 people is selected. How many different committees are possible?

B.4 Simulations

Learning Target: Design and use simulations to find probabilities of compound events.

Success Criteria:
- I can design a simulation to model a real-life situation.
- I can recognize favorable outcomes in a simulation.
- I can use simulations to find experimental probabilities.

EXPLORATION 1

Using a Simulation

Work with a partner. A basketball player makes 80% of her free throw attempts.

a. Is she likely to make at least two of her next three free throws? Explain your reasoning.

b. The table shows 30 randomly generated numbers from 0 to 999. Let each number represent three shots. How can you use the digits of these numbers to represent made shots and missed shots?

838	617	282	341	785
747	332	279	082	716
937	308	800	994	689
198	025	853	591	813
672	289	518	649	540
865	631	227	004	840

c. Use the table to estimate the probability that of her next three free throws, she makes

- exactly two free throws.

- at most one free throw.

- at least two free throws.

- at least two free throws in a row.

Math Practice

Choose Tools
What tools can you use to randomly generate data?

d. The experiment used in parts (b) and (c) is called a *simulation*. Another player makes $\frac{3}{5}$ of her free throws. Describe a simulation that can be used to estimate the probability that she makes three of her next four free throws.

A **simulation** is an experiment that is designed to reproduce the conditions of a situation or process. Simulations allow you to study situations that are impractical to create in real life.

EXAMPLE 1 **Simulating Outcomes That Are Equally Likely**

A dog has three puppies. The gender of each puppy is equally likely.

a. **Design a simulation involving 20 trials that you can use to model the genders of the puppies.**

Choose an experiment that has two equally likely outcomes for each event (gender), such as flipping three coins. Let heads (H) represent a male and tails (T) represent a female.

Math Practice

Communicate Precisely
Describe a simulation involving a number cube that you can use to find the probability in part (b).

b. **Use your simulation to find the experimental probability that all three puppies are males.**

To find the experimental probability, perform 20 trials of the simulation. The table shows the results. Find the number of outcomes that represent 3 males, HHH.

HTH	HTT	HTT	HTH	HTT
TTT	HTT	HHH	TTT	HTT
HTH	HTT	HHH	HTH	HTT
HTT	HTH	TTT	HTT	HTH

HHH occurred 2 times.

$$P(\text{three males}) = \frac{2}{20} = \frac{1}{10}$$

There is a total of 20 trials.

▷ The experimental probability is $\frac{1}{10}$, 0.1, or 10%.

Try It

1. You randomly guess the answers to four true-false questions.

 a. Design a simulation that you can use to model the answers.

 b. Use your simulation to find the experimental probability that you answer all four questions correctly.

EXAMPLE 2 **Simulating Outcomes That Are Not Equally Likely**

You have a 60% chance of winning a board game and a 20% chance of winning a card game. Design and use a simulation involving 50 randomly generated numbers to estimate the probability of winning both games.

Use a simulation with randomly generated numbers from 0 to 99. Let the digits 1 through 6 in the tens place represent winning the board game. Let the digits 1 and 2 in the ones place represent winning the card game.

Use the random number generator on a graphing calculator to generate the numbers. The table shows the results. Find the number of outcomes that represent winning both games.

> The digits 1–6 and 1–2 are chosen because they have a 60% and 20% chance of being randomly generated for each digit.

```
randInt(0,99,50)
{52 66 73 68 75...
```

(52)	66	73	68	75	28	35	47	48	02
16	68	49	03	77	35	92	78	06	06
58	18	89	39	24	80	(32)	(41)	77	(21)
(32)	40	96	59	86	01	(12)	00	94	73
40	71	28	(61)	01	24	37	25	03	25

$$P(\text{win both games}) = \frac{7}{50}$$

> 7 numbers meet the criteria.

> There is a total of 50 trials.

▶ The experimental probability is $\frac{7}{50}$, 0.14, or 14%.

Try It

2. A baseball team wins 70% of the time. Design and use a simulation to estimate the probability that the team wins the next three games.

Self-Assessment for Concepts & Skills

Solve each exercise. Then rate your understanding of the success criteria in your journal.

3. **SIMULATING OUTCOMES** Four multiple-choice questions on a quiz each have five answer choices. You randomly guess the answer to each question. Design and use a simulation to find the experimental probability that you answer all of the questions correctly.

4. **SIMULATING OUTCOMES** You select a marble from a bag and a chip from a box. You have a 20% chance of choosing a green marble and a 90% chance of choosing a red chip. Estimate the probability that you choose a green marble and a red chip.

EXAMPLE 3 **Modeling Real Life**

Each school year, there is a 40% chance that weather causes one or more days of school to be canceled. Estimate the probability that weather causes a cancellation at least 3 years in a row in the next 4 years.

Use a simulation involving 50 randomly generated four-digit numbers to estimate the probability. Let the digits 1 through 4 represent years with a cancellation.

Use a random number table in a spreadsheet to generate the numbers. The spreadsheet shows the results. Find the number of outcomes in which the digits 1 through 4 occur at least three times in a row.

To create a four-digit random number table in a spreadsheet, enter

=INT(RAND()*10000)

into each cell.

	A	B	C	D	E	F
1	6527	4621	7810	3510	1408	
2	8141	0676	2535	8172	4095	
3	3450	7780	6435	8672	7537	
4	5063	1925	5137	9485	9437	
5	3299	2364	8034	8063	1323	
6	2556	1519	2735	2796	3987	
7	3771	7417	9177	4308	2723	
8	7593	7289	5091	0351	2179	
9	1479	0511	4550	8242	9407	
10	6910	8079	6142	6823	6138	
11						

$$P\left(\begin{array}{l}\text{cancellation at least 3 years}\\ \text{in a row in the next 4 years}\end{array}\right) = \frac{4}{50} = \frac{2}{25}$$

4 numbers meet the criteria.

There is a total of 50 trials.

▷ The experimental probability is $\frac{2}{25}$, 0.08, or 8%.

 Self-Assessment for Problem Solving

Solve each exercise. Then rate your understanding of the success criteria in your journal.

5. Each day there is a 50% chance that your tablet overheats. Estimate the probability that your tablet overheats on exactly 2 of the next 3 days.

6. **DIG DEEPER!** The probability that a homeowner needs a plumber this year is 22%. The probability that the homeowner needs a septic tank specialist is 14%. Estimate the probability that the homeowner needs a plumber, but not a septic tank specialist.

B.4 Practice

 Go to *BigIdeasMath.com* to get HELP with solving the exercises.

▶ Review & Refresh

You flip a coin and roll the 20-sided figure. Find the probability of the compound event.

1. Flipping tails and rolling at least a 14

2. Flipping heads and rolling less than 3

Simplify the expression.

3. $5(a - 2)$

4. $-7(1 + 3x)$

5. $-1(3p - 8)$

▶▶ Concepts, Skills, & Problem Solving

USING A SIMULATION A medicine is effective for 80% of patients. The table shows 30 randomly generated numbers from 0 to 999. Use the table to estimate the probability of the event. (See Exploration 1, p. 545.)

463	013	231	898	139
365	492	565	188	465
438	751	961	646	598
045	241	940	901	467
151	774	538	380	509
251	924	401	549	859

6. The medicine is effective on each of three patients.

7. The medicine is effective on fewer than two of the next three patients.

SIMULATING OUTCOMES Design and use a simulation to find the experimental probability.

8. In your indoor garden, 50% of seeds sprout. What is the experimental probability that at least one of your next three seeds sprouts?

9. An archer hits a target 50% of the time. What is the experimental probability that the archer hits the target exactly four of the next five times?

10. A bank randomly selects one of four free gifts to send to each new customer. Gifts include a calculator, a keychain, a notepad, and a pen. What is the experimental probability that the next two new customers both receive calculators? that neither receives a calculator?

11. Employees spin a reward wheel. The wheel is equally likely to stop on each of six rewards labeled A–F. What is the experimental probability that fewer than two of the next three spins land on reward A?

USING NUMBER CUBES Design and use a simulation with number cubes to estimate the probability.

12. Your lawn mower does not start on the first try $\frac{1}{6}$ of the time. Estimate the probability that your lawn mower will not start on the first try exactly one of the next two times you mow the lawn.

13. An application on your phone correctly identifies four out of every six songs. Estimate the probability that at least three of the next four songs are correctly identified.

SIMULATING OUTCOMES Design and use a simulation to find the experimental probability.

14. Two beakers are used in a lab test. What is the experimental probability that there are reactions in both beakers during the lab test?

Probability of Reaction	
Beaker 1	80%
Beaker 2	50%

15. You use a stain remover on two separate stains on a shirt. What is the experimental probability that the stain remover removes both the mud stain and the food stain?

Probability of Stain Removal	
Mud	90%
Food	80%

16. **DIG DEEPER!** The probability that a computer crashes one or more times in a month is 10%. Estimate the probability that the computer crashes at least one or more times per month for two months in a row during the first half of the year.

17. **MP MODELING REAL LIFE** You visit an orchard. The probability that you randomly select a ripe apple is 92%. The probability that you randomly select a ripe cherry is 86%. Estimate the probability that you pick an apple that is ripe and a cherry that is not ripe.

18. **CRITICAL THINKING** You use a simulation to find an experimental probability. How does the experimental probability compare to the theoretical probability as the number of trials increases?

19. **MP LOGIC** At a restaurant, 30% of customers donate to charity in exchange for a coupon. Estimate the probability that it will take at least four customers to find one who donates.

Connecting Concepts

▶ *Using the Problem-Solving Plan*

1. In an Internet contest, gift cards and bicycles are given as prizes in the ratio 9 : 1. Estimate the probability that at least two of three randomly selected winners receive bicycles.

Understand the problem. You know the ratio of gift cards to bicycles awarded in the contest. You want to find the probability that at least two of three randomly selected winners receive bicycles.

Make a plan. Use the ratio to find the theoretical probability that a randomly selected winner receives a bicycle. Then use a simulation involving 50 randomly generated three-digit numbers to estimate the probability that at least two of three randomly selected winners receive bicycles.

Solve and check. Use the plan to solve the problem. Then check your solution.

2. A board game uses the spinner shown.

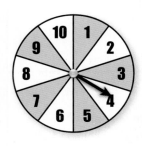

   a. Use theoretical probability to predict the number of times you will spin a number greater than or equal to 8 in 30 spins.

   b. You play the game and record the results of 30 spins. Find the percent error of your prediction in part (a).

Number Spun	1	2	3	4	5	6	7	8	9	10
Frequency	2	2	3	1	3	3	4	3	4	5

3. The tiles shown are placed in a bag. You randomly select one of the tiles, return it to the bag, and then randomly select another tile. What is the probability that the product of the numbers on the tiles selected is greater than zero? Justify your answer.

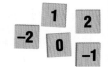

Performance Task

Fair and Unfair Carnival Games

At the beginning of this chapter, you watched a STEAM Video called "Massively Multiplayer Rock Paper Scissors." You are now ready to complete the performance task related to this video, available at *BigIdeasMath.com*. Be sure to use the problem-solving plan as you work through the performance task.

▶ Review Vocabulary

Write the definition and give an example of each vocabulary term.

experiment, *p. 522*
outcomes, *p. 522*
event, *p. 522*
favorable outcomes, *p. 522*
probability, *p. 523*

relative frequency, *p. 524*
experimental probability,
  p. 530
theoretical probability, *p. 530*
sample space, *p. 538*

Fundamental Counting
  Principle, *p. 538*
compound event, *p. 540*
simulation, *p. 546*

▶ Graphic Organizers

You can use a **Four Square** to organize information about a concept. Each of the four squares can be a category, such as definition, vocabulary, example, non-example, words, algebra, table, numbers, visual, graph, or equation. Here is an example of a Four Square for *probability*.

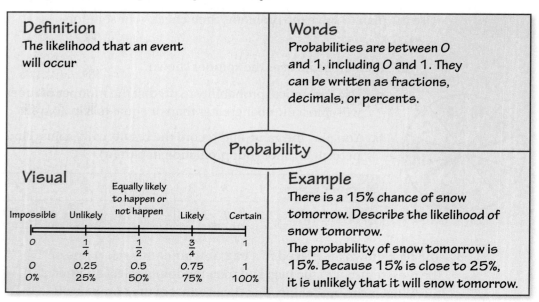

Choose and complete a graphic organizer to help you study the concept.

1. favorable outcomes

2. relative frequency

3. experimental probability

4. theoretical probability

5. Fundamental Counting Principle

6. compound event

7. simulation

"My **Four Square** shows that my new red skateboard is faster than my old blue skateboard."

▶ Chapter Self-Assessment

As you complete the exercises, use the scale below to rate your understanding of the success criteria in your journal.

1	**2**	**3**	**4**
I do not understand.	I can do it with help.	I can do it on my own.	I can teach someone else.

B.1 Probability *(pp. 521–528)*

Learning Target: Understand how the probability of an event indicates its likelihood.

You randomly choose one toy race car.

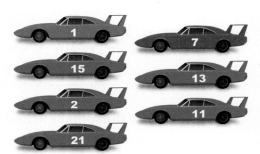

1. How many possible outcomes are there?

2. What are the favorable outcomes of choosing a car that is *not* green?

3. In how many ways can choosing a green car occur?

You spin the spinner. (a) Find the number of ways the event can occur. (b) Find the favorable outcomes of the event.

4. spinning a 1

5. spinning a 3

6. spinning an odd number

7. spinning an even number

8. spinning a number greater than 0

9. spinning a number less than 3

Describe the likelihood of the event given its probability.

10. There is a 0% chance of snow in July for Florida.

11. The probability that you are called on to answer a question in class is $\frac{1}{25}$.

12. There is an 85% chance the bus is on time.

13. The probability of flipping heads on a coin is 0.5.

14. During a basketball game, you record the number of rebounds from missed shots for each team. (a) Describe the likelihood that your team rebounds the next missed shot. (b) How many rebounds should your team expect to have in 15 missed shots?

Your Team	ЖІІ II
Opposing Team	III

B.2   Experimental and Theoretical Probability   (pp. 529–536)

Learning Target: Develop probability models using experimental and theoretical probability.

The bar graph shows the results of spinning a spinner 100 times. Use the bar graph to find the experimental probability of the event.

15. spinning a 2

16. spinning an even number

17. *not* spinning a 5

18. spinning a number less than 3

19. In Exercise 16, how does the experimental probability of spinning an even number compare with the theoretical probability?

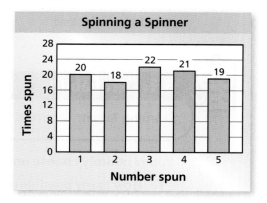

Use the spinner to find the theoretical probability of the event.

20. spinning blue

21. spinning a 1

22. spinning an even number

23. spinning a 4

24. The theoretical probability of choosing a red grape from a bag of grapes is $\frac{2}{9}$. There are 8 red grapes in the bag. How many grapes are in the bag?

25. The theoretical probability of choosing Event A is $\frac{2}{7}$. What is the theoretical probability of *not* choosing Event A? Explain your reasoning.

B.3   Compound Events   (pp. 537–544)

Learning Target: Find sample spaces and probabilities of compound events.

26. You have 6 bracelets and 15 necklaces. Find the number of ways you can wear one bracelet and one necklace.

27. Use a tree diagram to find how many different home theater systems you can make from 6 DVD players, 8 TVs, and 3 brands of speakers.

28. A red, green, and blue book are on a shelf. You randomly pick one of the books. Without replacing the first book, you choose another book. What is the probability that you picked the red and blue book?

29. You flip two coins and roll a number cube. What is the probability of flipping two tails and rolling an even number?

30. Describe a compound event that has a probability between 50% and 80%.

31. Your science teacher sets up six flasks. Two of the flasks contain water and four of the flasks contain hydrogen peroxide. A reaction occurs when you add yeast to hydrogen peroxide. You add yeast to two of the flasks. What is the probability that at least one reaction will occur?

B.4 Simulations *(pp. 545–550)*

Learning Target: Design and use simulations to find probabilities of compound events.

32. You select a marble from two different bags. You have a 30% chance of choosing a blue marble from the first bag and a 70% chance of choosing a blue marble from the second bag. Design and use a simulation to estimate the probability that you choose a blue marble from both bags.

33. A cereal company is including a prize in each box. There are 5 different prizes, all of which are equally likely.

    a. Describe a simulation involving 50 trials that you can use to model the prizes in the next 3 boxes of cereal you buy.

    b. Use your simulation to find the experimental probability that all three boxes contain a different prize.

34. In the past month, your cell phone has lost its entire charge on 40% of days. Design and use a simulation to estimate the experimental probability that your cell phone loses its entire charge on exactly 2 of the next 5 days.

35. You and your friends form a team in gym class. You have an 80% chance of winning a game of basketball and a 10% chance of winning a game of soccer. Design and use a simulation involving 50 randomly generated numbers to estimate the probability of winning both games.

You randomly choose one game piece. (a) Find the number of ways the event can occur. (b) Find the favorable outcomes of the event.

1. choosing green

2. choosing *not* yellow

Find the sample space and the total number of possible outcomes.

3.

Sunscreen	
SPF	10, 15, 30, 45, 50
Type	Lotion, Spray, Gel

4.

Calculator	
Type	Basic display, Scientific, Graphing, Financial
Color	Black, White, Silver

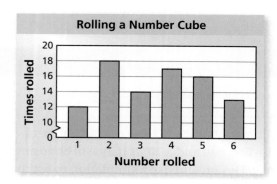

Use the bar graph to find the experimental probability of the event.

5. rolling a 1 or a 2

6. rolling an odd number

7. *not* rolling a 5

8. rolling a number less than 7

Use the spinner to find the theoretical probability of the event(s).

9. spinning an even number

10. spinning a 1 and then a 2

11. You randomly choose one of the pens shown. What is the theoretical probability of choosing a black pen?

12. You randomly choose one of the pens shown. Your friend randomly chooses one of the remaining pens. What is the probability that you and your friend both choose a blue pen?

13. There is an 80% chance of a thunderstorm on Saturday. Describe the likelihood that there is *not* a thunderstorm on Saturday.

14. You are helping to remodel a bathroom. The probability that a randomly selected tile is cracked is 40%. For every 10 boards, there is 1 that is warped. Design and use a simulation to estimate the experimental probability that the next tile you select is cracked and the next board you select is *not* warped.

Cumulative Practice

1. A school athletic director asked each athletic team member to name his or her favorite professional sports team. The results are below:

   - D.C. United: 3
   - Florida Panthers: 8
   - Jacksonville Jaguars: 26
   - Jacksonville Sharks: 7
   - Miami Dolphins: 22
   - Miami Heat: 15
   - Miami Marlins: 20
   - Minnesota Lynx: 4
   - New York Knicks: 5
   - Orlando Magic: 18
   - Tampa Bay Buccaneers: 17
   - Tampa Bay Lightning: 12
   - Tampa Bay Rays: 28
   - Other: 6

One athletic team member is picked at random. What is the likelihood that this team member's favorite professional sports team is *not* located in Florida?

   A. certain

   B. likely, but not certain

   C. unlikely, but not impossible

   D. impossible

2. Each student in your class voted for his or her favorite day of the week. Their votes are shown in the circle graph:

Favorite Day of the Week

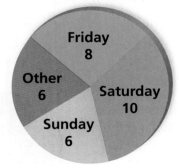

A student from your class is picked at random. What is the probability that this student's favorite day of the week is Sunday?

3. What value makes the equation $11 - 3x = -7$ true?

   F. -6 **G.** $-\dfrac{4}{3}$

   H. 6 **I.** 54

4. Your friend solved the proportion in the box below.

$$\frac{16}{40} = \frac{p}{27}$$

$$16 \cdot p = 40 \cdot 27$$

$$16p = 1080$$

$$\frac{16p}{16} = \frac{1080}{16}$$

$$p = 67.5$$

What should your friend do to correct the error that he made?

   A. Add 40 to 16 and 27 to p.

   B. Subtract 16 from 40 and 27 from p.

   C. Multiply 16 by 27 and p by 40.

   D. Divide 16 by 27 and p by 40.

5. Which value is a solution of the inequality?

$$3 - 2y < 7$$

   F. -6 **G.** -3

   H. -2 **I.** -1

6. A spinner is divided into eight equal sections, as shown. You spin the spinner twice. What is the probability that the arrow will stop in a yellow section both times?

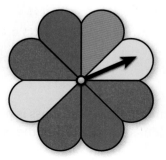

7. A pair of running shoes is on sale for 25% off the original price. Which price is closest to the sale price of the running shoes?

ORIGINAL PRICE
$123.75

A. $93

B. $99

C. $124

D. $149

8. The value of a baseball card was $6 when it was sold. The value of this card is now $15. What is the percent increase in the value of the card?

F. 40%

G. 90%

H. 150%

I. 250%

9. You roll a number cube twice. You want to roll two even numbers.

Think
Solve
Explain

Part A Find the number of favorable outcomes and the number of possible outcomes of each roll.

Part B Find the probability of rolling two even numbers. Explain your reasoning.

10. You put $600 into an account. The account earns 5% simple interest per year. What is the balance after 4 years?

A. $120

B. $720

C. $1800

D. $12,600

11. You are comparing the prices of four boxes of cereal. Two of the boxes contain free extra cereal.

- Box F costs $3.59 and contains 16 ounces.
- Box G costs $3.79 and contains 16 ounces, plus an additional 10% for free.
- Box H costs $4.00 and contains 500 grams.
- Box I costs $4.69 and contains 500 grams, plus an additional 20% for free.

Which box has the least unit cost?

F. Box F

G. Box G

H. Box H

I. Box I

C Statistics

Chapter Learning Target:
Understand statistics.

Chapter Success Criteria:
- ☐ I can determine the validity of a conclusion.
- ☐ I can explain variability in samples of a population.
- ☐ I can solve a problem using statistics.
- ☐ I can compare populations.

STEAM Video: "Comparing Dogs"

STEAM Video

Comparing Dogs

Although dogs and wolves are the same species, they can have very different characteristics. How are dogs and wolves similar?

Watch the STEAM Video "Comparing Dogs." Then answer the following questions.

1. In the video, the dogs Devo and Etta are walking in a park. Describe the *population* of the dogs shown in the video. Then describe a *sample* of the dogs shown in the video. Explain your reasoning.

2. Dogs, wolves, and dingos are all the same species. This species is called *Canis lupus.*

    a. Describe one possible sample of the *Canis lupus* species. Explain your reasoning.

    b. You want to know the average height of an animal in the Canis lupus species. Would you use the entire population of the species or would you use a sample to gather data? Explain.

    c. The entire *Canis lupus* species is a sample of what population? Explain.

Performance Task

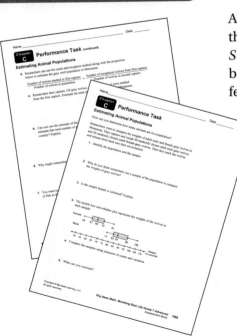

Estimating Animal Populations

After completing this chapter, you will be able to use the concepts you learned to answer the questions in the *STEAM Video Performance Task.* You will be given a double box-and-whisker plot that represents the weights of male and female gray wolves.

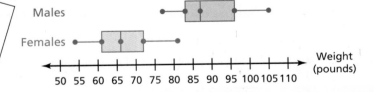

You will be asked to compare the weights of male and female gray wolves. Why might a researcher want to compare data from two different groups of wildlife?

561

Getting Ready for Chapter

Chapter Exploration

A **population** is an entire group of people or objects. A **sample** is a part of the population. You can use a sample to make an *inference*, or conclusion about a population.

Identify a population.	Select a sample.	Interpret the data in the sample.	Make an inference about the population.
(Population) →	(Sample) →	(Interpretation) →	(Inference)

1. **Work with a partner. Identify the population and the sample in each pair.**

   a.

   The students in a school   The students in a math class

   b.

   The grizzly bears with GPS collars in a park   The grizzly bears in a park

   c.

   150 quarters   All quarters in circulation

   d.

   All fiction books in the library   10 fiction books in the library

2. **Work with a partner. When a sample is random, each member of the population is equally likely to be selected. You want to know the favorite activity of students at your school. Tell whether each sample is random. Explain your reasoning.**

   a. members of the school band
   b. students in your math class
   c. students who enter your school in a morning
   d. school newspaper readers

Vocabulary

The following vocabulary terms are defined in this chapter. Think about what each term might mean and record your thoughts.

population
sample

unbiased sample
biased sample

C.1 Samples and Populations

A **population** is an entire group of people or objects. A **sample** is a part of a population. You can gain information about a population by examining samples of the population.

EXPLORATION 1

Using Samples of Populations

Work with a partner. You want to make conclusions about the favorite extracurricular activities of students at your school.

a. Identify the population. Then identify five samples of the population.

b. When a sample is selected *at random*, each member of the population is equally likely to be selected. Are any of the samples in part (a) selected at random? Explain your reasoning.

c. How are the samples below different? Is each conclusion valid? Explain your reasoning.

> You ask 20 members of the school band about their favorite activity. The diagram shows the results. You conclude that band is the favorite activity of 70% of the students in your school.

Favorite Activity

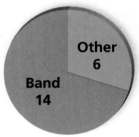

Other 6

Band 14

> You ask every eighth student who enters the school about their favorite activity. One student says glee club for every nine that name a different activity. You conclude that glee club is the favorite activity of 10% of the students in your school.

Math Practice

Maintain Oversight

Can the size of a sample affect the validity of a conclusion about a population? Explain.

d. **MP** **CHOOSE TOOLS** Write a survey question about a topic that interests you. How can you choose people to survey so that you can use the results to make a valid conclusion?

Key Vocabulary 🔊
population, *p. 563*
sample, *p. 563*
unbiased sample,
   p. 564
biased sample, *p. 564*

An **unbiased sample** is representative of a population. It is selected at random and is large enough to provide accurate data.

A **biased sample** is not representative of a population. One or more parts of the population are favored over others.

EXAMPLE 1 Identifying an Unbiased Sample

You want to estimate the number of students in a high school who ride a bus to school. Which sample is unbiased?

  A. 4 students in the hallway

  B. all students on the soccer team

  C. 50 twelfth-grade students at random

  D. 100 students at random during lunch

Choice A is not large enough to provide accurate data.

Choice B is not selected at random.

Choice C is not representative of the population because twelfth-grade students are favored over other students.

Choice D is representative of the population because it is selected at random and is large enough to provide accurate data.

Math Practice

Communicate Precisely
Explain why conclusions made from the sample in Choice C may be inaccurate. Is the sample biased for any possible population? Explain.

 So, the correct answer is **D**.

Try It

1. **WHAT IF?** You want to estimate the number of twelfth-grade students in a high school who ride a bus to school. Which sample is unbiased? Explain.

2. You want to estimate the number of eighth-grade students in your school who find it relaxing to listen to music. You consider two samples.

   • fifteen randomly selected members of the band

   • every fifth student whose name appears on an alphabetical list of eighth-grade students

   Which sample is unbiased? Explain.

🔊 *Multi-Language Glossary at BigIdeasMath.com*

The results of an unbiased sample are proportional to the results of the population. So, you can use unbiased samples to make conclusions about a population. Biased samples are not representative of a population. So, you should not use them to make conclusions about a population.

EXAMPLE 2 **Determining Whether Conclusions Are Valid**

You want to know how the residents of your town feel about adding a new landfill. Determine whether each conclusion is valid.

a. **You survey the 100 residents who live closest to the new landfill. The diagram shows the results. You conclude that 10% of the residents of your town support the new landfill.**

New Landfill

For 10

Against 90

The sample is not representative of the population because residents who live close to the landfill may be less likely to support it.

▷ So, the sample is biased, and the conclusion is not valid.

New Landfill	
Support	40
Do Not Support	60

b. **You survey 100 residents at random. The table shows the results. You conclude that 60% of the residents of your town do not support the new landfill.**

The sample is representative of the population because it is selected at random and is large enough to provide accurate data.

▷ So, the sample is unbiased, and the conclusion is valid.

Try It

3. Four out of five randomly chosen teenagers support the new landfill. So, you conclude that 80% of the residents of your town support the new landfill. Is the conclusion valid? Explain.

Self-Assessment for Concepts & Skills

Solve each exercise. Then rate your understanding of the success criteria in your journal.

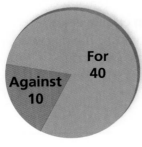

New Musical

For 40

Against 10

4. **WRITING** You want to estimate the number of students in your school who play a school sport. You ask 40 honors students at random whether they play a school sport. Is this sample biased or unbiased? Explain.

5. **ANALYZING A CONCLUSION** You survey 50 randomly chosen audience members at a theater about whether the theater should produce a new musical. The diagram shows the results. You conclude that 80% of the audience members support production of a new musical. Is your conclusion valid? Explain.

EXAMPLE 3 **Modeling Real Life**

You ask 75 randomly chosen students at a school how many movies they watch each week. There are 1200 students in the school. Estimate the number of students in the school who watch one movie each week.

Movies per Week

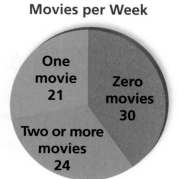

One movie 21
Zero movies 30
Two or more movies 24

Understand the problem.

You are given the numbers of movies watched each week by a sample of 75 students. You are asked to make an estimate about the population, all students in the school.

Make a plan.

The sample is representative of the population because it is selected at random and is large enough to provide accurate data. So, the sample is unbiased and its results are proportional to the results of the population. Use a ratio table to estimate the number of students in the school who watch one movie each week.

Solve and check.

$\times 4$ $\times 4$

Students (one movie)	21	84	336
Total Students	75	300	1200

$\times 4$ $\times 4$

Another Method
Use a proportion.

$$\frac{21}{75} = \frac{n}{1200}$$

$336 = n$ ✓

▷ So, about 336 students in the school watch one movie each week.

 Self-Assessment for Problem Solving

Solve each exercise. Then rate your understanding of the success criteria in your journal.

6. You want to estimate the mean photo size on your cell phone. You choose 30 photos at random from your phone. The total size of the sample is 186 megabytes. Explain whether you can use the sample to estimate the mean size of photos on your cell phone. If so, what is your estimate?

Books per Month

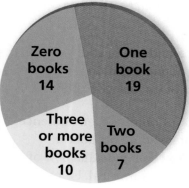

Zero books 14
One book 19
Three or more books 10
Two books 7

7. **DIG DEEPER!** You ask 50 randomly chosen employees of a company how many books they read each month. The diagram shows the results. There are 600 people employed by the company. Estimate the number of employees who read at least one book each month.

C.1 Practice

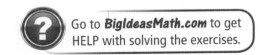

Go to *BigIdeasMath.com* to get HELP with solving the exercises.

▶ Review & Refresh

Design a simulation that you can use to model the situation. Then use your simulation to find the experimental probability.

1. The probability that a meal at a restaurant is overcooked is 10%. Estimate the probability that exactly 1 of the next 2 meals is overcooked.

2. The probability that you see a butterfly during a nature center tour is 80%. The probability that you see a turtle is 40%. What is the probability of seeing both?

Solve the inequality. Graph the solution.

3. $2x - 5 < 9$

4. $5q + 2 \geq -13$

5. $2 > 6 - 3r$

▶▶ Concepts, Skills, & Problem Solving

USING SAMPLES OF POPULATIONS **You ask 50 randomly chosen artists in your town about their favorite art form. Determine whether your conclusion is valid. Justify your answer.** (See Exploration 1, p. 563.)

6. You conclude that drawing is the favorite art form of 60% of artists in your town.

7. You conclude that ceramics is the favorite art form of 10% of people in your town.

Favorite Art Form

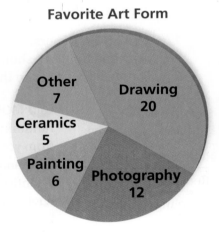

IDENTIFYING POPULATIONS AND SAMPLES **Identify the population and the sample.**

8.
Residents of New Jersey   Residents of Ocean County

9.

4 cards

All cards in a deck

IDENTIFYING BIASED AND UNBIASED SAMPLES **Determine whether the sample is *biased* or *unbiased*. Explain.**

10. You want to estimate the number of books students in your school read over the summer. You survey every fourth student who enters the school.

11. You want to estimate the number of people in a town who think that a park needs to be remodeled. You survey every 10th person who enters the park.

Section C.1   Samples and Populations   **567**

12. **MP MODELING REAL LIFE** You want to determine the number of students in your school who have visited a science museum. You survey 50 students at random. Twenty have visited a science museum, and thirty have not. So, you conclude that 40% of the students in your school have visited a science museum. Is your conclusion valid? Explain.

13. **USING A SAMPLE** Which sample is better for making an estimate? Explain.

Estimate the number of defective pencils produced per day.	
Sample A	A random sample of 500 pencils from 20 machines
Sample B	A random sample of 500 pencils from 1 machine

CONDUCTING SURVEYS Determine whether you should survey the population or a sample. Explain.

14. You want to know the average height of seventh graders in the United States.

15. You want to know the favorite types of music of students in your homeroom.

16. **CRITICAL THINKING** Does increasing the size of a sample necessarily make the sample more representative of a population? Give an example to support your explanation.

17. **MP LOGIC** A person surveys residents of a town to determine whether a skateboarding ban should be overturned. Describe how the person can conduct the survey so that the sample is biased toward overturning the ban.

Favorite Way to Eliminate Waste	
Reducing	14
Reusing	4
Recycling	2

18. **MP MODELING REAL LIFE** You ask 20 randomly chosen environmental scientists from your state to name their favorite way to eliminate waste. There are 200 environmental scientists in your state. Estimate the number of environmental scientists in your state whose favorite way to eliminate waste is recycling.

Candidate Preference

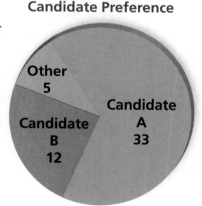

19. **MP MODELING REAL LIFE** To predict the result of a mayoral election, you survey 50 likely voters at random. The diagram shows the results. Describe whether the sample can be used to predict the outcome of the election. If so, what is your prediction for the number of votes received by the winner assuming that 500 people vote?

Number of Dogs	Frequency
1	54
2	38
3	3
4	1
5	4

20. **DIG DEEPER!** You ask 100 randomly chosen dog owners in your town how many dogs they own. The results are shown in the table. There are 500 dog owners in your town.

   a. Estimate the median number of dogs per dog owner in your town. Justify your answer.

   b. Estimate the mean number of dogs per dog owner in your town. Justify your answer.

Using Random Samples to Describe Populations

Learning Target: Understand variability in samples of a population.

Success Criteria:
- I can use multiple random samples to make conclusions about a population.
- I can use multiple random samples to examine variation in estimates.

EXPLORATION 1

Exploring Variability in Samples

Work with a partner. Sixty percent of all seventh graders have visited a planetarium.

a. Design a simulation using packing peanuts. Mark 60% of the packing peanuts and put them in a paper bag. What does choosing a marked peanut represent?

Math Practice

Make Conjectures
How many marked peanuts do you expect to draw in 30 trials? Explain your reasoning.

b. Simulate a sample of 25 students by choosing peanuts from the bag, replacing the peanut each time. Record the results.

c. Find the percent of students in the sample who have visited a planetarium. Compare this value to the actual percent of all seventh graders who have visited a planetarium.

d. Record the percent in part (c) from each pair in the class. Use a dot plot to display the data. Describe the variation in the data.

You have used unbiased samples to make conclusions about populations. Different samples often give slightly different conclusions due to variability in the sample data.

EXAMPLE 1 **Using Multiple Random Samples**

You and a group of friends want to know how many students in your school prefer pop music. There are 840 students in your school. Each person in the group randomly surveys 20 students. The table shows the results.

	Favorite Type of Music			
	Country	Pop	Rock	Rap
You	2	13	4	1
Friend A	3	8	7	2
Friend B	4	10	5	1
Friend C	5	10	4	1
Friend D	5	9	3	3

a.   **Use each sample to make an estimate for the number of students in your school who prefer pop music.**

In your sample, 13 out of 20, or 65% of the students chose pop music. So, you can estimate that 0.65(840) = 546 students in your school prefer pop music. Make estimates for the other samples.

	You	Friend A	Friend B	Friend C	Friend D
Estimate	546	336	420	420	378

> So, the estimates are that 336, 378, 420, 420, and 546 students prefer pop music.

b.   **Describe the center and the variation of the estimates.**

> The estimates have a median of 420 students and a range of 546 − 336 = 210 students.

Try It

1.   Use each sample to make an estimate for the number of students in your school who prefer rap music. Describe the center and the variation of the estimates.

EXAMPLE 2 **Estimating an Average of a Population**

Hours Worked Each Week

A: 6, 8, 6, 6, 7, 4, 10, 8, 7, 8

B: 10, 4, 4, 6, 8, 6, 7, 12, 8, 8

C: 10, 9, 8, 6, 5, 8, 6, 6, 9, 10

D: 4, 8, 4, 4, 5, 4, 4, 6, 5, 6

E: 6, 8, 8, 6, 12, 4, 10, 8, 6, 12

F: 10, 4, 8, 9, 6, 8, 7, 12, 16, 10

You want to know the mean number of hours students with part-time jobs work each week. At each of six schools you randomly survey 10 students with part-time jobs. Your results are shown.

a. Use each sample to make an estimate for the mean number of hours students with part-time jobs work each week. Describe the variation of the estimates.

Find the mean of each sample.

Sample	A	B	C	D	E	F
Mean	$\frac{70}{10} = 7$	$\frac{73}{10} = 7.3$	$\frac{77}{10} = 7.7$	$\frac{50}{10} = 5$	$\frac{80}{10} = 8$	$\frac{90}{10} = 9$

> So, the six estimates are that students with part-time jobs work 5, 7, 7.3, 7.7, 8, and 9 hours each week. The estimates have a range of $9 - 5 = 4$ hours.

b. Use all six samples to make one estimate for the mean number of hours students with part-time jobs work each week.

The mean of all sample data is $\frac{440}{60} = 7.\overline{3}$ hours.

> So, you can estimate that students with part-time jobs work $7.\overline{3}$ hours each week.

Try It

2. Repeat Example 2, but estimate the medians instead of the means.

Self-Assessment for Concepts & Skills

Solve each exercise. Then rate your understanding of the success criteria in your journal.

3. USING MULTIPLE RANDOM SAMPLES Use each sample in Example 1 to make an estimate for the number of students in your school who prefer rock music. Describe the variation of the estimates.

Hours Practiced Each Week

A: 6, 5, 5, 6, 4, 6, 8, 5, 2, 6

B: 0, 6, 6, 5, 4, 5, 6, 3, 4, 9

C: 4, 5, 6, 4, 3, 2, 2, 3, 12, 1

4. ESTIMATING AN AVERAGE OF A POPULATION You want to know the mean number of hours music students at your school practice each week. At each of three music classes you randomly survey 10 students. Your results are shown. Use all three samples to make one estimate for the mean number of hours music students practice each week.

You can use technology to perform simulations with large numbers of trials.

EXAMPLE 3 Modeling Real Life

As stated in Exploration 1, 60% of all seventh graders have visited a planetarium. Use technology to simulate choosing 200 random samples of 50 students each. How closely do the samples estimate the percent of all seventh graders who have visited a planetarium?

The actual percentage is 60%, the number of samples is 200, and the sample size is 50. Use technology to run the simulation.

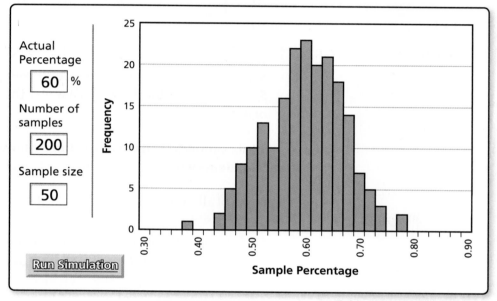

Math Practice

Make Sense of Quantities
What does each bar in the graph represent?

Available at *BigIdeasMath.com*

The estimates are clustered around 60%. Most are between 45% and 70%.

▷ So, most of the samples are within 15% of the actual percentage.

 Self-Assessment for Problem Solving

Solve each exercise. Then rate your understanding of the success criteria in your journal.

5. Repeat Example 3 with the assumption that 50% of all seventh graders have visited a planetarium.

6. Forty percent of all seventh graders have visited a state park. How closely do 200 random samples of 50 students estimate the percent of seventh graders who have visited a state park? Use a simulation to support your answer.

C.2 Practice

Go to **BigIdeasMath.com** to get HELP with solving the exercises.

Review & Refresh

You ask 100 randomly chosen high school students whether they support a new college in your town. Determine whether your conclusion is valid.

New College	
Support	85
Do not support	15

1. You conclude that 85% of high school students in your town support the new college.
2. You conclude that 15% of residents in your town do not support the new college.

Write and solve a proportion to answer the question.

3. What percent of 30 is 12?
4. 17 is what percent of 68?

Concepts, Skills, & Problem Solving

EXPLORING VARIABILITY IN SAMPLES **Thirty percent of all seventh graders own a bracelet. Explain whether the sample closely estimates the percentage of seventh graders who own a bracelet.** (See Exploration 1, p. 569.)

5. 50 seventh graders, 14 own a bracelet
6. 30 seventh graders, 3 own a bracelet

	Vegetable Preference	
	Fresh	Canned
A	11	9
B	14	6
C	12	8

7. USING MULTIPLE RANDOM SAMPLES A store owner wants to know how many of her 600 regular customers prefer canned vegetables. Each of her three cashiers randomly surveys 20 regular customers. The table shows the results.
   a. Use each sample to make an estimate for the number of regular customers of the store who prefer fresh vegetables.
   b. Describe the variation of the estimates.

8. USING MULTIPLE RANDOM SAMPLES An arcade manager wants to know how many of his 750 regular customers prefer to visit in the winter. Each of five staff members randomly surveys 25 regular customers. The table shows the results.
   a. Use each sample to make an estimate for the number of regular customers who prefer to visit in the winter.
   b. Describe the variation of the estimates.

	Preferred Season to Visit the Arcade			
	Spring	Summer	Fall	Winter
A	4	4	6	11
B	5	3	7	10
C	6	5	5	9
D	4	5	6	10
E	4	4	5	12

9. **ESTIMATING A MEAN OF A POPULATION** A park ranger wants to know the mean number of nights students in your school plan to camp next summer. The park ranger randomly surveys 10 students from each class. The results are shown.

Nights Camping
A: 0, 5, 2, 3, 0, 6, 0, 10, 3, 0
B: 14, 0, 0, 6, 5, 0, 1, 2, 2, 5
C: 8, 8, 2, 3, 4, 1, 0, 0, 0, 6
D: 10, 10, 5, 6, 1, 0, 0, 0, 4, 0

a. Use each sample to make an estimate for the mean number of nights students in your school plan to camp next summer. Describe the variation of the estimates.

b. Use all four samples to make one estimate for the mean number of nights students plan to camp next summer.

10. **ESTIMATING A MEDIAN OF A POPULATION** Repeat Exercise 9, but estimate the medians instead of the means.

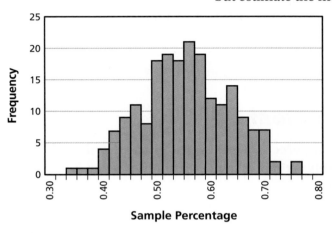

11. **DESCRIBING SAMPLE VARIATION** Fifty-five percent of doctors at a hospital prescribe a particular medication. A simulation with 200 random samples of 50 doctors each is shown. Describe how the sample percentages vary.

12. **MP MODELING REAL LIFE** Sixty percent of vacationers enjoy water parks. Use technology to generate 20 samples of size 100. How closely do the samples estimate the percent of all vacationers who enjoy water parks?

13. **MP MODELING REAL LIFE** Thirty percent of all new wooden benches have a patch of chipped paint. Use technology to simulate 100 random samples of 10 wooden benches. How closely do the samples estimate the percent of all wooden benches with a patch of chipped paint?

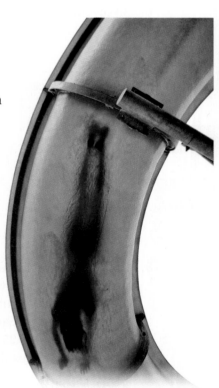

14. **DIG DEEPER!** You want to predict whether a proposal will be accepted by likely voters. You randomly sample 3 different groups of 100 likely voters. The results are shown. Do you expect the proposal to be accepted? Justify your answer.

	Proposal	
	Support	**Oppose**
Sample A	48	52
Sample B	52	48
Sample C	47	53

15. **CRITICAL THINKING** Explain why public opinion polls use sample sizes of more than 1000 people instead of using a smaller sample size.

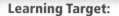
Learning Target: Compare populations using measures of center and variation.

Success Criteria:
• I can find the measures of center and variation of a data set.
• I can describe the visual overlap of two data distributions numerically.
• I can determine whether there is a significant difference in the measures of center of two data sets.

EXPLORATION 1

Comparing Two Data Distributions

Work with a partner.

a. Does each data display show *overlap*? Explain.

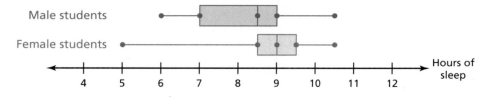

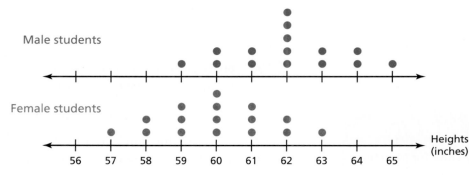

Math Practice

Recognize Usefulness of Tools

What are the advantages of each type of data display? Which do you prefer? Explain.

Ages of People in Two Exercise Classes

10:00 A.M. Class								8:00 P.M. Class
							1	8 9
							2	1 2 2 7 9 9
							3	0 3 4 5 7
9	7	3	2	2	2		4	0
		7	5	4	3	1	5	
				7	0	0	6	
						0	7	

Key: 2 | 4 | 0 = 42 and 40 years

b. How can you describe the overlap of two data distributions using words? How can you describe the overlap numerically?

c. In which pair of data sets is the difference in the measures of center the most significant? Explain your reasoning.

Use the mean and the mean absolute deviation (MAD) to compare two populations when both distributions are symmetric. Use the median and the interquartile range (IQR) when either one or both distributions are skewed.

EXAMPLE 1 Comparing Populations

Two data sets contain an equal number of values. The double box-and-whisker plot represents the values in the data sets.

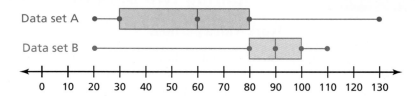

a. Compare the data sets using measures of center and variation.

Both distributions are skewed. Use the median and the IQR.

Data set A	Data set B
Median = 60	Median = 90
IQR = 80 − 30 = 50	IQR = 100 − 80 = 20

> So, Data set B has a greater measure of center, and Data set A has a greater measure of variation.

b. Which data set is more likely to contain a value of 95?

About 25% of the data values in Data set A are between 80 and 130. About 50% of the data values in Data set B are between 80 and 100.

> So, Data set B is more likely to contain a value of 95.

c. Which data set is more likely to contain a value that differs from the center by at least 30?

The IQR of Data set A is 50 and the IQR of Data set B is 20. This means it is more common for a value to differ from the center by 30 in Data set A than in Data set B.

> So, Data set A is more likely to contain a value that differs from the center by at least 30.

Math Practice

Look for Structure
Explain how you know that about 50% of the data values in Data set B are between 80 and 100.

Try It

1. Which data set is more likely to contain a value of 70?

2. Which data set is more likely to contain a value that differs from the center by no more than 3?

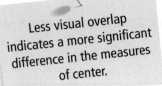

Less visual overlap indicates a more significant difference in the measures of center.

When two populations have similar variabilities, the visual overlap of the data can be described by writing the difference in the measures of center as a multiple of the measure of variation. Greater values indicate less visual overlap.

EXAMPLE 2 Describing Visual Overlap

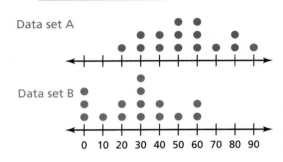

Data set A

Data set B

The double dot plot shows two data sets. Express the difference in the measures of center as a multiple of the measure of variation.

Both distributions are approximately symmetric. Use the mean and the MAD to describe the centers and variations.

Data set A

$$\text{Mean} = \frac{810}{15} = 54$$

$$\text{MAD} = \frac{244}{15} \approx 16$$

$$\frac{\text{difference in means}}{\text{MAD}} = \frac{26}{16} \approx 1.6$$

Data set B

$$\text{Mean} = \frac{420}{15} = 28$$

$$\text{MAD} = \frac{236}{15} \approx 16$$

 So, the difference in the means is about 1.6 times the MAD.

Try It

3. **WHAT IF?** Each value in the dot plot for Data set A increases by 30. How does this affect your answers? Explain.

 Self-Assessment *for Concepts & Skills*

Solve each exercise. Then rate your understanding of the success criteria in your journal.

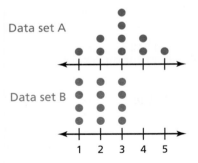

Data set A

Data set B

4. **COMPARING POPULATIONS** The double dot plot shows two data sets. Compare the data sets using measures of center and variation. Then express the difference in the measures of center as a multiple of the measure of variation.

5. **WHICH ONE DOESN'T BELONG?** You want to compare two populations represented by skewed distributions. Which measure does *not* belong with the other three? Explain your reasoning.

| Median of first data set | Median of second data set |

| IQR of first data set | MAD of second data set |

When the difference in the measures of center is at least 2 times the measure of variation, the difference is significant.

EXAMPLE 3 **Modeling Real Life**

The double box-and-whisker plot represents the heights of rollercoasters at two amusement parks. Are the rollercoasters significantly taller at one park than at the other park?

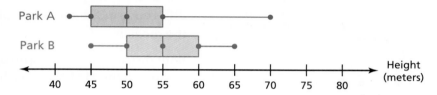

The distribution for Park A is skewed, so use the median and the IQR to describe the centers and variations.

Park A	Park B
Median = 50	Median = 55
IQR = 55 − 45 = 10	IQR = 60 − 50 = 10

Because the variabilities are similar, you can describe the visual overlap by expressing the difference in the medians as a multiple of the IQR.

$$\frac{\text{difference in medians}}{\text{IQR}} = \frac{5}{10} = 0.5$$

Because the quotient is less than 2, the difference in the medians is not significant.

▷ The rollercoasters are not significantly taller at one park than at the other park.

 Self-Assessment for *Problem Solving*

Solve each exercise. Then rate your understanding of the success criteria in your journal.

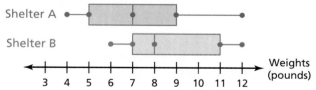

6. The double box-and-whisker plot represents the weights of cats at two shelters. Are the cats significantly heavier at one shelter than at the other? Explain.

7. **DIG DEEPER!** Tornadoes in Region A travel significantly farther than tornadoes in Region B. The tornadoes in Region A travel a median of 10 miles. Create a double box-and-whisker plot that can represent the distances traveled by the tornadoes in the two regions.

C.3 Practice

? Go to *BigIdeasMath.com* to get HELP with solving the exercises.

▶ Review & Refresh

Twenty percent of all seventh graders have watched a horse race. Explain whether the sample closely estimates the percentage of seventh graders who have watched a horse race.

1. In a sample of 15 seventh graders, 4 have watched a horse race.

2. In a sample of 10 seventh graders, 6 have watched a horse race.

Find the unit rate.

3. 60 kilometers in 2 hours

4. $11.40 for 5 cans

▶▶ Concepts, Skills, & Problem Solving

COMPARING TWO DATA DISTRIBUTIONS The double box-and-whisker plot represents the values in two data sets. (See Exploration 1, p. 575.)

5. Does the data display show *overlap*? Explain.

6. Is there a significant difference in the measures of center for the pair of data sets? Explain.

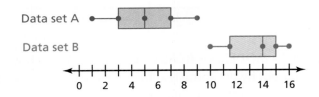

COMPARING POPULATIONS Two data sets contain an equal number of values. The double box-and-whisker plot represents the values in the data sets.

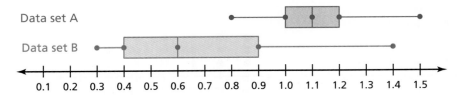

7. Compare the data sets using measures of center and variation.

8. Which data set is more likely to contain a value of 1.1?

9. Which data set is more likely to contain a value that differs from the center by 0.3?

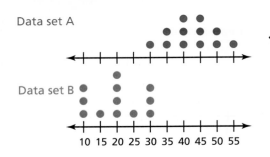

10. **DESCRIBING VISUAL OVERLAP** The double dot plot shows the values in two data sets. Express the difference in the measures of center as a multiple of the measure of variation.

11. **MP YOU BE THE TEACHER** The distributions of attendance at basketball games and volleyball games at your school are symmetric. Your friend makes a conclusion based on the calculations shown below. Is your friend correct? Explain your reasoning.

> Volleyball Game Attendance: Mean = 80, MAD = 20
>
> Basketball Game Attendance: Mean = 160, MAD = 20
>
> The difference in means is four times the MAD, so attendance at basketball games is significantly greater than attendance at volleyball games.

12. **MP MODELING REAL LIFE** The double box-and-whisker plot represents the goals scored per game by two hockey teams during a 20-game season. Is the number of goals scored per game significantly greater for one team than the other? Explain.

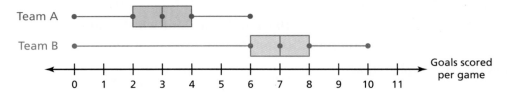

13. **MP MODELING REAL LIFE** The dot plots show the test scores for two classes taught by the same teacher. Are the test scores significantly greater for one class than the other? Explain.

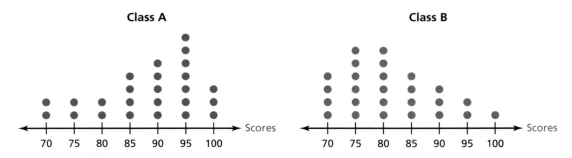

14. **MP PROBLEM SOLVING** A scientist experiments with mold colonies of equal area. She adds a treatment to half of the colonies. After a week, she measures the area of each colony. If the areas are significantly different, the scientist will repeat the experiment. The results are shown. Should the scientist repeat the experiment? Justify your answer.

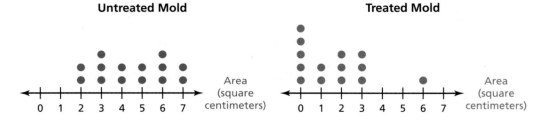

HSC C.4 Using Random Samples to Compare Populations

Learning Target: Use random samples to compare populations.

Success Criteria:
- I can compare random samples using measures of center and variation.
- I can recognize whether random samples are likely to be representative of a population.
- I can compare populations using multiple random samples.

EXPLORATION 1

Using Random Samples

Work with a partner. You want to compare the numbers of hours spent on homework each week by male and female students in your state. You take a random sample of 15 male students and 15 female students throughout the state.

Male Students				
1.5	3	0	2.5	1
8	2.5	1	3	0
6.5	1	5	0	5

Female Students				
4	0	3	1	1
5	1	3	5.5	10
2	0	6	3.5	2

a. Compare the data in each sample.

b. Are the samples likely to be representative of all male and female students in your state? Explain.

c. You take 100 random samples of 15 male students in your state and 100 random samples of 15 female students in your state and record the median of each sample. The double box-and-whisker plot shows the distributions of the sample medians. Compare the distributions in the double box-and-whisker plot with the distributions of the data in the tables.

Math Practice

Build Arguments

How does taking multiple random samples allow you to make conclusions about two populations?

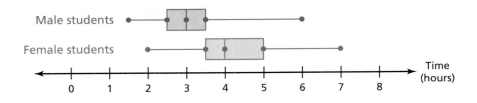

d. What can you conclude from the double box-and-whisker plot? Explain.

e. How can you use random samples to make accurate comparisons of two populations?

You do not need to have all of the data from two populations to make comparisons. You can use random samples to make comparisons.

EXAMPLE 1 **Comparing Random Samples**

Two bags each contain 1000 numbered tiles. The double box-and-whisker plot represents a random sample of 12 numbers from each bag. Compare the samples using measures of center and variation. Can you determine which bag contains tiles with greater numbers?

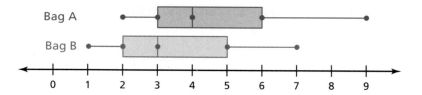

Both distributions are skewed right, so use the median and the IQR.

Bag A	**Bag B**
Median = 4	Median = 3
IQR = 6 − 3 = 3	IQR = 5 − 2 = 3

> You are more likely to make valid comparisons when the sample size is large and there is little variability in the data.

The variation in the samples is about the same, but the sample from Bag A has a greater median. The sample size is too small, however, to conclude that tiles in Bag A generally have greater numbers than tiles in Bag B.

Try It

1. The double dot plot shows the weekly reading habits of a random sample of 10 students in each of two schools. Compare the samples using measures of center and variation. Can you determine which school's students read less? Explain.

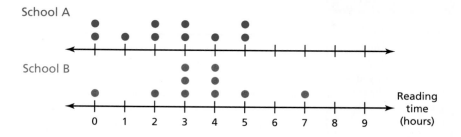

EXAMPLE 2 **Using Multiple Random Samples**

The double box-and-whisker plot represents the medians of 50 random samples of 12 numbers from each bag in Example 1. Compare the variability of the sample medians to the variability of the samples in Example 1. Can you determine which bag contains tiles with greater numbers?

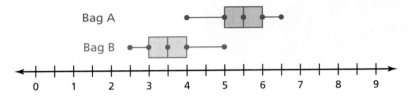

Bag A
Median = 5.5
IQR = 6 − 5 = 1

Bag B
Median = 3.5
IQR = 4 − 3 = 1

The IQR of the sample medians for each bag is 1, which is less than the IQR of the samples in Example 1. Most of the sample medians for Bag A are greater than the sample medians for Bag B. So, tiles in Bag A generally have greater numbers than tiles in Bag B.

Try It

2. **WHAT IF?** Each value in the box-and-whisker plot of the sample medians for Bag A decreases by 2. Does this change your answer?

 Self-Assessment for Concepts & Skills

Solve each exercise. Then rate your understanding of the success criteria in your journal.

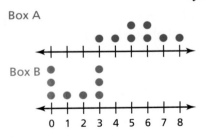

3. **COMPARING RANDOM SAMPLES** Two boxes each contain 600 numbered tiles. The double dot plot shows a random sample of 8 numbers from each box. Compare the samples using measures of center and variation. Can you determine which box contains tiles with greater numbers? Explain.

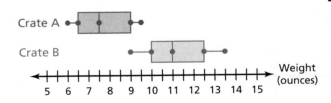

4. **USING MULTIPLE RANDOM SAMPLES** Two crates each contain 750 objects. The double box-and-whisker plot shows the median weights of 50 random samples of 10 objects from each crate. Can you determine which crate weighs more? Explain.

EXAMPLE 3 **Modeling Real Life**

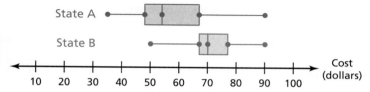

The double box-and-whisker plot represents the medians of 50 random samples of 10 speeding tickets issued in two states. Compare the costs of speeding tickets in the two states.

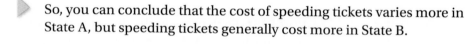

There is enough data to draw conclusions about the costs of speeding tickets in the two states. Find the measures of center and variation for the sample medians from each state. Then compare the data.

State A	**State B**
Median ≈ 54	Median = 70
IQR ≈ 67 − 48 = 19	IQR ≈ 77 − 67 = 10

The variation for State A is greater than the variation for State B, and the measure of center for State B is greater than the measure of center for State A.

▷ So, you can conclude that the cost of speeding tickets varies more in State A, but speeding tickets generally cost more in State B.

 Self-Assessment for *Problem Solving*

Solve each exercise. Then rate your understanding of the success criteria in your journal.

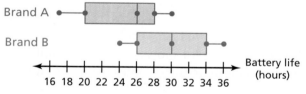

5. The double box-and-whisker plot represents the medians of 100 random samples of 20 battery lives for two cell phone brands. Compare the battery lives of the two brands.

6. The double box-and-whisker plot represents the medians of 50 random samples of 10 wait times at two patient care facilities. Which facility should you choose? Explain your reasoning.

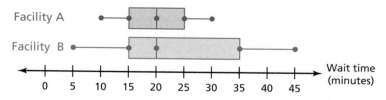

C.4 Practice

? Go to *BigIdeasMath.com* to get HELP with solving the exercises.

▶ Review & Refresh

The double dot plot shows the values in two data sets.

1. Compare the data sets using measures of center and variation.

2. Are the values of one data set significantly greater than the values of the other data set? Explain.

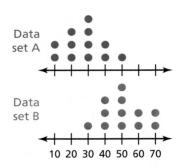

Solve the equation. Check your solution.

3. $5b - 3 = 22$

4. $1.5d + 3 = -4.5$

5. $4 = 9z - 2$

▶▶ Concepts, Skills, & Problem Solving

USING RANDOM SAMPLES You want to compare the numbers of hours spent on recreation each week by teachers and non-teachers in your state. You take 100 random samples of 15 teachers and 100 random samples of 15 non-teachers throughout the state and record the median value of each sample. The double box-and-whisker plot shows the distributions of sample medians. *(See Exploration 1, p. 581.)*

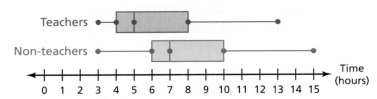

6. Are the samples likely to be representative of all teachers and non-teachers in your state?

7. What can you conclude from the double box-and-whisker plot? Explain.

8. **COMPARING RANDOM SAMPLES** The double dot plot shows the weekly running habits of athletes at two colleges. Compare the samples using measures of center and variation. Can you determine which college's athletes spend more time running? Explain.

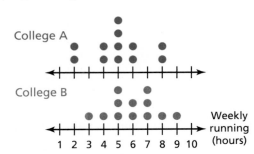

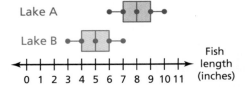

9. **USING MULTIPLE RANDOM SAMPLES** Two lakes each contain about 2000 fish. The double box-and-whisker plot shows the medians of 50 random samples of 14 fish lengths from each lake. Can you determine which lake contains longer fish? Explain.

10. **(MP) MODELING REAL LIFE** Two laboratories each produce 800 chemicals. A chemist takes 10 samples of 15 chemicals from each lab, and records the number that pass an inspection. Are the samples likely to be representative of all the chemicals for each lab? If so, which lab has more chemicals that will pass the inspection? Justify your answer.

Research Lab A				
14	13	15	15	14
14	15	15	13	12

Research Lab B				
12	10	12	14	11
9	14	11	11	15

11. **(MP) MODELING REAL LIFE** A farmer grows two types of corn seedlings. There are 1000 seedlings of each type. The double box-and-whisker plot represents the median growths of 50 random samples of 7 corn seedlings of each type. Compare the growths of each type of corn seedling. Justify your result.

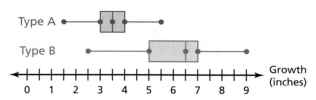

12. **DIG DEEPER!** You want to compare the number of words per sentence in a sports magazine to the number of words per sentence in a political magazine.

  a. The data represent random samples of the number of words in 10 sentences from each magazine. Compare the samples using measures of center and variation. Can you use the data to make a valid comparison about the magazines? Explain.

    Sports magazine: 9, 21, 15, 14, 25, 26, 9, 19, 22, 30

    Political magazine: 31, 22, 17, 5, 23, 15, 10, 20, 20, 17

  b. The double box-and-whisker plot represents the means of 200 random samples of 20 sentences from each magazine. Compare the variability of the sample means to the variability of the sample numbers of words in part (a).

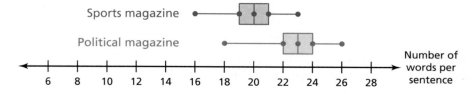

  c. Make a conclusion about the numbers of words per sentence in each magazine.

13. **PROJECT** You want to compare the average amounts of time students in sixth, seventh, and eighth grade spend on homework each week.

  a. Design an experiment involving random sampling that can help you make a comparison.

  b. Perform the experiment. Can you make a conclusion about which grade spends the most time on homework? Explain your reasoning.

Connecting Concepts

▶ Using the Problem-Solving Plan

1. In a city, 1500 randomly chosen residents are asked how many sporting events they attend each month. The city has 80,000 residents. Estimate the number of residents in the city who attend at least one sporting event each month.

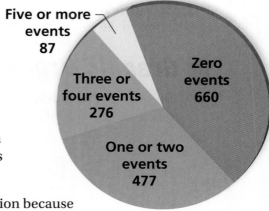

Sporting Events per Month

Five or more events 87

Zero events 660

Three or four events 276

One or two events 477

Understand the problem. You are given the numbers of sporting events attended each month by a sample of 1500 residents. You are asked to make an estimate about the population, all residents of the city.

Make a plan. The sample is representative of the population because it is selected at random and is large enough to provide accurate data. So, find the percent of people in the survey that attend at least one sporting event each month, and use the percent equation to make an estimate.

Solve and check. Use the plan to solve the problem. Then check your solution.

2. The dot plots show the values in two data sets. Is the difference in the measures of center for the data sets significant?

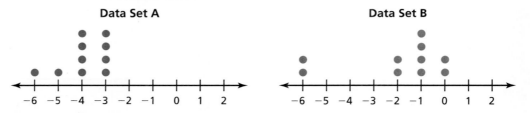

Data Set A

Data Set B

Yes	No
42	18

3. You ask 60 randomly chosen students whether they support a later starting time for school. The table shows the results. Estimate the probability that at least two out of four randomly chosen students do not support a later starting time.

Performance Task

Estimating Animal Populations

At the beginning of the this chapter, you watched a STEAM Video called "Comparing Dogs." You are now ready to complete the performance task related to this video, available at *BigIdeasMath.com*. Be sure to use the problem-solving plan as you work through the performance task.

Go to *BigIdeasMath.com* to download blank graphic organizers.

▶ Review Vocabulary

Write the definition and give an example of each vocabulary term.

population, *p. 563*
sample, *p. 563*

unbiased sample, *p. 564*
biased sample, *p. 564*

▶ Graphic Organizers

You can use a **Definition and Example Chart** to organize information about a concept. Here is an example of a Definition and Example Chart for the vocabulary term *sample*.

Sample: part of a population

Example

unbiased sample: 100 seventh-grade students selected randomly during lunch

Example

biased sample: the seventh-grade students at your lunch table

Choose and complete a graphic organizer to help you study each topic.

1. population

2. shape of a distribution

3. mean absolute deviation (MAD)

4. interquartile range (IQR)

5. double box-and-whisker plot

6. double dot plot

"Here is my Definition and Example Chart. I read in the news that a cat once floated over this waterfall in a barrel."

Chapter Self-Assessment

As you complete the exercises, use the scale below to rate your understanding of the success criteria in your journal.

1	**2**	**3**	**4**
I do not understand.	I can do it with help.	I can do it on my own.	I can teach someone else.

C.1 Samples and Populations (pp. 563–568)

Learning Target: Understand how to use random samples to make conclusions about a population.

1. You want to estimate the number of students in your school whose favorite subject is biology. You survey the first 10 students who arrive at biology club. Determine whether the sample is *biased* or *unbiased*. Explain.

2. You want to estimate the number of athletes who play soccer. Give an example of a biased sample. Give an example of an unbiased sample.

3. You want to know how the residents of your town feel about building a new baseball stadium. You randomly survey 100 people who enter the current stadium. Eighty support building a new stadium, and twenty do not. So, you conclude that 80% of the residents of your town support building a new baseball stadium. Is your conclusion valid? Explain.

4. Which sample is better for making an estimate? Explain.

Predict the number of students in a school who like gym class.	
Sample A	A random sample of 8 students from the yearbook
Sample B	A random sample of 80 students from the yearbook

5. You ask 125 randomly chosen students to name their favorite beverage. There are 1500 students in the school. Predict the number of students in the school whose favorite beverage is a sports drink.

6. You want to know the number of students in your state who have summer jobs. Determine whether you should survey the population or a sample. Explain.

Favorite Beverage	
Sports drink	58
Soda	36
Water	14
Other	17

C.2 Using Random Samples to Describe Populations (pp. 569–574)

Learning Target: Understand variability in samples of a population.

7. To pass a quality control inspection, the products at a factory must contain no critical defects, no more than 2.5% of products can contain major defects, and no more than 4% of products can contain minor defects. There are 40,000 products being shipped from a factory. Each inspector randomly samples 125 products. The table shows the results.

   a. Use each sample to make an estimate for the number of products with minor defects at the factory. Describe the center and the variation of the estimates.

   b. Use the samples to make an estimate for the percent of products with minor defects, with major defects, and with critical defects at the factory. Does the factory pass inspection? Explain.

	Type of Defect		
	Critical	**Major**	**Minor**
Inspector A	0	2	5
Inspector B	0	1	6
Inspector C	0	3	3
Inspector D	0	5	6

8. A scientist determines that 35% of packages of a food product contain a specific bacteria. Use technology to simulate choosing 100 random samples of 20 packages. How closely do the samples estimate the percent of all packages with the specific bacteria?

C.3 Comparing Populations (pp. 575–580)

Learning Target: Compare populations using measures of center and variation.

9. The double box-and-whisker plot represents the points scored per game by two football teams during the regular season.

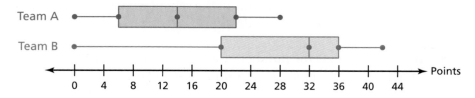

   a. Compare the data sets using measures of center and variation.

   b. Which team is more likely to score 18 points in a game?

10. The dot plots show the ages of campers at two summer camps.

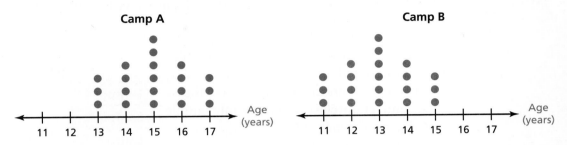

a. Express the difference in the measures of center as a multiple of the measure of variation.

b. Are the ages of campers at one camp significantly greater than at the other? Explain.

C.4 Using Random Samples to Compare Populations *(pp. 581–586)*

Learning Target: Use random samples to compare populations.

11. The double dot plot shows the median gas mileages of 10 random samples of 50 vehicles for two car models. Compare the samples using measures of center and variation. Can you determine which car model has a better gas mileage? Explain.

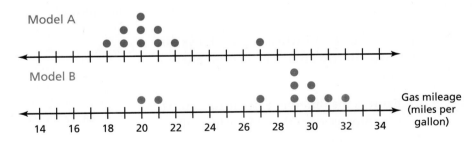

12. You compare the average amounts of time people in their twenties and thirties spend driving each week. The double box-and-whisker plot represents the medians of 100 random samples of 8 people from each age group. Can you determine whether one age group drives more than the other? Explain.

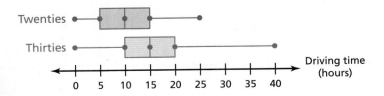

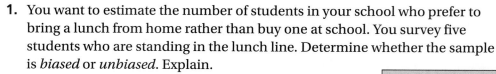

Practice Test

1. You want to estimate the number of students in your school who prefer to bring a lunch from home rather than buy one at school. You survey five students who are standing in the lunch line. Determine whether the sample is *biased* or *unbiased*. Explain.

2. You want to predict which candidate will likely be voted Seventh Grade Class President. There are 560 students in the seventh grade class. You randomly sample 3 different groups of 50 seventh-grade students. The results are shown.

	Candidate Preference	
	Candidate A	**Candidate B**
Sample 1	27	23
Sample 2	22	28
Sample 3	15	35

   a. Use each sample to make an estimate for the number of students in seventh grade that vote for Candidate A.

   b. Who do you expect to be voted Seventh Grade Class President? Explain.

3. Of 60 randomly chosen students from a school surveyed, 16 chose the aquarium as their favorite field trip. There are 720 students in the school. Predict the number of students in the school who choose the aquarium as their favorite field trip.

4. The double box-and-whisker plot shows the ages of the viewers of two television shows in a small town.

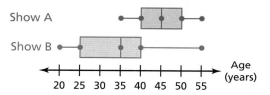

   a. Compare the data sets using measures of center and variation.

   b. Which show is more likely to have a 44-year-old viewer?

5. The double box-and-whisker plot shows the test scores for two French classes taught by the same teacher.

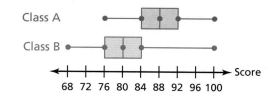

   a. Express the difference in the measures of center as a multiple of the measure of variation.

   b. Are the scores for one class significantly greater than for the other? Explain.

6. Two airplanes each hold about 400 pieces of luggage. The double dot plot shows a random sample of 8 pieces of luggage from each plane. Compare the samples using measures of center and variation. Can you determine which plane has heavier luggage? Explain.

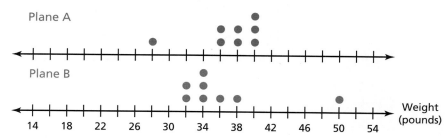

Cumulative Practice

1. Which of the ratios form a proportion?

   A. 5 to 2 and 4 to 10

   B. 2 : 3 and 7 : 8

   C. 3 to 2 and 15 to 10

   D. 12 : 8 and 8 : 4

2. A student scored 600 the first time she took the mathematics portion of a college entrance exam. The next time she took the exam, she scored 660. Her second score represents what percent increase over her first score?

   F. 9.1%   G. 10%

   H. 39.6%   I. 60%

3. You ask 100 randomly chosen students to name their favorite food. There are 1250 students in the school. Based on this sample, what is the number of students in the school whose favorite food is chicken?

Favorite Food	
Pizza	38
Tacos	36
Chicken	8
Other	18

   A. 100   B. 225

   C. 450   D. 475

4. Which value of p makes the equation $p + 6 = 5$ true?

   F. −1   G. 1

   H. 11   I. 30

5. The table shows the costs for four cans of tomato soup. Which can has the lowest cost per ounce?

	Cost (dollars)	Number of Ounces
Can A	1.95	26
Can B	0.72	8
Can C	0.86	10.75
Can D	2.32	23.2

A. Can A

B. Can B

C. Can C

D. Can D

6. What value of *y* makes the equation $-3y = -18$ true?

7. The double dot plot shows the values in two data sets. Which sentence best represents the difference in the measures of center as a multiple of the measure of variation?

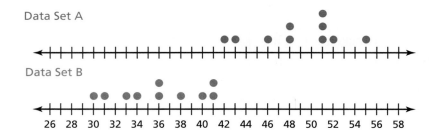

F. The difference of the means is about 3.3 times the MAD.

G. The difference of the means is about 3.8 times the MAD.

H. The difference of the means is 36 times the MAD.

I. The difference of the means is 48.7 times the MAD.

8. What is the missing value in the ratio table?

x	y
$\frac{2}{3}$	5
2	15
$\frac{8}{3}$	
8	60

9. You are selling tomatoes. What is the minimum number of pounds of tomatoes you need to sell to earn at least $44?

A. 11

B. 12

C. 40

D. 176

$4 per pound

10. You and a group of friends want to know how many students in your school prefer science. There are 900 students in your school. Each person randomly surveys 20 students. The table shows the results. Which subject do students at your school prefer?

Think
Solve
Explain

	Favorite Subject			
	English	**Math**	**Science**	**History**
You	4	5	6	5
Friend A	2	4	7	7
Friend B	7	4	8	1
Friend C	3	6	5	6
Friend D	6	7	2	5

Part A Use each sample to make an estimate for the number of students in your school who prefer science.

Part B Describe the variation of the estimates.

Part C Use the samples to make one estimate for the number of students who prefer science in your school.

D Geometric Shapes and Angles

Chapter Learning Target:
Understand geometry.

Chapter Success Criteria:
- ■ I can explain how to find the circumference of a circle.
- ■ I can find the areas of circles and composite figures.
- ■ I can solve problems involving angle measures.
- ■ I can construct a polygon.

STEAM Video: "Track and Field"

Track and Field

Different lanes on a race track have different lengths. How can competitors run in different lanes and have the same finish line?

Watch the STEAM Video "Track and Field." Then answer the following questions.

1. A track consists of a rectangle and two semicircles. The dimensions of the rectangle formed by the innermost lane are shown. What is the distance around each semicircle on the 400-meter, innermost lane?

2. How does the width of the rectangle, 63.7 meters, compare to the distance around each semicircle? Explain.

Finding the Area and Perimeter of a Track

After completing this chapter, you will be able to use the concepts you learned to answer the questions in the *STEAM Video Performance Task*. You will be given the dimensions of a race track.

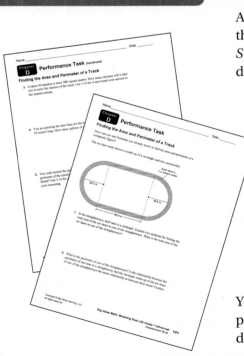

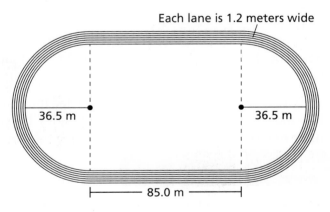

You will be asked to solve various perimeter and area problems about the track. Given a race track, what measures do you need to find the outer perimeter?

Getting Ready for Chapter

Chapter Exploration

Work with a partner.

1. Perform the steps for each of the figures.

- Measure the perimeter of the larger polygon to the nearest millimeter.
- Measure the diameter of the circle to the nearest millimeter.
- Measure the perimeter of the smaller polygon to the nearest millimeter.
- Calculate the value of the ratio of the two perimeters to the diameter.
- Take the average of the ratios. This average is the approximation of π (the Greek letter *pi*).

a.

Large Hexagon

Small Hexagon

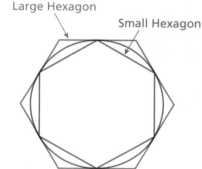

b.

Large Octagon

Small Octagon

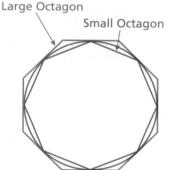

c.

Large Decagon

Small Decagon

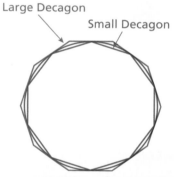

Sides	Large Perimeter	Diameter of Circle	Small Perimeter	Large Perimeter / Diameter	Small Perimeter / Diameter	Average of Ratios
6						
8						
10						

2. Based on the table, what can you conclude about the value of π? Explain your reasoning.

3. The Greek mathematician Archimedes used the above procedure to approximate the value of π. He used polygons with 96 sides. Do you think his approximation was more or less accurate than yours? Explain your reasoning.

Vocabulary

The following vocabulary terms are defined in this chapter. Think about what each term might mean and record your thoughts.

diameter of a circle   semicircle   adjacent angles
circumference   composite figure   vertical angles

D.1 Circles and Circumference

Learning Target: Find the circumference of a circle.

Success Criteria:
- I can explain the relationship between the diameter and circumference of a circle.
- I can use a formula to find the circumference of a circle.

EXPLORATION 1

Using a Compass to Draw a Circle

Work with a partner. Set a compass to 2 inches and draw a circle.

a. Draw a line from one side of the circle to the other that passes through the center. What is the length of the line? This is called the *diameter* of the circle.

b. **MP CHOOSE TOOLS** Estimate the distance around the circle. This is called the *circumference* of the circle. Explain how you found your answer.

EXPLORATION 2

Exploring Diameter and Circumference

Work with a partner.

Math Practice

Calculate Accurately
What other methods can you use to calculate the circumference of a circle? Which methods are more accurate?

a. Roll a cylindrical object on a flat surface to find the circumference of the circular base.

b. Measure the diameter of the circular base. Which is greater, the diameter or the circumference? how many times greater?

c. Compare your answers in part (b) with the rest of the class. What do you notice?

d. Without measuring, how can you find the circumference of a circle with a given diameter? Use your method to estimate the circumference of the circle in Exploration 1.

Key Vocabulary 🔊
circle, *p. 600*
center, *p. 600*
radius, *p. 600*
diameter, *p. 600*
circumference, *p. 601*
pi, *p. 601*
semicircle, *p. 602*

A **circle** is the set of all points in a plane that are the same distance from a point called the **center**.

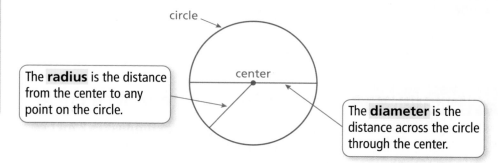

circle

center

The **radius** is the distance from the center to any point on the circle.

The **diameter** is the distance across the circle through the center.

 Key Idea

Radius and Diameter

Words   The diameter *d* of a circle is twice the radius *r*. The radius *r* of a circle is one-half the diameter *d*.

Algebra   **Diameter:** $d = 2r$ **Radius:** $r = \dfrac{d}{2}$

EXAMPLE 1   **Finding a Radius and a Diameter**

a. The diameter of a circle is 20 feet. Find the radius.

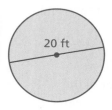

20 ft

$r = \dfrac{d}{2}$ Radius of a circle

$ = \dfrac{20}{2}$ Substitute 20 for *d*.

$ = 10$ Divide.

▷ The radius is 10 feet.

b. The radius of a circle is 7 meters. Find the diameter.

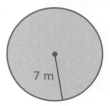

7 m

$d = 2r$ Diameter of a circle

$ = 2(7)$ Substitute 7 for *r*.

$ = 14$ Multiply.

▷ The diameter is 14 meters.

Try It

1. The diameter of a circle is 16 centimeters. Find the radius.

2. The radius of a circle is 9 yards. Find the diameter.

The distance around a circle is called the **circumference**. The ratio of the circumference to the diameter is the same for *every* circle and its value is represented by the Greek letter π, called **pi**. Two approximations for the value of π are 3.14 and $\dfrac{22}{7}$.

When the radius or diameter is a multiple of 7, it is easier to use $\dfrac{22}{7}$ as the estimate of π.

🔑 Key Idea

Circumference of a Circle

Words The circumference C of a circle is equal to π times the diameter d or π times twice the radius r.

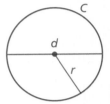

Algebra $C = \pi d$ or $C = 2\pi r$

EXAMPLE 2 Finding Circumferences of Circles

a. **Find the circumference of the flying disc. Use 3.14 for π.**

5 in.

$C = 2\pi r$ Write formula for circumference.

$\approx 2 \cdot 3.14 \cdot 5$ Substitute 3.14 for π and 5 for r.

$= 31.4$ Multiply.

▷ The circumference is about 31.4 inches.

b. **Find the circumference of the watch face. Use $\dfrac{22}{7}$ for π.**

28 mm

$C = \pi d$ Write formula for circumference.

$\approx \dfrac{22}{7} \cdot 28$ Substitute $\dfrac{22}{7}$ for π and 28 for d.

$= 88$ Multiply.

▷ The circumference is about 88 millimeters.

Try It **Find the circumference of the object. Use 3.14 or $\dfrac{22}{7}$ for π.**

3.
2 cm

4.

14 ft

5.

9 in.

EXAMPLE 3 **Finding the Perimeter of a Semicircular Region**

A semicircle is one-half of a circle. Find the perimeter of the semicircular region.

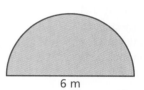

The straight side is 6 meters long. The distance around the curved part is one-half the circumference of a circle with a diameter of 6 meters.

6 m

$$\frac{C}{2} = \frac{\pi d}{2}$$ Divide the circumference by 2.

$$\approx \frac{3.14 \cdot 6}{2}$$ Substitute 3.14 for π and 6 for d.

$$= \frac{18.84}{2}$$ Multiply.

$$= 9.42$$ Divide.

▷ So, the perimeter is about $6 + 9.42 = 15.42$ meters.

Try It **Find the perimeter of the semicircular region.**

6.

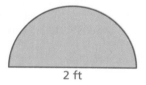

2 ft

7.

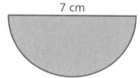

7 cm

8.

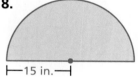

├─15 in.─┤

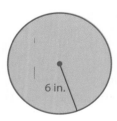

Self-Assessment for Concepts & Skills

Solve each exercise. Then rate your understanding of the success criteria in your journal.

9. **WRITING** Are there circles for which the value of the ratio of circumference to diameter is not equal to π? Explain.

10. **FINDING A PERIMETER** Find the perimeter of a semicircular region with a straight side that is 8 yards long.

11. **DIFFERENT WORDS, SAME QUESTION** Which is different? Find "both" answers.

6 in.

What is the distance around the circle?

What is π times the radius?

What is the circumference of the circle?

What is π times the diameter?

EXAMPLE 4 **Modeling Real Life**

The circumference of the roll of caution tape decreases 10.5 inches after a firefighter uses some of the tape. What is the radius of the roll after the firefighter uses the tape?

C = 31.4 in.

The radius and circumference of the roll are the radius and circumference of the circular bases of the roll. After the decrease, the circumference is $31.4 - 10.5 = 20.9$ inches.

Use the formula for the circumference of a circle to find the radius of a circle with a circumference of 20.9 inches.

$C = 2\pi r$	Write formula for circumference.
$20.9 \approx 2(3.14)r$	Substitute 20.9 for C and 3.14 for π.
$20.9 = 6.28r$	Multiply.
$3.3 \approx r$	Divide each side by 6.28.

▷ So, the radius of the roll is about 3.3 inches.

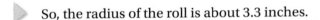

Self-Assessment for Problem Solving

Solve each exercise. Then rate your understanding of the success criteria in your journal.

12. The wheels of a monster truck are 66 inches tall. Find the distance the monster truck travels when the tires make one 360-degree rotation.

66 in.

13. **DIG DEEPER!** The radius of a dog's collar should be at least 0.5 inch larger than the radius of the dog's neck. A dog collar adjusts to a circumference of 10 to 14 inches. Should the collar be worn by a dog with a neck circumference of 12.5 inches? Explain.

14. You resize a picture so that the radius of the midday Sun appears four times larger. How much larger does the circumference of the Sun appear? Explain.

D.1 Practice

Go to *BigIdeasMath.com* to get
HELP with solving the exercises.

▶ Review & Refresh

Two jars each contain 1000 numbered tiles. The double box-and-whisker plot represents a random sample of 10 numbers from each jar.

1. Compare the samples using measures of center and variation.

2. Can you determine which jar contains greater numbers? Explain.

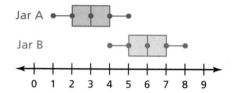

3. Find the percent of change from 24 to 18.

   A. 25% decrease   **B.** 25% increase   **C.** 75% increase   **D.** 75% decrease

▶▶ Concepts, Skills, & Problem Solving

EXPLORING DIAMETER AND CIRCUMFERENCE **Estimate the circumference of the circular base of the object.** (See Exploration 2, p. 599.)

4. tube of lip balm with radius 0.5 mm   5. D battery with radius 0.65 in.

FINDING A RADIUS **Find the radius of the button.**

6.  5 cm

7. 28 mm

8. 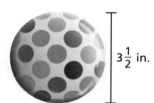 $3\frac{1}{2}$ in.

FINDING A DIAMETER **Find the diameter of the object.**

9. 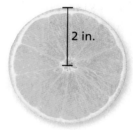 2 in.

10.  0.8 ft

11.  $\frac{3}{5}$ cm

FINDING A CIRCUMFERENCE **Find the circumference of the object. Use 3.14 or $\frac{22}{7}$ for π.**

12. 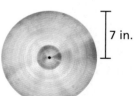 7 in.

13.  6 cm

14. 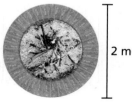 2 meters

FINDING THE PERIMETER OF A SEMICIRCULAR REGION **Find the perimeter of the window.**

15.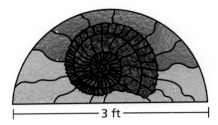

├─────── 3 ft ───────┤

16.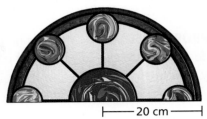

├───── 20 cm ─────┤

ESTIMATING A RADIUS **Estimate the radius of the object.**

17.

C = 8.9 mm

18.

C = 122 in.

19. **MP** **MODELING REAL LIFE** A circular sinkhole has a circumference of 75.36 meters. A week later, it has a circumference of 150.42 meters.

   a. Estimate the diameter of the sinkhole each week.

   b. How many times greater is the diameter of the sinkhole a week later?

20. **MP** **REASONING** Consider the circles *A*, *B*, *C*, and *D*.

A.
8 ft

B.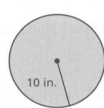
10 in.

C.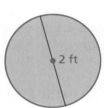
2 ft

D.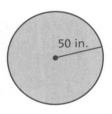
50 in.

   a. Without calculating, which circle has the greatest circumference? Explain.

   b. Without calculating, which circle has the least circumference? Explain.

FINDING CIRCUMFERENCES **Find the circumferences of both circles.**

21.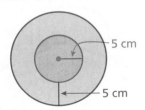
5 cm
5 cm

22.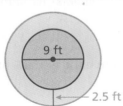
9 ft
2.5 ft

23.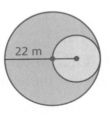
22 m

24. **MP** **MODELING REAL LIFE** A satellite is in an approximately circular orbit 36,000 kilometers from Earth's surface. The radius of Earth is about 6400 kilometers. What is the circumference of the satellite's orbit?

25. **(MP) STRUCTURE** The ratio of circumference to diameter is the same for every circle. Is the ratio of circumference to radius the same for every circle? Explain.

26. **(MP) PROBLEM SOLVING** A wire is bent to form four semicircles. How long is the wire? Justify your answer.

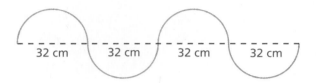

32 cm   32 cm   32 cm   32 cm

27. **CRITICAL THINKING** Explain how to draw a circle with a circumference of π^2 inches. Then draw the circle.

28. **DIG DEEPER!** "Lines" of latitude on Earth are actually circles. The Tropic of Cancer is the northernmost line of latitude at which the Sun appears directly overhead at noon. The Tropic of Cancer has a radius of 5854 kilometers.

To qualify for an around-the-world speed record, a pilot must cover a distance no less than the circumference of the Tropic of Cancer, cross all meridians, and land on the same airfield where the flight began.

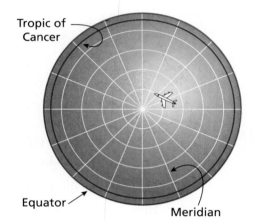

Tropic of Cancer

Equator

Meridian

a. What is the minimum distance that a pilot must fly to qualify for an around-the-world speed record?

b. **RESEARCH** Estimate the time it will take for a pilot to qualify for the speed record. Explain your reasoning.

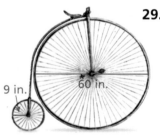

9 in.   60 in.

29. **(MP) PROBLEM SOLVING** Bicycles in the late 1800s looked very different than they do today.

a. How many rotations does each tire make after traveling 600 feet? Round your answers to the nearest whole number.

b. Would you rather ride a bicycle made with two large wheels or two small wheels? Explain.

30. **(MP) LOGIC** The length of the minute hand is 150% of the length of the hour hand.

a. What distance will the tip of the minute hand move in 45 minutes? Justify your answer.

b. In 1 hour, how much farther does the tip of the minute hand move than the tip of the hour hand? Explain how you found your answer.

36 mm

D.2 Areas of Circles

Learning Target: Find the area of a circle.

Success Criteria:
- I can estimate the area of a circle.
- I can use a formula to find the area of a circle.

Estimating the Area of a Circle

Work with a partner. Each grid contains a circle with a diameter of 4 centimeters. Use each grid to estimate the area of the circle. Which estimate should be closest to the actual area? Explain.

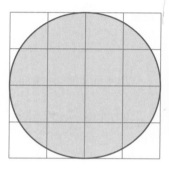 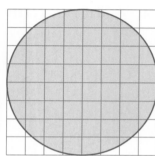 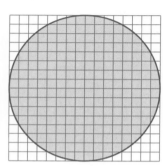

Writing a Formula for the Area of a Circle

Work with a partner. A student draws a circle with radius *r* and divides the circle into 24 equal sections. The student cuts out each section and arranges the sections to form a shape that resembles a parallelogram.

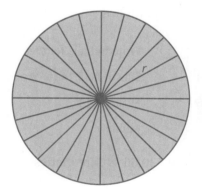 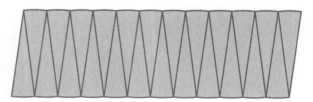

Math Practice

Interpret a Solution

Describe the relationship between the radius and the area of a circle.

a. Use the diagram to write a formula for the area *A* of a circle in terms of the radius *r*. Explain your reasoning.

b. Use the formula to check your estimates in Exploration 1.

Key Idea

Area of a Circle

Words The area A of a circle is the product of π and the square of the radius r.

Algebra $A = \pi r^2$

EXAMPLE 1 **Finding Areas of Circles**

a. Find the area of the circle. Use $\dfrac{22}{7}$ for π.

Estimate

$3 \times 7^2 \approx 3 \times 50$

$= 150$

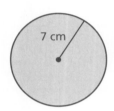

7 cm

$A = \pi r^2$ Write formula for area.

$\approx \dfrac{22}{7} \cdot 7^2$ Substitute $\dfrac{22}{7}$ for π and 7 for r.

$= \dfrac{22}{\overset{}{\underset{1}{\cancel{7}}}} \cdot \overset{7}{\cancel{49}}$ Evaluate 7^2. Divide out the common factor.

$= 154$ Multiply.

▷ The area is about 154 square centimeters.

Reasonable?

$154 \approx 150$ ✓

b. Find the area of the circle. Use 3.14 for π.

The radius is $26 \div 2 = 13$ inches.

Estimate

$3 \times 13^2 \approx 3 \times 170$

$= 510$

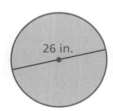

26 in.

$A = \pi r^2$ Write formula for area.

$\approx 3.14 \cdot 13^2$ Substitute 3.14 for π and 13 for r.

$= 3.14 \cdot 169$ Evaluate 13^2.

$= 530.66$ Multiply.

▷ The area is about 530.66 square inches.

Reasonable?

$530.66 \approx 510$ ✓

Try It

1. Find the area of a circle with a radius of 6 feet. Use 3.14 for π.

2. Find the area of a circle with a diameter of 28 meters. Use $\dfrac{22}{7}$ for π.

EXAMPLE 2 **Finding the Area of a Semicircle**

Find the area of the semicircle.

The area of the semicircle is one-half the area of a circle with a diameter of 30 feet. The radius of the circle is $30 \div 2 = 15$ feet.

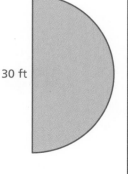

$$\frac{A}{2} = \frac{\pi r^2}{2} \qquad \text{Divide the area by 2.}$$

30 ft

$$\approx \frac{3.14 \cdot 15^2}{2} \qquad \text{Substitute 3.14 for } \pi \text{ and 15 for } r.$$

$$= \frac{3.14 \cdot 225}{2} \qquad \text{Evaluate } 15^2.$$

$$= 353.25 \qquad \text{Simplify.}$$

▷ So, the area of the semicircle is about 353.25 square feet.

Math Practice

Find General Methods

How can you find the area of one-fourth of a circle? three-fourths of a circle?

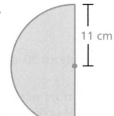

Try It **Find the area of the semicircle.**

3.

11 cm

4.

8 m

5. 5 yd

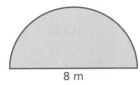 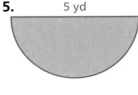

Self-Assessment *for Concepts & Skills*

Solve each exercise. Then rate your understanding of the success criteria in your journal.

6. ESTIMATING AN AREA The grid contains a circle with a diameter of 2 centimeters. Use the grid to estimate the area of the circle. How can you change the grid to improve your estimate? Explain.

7. WRITING Explain the relationship between the circumference and area of a circle.

8. DIFFERENT WORDS, SAME QUESTION Which is different? Find "both" answers.

> What is the area of a circle with a diameter of 1 m?

> What is the area of a circle with a diameter of 100 cm?

> What is the area of a circle with a radius of 100 cm?

> What is the area of a circle with a radius of 500 mm?

EXAMPLE 3 **Modeling Real Life**

A tsunami warning siren can be heard up to 2.5 miles away in all directions. From how many square miles can the siren be heard?

 Understand the problem.

You are given the description of a region in which a siren can be heard. You are asked to find the number of square miles within the range of the siren.

 Make a plan.

Two and a half miles from the siren in all directions is a circular region with a radius of 2.5 miles. So, find the area of a circle with a radius of 2.5 miles.

 **Solve and check.**

$A = \pi r^2$	Write formula for area.
$\approx 3.14 \cdot 2.5^2$	Substitute 3.14 for π and 2.5 for r.
$= 3.14 \cdot 6.25$	Evaluate 2.5^2.
$= 19.625$	Multiply.

So, the siren can be heard from about 20 square miles.

> **Check Reasonableness** The number of square miles should be greater than $3 \cdot 2^2 = 12$, but less than $4 \cdot 3^2 = 36$.
> Because $12 < 20 < 36$, the answer is reasonable. ✓

 Self-Assessment for *Problem Solving*

Solve each exercise. Then rate your understanding of the success criteria in your journal.

9. A local event planner wants to cover a circular region with mud for an obstacle course. The region has a circumference of about 157 feet. The cost to cover 1 square foot with mud is $1.50. Approximate the cost to cover the region with mud.

10. **DIG DEEPER!** A manufacturer recommends that you use a frying pan with a radius that is within 1 inch of the radius of your stovetop burner. The area of the bottom of your frying pan is 25π square inches. The circumference of your cooktop burner is 9π inches. Does your frying pan meet the manufacturer's recommendation?

D.2 Practice

Go to *BigIdeasMath.com* to get
HELP with solving the exercises.

▶ Review & Refresh

Find the circumference of the object. Use 3.14 or $\frac{22}{7}$ for π.

1.  9 cm

2.  7 in.

You spin the spinner shown.

3. How many possible outcomes are there?

4. In how many ways can spinning an odd number occur?

▶▶ Concepts, Skills, & Problem Solving

ESTIMATING AN AREA **Use the grid to estimate the area of the circle.** (See Exploration 1, p. 607.)

5. diameter of 3 centimeters

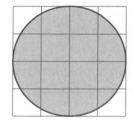

6. diameter of 1.6 inches

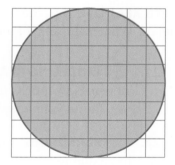

FINDING AN AREA **Find the area of the circle. Use 3.14 or $\frac{22}{7}$ for π.**

7.  9 mm

8.  14 cm

9. 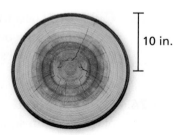 10 in.

10. 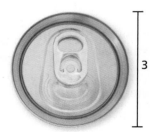 3 in.

11. 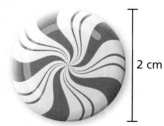 2 cm

12. 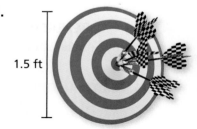 1.5 ft

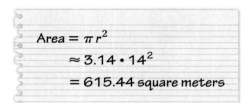

$$\text{Area} = \pi r^2$$
$$\approx 3.14 \cdot 14^2$$
$$= 615.44 \text{ square meters}$$

13. **MP YOU BE THE TEACHER** Your friend finds the area of a circle with a diameter of 7 meters. Is your friend correct? Explain.

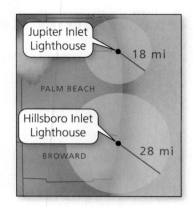

Jupiter Inlet Lighthouse — 18 mi

PALM BEACH

Hillsboro Inlet Lighthouse — 28 mi

BROWARD

14. **MP MODELING REAL LIFE** The diameter of a flour tortilla is 12 inches. What is the total area of two tortillas?

15. **MP MODELING REAL LIFE** The diameter of a coaster is 7 centimeters. What is the total area of five coasters?

16. **MP PROBLEM SOLVING** The Hillsboro Inlet Lighthouse lights up how much more area than the Jupiter Inlet Lighthouse?

FINDING THE AREA OF A SEMICIRCLE **Find the area of the semicircle.**

17.

├─── 20 cm ───┤

18.

├──── 24 in. ────┤

19.

├──── 2 ft ────┤

20. **MP MODELING REAL LIFE** The plate for a microscope has a circumference of 100π millimeters. What is the area of the plate?

20 ft

21. **MP MODELING REAL LIFE** A dog is leashed to the corner of a house. How much running area does the dog have? Explain how you found your answer.

22. **MP REASONING** Target A has a circumference of 20 feet. Target B has a diameter of 3 feet. Both targets are the same distance away. Which target is easier to hit? Explain your reasoning.

23. **MP MODELING REAL LIFE** A circular oil spill has a radius of 2 miles. After a day, the radius of the oil spill increases by 3 miles. By how many square miles does the area of the oil spill increase?

24. **FINDING AN AREA** Find the area of the circle in square yards.

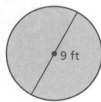

9 ft

25. **MP REPEATED REASONING** What happens to the circumference and the area of a circle when you double the radius? triple the radius? Justify your answer.

26. **CRITICAL THINKING** Is the area of a semicircle with a diameter of x *greater than*, *less than*, or *equal to* the area of a circle with a diameter of $\frac{1}{2}x$? Explain.

D.3 Perimeters and Areas of Composite Figures

Learning Target: Find perimeters and areas of composite figures.

Success Criteria:
- I can use a grid to estimate perimeters and areas.
- I can identify the shapes that make up a composite figure.
- I can find the perimeters and areas of shapes that make up composite figures.

EXPLORATION 1

Submitting a Bid

Work with a partner. You want to bid on a project for the pool shown. The project involves ordering and installing the brown tile that borders the pool, and ordering a custom-made tarp to cover the surface of the pool. In the figure, each grid square represents 1 square foot.

- You pay $5 per linear foot for the tile.
- You pay $4 per square foot for the tarp.
- It takes you about 15 minutes to install each foot of tile.

a. Estimate the total cost for the tile and the tarp.

b. Write a bid for how much you will charge for the project. Include the hourly wage you will receive. Estimate your total profit.

Math Practice

Simplify a Situation

How does using a grid help you make approximations for the perimeter and area of the pool?

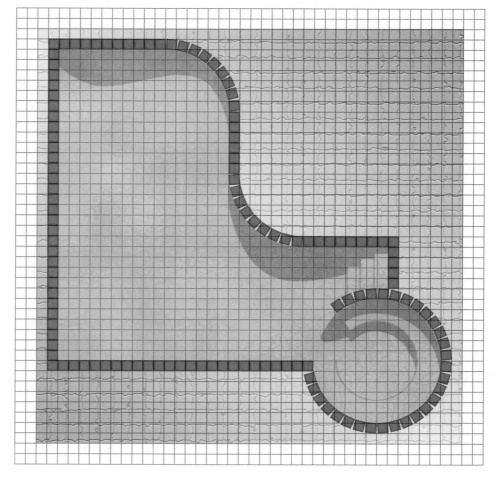

Key Vocabulary 🔊

composite figure,
p. 614

A **composite figure** is made up of triangles, squares, rectangles, semicircles, and other two-dimensional figures.

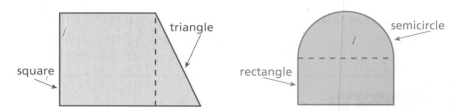

To find the perimeter of a composite figure, find the distance around the figure. To find the area of a composite figure, separate it into figures with areas you know how to find. Then find the sum of the areas of those figures.

EXAMPLE 1 **Estimating Perimeter and Area**

Estimate (a) the perimeter and (b) the area of the arrow.

a.

Count the number of grid square lengths around the arrow. There are 14.

Count the number of diagonal lengths around the arrow. There are 4.

Estimate the diagonal length to be 1.5 units.

Length of 14 grid square lengths: $14 \times 1 = 14$ units

Length of 4 diagonal lengths: $4 \times 1.5 = 6$ units

▷ So, the perimeter is about $14 + 6 = 20$ units.

b.

Count the number of squares that lie entirely in the figure. There are 12.

Count the number of half squares in the figure. There are 4.

Area of 12 squares: $12 \times 1 = 12$ square units

Area of 4 half squares: $4 \times 0.5 = 2$ square units

▷ So, the area is $12 + 2 = 14$ square units.

Try It

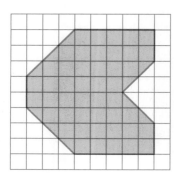

1. Estimate the perimeter and the area of the figure.

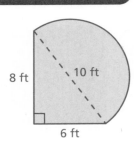

EXAMPLE 2 **Finding Perimeter and Area**

Find (a) the perimeter and (b) the area of the figure.

a. The figure is made up of a triangle and a semicircle.

The distance around the triangular part of the figure is $6 + 8 = 14$ feet. The distance around the semicircle is one-half the circumference of a circle with a diameter of 10 feet.

$$\frac{C}{2} = \frac{\pi d}{2}$$ Divide the circumference by 2.

$$\approx \frac{3.14 \cdot 10}{2}$$ Substitute 3.14 for π and 10 for d.

$$= 15.7$$ Simplify.

▷ So, the perimeter is about $14 + 15.7 = 29.7$ feet.

b. Find the area of the triangle and the area of the semicircle.

Area of Triangle

$$A = \frac{1}{2}bh$$

$$= \frac{1}{2}(6)(8)$$

$$= 24$$

Area of Semicircle

$$A = \frac{\pi r^2}{2}$$

$$\approx \frac{3.14 \cdot 5^2}{2}$$

$$= 39.25$$

The semicircle has a radius of $\frac{10}{2} = 5$ feet.

▷ So, the area is about $24 + 39.25 = 63.25$ square feet.

Try It

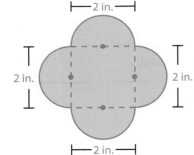

2. Find the perimeter and the area of the figure.

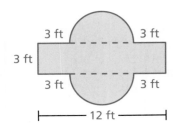

Self-Assessment *for Concepts & Skills*

Solve each exercise. Then rate your understanding of the success criteria in your journal.

3. ESTIMATING PERIMETER AND AREA
Estimate the perimeter and area of the figure at the right.

4. FINDING PERIMETER AND AREA Identify the shapes that make up the figure at the left. Then find the perimeter and area of the figure.

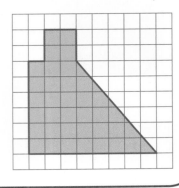

 **EXAMPLE 3** **Modeling Real Life** ─────────

The center circle of the basketball court has a radius of 3 feet and is painted blue. The rest of the court is stained brown. One gallon of wood stain covers 150 square feet. How many gallons of wood stain do you need to cover the brown portions of the court?

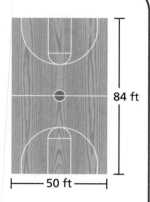

Understand the problem.

You are given dimensions of a basketball court. You are asked to determine the number of gallons of wood stain needed to stain the brown portions of the court when one gallon of wood stain covers 150 square feet.

Make a plan.

Find the entire area of the rectangular court. Then subtract the area of the center circle and divide by 150.

 Solve and check.

Area of Rectangle	*Area of Circle*
$A = \ell w$	$A = \pi r^2$
$= 84(50)$	$\approx 3.14 \cdot 3^2$
$= 4200$	$= 28.26$

Check Reasonableness
The circle covers a small area of the court. So, it makes sense that you need just less than $\frac{84(50)}{150} = 28$ gallons of wood stain. ✔

The area that is stained is about $4200 - 28.26 = 4171.74$ square feet.

> Because one gallon of wood stain covers 150 square feet, you need $4171.74 \div 150 \approx 27.8$ gallons of wood stain.

 Self-Assessment *for Problem Solving* ─────────

Solve each exercise. Then rate your understanding of the success criteria in your journal.

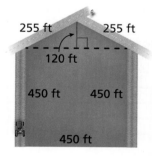

255 ft   255 ft
120 ft
450 ft   450 ft
450 ft

5. A farmer wants to seed and fence a section of land. Fencing costs $27 per yard. Grass seed costs $2 per square foot. How much does it cost to fence and seed the pasture?

6. **DIG DEEPER!** In each room shown, you plan to put down carpet and add a wallpaper border around the ceiling. Which room needs more carpeting? more wallpaper?

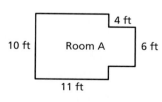

10 ft   Room A   6 ft   4 ft
11 ft

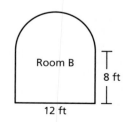

Room B   8 ft
12 ft

D.3 Practice

Go to *BigIdeasMath.com* to get HELP with solving the exercises.

▶ Review & Refresh

Find the area of the circle. Use 3.14 or $\frac{22}{7}$ for π.

1.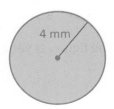
4 mm

2.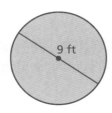
9 ft

Find the missing dimension. Use the scale 1 : 5.

	Item	Model	Actual
3.	House	Height: 6 ft	Height: _____ ft
4.	Garden hose	Length: _____ ft	Length: 20 yd
5.	Fountain	Depth: 20 cm	Depth: _____ m
6.	Bicycle wheel	Diameter: _____ in.	Diameter: 2 ft

▶▶ Concepts, Skills, & Problem Solving

ESTIMATING PERIMETER AND AREA You build a patio with a brick border. (See Exploration 1, p. 613.)

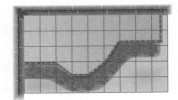

7. Estimate the perimeter of the patio.

8. Estimate the area of the patio.

ESTIMATING PERIMETER AND AREA Estimate the perimeter and the area of the shaded figure.

9.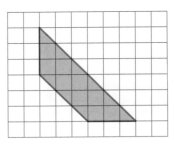

10.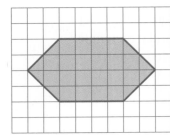

11.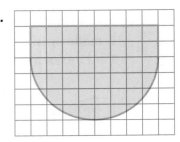

12.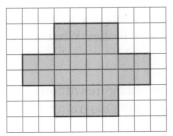

13.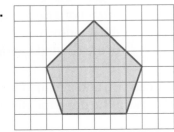

14.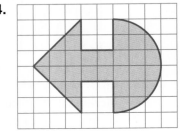

FINDING PERIMETER AND AREA **Find the perimeter and the area of the figure.**

15.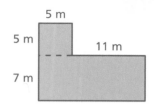

5 m

5 m

11 m

7 m

16.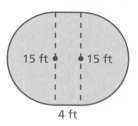

15 ft   15 ft

4 ft

17.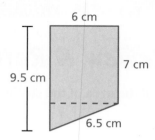

6 cm

7 cm

9.5 cm

6.5 cm

18. **MP YOU BE THE TEACHER** Your friend finds the perimeter of the figure. Is your friend correct? Explain your reasoning.

Perimeter = 4 + 3 + 4 + 5 + 4 + 5

= 25 in.

4 in.

4 in.

5 in.   5 in.

3 in.

4 in.

19. **MP LOGIC** A running track has six lanes. Explain why the starting points for the six runners are staggered. Draw a diagram as part of your explanation.

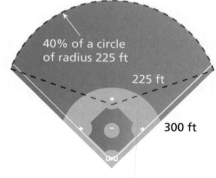

40% of a circle of radius 225 ft

225 ft

300 ft

20. **MP PROBLEM SOLVING** You run around the perimeter of the baseball field at a rate of 9 feet per second. How long does it take you to run around the baseball field?

21. **MP STRUCTURE** The figure at the right is made up of a square and a rectangle. Find the area of the shaded region.

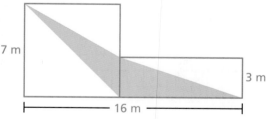

7 m

3 m

16 m

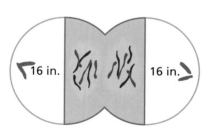

16 in.   16 in.

22. **DIG DEEPER!** Your friend makes a two-dimensional model of a dividing cell as shown. The total area of the dividing cell is 350 square inches. What is the area of the shaded region?

23. **CRITICAL THINKING** How can you add a figure to a composite figure without increasing its perimeter? Can this be done for all figures? Draw a diagram to support your answer.

D.4 Constructing Polygons

Learning Target: Construct a polygon with given measures.

Success Criteria:
- I can use technology to draw polygons.
- I can determine whether given measures result in one triangle, many triangles, or no triangle.
- I can draw polygons given angle measures or side lengths.

EXPLORATION 1   Using Technology to Draw Polygons

Work with a partner.

a. Use geometry software to draw each polygon with the given side lengths or angle measures, if possible. Complete the table.

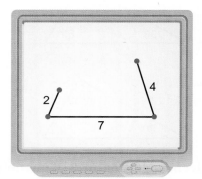

Side Lengths or Angle Measures	How many figures are possible?
i. 4 cm, 6 cm, 7 cm	
ii. 2 cm, 6 cm, 7 cm	
iii. 2 cm, 4 cm, 7 cm	
iv. 2 cm, 4 cm, 6 cm	
v. 2 in., 3 in., 3 in., 5 in.	
vi. 1 in., 1 in., 3 in., 6 in.	
vii. 1 in., 1 in., 3 in., 4 in.	
viii. 90°, 60°, 30°	
ix. 100°, 40°, 20°	
x. 50°, 60°, 70°	
xi. 20°, 80°, 100°	
xii. 20°, 50°, 50°, 60°	
xiii. 30°, 80°, 120°, 130°	
xiv. 60°, 60°, 120°, 120°	

b. Without constructing, how can you tell whether it is possible to draw a triangle given three angle measures? three side lengths? Explain your reasoning.

c. Without constructing, how can you tell whether it is possible to draw a quadrilateral given four angle measures? four side lengths? Explain your reasoning.

You can draw a triangle with three given angle measures when the sum of the angle measures is 180°.

EXAMPLE 1 Constructing Triangles Using Angle Measures

Draw a triangle with angle measures of 30°, 60°, and 90°, if possible.

Because 30° + 60° + 90° = 180°, you can draw a triangle with the given angle measures.

Step 1: Draw the 30° angle.　　　　**Step 2:** Draw the 60° angle.

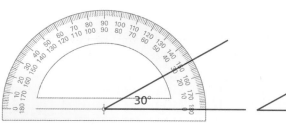

Step 3: Measure the remaining angle. The angle measure is 90°.

Try It **Draw a triangle with the given angle measures, if possible.**

1. 45°, 45°, 90°　　　　**2.** 100°, 55°, 25°　　　　**3.** 60°, 60°, 80°

EXAMPLE 2 Constructing Triangles Using Angles and Sides

Draw a triangle with side lengths of 3 centimeters and 4 centimeters that meet at a 20° angle.

Step 1: Draw a 20° angle.

Step 2: Use a ruler to mark 3 centimeters on one ray and 4 centimeters on the other ray.

Step 3: Draw the third side to form the triangle.

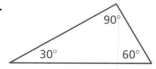

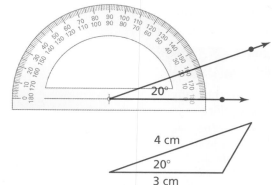

In Example 1, you can change the lengths of the sides to create many different triangles that meet the criteria. In Example 2, only one triangle is possible.

Try It

4. Draw a triangle with side lengths of 1 inch and 2 inches that meet at a 60° angle.

You can draw a triangle with three given side lengths when the sum of the lengths of any two sides is greater than the length of the third side.

EXAMPLE 3 Constructing Triangles Using Side Lengths

Draw a triangle with the given side lengths, if possible.

a. **4 cm, 2 cm, 3 cm**

The sum of the lengths of any two sides is greater than the length of the third side.

$$4 \text{ cm} + 2 \text{ cm} > 3 \text{ cm} \qquad 4 \text{ cm} + 3 \text{ cm} > 2 \text{ cm} \qquad 2 \text{ cm} + 3 \text{ cm} > 4 \text{ cm}$$

So, you can draw a triangle with the given side lengths.

Step 1: Draw a 4-centimeter side.

Step 2: Use a compass to determine where the 2-centimeter side and the 3-centimeter side meet.

Step 3: The third vertex can be at either intersection point. Draw the triangle.

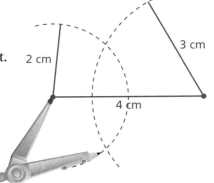

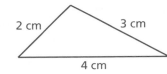

> In Example 3, only one triangle is possible. You can start with a different side length in Step 1, but the resulting triangle will have the same size and shape.

b. **2.5 in., 1 in., 1 in.**

Because 1 in. + 1 in. < 2.5 in., it is not possible to draw the triangle.

Check Try to draw the triangle. Draw a 2.5-inch side. Use a compass to show that the 1-inch sides cannot intersect.

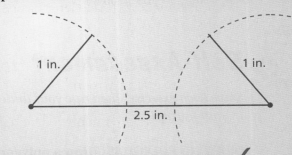

So, it is not possible to draw the triangle. ✓

Math Practice

Look for Structure
How can you change one of the side lengths in part (b) so that they form a triangle? Compare answers with a classmate.

Try It **Draw a triangle with the given side lengths, if possible.**

5. 2 cm, 2 cm, 5 cm   6. 4 cm, 3 cm, 3 cm   7. 1 cm, 4 cm, 5 cm

You can draw a quadrilateral with four given angle measures when the sum of the angle measures is 360°.

EXAMPLE 4 **Constructing a Quadrilateral**

Draw a quadrilateral with angle measures of 60°, 120°, 70°, and 110°, if possible.

Because 60° + 120° + 70° + 110° = 360°, you can draw a quadrilateral with the given angle measures.

Step 1: Draw a 60° angle and a 120° angle that each have one side on a line.

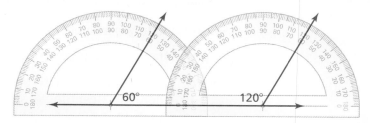

Step 2: Draw the remaining side at a 70° angle.

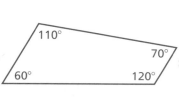

Step 3: Measure the remaining angle. The angle measure is 110°.

Try It **Draw a quadrilateral with the given angle measures, if possible.**

8. 100°, 90°, 65°, 105°

9. 100°, 40°, 20°, 20°

Self-Assessment *for Concepts & Skills*

Solve each exercise. Then rate your understanding of the success criteria in your journal.

DRAWING POLYGONS **Draw a polygon with the given side lengths or angle measures, if possible.**

10. 25 mm, 36 mm, 38 mm

11. 10°, 15°, 155°

12. 20°, 45°, 50°, 65°

13. 50°, 90°, 110°, 110°

14. USING SIDE LENGTHS Can you construct *one*, *many*, or *no* triangle(s) with side lengths of 3 inches, 4 inches, and 8 inches? Explain.

EXAMPLE 5 **Modeling Real Life**

You enclose a flower bed using landscaping boards with lengths of 3 yards, 4 yards, and 5 yards. Estimate the area of the flower bed.

Understand the problem.

You know the lengths of boards used to enclose a triangular region. You are asked to estimate the area of the triangular region.

Make a plan.

Draw a triangle with side lengths of 3 yards, 4 yards, and 5 yards using a scale of 1 cm : 1 yd. Use the drawing to estimate the base and height of the flower bed. Then use the formula for the area of a triangle to estimate the area.

Solve and check.

Draw the triangle.

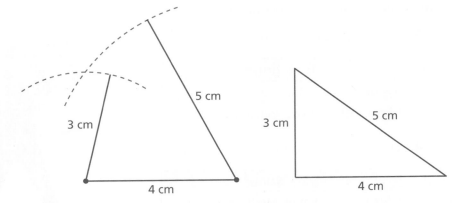

Another Method
Using a ruler, the height from the largest angle to the 5-centimeter side is about 2.4 centimeters. So, the area is about $\frac{1}{2}(2.4)(5) = 6 \text{ yd}^2$. ✓

The shape of the flower bed appears to be a right triangle with a base length of 4 yards and a height of 3 yards.

So, the area of the flower bed is about $A = \frac{1}{2}(4)(3) = 6$ square yards.

Self-Assessment for Problem Solving

Solve each exercise. Then rate your understanding of the success criteria in your journal.

15. A triangular pen has fence lengths of 6 feet, 8 feet, and 10 feet. Create a scale drawing of the pen.

16. The front of a cabin is the shape of a triangle. The angles of the triangle are 40°, 70°, and 70°. Can you determine the height of the cabin? If not, what information do you need?

17. **DIG DEEPER!** Two rooftops have triangular patios. One patio has side lengths of 9 meters, 10 meters, and 11 meters. The other has side lengths of 6 meters, 10 meters, and 15 meters. Which patio has a greater area? Explain.

D.4 Practice

Go to *BigIdeasMath.com* to get HELP with solving the exercises.

▶ Review & Refresh

Find the perimeter and area of the figure.

1.

2 in.

2 in.   2 in.

2 in.

1 in.

2.

4 cm   5 cm

3 cm

Use a tree diagram to find the sample space and the total number of possible outcomes of the indicated event.

3. choosing a toothbrush

Toothbrush	
Type	Electric, Traditional
Strength	Extra soft, Soft, Medium

4. choosing a toy hoop

Toy Hoop	
Size	Small, Medium, Large
Color	Blue, Green, Orange, Pink, Purple, Yellow

▶▶ Concepts, Skills, & Problem Solving

USING TECHNOLOGY TO DRAW POLYGONS Use geometry software to draw the polygon with the given side lengths or angle measures, if possible. (See Exploration 1, p. 619.)

5. $30°, 65°, 85°$

6. 2 in., 3 in., 5 in.

7. $80°, 90°, 100°, 110°$

8. 2 cm, 2 cm, 5 cm, 5 cm

CONSTRUCTING TRIANGLES USING ANGLE MEASURES Draw a triangle with the given angle measures, if possible.

9. $40°, 50°, 90°$

10. $20°, 40°, 120°$

11. $38°, 42°, 110°$

12. $54°, 60°, 66°$

13. **MP YOU BE THE TEACHER** Your friend determines whether he can draw a triangle with angle measures of $10°$, $40°$, and $130°$. Is your friend correct? Explain your reasoning.

> $10° + 40° < 130°$
>
> Because the sum of the measure of two angles is not greater than the measure of the third angle, you cannot draw a triangle.

CONSTRUCTING TRIANGLES USING ANGLES AND SIDES Draw a triangle with the given description.

14. side lengths of 1 inch and 2 inches meet at a 50° angle

15. side lengths of 7 centimeters and 9 centimeters meet at a 120° angle

16. a 95° angle connects to a 15° angle by a side of length 2 inches

17. a 70° angle connects to a 70° angle by a side of length 4 centimeters

CONSTRUCTING TRIANGLES USING SIDE LENGTHS Draw a triangle with the given side lengths, if possible.

18. 4 in., 5 in., 10 in.

19. 10 mm, 30 mm, 50 mm

20. 5 cm, 5 cm, 8 cm

21. 8 mm, 12 mm, 13 mm

22. **MP** **MODELING REAL LIFE** Can you construct a triangular case using two pieces of wood that are 12 inches long and one piece of wood that is 25 inches long? Explain.

23. **MP** **MODELING REAL LIFE** Can you construct a warning triangle using three pieces of plastic that are each 6 inches long? Explain.

24. **MP** **LOGIC** You are constructing a triangle. You draw the first angle, as shown. Your friend says that you must be constructing an acute triangle. Is your friend correct? Explain your reasoning.

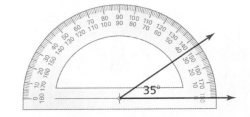

USING ANGLES AND SIDES Determine whether you can construct *one, many,* or *no* triangle(s) with the given description. Explain your reasoning.

25. a triangle with one angle measure of 60° and one side length of 4 centimeters

26. a scalene triangle with side lengths of 3 centimeters and 7 centimeters

27. an isosceles triangle with two side lengths of 4 inches that meet at an 80° angle

28. a triangle with one angle measure of 60°, one angle measure of 70°, and a side length of 10 centimeters between the two angles

29. a triangle with one angle measure of 20°, one angle measure of 35°, and a side of length 3 inches that is between the two angles

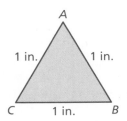

30. **MP** **REASONING** A triangle is shown.

    a. Construct a triangle with side lengths twice those of the triangle shown. Does the new triangle have the same angle measures?

    b. How can you change the side lengths of the triangle so that the measure of ∠A increases?

CONSTRUCTING QUADRILATERALS **Draw a quadrilateral with the given angle measures, if possible.**

31. 60°, 60°, 120°, 120°

32. 50°, 60°, 110°, 150°

33. 20°, 30°, 150°, 160°

34. 10°, 10°, 10°, 150°

CONSTRUCTING SPECIAL QUADRILATERALS **Construct a quadrilateral with the given description.**

35. a rectangle with side lengths of 1 inch and 2 inches

36. a kite with side lengths of 4 centimeters and 7 centimeters

37. a trapezoid with base angles of 40°

38. a rhombus with side lengths of 10 millimeters

39. **MP** **REASONING** A quadrilateral has side lengths of 6 units, 2 units, and 3 units as shown. How many quadrilaterals can be formed given a fourth side with a fixed length? Explain.

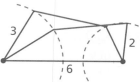

40. **MP** **REASONING** What types of quadrilaterals can you form using four side lengths of 7 units? Use drawings to support your conclusion.

41. **MP** **MODELING REAL LIFE** A triangular section of a farm is enclosed by fences that are 2 meters, 6 meters, and 7 meters long. Estimate the area of the section.

42. **MP** **MODELING REAL LIFE** A chemical spill expert sets up a triangular caution zone using cones. Cones A and B are 14 meters apart. Cones B and C are 22 meters apart. Cones A and C are 34 meters apart. Estimate the area of the caution zone.

43. **MP** **MODELING REAL LIFE** A search region is in the shape of an equilateral triangle. The measure of one side of the region is 20 miles. Make a scale drawing of the search region. Estimate the area of the search region.

44. **MP** **REASONING** A triangle has fixed side lengths of 2 and 14.

  a. How many triangles can you construct? Use the figure below to explain your reasoning.

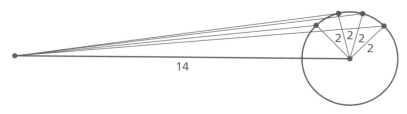

  b. Is the unknown side length of the triangle also fixed? Explain.

D.5 Finding Unknown Angle Measures

Learning Target: Use facts about angle relationships to find unknown angle measures.

Success Criteria:
- I can identify adjacent, complementary, supplementary, and vertical angles.
- I can use equations to find unknown angle measures.
- I can find unknown angle measures in real-life situations.

EXPLORATION 1

Using Rules About Angles

Work with a partner. The diagram shows pairs of *adjacent* angles and *vertical* angles. Vertical angles cannot be adjacent.

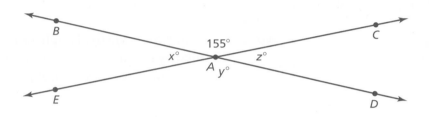

a. Which pair(s) of angles are adjacent angles? Explain.

b. Which pair(s) of angles are vertical angles? Explain.

c. Without using a protractor, find the values of x, y, and z. Explain your reasoning.

d. Make a conjecture about the measures of any two vertical angles.

e. Test your conjecture in part (d) using the diagram below. Explain why your conjecture is or is *not* true.

Math Practice

Use Definitions

How can you use the definition of supplementary angles to explain why your conjecture is or is *not* true?

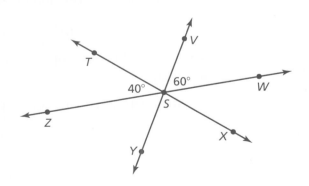

Key Ideas

Adjacent Angles

Words Two angles are **adjacent angles** when they share a common
side and have the same vertex.

Complementary Angles

Words Two angles are **complementary angles** when the sum of their
measures is 90°.

Supplementary Angles

Words Two angles are **supplementary angles** when the sum of their
measures is 180°.

Vertical Angles

Words Two angles are **vertical angles** when they are opposite angles
formed by the intersection of two lines. Vertical angles have the same
measure because they are both supplementary to the same angle.

Reading

Angles that have
the same measures
are called *congruent*
angles.

EXAMPLE 1 **Naming Angles**

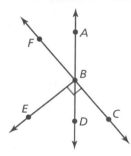

Name a pair of (a) adjacent angles, (b) complementary angles,
(c) supplementary angles, and (d) vertical angles in the figure.

a. ∠ABC and ∠ABF share a common side and have the same vertex B.

▶ So, ∠ABC and ∠ABF are adjacent angles.

b. ∠EBC is a right angle. This means that the sum of the measure of
∠EBD and the measure of ∠CBD is 90°.

▶ So, ∠EBD and ∠CBD are complementary angles.

c. ∠ABC and ∠DBC make up a straight angle. This means that the sum
of the measure of ∠ABC and the measure of ∠DBC is 180°.

▶ So, ∠ABC and ∠DBC are supplementary angles.

d. ∠ABF and ∠CBD are opposite angles formed by the intersection
of two lines.

▶ So, ∠ABF and ∠CBD are vertical angles.

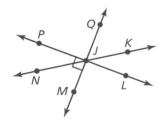

Try It

1. Name a pair of (a) adjacent angles, (b) complementary angles,
(c) supplementary angles, and (d) vertical angles in the figure.

EXAMPLE 2 **Using Pairs of Angles**

Classify each pair of angles. Then find the value of *x*.

a.

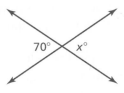

The angles are vertical angles. Vertical angles have the same measure.

▷ So, the value of *x* is 70.

Remember

When two or more adjacent angles form a larger angle, the sum of the measures of the smaller angles is equal to the measure of the larger angle.

b.

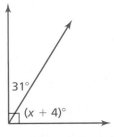

The angles are adjacent angles. Because the angles make up a right angle, the angles are also complementary angles, and the sum of their measures is 90°.

$(x + 4) + 31 = 90$ Write equation.

$x + 35 = 90$ Combine like terms.

$x = 55$ Subtract 35 from each side.

▷ So, the value of *x* is 55.

c.

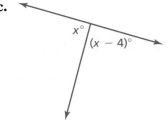

The angles are adjacent angles. Because the angles make up a straight angle, the angles are also supplementary angles, and the sum of their measures is 180°.

$x + (x - 4) = 180$ Write equation.

$2x - 4 = 180$ Combine like terms.

$2x = 184$ Add 4 to each side.

$x = 92$ Divide each side by 2.

▷ So, the value of *x* is 92.

Try It Classify the pair of angles. Then find the value of *x*.

2.

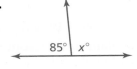

3.

4.

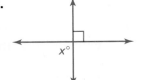

EXAMPLE 3 **Finding an Angle Measure**

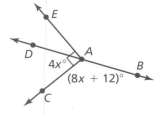

Remember

The sum of the measures of the angles around a point is equal to 360°.

Find the measure of ∠EAB.

To find the measure of ∠EAB, subtract the sum of the measures of ∠BAC and ∠EAC from 360°.

To find the measure of ∠BAC, find the value of x. ∠DAC and ∠BAC are supplementary angles. So, the sum of their measures is 180°.

$4x + (8x + 12) = 180$	Write equation.
$12x + 12 = 180$	Combine like terms.
$12x = 168$	Subtract 12 from each side.
$x = 14$	Divide each side by 12.

So, the measure of ∠BAC is $8(14) + 12 = 124°$.

Because ∠EAC is a right angle, it has a measure of 90°.

▷ So, the measure of ∠EAB is $360 - (124 + 90) = 146°$.

Try It **Find the measure of the indicated angle in the diagram.**

5. ∠NJM   **6.** ∠KJP   **7.** ∠KJM

Self-Assessment for Concepts & Skills

Solve each exercise. Then rate your understanding of the success criteria in your journal.

8. NAMING ANGLES Name a pair of (a) adjacent angles, (b) complementary angles, (c) supplementary angles, and (d) vertical angles in the figure at the left.

FINDING ANGLE MEASURES **Find the value of x.**

9.

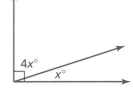

10.

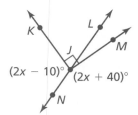

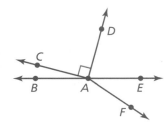

11. WHICH ONE DOESN'T BELONG? Which pair of angles does *not* belong with the other three? Explain your reasoning.

∠FBA, ∠FBE	∠CBD, ∠DBF	∠DBE, ∠DBC	∠FBA, ∠EBD

EXAMPLE 4 **Modeling Real Life**

A city worker designs an intersection of three roads that will be constructed next year. The measure of the angle between any two roads must be at least 60° in order for vehicles to turn safely. Does the design shown meet the requirement?

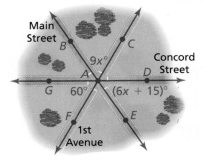

Because ∠GAF and ∠DAC are vertical angles, you know that the measure of ∠DAC is 60°. Because ∠BAC, ∠DAC, and ∠EAD make up a straight angle, you know that the sum of their measures is 180°. Use this information to write and solve an equation for x. Then determine whether any of the angle measures between two roads is less than 60°.

$$9x + 60 + (6x + 15) = 180 \qquad \text{Write equation.}$$
$$15x + 75 = 180 \qquad \text{Combine like terms.}$$
$$15x = 105 \qquad \text{Subtract 75 from each side.}$$
$$x = 7 \qquad \text{Divide each side by 15.}$$

∠EAD has a measure of $6(7) + 15 = 57°$.

So, the measure of ∠EAD is less than 60°, and the design does not meet the requirement.

Self-Assessment for Problem Solving

Solve each exercise. Then rate your understanding of the success criteria in your journal.

12. What is the angle between any two windmill blades in the windmill at the left? Justify your answer.

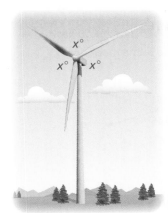

13. A hockey puck strikes a wall at an angle of 30°. The puck then travels away from the wall at the same angle. Find the value of y. Explain your reasoning.

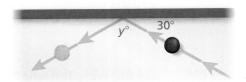

14. The laptop screen turns off when the angle between the keyboard and the screen is less than 20°. How many more degrees can the laptop screen close before the screen turns off?

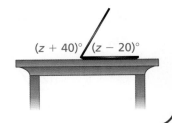

D.5 Practice

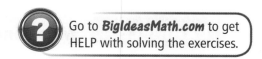

Go to *BigIdeasMath.com* to get
HELP with solving the exercises.

▶ Review & Refresh

Draw a triangle with the given side lengths, if possible.

1. 1 in., 3 in., 4 in.

2. 4 cm, 4 cm, 7 cm

Solve the inequality. Graph the solution.

3. $-8y \le 40$

4. $1.1z > -3.3$

5. $\frac{1}{3}x \ge 2.5$

▶▶ Concepts, Skills, & Problem Solving

USING RULES ABOUT ANGLES The diagram shows pairs of *adjacent* angles and *vertical* angles. (See Exploration 1, p. 627.)

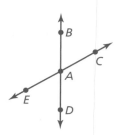

6. Which pair(s) of angles are adjacent angles? Explain.

7. Which pair(s) of angles are vertical angles? Explain.

NAMING ANGLES Use the figure shown.

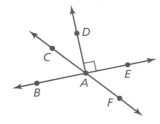

8. Name a pair of adjacent angles.

9. Name a pair of complementary angles.

10. Name a pair of supplementary angles.

11. Name a pair of vertical angles.

12. **MP YOU BE THE TEACHER** Your friend names a pair of angles with the same measure. Is your friend correct? Explain your reasoning.

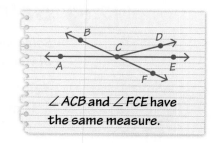

∠ACB and ∠FCE have the same measure.

ADJACENT AND VERTICAL ANGLES Tell whether the angles are *adjacent*, *vertical*, or *neither*. Explain.

13.

14.

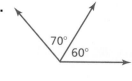

15.

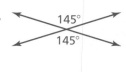

COMPLEMENTARY AND SUPPLEMENTARY ANGLES Tell whether the angles are *complementary*, *supplementary*, or *neither*. Explain.

16.

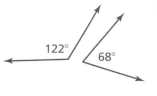

17.

18.

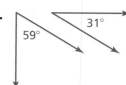

19. **MP** **YOU BE THE TEACHER** Your friend names a pair of supplementary angles. Is your friend correct? Explain.

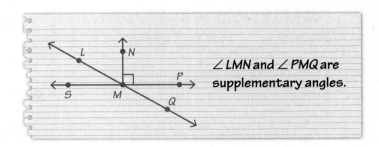

∠LMN and ∠PMQ are supplementary angles.

USING PAIRS OF ANGLES Classify the pair of angles. Then find the value of x.

20.

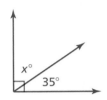

$x°$ 35°

21.

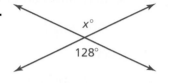

$x°$ 128°

22.

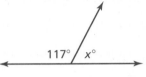

117° $x°$

23.

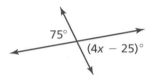

75° $(4x - 25)°$

24.

$4x°$ $2x°$

25.

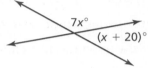

$7x°$ $(x + 20)°$

26.

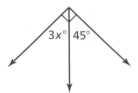

$3x°$ 45°

27.

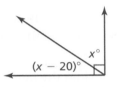

$x°$ $(x - 20)°$

28.

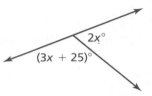

$2x°$ $(3x + 25)°$

29. **MP** **MODELING REAL LIFE** What is the measure of each angle formed by the intersection? Explain.

30. **MP** **MODELING REAL LIFE** A tributary joins a river at an angle. Find the value of x. Explain.

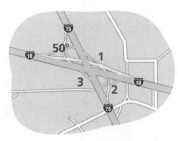

$x°$ $(2x + 21)°$

31. **MP** **MODELING REAL LIFE** The iron cross is a skiing trick in which the tips of the skis are crossed while the skier is airborne. Find the value of x in the iron cross shown.

127° $(2x + 41)°$

FINDING ANGLE MEASURES Find all angle measures in the diagram.

32.

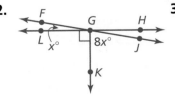

$x°$ $8x°$

33.

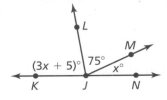

$(3x + 5)°$ 75° $x°$

34.

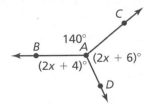

140° $(2x + 6)°$ $(2x + 4)°$

OPEN-ENDED Draw a pair of adjacent angles with the given description.

35. Both angles are acute.

36. One angle is acute, and one is obtuse.

37. The sum of the angle measures is 135°.

(MP) REASONING Copy and complete each sentence with *always, sometimes,* or *never*.

38. If *x* and *y* are complementary angles, then both *x* and *y* are_____ acute.

39. If *x* and *y* are supplementary angles, then *x* is_____ acute.

40. If *x* is a right angle, then *x* is_____ acute.

41. If *x* and *y* are complementary angles, then *x* and *y* are _____ adjacent.

42. If *x* and *y* are supplementary angles, then *x* and *y* are_____ vertical.

43. **(MP) REASONING** Draw a figure in which ∠1 and ∠2 are acute vertical angles, ∠3 is a right angle adjacent to ∠2, and the sum of the measure of ∠1 and the measure of ∠4 is 180°.

44. **(MP) STRUCTURE** Describe the relationship between the two angles represented by the graph shown at the right.

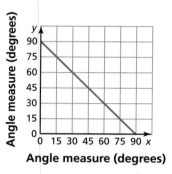

45. **(MP) STRUCTURE** Consider the figure shown at the left. Use a ruler to extend both rays into lines. What do you notice about the three new angles that are formed?

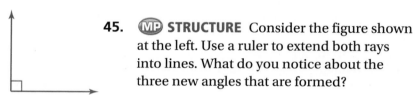

46. **OPEN-ENDED** Give an example of an angle that can be a supplementary angle but cannot be a complementary angle to another angle. Explain.

47. **(MP) MODELING REAL LIFE** The *vanishing point* of the picture is represented by point *B*.

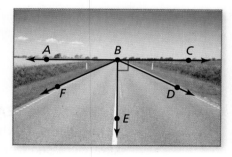

  a. The measure of ∠*ABD* is 6.2 times greater than the measure of ∠*CBD*. Find the measure of ∠*CBD*.

  b. ∠*FBE* and ∠*EBD* are congruent. Find the measure of ∠*FBE*.

48. **CRITICAL THINKING** The measures of two complementary angles have a ratio of 3 : 2. What is the measure of the larger angle?

49. **(MP) REASONING** Two angles are vertical angles. What are their measures if they are also complementary angles? supplementary angles?

50. **(MP) PROBLEM SOLVING** Find the values of *x* and *y*.

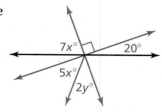

Connecting Concepts

▶ Using the Problem-Solving Plan

1. A dart is equally likely to hit any point on the board shown. Find the theoretical probability that a dart hitting the board scores 100 points.

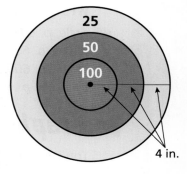

4 in.

Understand the problem. You are given the dimensions of a circular dart board. You are asked to find the theoretical probability of hitting the center circle.

Make a plan. Find the area of the center circle and the area of the entire dart board. To find the theoretical probability of scoring 100 points, divide the area of the center circle by the area of the entire dart board.

Solve and check. Use the plan to solve the problem. Then check your solution.

2. A scale drawing of a window is shown. Find the perimeter and the area of the actual window. Justify your answer.

1 cm : 2 ft

3. $\angle CAD$ makes up 20% of a pair of supplementary angles. Find the measure of $\angle DAE$. Justify your answer.

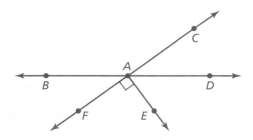

Finding the Area and Perimeter of a Track

At the beginning of the this chapter, you watched a STEAM video called "Track and Field". You are now ready to complete the performance task related to this video, available at *BigIdeasMath.com*. Be sure to use the problem-solving plan as you work through the performance task.

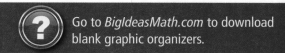

▶ Review Vocabulary

Write the definition and give an example of each vocabulary term.

circle, *p. 600*	circumference, *p. 601*	adjacent angles, *p. 628*
center, *p. 600*	pi, *p. 601*	complementary angles, *p. 628*
radius, *p. 600*	semicircle, *p. 602*	supplementary angles, *p. 628*
diameter, *p. 600*	composite figure, *p. 614*	vertical angles, *p. 628*

▶ Graphic Organizers

You can use a **Four Square** to organize information about a concept. Each of the four squares can be a category, such as definition, vocabulary, example, non-example, words, algebra, table, numbers, visual, graph, or equation. Here is an example of a Four Square for *circumference*.

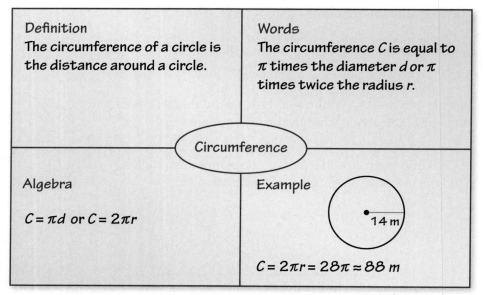

Definition
The circumference of a circle is the distance around a circle.

Words
The circumference *C* is equal to π times the diameter *d* or π times twice the radius *r*.

Circumference

Algebra

$C = \pi d$ or $C = 2\pi r$

Example

14 m

$C = 2\pi r = 28\pi \approx 88$ m

Choose and complete a graphic organizer to help you study each topic.

1. area of a circle
2. semicircle
3. composite figure
4. constructing triangles
5. constructing quadrilaterals
6. complementary angles
7. supplementary angles
8. vertical angles

Definition
A toy duck that floats in the bathtub

Color
Body = Yellow
Bill = Orange

Rubber Ducky

Visual

Fact
Rubber duckies are made so that they float in water.

I'd say that's an unlucky ducky!

"How do you like my Four Square on rubber duckies? Whenever I have my doggy bath, I insist that my ducky is with me."

Chapter Self-Assessment

As you complete the exercises, use the scale below to rate your understanding of the success criteria in your journal.

1 I do not understand.

2 I can do it with help.

3 I can do it on my own.

4 I can teach someone else.

D.1 Circles and Circumference (pp. 599–606)

Learning Target: Find the circumference of a circle.

1. What is the radius of a circular lid with a diameter of 5 centimeters?

2. The radius of a circle is 25 millimeters. Find the diameter.

Find the circumference of the object. Use 3.14 or $\frac{22}{7}$ for π.

3.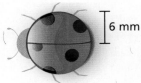
6 mm

4.
1.5 ft

5.
7 cm

6. You are placing non-slip tape along the perimeter of the bottom of a semicircle-shaped doormat. How much tape will you save applying the tape to the perimeter of the inside semicircle of the doormat? Justify your answer.

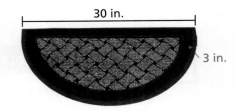
30 in.

3 in.

7. You need to carry a circular cake through a 32-inch wide doorway without tilting it. The circumference of the cake is 100 inches. Will the cake fit through the doorway? Explain.

C = 44 m

8. Estimate the radius of the Big Ben clock face in London.

9. Describe and solve a real-life problem that involves finding the circumference of a circle.

D.2 Areas of Circles *(pp. 607–612)*

Learning Target: Find the area of a circle.

Find the area of the circle. Use 3.14 or $\frac{22}{7}$ for π.

10.

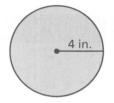

4 in.

11.

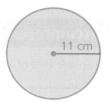

11 cm

12.

42 mm

13. A desktop is shaped like a semicircle with a diameter of 28 inches. What is the area of the desktop?

14. An ecologist is studying an algal bloom that has formed on the entire surface of a circular pond. What is the area of the surface of the pond covered by the algal bloom?

28 ft

15. A knitted pot holder is shaped like a circle. Its radius is 3.5 inches. What is its area?

D.3 Perimeters and Areas of Composite Figures *(pp. 613–618)*

Learning Target: Find perimeters and areas of composite figures.

Find the perimeter and the area of the figure.

16.

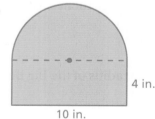

4 in.

10 in.

17.

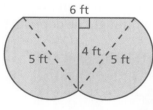

6 ft

5 ft   4 ft   5 ft

18. **GARDEN** You want to fence part of a yard to make a vegetable garden. How many feet of fencing do you need to surround the garden?

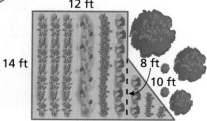

12 ft

14 ft

8 ft

10 ft

18 ft

D.4 Constructing Polygons (pp. 619–626)

Learning Target: Construct a polygon with given measures.

Draw a triangle with the given description, if possible.

19. a triangle with angle measures of 15°, 75°, and 90°

20. a triangle with a 3-inch side and a 4-inch side that meet at a 30° angle

21. a triangle with side lengths of 5 centimeters, 8 centimeters, and 2 centimeters

Draw a quadrilateral with the given angle measures, if possible.

22. 110°, 80°, 70°, 100°   **23.** 105°, 15°, 20°, 40°

D.5 Finding Unknown Angle Measures (pp. 627–634)

Learning Target: Use facts about angle relationships to find unknown angle measures.

Use the figure shown.

24. Name a pair of adjacent angles.

25. Name a pair of complementary angles.

26. Name a pair of supplementary angles.

27. Name a pair of vertical angles.

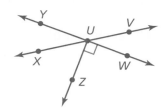

Classify the pair of angles. Then find the value of x.

28.

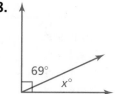

29.

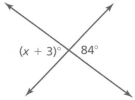

30.

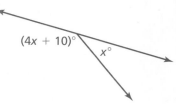

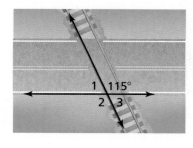

31. Describe two ways to find the measure of $\angle 2$.

32. Using the diagram from Exercises 24–27, find all the angle measures when $\angle XUY = 40°$.

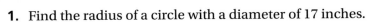

1. Find the radius of a circle with a diameter of 17 inches.

Find (a) the circumference and (b) the area of the circle. Use 3.14 or $\frac{22}{7}$ for π.

2.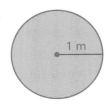

1 m

3.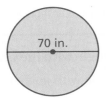

70 in.

Find (a) the perimeter and (b) the area of the figure. Use 3.14 or $\frac{22}{7}$ for π.

4.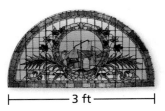

├── 3 ft ──┤

5.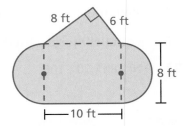

8 ft   6 ft

8 ft

├── 10 ft ──┤

Draw a figure with the given description, if possible.

6. a triangle with sides of length 5 inches and 6 inches that meet at a 50° angle

7. a triangle with side lengths of 3 inches, 4 inches, and 5 inches

8. a quadrilateral with angle measures of 90°, 110°, 40°, and 120°

Classify each pair of angles. Then find the value of x.

9.

$(8x + 2)°$ 74°

10.

$(x + 6)°$

56°

11.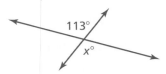

113°

$x°$

12. A museum plans to rope off the perimeter of the L-shaped exhibit. How much rope does it need?

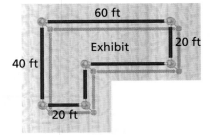

60 ft

Exhibit   20 ft

40 ft

20 ft

13. Draw a pair of adjacent angles that are neither complementary nor supplementary.

14. The circumference of a circle is 36.2 centimeters. What is the length of the diameter of the circle?

├── 15 ft ──┤

15. The circular rug is placed on a square floor. The rug touches all four walls. How much of the floor space is *not* covered by the rug?

1. To make 6 servings of soup, you need 5 cups of chicken broth. You want to know how many servings you can make with 2 quarts of chicken broth. Which proportion should you use?

   A. $\dfrac{6}{5} = \dfrac{2}{x}$

   B. $\dfrac{6}{5} = \dfrac{x}{2}$

   C. $\dfrac{6}{5} = \dfrac{x}{8}$

   D. $\dfrac{5}{6} = \dfrac{x}{8}$

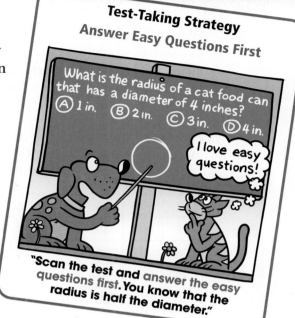
2. What is the value of x?

   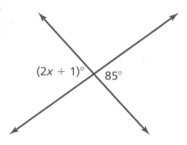

   $(2x + 1)°$ $85°$

3. Your mathematics teacher described an inequality in words.

   > "5 less than the product of 7 and an unknown number is greater than 42."

   Which inequality matches your mathematics teacher's description?

   F. $7n - 5 < 42$

   G. $(7 - 5)n > 42$

   H. $5 - 7n > 42$

   I. $7n - 5 > 42$

4. What is the approximate area of the circle below? $\left(\text{Use } \dfrac{22}{7} \text{ for } \pi.\right)$

   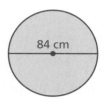

   84 cm

   A. 132 cm^2

   B. 264 cm^2

   C. 5544 cm^2

   D. 22,176 cm^2

5. You have a 50% chance of selecting a blue marble from Bag A and a 20% chance of selecting a blue marble from Bag B. Use the provided simulation to answer the question, "What is the estimated probability of selecting a blue marble from both bags?"

The digits 1 through 5 in the tens place represent selecting a blue marble from Bag A. The digits 1 and 2 in the ones place represent selecting a blue marble from Bag B.

52	66	73	68	75	28	35	47	48	02
16	68	49	03	77	35	92	78	06	06
58	18	89	39	24	80	32	41	77	21
32	40	96	59	86	01	12	00	94	73
40	71	28	61	01	24	37	25	03	25

F. 12%

G. 16%

H. 24%

I. 88%

6. Which proportion represents the problem?

"What number is 12% of 125?"

A. $\dfrac{n}{125} = \dfrac{12}{100}$

B. $\dfrac{12}{125} = \dfrac{n}{100}$

C. $\dfrac{125}{n} = \dfrac{12}{100}$

D. $\dfrac{12}{n} = \dfrac{125}{100}$

7. What is the approximate perimeter of the figure below? (Use 3.14 for π.)

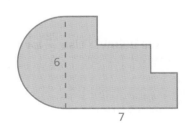

6

7

8. A savings account earns 2.5% simple interest per year. The principal is $850. What is the balance after 3 years?

F. $63.75

G. $871.25

H. $913.75

J. $7225

9. Two ponds each contain about 400 fish. The double box-and-whisker plot represents the weights of a random sample of 12 fish from each pond. Which statement about the measures of center and variation is true?

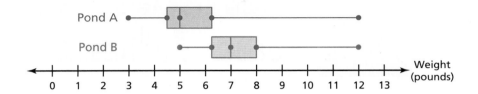

A. The variation in the samples is about the same, but the sample from Pond A has a greater median.

B. The variation in the samples is about the same, but the sample from Pond B has a greater median.

C. The measures of center and variation are about the same for both samples.

D. Neither the measures of center nor variation are the same for the samples.

10. A lawn sprinkler sprays water onto part of a circular region, as shown below.

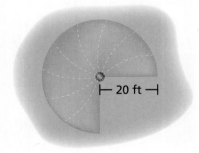

Part A What is the area, in square feet, of the region that the sprinkler sprays with water? Explain your reasoning. (Use 3.14 for π.)

Part B What is the perimeter, in feet, of the region that the sprinkler sprays with water? Explain your reasoning. (Use 3.14 for π.)

11. What is the least value of x for which $x - 12 \geq -8$ is true?

F. -20 **G.** -4

H. 4   **I.** 5

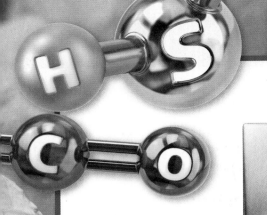

E Surface Area and Volume

Chapter Learning Target:
Understand surface area and volume.

Chapter Success Criteria:
- ▢ I can describe the surface area and volume of different shapes.
- ▢ I can use formulas to find surface areas and volumes of solids.
- ■ I can solve real-life problems involving surface area and volume.
- ■ I can describe cross sections of solids.

STEAM Video: "Paper Measurements"

STEAM Video

Paper Measurements

The thickness of a single piece of paper cannot be precisely measured using a ruler. What other method can you use to measure the thickness of a piece of paper?

**Watch the STEAM Video "Paper Measurements."
Then answer the following questions.**

1. A stack of 500 pieces of paper is 2 inches tall. How tall is a stack of 250 pieces? 100 pieces? 10 pieces? How thick is a single piece of paper?

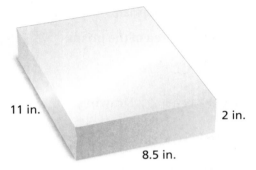

11 in.   2 in.

8.5 in.

2. You have a circular notepad. How can you find the volume of one piece of paper in the notepad?

Performance Task

Volumes and Surface Areas of Small Objects

After completing this chapter, you will be able to use the concepts you learned to answer the questions in the *STEAM Video Performance Task*. You will be given the dimensions of a shipping box and the number of bouncy balls that fit in the box.

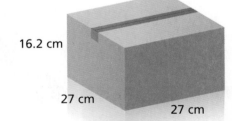

16.2 cm

27 cm

27 cm

You will be asked to use the box to estimate the volume of each bouncy ball. Why might it be helpful to use the volume of a container of objects to estimate the volume of one of the objects?

Getting Ready for Chapter

Chapter Exploration

1. Work with a partner. Perform each step for each of the given dimensions.

   - Use 24 one-inch cubes to form a rectangular prism that has the given dimensions.
   - Make a sketch of the prism.
   - Find the surface area of the prism.

   a. $4 \times 3 \times 2$ **Drawing**   **Surface Area**

                                               ▨ in.^{2}

   b. $1 \times 1 \times 24$ **c.** $1 \times 2 \times 12$ **d.** $1 \times 3 \times 8$

   e. $1 \times 4 \times 6$ **f.** $2 \times 2 \times 6$ **g.** $2 \times 4 \times 3$

2. **MP REASONING** Work with a partner. If two blocks of ice have the same volume, the block with the greater surface area will melt faster. The blocks below have equal volumes. Which block will melt faster? Explain your reasoning.

1 ft

1 ft

1 ft

0.5 ft

1 ft

2 ft

Vocabulary

The following vocabulary terms are defined in this chapter. Think about what each term might mean and record your thoughts.

lateral surface area   slant height of a pyramid

regular pyramid   cross section

E.1 Surface Areas of Prisms

Learning Target: Find the surface area of a prism.

Success Criteria:
- I can use a formula to find the surface area of a prism.
- I can find the lateral surface area of a prism.

EXPLORATION 1   Writing a Formula for Surface Area

Work with a partner.

   a.   Use the diagrams to write a formula for the surface area of a rectangular prism. Explain your reasoning.

Math Practice

View as Components
Explain the meaning of each term in your formula.

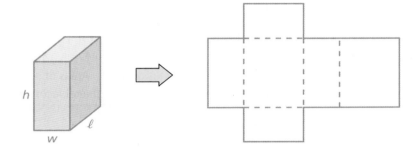

   b.   Choose dimensions for a rectangular prism. Then draw the prism and use your formula in part (a) to find the surface area.

EXPLORATION 2   Surface Areas of Prisms

Work with a partner.

   a.   Identify the solid represented by the net. Then find the surface area of the solid.

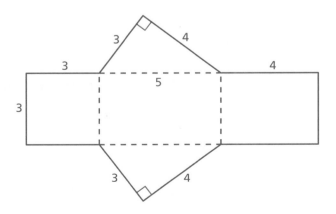

   b.   Describe a method for finding the surface area of any prism.

Key Vocabulary
lateral surface area,
p. 650

Key Idea

Surface Area of a Rectangular Prism

Words The surface area S of a rectangular prism is the sum of the areas of the bases and the lateral faces.

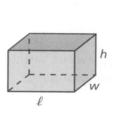

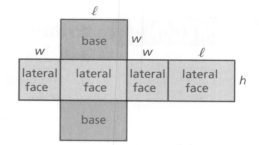

Algebra $S = 2\ell w + 2\ell h + 2wh$

Areas of bases

Areas of lateral faces

EXAMPLE 1 **Finding the Surface Area of a Rectangular Prism**

Find the surface area of the prism.

Draw a net.

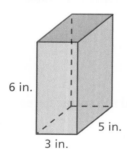

$$S = 2\ell w + 2\ell h + 2wh$$

$$= 2(3)(5) + 2(3)(6) + 2(5)(6)$$

$$= 30 + 36 + 60$$

$$= 126$$

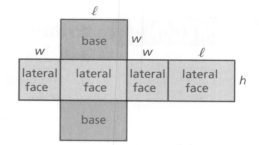

▷ The surface area is 126 square inches.

Try It **Find the surface area of the prism.**

1.
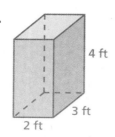

2.
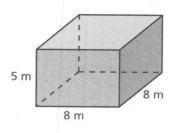

Key Idea

Surface Area of a Prism

The surface area S of any prism is the sum of the areas of the bases and the lateral faces.

$$S = \text{areas of bases} + \text{areas of lateral faces}$$

EXAMPLE 2 **Finding the Surface Area of a Prism**

Find the surface area of the prism.

Draw a net.

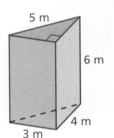

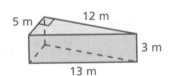

Area of a Base

Red base: $\frac{1}{2} \cdot 3 \cdot 4 = 6$

Areas of Lateral Faces

Green lateral face: $3 \cdot 6 = 18$

Purple lateral face: $5 \cdot 6 = 30$

Blue lateral face: $4 \cdot 6 = 24$

$S = \text{areas of bases} + \text{areas of lateral faces}$

$= 6 + 6 + 18 + 30 + 24 = 84$

> There are two identical bases. Count the area twice.

▷ The surface area is 84 square meters.

Try It

3. Find the surface area of the prism at the left.

Self-Assessment for Concepts & Skills

Solve each exercise. Then rate your understanding of the success criteria in your journal.

4. WRITING Explain the meaning of each term in the formula for the surface area of a rectangular prism.

5. DIFFERENT WORDS, SAME QUESTION Which is different? Find "both" answers.

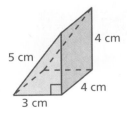

Find the surface area of the prism.	Find the area of the bases of the prism.
Find the area of the net of the prism.	Find the sum of the areas of the bases and the lateral faces of the prism.

The **lateral surface area** of a solid is the sum of the areas of each lateral face.

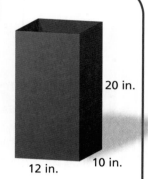
20 in.
12 in.   10 in.

EXAMPLE 3   Modeling Real Life

The outsides of purple traps are coated with glue to catch emerald ash borers. You make your own trap in the shape of a rectangular prism with an open top and bottom. What is the surface area that you need to coat with glue?

Use the formula for the surface area of a rectangular prism. To find the lateral surface area, do not include the areas of the bases in the formula.

$S = 2\ell h + 2wh$ Write the formula.

$= 2(12)(20) + 2(10)(20)$ Substitute.

$= 480 + 400$ Multiply.

$= 880$ Add.

▷ So, you need to coat 880 square inches with glue.

✓ Self-Assessment for Problem Solving

Solve each exercise. Then rate your understanding of the success criteria in your journal.

6. You want to stain the lateral faces of the wooden chest shown. Find the area that you want to stain in *square inches*.

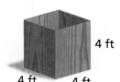
4 ft
4 ft   4 ft

3 in.
13 in.
9 in.

7. One can of frosting covers about 280 square inches. Is one can of frosting enough to frost the cake? Explain.

8. **DIG DEEPER!** Find the surface area of the bench shown. Justify your answer.

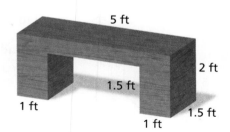
5 ft
2 ft
1.5 ft
1 ft   1.5 ft
1 ft

E.1 Practice

 Go to *BigIdeasMath.com* to get HELP with solving the exercises.

Review & Refresh

Classify the pair of angles. Then find the value of *x*.

1.
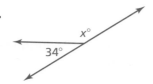

34° *x*°

2.
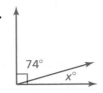

74° *x*°

3.
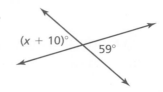

(*x* + 10)° 59°

Find the area of a circle with the indicated dimensions. Use 3.14 or $\frac{22}{7}$ for π.

4. radius: 21 in. **5.** diameter: 36 mm **6.** radius: 8.5 m

Concepts, Skills, & Problem Solving

SURFACE AREA OF A PRISM Identify the solid represented by the net. Then find the surface area of the solid. (See Explorations 1 & 2, p. 647.)

7.
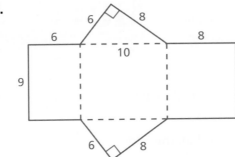

6 8
6 8
10
9
6 8

8.
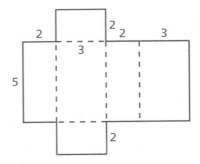

2 2 2 3
3
5
2

FINDING THE SURFACE AREA OF A PRISM Find the surface area of the prism.

9.
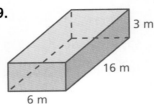

3 m
16 m
6 m

10.
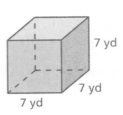

7 yd
7 yd
7 yd

11.
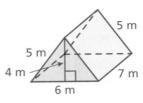

5 m
5 m
4 m 7 m
6 m

12.
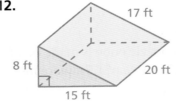

17 ft
8 ft 20 ft
15 ft

13.
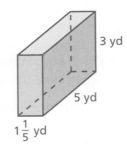

3 yd
5 yd
$1\frac{1}{5}$ yd

14.
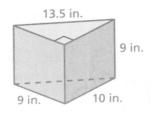

13.5 in.
9 in.
9 in. 10 in.

15. **MP YOU BE THE TEACHER** Your friend finds the surface area of the prism. Is your friend correct? Explain your reasoning.

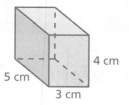
4 cm
5 cm
3 cm

$S = 2(5)(3) + 2(3)(4) + 2(5)(3)$

$= 30 + 24 + 30$

$= 84 \text{ cm}^2$

16. **MP MODELING REAL LIFE** A cube-shaped satellite has side lengths of 10 centimeters. What is the least amount of aluminum needed to cover the satellite?

FINDING SURFACE AREA Find the surface area of the prism.

17.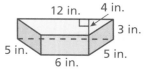
12 in.   4 in.
3 in.
5 in.
6 in.   5 in.

18.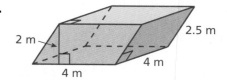
2.5 m
2 m
4 m
4 m

19. **OPEN-ENDED** Draw and label a rectangular prism that has a surface area of 158 square yards.

3 in.
2 in.
2 in.
x in.

20. **DIG DEEPER!** A label that wraps around a box of golf balls covers 75% of its lateral surface area. What is the value of x?

21. **MP STRUCTURE** You are painting the prize pedestals shown (including the bottoms). You need 0.5 pint of paint to paint the red pedestal.

a. The edge lengths of the green pedestal are one-half the edge lengths of the red pedestal. How much paint do you need to paint the green pedestal?

b. The edge lengths of the blue pedestal are triple the edge lengths of the green pedestal. How much paint do you need to paint the blue pedestal?

c. Compare the ratio of paint volumes to the ratio of edge lengths for the green and red pedestals. Repeat for the green and blue pedestals. What do you notice?

24 in.
16 in.
16 in.

22. **MP NUMBER SENSE** A keychain-sized puzzle cube is made up of small cubes. Each small cube has a surface area of 1.5 square inches.

a. What is the edge length of each small cube?

b. What is the surface area of the entire puzzle cube?

E.2 Surface Areas of Cylinders

Learning Target: Find the surface area of a cylinder.

Success Criteria:
- I can use a formula to find the surface area of a cylinder.
- I can find the lateral surface area of a cylinder.

A *cylinder* is a solid that has two parallel, identical circular bases.

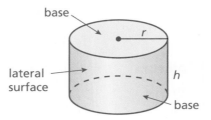

EXPLORATION 1

Finding the Surface Area of a Cylinder

Work with a partner.

a. Make a net for the can. Name each shape in the net.

b. How are the dimensions of the paper related to the dimensions of the can?

c. Write a formula that represents the surface area of a cylinder with a height of h and bases with a radius of r.

d. Estimate the dimensions of each can. Then use your formula in part (c) to estimate the surface area of each can.

Math Practice

Specify Units
What units did you use in your estimations in part (d)? What are the units for the surface areas of the cans?

Key Idea

Surface Area of a Cylinder

Words The surface area S of a cylinder is the sum of the areas of the bases and the lateral surface.

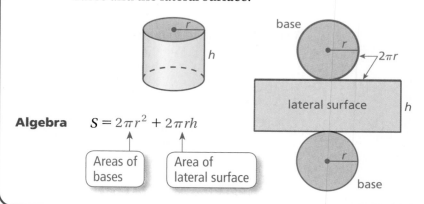

Algebra $S = 2\pi r^2 + 2\pi rh$

Areas of bases

Area of lateral surface

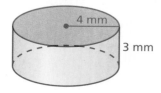

Remember

Pi can be approximated as 3.14 or $\frac{22}{7}$.

EXAMPLE 1 **Finding the Surface Area of a Cylinder**

Find the surface area of the cylinder.

Draw a net.

$$S = 2\pi r^2 + 2\pi rh$$

$$= 2\pi(4)^2 + 2\pi(4)(3)$$

$$= 32\pi + 24\pi$$

$$= 56\pi$$

$$\approx 176$$

▶ The surface area is about 176 square millimeters.

4 mm

3 mm

4 mm

4 mm

3 mm

Try It **Find the surface area of the cylinder. Round your answer to the nearest tenth if necessary.**

1.

6 yd

9 yd

2.

3 cm

18 cm

EXAMPLE 2 **Finding the Lateral Surface Area of a Cylinder**

Find the lateral surface area of the cylinder.

Use the formula for the surface area of a cylinder. To find the lateral surface area, do not include the areas of the circular bases in the formula.

The radius is $8 \div 2 = 4$ feet.

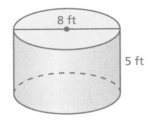

$S = 2\pi rh$	Write the formula.
$= 2\pi(4)(5)$	Substitute 4 for r and 5 for h.
$= 40\pi$	Multiply.
≈ 125.6	Use 3.14 for π.

> The lateral surface area is about 125.6 square feet.

Math Practice

Look for Structure
Explain why the area of the lateral face is the product of the height of the cylinder and the circumference of the base.

Try It **Find the lateral surface area of the cylinder. Round your answer to the nearest tenth.**

3.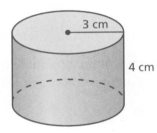

4.

 Self-Assessment **for Concepts & Skills**

Solve each exercise. Then rate your understanding of the success criteria in your journal.

5. WRITING Which part of the formula $S = 2\pi r^2 + 2\pi rh$ represents the lateral surface area of a cylinder? the areas of the bases?

6. CRITICAL THINKING You are given the height of a cylinder and the circumference of its base. Describe how to find the surface area of the cylinder.

7. FINDING A SURFACE AREA Find the surface area of the cylinder at the left. Round your answer to the nearest tenth.

8. FINDING A LATERAL SURFACE AREA Find the lateral surface area of the cylinder at the right. Round your answer to the nearest tenth.

EXAMPLE 3 **Modeling Real Life**

The iced tea can is made from a sheet of aluminum that weighs 0.01 ounce per square inch. You receive $0.40 per pound of aluminum that you recycle. How much do you earn for recycling 24 iced tea cans?

1.5 in.

7 in.

12 FL OZ

Understand the problem.

You are given a unit rate in dollars per pound for recycled aluminum, the weight of one square inch of an aluminum can, and the dimensions of the can. You are asked to find how much you earn for recycling 24 cans.

Make a plan.

Find the surface area of one can and use it to find the weight of 24 cans. Then use the unit rate given in dollars per pound to find the value of the cans.

Solve and check.

$$S = 2\pi r^2 + 2\pi rh$$ Write the formula.

$$= 2\pi(1.5)^2 + 2\pi(1.5)(7)$$ Substitute 1.5 for r and 7 for h.

$$= 4.5\pi + 21\pi$$ Simplify.

$$= 25.5\pi$$ Add.

$$\approx 80$$ Use 3.14 for π.

Check Reasonableness
19.2 ounces is greater than 16 ounces, or 1 pound, so the value should be greater than $0.40. Because $0.48 > $0.40, the answer is reasonable. ✓

The surface area of one can is about 80 square inches. So, 24 cans weigh about $24(80)(0.01) = 19.2$ ounces. This has a value of

$$19.2 \text{ oz} \times \frac{1 \text{ lb}}{16 \text{ oz}} \times \frac{\$0.40}{1 \text{ lb}} = \$0.48.$$

So, you earn about $0.48 for recycling 24 cans.

Self-Assessment for *Problem Solving*

Solve each exercise. Then rate your understanding of the success criteria in your journal.

9. You remove the lid of the can. What is the percent of change in the surface area of the can?

10. After burning half of a cylindrical candle, the surface area is 176 square inches. The radius of the candle is 2 inches. What was the original height of the candle?

40 mm

85 mm

11. **DIG DEEPER!** The area of the sheet of wrapping paper is equal to the lateral surface area of a cylindrical tube. The tube is 14 inches tall. What is the surface area of the tube, including the bases? Explain your reasoning.

Length 26 in.

Width 14 in.

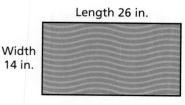

E.2 Practice

Go to *BigIdeasMath.com* to get
HELP with solving the exercises.

▶ Review & Refresh

Find the surface area of the prism.

1.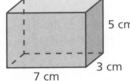

5 cm
3 cm
7 cm

2.

29 ft
21 ft
30 ft
20 ft

3. Which of the following is equivalent to 0.625?

A. $\frac{5}{8}$ **B.** $\frac{625}{100}$ **C.** 0.625%   **D.** 6.25%

▶▶ Concepts, Skills, & Problem Solving

FINDING SURFACE AREA **Find the surface area of the cylinder.**
(See Exploration 1, p. 653.)

4. a can with a radius of 60 millimeters and a height of 160 millimeters

5. a hay bale with a diameter of 30 inches and a height of 72 inches

FINDING SURFACE AREA **Find the surface area of the cylinder. Round your answer to the nearest tenth if necessary.**

6.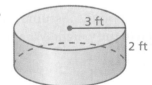
3 ft
2 ft

7.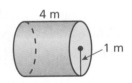
4 m
1 m

8.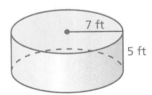
7 ft
5 ft

9.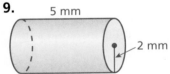
5 mm
2 mm

10.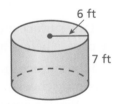
6 ft
7 ft

11.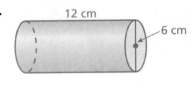
12 cm
6 cm

FINDING LATERAL SURFACE AREA **Find the lateral surface area of the cylinder. Round your answer to the nearest tenth if necessary.**

12.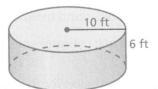
10 ft
6 ft

13.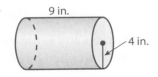
9 in.
4 in.

14.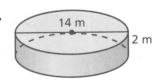
14 m
2 m

15. **MP** **YOU BE THE TEACHER**
Your friend finds the
surface area of the cylinder.
Is your friend correct?
Explain your reasoning.

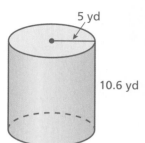

5 yd

10.6 yd

$$S = \pi r^2 + 2\pi rh$$
$$= \pi(5)^2 + 2\pi(5)(10.6)$$
$$= 25\pi + 106\pi$$
$$= 131\pi$$
$$\approx 411.3 \text{ yd}^2$$

16. **MP** **MODELING REAL LIFE**
The tank of a tanker truck is a
stainless steel cylinder. Find
the surface area of the tank.

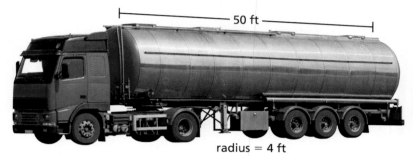

50 ft

radius = 4 ft

17. **MP** **MODELING REAL LIFE** The Petri dish shown has no lid.
What is the surface area of the outside of the Petri dish?

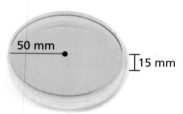

50 mm

15 mm

18. **MP** **REASONING** You have two 8.5-by-11-inch pieces of paper.
You form the lateral surfaces of two different cylinders by taping
together a pair of opposite sides on each piece of paper so that
one cylinder has a height of 8.5 inches and the other has a height
of 11 inches. Without calculating, compare the surface areas of
the cylinders (including the bases). Explain.

10 cm

3.5 cm

24.5 cm

5.5 cm

19. **DIG DEEPER!** A *ganza* is a percussion instrument
used in samba music.

    a. Find the surface area of each of the two labeled ganzas.

    b. The smaller ganza weighs 1.1 pounds. Assume that the
surface area is proportional to the weight. What is the
weight of the larger ganza?

20. **MP** **PROBLEM SOLVING** The wedge
is one-eighth of the wheel of cheese.

    a. Find the surface area of
the cheese before it is cut.

    b. Find the surface area of the
remaining cheese after
the wedge is removed.
Did the surface area increase,
decrease, or remain the same?

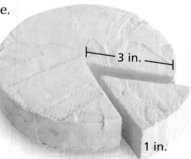

3 in.

1 in.

r

h

21. **MP** **REPEATED REASONING** A cylinder has radius *r* and height *h*.

    a. How many times greater is the surface area of a cylinder when both
dimensions are multiplied by 2? 3? 5? 10?

    b. Describe the pattern in part (a). Write an expression for the surface area
of the cylinder when both dimensions are multiplied by a number *x*.

E.3 Surface Areas of Pyramids

Learning Target: Find the surface area of a pyramid.

Success Criteria:
• I can use a net to find the surface area of a regular pyramid.
• I can find the lateral surface area of a regular pyramid.

Many well-known pyramids have square bases, however, the base of a pyramid can be any polygon.

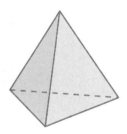

Triangular Base

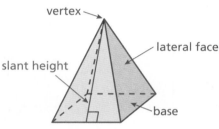

vertex

lateral face

slant height

base

Square Base

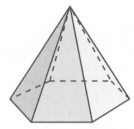

Hexagonal Base

EXPLORATION 1

Making a Scale Model

Work with a partner. Each pyramid below has a square base.

Cheops Pyramid in Egypt

Side ≈ 230 m, Slant height ≈ 186 m

Louvre Pyramid in Paris

Side ≈ 35 m, Slant height ≈ 28 m

Math Practice

Analyze Relationships

What is the relationship between the lateral surface area of your scale model and the lateral surface area of the real-life pyramid?

a. Draw a net for a scale model of one of the pyramids. Describe the scale factor.

b. Find the lateral surface area of the real-life pyramid that you chose in part (a). Explain how you found your answer.

c. Draw a net for a pyramid with a non-rectangular base and find its lateral surface area. Explain how you found your answer.

E.3 Lesson

Key Vocabulary
regular pyramid,
    p. 660
slant height, p. 660

A **regular pyramid** is a pyramid whose base is a regular polygon. The lateral faces are triangles. The height of each triangle is the **slant height** of the pyramid.

Key Idea

Surface Area of a Pyramid

The surface area S of a pyramid is the sum of the areas of the base and the lateral faces.

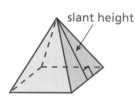

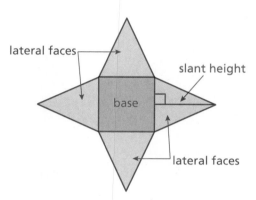

S = area of base + areas of lateral faces

Remember

In a regular polygon, all the sides are identical and all the angles are identical.

EXAMPLE 1 — Finding the Surface Area of a Square Pyramid

Find the surface area of the regular pyramid.

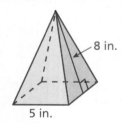

Draw a net.

Area of Base	*Area of a Lateral Face*
$5 \cdot 5 = 25$	$\frac{1}{2} \cdot 5 \cdot 8 = 20$

Find the sum of the areas of the base and the lateral faces.

S = area of base + areas of lateral faces

$\quad = 25 + 20 + 20 + 20 + 20$

$\quad = 105$

> There are 4 identical lateral faces. Count the area 4 times.

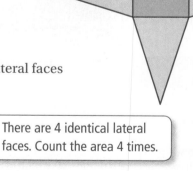

▷ The surface area is 105 square inches.

Try It

1. What is the surface area of a square pyramid with a base side length of 9 centimeters and a slant height of 7 centimeters?

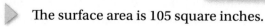

◀)) Multi-Language Glossary at BigIdeasMath.com

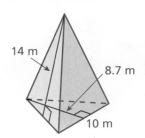

EXAMPLE 2 **Finding the Surface Area of a Triangular Pyramid**

Find the surface area of the regular pyramid.

Draw a net.

Area of Base

$$\frac{1}{2} \cdot 10 \cdot 8.7 = 43.5$$

Area of a Lateral Face

$$\frac{1}{2} \cdot 10 \cdot 14 = 70$$

Find the sum of the areas of the base and the lateral faces.

$$S = \text{area of base} + \text{areas of lateral faces}$$

$$= 43.5 + \underbrace{70 + 70 + 70}$$

$$= 253.5$$

> There are 3 identical lateral faces. Count the area 3 times.

▷ The surface area is 253.5 square meters.

Try It

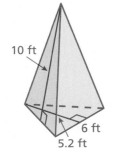

2. Find the surface area of the regular pyramid at the left.

Self-Assessment for Concepts & Skills

Solve each exercise. Then rate your understanding of the success criteria in your journal.

3. **VOCABULARY** Can a pyramid have rectangles as lateral faces? Explain.

FINDING THE SURFACE AREA OF A PYRAMID Find the surface area of the regular pyramid.

4.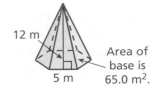

5.

6. **WHICH ONE DOESN'T BELONG?** Which description of the solid does *not* belong with the other three? Explain your reasoning.

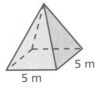

| square pyramid | regular pyramid |
| rectangular pyramid | triangular pyramid |

EXAMPLE 3 **Modeling Real Life**

The roof is shaped like a square pyramid. One bundle of shingles covers 25 square feet. How many bundles should you buy to cover the roof?

 Understand the problem.

You are given the dimensions of a roof that is shaped like a square pyramid. You are asked to find the number of bundles of shingles you should buy to cover the roof when each bundle covers 25 square feet.

 Make a plan.

The base of the roof does not need shingles. So, find the sum of the areas of the lateral faces of the pyramid. Then divide the area by 25 square feet to find the number of bundles needed to cover the roof.

 Solve and check.

Area of a Lateral Face

$$\frac{1}{2} \cdot 18 \cdot 15 = 135$$

There are four identical lateral faces. So, the lateral surface area is

$$135 + 135 + 135 + 135 = 540 \text{ square feet.}$$

Because one bundle of shingles covers 25 square feet, it will take $540 \div 25 = 21.6$ bundles to cover the roof.

 So, you should buy 22 bundles of shingles.

Check Reasonableness
20 bundles cover
$20 \times 25 = 500$ square feet
and 25 bundles cover
$25 \times 25 = 625$ square feet.
Your answer is
reasonable because
$500 < 540 < 625.$ ✓

Self-Assessment for Problem Solving

Solve each exercise. Then rate your understanding of the success criteria in your journal.

7. A building in the shape of a square pyramid is covered with solar panels. The building has a slant height of 12 feet and a base with side lengths of 15 feet. The solar panels cost $70 per square foot to install. How much does it cost to install enough solar panels to cover the entire surface of the building?

8. You use the glass pyramid shown to display rainbows on the walls of a room. The pyramid is regular and has a surface area of 105.35 square centimeters. Find the height of each triangular face. Justify your answer.

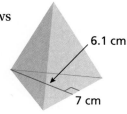

E.3 Practice

? Go to *BigIdeasMath.com* to get HELP with solving the exercises.

▶ Review & Refresh

Find the surface area of the cylinder. Round your answer to the nearest tenth.

1.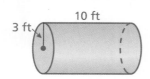
3 ft
10 ft

2.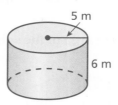
5 m
6 m

3.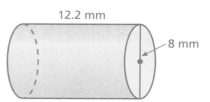
12.2 mm
8 mm

4. The ratio of the distance between bases on a professional baseball field to the distance between bases on a youth baseball field is 3 : 2. Bases on a professional baseball field are 90 feet apart. What is the distance between bases on a youth baseball field?

 A. 30 ft **B.** 45 ft **C.** 60 ft **D.** 135 ft

▶▶ Concepts, Skills, & Problem Solving

USING A NET Use the net to find the surface area of the regular pyramid.
(See Exploration 1, p. 659.)

5.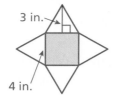
3 in.
4 in.

6.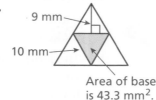
9 mm
10 mm
Area of base is 43.3 mm².

7.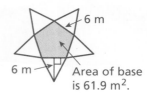
6 m
6 m
Area of base is 61.9 m².

FINDING THE SURFACE AREA OF A PYRAMID Find the surface area of the regular pyramid.

8.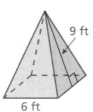
9 ft
6 ft

9.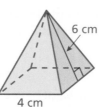
6 cm
4 cm

10.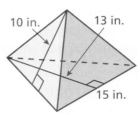
10 in.
13 in.
15 in.

11.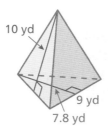
10 yd
9 yd
7.8 yd

12.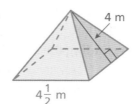
4 m
$4\frac{1}{2}$ m

13.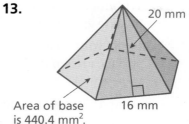
20 mm
16 mm
Area of base is 440.4 mm².

14. 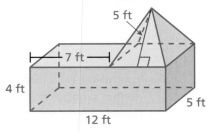 **🅜🅟 MODELING REAL LIFE** The base of the lampshade is a regular hexagon with side lengths of 8 inches. Estimate the amount of glass needed to make the lampshade.

15. **GEOMETRY** The surface area of a square pyramid is 85 square meters. The side length of the base is 5 meters. What is the slant height?

FINDING SURFACE AREA Find the surface area of the solid.

16.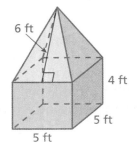

17.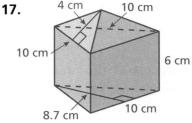

18.

19. **GEOMETRY** A tetrahedron is a triangular pyramid with four faces that are identical equilateral triangles. The total lateral surface area of a tetrahedron is 93 square centimeters. Find the surface area of the tetrahedron.

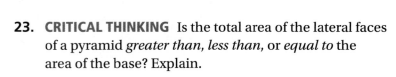

20. **🅜🅟 PROBLEM SOLVING** You are making an umbrella that is shaped like a regular octagonal pyramid.

    a. Estimate the amount of fabric that you need to make the umbrella.

    b. The fabric comes in rolls that are 60 inches wide. Draw a diagram of how you can cut the fabric from rolls that are 10 feet long.

    c. How much fabric is wasted?

21. **🅜🅟 REASONING** The *height* of a pyramid is the perpendicular distance between the base and the top of the pyramid. Which is greater, the height of a pyramid or the slant height? Explain your reasoning.

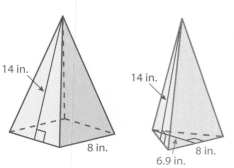

22. **🅜🅟 REASONING** Both pyramids at the right have regular bases.

    a. Without calculating, determine which pyramid has the greater surface area. Explain.

    b. Verify your answer to part (a) by finding the surface area of each pyramid.

23. **CRITICAL THINKING** Is the total area of the lateral faces of a pyramid *greater than*, *less than*, or *equal to* the area of the base? Explain.

E.4 Volumes of Prisms

Learning Target: Find the volume of a prism.

Success Criteria:
- I can use a formula to find the volume of a prism.
- I can use the formula for the volume of a prism to find a missing dimension.

EXPLORATION 1

Finding a Formula for Volume

Work with a partner.

a. In the figures shown, each cube has a volume of 1 cubic unit. Compare the volume V (in cubic units) of each rectangular prism to the area B (in square units) of its base. What do you notice?

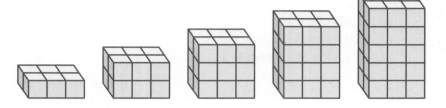

b. Repeat part (a) using the prisms below.

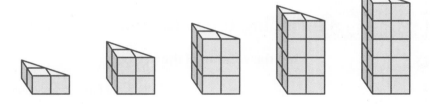

c. Use what you learned in parts (a) and (b) to write a formula that gives the volume of any prism.

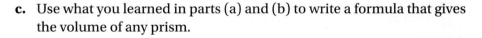

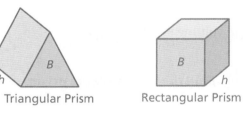

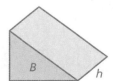
Triangular Prism

Rectangular Prism

Pentagonal Prism

Triangular Prism

Hexagonal Prism

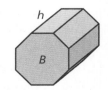
Octagonal Prism

Math Practice

Make Conjectures
How can you find the volume of the prism shown? Explain your reasoning.

E.4 Lesson

The *volume* of a three-dimensional figure is a measure of the amount of space that it occupies. Volume is measured in cubic units.

 **Key Idea**

Volume of a Prism

Words The volume *V* of a prism is the product of the area of the base and the height of the prism.

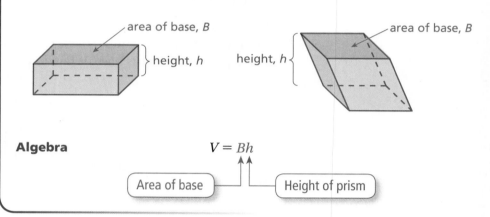

> The slanted figure is called an *oblique prism*. Volumes of oblique prisms are calculated in the same way as volumes of right prisms.

Algebra $V = Bh$

Area of base ⟶ ⟵ Height of prism

EXAMPLE 1 **Finding the Volume of a Rectangular Prism**

Find the volume of the prism.

> The area of the base of a rectangular prism is the product of the length ℓ and the width *w*. You can use $V = \ell wh$ to find the volume of a rectangular prism.

$V = Bh$	Write the formula for volume.
$= 6(8) \cdot 15$	Substitute.
$= 48 \cdot 15$	Simplify.
$= 720$	Multiply.

▷ The volume is 720 cubic yards.

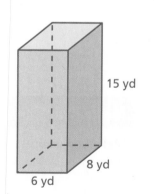

Try It Find the volume of the prism.

1.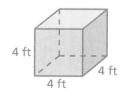

2.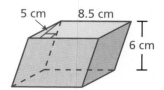

EXAMPLE 2 **Finding the Volume of a Triangular Prism**

Find the volume of the prism.

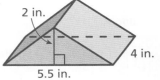

$V = Bh$ Write the formula for volume.

$= \dfrac{1}{2}(5.5)(2) \cdot 4$ Substitute.

$= 5.5 \cdot 4$ Simplify.

$= 22$ Multiply.

▷ The volume is 22 cubic inches.

Math Practice

Check Progress
How can you use a cube with edge lengths of 1 foot to check the reasonableness of the volume in Example 2?

Try It **Find the volume of the prism.**

3.

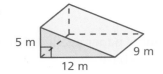

4.

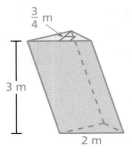

 Self-Assessment *for Concepts & Skills*

Solve each exercise. Then rate your understanding of the success criteria in your journal.

FINDING THE VOLUME OF A PRISM **Find the volume of the prism.**

5.

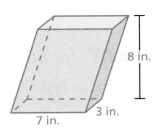

6.

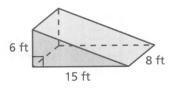

7.

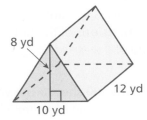

8.

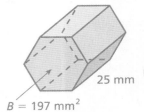

9. OPEN-ENDED Draw and label a prism with a volume of 144 cubic inches. Justify your answer.

EXAMPLE 3 **Modeling Real Life**

Each popcorn bag shown holds exactly 96 cubic inches of popcorn. Which bag should a movie theater choose in order to use less paper when making popcorn bags?

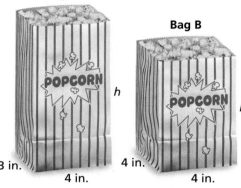

Bag A

Bag B

3 in.
4 in.
4 in.
4 in.

Use the formula for volume to find the height of each bag.

Bag A	**Bag B**
$V = Bh$	$V = Bh$
$96 = 4(3)(h)$	$96 = 4(4)(h)$
$96 = 12h$	$96 = 16h$
$8 = h$	$6 = h$

To determine the amount of paper needed, find the surface area of each bag. Do not include the top base.

Bag A	**Bag B**
$S = \ell w + 2\ell h + 2wh$	$S = \ell w + 2\ell h + 2wh$
$= 4(3) + 2(4)(8) + 2(3)(8)$	$= 4(4) + 2(4)(6) + 2(4)(6)$
$= 12 + 64 + 48$	$= 16 + 48 + 48$
$= 124 \text{ in.}^2$	$= 112 \text{ in.}^2$

▷ The surface area of Bag B is less than the surface area of Bag A. So, the movie theater should choose Bag B.

Self-Assessment for Problem Solving

Solve each exercise. Then rate your understanding of the success criteria in your journal.

10. **DIG DEEPER!** You visit an aquarium. One of the tanks at the aquarium holds 450 gallons of water. Draw a diagram to show one possible set of dimensions of the tank. Justify your answer. ($1 \text{ gal} = 231 \text{ in.}^3$)

11. A stack of paper contains 400 sheets. The volume of the stack is 140.25 cubic inches. Each sheet of paper is identical, with a length of 11 inches and a width of 8.5 inches. Find the height of each sheet of paper. Justify your answer.

E.4 Practice

Go to *BigIdeasMath.com* to get HELP with solving the exercises.

▶ Review & Refresh

Find the surface area of the regular pyramid.

1.

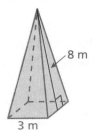

8 m

3 m

2.

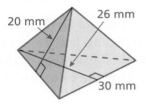

20 mm   26 mm

30 mm

3.

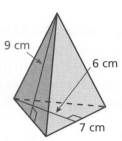

9 cm   6 cm

7 cm

Find the selling price.

4. Cost to store: $75
   Markup: 20%

5. Cost to store: $90
   Markup: 60%

6. Cost to store: $130
   Markup: 85%

▶▶ Concepts, Skills, & Problem Solving

MP USING TOOLS In the figure, each cube has a volume of 1 cubic unit. Find the volume of the figure and the area of its base. (See Exploration 1, p. 665.)

7.

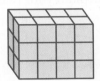

8.

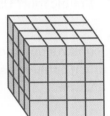

9.

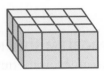

FINDING THE VOLUME OF A PRISM Find the volume of the prism.

10.

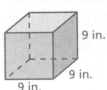

9 in.

9 in.

9 in.

11.

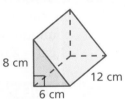

8 cm

6 cm

12 cm

12.

$8\frac{1}{2}$ m

7 m

4 m

13.

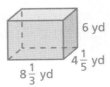

6 yd

$4\frac{1}{5}$ yd

$8\frac{1}{3}$ yd

14.

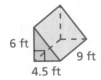

6 ft

9 ft

4.5 ft

15.

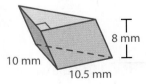

8 mm

10 mm

10.5 mm

16.

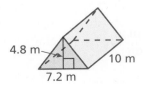

4.8 m

10 m

7.2 m

17.

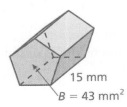

15 mm

$B = 43$ mm^2

18.

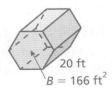

20 ft

$B = 166$ ft^2

19. **MP YOU BE THE TEACHER** Your friend finds the volume of the triangular prism. Is your friend correct? Explain your reasoning.

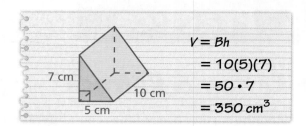

$V = Bh$
$= 10(5)(7)$
$= 50 \cdot 7$
$= 350 \, cm^3$

7 cm
10 cm
5 cm

20. **MP MODELING REAL LIFE** A battery for an underwater drone is in the shape of a square prism. It is designed to draw in seawater that is then used to produce energy. The base of the battery has side lengths of 15 centimeters and the height of the battery is 10 centimeters. Find the volume of the battery.

School Locker

Gym Locker

60 in.

48 in.

12 in.

12 in.

10 in.

15 in.

21. **MP MODELING REAL LIFE** A cereal box has a volume of 225 cubic inches. The length of the base is 9 inches and the width of the base is 2.5 inches. What is the height of the box? Justify your answer.

22. **MP REASONING** Each locker is shaped like a rectangular prism. Which has more storage space? Explain.

23. **MP USING TOOLS** How many cubic inches are in 1 cubic foot? Use a sketch to explain your reasoning.

24. **MP PROBLEM SOLVING** A concrete construction block has the measurements shown. How much concrete is used to make the block? Justify your answer.

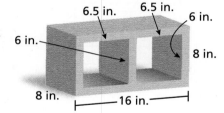

6.5 in.   6.5 in.
6 in.   6 in.
6 in.   8 in.
8 in.   16 in.

25. **RESEARCH** The gas tank is 20% full. Use the current price of regular gasoline in your community to find the cost to fill the tank. (1 gal = 231 in.^{3})

26. **DIG DEEPER!** Two liters of water are poured into an empty vase shaped like an octagonal prism. The base area is 100 square centimeters. What is the height of the water? (1 L = 1000 cm^3)

11 in.

1.25 ft

1.75 ft

27. **MP LOGIC** Two prisms have the same volume. Do they *always*, *sometimes*, or *never* have the same surface area? Justify your answer.

28. **CRITICAL THINKING** How many times greater is the volume of a triangular prism when one of its dimensions is doubled? when all three dimensions are doubled?

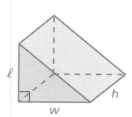

ℓ

h

w

E.5 Volumes of Pyramids

Learning Target: Find the volume of a pyramid.

Success Criteria:
- I can use a formula to find the volume of a pyramid.
- I can use the volume of a pyramid to solve a real-life problem.

EXPLORATION 1

Finding a Formula for the Volume of a Pyramid

Work with a partner. Draw the two nets on cardboard and cut them out. Fold and tape the nets to form an open cube and an open square pyramid. Both figures should have the same size square base and the same height.

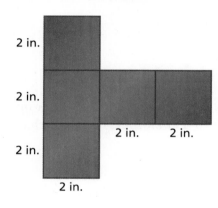

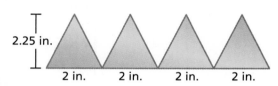

a. Compare the volumes of the figures. What do you notice?

b. Use your observations in part (a) to write a formula for the volume of a pyramid.

Math Practice

Interpret a Solution

How do your calculations in part (c) help you verify that your formula is correct?

c. The rectangular prism below can be cut to form three pyramids. Use your formula in part (b) to show that the sum of the volumes of the three pyramids is equal to the volume of the prism.

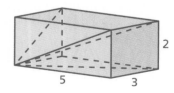

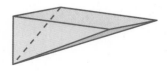

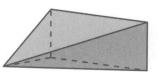

E.5 Lesson

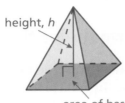

🔑 Key Idea

Volume of a Pyramid

Words The volume V of a pyramid is one-third the product of the area of the base and the height of the pyramid.

> Volumes of oblique pyramids are calculated the same way as volumes of right pyramids.

height, h

area of base, B

height, h

area of base, B

Area of base

Algebra $V = \dfrac{1}{3}Bh$

Height of pyramid

EXAMPLE 1 **Finding the Volume of a Pyramid**

Find the volume of the pyramid.

$V = \dfrac{1}{3}Bh$ Write the formula for volume.

$= \dfrac{1}{3}(48)(9)$ Substitute.

$= 144$ Multiply.

▷ The volume is 144 cubic millimeters.

9 mm

$B = 48 \text{ mm}^2$

Try It **Find the volume of the pyramid.**

1.

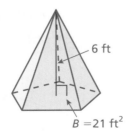

6 ft

$B = 21 \text{ ft}^2$

2.

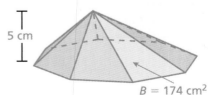

5 cm

$B = 174 \text{ cm}^2$

EXAMPLE 2 **Finding the Volume of a Pyramid**

Find the volume of the pyramid.

a.

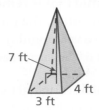

7 ft
4 ft
3 ft

$$V = \frac{1}{3}Bh$$

$$= \frac{1}{3}(4)(3)(7)$$

$$= 28$$

▷ The volume is
28 cubic feet.

b.

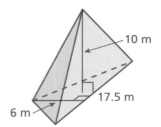

10 m
17.5 m
6 m

$$V = \frac{1}{3}Bh$$

$$= \frac{1}{3}\left(\frac{1}{2}\right)(17.5)(6)(10)$$

$$= 175$$

▷ The volume is
175 cubic meters.

> The area of the base of a rectangular pyramid is the product of the length ℓ and the width w.
> You can use $V = \frac{1}{3}\ell wh$ to find the volume of a rectangular pyramid.

Try It **Find the volume of the pyramid.**

3.

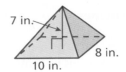

7 in.
8 in.
10 in.

4.

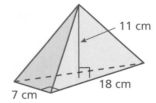

11 cm
18 cm
7 cm

Self-Assessment *for Concepts & Skills*

Solve each exercise. Then rate your understanding of the success criteria in your journal.

5. **WRITING** How is the formula for the volume of a pyramid different from the formula for the volume of a prism?

6. **MP** **PROBLEM SOLVING** How many different pyramids can you draw with the same height and volume? Explain.

FINDING THE VOLUME OF A PYRAMID **Find the volume of the pyramid.**

7.

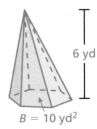

6 yd
$B = 10$ yd^2

8.

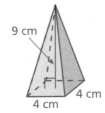

9 cm
4 cm
4 cm

Section E.5   Volumes of Pyramids   **673**

EXAMPLE 3 **Modeling Real Life**

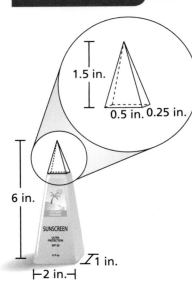

1.5 in.

0.5 in. 0.25 in.

6 in.

1 in.

2 in.

Suncreen $9.96

The diagram shows the portion of a rectangular pyramid that is removed to make a sunscreen bottle. The portion that is removed is also a rectangular pyramid. Find the unit cost of the sunscreen.

Find the volume of the original pyramid and subtract the volume of the smaller pyramid.

Original Pyramid	*Smaller Pyramid*
$V = \frac{1}{3}Bh$	$V = \frac{1}{3}Bh$
$= \frac{1}{3}(2)(1)(6)$	$= \frac{1}{3}(0.5)(0.25)(1.5)$
$= 4 \text{ in.}^3$	$= 0.0625 \text{ in.}^3$

The volume of sunscreen in the bottle is $4 - 0.0625 = 3.9375$ cubic inches. The bottle of sunscreen costs $9.96. Find the unit rate.

$9.96 per 3.9375 cubic inches: $\frac{9.96}{3.9375} \approx \$2.53$ per cubic inch.

▷ So, the unit cost of the sunscreen is about $2.53 per cubic inch.

 Self-Assessment for Problem Solving

Solve each exercise. Then rate your understanding of the success criteria in your journal.

9. A resort features a square pyramid with a water slide. The length of the water slide is 90% of the height of the pyramid. The base of the pyramid has side lengths of 60 feet. The volume of the pyramid is 60,000 cubic feet. What is the length of the water slide?

10. **DIG DEEPER!** To make a candle, you use a mold to create the wax pyramid shown. You cut off the top 3 centimeters of the pyramid to make space for a wick. If the base area of the removed portion is 5.4 square centimeters, what percentage of the wax did you remove?

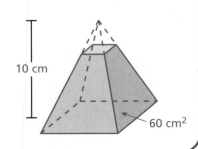

10 cm

60 cm²

E.5 Practice

Go to *BigIdeasMath.com* to get
HELP with solving the exercises.

▶ Review & Refresh

Find the volume of the prism.

1.

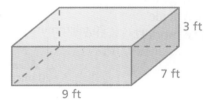

3 ft
7 ft
9 ft

2.

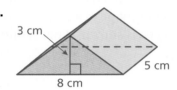

3 cm
5 cm
8 cm

Solve the inequality. Graph the solution.

3. $r + 0.5 < -0.4$ **4.** $z - 2.4 \geq -0.6$ **5.** $h - 5 \leq -3.7$

▶▶ Concepts, Skills, & Problem Solving

VOLUMES OF PYRAMIDS The rectangular prism is cut to form three pyramids.
**Show that the sum of the volumes of the three pyramids is equal to the volume
of the prism.** (See Exploration 1, p. 671.)

6.

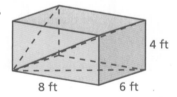

4 ft
8 ft
6 ft

7.

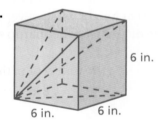

6 in.
6 in.
6 in.

FINDING THE VOLUME OF A PYRAMID Find the volume of the pyramid.

8.

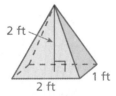

2 ft
1 ft
2 ft

9.

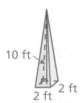

10 ft
2 ft
2 ft

10.

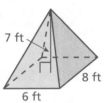

7 ft
8 ft
6 ft

11.

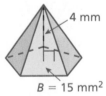

4 mm
$B = 15 \text{ mm}^2$

12.

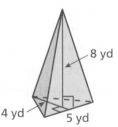

8 yd
4 yd
5 yd

13.

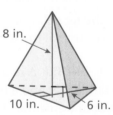

8 in.
10 in.
6 in.

14.

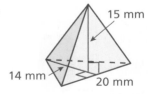

15 mm
14 mm
20 mm

15.

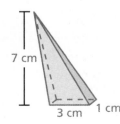

7 cm
3 cm
1 cm

16.

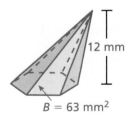

12 mm
$B = 63 \text{ mm}^2$

17. **MP YOU BE THE TEACHER** Your friend finds the volume of the pyramid. Is your friend correct? Explain your reasoning.

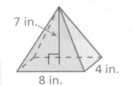

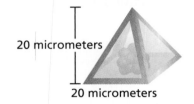

$V = Bh$

$\quad = 8(4)(7)$

$\quad = 224$ cubic inches

18. **MP MODELING REAL LIFE** A researcher develops a cage for a living cell in the shape of a square-based pyramid. A scale model of the cage is shown. What is the volume of the model?

20 micrometers

20 micrometers

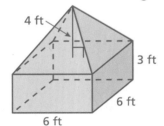

19. **FINDING VOLUME** Find the volume of the composite solid. Justify your answer.

20. **MP MODELING REAL LIFE** In 1483, Leonardo da Vinci designed a parachute. It is believed that this was the first parachute ever designed. In a notebook, he wrote, "If a man is provided with a length of gummed linen cloth with a length of 12 yards on each side and 12 yards high, he can jump from any great height whatsoever without injury." Find the volume of air inside Leonardo's parachute.

Not drawn to scale

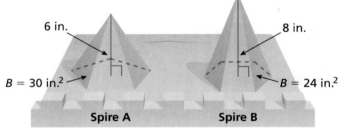

Spire A   Spire B

21. **MP MODELING REAL LIFE** Which sandcastle spire has a greater volume? How much more sand do you need to make the spire with the greater volume?

22. **MP PROBLEM SOLVING** Use the photo of the tepee.

    a. What is the shape of the base? How can you tell?

    b. The tepee's height is about 10 feet. Estimate the volume of the tepee.

23. **OPEN-ENDED** A rectangular pyramid has a volume of 40 cubic feet and a height of 6 feet. Find one possible set of dimensions of the base.

24. **MP REASONING** Do the two solids have the same volume? Explain.

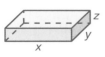

E.6 Cross Sections of Three-Dimensional Figures

Learning Target: Describe the cross sections of a solid.

Success Criteria:
- I can explain the meaning of a cross section.
- I can describe cross sections of prisms and pyramids.
- I can describe cross sections of cylinders and cones.

EXPLORATION 1

Describing Cross Sections

Work with a partner. A baker is thinking of different ways to slice zucchini bread that is in the shape of a rectangular prism. The shape that is formed by the cut is called a *cross section*.

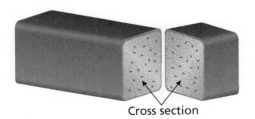

Cross section

a. What is the shape of the cross section when the baker slices the bread vertically, as shown above?

b. What is the shape of the cross section when the baker slices the bread horizontally?

c. What is the shape of the cross section when the baker slices off a corner of the bread?

Math Practice

Justify Conclusions

How can you use real-life objects to justify your conclusions in parts (d) and (e)?

d. Is it possible to obtain a cross section that is a trapezoid? Explain.

e. Name at least 3 cross sections that are possible to obtain from a rectangular pyramid. Explain your reasoning.

E.6 Lesson

Key Vocabulary 🔊
cross section, *p. 678*

Consider a plane "slicing" through a solid. The intersection of the plane and the solid is a two-dimensional shape called a **cross section**. For example, the diagram shows that the intersection of the plane and the rectangular prism is a rectangle.

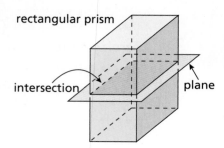

rectangular prism

intersection

plane

EXAMPLE 1 **Describing Cross Sections of Prisms and Pyramids**

Describe the intersection of the plane and the solid.

a.

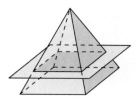

▷ The diagram shows the intersection of a plane and a rectangular pyramid. The intersection is a rectangle.

b.

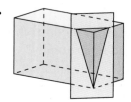

▷ The diagram shows the intersection of a plane and a rectangular prism. The intersection is a triangle.

Try It **Describe the intersection of the plane and the solid.**

1.

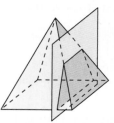

2.

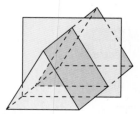

🔊 Multi-Language Glossary at *BigIdeasMath.com*

Example 1 shows how a plane intersects a polyhedron. Now consider the intersection of a plane and a solid having a curved surface, such as a cylinder or cone. As shown, a *cone* is a solid that has one circular base and one vertex.

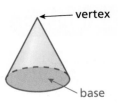

vertex

base

EXAMPLE 2 **Describing Cross Sections of Cylinders and Cones**

Describe the intersection of the plane and the solid.

a.

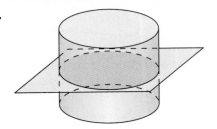

▷ The diagram shows the intersection of a plane and a cylinder. The intersection is a circle.

b.

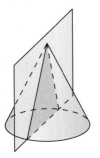

▷ The diagram shows the intersection of a plane and a cone. The intersection is a triangle.

Math Practice

Communicate Precisely
Can a cross section be three dimensional? Explain your reasoning.

Try It **Describe the intersection of the plane and the solid.**

3.

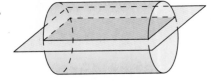

4.

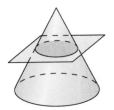

Self-Assessment *for Concepts & Skills*

Solve each exercise. Then rate your understanding of the success criteria in your journal.

5. **VOCABULARY** What is a cross section?

6. **DESCRIBING CROSS SECTIONS** Describe the intersection of the plane and the solid at the left.

7. **MP** **REASONING** Name all possible cross sections of a cylinder.

8. **WHICH ONE DOESN'T BELONG?** You slice a square prism. Which cross section does *not* belong with the other three? Explain your reasoning.

| circle | square | triangle | rectangle |

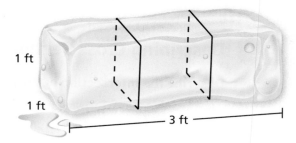

EXAMPLE 3   Modeling Real Life

An ice sculptor cuts the block of ice into 3 identical pieces. What is the percent of increase in the surface area of the ice?

1 ft

1 ft

3 ft

Find the surface area of the ice before it is cut.

$S = 2\ell w + 2\ell h + 2wh$	Write the formula.
$= 2(1)(1) + 2(1)(3) + 2(1)(3)$	Substitute 1 for ℓ, 1 for w, and 3 for h.
$= 2 + 6 + 6$	Simplify.
$= 14 \text{ ft}^2$	Add.

When the ice is cut, the cross sections are squares with side lengths of 1 foot. The ice is cut into three cubes, each with edge lengths of 1 foot. Find the total surface area of the three cubes.

Remember

The surface area S of a cube with an edge length of s is $S = 6s^2$.

$S = 3(6s^2)$

$\quad = 3(6 \cdot 1^2)$

$\quad = 3(6)$

$\quad = 18 \text{ ft}^2$

 1 ft

1 ft

1 ft

 1 ft

▷ So, the percent of increase in the surface area of the ice is $\dfrac{18 - 14}{14} \approx 29\%$.

Self-Assessment for Problem Solving

Solve each exercise. Then rate your understanding of the success criteria in your journal.

9. A steel beam that is 12 meters long is cut into four equal parts. The cross sections are rectangles with side lengths of 1 meter and 2 meters.

   a. What is the perimeter of each cross section?

   b. What is the area of each cross section?

   c. What is the volume of the original beam?

10. **DIG DEEPER!**   A lumberjack saws a cylindrical tree trunk at an angle. Is the cross section a circle? Explain your reasoning.

E.6 Practice

▶ Review & Refresh

Find the volume of the pyramid.

1.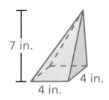
7 in.
4 in.
4 in.

2.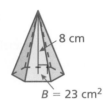
8 cm
$B = 23$ cm²

Find the sum.

3. $(w - 7) + (-6w - 5)$

4. $(8 - b) + (5b + 6)$

▶▶ Concepts, Skills, & Problem Solving

DESCRIBING CROSS SECTIONS **Determine whether it is possible to obtain the cross section from a cube.** (See Exploration 2, p. 677.)

5. circle

6. square

7. equilateral triangle

8. pentagon

9. non-rectangular parallelogram

10. octagon

DESCRIBING CROSS SECTIONS OF PRISMS AND PYRAMIDS **Describe the intersection of the plane and the solid.**

11.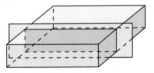

12.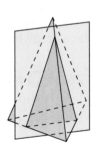

13.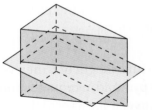

14.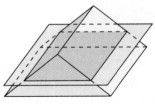

DESCRIBING CROSS SECTIONS OF CYLINDERS AND CONES **Describe the intersection of the plane and the solid.**

15.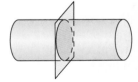

16.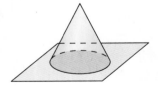

DESCRIBING CROSS SECTIONS Describe the shape that is formed by the cut in the food.

17.

18.

19.

20. **DESCRIBING CROSS SECTIONS** Describe the intersection of the plane and the cylinder.

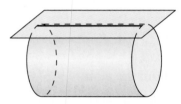

MP **REASONING** Determine whether the given intersection is possible. If so, draw the solid and the cross section.

21. The intersection of a plane and a cone is a rectangle.

22. The intersection of a plane and a square pyramid is a triangle.

23. **MP** **REASONING** A plane that intersects a prism is parallel to the bases of the prism. Describe the intersection of the plane and the prism.

24. **MP** **REASONING** Explain how a plane can be parallel to the base of a cone and intersect the cone at exactly one point.

25. **MP** **MODELING REAL LIFE** An artist plans to paint bricks.

    a. Find the surface area of the brick.

    b. The artist cuts along the length of the brick to form two bricks, each with a width of 2 inches. What is the percent of increase in the surface area? Justify your answer.

3 in.

10 in.

4 in.

26. **MP** **MODELING REAL LIFE** A cross section of an artery is shown.

    a. Describe the cross section of the artery.

    b. The radius of the artery is 0.22 millimeter. What is the circumference of the artery?

27. **MP** **REASONING** Three identical square pyramids each with a height of h meters and a base area of 100 square meters are shown. For each pyramid, a cross section parallel to the base is shown. Describe the relationship between the area of the base and the area of any cross section parallel to the base.

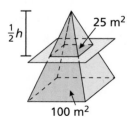

$\frac{1}{2}h$ 25 m²

100 m²

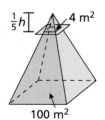

$\frac{1}{5}h$ 4 m²

100 m²

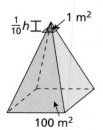

$\frac{1}{10}h$ 1 m²

100 m²

Connecting Concepts

Using the Problem-Solving Plan

1. A store pays $2 per pound for popcorn kernels. One cubic foot of kernels weighs about 45 pounds. What is the selling price of the container shown when the markup is 30%?

6 in.

4 in.

4 in.

Understand the problem. You are given the dimensions of a container of popcorn kernels and the price that a store pays for the kernels. You also know the weight of one cubic foot of popcorn kernels. You are asked to find the selling price of the container when the markup is 30%.

Make a plan. Use the volume of the container to find the weight of the kernels. Then use the weight of the kernels to find the cost to the store. Finally, use the percent markup to find the selling price of the container.

Solve and check. Use the plan to solve the problem. Then check your solution.

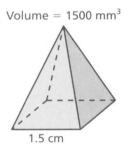

Volume = 1500 mm³

1.5 cm

2. The pyramid shown has a square base. What is the height of the pyramid? Justify your answer.

3. A cylindrical can of soup has a height of 7 centimeters and a lateral surface area of 63π square centimeters. The can is redesigned to have a lateral surface area of 45π square centimeters without changing the radius of the can. What is the height of the new design? Justify your answer.

Performance Task

WIDTH 8.5 IN. LENGTH 11 IN. HEIGHT 2 IN.

Volumes and Surface Areas of Small Objects

At the beginning of this chapter, you watched a STEAM Video called "Paper Measurements." You are now ready to complete the performance task related to this video, available at *BigIdeasMath.com*. Be sure to use the problem-solving plan as you work through the performance task.

Chapter Review

 Go to *BigIdeasMath.com* to download blank graphic organizers.

▶ Review Vocabulary

Write the definition and give an example of each vocabulary term.

lateral surface area, *p. 650*

regular pyramid, *p. 660*

slant height, *p. 660*

cross section, *p. 678*

▶ Graphic Organizers

You can use an **Information Frame** to help organize and remember a concept. Here is an example of an Information Frame for *Surface Areas of Rectangular Prisms*.

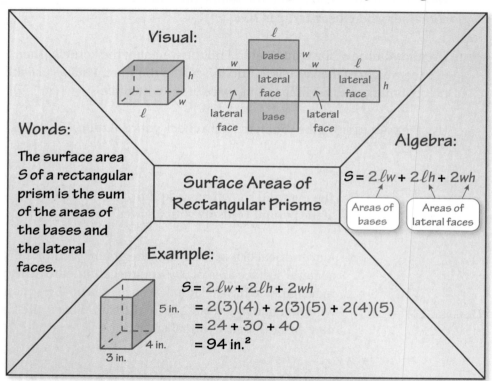

Choose and complete a graphic organizer to help you study the concept.

1. surface areas of prisms

2. surface areas of cylinders

3. surface areas of pyramids

4. volumes of prisms

5. volumes of pyramids

6. cross sections of three-dimensional figures

"I'm having trouble thinking of a good title for my **Information Frame***."*

▶ Chapter Self-Assessment

As you complete the exercises, use the scale below to rate your understanding of the success criteria in your journal.

1	**2**	**3**	**4**
I do not understand.	I can do it with help.	I can do it on my own.	I can teach someone else.

E.1 Surface Areas of Prisms *(pp. 647–652)*

Learning Target: Find the surface area of a prism.

Find the surface area of the prism.

1.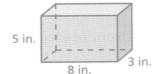
5 in.
8 in.
3 in.

2.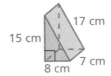
17 cm
15 cm
8 cm
7 cm

3.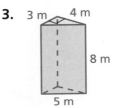
3 m   4 m
8 m
5 m

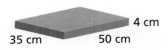
4 cm
35 cm   50 cm

4. You want to wrap the box using a piece of wrapping paper that is 76 centimeters long by 56 centimeters wide. Do you have enough wrapping paper to wrap the box? Explain.

5. To finish a project, you need to paint the lateral surfaces of a cube with side length 2.5 inches. Find the area that you need to paint.

E.2 Surface Areas of Cylinders *(pp. 653–658)*

Learning Target: Find the surface area of a cylinder.

Find the surface area and lateral surface area of the cylinder. Round your answers to the nearest tenth.

6.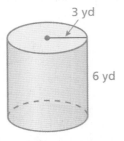
3 yd
6 yd

7.
1.6 cm
Lip Balm
Protects your lips from the sun and wind
Lip Balm
6 cm

8. The label covers the entire lateral surface area of the can. How much of the can is *not* covered by the label?

4 cm
Sunnyview Farms
Mandarin
ORANGE SEGMENTS
11 cm
NET WT. 16 OZ

E.3 Surface Areas of Pyramids (pp. 659–664)

Learning Target: Find the surface area of a pyramid.

Find the surface area of the regular pyramid.

9.
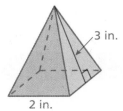
3 in.
2 in.

10.
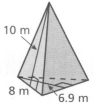
10 m
8 m
6.9 m

11.
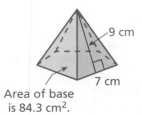
9 cm
7 cm
Area of base
is 84.3 cm².

12. The tent is shaped like a square pyramid. There is no fabric covering the ground.

6 ft
3 ft

    a. Estimate the amount of fabric needed to make the tent.

    b. Fabric costs $5.25 per square yard. How much will it cost to make the tent?

E.4 Volumes of Prisms (pp. 665–670)

Learning Target: Find the volume of a prism.

Find the volume of the prism.

13.
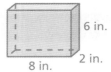
6 in.
2 in.
8 in.

14.
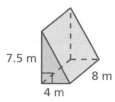
7.5 m
8 m
4 m

15.
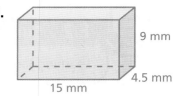
9 mm
4.5 mm
15 mm

16.
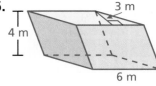
3 m
4 m
6 m

17.
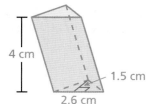
4 cm
1.5 cm
2.6 cm

18.
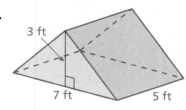
3 ft
7 ft
5 ft

19. Two cereal boxes each hold exactly 192 cubic inches of cereal. Which box should a manufacturer choose to minimize the amount of cardboard needed to make the cereal boxes?

BRAN FLAKES
h
2 in.
8 in.

BRAN FLAKES
h
3 in.
8 in.

E.5 Volumes of Pyramids *(pp. 671–676)*

Learning Target: Find the volume of a pyramid.

Find the volume of the pyramid.

20.

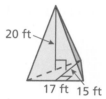

20 ft

17 ft 15 ft

21.

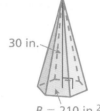

30 in.

$B = 210$ in.^{2}

22.

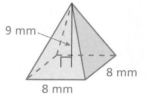

9 mm

8 mm

8 mm

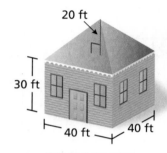

20 ft

30 ft

40 ft 40 ft

23. A pyramid-shaped hip roof is a good choice for a house in an area with many hurricanes.

   a. What is the volume of the roof to the nearest tenth of a foot?

   b. What is the volume of the entire house, including the roof?

24. A laboratory creates calcite crystals for use in the study of light. The crystal is made up of two pieces of calcite that form a square pyramid. The base length of the top piece is 2 inches.

   a. Find the volume of the entire pyramid.

   b. Find the volume of each piece of the pyramid.

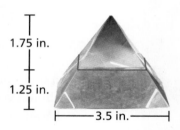

1.75 in.

1.25 in.

3.5 in.

E.6 Cross Sections of Three-Dimensional Figures *(pp. 677–682)*

Learning Target: Describe the cross sections of a solid.

Describe the intersection of the plane and the solid.

25.

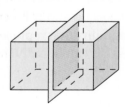

26.

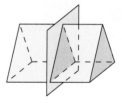

Sketch how a plane can intersect with a cylinder to form a cross section of the given shape.

27. rectangle   **28.** circle   **29.** line segment

Find the surface area of the prism or regular pyramid.

1.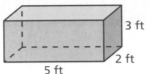
3 ft
2 ft
5 ft

2.
2 in.
1 in.

3.
15 m
11 m
9.5 m

Find the surface area and lateral surface area of the cylinder. Round your answers to the nearest tenth.

4.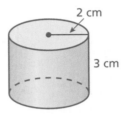
2 cm
3 cm

5.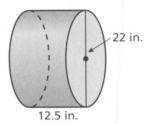
22 in.
12.5 in.

Find the volume of the solid.

6.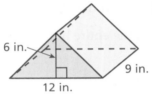
6 in.
9 in.
12 in.

7.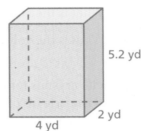
5.2 yd
2 yd
4 yd

8.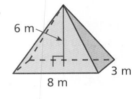
6 m
3 m
8 m

9. A quart of paint covers 80 square feet. How many quarts should you buy to paint the ramp with two coats? (Assume you will not paint the bottom of the ramp.)

15.2 ft
6 ft
19.5 ft
14 ft

GRAHAM CRACKERS
"With the taste of REAL honey in every bite"

$h = 9$ in.
$\ell = 6$ in. $w = 2$ in.

10. A manufacturer wants to double the volume of the graham cracker box. The manufacturer will either double the height or double the width.

   a. What is the volume of the new graham cracker box?

   b. Which option uses less cardboard? Justify your answer.

   c. A graham cracker takes up about 1.5 cubic inches of space. Write an inequality that represents the numbers of graham crackers that can fit in the new box.

11. The label on the can of soup covers about 354.2 square centimeters. What is the height of the can? Round your answer to the nearest whole number.

4.7 cm
TOMATO SOUP

12. A lumberjack splits the cylindrical log from top to bottom with an ax, dividing it in half. Describe the shape that is formed by the cut.

Cumulative Practice

1. A gift box and its dimensions are shown.

8 in.   2 in.   4 in.

What is the least amount of wrapping paper that you need to wrap the box?

A. 20 in.^{2}

B. 56 in.^{2}

C. 64 in.^{2}

D. 112 in.^{2}

2. James is getting ready for wrestling season. As part of his preparation, he plans to lose 5% of his body weight. James currently weighs 160 pounds. How much will he weigh, in pounds, after he loses 5% of his weight?

3. How far will the tip of the hour hand of the clock travel in 2 hours? (Use $\frac{22}{7}$ for π.)

84 mm

F. 44 mm

G. 88 mm

H. 264 mm

I. 528 mm

4. Which value of x makes the equation true?

$$5x - 3 = 11$$

A. 1.6

B. 2.8

C. 40

D. 70

5. A hockey rink contains 5 face-off circles. Each of these circles has a radius of 15 feet. What is the total area of all the face-off circles? (Use 3.14 for π.)

F. 706.5 ft^2

G. 2826 ft^2

H. 3532.5 ft^2

I. 14,130 ft^2

6. How much material is needed to make the popcorn container?

4 in.

9.5 in.

A. 76π in.^{2}

B. 84π in.^{2}

C. 92π in.^{2}

D. 108π in.^{2}

7. What is the surface area of the square pyramid?

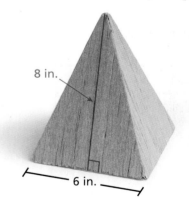

8 in.

6 in.

F. 24 in.^{2}

G. 96 in.^{2}

H. 132 in.^{2}

I. 228 in.^{2}

8. A rectangular prism and its dimensions are shown.

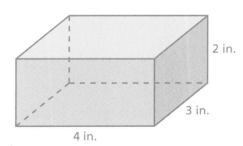

2 in.

3 in.

4 in.

What is the volume, in cubic inches, of a rectangular prism whose dimensions are three times greater?

9. What is the value of x?

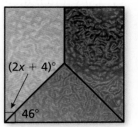

$(2x + 4)°$

$46°$

A. 20

B. 43

C. 44

D. 65

10. Which of the following are possible angle measures of a triangle?

F. $60°, 50°, 20°$

G. $40°, 80°, 90°$

H. $30°, 60°, 90°$

I. $0°, 90°, 90°$

11. The table shows the costs of buying matinee movie tickets.

Think
Solve
Explain

Matinee Tickets, x	2	3	4	5
Cost, y	$9	$13.50	$18	$22.50

Part A   Graph the data.

Part B   Find and interpret the constant of proportionality for the graph of the line.

Part C   How much does it cost to buy 8 matinee movie tickets?

Selected Answers

Chapter 1

Section 1.1
Review & Refresh

1. 5   **3.** 112

5. terms: $h, 9, g$
coefficients: 1, 1
constant: 9

7. $\dfrac{22}{a}$

Concepts, Skills, & Problem Solving

9. Addition Property of Equality; $x = 4$; Add 5 to each side of the equation $x - 5 = -1$.

11. $x = -5$ **13.** $p = 21$

15. $x = 9\pi$ **17.** $d = \dfrac{2}{3}$

19. $n = -4.9$

21. **a.** $x + 8 = 65$; 57

   b. you; your friend's score: $2(65) = 130$; your score: $57 + 80 = 137$

23. $n = -5$ **25.** $m = 7.3\pi$

27. $k = 1\dfrac{2}{3}$ **29.** $p = -2\dfrac{1}{3}$

31. no; Your friend should have added 1.5 to each side.

33. \$6.50 per hour   **35.** \$60

37. 145 ft   **39.** $w = 19$

41. $d = 0$ **43.** $p = -\dfrac{1}{12}$

45. $x + 45 = 90$; $x = 45$

47. $+$ and $-$ are inverses; Adding a number and subtracting that same number cancel each other out.

$\times$ and $\div$ are inverses; Multiplying by a number and dividing by that same number cancel each other out.

49. *Sample answer:* $x - 2 = -4, \dfrac{x}{2} = -1$;

$$(-2) - 2 \overset{?}{=} -4 \qquad \dfrac{-2}{2} \overset{?}{=} -1$$
$$-4 = -4 \qquad -1 = -1$$

51. 120 students

53. **a.** \$18, \$27, \$45

   b. *Sample answer:* Everyone did not do an equal amount of painting.

Section 1.2
Review & Refresh

1. $y = -5$ **3.** $n = -2\dfrac{1}{2}$

5. $-\dfrac{1}{5}$ **7.** $-\dfrac{227}{500}$

Concepts, Skills, & Problem Solving

9. $20°, 24°, 136°$; $20 + (y - 10) + 4y = 180, y = 34$

11. $x = 3$ **13.** $x = 2$

15. $x = -2$ **17.** $v = 2$

19. $d = 2$

21. no; Your friend did not distribute the -2 properly.

23. 20 watches   **25.** 29 mL

27. 6 in.   **29.** 3500 people

Section 1.3
Review & Refresh

1. $z = -1$ **3.** $x = -11$

5. 27 cm^3 **7.** 24 in.^3

Concepts, Skills, & Problem Solving

9. $x = 7.2$; $26x + 72 = 36x, x = 7.2$

11. $m = -4$ **13.** $x = 22$

15. $w = 2$ **17.** $z = 1.6$

19. $d = 14$

21. $20 + 0.5m = 30 + 0.25m$; 40 mi

23. $x = \dfrac{1}{3}$ **25.** $x = 0$

27. $x = 6$ **29.** $x = 2$

31. infinitely many solutions

33. infinitely many solutions

35. *Sample answer:* $8x + 2 = 8x$; The number $8x$ cannot be equal to 2 more than itself.

37. The total number of crusts made by the pizza parlor is always twice the total number of crusts made by the diner.

39. 3 units

41. 232 units

43. fractions; $\dfrac{1}{3}$ written as a decimal is repeating.

45. *Sample answer:*
one solution: $7x + 3x + 10 = -2(7x + 4)$
no solution: $7x + 3x + 10 = -2(-5x + 4)$
infinitely many solutions:
$7x + 3x + 10 = -2(-5x + (-5))$

47. 25 g;
$$x = 21 + 0.16x$$
$$0.84x = 21$$
$$x = 25$$

49. $a - b = 1, c = 0$ and $a \neq b, c = 0$;

$a - b = 1, c = 0$	$a = b, c \neq 0$
$c = ax - bx$	$c = ax - bx$
$c = x(a - b)$	$c = ax - ax$
$0 = x(1)$	$c = 0$, where $c \neq 0$
$0 = x$	no solution
one solution	

$a = b, c = 0$
$c = ax - bx$
$0 = ax - ax$
$0 = 0$
infinitely many solutions

$a \neq b, c = 0$
$c = ax - bx$
$0 = x(a - b)$, where $a - b \neq 0$
$\dfrac{0}{a - b} = \dfrac{x(a - b)}{a - b}$
$0 = x$
one solution

Section 1.4
Review & Refresh
1. $x = -5$
3. no solution
5. 12 mi per h
7. 1.5 lb per crate

Concepts, Skills, & Problem Solving
9. $h = \dfrac{V}{B}$; 6 in.

11. yes; The equation contains 2 variables.

13. $y = 4 - \dfrac{1}{3}x$ **15.** $y = \dfrac{2}{3} - \dfrac{4}{9}x$

17. $y = 3x - 1.5$

19. no; When $2x$ is subtracted from each side of the equation, the result should be $-y = -2x + 5$.

21. $m = \dfrac{e}{c^2}$ **23.** $a = P - b - c$

25. $V = \dfrac{m}{D}$

27. a. $t = \dfrac{I}{Pr}$

    b. 3 yr

29. a. $F = 32 + \dfrac{9}{5}(K - 273.15)$

    b. $-457.96°F$

    c. liquid nitrogen

31. 6 ft; $V = \dfrac{Bh}{3}$, $B = \dfrac{3V}{h} = \dfrac{3(360)}{30} = 36$. Because B is the area of the square base, the side lengths of the base are 6 feet.

Chapter 2
Section 2.1
Review & Refresh
1. $y = -6x + 12$ **3.** $y = -\dfrac{1}{6}x + 4$

Concepts, Skills, & Problem Solving
5. 6 units right and 3 units down
7. yes   **9.** no
11. yes

13. 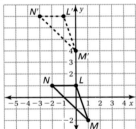   **15.**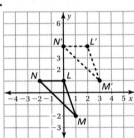

17. no; The translations for the x- and y-coordinates were reversed.

19. $A'(-3, 0), B'(0, -1), C'(1, -4), D'(-3, -5)$

21. 5 units right and 9 units up

23. $A'(5, -5), B'(5, 2), C'(8, 2), D'(8, -5)$

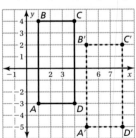

25. yes; *Sample answer:* You can write one translation to get from the original triangle to the final triangle, which is $(x + 2, y - 10)$. So, the triangles are identical.

Section 2.2

Review & Refresh

1.

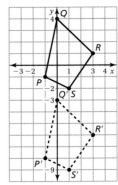

3.

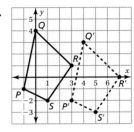

5. neither

7. neither

Concepts, Skills, & Problem Solving

9. reflection in the x-axis

11. reflection in the y-axis

13. yes

15. no

17. no

19.

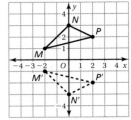

$M'(-2, -1), N'(0, -3), P'(2, -2)$

21.

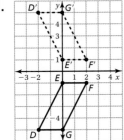

$D'(-2, 5), E'(0, 1), F'(2, 1), G'(0, 5)$

23.

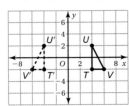

$T'(-4, -2), U'(-4, 2), V'(-6, -2)$

25.

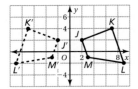

$J'(-2, 2), K'(-7, 4), L'(-9, -2), M'(-3, -1)$

27. x-axis   **29.** $x = 1$

31. $R''(3, -4), S''(3, -1), T''(1, -4)$

33. yes; *Sample answer:* Translations and reflections produce images that are identical to the original figure.

35.

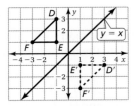

The x-coordinate and y-coordinate for each point are switched in the image.

Section 2.3

Review & Refresh

1. yes   **3.** about 88 cm

5. about 3.14 ft

Concepts, Skills, & Problem Solving

7. rotation of 90° counterclockwise about the origin

9. no

11. yes; 180° clockwise or counterclockwise

13. $A'(2, 2), B'(1, 4), C'(3, 4), D'(4, 2)$

15. $J'(1, 4), K'(1, 2), L'(-3, 4)$

17. $W'(-2, 6), X'(-2, 2), Y'(-6, 2), Z'(-6, 5)$

19. no; Your friend found the coordinates of the image after a rotation 90° counterclockwise, not clockwise.

21. yes; The figure only needs to rotate 120° to produce an identical image.

23. yes; The figure only needs to rotate 180° to produce an identical image.

25. $J''(4, 4), K''(3, 4), L''(1, 1), M''(4, 1)$

27. *Sample answer:* Rotate 90° counterclockwise about the origin and then translate 1 unit left and 1 unit down; Reflect in the x-axis and then translate 4 units left and 2 units up.

29. $D'(2, 1), E'(5, 1), F'(-1, -2)$

31. $W'(-5, 0), X'(-1, -4), Y'(-6, -8), Z'(-9, -5)$

33. (1) Rotate 180° about the origin.
(2) Rotate 90° counterclockwise about the origin.
(3) Reflect in the y-axis.
(4) Translate 1 unit right and 1 unit up.

Section 2.4
Review & Refresh
1. $A'(-3, 1), B'(-5, 2), C'(-5, 3), D'(-3, 2)$

3. $4(n - 8)$ **5.** $2(y - 9)$

Concepts, Skills, & Problem Solving
7. yes

9. Figure $EFGH$ and Figure $BCDA$

11. *Sample answer:* Rotate the red figure 180° about the origin and then translate the image 1 unit right and 1 unit down.

13. $\angle A$ and $\angle E$, $\angle B$ and $\angle F$, $\angle C$ and $\angle G$, $\angle D$ and $\angle H$; $\overline{AB}$ and $\overline{EF}$, $\overline{BC}$ and $\overline{FG}$, $\overline{CD}$ and $\overline{GH}$, $\overline{DA}$ and $\overline{HE}$

15. *Sample answer:* Use a reflection in a vertical line followed by a 90° clockwise rotation.

17. **a.** 32 ft

    b. $\angle M$

    c. 20 ft; 96 ft

Section 2.5
Review & Refresh
1. *Sample answer:* Rotate the blue figure 90° counterclockwise about the origin and then translate the image 1 unit left and 4 units down.

3. no   **5.** yes

Concepts, Skills, & Problem Solving
7. dilation with respect to the origin by a scale factor of $\frac{1}{4}$

9. yes   **11.** no

13. yes

15.

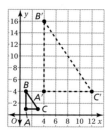

enlargement

17.

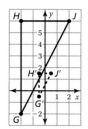

reduction

19.

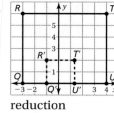

reduction

21. yes; Each x- and y-coordinate was multiplied by the scale factor 2.

23. reduction; $\frac{1}{4}$

25. reduction; $\frac{1}{2}$

27. $F''(-6, 0), G''(-2, 2), H''(-2, 0)$

29. **a.** enlargement

    b. center of dilation

    c. $\frac{4}{3}$

    d. The shadow on the wall becomes larger; The scale factor becomes larger.

31. The transformations are a dilation with a scale factor of 2 and then a translation of 4 units right and 3 units down; no; The dilation does not produce a congruent figure, so the final image is not congruent.

33. The transformations are a dilation with a scale factor of $\frac{1}{3}$ and then a reflection in the x-axis; no; The dilation does not produce a congruent figure, so the final image is not congruent.

35. $(x, y) \rightarrow \left(\frac{1}{4}x, \frac{1}{2}y\right)$; Each x-coordinate is multiplied by $\frac{1}{4}$ and each y-coordinate is multiplied by $\frac{1}{2}$.

37. $A'(-2, 3), B'(6, 3), C'(12, -7), D'(-2, -7)$; Check students' work.

Section 2.6
Review & Refresh
1. no   **3.** C

Concepts, Skills, & Problem Solving
5. no

7. no; There is no similarity transformation between $\triangle ABC$ and $\triangle JKL$.

9.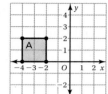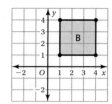

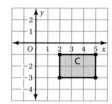

A and B; *Sample answer:* Obtain B from A by dilating A using a scale factor of $\frac{3}{2}$ and then translating the image 7 units right and 1 unit up.

11. *Sample answer:* Dilate the red figure using a scale factor of 3 and then translate the image 11 units left and 11 units up.

13. a. sometimes; They are similar only when corresponding side lengths are proportional and corresponding angles are congruent.

  b. always; All angles are congruent and all sides are proportional.

  c. sometimes; Corresponding angles are always congruent, but corresponding side lengths are not always proportional.

15. a. yes; *Sample answer:* The new sign is a dilation of the original sign using a scale factor of 1.2.

  b. no; *Sample answer:* Because the length and width are different, adding 6 to each side length does not produce an equivalent ratio. So, corresponding side lengths are not proportional.

17. a. yes

  b. yes; The ratios are equivalent because the heights are multiplied by the same amount as the sides.

Section 2.7
Review & Refresh

1. *Sample answer:* Dilate the red figure using a scale factor of 3 and then reflect the image in the *y*-axis.

3. 144 cm² **5.** 35 km²

Concepts, Skills, & Problem Solving

7. $\frac{1}{2}; \frac{1}{4}$ **9.** $\frac{5}{8}; \frac{25}{64}$

11. $\frac{14}{9}; \frac{196}{81}$ **13.** 25.6

15. 108 yd

17. a. 400 times greater; The value of the ratio of the corresponding lengths is $\frac{120 \text{ in.}}{6 \text{ in.}} = \frac{20}{1}$. So, the value of the ratio of the areas is $\left(\frac{20}{1}\right)^2 = \frac{400}{1}$.

  b. 1250 ft²

19. 15 m

21. $2177.\overline{7}$ cm²; *Sample answer:* The side length of Mirror C is $280 \div 4 = 70$ cm. So, the area of Mirror C is 4900 cm².

$$\frac{\text{Area of Mirror B}}{4900} = \frac{16}{25}$$

Area of Mirror B = 3136 cm²

$$\frac{\text{Area of Mirror A}}{3136} = \left(\frac{5}{6}\right)^2$$

Area of Mirror A = $2177.\overline{7}$ cm²

Chapter 3

Section 3.1
Review & Refresh

1. $\frac{3}{5}; \frac{9}{25}$ **3.** 13

5. 51

Concepts, Skills, & Problem Solving

7. no

9. $\angle 3 = 95°$; $\angle 3$ and the given angle are corresponding angles.
$\angle 4 = 85°$; $\angle 3$ and $\angle 4$ are supplementary.

11. no; The two lines are not parallel, so $\angle 5 \neq \angle 6$.

13. *Sample answer:* Railroad tracks are parallel, and the out of bounds lines on a football field are parallel.

15. $\angle 1 = 81°$, $\angle 2 = 99°$, $\angle 3 = 81°$, $\angle 4 = 99°$, $\angle 5 = 81°$, $\angle 6 = 99°$, $\angle 7 = 81°$

17. 56°; *Sample answer:* $\angle 1$ and $\angle 8$ are corresponding angles and $\angle 8$ and $\angle 4$ are supplementary.

19. 55°; $\angle 4$ and $\angle 2$ are alternate interior angles.

21. 129.5°; *Sample answer:* $\angle 7$ and $\angle 5$ are alternate exterior angles and $\angle 5$ and $\angle 6$ are supplementary.

23. 40°

25. Perpendicular lines form 90° angles.

27. *Sample answer:* 1) ∠1 and ∠7 are congruent because they are alternate exterior angles.
2) ∠1 and ∠5 are congruent because they are corresponding angles. ∠5 and ∠7 are congruent because they are vertical angles. So, ∠1 and ∠7 are congruent.

29. 115

31. a. no; They look like they are spreading apart.

   b. Check students' work.

Section 3.2
Review & Refresh

1. 82°; ∠2 and the given angle are alternate exterior angles.

3. 82°; *Sample answer:* ∠4 and the given angle are corresponding angles.

5. 1, 2, 3

Concepts, Skills, & Problem Solving

7. ∠A = 30°, ∠B = 105°, ∠C = 45°, ∠D = 150°, ∠E = 75°, ∠F = 105°, ∠G = 30°

9. 30°, 60°, 90°

11. 35°, 45°, 100°

13. 44°, 48°, 88°

15. 128°

17. 108°

19. no; The measure of the exterior angle is equal to the sum of the measures of the two nonadjacent interior angles. The sum of all three angles is not 180°.

21. 126°

23. sometimes; The sum of the angle measures must equal 180°.

25. never; If a triangle had more than one vertex with an acute exterior angle, then it would have to have more than one obtuse interior angle, which is impossible.

Section 3.3
Review & Refresh

1. 60

3. 113

5. x = 2

Concepts, Skills, & Problem Solving

7. 360°

9. 540°

11. 1080°

13. no; The right side of the formula should be (n − 2) • 180°, not n • 180°.

15. 135

17. 60°

19. 150°

21. a. 108°

   b. *Sample answer:* to deter people from tampering with fire hydrants, because most wrenches are hexagonal

23. hexagon;
number of interior angles = number of sides = n
120 • n = (n − 2) • 180
   n = 6;
no; *Sample answer:* The sides do not have to be the same length.

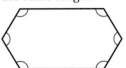

25. 45°, 67.5°, 67.5°

27. 135°, 135°, 135°, 135°, 120°, 120°, 120°

Section 3.4
Review & Refresh

1. 135°

3. 160°

5. x = 6

Concepts, Skills, & Problem Solving

7. When two angles in one triangle are congruent to two angles in another triangle, the third angles are also congruent and triangles are similar.

9. yes; The triangles have two pairs of congruent angles.

11. no; The triangles do not have the same angle measures.

13. the leftmost and rightmost; They both are right triangles with two 45° angles.

15. no; The triangles do not have the same angle measures.

17. yes; *Sample answer:* ∠ACB and ∠ECD are vertical angles, and ∠B and ∠D are congruent alternate interior angles.

19. Because the triangles have a pair of vertical angles and a pair of right angles, the triangles have the same interior angle measures; 100 steps

21. Check students' work.

23. △ABG ~ △ACF, △ABG ~ △ADE, △ACF ~ △ADE; 2 ft; 4 ft

Chapter 4

Section 4.1
Review & Refresh

1. yes; The triangles have the same angle measures, 95°, 46°, and 39°.

3. 2 units right and 4 units up

5. 13 units left and 5 units up

Concepts, Skills, & Problem Solving

7.

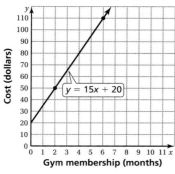

9. *Sample answer:*

x	0	3
$y = \frac{1}{3}x + 2$	2	3

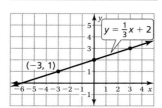

11.

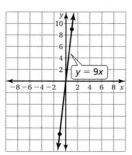

13.

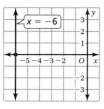

15.

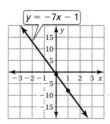

17.

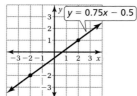

19.

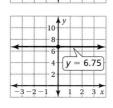

21.

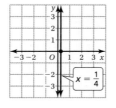

23.

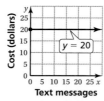

Sample answer: No matter how many text messages are sent, the cost is $20.

25. $y = 3x + 1$

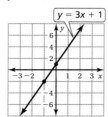

27. $y = 12x - 9$

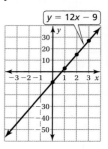

29. 0.8 in.;

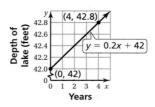

31. a.

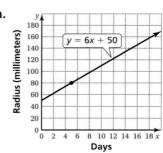

b. about 56,381.84 mm²; *Sample answer:* After 14 days, the radius is $6(14) + 50 = 134$ mm.

$$A = \pi r^2$$
$$= \pi(134)^2$$
$$= 17{,}956\pi \text{ mm}^2$$
$$\approx 56{,}381.84 \text{ mm}^2$$

33. a.

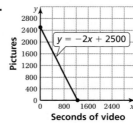

b. 2320 pictures

Section 4.2
Review & Refresh

1.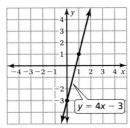

3.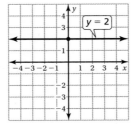

5.

Yards	1	$3\frac{1}{3}$	5	7
Feet	3	10	15	21

Concepts, Skills, & Problem Solving

7. $-\dfrac{1}{2}$ **9.** $\dfrac{3}{4}$

11. $-\dfrac{3}{5}$ **13.** 0

15. 0 **17.** undefined

19. $-\dfrac{11}{6}$

21. no; Both lines have the same slope, so the lines are parallel.

23. blue and red; They both have a slope of -3.

25. yes; Both lines are horizontal and have a slope of 0.

27. yes; Both lines are vertical and have an undefined slope.

29. $\dfrac{2}{5}$

31. **a.** Check students' work.

   b. *Sample answer:*

33. $k = 4$ **35.** $k = 8$

37. the boat ramp; It has a 16.67% grade.

39. $2750 per month; $\dfrac{17,500 - 6500}{5 - 1} = \dfrac{11,000}{4} = 2750$

41. **a.** 0.65

   b. The slope increases because the vertical distance for the main portion of the slide increases and the horizontal distance stays the same.

Section 4.3
Review & Refresh

1. 1 **3.** 4

5. $x = \dfrac{23}{18}$

Concepts, Skills, & Problem Solving

7.

Water (cups), x	3	6	9
Flour (cups), y	5	10	15

For every increase of 5 cups of flour, there is an increase of 3 cups of water. The slope is $\dfrac{5}{3}$.

9.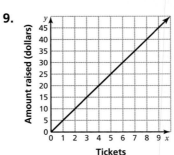

Each ticket costs $5.

11. yes; The line passes through the origin; $y = 4x$

13. no; The rate of change in the table is not constant.

15. **a.** car; *Sample answer:* Compare unit rates. 25 mpg > 18 mpg

   b. 56 mi

17. it is the same

19. yes; The equation is $d = 50r$, which represents a proportional relationship.

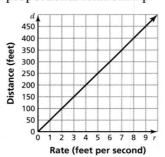

Section 4.4
Review & Refresh

1. no; The line does not pass through the origin.

3. $y = \dfrac{1}{4}x + \dfrac{1}{2}$

5. $y = -\dfrac{4}{5}x - 3$ **7.** $y = -3x - 4$

Concepts, Skills, & Problem Solving

9.

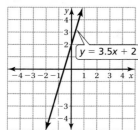

11. B; slope: 2; y-intercept: 1

13. C; slope: $-\dfrac{2}{3}$; y-intercept: 1

15. slope: -7; y-intercept: 12

17. slope: 2.25; y-intercept: 3

19. slope: $\dfrac{3}{8}$; y-intercept: 6

21. slope: $-\dfrac{1}{2}$; y-intercept: -5

23. no; The y-intercept should be -3.

25.

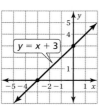

x-intercept: -3

27.

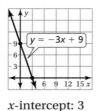

x-intercept: 3

29.

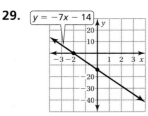

x-intercept: -2

31. a. $y = 0.75x + 5$; The cost of going to the festival is the sum of the cost of picking x pounds of apples, $0.75x$, and the cost of admission, 5.

b.

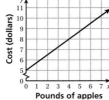

33. a.

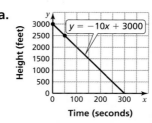

b. The slope of -10 means that the skydiver falls to the ground at a rate of 10 feet per second. The y-intercept of 3000 means the initial height of the skydiver is 3000 feet above the ground. The x-intercept of 300 means the skydiver lands on the ground after 300 seconds.

Section 4.5

Review & Refresh

1. slope: 1; y-intercept: -1

3. slope: $\dfrac{8}{9}$; y-intercept: -8

5. yes

Concepts, Skills, & Problem Solving

7. x = pounds of peaches
y = pounds of apples
$$y = -\frac{4}{3}x + 10$$

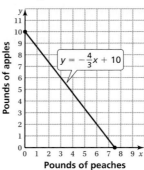

9. $y = -2x + 17$

11. $y = \dfrac{1}{2}x + 10$

13.

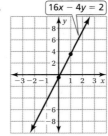

15. B

17. C

19. a.

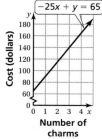

b. $140

21.

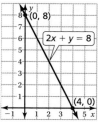

23.

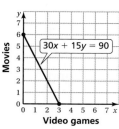

The x-intercept shows that your cousin can purchase 3 video games if no movies are purchased. The y-intercept shows that your cousin can purchase 6 movies if no video games are purchased.

25. a. $9.45x + 3.78y = 113.4$

b.

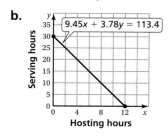

27. a. $y = 40x + 70$

b. x-intercept: $-\dfrac{7}{4}$; no; You cannot have a negative time.

c.

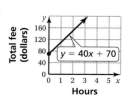

Section 4.6

Review & Refresh

1. $y = -4x + 1$

3. $y = \dfrac{1}{3}x - \dfrac{7}{2}$

5 and 7.

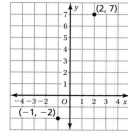

Concepts, Skills, & Problem Solving

9. $y = 10x + 15$

11. $y = x + 4$

13. $y = \dfrac{1}{4}x + 1$

15. $y = \dfrac{1}{3}x - 3$

17. $y = -2x + 2$

19. $x = 0$

21. $y = \dfrac{2}{3}x + \dfrac{3}{2}$

23. The slope of 200 represents the additional fee per tooth removal. The y-intercept of 100 represents the initial fee for an office visit.

25. $y = -140x + 500$

Section 4.7

Review & Refresh

1. $y = \dfrac{1}{2}x + 5$

3. no solution

5. $x = 4$

Concepts, Skills, & Problem Solving

7. $V = -4000t + 30{,}000$

9. $y - 8 = \dfrac{3}{4}(x - 4)$

11. $y + 5 = -\dfrac{1}{7}(x - 7)$

13. $y + 4 = -2(x + 1)$

15. $y = 2x$

17. $y = \dfrac{1}{4}x$

19. $y = x + 1$

21. *Sample answer:* $y = x + 2.5$; Explanations will vary.

23. *Sample answer:* $y = -3x + 1.5$; Explanations will vary.

25. *Sample answer:* $y = \dfrac{2}{3}x + 1$; Explanations will vary.

27. $y = 4x - 30$

29. a. 65°F

    b. 224 chirps;
$$96 = 0.25x + 40$$
$$56 = 0.25x$$
$$224 = x$$

Chapter 5

Section 5.1

Review & Refresh

1. $y + 4 = 1(x - 3)$ **3.** $y - 0 = -\dfrac{1}{4}(x - 1)$

5. $y = 4$

Concepts, Skills, & Problem Solving

7.

x (weeks)	1	2	3	4	5
y (Country)	160	170	180	190	200
y (Pop)	135	155	175	195	215

x (weeks)	6	7	8	9	10
y (Country)	210	220	230	240	250
y (Pop)	235	255	275	295	315

Sample answer: Initially, the ticket sales for the Country Music Festival are greater than the ticket sales for the Pop Music Festival, but they increase slower and are less than the ticket sales for the Pop Music Festival for weeks 4 through 10.

9. $(-1, 7)$ **11.** $(-4, -3)$

13. $(5, 22)$ **15.** $(5, 1.5)$

17. $(-6, 2)$

19. 26 math problems, 16 science problems;
$x + y = 42$
$x = y + 10$
Solution: $(26, 16)$

21. a. 1.25 h

    b. 0.5 mi

23. *Sample answer:* $y = x - 4$
$$y = \frac{1}{3}x - 2$$

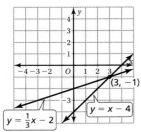

25. a. $y = 0.5x + 2.5$
$y = 0.4x + 5.8$

    b. yes; month 33

27. 14 ft

Section 5.2

Review & Refresh

1. $(4, 5)$ **3.** $(3, -5)$

Concepts, Skills, & Problem Solving

5. $\moon = 7$, $\bigstar = 4$ **7.** $(2, -2)$

9. $\left(-2, -\dfrac{9}{2}\right)$ **11.** $(-6.5, -3)$

13. $(-3, -3)$ **15.** $(6, -3)$

17. a. $x = 2y$
$64x + 132y = 1040$

    b. adult tickets: $8, student tickets: $4

19. $(1, 5)$; Explanations will vary.

21. $(-1, 3)$; Explanations will vary.

23. $y = 2.5x$
$2x + y = 180$;
acute angles: 40°, obtuse angle: 100°

25. 63 nurses; 14 doctors

Section 5.3

Review & Refresh

1. $(4, 1)$ **3.** $(22, -4)$

5.

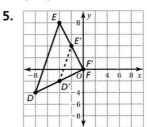

reduction

Concepts, Skills, & Problem Solving

7. Multiply Equation 2 by -2, then add the equations.

9. $(2, 1)$ **11.** $(1, -3)$

13. $(3, 2)$

15. no; Your friend should have added the x-terms and the constants, not subtracted them.

17. $2x + y = 10$
$2x + 3y = 22$;
6 min

19. $(5, -1)$ **21.** $(-2, -1)$

23. $(4, 3)$

25. $(4, 0)$; Explanations will vary.

27. $\left(\dfrac{8}{5}, -\dfrac{4}{5}\right)$; Explanations will vary.

29. $\left(-\dfrac{14}{5}, -\dfrac{8}{5}\right)$; Explanations will vary.

31. *Sample answer:* -4; When $a = -4$, the coefficients of the x-terms are opposites.

33. no; The lines are parallel.

35. $y = 2x$

$y = -\dfrac{1}{3}x + 14$;

Solution: $(6, 12)$

37. multiple choice: 2 points each, short response: 4 points each

39. $95

41. 90% gold alloy: 5 g, 50% gold alloy: 3 g

43. $x = -1, y = 2, z = 1$

Section 5.4
Review & Refresh

1. $(-8, 6)$ **3.** $(2, 1)$

5. $y = 2x - 3$

Concepts, Skills, & Problem Solving

7. no solution   **9.** one solution

11. $(-1, -2)$; Explanations will vary.

13. infinitely many solutions; Explanations will vary.

15. $(-2.4, -3.5)$; Explanations will vary.

17. $\left(\dfrac{1}{10}, \dfrac{9}{10}\right)$; Explanations will vary.

19. no; The lines have different y-intercepts, so the system has no solution.

21. one solution; The lines have different slopes.

23. **a.** 6 h

b. You both work the same number of hours.

25. $7.50; $11

27. no;
$36x + 18y = 684$
$24x + 12y = 456$
infinitely many solutions
yes;
$36x + 18y = 684$
$18x + 18y = 432$
Solution: $(14, 10)$

Chapter 6

Section 6.1
Review & Refresh

1. no solution   **3.** $\left(\dfrac{4}{5}, -\dfrac{4}{5}\right)$

Concepts, Skills, & Problem Solving

5.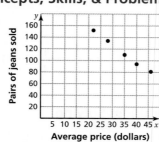

7.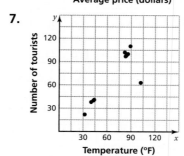

outlier: $(102, 63)$; gap: from $44°F$ to $82°F$; cluster: from $82°F$ to $89°F$

9. negative linear relationship; outlier: $(15, 10)$; gap: from $x = 15$ to $x = 25$; no clusters

11. no relationship; no outliers, gaps, or clusters

13. positive linear relationship

15. **a.** *Sample answer:* 3.5 h

b. *Sample answer:* $85

c. positive linear relationship

17. **a.** 2014

b. *Sample answer:* 950 scooters

c. negative linear relationship

d. *Sample answer:* 2019

Section 6.2
Review & Refresh

1. negative linear relationship; outlier: $(6, 10)$; no gaps or clusters

3. positive linear relationship; no outliers or gaps; cluster: from $x = 11$ to $x = 15$

5. $0.28, 28\%$

Concepts, Skills, & Problem Solving

7. *Sample answer:*

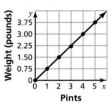

9. a. *Sample answer:*

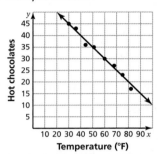

b. *Sample answer:* $y = -0.5x + 60$

c. *Sample answer:* You could expect that 60 hot chocolates are sold when the temperature is 0°F, and the sales decrease by 1 hot chocolate for every 2°F increase in temperature.

11. $y = -4.9x + 1042$; about -0.969; strong negative correlation

13. a. $y = 1.3x + 2$; about 0.9995; strong positive correlation

b. The number of electoral votes increases by 1.3 for every increase of 1 million people in the state.

c. A state with a population of 0 has 2 electoral votes.

d. *Sample answer:* The number of electoral votes a state has is based on the number of members that state has in Congress. Each state has 2 Senators, plus a number of members of the House of Representatives based on its population. So, the y-intercept is 2 because a hypothetical state with no population would still have 2 Senators.

15. a. 251 ft

b. The height of the baseball is not linear.

Section 6.3
Review & Refresh

1. $y = 12.6x + 75.8$

3.

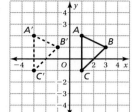

5.

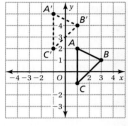

Concepts, Skills, & Problem Solving

7. 0 shirts   **9.** 51 female students

11. 71 students are juniors; 75 students are seniors; 93 students will attend the school play; 53 students will not attend the school play; 146 students were surveyed.

13.

	Treatment		
	Yes	**No**	**Total**
Improved	34	12	46
Did Not Improve	10	29	39
Total	44	41	85

(Condition)

15.

	Eye Color		
	Green	**Blue**	**Brown**
Male	10.4%	33.3%	56.3%
Female	7.5%	47.5%	45%

(Gender)

17.

		Age		
		20–29	**30–39**	**40–49**
Yes		28%	45%	62.5%
No		72%	55%	37.5%

(Saved at Least $1000)

Yes, the table shows that as age increases, people are more likely to have at least $1000 in savings.

Section 6.4
Review & Refresh

1. 24 male students; 9 female students

3. slope: 4; y-intercept: 10

5. slope: -1; y-intercept: 8

Concepts, Skills, & Problem Solving

7. *Sample answer:* stem-and-leaf plot; shows how data is distributed

9. *Sample answer:* dot plot; shows the number of times each outcome occurs

11. a. yes; The circle graph shows the data as parts of the whole.

   b. no; The bar graph shows the number of students, not the portion of students.

13. when the data are in terms of intervals of one category, as opposed to multiple categories; *Sample answer:* You can use a histogram to display the frequencies of voters in the last election by age group.

15. the graph on the right; The interval for the third bar is greater than the interval for the other two bars, which makes it seem like there is an increasing trend.

17. no; The tickets vary in width and the vertical axis has a break, which makes it seem like the ticket price for Group C is more than double the ticket price for Group A. The ticket price for Group A is actually about \$40, and the ticket price for Group C is actually about \$53.

19. a. The percents do not sum to 100%.

   b. *Sample answer:* bar graph; It would show the frequency of each sport.

Chapter 7

Section 7.1

Review & Refresh

1. *Sample answer:* histogram; shows frequencies of data values in intervals of the same size

3. 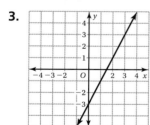 **5.**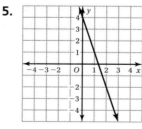

Concepts, Skills, & Problem Solving

7. As the input increases by 1, the output decreases by 4; output: -17; input: 6; The input 5 only has one possible output, and the output -21 only has one possible input.

9. (0, 4), (3, 5), (6, 6), (9, 7)

11. (6, -5), (7, -5), (8, -10), (9, -10)

13. function

15. no; In order for a relation to be a function, each input must be paired with exactly one output. So, the relation is not a function.

17. Input   Output

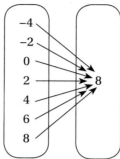

function; Each input has exactly one output.

19. a. 4 ATM; 5 ATM; 6 ATM

   b. yes

   c. The pressure increases by 1 ATM for each 10-meter increase in the depth.

   d. (0, 1), (10, 2), (20, 3), (30, 4), (40, 5), (50, 6);

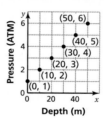

   Sample answer: The points lie on a line.

   e. *Sample answer:* A beginner scuba diver should not go below 30 meters; The safe limit for an experienced scuba diver should be around 60 meters.

21. 1025

Section 7.2

Review & Refresh

1. function   **3.** not a function

5. $-\dfrac{5}{2}$

Concepts, Skills, & Problem Solving

7. false   **9.** $y = \dfrac{1}{2}x$

11. $y = x - 3$ **13.** $y = 6x$

15. 8   **17.** -17

19. 54

21.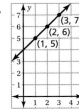

23.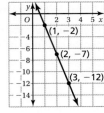

25.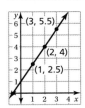

27. B

29. A

31. a. $p = 30d$

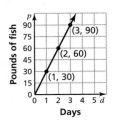

    b. 900 lb

33. -3

35. 36

37. a. $y = 0.4x$

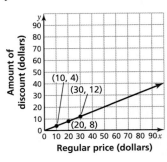

    b. $51

39. 17

41. 44 square units; 45 square units; *Sample answer:* The "green area" of an even numbered square is equal to four more than twice the square number. The "green area" of an odd numbered square is equal to three more than twice the square number.

Section 7.3

Review & Refresh

1. $y = x - 10$

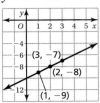

3. $(-1, 4)$ **5.** $(-5, -2)$

Concepts, Skills, & Problem Solving

7. x is diameter of the circle; y is the circumference; $y = \pi x$; yes; *Sample answer:* The function is in slope-intercept form.

9. $y = 3$ **11.** $y = \dfrac{2}{3}x + 5$

13. a. $y = -0.2x + 1$

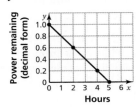

    b. The slope indicates that the power decreases by 20% per hour. The x-intercept indicates that the battery lasts 5 hours. The y-intercept indicates that the battery power is at 100% when you turn on the laptop.

    c. 1.25 h

15. $y = 19x$; You win when the race is longer than 190 feet. You catch up to your friend after you run 190 feet, so you will be ahead of your friend for any distance greater than 190 feet.

17. no; Any linear equation of the form $x = a$ is not a linear function because its graph is a vertical line.

Section 7.4

Review & Refresh

1. $y = x - 2$

3.

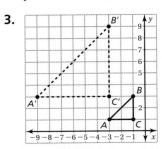

enlargement

Concepts, Skills, & Problem Solving

5.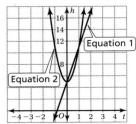

Equation 1: linear; Equation 2: nonlinear

7. linear; As x increases by 1, y increases by 4.

9. linear; You can rewrite the equation in slope-intercept form.

11. nonlinear; You cannot rewrite the equation in slope-intercept form.

13. nonlinear; The graph is not a line.

15. nonlinear

17. a. nonlinear; As h increases by 6, x increases by different amounts.

b. the birch tree; After 10 years, the birch tree will be 29 feet tall. The willow tree grew 6 feet in the last 5 years, so it will likely grow less than 6 feet in the next year and will not reach 29 feet.

19. a.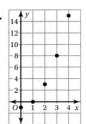

As x increases by 1, y increases by 2 more than the previous increase; nonlinear

b. $y = x^2 - 1$

Section 7.5
Review & Refresh

1. linear; As x increases by 4, y decreases by 2.

3. 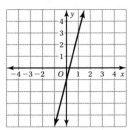 **5.**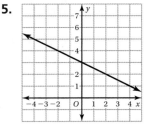

Concepts, Skills, & Problem Solving

7. D   **9.** B

11. Sales decrease at a constant rate and then increase at a constant rate.

13. Grams decrease at a decreasing rate.

15. The loan balance remains constant, then decreases instantly, then remains constant, then decreases instantly, and then remains constant.

17. a. The usage decreases at an increasing rate.

b. The usage decreases at a decreasing rate.

19. 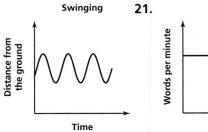   **21.**

23. a. Bowler A's average score increased at an increasing rate. Bowler B's average score increased at a decreasing rate.

b. Bowler B; Bowler A

c. *Sample answer:* Bowler A starts to practice more often. Bowler B starts to practice less often.

Chapter 8

Section 8.1
Review & Refresh

1.

3. $A'(-4, 0)$, $B'(-1, 0)$, $C'(-1, -2)$

Concepts, Skills, & Problem Solving

5. $4 \cdot 4 \cdot 4 \cdot 4$; 256

7. $(-2) \cdot (-2) \cdot (-2)$; -8

9. $(-6)^2$ **11.** $\left(\dfrac{1}{3}\right)^3$

13. $(-4)^3 y^2$ **15.** $(-t)^5$

17. $-\left(\dfrac{1}{4}\right)^4$ **19.** -1331

21. $\dfrac{1}{64}$ **23.** $-\dfrac{1}{729}$

25. $3^3 \cdot 5^2$ **27.** $3 \cdot 11^2$

29. 29   **31.** 5

33. 66   **35.** 3

37. -4

39. a. about 99.95 g   **b.** 99.95%

Section 8.2
Review & Refresh
1. 11^5 **3.** -28

5. 1

Concepts, Skills, & Problem Solving
7. $5 \cdot 5 \cdot 5 \cdot 5 \cdot 5 \cdot 5 \cdot 5 \cdot 5 \cdot 5$; 5^9

9. $(-8) \cdot (-8) \cdot (-8) \cdot (-8) \cdot (-8) \cdot (-8) \cdot (-8)$; $(-8)^7$

11. 8^{14} **13.** $(-3)^8$

15. h^7 **17.** $\left(\dfrac{2}{3}\right)^8$

19. n^{15} **21.** $\left(-\dfrac{5}{7}\right)^{17}$

23. no; The exponents should be multiplied, not added.

25. $-243v^5$ **27.** $2.0736m^4$

29. $-\dfrac{27}{64}p^3$

31. a. $(3w)^3$ **b.** $27w^3$

33. 3^9 ft

35. $2^{12} \cdot 3^5 \cdot 5^5$ pieces of mail

37. a. 3   **b.** 4

Section 8.3
Review & Refresh
1. 4^5 **3.** x^7y^7

5. *Sample answer:* Dilate the red figure using a scale factor of $\dfrac{1}{2}$ and then reflect the image in the x-axis.

Concepts, Skills, & Problem Solving
7. $\dfrac{(-4.5) \cdot (-4.5) \cdot (-4.5) \cdot (-4.5) \cdot (-4.5) \cdot (-4.5)}{(-4.5) \cdot (-4.5)}$; $(-4.5)^4$

9. 6^6 **11.** $(-3)^3$

13. 64   **15.** $(-6.4)^2$

17. no; The exponents should be subtracted, not divided.

19. 6^7 **21.** π^8

23. z^6 **25.** $(-4)^5$

27. 3^{10} **29.** x^6

31. a. 4 times more storage

b. no; As the price increases by \$20, the storage capacity doubles.

33. 10^{13} galaxies

Section 8.4
Review & Refresh
1. 10^4 **3.** $(-3)^9$

5. no; The triangles do not have the same angle measures.

Concepts, Skills, & Problem Solving
7. 7^{-4+4}; 7^0; 1

9. 1   **11.** 1

13. $\dfrac{1}{36}$ **15.** $\dfrac{1}{16}$

17. $\dfrac{1}{4}$ **19.** $\dfrac{1}{125}$

21. no; The negative sign goes with the exponent, not the base.

23. 5^{-5}, 5^0, 5^4; Each base is 5, so order the exponents.

25. $\dfrac{a^7}{64}$ **27.** $5b$

29. 12   **31.** $\dfrac{w^6}{9}$

33. 100 mm   **35.** 1,000,000 nanometers

37. a. 10^{-7} m   **b.** less than

39. Write the power as 1 divided by a power with the same base and a negative exponent;
$$a^n = a^{-(-n)} = \dfrac{1}{a^{-n}}$$

Section 8.5
Review & Refresh
1. $\dfrac{3}{x^5}$ **3.** $\dfrac{1}{2a^5}$

5. $y - 4 = \dfrac{3}{4}(x - 3)$

Concepts, Skills, & Problem Solving
7. B   **9.** C

11. 4×10^{11} **13.** 3×10^{10}

15. 1×10^{12} **17.** 5×10^8 dollars

19. 4×10^{-5} **21.** 6×10^{-4}

23. 1×10^{-9} **25.** 7×10^6 words

27. 9×10^{10} **29.** 10 times more pixels

31. a. cow, buffalo, camel, donkey, rat

   b. *Sample answer:* millimeters; A millimeter is a common unit used to represent small quantities.

33. 5,305,004; 5,305,004 is closer to 5×10^6.

Section 8.6
Review & Refresh

1. 1×10^{-6} **3.** 2×10^{-7}

5. 4^5 **7.** $(-2)^3$

Concepts, Skills, & Problem Solving

9. 10,240,000,000,000   **11.** 5.43×10^6

13. 6.25×10^{-6} **15.** 1.07×10^7

17. 9.256×10^{-12} **19.** 70,000,000

21. 500   **23.** 0.000044

25. 1,660,000,000   **27.** 9,725,000

29. 0.00025 ft; 0.003 in.

31. D   **33.** A

35. The value of the number is 10 times greater.

37. 5×10^{12} km^2

39. fastest: vacuum; slowest: glass

Section 8.7
Review & Refresh

1. 3.8×10^{-3} **3.** 4.75×10^{-5}

5. $\dfrac{3}{2}; \dfrac{9}{4}$

Concepts, Skills, & Problem Solving

7. sum: 7.5×10^{-4}; difference: 4.5×10^{-4}; product: 9×10^{-8}; quotient: 4×10^0

9. 1.83×10^{-9} **11.** 1.264×10^{-5}

13. 2.51×10^{-3} **15.** 1.85×10^{-1}

17. 3.5×10^8 **19.** 3×10^{-6}

21. 5×10^{-1} **23.** 9.1×10^3

25. C   **27.** D

29. about 12 times greater

31. 4.006×10^9 **33.** 1.962×10^8 cm

35. *Answer should include, but is not limited to:* Make sure calculations using scientific notation are done correctly.

Chapter 9
Section 9.1
Review & Refresh

1. 6.7×10^3 **3.** 6.3×10^{-1}

5.

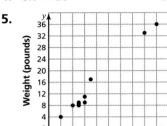

outliers: (8, 33) and (9, 36); gap: from 3.5 meters to 8 meters; cluster: from 2 meters to 3 meters

Concepts, Skills, & Problem Solving

7. 21 cm   **9.** $\dfrac{6}{7}$ yd

11. 8 and -8 **13.** 12 and -12

15. -14 and 14   **17.** -50 and 50

19. $\dfrac{7}{24}$ **21.** $-\dfrac{3}{10}$

23. 2.7   **25.** -1.5

27. 1.5 in.

29. >   **31.** <

33. -116 **35.** 9

37. 25   **39.** 40

41. $x = -10$ and $x = 10$ **43.** $z = -6$ and $z = 6$

45. $r = -14$ and $r = 14$

47. yes; The solution is correct.

49. 9 ft   **51.** 8 m/sec

53. 2.5 ft; $355 = \dfrac{n^2}{5} + 175$, so $n = 30$ in. and $\dfrac{30}{12} = 2.5$ ft.

55. 8 cm   **57.** 2

59. 0

Section 9.2
Review & Refresh

1. $z = -6$ and $z = 6$ **3.** $n = -8$ and $n = 8$

Concepts, Skills, & Problem Solving

5. 10   **7.** 29 km

9. 9 in.   **11.** 24 cm

13. no; The length of the hypotenuse should be substituted for c, not b.

15. 50 in.

17. 6 cm

19. 5 units

21. 29 units

23. 30.5 units

25. 37 mm

27. yes; The distance from the player's mouth to the referee's ear is 25 feet.

29. Check students' work.

31. **a.** *Sample answer:*

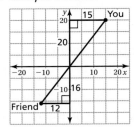

    b. 45 ft

33. no; The rod is 135 inches long, and the diagonal from a top corner to the opposite bottom corner is 130 inches long.

35. $\sqrt{18}$; 4.24 units

Section 9.3

Review & Refresh

1. 40 m

3. C

Concepts, Skills, & Problem Solving

5. $\frac{1}{3}$ ft

7. 9

9. -10

11. $-\frac{1}{8}$

13. -9

15. 21

17. 38

19. 55

21. 135

23. $t = -7$

25. $z = 6$

27. $k = -15$

29. **a.** 40 in.

    b. 9600 in.²

31. $>$

33. $<$

35. **a.** true; The square of a positive or negative number is never negative; not true; *Sample answer:* $\sqrt[3]{-8} = -2$

    b. true; The square of a number equals the square of its opposite; not true; *Sample answer:* 64 only has a positive cube root.

37. 25

39. $x = \frac{3}{2}$

Section 9.4

Review & Refresh

1. 5

3. 23

---

5. 40°, 60°, 80°

Concepts, Skills, & Problem Solving

7. $\frac{7}{9}$

9. $\frac{23}{99}$

11. $9.08\overline{3}$

13. 6.025

15. $-2.3\overline{8}$

17. $-\frac{5}{9}$

19. $-\frac{353}{990}$

21. $\frac{103}{550}$

23. $\frac{8}{9}$

25. $3.\overline{142857}$

27. $0.999\overline{8}; \frac{8999}{9000}$; 2 germs

29. Account C;

Account A interest rate: $\frac{\$4.00}{\$90.00} = 0.0\overline{4} = 4.\overline{4}\%$

Account B interest rate: $\frac{\$5.50}{\$120.00} = 0.0458\overline{3}$ $= 4.58\overline{3}\%$

Account C interest rate: $\frac{\$4.80}{\$100.00} = 0.048 = 4.8\%$

31. equal; $9 \div 22 = 0.40909\ldots$

33. equal; $135 \div 90 = 1.5$

35. $-\frac{58}{99}$ or $-0.\overline{58}$

37. $-\frac{1}{99}$ or $-0.\overline{01}$

Section 9.5

Review & Refresh

1. $\frac{4}{9}$

3. $\frac{25}{33}$

5. 5^8

7. a^9

Concepts, Skills, & Problem Solving

9. $\sqrt{18}$; 4 and 5

11. whole, integer, rational

13. irrational

15. rational

17. irrational

19. no; 144 is a perfect square. So, $\sqrt{144}$ is rational.

21. **a.** If the last digit is 0, place it in the set of whole numbers. Otherwise, place it in the set of natural numbers.

    b. irrational number

    c. irrational number

23. **a.** -10 **b.** -10.2

25. **a.** 7   **b.** 6.8

27. **a.** -13 **b.** -12.9

29. $\sqrt{22}$; $\sqrt{22}$ is to the right of $\sqrt[3]{34}$ on a number line.

31. π; π is to the right of $\sqrt{5}$ on a number line.

33. $-\sqrt{38}$; $-\sqrt{38}$ is to the right of $\sqrt[3]{-250}$ on a number line.

35. true

37. 7.2 units

39. 6.3 units

41. 8.5 units

43. **a.** 5.8 km   **b.** 8.6 km

    c. 7.1 km   **d.** 11.7 km

45. 8 ft

47. 12 in.;
    edge length of cube $= \sqrt[3]{340} \approx 7$ in.
    length of diagonal of base $\approx \sqrt{7^2 + 7^2} = \sqrt{98} \approx 10$ in.
    $d \approx \sqrt{7^2 + 10^2} = \sqrt{149} \approx 12$ in.

49. 0.6

51. 1.2

53. 30.1 m/sec

55. **a.** 5.2 astronomical units

    b. 29.3 yr

57. **a.** always; If $\dfrac{a}{b}$ and $\dfrac{c}{d}$ are rational numbers, then ac and bd are integers and $bd \neq 0$. So, $\dfrac{ac}{bd}$ is rational.

    b. sometimes; *Sample answer:* $\pi \cdot 0 = 0$ is rational, but $2 \cdot \sqrt{3}$ is irrational.

    c. sometimes; *Sample answer:* $\sqrt{2} \cdot \pi$ is irrational, but $\pi \cdot \dfrac{1}{\pi}$ is rational.

Section 9.6

Review & Refresh

1. **a.** 6   **b.** 5.6

3. **a.** 3   **b.** 2.9

5. 4.5

Concepts, Skills, & Problem Solving

7. If *ABCD* is a parallelogram, then *ABCD* is a square; statement: true; A square is a parallelogram; converse: false; Not all parallelograms have 4 right angles and 4 congruent sides.

9. yes

11. no

13. yes

15. no; $(12.6)^2 + (12.6)^2 \neq (12.6)^2$

17. no

19. no; The length of the longest side, $\sqrt{58}$, should be substituted for c, and the lengths of the two shorter sides, 3 and 7, should be substituted for a and b.

21. no

23. no

25. no

27. no; The side lengths are $\sqrt{5000}$, $\sqrt{3700}$, and $\sqrt{8500}$, and $(\sqrt{5000})^2 + (\sqrt{3700})^2 \neq (\sqrt{8500})^2$.

29. yes

Chapter 10

Section 10.1

Review & Refresh

1. yes

3. no

5. 0.000067

7. C

Concepts, Skills, & Problem Solving

9. 50π cubic units

11. $486\pi \approx 1526.8$ ft^3

13. $245\pi \approx 769.7$ ft^3

15. $256\pi \approx 804.2$ cm^3

17. the cube; The cylinder could fit inside the cube with room to spare.

19. 8 cm

21. $6.75\pi \approx 21$ gal

23. about 4 square bales

25. $8325 - 729\pi \approx 6035$ m^3

27. **a–b.** Check students' work.

Section 10.2

Review & Refresh

1. $63\pi \approx 197.9$ cm^3

3. $500\pi \approx 1570.8$ yd^3

5. $y = -2$

Concepts, Skills, & Problem Solving

7. 8π cubic units

9. $\dfrac{16}{3}\pi \approx 16.8$ in.^{3}

11. $\dfrac{250}{3}\pi \approx 261.8$ mm^3

13. $\dfrac{200}{3}\pi \approx 209.4$ cm^3

15. $\dfrac{112}{3}\pi \approx 117.3$ ft^3

17. $\dfrac{32}{3}\pi \approx 33.5$ cm^3

19. 1.5 ft

21. 0.9 in.

23. about 24 min

25. $3y$

27. The volume is 8 times the original volume.

Section 10.3

Review & Refresh

1. $8\pi \approx 25.1$ ft^3

3. $27\pi \approx 84.8$ m^3

5. 5×10^{-11}

Concepts, Skills, & Problem Solving

7. 288π cubic units

9. $\dfrac{4000}{3}\pi$ cubic units

11. $\dfrac{1372}{3}\pi \approx 1436.8$ ft^3

13. $288\pi \approx 904.8$ yd^3

15. $\dfrac{10{,}976}{3}\pi \approx 11{,}494.0 \text{ m}^3$

17. 1.5 cm

19. $\dfrac{8788}{3}\pi \approx 9203 \text{ cm}^3$

21. $r = \dfrac{3}{4}h$

23. $384\pi \approx 1206.4 \text{ ft}^3$

25. $54\pi \approx 170 \text{ cm}^3$

27. $3958 \text{ mi}; 581{,}000{,}000\pi = \dfrac{4}{3}\pi r^3$, so
$r = \sqrt[3]{435{,}750{,}000} \text{ mi}$, and
$3200 + \sqrt[3]{435{,}750{,}000} \approx 3958 \text{ mi}$.

Section 10.4
Review & Refresh

1. $\dfrac{5324}{3}\pi \approx 5575.3 \text{ cm}^3$

3. $288\pi \approx 904.8 \text{ mm}^3$

Concepts, Skills, & Problem Solving

5. 25 times greater; 125 times greater

7. yes

9. yes

11. $d = 2.5 \text{ ft}$

13. $\ell = 11.5 \text{ mm}; w = 11.5 \text{ mm}$

15. 90 m^2

17. 673.75 cm^2

19. $13{,}564.8 \text{ ft}^3$

21. 204 mm^2

23. a. 9483 lb; The ratio of the height of the original statue to the height of the small statue is $84:10$.
So, solve the proportion $\dfrac{x}{16} = \left(\dfrac{84}{10}\right)^3$.

b. 221,184 lb

25. a. yes; Because all circles are similar, the slant height and the circumference of the base of the cones are proportional.

b. no; Your cone holds about 2.2 times as much.

Chapter A
Section A.1
Review & Refresh

1. $4(x - 5)$

3. $-\dfrac{2}{5}(w - 2)$

5. -56

7. -9

9. B

Concepts, Skills, & Problem Solving

11. $x = -2$; Add three $+1$ tiles to each side of the equation.

13. $a = 19$

15. $k = -20$

17. $g = -10$

19. $w = -15.4$

21. $p = \dfrac{2}{3}$

23. $y = -2.08$

25. $q = \dfrac{5}{18}$

27. $w = -1\dfrac{13}{24}$

29. $n - 4 = -15; n = -11$

31. $y + (-3) = -8; y = -5$

33. $t - 184.9 = -109.3; 75.6°\text{F}$

35. $10\dfrac{3}{4} \text{ m}$; The solution of $h - \left(-7\dfrac{3}{4}\right) = 18\dfrac{1}{2}$ is $h = 10\dfrac{3}{4}$.

37. 3.8 in.

39. 152 ft; The solution of $305 = h + 153$ is $152 = h$.

41. $41\dfrac{4}{15} \text{ km}$; The solution of $65\dfrac{3}{5} = d + 24\dfrac{1}{3}$ is
$41\dfrac{4}{15} = d$.

43. 74.36

45. $2, -2$

47. $13, -13$

Section A.2
Review & Refresh

1. $n = -3$

3. $h = -15.1$

5. -9

7. -9

Concepts, Skills, & Problem Solving

9. $x = -4$; Divide each side into 4 equal groups.

11. $x = 4$; Divide each side into 5 equal groups, then add a $+$ variable and four $+1$ tiles to each side of the equation.

13. $t = 9$

15. $k = -27$

17. $t = -4$

19. $b = 40$

21. $d = -9$

23. $p = 24$

25. $c = -20$

27. $y = -16\dfrac{1}{4}$

29. $\dfrac{x}{-9} = -16; x = 144$

31. $15x = -75; x = -5$

33. $0.75n = 36; 48 \text{ bracelets}$

35 and 37. Sample answers are given.

35. a. $3x = -9$

b. $\dfrac{x}{2} = -1.5$

37. a. $5x = -\dfrac{5}{2}$

b. $\dfrac{x}{2} = -\dfrac{1}{4}$

39. All of them except "multiply each side by $-\dfrac{2}{3}$."

41. 1952 students; The solution of $\dfrac{3}{4}s = 1464$ is
$s = 1952$.

43. \$30.12; The solution of $150.60 = \frac{5}{6}x$ is $180.72 = x$ and $180.72 - 150.60 = \$30.12$.

45. $1\frac{3}{5}$ days; The solution of $\frac{5}{7}d = 4$ is $d = 5\frac{3}{5}$ and $5\frac{3}{5} - 4 = 1\frac{3}{5}$.

Section A.3

Review & Refresh

1. $z = 6$
3. $m = -20$
5. -34.72
7. $-3\frac{1}{8}$
9. C

Concepts, Skills, & Problem Solving

11. $-3x + 4 = -11$; $x = 5$
13. $b = -3$
15. $t = -4$
17. $g = 4.22$
19. $p = 3\frac{1}{2}$
21. $h = -8.5$
23. $y = -6.4$
25. no; *Sample answer:* Use the Distributive Property first.
27. $a = 1\frac{1}{3}$
29. $b = 13\frac{1}{2}$
31. $v = -\frac{1}{30}$
33. $v = -5$
35. $d = -12$
37. 3 games; The solution of $2.5 + 2.25x = 9.25$ is $x = 3$.
39. $h = 9$
41. **a.** $\frac{x - 5}{3} = 9$; 32 insects

   b. 32 insects; *Sample answer:* $3 \cdot 9 + 5 = 32$

   c. *Sample answers:* The length of a rectangle is 3 inches more than 2 times the width. The perimeter is 52 inches. Find the length; You currently have 13 coins after a classmate gave you 5 coins. How many coins did you start with?

Section A.4

Review & Refresh

1. $p = 11$
3. $x = -7$
5. $n = 5$
7. C

Concepts, Skills, & Problem Solving

9. *Sample answer:* 21; all integers greater than or equal to 20

11. *Sample answer:* -600; all values less than -400
13. $w + 2.3 > 18$
15. $b - 4.2 < -7.5$
17. yes; The inequality is correct.
19. no
21. yes
23. no

25.

27.

29. no
31. no

33. **a.** $1.25x > 35$

   b. yes; It cost \$56.25 for 45 trips, which is more than the \$35 monthly pass.

35.

Section A.5

Review & Refresh

1. $p > 5$
3. $n + \frac{2}{3} \geq 5\frac{1}{3}$
5. $w = -27$
7. $h = 80$

Concepts, Skills, & Problem Solving

9. $-1 < 4$; yes; $1 < 6$
11. $-4 < -1$; yes; $-2 < 1$
13. $a > 6$

15. $k \leq -11$

17. $n < 9$

19. $p \geq 1\frac{3}{4}$

21. $z \geq 3.1$

23. $-\frac{4}{5} > s$

25. $r < -0.9$

27. no; The graph should have an open circle at 5.

29. **a.** $15 + p \leq 44; p \leq 29$ passengers

   b. no; Only 29 more passengers can board the plane.

31. $x > 5$ in.   **33.** 4

35. **a.** $x \leq 1350$ watts

   b. *Sample answer:* aquarium and television; yes;
   $200 + 150 = 350$ watts,
   $200 + 1100 = 1300$ watts

Section A.6

Review & Refresh

1. $h < 2$

3. $n \geq -\dfrac{1}{10}$

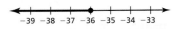

5. $v = 45$ **7.** $m = 4$

Concepts, Skills, & Problem Solving

9. $-2 < 5$; yes; no; $-4 < 10, 4 \not< -10$

11. $6 > -3$; yes; no; $12 > -6, -12 \not> 6$

13. $c \leq -36$

15. $x < -32$

17. $k > 2$

19. $y \leq -3$

21. $9.2x \geq 299; x \geq 32.5$ h

23. $n \geq -3$

25. $h \leq -24$

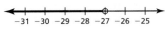

27. $y > \dfrac{14}{3}$

29. $m < -27$

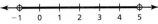

31. $b > 6$

33. yes; The properties of inequalities were all used correctly to find the solution.

35. $\dfrac{p}{7} < -3; p < -21$ **37.** $-2x > 30; x < -15$

39. $-2.5s < -20; s > 8$ sec

41. $10x \geq 120; x \geq 12$ cm

43. at least 5 days; The solution of $37d \geq 185$ is $d \geq 5$.

45. **a–c.** Answers will vary.

47. $m > -1$ and $m < 5$

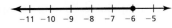

49. $x \geq 3$

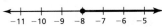

Section A.7

Review & Refresh

1. $x \leq -6$

3. $g \geq -8$

5.

Boys	6	3	30
Girls	10	5	50

$6 : 10, 3 : 5, 30 : 50$

Concepts, Skills, & Problem Solving

7. $2x + 4 \geq -6; x \geq -5$

9. $y < 1$

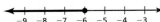

11. $h > \dfrac{9}{2}$

13. $b \leq -6$

15. $g > -1$

17. $k \geq -18$

19. $n < -0.6$

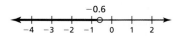

21. no; *Sample answer:* 4 should be multiplied by 3.

23. $n \geq 8$ additional jumps

25. $d > 6$

27. at least 6 lb

29. a. $150x + 450 \leq 1000;\ x \leq 3\frac{2}{3}$

   b. 0, 1, 2, 3; *Sample answer:* Only nonnegative integers make sense for the problem.

Chapter B

Section B.1

Review & Refresh

1. $84   **3.** $36

5. $2 : \frac{1}{2}$; The amount of rolled oats in the recipe is 4 times the amount of chopped peanuts.

7. $\frac{1}{4} : 2$; The amount of pumpkin seeds in the recipe is $\frac{1}{8}$ the amount of rolled oats.

9. $b \geq -5$

11. $g \leq -3$

Concepts, Skills, & Problem Solving

13. equal chance; *Sample answer:* All numbers have the same area, so you are equally likely to spin each number.

15. 1, 2, 3   **17.** 4 ways

19. a. 1 way   **b.** green

21. a. 1 way   **b.** yellow

23. a. 7 ways

   b. red, red, red, purple, purple, green, yellow

25. false; red   **27.** true

29. likely   **31.** certain

33. You are equally likely to be chosen or not chosen.

35. a. likely

   b. unlikely

   c. no; *Sample answer:* A fair coin would result in an equal number of heads and tails for the relative frequency.

37. a. unlikely; Rolling a 1 has a probability of $\frac{1}{12}$, or $8.\overline{3}\%$, which is unlikely.

   b. unlikely; Rolling a multiple of 3 has a probability of $\frac{1}{3}$, or $33.\overline{3}\%$, which is unlikely.

   c. equally likely to happen or not happen; Rolling a number greater than 6 has a probability of $\frac{1}{2}$, or 50%, which is equally likely to happen or not happen.

39. With all five cards available, the number of possible outcomes is 5. With only four cards left, the number of possible outcomes is reduced to 4.

41. $\frac{3}{4}$, or 75%

Section B.2

Review & Refresh

1. unlikely   **3.** 4%

5. no

Concepts, Skills, & Problem Solving

7. $\frac{7}{50}$, or 14%   **9.** $\frac{7}{25}$, or 28%

11. $\frac{17}{50}$, or 34%

13. no; Your friend found the theoretical probability.

15. $\frac{1}{3}$, or about 33.3%   **17.** $\frac{1}{2}$, or 50%

19. 1, or 100%   **21.** $\frac{25}{26}$, or about 96.2%

23. theoretical: $\frac{1}{5}$, or 20%; experimental: $\frac{39}{200}$, or 19.5%; The experimental probability is close to the theoretical probability.

25. theoretical: $\frac{3}{5}$, or 60%; experimental: $\frac{120}{200}$, or 60%; The probabilities are equal.

27. 38 vowels

29. a. $\frac{4}{9}$, or about 44.4%   **b.** 5 males

31. a.

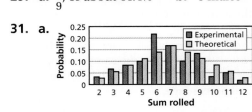

b. As the number of trials increases, the most likely sum will change from 6 to 7.

c. *Sample answer:* The experimental probability should approach the theoretical probability.

Section B.3
Review & Refresh

1. $\frac{19}{100}$, or 19%   **3.** $\frac{71}{100}$, or 71%

5. 6   **7.** 12

Concepts, Skills, & Problem Solving

9. a password with 6 numbers

11. Sample space: Realistic Lion, Realistic Bear, Realistic Hawk, Realistic Dragon, Cartoon Lion, Cartoon Bear, Cartoon Hawk, Cartoon Dragon; 8 possible outcomes

13. Sample space: Cube Metal, Cube Plastic, Cube Rubber, Necklace Metal, Necklace Plastic, Necklace Rubber, Spinner Metal, Spinner Plastic, Spinner Rubber; 9 possible outcomes

15. 12 possible outcomes

17. 24 possible outcomes

19. a. tree diagram or the Fundamental Counting Principle

b. 12 possible outcomes

21. $\frac{1}{10}$, or 10%   **23.** $\frac{1}{5}$, or 20%

25. $\frac{2}{5}$, or 40%   **27.** $\frac{1}{18}$, or $5\frac{5}{9}$%

29. $\frac{1}{9}$, or $11\frac{1}{9}$%

31. a. $\frac{1}{9}$, or about 11.1%

b. It increases the probability that your guesses are correct to $\frac{1}{4}$, or 25%, because you are only choosing between 2 choices for each question.

33. There are 1000 possible combinations. With 5 tries, you would guess 5 out of the 1000 possibilities. So, the probability of getting the correct combination is $\frac{5}{1000}$, or 0.5%.

35. a. Fundamental Counting Principle; The Fundamental Counting Principle is more efficient. A tree diagram would be too large.

b. 1,000,000,000 or one billion

c. *Sample answer:* Not all possible number combinations are used for Social Security Numbers (SSN). SSNs are coded into geographical, group, and serial numbers. Some SSNs are reserved for commercial use and some are forbidden for various reasons.

37. 10 ways

Section B.4
Review & Refresh

1. $\frac{7}{40}$, or 17.5%   **3.** $5a - 10$

5. $-3p + 8$

Concepts, Skills, & Problem Solving

7. $\frac{2}{15}$, or $13.\overline{3}$%

9. Answers will vary, but the theoretical probability is $\frac{5}{32}$, 0.15625, or 15.625%.

11. Answers will vary, but the theoretical probability is $\frac{25}{27}$, about 0.9259, or about 92.59%.

13. Answers will vary, but the theoretical probability is $\frac{16}{27}$, about 0.5926, or about 59.26%.

15. Answers will vary, but the theoretical probability is $\frac{18}{25}$, 0.72, or 72%.

17. Answers will vary, but the theoretical probability is $\frac{161}{1250}$, 0.1288, or 12.88%.

19. Answers will vary, but the theoretical probability is $\frac{343}{1000}$, 0.343, or 34.3%.

Chapter C

Section C.1
Review & Refresh

1. Answers will vary, but the theoretical probability is $\frac{9}{50}$, 0.18, or 18%.

3. $x < 7$

5. $r > \frac{4}{3}$

Concepts, Skills, & Problem Solving

7. yes; $\frac{5}{50} = 0.1 = 10\%$

9. Population: All cards in a deck, Sample: 4 cards

11. biased; The sample is not representative of the population because people who go to a park are more likely to think that the park needs to be remodeled.

13. Sample A; It is representative of the population.

15. a population; There are few enough students in your homeroom to not make the surveying difficult.

17. *Sample answer:* The person could ask, "Do you agree with the town's unfair ban on skateboarding on public property?"

19. yes; The sample is representative of the population, selected at random, and large enough to provide accurate data; 330 votes

Section C.2
Review & Refresh

1. valid

3. $\frac{x}{100} = \frac{12}{30}$; 40%

Concepts, Skills, & Problem Solving

5. yes; $\frac{14}{50} = 28\%$, which is close to 30%

7. **a.** 330, 360, 420

   b. median: 360 customers; range: 90 customers

9. **a.** 2.9, 3.5, 3.2, 3.6; median: 3.35 nights; range: 0.7 night

   b. 3.3 nights

11. *Sample answer:* Most of the samples are within 15% of the actual percentage.

13. Answers will vary.

15. *Sample answer:* The larger the sample size, the closer the sample estimate will be to the theoretical percentage.

Section C.3
Review & Refresh

1. yes; $\frac{4}{15}$, or $26.\overline{6}\%$, is close to 20%.

3. 30 kilometers per hour

Concepts, Skills, & Problem Solving

5. no; *Sample answer:* none of the sets have similar values

7. Data set A has a greater median and Data set B has a greater range and greater IQR.

9. Data set B

11. yes; Because the difference in means is greater than two times the MAD, the attendance is significantly greater.

13. no; The difference in the medians is 0.8 to 1 times the IQR.

Section C.4
Review & Refresh

1. Data set B has a greater median and a greater IQR.

3. $b = 5$

5. $z = \frac{2}{3}$

Concepts, Skills, & Problem Solving

7. non-teachers spend more time on recreation each week than teachers; *Sample answer:* 75% of non-teachers spend at least 6 hours on recreation. 50% of teachers spend less than 5 hours on recreation.

9. yes; *Sample answer:* The variation for Lake A and Lake B are the same, but the measure of center for Lake A is greater than the measure of center for Lake B. You can conclude that Lake A generally contains larger fish than Lake B.

11. *Sample answer:* The measures of center and variation for Type B are greater than Type A. You can conclude that growths of the Type B corn seedlings are larger and vary by more than the Type A corn seedlings.

13. a. Check students' work. Experiments should include taking many samples of a manageable size from each grade level. This will be more doable if the work of sampling is divided among the whole class, and the results are pooled together.

b. Check students' work. The data may or may not support a conclusion.

Chapter D

Section D.1

Review & Refresh

1. Jar A: Median: 3, IQR: 2; Jar B: Median: 6, IQR: 2

3. A

Concepts, Skills, & Problem Solving

5. about 4.08 in. **7.** 14 mm

9. 4 in. **11.** $1\frac{1}{5}$ cm

13. about 18.84 cm

15. about 7.71 ft

17. about 1.42 mm

19. a. about 25 m; about 50 m

b. about 2 times greater

21. about 31.4 cm; about 62.8 cm

23. about 69.08 m; about 138.16 m

25. yes; Because $\dfrac{\text{circumference}}{\text{radius}} = \dfrac{2\pi r}{r} = 2\pi$, the ratio is the same for every circle.

27. The circle has a diameter of π inches, so use a diameter of about 3.1 inches.

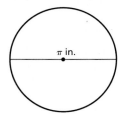

π in.

29. a. small tire: about 127 rotations; large tire: about 38 rotations

b. *Sample answer:* A bicycle with large wheels would allow you to travel farther with each rotation of the pedal.

Section D.2

Review & Refresh

1. about 28.26 cm

3. 3 possible outcomes

Concepts, Skills, & Problem Solving

5. about 6.75 cm^2

7. about 254.34 mm^2

9. about 314 in.^{2}

11. about 3.14 cm^2

13. no; The diameter was doubled instead of taking half of the diameter to find the radius.

15. about 192.33 cm^2

17. about 628 cm^2

19. about 1.57 ft^2

21. about 942 ft^2; *Sample answer:* The running area is $\dfrac{3}{4}$ the area of a circle with a radius of 20 feet.

23. about 65.94 mi^2

25. circumference doubles and area quadruples; circumference triples and area is 9 times greater; double the radius: circumference $= 2\pi(2r) = 4\pi r$, $\dfrac{4\pi r}{2\pi r} = 2$ times larger, area $= \pi(2r)^2 = 4\pi r^2$, $\dfrac{4\pi r^2}{\pi r^2} = 4$ times larger;

triple the radius: circumference $= 2\pi(3r) = 6\pi r$, $\dfrac{6\pi r}{2\pi r} = 3$ times larger, area $= \pi(3r)^2 = 9\pi r^2$, $\dfrac{9\pi r^2}{\pi r^2} = 9$ times larger

Section D.3

Review & Refresh

1. about 50.24 mm^2

3. 30 ft

5. 1 m

Concepts, Skills, & Problem Solving

7. *Sample answer:* about 24 units

9. about 19.5 units; 13.5 units^2

11. about 24.6 units; about 41.1 units^2

13. about 19 units; 24 units^2

15. 56 m; 137 m^2

17. 29 cm; 49.5 cm^2

19. The starting points are staggered so that each runner can run the same distance and use the same finish line. This is necessary because the circumference is different for each lane. The diagram shows this because the diameter is greater in the outer lanes.

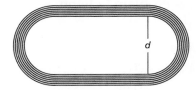

21. 24 m²

23. *Sample answer:* By adding the triangle shown by the dashed line to the L-shaped figure, you *reduce* the perimeter.

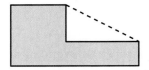

no; For the composite figure below, adding any figure increases its perimeter.

Section D.4

Review & Refresh

1. 14 in.; 8 in.²

3. Electric Extra Soft, Electric Soft, Electric Medium, Traditional Extra Soft, Traditional Soft, Traditional Medium; 6 possible outcomes

Concepts, Skills, & Problem Solving

5.

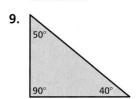

7. not possible

9.

11. not possible

13. no; *Sample answer:* Your friend was using the rule for side lengths. Because the sum of the angle measures is 180°, you can draw the triangle.

15.

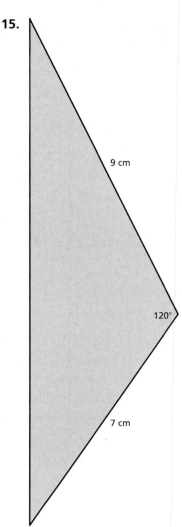

17.

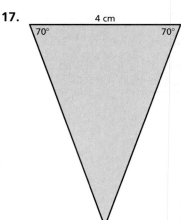

19. not possible

21.

23. yes; *Sample answer:* The sum of the lengths of any two sides is 12 inches, which is greater than the length of the third side, 6 inches.

25. many; With only 1 angle measure and 1 side length given, many triangles can be created.

27. one; Only one line segment can be drawn between the endpoints of the two given sides.

29. one; The other angle measure will be 125°. You can draw the two angles that connect to the given side length. The other two sides will only intersect at one possible point.

31. *Sample answer:*

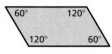

33. *Sample answer:*

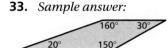

35.

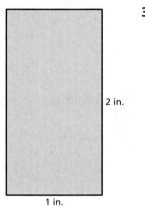

37.

39. infinitely many; *Sample answer:* The fourth side is a fixed length, but the angles are not fixed.

41. about 5.56 m²

43. *Sample answer:*

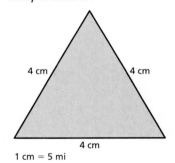

about 173.2 mi²

Section D.5
Review & Refresh

1. not possible

3. $y \geq -5$

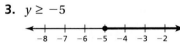

5. $x \geq 7.5$

Concepts, Skills, & Problem Solving

7. ∠*BAC* and ∠*EAD*, ∠*BAE* and ∠*CAD*; *Sample answer:* All vertical angles are opposite angles formed by the intersection of two lines.

9. *Sample answer:* ∠*BAC* and ∠*CAD*

11. *Sample answer:* ∠*EAF* and ∠*CAB*

13. neither; The angles do not share a common side (adjacent) nor are they opposite angles formed by two intersecting lines (vertical).

15. vertical; The angles are opposite angles formed by the intersection of two lines.

17. complementary; The sum of the measures of the angles is 90°.

19. no; ∠*LMN* and ∠*PMQ* are complementary, not supplementary.

21. vertical; 128   **23.** vertical; 25

25. supplementary; 20   **27.** complementary; 55

29. ∠1 = 130°, ∠2 = 50°, ∠3 = 130°; *Sample answer:* ∠2 is a vertical angle to 50°, ∠1 and ∠2 are supplementary angles, ∠1 and ∠3 are vertical angles.

31. 43

33. ∠*KJL* = 80°, ∠*NJM* = 25°, ∠*MJL* = 75°

35. *Sample answer:*

37. *Sample answer:*

39. sometimes   **41.** sometimes

43.

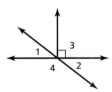

45. They are right angles.

47. a. 25°   **b.** 65°

49. 45°; 90°

Chapter E

Section E.1
Review & Refresh

1. supplementary; 146   **3.** vertical; 49

5. about 1017.36 mm²

Concepts, Skills, & Problem Solving

7. triangular prism; 264 units²

9. 324 m²   **11.** 136 m²

13. 49.2 yd^2

15. no; The area of the 3 × 5 face is used 4 times rather than just twice.

17. 156 in.^{2}

19. *Sample answer:*

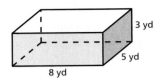

21. a. 0.125 pint

b. 1.125 pints

c. red and green: The ratio of the paint volumes (red to green) is 4 : 1 and the ratio of the edge lengths is 2 : 1.

green and blue: The ratio of the paint volumes (blue to green) is 9 : 1 and the ratio of the edge lengths is 3 : 1.

The ratio of the paint volumes is the square of the ratio of the edge lengths.

Section E.2

Review & Refresh

1. 142 cm^2 **3.** A

Concepts, Skills, & Problem Solving

5. about 8195.4 in.^{2} **7.** about 31.4 m^2

9. about 87.9 mm^2 **11.** about 282.6 cm^2

13. about 226.1 in.^{2}

15. no; The area of only one base is added. The first term should have a factor of 2.

17. about 12,560 mm^2

19. a. about 129.1 cm^2, about 470.6 cm^2

b. about 4.0 lb

21. a. 4 times greater; 9 times greater; 25 times greater; 100 times greater

b. When both dimensions are multiplied by a factor of x, the surface area increases by a factor of x^2; $x^2(2\pi r^2 + 2\pi rh)$

Section E.3

Review & Refresh

1. about 244.9 ft^2 **3.** about 406.9 mm^2

Concepts, Skills, & Problem Solving

5. 40 in.^{2} **7.** 151.9 m^2

9. 64 cm^2 **11.** 170.1 yd^2

13. 1240.4 mm^2 **15.** 6 m

17. 283.5 cm^2 **19.** 124 cm^2

21. the slant height; The height is the distance between the top and the point on the base directly beneath it. The distance from the top to any other point on the base is greater than the height.

23. greater than; If it is less than or equal to, then the lateral face could not meet at a vertex to form a solid.

Section E.4

Review & Refresh

1. 57 m^2 **3.** 115.5 cm^2

5. $144

Concepts, Skills, & Problem Solving

7. $V = 24$ units^3; $B = 8$ units^2

9. $V = 24$ units^3; $B = 12$ units^2

11. 288 cm^3 **13.** 210 yd^3

15. 420 mm^3 **17.** 645 mm^3

19. no; The area of the base is wrong.

21. 10 in.; *Sample answer:*

$$V = \ell \cdot w \cdot h$$
$$225 = (9)(2.5)h$$
$$225 = 22.5h$$
$$10 = h$$

23. 1728 in.^{3}

$1 \times 1 \times 1 = 1$ ft^3 $12 \times 12 \times 12 = 1728$ in.^{3}

25. Check students' work.

27. sometimes; The prisms in Example 3 have different surface areas but the same volume. Two prisms that are exactly the same will have the same surface area.

Section E.5

Review & Refresh

1. 189 ft^3

3. $r < -0.9$

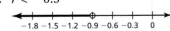

5. $h \le 1.3$

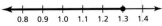

Concepts, Skills, & Problem Solving

7. Volume of prism $= 6 \cdot 6 \cdot 6 = 216$ in.^{3}

$$V = \frac{1}{3}(6 \cdot 6)(6) = 72 \text{ in.}^3$$

$$V = \frac{1}{3}(6 \cdot 6)(6) = 72 \text{ in.}^3$$

$$V = \frac{1}{3}(6 \cdot 6)(6) = 72 \text{ in.}^3$$

$$72 + 72 + 72 = 216 \text{ in.}^3$$

9. $13\frac{1}{3}$ ft^3 **11.** 20 mm^3

13. 80 in.^{3} **15.** 7 cm^3

17. no; Your friend forgot to multiply by $\frac{1}{3}$.

19. 156 ft^3; *Sample answer:*
Total volume = volume of rectangular prism
                + volume of rectangular pyramid

$$= 6 \cdot 6 \cdot 3 + \frac{1}{3}(6 \cdot 6) \cdot 4$$

$$= 108 + 48$$

$$= 156$$

21. Spire B; 4 in.^{3}

23. *Sample answer:* 5 ft by 4 ft

Section E.6

Review & Refresh

1. $37\frac{1}{3}$ in.^{3} **3.** $-5w - 12$

Concepts, Skills, & Problem Solving

5. not possible   **7.** possible

9. possible   **11.** rectangle

13. triangle   **15.** circle

17. circle   **19.** circle

21. not possible

23. The intersection is the shape of the base.

25. **a.** 164 in.^{2}

     b. about 37%;
Brick before cut:
$S = 2(10 \cdot 4) + 2(10 \cdot 3) + 2(4 \cdot 3) = 164$ in.^{2}
Bricks after cut:
$S = 2[2(10 \cdot 2) + 2(10 \cdot 3) + 2(2 \cdot 3)] = 224$ in.^{2}

$$\frac{224 - 164}{164} = \frac{60}{164} \approx 0.37 \text{ or } 37\%$$

27. *Sample answer:* The area of a cross section is the square of the coefficient of h times the area of the base.

English-Spanish Glossary

English

Spanish

A

adjacent angles *(p. 628)* Two angles that share a common side and have the same vertex

ángulos adyacentes *(p. 628)* Dos ángulos que tienen el vértice y un lado en común

angle of rotation *(p. 56)* The number of degrees a figure rotates about a point

ángulo de rotación *(p. 56)* El número de grados que gira una figura sobre un punto

B

base (of a power) *(p. 320)* The base of a power is the repeated factor.

base (de una potencia) *(p. 320)* La base de una potencia es el factor repetido.

biased sample *(p. 564)* A sample that is not representative of a population

muestra sesgada *(p. 564)* Una muestra que no es representiva de una población

C

center (of a circle) *(p. 600)* The point inside a circle that is the same distance from all points on the circle

centro (de un círculo) *(p. 600)* El punto dentro de un círculo que está a la misma distancia de todos los puntos en el círculo

center of dilation *(p. 70)* A point with respect to which a figure is dilated.

centro de dilatación *(p. 70)* Un punto con respecto al cual se dilata una figura

center of rotation *(p. 56)* The point about which a figure is rotated.

centro de rotación *(p. 56)* El punto sobre del cualse rota una figura

circle *(p. 600)* The set of all points in a plane that are the same distance from a point called the center

círculo *(p. 600)* El conjunto de todos los puntos en un plano que están a la misma distancia de un punto llamado el centro

circumference *(p. 601)* The distance around a circle

circunferencia *(p. 601)* La distancia alrededor de un círculo

complementary angles *(p. 628)* Two angles whose measures have a sum of 90°

ángulos complementarios *(p. 628)* Dos ángulos cuyas medidas tienen una suma de 90°

composite figure *(p. 614)* A figure made up of triangles, squares, rectangles, and other two-dimensional figures

figura compuesta *(p. 614)* Una figura hecha de triángulos, cuadros, rectángulos, y otras figuras bidimensionales

compound event *(p. 540)* A compound event consists of one or more events. The probability of a compound event is the quotient of the number of favorable outcomes and the number of possible outcomes.

evento compuesto *(p. 540)* Un evento compuesto consiste de uno o más eventos. La probabilidad de un evento compuesto es el cociente del número de resultados favorables y el número de resultados posibles.

cone *(p. 433)* A solid that has one circular base and one vertex

cono *(p. 433)* Un sólido que tiene una base circular y una vértice

congruent angles *(p. 64)* Angles that have the same measure

ángulos congruentes *(p. 64)* Ángulos que miden lo mismo

congruent figures *(p. 64)* Figures that have the same size and the same shape

figuras congruentes *(p. 64)* Figuras que tienen el mismo tamaño y la misma forma

congruent sides *(p. 64)* Sides that have the same length

lados congruentes *(p. 64)* Lados con la misma longitud

cross section *(p. 678)* The intersection of a plane and a solid

sección transversal *(p. 678)* La intersección de un plano y un sólido

cube root *(p. 390)* A number that, when multiplied by itself, and then multiplied by itself again, equals a given number.

raíz cúbica *(p. 390)* Un número que, al multiplicarse por sí mismo, y luego al multiplicarse de nuevo por sí mismo, es igual a un número dado

---

D

---

diameter *(p. 600)* The distance across a circle through the center

diámetro *(p. 600)* La distancia a través de un círculo, pasando por el centro

dilation *(p. 70)* A transformation in which a figure is made larger or smaller with respect to a fixed point called the center of dilation

dilatación *(p. 70)* Una transformación en la que una figura se hace más grande o más pequeña con respecto a un punto fijo llamado el centro de dilatación

---

E

---

equivalent equations *(p. 466)* Equations that have the same solutions

ecuaciones equivalentes *(p. 466)* Ecuaciones que tienen las mismas soluciones

event *(p. 522)* A collection of one or more outcomes

evento *(p. 522)* Un grupo de una o más resultadas

experiment *(p. 522)* An investigation or a procedure that has varying results

experimento *(p. 522)* Una investigación o un método que tiene resultados variados

experimental probability *(p. 530)* A probability based on repeated trials of an experiment

probabilidad experimenta *(p. 530)* Una probabilidad basada en ensayos repetidos de un experimento

exponent *(p. 320)* The exponent of a power indicates the number of times a base is used as a factor.

exponente *(p. 320)* El exponente de una potencia indica cuantas veces una base es usada como un factor.

exterior angles *(p. 105)* When two parallel lines are cut by a transversal, four exterior angles are formed on the outside of the parallel lines.

ángulos externos *(p. 105)* Cuando una transversal corta dos rectas paralelas, se forman cuatro ángulos externos por fuera de las rectas paralelas.

exterior angles of a polygon *(p. 112)* The angles adjacent to the interior angles when the sides of a polygon are extended

angulos exteriores de un polígono *(p. 112)* Los ángulos adyacentes a los ángulos interiores cuando los lados de una polígono están extendidos

favorable outcomes *(p. 522)* The outcomes of a specific event

resultados favorables *(p. 522)* Los resultados de un evento especifico

function *(p. 277)* A relation that pairs each input with exactly one output

función *(p. 277)* Una relación que asocia cada entrada con una sola salida

function rule *(p. 282)* An equation that describes the relationship between inputs (independent variable) and outputs (dependent variable)

regla de la función *(p. 282)* Una ecuación que describe la relación entre entradas (variable independiente) y salidas (variable dependiente)

Fundamental Counting Principle *(p. 538)* A way to find the total number of possible outcomes

Principio de conteo fundamental *(p. 538)* Un método para descubrir el número total de resultados posibles

graph of an inequality *(p. 486)* A graph that shows all the solutions of an inequality on a number line

gráfica de una desigualdad *(p. 486)* Una gráfica que muestra todas las soluciones de una desigualdad en una recta numérica

hemisphere *(p. 442)* One-half of a sphere

hemisferio *(p. 442)* La mitad de una esfera

hypotenuse *(p. 382)* The side of a right triangle that is opposite the right angle

hipotenusa *(p. 382)* El lado de un triángulo rectángulo opuesto al ángulo recto

image *(p. 44)* The new figure produced when a figure is transformed

imagen *(p. 44)* La nueva figura producida cuando una figura esta transformada

indirect measurement *(p. 126)* Indirect measurement uses similar figures to find a missing measure when the measurement is difficult to find directly.

medida indirecta *(p. 126)* Medida indirecta usa figuras similares para hallar una medida que falta cuando la medida es dificil de hallar directamente.

inequality *(p. 484)* A mathematical sentence that compares expressions; contains the symbols <, >, ≤, or ≥

desigualdad *(p. 484)* Una oración matemática que compara las expresiones; contiene los símbolos <, >, ≤, or ≥

input *(p. 276)* In a relation, inputs are values associated with outputs.

entrada *(p. 276)* En una relación, entradas son valores asociadas con salidas.

interior angles *(p. 105)* When two parallel lines are cut by a transversal, four interior angles are formed on the inside of the parallel lines.

ángulos internos *(p. 105)* Cuando una transversal corta dos rectas paralelas, se forman cuatro ángulos internos dentro de las rectas paralelas.

interior angles of a polygon *(p. 112)* The angles inside a polygon

ángulos interiores de un polígono *(p. 112)* Los ángulos que están dentro de un polígono

irrational number *(p. 402)* A number that cannot be written as the ratio of two integers

número irracional *(p. 402)* Un número que no puede escribirse como la razón de dos números enteros

J

joint frequency *(p. 250)* Each entry in a two-way table

frecuencia conjunta *(p. 250)* Cada valor en una tabla de doble entrada

L

lateral surface area (of a prism) *(p. 650)* The sum of the areas of the lateral faces of a prism

área de superficie lateral (de un prisma) *(p. 650)* La suma de las áreas de las caras laterales de un prisma

legs *(p. 382)* The two sides of a right triangle that form the right angle

catetos *(p. 382)* Los dos lados de un triángulo rectángulo que forman el ángulo recto

line of best fit *(p. 245)* Out of all possible lines of fit, the line that best models a set of data

línea de mejor ajuste *(p. 245)* De todas las líneas de ajuste posibles, la línea que mejor modela un conjunto de datos

line of fit *(p. 244)* A line drawn on a scatter plot close to most of the data points; The line can be used to estimate data on a graph.

línea de ajuste *(p. 244)* Una línea dibujada en un diagrama de dispersión, cerca de la mayoría de los puntos de datos; La línea se puede usar para estimar datos en una gráfica.

line of reflection *(p. 50)* A line in which a transformed figure is reflected

línea de reflexión *(p. 50)* Una línea en donde una figura transformada está reflejada

linear equation *(p. 142)* An equation whose graph is a line

ecuación lineal *(p. 142)* Una ecuación cuya gráfica es una línea

linear function *(p. 290)* A function whose graph is a non-vertical line; A linear function has a constant rate of change.

función lineal *(p. 290)* Una función cuya gráfica es una línea no vertical; Una función lineal tiene una tasa de cambio constante.

literal equation *(p. 26)* An equation that has two or more variables

ecuación literal *(p. 26)* Una ecuación que tiene dos o más variables

M

mapping diagram *(p. 276)* A way to represent a relation

diagrama de función *(p. 276)* Una manera para representar una relación

marginal frequency *(p. 250)* The sums of the rows and columns in a two-way table

frecuencia marginal *(p. 250)* Las sumas de las hileras y columnas en una tabla de doble entrada

N

nonlinear function *(p. 296)* A function that does not have a constant rate of change; a function whose graph is not a line

función no lineal *(p. 296)* Una función que no tiene una tasa constante de cambio; una función cuya gráfica no es una línea

outcomes *(p. 522)* The possible results of an experiment

resultados *(p. 522)* Los resultados posibles de un experimento

output *(p. 276)* In a relation, outputs are the values associated with inputs.

salida *(p. 276)* En una relación, salidas son los valores asociadas con entradas.

perfect cube *(p. 390)* A number that can be written as the cube of an integer

cubo perfecto *(p. 390)* Un número que puede escribirse como el cubo de un entero

perfect square *(p. 374)* A number with integers as its square roots

cuadrado perfecto *(p. 374)* Un número cuyas raíces cuadradas son números enteros

pi (π) *(p. 601)* The ratio of the circumference of a circle to its diameter

pi (π) *(p. 601)* La razón de la circunferencia de un círculo a su diámetro

point-slope form *(p. 180)* A linear equation written in the form $y - y_1 = m(x - x_1)$; The graph of the equation is a line that passes through the point (x_1, y_1) and has the slope m.

forma punto-pendiente *(p. 180)* Una ecuación lineal escrita en la forma $y - y_1 = m(x - x_1)$; El grafico de la ecuación es una linea que pasa por el punto (x_1, y_1) y tiene la pendiente m.

population *(p. 563)* A population is an entire group of people or objects.

población *(p. 563)* Una población es un grupo entero de personas u objetos.

power *(p. 320)* A product of repeated factors

potencia *(p. 320)* Un producto de factores repetidos

probability *(p. 523)* A measure of the likelihood, or chance, that an event will occur

probabilidad *(p. 523)* Una medida de la probabilidad o posibilidad de que ocurrirá un evento

Pythagorean Theorem *(p. 382)* In any right triangle, the sum of the squares of the lengths of the legs is equal to the square of the length of the hypotenuse: $a^2 + b^2 = c^2$.

Teorema de Pitágoras *(p. 382)* En cualquier triángulo rectángulo, la suma de los largos de los catetos es igual al cuadrado del largo de la hipotenusa: $a^2 + b^2 = c^2$.

radical sign *(p. 374)* The symbol $\sqrt{\ }$ which is used to represent a square root

símbolo radical *(p. 374)* El símbolo $\sqrt{\ }$ que es usado para representar una raíz cuadrada

radicand *(p. 374)* The number under a radical sign

radicando *(p. 374)* El número bajo un símbolo radical

radius *(p. 600)* The distance from the center of a circle to any point on the circle

radio *(p. 600)* La distancia desde el centro de un círculo hasta cualquier punto del círculo

real numbers *(p. 402)* The set of all rational and irrational numbers

números reales *(p. 402)* El conjunto de todos los números racionales e irracionales

reflection *(p. 50)* A flip; a transformation in which a figure is reflected in a line called the line of reflection; A reflection creates a mirror image of the original figure.

reflexión *(p. 50)* Un reflejo; una tranformación en la que una figura se refleja en una línea llamada la línea de reflexión; Una reflexión crea un reflejo exacto de la figura original.

regular polygon *(p. 120)* A polygon in which all the side are congruent, and all the interior angles are congruent

regular pyramid *(p. 660)* A pyramid whose base is a regular polygon

relation *(p. 276)* A pairing of inputs with outputs; can be represented by ordered pairs or a mapping diagram

relative frequency *(p. 524)* The fraction or percent of the time that an event occurs in an experiment

rigid motion *(p. 64)* A transformation that preserves length and angle measure

rise *(p. 148)* The change in *y* between any two points on a line

rotation *(p. 56)* A turn; a transformation in which a figure is rotated about a point

run *(p. 148)* The change in *x* between any two points on a line

polígono regular *(p. 120)* Un polígono en el que todos los lados son congruentes, y todos los ángulos interiores son congruentes

pirámide regular *(p. 660)* Una pirámide cuya base es un polígono regular

relación *(p. 276)* Una pareja de entradas con salidas; se puede representar por pares ordenados o un diagrama de funciones

frecuencia relativa *(p. 524)* La fracción o porcentaje de tiempo en que un evento ocurre en un experimento

movimiento rígido *(p. 64)* Una transformación que preserva la longitud y medida del ángulo

desplazamiento vertical *(p. 148)* El cambio en *y* entre dos puntos cualesquiera de una línea

rotación *(p. 56)* Una vuelta; una transformación en donde una figura se rota sobre de un punto

desplazamiento horizontal *(p. 148)* El cambio en *x* entre dos puntos cualesquiera de una línea

---

S

---

sample *(p. 563)* A part of a population

sample space *(p. 538)* The set of all possible outcomes of one or more events

scale factor (of a dilation) *(p. 70)* The value of the ratio of the side lengths of the image to the corresponding side lengths of the original figure

scatter plot *(p. 238)* A data display that shows the relationship between two data sets using ordered pairs in a coordinate plane

scientific notation *(p. 350)* A number is written in scientific notation when it is represented as the product of a factor and a power of 10. The factor must be greater than or equal to 1 and less than 10.

semicircle *(p. 602)* One-half of a circle

muestra *(p. 563)* Una parte de una población

espacio de muestra *(p. 538)* El conjunto de todas los resultados posibles de uno o más eventos

factor de escala (de una dilatación) *(p. 70)* El valor de la razón de las longitudes de los lados de la imagen a las longitudes de los lados correspondientes de la figura inicial

diagrama de dispersión *(p. 238)* Una presentación de datos que muestra la relación entre dos conjuntos de datos, usando pares ordenados en un plano de coordenadas

notación científica *(p. 350)* Un número está escrito en notación científica cuando se representa como el producto de un factor y una potencia de 10. El factor debe ser mayor o igual que 1 e inferior a 10.

semicírculo *(p. 602)* La mitad de un círculo

similar figures *(p. 78)* Figures that have the same shape but not necessarily the same size; Two figures are similar when corresponding side lengths are proportional and corresponding angles are congruent.

figuras semejantes *(p. 78)* Figuras que tienen la misma forma pero no necesariamente el mismo tamaño; Dos figuras son semejantes cuando las longitudes de sus lados correspondientes son proporcionales y los ángulos correspondientes son congruentes.

similar solids *(p. 446)* Two solids of the same type with equal ratios of corresponding linear measures

sólidos similares *(p. 446)* Dos sólidos del mismo tipo con razones iguales de medidas lineales correspondientes

similarity transformation *(p. 78)* A dilation or a sequence of rigid motions and dilations

transformación de similitud *(p. 78)* Una dilatación o secuencia de movimientos rígidos y dilataciones

simulation *(p. 546)* An experiment that is designed to reproduce the conditions of a situation or process so that the simulated outcomes closely match the real-world outcomes

simulación *(p. 546)* Un experimento que es diseñado para reproducir las condiciones de una situación o proceso, de tal manera que los resultados posibles simulados coincidan en gran medida con los resultados del mundo real

slant height (of a pyramid) *(p. 660)* The height of each lateral triangular face of a pyramid

apotema lateral (de una pirámide) *(p. 660)* La altura de cada cara lateral triangular de una pirámide

slope *(p. 148)* The value of a ratio of the change in y (the rise) to the change in x (the run) between any two points on a line; Slope is a measure of the steepness of a line.

pendiente *(p. 148)* El valor de una razón entre el cambio en y (desplazamiento vertical) y el cambio en x (desplazamiento horizontal), entre dos puntos de una línea; Pediente es una medida de la inclinación de una línea.

slope-intercept form *(p. 162)* A linear equation written in the form $y = mx + b$; The graph of the equation is a line that has a slope of m and a y-intercept of b.

forma intersección-pendiente *(p. 162)* Una ecuación lineal escrita en la forma $y = mx + b$; El grafico de la ecuación es una linea que tiene una pendiente de m y una intersección y de b.

solution of an inequality *(p. 484)* A value that makes an inequality true

solución de una desigualdad *(p. 484)* Un valor que hace una desigualdad verdadera

solution of a linear equation *(p. 142)* An ordered pair (x, y) that makes an equation true

solución de una ecuación lineal *(p. 142)* Un par ordenado (x, y) que hace que una ecuación sea verdadera

solution set *(p. 484)* The set of all solutions of an inequality

conjunto solución *(p. 484)* El conjunto de todas las soluciones de una desigualdad

solution of a system of linear equations (in two variables) *(p. 200)* An ordered pair that is a solution of each equation in the system

solución de un sistema de ecuaciones lineales (en dos variables) *(p. 200)* Un par ordenado que es una solución de cada ecuación en el sistema

sphere *(p. 439)* The set of all points in space that are the same distance from a point called the center

square root *(p. 374)* A number that, when multiplied by itself, equals a given number

standard form *(p. 168)* The standard form of a linear equation is $Ax + By = C$, where A and B are not both zero.

supplementary angles *(p. 628)* Two angles whose measures have a sum of 180°

system of linear equations *(p. 200)* A set of two or more linear equations in the same variables

esfera *(p. 439)* El conjunto de todos los pontos en el espacio que están a la misma distancia de un punto llamado centro

raíz cuadrada *(p. 374)* Un número que, multiplicado por sí mismo, es igual a un número dado

forma estándar *(p. 168)* La forma estándar de una ecuación lineal es $Ax + By = C$, donde A y B no son ambos cero.

ángulos suplementarios *(p. 628)* Dos ángulos cuyas medidas tienen una suma de 180°

sistema de ecuaciones lineales *(p. 200)* Un conjunto de dos o más ecuaciones lineales en las mismas variables

---

T

---

theorem *(p. 381)* A rule in mathematics

theoretical probability *(p. 530)* The quotient of the number of favorable outcomes and the number of possible outcomes when all possible outcomes are equally likely

transformation *(p. 44)* A change in the size, shape, position, or orientation of a figure

translation *(p. 44)* A slide; a transformation that shifts a figure horizontally and/or vertically, but does not change its size, shape, or orientation

transversal *(p. 104)* A line that intersects two or more lines

two-way table *(p. 250)* A frequency table that displays two categories of data collected from the same source

teorema *(p. 381)* Un enunciado que afirma una verdad demostrable

probabilidad teórica *(p. 530)* El cociente del número de resultados favorables y el número de posibles resultados cuando todos los resultados posibles son igualmente probables

transformación *(p. 44)* Un cambio en el tamaño, forma, posición u orientación de una figura

traslación *(p. 44)* Un deslice; una transformación que desplaza una figura horizontal y/o verticalmente, pero no cambia su tamaño, forma u orientación

transversal *(p. 104)* Una recta que interseca dos o más rectas

tabla de doble entrada *(p. 250)* Una tabla de frecuencia que muestra dos categorias de datos recogidos de la misma fuente

---

U

---

unbiased sample *(p. 564)* A sample that is representative of a population

muestra no sesgada *(p. 564)* Una muestra que es representativa de una población

---

V

---

vertical angles *(p. 628)* Opposite angles formed by the intersection of two lines

ángulos verticales *(p. 628)* Ángulos opuestos formados por la intersección de dos líneas

x-intercept *(p. 162)* The *x*-coordinate of the point where a line crosses the *x*-axis

intersección x *(p. 162)* La coordenada *x* del punto donde una línea cruza el eje *x*

y-intercept *(p. 162)* The *y*-coordinate of the point where a line crosses the *y*-axis

intersección y *(p. 162)* La coordenada *y* del punto donde una línea cruza el eje *y*

English-Spanish Glossary

Index

A

Absolute value, of exponents, 351
Addition
    Distributive Property over (*See* Distributive Property)
    in scientific notation, 355, 356
    solving equations using, 465–470
    solving inequalities using, 489–494
Addition Property of Equality, solving equations with, 3, 4, 12, 18, 19, 465, 466, 478, 510
Addition Property of Inequality, solving inequalities with, 490, 504, 505
Adjacent angles, 627, 628, 629
Algebra tiles, 3, 465, 471, 477, 503
Alternate exterior angles, 105, 106
Alternate interior angles, 105, 106
Angle(s)
    adjacent, 627, 628, 629
    alternate exterior, 105, 106
    alternate interior, 105, 106
    complementary, 628, 629
    congruent, 64, 104, 105, 628
    corresponding, 104, 105
    drawing triangles using, 620
    exterior, 105
    identifying relationships of, 106
    interior, 105
    naming, 628
    pairs of, 629
    of polygons, 112, 117–122
    right (*See* Right angles)
    of rotation, 56
    of similar figures, 78
    of similar triangles, 124, 125
    supplementary, 105, 627, 628, 629
    transversals forming, 104, 105, 106, 111
    of triangles, 111–116, 124, 125
    using rules about, 627
    vertical, 105, 627, 628, 629
Angle measures
    constructing quadrilaterals using, 622
    constructing triangles using, 620
    drawing triangles from, 123
    finding unknown, 11, 104, 119, 627–634
    sum of
        in polygons, 118
        in triangle, 112

Approximation
    of cube roots, 403
    of irrational numbers, 403
    of numbers, 343
    of square roots, 401, 403
Areas. *See also* Surface areas
    of bases, 427, 428, 434, 649, 654, 660, 661, 666, 672
    of circles, 20, 377, 607–612, 616
    of composite figures, 613–618
    estimating, 614
    of lateral faces, 649, 660, 661
    of lateral surface, 650, 654, 655
    of rectangles, 616
    of semicircles, 615
    of similar figures, 84, 85
    of triangles, 615
Associative Property of Multiplication, 356
Axes, labeling, 295

B

Bar graphs, 256, 257
Bases (in exponential expressions)
    definition of, 319, 320
    dividing powers with same, 332
    multiplying powers with same, 326
    negative, 320
Bases (in geometry), areas of, 427, 428, 434, 649, 654, 660, 661, 666, 672
    in cylinder area formula, 654
    in prism volume formula, 666
    in pyramid volume formula, 672
    of pyramids, 659, 660, 661
    in surface area formula, 648, 649
Biased sample, 564, 565
Box-and-whisker plots, 256, 576, 578, 581, 582, 583, 584

C

Celsius, converting Fahrenheit to, 27
Center
    of circle, 600
    of dilation, 70
    of rotation, 56
    of sphere, 439
Challenge. *See* Dig Deeper
Change, rate of, 296
Chapter Exploration, *In every chapter. For example, see:* 2, 42, 102, 140, 198, 236, 274, 318, 372, 426

Chapter Practice, *In every chapter. For example, see:* 8–10, 47–48, 108–110, 145–146, 203–204, 241–242, 279–280, 323–324, 378–380, 431–432
Chapter Review, *In every chapter. For example, see:* 32–35, 90–95, 130–133, 186–191, 226–229, 264–267, 308–311, 362–365, 416–419, 454–457
Check Your Answer, *Throughout. For example, see:* 4, 46, 114, 164, 200, 252, 346, 356, 377
Choose Tools, *Throughout. For example, see:* 154, 255, 543
Circle(s), 599–606
    areas of, 20, 377, 607–612, 616
    circumference of (*See* Circumference)
    definition of, 600
    diameter of, 599, 600
    drawing, using compass for, 599
    radius of, 600
Circle graphs, 256
Circumference, 599–606
    definition of, 601
    exploring, 599
    finding, 601
    four square for, 636
Clockwise, rotating figure, 56, 57
Clusters, on scatter plots, 238
Common Error, *Throughout. For example, see:* T-47, 58, 64, 78, T-227, 326, 332, 345, T-372, 410
Commutative Property of Multiplication, 356
Comparison, of similar figures, 83, 84, 85
Compass, 599, 621
Complementary angles, 628, 629
Composite figures
    areas of, 613–618
    definition of, 614
    perimeters of, 613–618
Composite solids, 442
Compound events, 537–544
Conclusions, determining validity of, 565
Cones
    cross sections of, 679
    definition of, 433
    height of, 434
    radius of, 435

definition of, 396
as real numbers, 402
Reading, *Throughout. For example, see:* 44, 64, 78, 118, 148
Real numbers
classifying, 402
definition of, 402
Real World. *See* Modeling Real Life
Reasonableness, checking for, 246, 292, 442, 525, 610, 616, 656, 662
Reasoning, *Throughout. For example, see:* 10, 48, 109, 153, 204, 280, 330, 380, 431
Rectangles
area of, 616
congruent, 65
dilating, 71
finding missing measures in, 17
reflections of, 49
rotating, 58
similar, 83, 84
writing formula for length of, 25
Rectangular prisms
finding missing measures in, 17
similar, 446
surface area of, 647, 648, 684
volume of, 427, 666
writing formula for height of, 25
writing formula for length of, 25
Rectangular pyramids, volume of, 673
Reduction, 71
Reflections, 49–54
definition of, 50
identifying, 50
line of, 50
as rigid motions, 64
Regular polygons, 120
Regular pyramid, 660
Relations, 275–280
definition of, 276
as functions, 277
ordered pairs of, 276
Relationships between data
analyzing, 275, 301
describing
between quantities, 275
using graphs, 281, 301, 302, 303
using table, 281
using two-way table, 252
finding, 237
identifying, 239, 245
proportional (*See* Proportional relationships)
on scatter plots, 238–239, 244–245
types of, 239
Relative frequency, 524

Remember, *Throughout. For example, see:* 4, 5, 26, 142, 174, 175, 282, 402, 428
Repeated Reasoning, *Throughout. For example, see:* 88, 117, 210, 280, 452
Repeating decimals
definition of, 396
writing, as fractions, 395, 397, 474
Response to Intervention, *Throughout. For example, see:* T-0B, T-60, T-129, T-138B, T-206, T-241, T-272B, T-341, T-415, T-424B
Review & Refresh, *In every lesson. For example, see:* 8, 47, 108, 145, 203, 241, 279, 323, 378, 431
Right angles
lines intersecting at, 104
in right triangles, 382
Right prism, 666
Right pyramids, 672
Right triangles. *See also* Pythagorean Theorem
identifying, 410, 411
sides of, 382
using, 147
Rigid motions
definition of, 64
describing sequence of, 65
Rise, 148
Rotational symmetry, 61
Rotations, 55–62
center of, 56
clockwise, 56, 57
counterclockwise, 57
definition of, 56
identifying, 56
as rigid motions, 64
Rounding numbers, 344, 345
Ruler, 620, 623
Run, 148

S

Sample(s) 563–568
biased, 564, 565
definition of, 563
definition and example chart for, 588
random (*See* Random samples)
unbiased, 564, 565
using, 563
variability in, 569
Sample space
definition of, 538
finding, 538, 539

Scaffolding Instruction, *In every lesson. For example, see:* T-4, T-64, T-112, T-174, T-225, T-244, T-276, T-344, T-390, T-453
Scale,
in similar figures, 84
Scale drawings,
as dilations, 70
similar figures as, 84
Scale factor
of dilation, 70
in scale drawings, 84
Scale models,
making, 659
Scatter plots, 237–242
definition of, 238
function of, 256
information frame for, 264
line of fit on, 243–248
making, 238
Scientific notation, 349–354
converting, to standard form, 351
definition of, 350
operations in, 355–360
writing numbers in, 350
Self-Assessment for Concepts & Skills, *In every lesson. For example, see:* 6, 45, 106, 143, 201, 239, 277, 321, 376, 429
Self-Assessment for Problem Solving, *In every lesson. For example, see:* 7, 46, 107, 144, 202, 240, 278, 322, 377, 430
Semicircles
area of, 615
definition of, 602
Semicircular region, perimeter of, 602
Side(s)
congruent, 64, 120
drawing triangles using, 620, 621
of pyramids, 659
Side lengths
finding, 155, 373
of right triangles, 382 (*See also* Pythagorean Theorem)
of similar figures, 78
Similar figures, 77–82
areas of, 84, 85
comparing, 83, 84, 85
definition of, 78
describing, 79
identifying, 78
indirect measurement of, 126
perimeters of, 84
symbol of, 78

Credits

Chapter 8

316 *top* zentilia/Shutterstock.com; *bottom* OnstOn/iStock/Getty Images Plus; **317** tawan/Shutterstock.com; **318** *a.* ©iStockphoto.com/Manfred Konrad; *b.* alex-mit/iStock/Getty Images Plus; *c.* macrovector/iStock/Getty Images Plus; *d.* Kilav/iStock/Getty Images Plus; *e.* Digital Vision./Photodisc/Getty Images; *f.* ZU_09/DigitalVision Vectors/Getty Images; *bottom* Stevyn Colgan; **319** ©iStockphoto.com/Franck Boston; **322** *top* Cecilie_Arcurs/E+/Getty Images; *bottom* photographer3431/iStock/Getty Images Plus; **324** *top* muratkoc/E+/Getty Images; *bottom* ©iStockphoto.com/Boris Yankov; **328** *left* MR1805/iStock/Getty Images Plus; *right* Nikitin Victor/Shutterstock.com; **330** *top* ©iStockphoto.com/VIKTORIIA KULISH; *bottom* DNY59/E+/Getty Images; **334** AndrewRafalsky/iStock/Getty Images Plus; **336** *top* ©iStockphoto.com/Petrovich9; *center* Okea/iStock/Getty Images Plus; *bottom* NASA/JPL-Caltech/L.Cieza (UT Austin); **340** *top* ILYA AKINSHIN/Shutterstock.com; *bottom* filipfoto/iStock/Getty Images Plus; **342** ©iStockphoto.com/Nancy Louie; **343** *Exploration 1a. and c.* Tom C Amon/Shutterstock.com; *Exploration 1b.* Olga Gabay/Shutterstock.com; *Exploration 1d.* HuHu/Shutterstock.com; **344** adventtr/E+/Getty Images; **347** Aslan Alphan/iStock/Getty Images Plus; **348** *right* AZ68/iStock/Getty Images Plus; *left* Crevis/Shutterstock.com; **352** *top* ©iStockphoto.com/Oliver Sun Kim; *bottom* BORTEL Pavel/Shutterstock.com; **353** John Baker; **354** *top* ©iStockphoto.com/Christian Jasiuk; *bottom* ©iStockphoto.com/cdascher; **358** *top* Sebastian Kaulitzki/Shutterstock.com; *bottom* asiseeit/iStock/Getty Images Plus; **361** *top* filo/DigitalVision Vectors/Getty Images; *bottom* OnstOn/iStock/Getty Images Plus; **363** FatCamera/E+/Getty Images; **364** T_A_P/E+/Getty Images; **366** TranceDrumer/Shutterstock.com

Chapter 9

370 *top* zentilia/Shutterstock.com; *bottom* OnstOn/iStock/Getty Images Plus; **371** uatp2/iStock/Getty Images Plus; **377** *top* Perfectblue97; *bottom* Ig0rZh/iStock/Getty Images Plus; **379** *top* seregam/iStock/Getty Images Plus; *bottom* MarisaPerez/iStock/Getty Images Plus; **380** *top* ©iStockphoto.com/iShootPhotos, LLC; *Exercise 52 left* popovaphoto/iStock/Getty Images Plus; *Exercise 52 right* Dkart/E+/Getty Images; **381** claudio zaccherini/Shutterstock.com; **385** gui00878/iStock/Getty Images Plus; **388** romeovip_md/Shutterstock.com; **394** *right* Gary Whitton/iStock/Getty Images Plus; *left* DonNichols/iStock/Getty Images Plus; **398** *top* RomoloTavani/iStock/Getty Images Plus; *bottom* tc397/E+/Getty Images; **399** NOAA; **400** *top* dial-a-view/E+/Getty Images; *center* atoss/iStock/Getty Images Plus; *bottom* Oktay Ortakcioglu/E+/Getty Images; **405** ©iStockphoto.com/iLexx; **408** ©iStockphoto.com/Marcio Silva; **412** *left* youngID/DigitalVision Vectors/Getty Images; *right* JulieVMac/E+/Getty Images; **414** twildlife/iStock/Getty Images Plus; **415** OnstOn/iStock/Getty Images Plus; **417** Vaniatos/iStock/Getty Images Plus; **418** *Exercise 17 right* DS70/iStock Unreleased/Getty Images Plus; *Exercise 17 left* kostsov/iStock/Getty Images Plus; *bottom* Rawpixel/iStock/Getty Images Plus; **419** supergenijalac/iStock/Getty Images Plus; **420** CD Lanzen/Shutterstock.com

Chapter 10

424 *top* zentilia/Shutterstock.com; *bottom* OnstOn/iStock/Getty Images Plus; **425** carlosgaw/E+/Getty Images; **430** *top* Alison Hancock/Shutterstock.com; *bottom* rasslava/iStock/Getty Images Plus; **432** *Exercise 18* ©iStockphoto.com/Prill Med: Mediendesigns & Fotografie; *Exercise 19* MileA/iStock/Getty Images Plus; *Exercise 20* ©iStockphoto.com/subjug; *Exercise 23* ©iStockphoto.com/Matthew Dixon; *Exercise 24* mladn61/E+/Getty Images; *bottom* ©iStockphoto.com/Jill Chen; **436** pixeldigits/iStock/Getty Images Plus; **438** *center* abu/E+/Getty Images; *bottom* rypson/iStock Editorial/Getty Images Plus; **422** *top* Donald Joski/Shutterstock.com; *bottom right* ©iStockphoto.com/Philippa Banks; *bottom left* Elenathewise/iStock/Getty Images Plus; **444** *top* ©iStockphoto.com/Yury Kosourov; *center* Carlos Caetano/Shutterstock.com; *bottom* johan63/iStock/Getty Images Plus; **449** Tammy616/E+/Getty Images; **452** *top* Neustockimages/E+/Getty Images; *Exercise 22* Ford; *Exercise 23* ©iStockphoto.com/wrangel; *Exercise 24* Vold77/iStock/Getty Images Plus; *bottom* alfocome/Shutterstock.com; **453** *top* loca4motion/iStock/Getty Images Plus; *bottom* OnstOn/iStock/Getty Images Plus; **456** Laures/iStock/Getty Images Plus

Chapter A

462 *top* zentilia/Shutterstock.com; *bottom* OnstOn/iStock/Getty Images Plus; **463** Georgethefourth/iStock/Getty Images Plus; **467** German-skydiver/iStock/Getty Images Plus; **470** ©iStockphoto.com/fotoVoyager; **476** *top* Alexander Mak/Shutterstock.com; *bottom* robertsrob/iStock/Getty Images Plus; **480** tolokonov/iStock/Getty Images Plus; **482** *top* zbruch/E+/Getty Images; *bottom* huePhotography/iStock/Getty Images Plus; **483** *top left* bitt24/Shutterstock.com; *top right* Amawasri/iStock/Getty Images Plus; *center left* mphillips007/E+/Getty Images; *bottom right* Creativ/iStock/Getty Images Plus; **486** gregepperson/iStock/Getty Images Plus; **488** Gregory James Van Raalte/Shutterstock.com; **492** ©iStockphoto.com/suriyasilsaksom; **494** *top* Khafizov Lvan Harisovich/Shutterstock.com; *bottom* Victoria_Novak/iStock/Getty Images Plus, Opka/iStock/Getty Images Plus; **499** *top* Ralph White/Corbis Documentary/Getty Images; *bottom* sweetmoments/E+/Getty Images; **500** LockStockBob/Shutterstock.com; **501** jacoblund/iStock/Getty Images Plus; **502** Jacek Chabraszewski/Shutterstock.com; **506** *top* GaryAlvis/E+/Getty Images; MaksTRV/iStock/Getty Images Plus; *bottom* graemenicholson/iStock/Getty Images Plus; **508** *top* ©Keddie. Image from BigStockPhoto.com; *bottom* GlobalP/iStock/Getty Images Plus; **509** OnstOn/iStock/Getty Images Plus; **511** urich84/iStock/Getty Images Plus; **514** ©iStockphoto.com/Jack Puccio

Chapter B

518 *top* zentilia/Shutterstock.com; *bottom* OnstOn/iStock/Getty Images Plus; **519** ©iStockphoto.com/ryasick; **520** ©iStockphoto.com/ryasick; **522** Sussenn/iStock/Getty Images Plus; **524** *top* Rattasak/iStock/Getty Images Plus, Oda_dao/iStock/Getty Images Plus, antoniotruzzi/iStock/Getty Images Plus; *bottom* Big Ideas Learning, LLC; **525** Roydee/E+/Getty Images; **527** 1550539/iStock/Getty Images Plus, Sussenn/iStock/Getty Images Plus; **528** RomoloTavani/iStock/Getty Images Plus; **529** *top* Meral Hydaverdi/Shutterstock.com; *bottom* Warren Goldswain/Shutterstock.com; **531** ©iStockphoto.com/Eric Ferguson; **532** maryloo/iStock/Getty Images Plus; **533** fatihhoca/E+/Getty Images; **534** gmnicholas/E+/Getty Images; **535** Juanmonino/iStock Unreleased/Getty Images; **536** Feng Yu/Shutterstock.com; **537** *top* FernandoMadeira/iStock/Getty Images Plus; *center* Krasyuk/iStock/Getty Images Plus; *bottom* Mark Aplet/Shutterstock.com; **538** the-lightwriter/iStock/Getty Images Plus; **539** Big Ideas Learning, LLC; **540** Rodrusoleg/iStock/Getty Images Plus; **541** *top* carlosalvarez/E+/Getty Images; *bottom* goir/iStock/Getty Images Plus; **543** Sussenn/iStock/Getty Images Plus; **544** *top left* basar17/iStock/Getty Images Plus; *top* ET-ARTWORKS/DigitalVision Vectors/Getty Images; *bottom* tele52/Shutterstock.com; **545** rbv/iStock/Getty Images Plus; **546** Dorottya_Mathe/iStock/Getty Images Plus; **548** ovro77/iStock/Getty Images Plus; **549** Kagenmi/iStock/Getty Images Plus; **550** *top* urbancow/E+/Getty Images; *bottom* IngaNielsen/iStock/Getty Images Plus; **551** *top* pioneer111/iStock/Getty Images Plus; *bottom* OnstOn/iStock/Getty Images Plus; **555** *top* asiseeit/iStock/Getty Images Plus; *bottom* monkeybusinessimages/iStock/Getty Images Plus

Chapter C

560 *top* zentilia/Shutterstock.com; *bottom* OnstOn/iStock/Getty Images Plus; **561** ©iStockphoto.com/Eric Isselée; **562** *a. left* ©iStockphoto.com/Shannon Keegan; *a. right* ©iStockphoto.com/Lorelyn Medina; *b. left* Joel Sartore/joelsartore.com; *b. right* Feng Yu/Shutterstock.com; *c. left* ©iStockphoto.com/kledge; *c. right* ©iStockphoto.com/spxChrome; *d.* ©iStockphoto.com/Alex Slobodkin; **563** 3bugsmom/iStock/Getty Images Plus; **564** sihuo0860371/iStock/Getty Images Plus; **566** macrovector/iStock/Getty Images Plus; **567** amwu/iStock/Getty Images Plus; **568** smontgom65/iStock Editorial/Getty Images Plus; **569** *top* DonNichols/E+/Getty Images; *bottom* BanksPhotos/iStock/Getty Images Plus; **570** RKaulitzki/iStock/Getty Images Plus; **572** zrfphoto/iStock/Getty Images Plus; **573** EVAfotografie/iStock/Getty Images Plus; **574** MariaBobrova/iStock/Getty Images Plus; **578** Aneese/iStock/Getty Images Plus; **579** EricFerguson/E+/Getty Images; **580** *top* Geerati/iStock/Getty Images Plus; *bottom* zhuzhu/iStock/Getty Images Plus; **584** ©iStockphoto.com/Rawpixel Ltd; **586** *right* rrocio/E+/Getty Images; *left* bdspn/iStock/Getty Images Plus; **587** OnstOn/iStock/Getty Images Plus; **589** DragonImages/iStock/Getty Images Plus; **591** funduck/iStock/Getty Images Plus; **595** Peter zijlstra/Shutterstock.com

Chapter D

596 *top* zentilia/Shutterstock.com; *bottom* OnstOn/iStock/Getty Images Plus; **597** peepo/E+/Getty Images; **599** *top* MichaelJay/iStock/Getty Images Plus; *bottom* urbancow/E+/Getty Images, johan10/iStock/Getty Images Plus, junce/iStock/Getty Images Plus; **603** *left* Mechanik/Shutterstock.com; *bottom right* mehmettorlak/E+/Getty Images; **604** *Exercise 6* ©iStockphoto.com/zentillia; *Exercise 7* Mr Doomits/Shutterstock.com; *Exercise 8* Nikolamirejovska/Shutterstock.com; *Exercise 9* ©iStockphoto.com/ALEAIMAGE; *Exercise 10* ©iStockphoto.com/iLexx; *Exercise 11* saicle/iStock/Getty Images Plus; *Exercise 12* boggy22/iStock/Getty Images Plus; *Exercise 13* wragg/iStock/Getty Images Plus; **605** *Exercise 17* akiyoko/iStock/Getty Images Plus; *Exercise 18* ZargonDesign/E+/Getty Images; *bottom* Inok/iStock/Getty Images Plus; **606** *left* ©iStockphoto.com/HultonArchive; *right* Dimedrol68/iStock/Getty Images Plus; **610** *top* trekandshoot/iStock/Getty Images Plus; *bottom* StockPhotoAstur/iStock/Getty Images Plus; **611** *Exercise 1* SergeBogomyako/iStock/Getty Images Plus; *Exercise 2* MileA/iStock/Getty Images Plus; *Exercise 7* ©iStockphoto.com/zentillia; *Exercise 8* boygovideo/iStock/Getty Images Plus; *Exercise 9* prmustafa/iStock/Getty Images Plus; *Exercise 10* ©iStockphoto.com/subjug; *Exercise 11* kulykt/iStock/Getty Images Plus; *Exercise 12* ©iStockphoto.com/7nuit; **618** ©iStockphoto.com/Scott Slattery; **623** asbe/iStock/Getty Images Plus; **624** Gino Santa Maria/Shutterstock.com; **626** Bliznetsov/E+/Getty Images; **633** mountainpix/Shutterstock.com; **634** ©iStockphoto.com/Jorgen Jacobsen; **635** OnstOn/iStock/Getty Images Plus; **637** *Exercise 3* ©iStockphoto.com/DivaNir4A; *Exercise 4* ©iStockphoto.com/Stacey Walker; *Exercise 5* JuSun/E+/Getty Images; *Exercise 6* simonkr/iStock/Getty Images Plus; *bottom* wrangel/iStock/Getty Images Plus; **638** StevenEllingson/iStock/Getty Images Plus; **640** Kalamazoo (Michigan) Public Library

Chapter E

644 *top* zentilia/Shutterstock.com; *bottom* OnstOn/iStock/Getty Images Plus; **645** tropper2000/iStock/Getty Images Plus; **646** ©iStockphoto.com/Remigiusz Załucki; **650** *left* Bob the Wikipedian/CC-BY-SA-3.0; *right* ©iStockphoto.com/Sherwin McGehee; **652** *top right* mihmihmal/iStock/Getty Images Plus; *center* kriangkrai_net/iStock/Getty Images Plus; *bottom left* ©iStockphoto.com/stevanovicigor; **656** Tsekhmister/iStock/Getty Images Plus; **658** *top* ©iStockphoto.com/Tomasz Pietryszek; *Exercise 17* 10174593_258/iStock/Getty Images Plus; *Exercise 19* Newcastle Drum Centre; *bottom* ©iStockphoto.com/scol22; **659** *left* ©iStockphoto.com/Luke Daniek; *right* vichie81/iStock Editorial/Getty Images Plus; **662** hxdyl/iStock/Getty Images Plus; **668** EuToch/iStock/Getty Images Plus; **674** Vladone/iStock/Getty Images Plus; **676** *top* ©iStockphoto.com/ranplett, Image © Courtesy of Museum of Science, Boston; *bottom* ©iStockphoto.com/Yails; **680** yocamon/iStock Editorial/Getty Images Plus; **682** *Exercise 17* ©iStockphoto.com/AlexStar; *Exercise 18* Knartz/Shutterstock.com; *Exercise 19* SOMMAI/Shutterstock.com; *Exercise 25* ©iStockphoto.com/Frank Wright; *bottom* 7activestudio/iStock/Getty Images Plus; **683** OnstOn/iStock/Getty Images Plus; **686** lucagal/iStock/Getty Images Plus; **687** Wimage72/iStock/Getty Images Plus; **688** Tevarak/iStock/Getty Images Plus; **690** ra-design/Shutterstock.com

Cartoon illustrations: Tyler Stout
Design Elements: ©iStockphoto.com/Gizmo; Valdis Torms; Juksy/iStock/Getty Images Plus

Mathematics Reference Sheet

Conversions

U.S. Customary
1 foot = 12 inches
1 yard = 3 feet
1 mile = 5280 feet
1 acre = 43,560 square feet
1 cup = 8 fluid ounces
1 pint = 2 cups
1 quart = 2 pints
1 gallon = 4 quarts
1 gallon = 231 cubic inches
1 pound = 16 ounces
1 ton = 2000 pounds
1 cubic foot ≈ 7.5 gallons

U.S. Customary to Metric
1 inch = 2.54 centimeters
1 foot ≈ 0.3 meter
1 mile ≈ 1.61 kilometers
1 quart ≈ 0.95 liter
1 gallon ≈ 3.79 liters
1 cup ≈ 237 milliliters
1 pound ≈ 0.45 kilogram
1 ounce ≈ 28.3 grams
1 gallon ≈ 3785 cubic centimeters

Time
1 minute = 60 seconds
1 hour = 60 minutes
1 hour = 3600 seconds
1 year = 52 weeks

Temperature
$$C = \frac{5}{9}(F - 32)$$

$$F = \frac{9}{5}C + 32$$

Metric
1 centimeter = 10 millimeters
1 meter = 100 centimeters
1 kilometer = 1000 meters
1 liter = 1000 milliliters
1 kiloliter = 1000 liters
1 milliliter = 1 cubic centimeter
1 liter = 1000 cubic centimeters
1 cubic millimeter = 0.001 milliliter
1 gram = 1000 milligrams
1 kilogram = 1000 grams

Metric to U.S. Customary
1 centimeter ≈ 0.39 inch
1 meter ≈ 3.28 feet
1 kilometer ≈ 0.62 mile
1 liter ≈ 1.06 quarts
1 liter ≈ 0.26 gallon
1 kilogram ≈ 2.2 pounds
1 gram ≈ 0.035 ounce
1 cubic meter ≈ 264 gallons

Number Properties

Commutative Properties of Addition and Multiplication
$$a + b = b + a$$
$$a \cdot b = b \cdot a$$

Associative Properties of Addition and Multiplication
$$(a + b) + c = a + (b + c)$$
$$(a \cdot b) \cdot c = a \cdot (b \cdot c)$$

Addition Property of Zero
$$a + 0 = a$$

Multiplication Properties of Zero and One
$$a \cdot 0 = 0$$
$$a \cdot 1 = a$$

Multiplicative Inverse Property
$$n \cdot \frac{1}{n} = \frac{1}{n} \cdot n = 1, n \neq 0$$

Distributive Property:
$$a(b + c) = ab + ac$$
$$a(b - c) = ab - ac$$

Properties of Equality

Addition Property of Equality
If $a = b$, then $a + c = b + c$.

Subtraction Property of Equality
If $a = b$, then $a - c = b - c$.

Multiplication Property of Equality
If $a = b$, then $a \cdot c = b \cdot c$.

Division Property of Equality
If $a = b$, then $a \div c = b \div c, c \neq 0$.

Squaring both sides of an equation
If $a = b$, then $a^2 = b^2$.

Cubing both sides of an equation
If $a = b$, then $a^3 = b^3$.

Properties of Inequality

Addition Property of Inequality
If $a > b$, then $a + c > b + c$.

Subtraction Property of Inequality
If $a > b$, then $a - c > b - c$.

Multiplication Property of Inequality
If $a > b$ and c is positive, then $a \cdot c > b \cdot c$.
If $a > b$ and c is negative, then $a \cdot c < b \cdot c$.

Division Property of Inequality
If $a > b$ and c is positive, then $a \div c > b \div c$.
If $a > b$ and c is negative, then $a \div c < b \div c$.

Properties of Exponents

Product of Powers Property: $a^m \cdot a^n = a^{m+n}$

Quotient of Powers Property: $\dfrac{a^m}{a^n} = a^{m-n}, a \neq 0$

Power of a Power Property: $\left(a^m\right)^n = a^{mn}$

Power of a Product Property: $(ab)^m = a^m b^m$

Zero Exponents: $a^0 = 1, a \neq 0$

Negative Exponents: $a^{-n} = \dfrac{1}{a^n}, a \neq 0$

Slope

$m = \dfrac{\text{rise}}{\text{run}}$

$= \dfrac{\text{change in } y}{\text{change in } x}$

$= \dfrac{y_2 - y_1}{x_2 - x_1}$

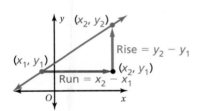

Pythagorean Theorem

$a^2 + b^2 = c^2$

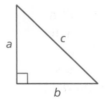

Converse of the Pythagorean Theorem

If the equation $a^2 + b^2 = c^2$ is true for the side lengths of a triangle, then the triangle is a right triangle.

Equations of Lines

Slope-intercept form
$y = mx + b$

Standard form
$Ax + By = C, A \neq 0, B \neq 0$

Point-slope form
$y - y_1 = m(x - x_1)$

Angles of Polygons

Interior Angle Measures of a Triangle

$x + y + z = 180$

Interior Angle Measures of a Polygon

The sum S of the interior angle measures of a polygon with n sides is $S = (n - 2) \cdot 180°$.

Circumference and Area of a Circle

$C = \pi d$ or $C = 2\pi r$

$A = \pi r^2$

$\pi \approx \dfrac{22}{7}$, or 3.14

Surface Area

Prism

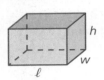 

$$S = 2\ell w + 2\ell h + 2wh$$

$S =$ areas of bases
+ areas of lateral faces

Pyramid

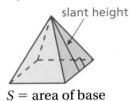

slant height

$S =$ area of base
+ areas of lateral faces

Cylinder

$$S = 2\pi r^2 + 2\pi rh$$

Volume

Prism

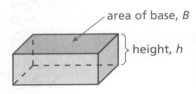

area of base, B

height, h

$$V = Bh$$

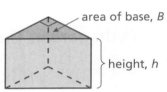

area of base, B

height, h

$$V = Bh$$

Pyramid

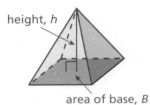

height, h

area of base, B

$$V = \frac{1}{3}Bh$$

Cylinder

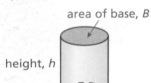

area of base, B

height, h

$$V = Bh = \pi r^2 h$$

Cone

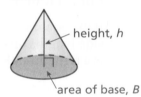

height, h

area of base, B

$$V = \frac{1}{3}Bh = \frac{1}{3}\pi r^2 h$$

Sphere

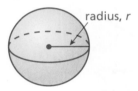

radius, r

$$V = \frac{4}{3}\pi r^3$$

Simple Interest

Simple interest formula

$$I = Prt$$